D1713413

Order and Innovation in the Middle Ages

Joseph R. Strayer (Photograph by Virginia Oliver)

# Order and Innovation
# in the Middle Ages:

*Essays in Honor of Joseph R. Strayer*

edited by
William C. Jordan
Bruce McNab
Teofilo F. Ruiz

PRINCETON UNIVERSITY PRESS
PRINCETON, NEW JERSEY

Contents

vi                           Contents

Contents

Foreword

The Middle Ages is a period which has been traditionally associated in the popular mind with static qualities. Faith and order, the twin pillars of Respublica Christiana, were once thought to have supported a rigid society which remained sterile and introspective during the long centuries between the end of classical civilization and the beginning of the Renaissance. This interpretation of history was largely discredited by the time Joseph R. Strayer began his scholarly career. But the replacement of it by a universal regard for the period as a time of great intellectual diversity and social vitality has been due in no small way to the work of the great historian in whose honor the present volume has been collected. His research, writing, and teaching during a forty-five-year career as a university professor and mentor to a whole generation of medievalists have illuminated the once supposedly stagnant Middle Ages and have demonstrated that within the order and hierarchy of medieval civilization there was a continuing process of successful innovation and experimentation, particularly in the fields of law, government administration, and finance, which have been his special interests. Although the theme of this volume of studies in honor of Professor Strayer echoes the pattern of his own work, a number of the articles themselves treat areas of medieval life and thought different from those which have been the subjects of his publications. This variety is an active testimony to Professor Strayer's multiplicity of interests and to his unfailing ability to guide and inspire his students and colleagues, even in areas apparently far removed from the sphere of his own research.

The first group of essays deals with organization and administration in medieval government. Frederic Kreisler's examination of the techniques employed in the compilation of the Domesday survey treats aspects of English administrative history with which Professor Strayer himself has been concerned; the same is true for Charles Radding's study of the administration of the aids in Normandy, which initiates the reader into the type of regional

study that paralleled Professor Strayer's early historical interests.
Broadly speaking, in this first section of the book, the writers
have analyzed different contexts within which administrative techniques developed in the Middle Ages.  Their analyses range from the
relatively simple techniques applied in eleventh-century England to
the sophisticated methods used in the diplomatic relations used for
an Italian city-state of the early Renaissance, as examined by
William Bowsky in his article on Siena.  Chronologically between
these two, Giles Constable's study of the organization of the Cluniac
order and John B. Freed's examination of the friars in Germany provide insights into that most medieval of institutions, the Church.

   In the second section of the volume, under the heading "Finance:
Money and Prices," the period is surveyed from a slightly different,
less institutional, point of view.  Philippe Wolff offers the
reader a conceptual framework for understanding the beginnings of
medieval monetary history, and Thomas Bisson ventures into the
hitherto uncharted waters of credit and prices in twelfth-century
Catalonia.  Richard Kaeuper and John Benton, with admirable clarity,
draw the reader into the complex problems of royal financial policy
in the late medieval period, where the twin themes of order and
innovation, now financial order and economic innovation, meet again.

   These cardinal themes continue to be explored in the third section
of the book, which treats medieval trade and urban life.  Archibald
Lewis begins the discussion with a panoramic view of the gradual
increase in the activities of northern traders in the Mediterranean
Sea.  There follows a detailed series of intensive studies, each
with a different emphasis, on the nature, extent, and social setting
of the trading experience in various areas of medieval Europe.  The
articles by William Jordan, Rhiman Rotz, and Robert Baker deal pre-
eminently with social and political questions affecting mercantile
activity.  The legal formulae of proxy (particularly as they are
used in documents of the Zaccaria connection) are examined by
Robert Lopez; cross-cultural influences on trade is the subject of
essays by Teofilo Ruiz and Raphael DeSoignie.

   Section four is, in one sense, an extension of these inquiries
into more general questions of the social order.  Bennett Hill

examines the still obscure question of the connection between the
early feudal nobility and religious foundations. Fredric Cheyette,
applying the relatively new research tool of aerial photography to
an area of southern France, opens the subject of thirteenth-century
fortifications (and related topics) to a more profound investigation
than has been thought possible before. Using more traditional
archival techniques, Jan Rogozinski and Bruce McNab discuss two
unsettling problems of French and English social history which
promise to provide material for much future research.

Nowhere is the diversity of emotions and aims in the Middle Ages
more evident than in the study of individual personalities and human
relationships. In the fifth and final section of the book, the con-
tributors explore topics which deal with the complex issues of personality and ethics. The psychology of a fiery reformer and the
tangled views of a rather pleasant heretic are critically examined
by Lester Little and Robert Lerner. The patient policy of kings
awaiting death is laid bare in an extraordinary article by Elizabeth
Brown, and the influence of immorality on law is explored with keen
wit by Charles Wood. There is a great deal of tension in these portraits and vignettes, a tension that penetrated philosophical discourse and had an uneasy resolution in the Middle Ages. The
thirteenth century was, of course, the great age of resolutions and
syntheses, but Gaines Post in his magisterial concluding essay shows
that intellectual tensions, even in that age of supposed stability
and harmony, were not really far below the surface. Professor Post
also demonstrates that the search for innovative solutions to problems even in a society which had a sense of certain agreed-upon
ideals (one might almost say "order") was a necessary prerequisite
for health and hope. It is still not a bad formula.

The editors wish to express their gratitude to all those who have
helped in one way or another with the preparation of this volume of
essays for publication. Collective thanks is due to the Department
of History of Princeton University for its continuing official help
and encouragement, and very special thanks to Professors Elizabeth
Brown, John Benton, Thomas Bisson, Karlfried Froehlich, Felix

Gilbert, Gaines Post, Jerrold Seigel, Brian Tierney, and Colonel
Lawrence Spellman for their scholarly judgments and good advice.  In
addition, we are boundlessly grateful to Mrs. Emily Lawyer and Mrs.
Christine Jordan for their cheerful and painstaking help in editing
and retyping the entire manuscript.

Finally, our deepest thanks go to Miss Miriam Brokaw, Associate
Director and Editor of Princeton University Press, and to Mrs. Arthur
Sherwood, our editor, without whose constant support and assistance
this project would not have been possible.

Princeton,                                              W.C.J.
September, 1974                                          B.M.
                                                        T.F.R.

Part I

Organization and Administration in Medieval Government

Chapter 1

Domesday Book and the Anglo-Norman Synthesis

Frederic F. Kreisler

Domesday criticism has made remarkable advances since J. H. Round
revolutionized the field with the publication of Feudal England in
1895. Among the most significant contributions were a series of
discoveries demonstrating the extreme complexity of the administrative process employed in the making of Domesday Book. Consequently
it has become clear that Round and his followers held a simplistic
view of the nature of the "original returns" to the Domesday Inquest.
He assumed the existence of a huge set of returns arranged in hundredal form, and he believed that these constituted the sole sources
for "Domesday Book in which their contents were (1) re-arranged on
a different system, (2) epitomized and partly omitted, (3) altered
in wording."[1] To Round's view of the administrative procedure,
Maitland added an interpretation of the purpose of the Inquest that
stressed its relationship to the assessment and collection of geld,
to the exclusion of all other motives.[2] Although the authority
associated with the names of Round and Maitland tended to discourage
challenge of their theories for decades,[3] the labors of a new generation of Domesday scholars have produced a more sophisticated
interpretation based upon evidence from a wide range of extant
sources.

Professor D. C. Douglas was one of the pioneers in developing a
revision of the Round-Maitland thesis, bringing to light fresh
evidence and daring to reopen questions considered closed since the
turn of the century. As early as 1929 he suggested the possibility
that religious houses took an active part in assembling information
about their own lands for the Domesday Commissioners, information
which they themselves could have used in the preparation of private
surveys. It was Douglas who repeatedly drew attention to the
Domesday Monachorum of Christ Church, Canterbury, insisted upon its
significance in the context of modern Domesday criticism, and

finally published a text in 1944. Coupled with his idea that the
Domesday survey was conducted at least in part for the purpose of
settling disputed land claims which threatened to disrupt the precarious stability of the Norman settlement, Douglas' studies of
monastic "satellite" texts marked a turning-point in Domesday
historiography.[4]

    The revolutionary argument that effectively undermined the classic
Round-Maitland thesis was formulated by Professor V. H. Galbraith
in an article[5] which became the center of thirty years' vigorous
debate and inaugurated a new golden era of Domesday scholarship.
Galbraith offered an entirely new frame of reference for the
Domesday problem. His central insight lay in exposing the contradiction inherent in the dual proposition that analysis and reform
of the geld assessment system had been the purpose of the Inquest
and that the form of the Exchequer Domesday adequately served that
purpose. He pointed out that the feudal arrangement of D.B. all
but destroyed its value as an administrative tool in the hands of
tax-collectors. If reassessment of the geld had indeed been the
primary purpose of the Inquest, and if the "original returns" had
really been arranged hundred by hundred and village by village,
then it is inconceivable that a record in the form of the Exchequer
Domesday should have been the end result. On these highly pragmatic grounds Galbraith affirmed what is now so very plain: that
the Normans had every intention of constructing a record of feudal
land tenure, and not a "geld-book." Adopting Round's "view that by
discovering _how_ the Domesday survey was made, we could best hope to
understand _why_ it was made,"[6] he then asked how the information
recorded in D.B. had been gathered and compiled. His work led to
an answer typically consistent with common sense: like all good
bureaucrats faced with the task of getting a difficult job done on
time, the Domesday Commissioners amassed as much information as
they could, as quickly as possible, from any sources at hand.
Having analyzed the texts of the Domesday volumes and related
materials, Galbraith concluded that the "original returns" were of
different types, including written statements as well as oral testimony furnished by land-holders themselves or their stewards. At the

formal sessions of the Inquest the hundred-jurors were asked to
swear to the accuracy of information which had already been compiled
in preliminary form.  Once having obtained public sanction for the
factual material, the Domesday officials produced a digest in feudal
form for each county and ultimately for each circuit.  Finally the
circuit recension was submitted to the Exchequer, where it was condensed into the uniform style of D.B. I.  For some reason (perhaps
the Conqueror's death) the return from the East Anglian circuit was
never abbreviated.

Once the scholarly community began thinking along these lines,
evidence supporting the basic elements of Galbraith's theory began
to accumulate.  In 1943 Lennard reported the existence of a Bath
Abbey text which, he concluded, was indeed a return of demesne
manors submitted to the Domesday Commissioners by the abbey.  With
this solid piece of evidence in hand, it became possible to speak
more confidently about separate written returns submitted by tenants-
in-chief concerning their own lands.[7]  More recently, Sawyer uncovered
an Evesham text consisting of Domesday information arranged in
hundredal order and supplied by tenants-in-chief directly; moreover
he showed that the tenants-in-chief themselves arranged the information in hundredal form, presumably in preparation for the formal
court session which, as they had been informed in advance, was to
be conducted in order of hundreds.[8]  Lennard furnished fresh evidence from one of Round's own favorite sources, the Inquisitio
Eliensis, to support Galbraith's contention that the "returns,"
whatever form they may have taken, were not sent to Winchester, but
remained in the counties.[9]  And it was Sawyer who supplied an additional tool of analysis for Domesday studies:  the examination of
the "hundredal order" of entries in lists of manors and land
surveys.[10]

Galbraith returned to the field in 1961 with The Making of
Domesday Book in which he marshaled all the available evidence in
support of his 1942 thesis, and effectively dealt with the counter-
arguments critics had offered in the intervening period.  Concerning
the "returns," he once again argued that behind the "engrossed
records" in feudal form lay not "engrossed records" in hundredal

form, but "a mass of preliminary notes and drafts, made before,
during, and after the formal sittings of the Inquest.... The function of the hundred juries at the formal sessions was apparently to
approve and check the information variously assembled...."[11]  The
"original" written returns, in any formal sense, were local
Domesdays, locally compiled.  Exon Domesday provides an example of
the preliminary recension of such a circuit return, Little Domesday
an example of a final version sent to Winchester for abbreviation
into Exchequer form.  The procedure followed may have been different
in each circuit, and apart from Cambridgeshire (which appears to
have been the exception rather than the rule) there is no indication
that written returns in hundredal form existed at any stage.  The
hundredal order apparent in many Domesday counties proves only that
the formal sessions of the Inquest must have followed such an order,
but reveals nothing about the written returns.[12]  Sawyer's Evesham
text fits perfectly into Galbraith's analysis, showing precisely
how a feudal return by a tenant-in-chief could nevertheless bear
the telltale marks of hundredal order without having been derived
from an "engrossed" hundredal return.  That such corroborative evidence should have been discovered after the initial formulation of
Galbraith's hypothesis speaks both for the acumen of its author and
for the power of the hypothesis as a stimulus to further discoveries.[13]

    In the light of these developments, the Domesday Monachorum of
Christ Church, Canterbury, assumes new significance, for it too
contains the text of a document used by the Commissioners of 1086
as a source in their work of compiling the necessary information
for Domesday Book.  It is the section beginning with the words "Rex
tenet Derteford."[14]  Douglas had overlooked the peculiar relationship of this text to the Kentish Domesday, as Lennard pointed out
immediately in his book review.[15]  A complete collation of RTD with
D.B. indicates beyond reasonable doubt that RTD was an "original"
source used by the Domesday clerks.[16]  The argument leading to this
conclusion is straightforward, the evidence compelling.  First, RTD
records a state of affairs earlier than that found in D.B., as
comparisons of incumbent tenants, geld assessment figures, and
place-name forms testify.  Second, the texts of RTD and the Kentish

Domesday are virtually identical in certain critical respects.
Verbal similarities and other textual features alone would suffice
to establish a presumption that they are indeed closely related.
The respective orders of manorial entries in the two texts leave no
room for doubt:  they are identical for the most part, and even
where the Domesday order differs from RTD, it is clear that the D.B.
order was derived from RTD by adherence to a simple set of tenurial
and geographical organizing principles.

   The importance of demonstrating this relationship need hardly be
stressed.  Since the texts are so closely related, and since RTD is
older than the Kentish Domesday, it is impossible to avoid the conclusion that RTD was one of the sources from which the Domesday
Commissioners drew information.  Even more startling is the logical
extension of this discovery to the claim that, in all likelihood,
the makers of D.B. used RTD (and perhaps other similar records) as
a model in planning the structural organization of the entire
Survey.[17]  It is this possibility that I propose to examine in the
remainder of this paper.

   If RTD was not derived from D.B., what then was its origin?
Sawyer, though arguing that RTD "records an earlier state of affairs
than that found in DB," believed that it was "clearly derived from
the Domesday enquiry but from an earlier stage than DB."[18]  He thus
assumed a compilation date no earlier than 1086, and inferred that
RTD must represent one of the early steps in the Domesday officials'
procedures for collecting information.  According to this view, RTD
should be considered one form of "original return" to the Domesday
Inquest.  Hoyt suggested, on the contrary, that RTD was compiled
independently of the Domesday Inquest, even before Domesday was
contemplated.  He characterized RTD as "an administrative document,
a 'public record' on the level of local administration, whose
deficiencies may well illustrate one of the reasons for the 'deep
speech at Gloucester' at Christmastide 1085, leading to a decision
to undertake the monumental task of surveying the whole of England
in detail."[19]  Thus the issue is clearly drawn, whether RTD is to be
viewed as a written "return" submitted to the royal clerks early in
the Domesday process, or whether it indicates that the Domesday

Commissioners allowed the use of existing administrative documents
as sources of information.

The issue would be decided if the year of RTD's compilation could
be established; unfortunately the evidence falls short of the
requirements for a definitive dating. A number of complementary,
though indirect, lines of inference, nevertheless, seem to favor
Hoyt's interpretation, which is based on an early date. Domesday
records as current tenants the heirs or successors of a few RTD
tenants. It is conceivable that these changes occurred in the
course of the Domesday Inquest, and that "news" was incorporated
into the Survey,[20] but there is no independent evidence to corrobo-
rate such "coincidences."

Furthermore, the sulungation figures of RTD correspond to the
T.R.E. figures quoted in D.B. Once again one might assume that
changes were instituted in the course of the year 1086 by the
Domesday Commissioners themselves, but this appears even less likely
than the replacement of RTD tenants during the Inquest. In the
first place, the purpose of the Inquest was to record existing conditions, not to carry out a far-reaching reassessment of geld-
liability. Second, there is good reason to believe that reassess-
ments did occur shortly after the Conquest. No consistent relationship can be established between the reductions in valuation of
certain Kentish manors devastated by the Conqueror's army and the
drastic reduction of Kent's overall geld assessment after 1066,
yet it seems quite possible that the Kentish tenants-in-chief justified a demand for tax-reduction by reference to the damage
inflicted on their estates by the Norman invaders. D.B. leaves no
doubt that many Kentish manors fell sharply in value early in the
Conqueror's reign, and gradually regained their former value
through a process of rehabilitation and restocking until, by 1086,
many had appreciated beyond their T.R.E. value. An alternative (or
perhaps correlative) explanation of the drop in assessment would
relate it to William's imposition of feudal military quotas, the
servicium debitum, on the lands of his tenants-in-chief, probably
c. 1070.[21] Hollister has argued convincingly that the Old English
fyrd obligation survived into the Norman period.[22] Whereas

elsewhere the provision of one fyrd-warrior rested on the five-hide
or six-carucate unit, in Kent the obligation probably fell on two-
sulung units.[23] With the imposition of feudal tenures owing knight-
service according to the Conqueror's quota system, the land was
saddled with a double military obligation. It might well be,
therefore, that the broad reductions in sulungation recorded in
the Kentish Domesday were granted in recognition of the burdensome
nature of such a double obligation.[24] The problem of precise dating
remains intractable, however. We cannot be sure when the manorial
assessments were reduced, or even whether the whole system was
revised at a single blow. Presumably the original of RTD was compiled before the assessment reductions, whenever they took place.
If Hollister's conjecture is correct, the reductions would not
have been made earlier than the imposition of the servicia debita,
c. 1070.

Another fixed event, which might help to establish the earliest
possible date of RTD, is an exchange of land which took place
between the abbot of St. Augustine's, Canterbury, and Odo of Bayeux.
The bishop received a "park" at "Wickham" in return for a number of
small pieces of territory which included a half sulung in the manor
of Leeds mentioned in D.B.[25] In RTD, however, no trace of such an
exchange is apparent;[26] independent charter evidence for the exchange
is lacking; neither Thorne nor Thomas of Elmham, the late chroniclers
of St. Augustine's, refers to it. Thus the clue in Domesday leads
nowhere.

One other possibility remains. We are fortunate in possessing a
series of documents which record the tenants of certain Kentish
manors at various times between the Conquest and Domesday. By comparing RTD with these texts it is possible to establish a relative
chronology. First, there are several reports of the Pennenden
Heath trial, which probably took place in 1072.[27] Douglas demonstrated that of all the properties listed in the various reports
only seven can be proved to have been recovered by their ecclesiastical claimants at the Pennenden trial itself: Detling, Preston,
Stoke, Denton, Ruckinge, Brooke, and 60 shillings' worth of pasture
in the Isle of Grain.[28] Comparison of tenants leaves no doubt that

RTD was compiled after the trial on Pennenden Heath, for D.B. records the same tenants as RTD. Finally, the royal memorandum[29] analyzed by Douglas also antedated RTD. It seems to record tenurial conditions in a long list of Kentish manors still disputed after the Pennenden Heath trial. By 1086, ecclesiastical claimants had recovered many of these manors from the tenants who had been in possession when the royal memorandum was drawn up. Douglas suggested "1078 or 1079" as the date of the memorandum, but offered no evidence other than a somewhat vague impression that it was compiled "about mid-way between the Pennenden Trial and the Domesday Inquisition."[30] To summarize, therefore, RTD can be dated with confidence to the ten-year period before the Domesday Inquest, but the quest for an exact terminus post quem remains unfulfilled.

If we accept Hoyt's view of RTD as a pre-Domesday "public record," it remains to explain how it was itself compiled and under what circumstances. It records tenurial conditions at some time between c. 1075 and 1086, yet its sulungation statistics coincide with the D.B. figures for T.R.E. This suggests that RTD's source of information for assessments was a geld-list, or "geld-roll," compiled soon after the Conquest, at a time when the T.R.E. assessments had not been altered significantly. This geld-list has not survived, but RTD does not stand in isolation as the only pre-Domesday document concerning geld; there are at least three other documents to which our Kentish sulungation list bears comparison in point of date, form, and content.[31] The provenance of RTD can be understood only when it is viewed in the context of what is known about geld-administration in the mid-eleventh century.

J. H. Round, in one of the miscellaneous chapters of Feudal England, first drew attention to the early-Norman document called the "Northamptonshire geld-roll." His most important discovery was the very existence of "a levy of Danegeld hitherto unknown."[32] It was this breakthrough that led eventually to the modern view that the geld was collected frequently, perhaps even annually, during the Conqueror's reign.[33] Between 1066 and 1086, as William's fiscal officials grappled continually with the task of collecting the customary geld-levy, the inefficiency of the assessment scheme they

had inherited from their English predecessors must have become
increasingly obvious to them.[34]

The date of the Northamptonshire geld-roll has not been established definitively;[35] of more immediate concern is the form of the
document and the reason for its compilation.  Whereas RTD is a
simple statement of the assessments assigned to all Kentish manors
at some moment in time, the Northamptonshire geld-roll records the
actual results of one particular geld-collection.  It consists of a
list of 32 hundreds, assessed at a total of 2663½ hides.  For each
hundred it records (1) the total number of hides assessed; (2) the
number of hides on which geld has been paid in the current collection; and (3) the number of hides on which nothing has been paid
either because they are exempt (as parts of "the king's own farm
land," as baronial "demesne," or as special concessions to persons
in the royal service) or because they lie "waste."  This last category of exemptions struck Round, who immediately associated the vast
tracts of "waste" with the effects of Earl Morcar's devastations in
Northamptonshire in 1065, which in turn necessitated a sweeping
reassessment of the county.[36]  Hence the geld-roll was compiled to
record de facto changes in the county's capacity to pay taxes, as a
result of war damage.  In addition, the Crown had in several cases
granted arbitrary reductions in the hundredal assessments by
increasing the amount of exempt "demesne" or "inland" to an even,
decimal figure.[37]  This first reduction of assessment occurred early
in the Conqueror's reign, i.e., before the compilation of the geld-
roll.  A second sweeping reduction in assessment occurred between
the time of the geld-roll and Domesday, carried out this time by an
arbitrary reduction in the assessment of hundreds which was passed
on to the assessment of individual manors by reducing the hidation
of each by a fixed percentage.[38]  Apparently the process continued
after Domesday, for only 1192¾ hides can be accounted for in the
Pipe Roll of 1130 for Northamptonshire.[39]  Hoyt added some refine-
ments to our knowledge of the meaning of "king's farm land," when
he showed that only the non-demesne portions of selected royal
manors were included.  This confirmed his demonstration that royal
lands were not different in principle from manors held in feudal

tenure with regard to geld exemption in the Conqueror's reign, since
exemptions required special citation, while certain royal manors
were actually subject to payment of geld.[40]

Only a short flight of the imagination is required to move
from the Northamptonshire geld-roll to an analogous document for
Kent.  Just as Round traced the path of Morcar's armies through
Northamptonshire in 1065 on the basis of Domesday figures indicating
sharp fluctuations in manorial valuations, so also Baring was able
to trace the movements of the Conqueror's army in Kent in 1066 by
the same method.[41]  Both counties suffered considerable damage,
though it was far more localized in Kent.  It would not be at all
surprising if a Kentish geld-roll had been drawn up, recognizing
the exemption of newly wasted land from the current geld levy.  The
total sulungation of manors and lathes would have remained at the
T.R.E. level, but of the total a larger number of sulungs would
have appeared as exempt.  The same period (the 1070's) saw the
complications of geld-administration in Kent compounded by tenurial
disputes between the parties of Lanfranc and Odo of Bayeux.  Judicial inquests were held and the results recorded in documents like
Douglas' memorandum.[42]  In light of this combination of geld-
reassessment and litigation over rights of tenure in Kent, the
compilation of a comprehensive list of manors, tenants, and sulunga-
tions would have been a useful administrative weapon in the hands
of royal officials, serving both as a checklist for subsequent geld-
collections and as a record of tenure as of the most recent judicial
determination.  It was precisely such a document, recording the
manors, tenants, and T.R.E. assessments of Kent, that served as a
source for the later compilation of RTD.

The suggestion that an early Kentish geld-roll could have served
as the source for a document as detailed as RTD might seem tenuous
were it based merely on an analogy to the Northamptonshire list.
After all, the latter contains scarcely any information on individual manors; all its statistics are composite figures covering
entire hundreds.  Such was not the case, however, in all pre-
Domesday geld accounts.  The geld-rolls in Exon Domesday, though

conforming to the same overall pattern as the Northamptonshire
geld-roll in stating the total hidage of each hundred, the number
of hides exempt from geld as baronial demesne land (or "inland"),
and the amount of money actually received in a particular geld-
collection, are infinitely more complex in their manorial breakdown
and in the detailed information supplied about both tenure and
assessment.  The conjunction of names of manors, names of tenants,
and assessment figures in each entry of a county-wide record con-
stitutes a dramatic advance over the rather simple, traditional summary in the Northamptonshire geld-roll.  Exactly the same combination of elements marks the fundamental difference between RTD and
the Northamptonshire record.[43]

   Nor are the Exon Domesday geld-rolls and RTD the sole examples of
geld-records combining information about manors, tenants, and
assessments.  The first of Douglas' "early surveys from the abbey
of Abingdon"[44] bears a striking resemblance to the Canterbury-
Rochester section of RTD.[45]  It is a list of Abingdon manors in
Berkshire giving the hidation of each manor; the holdings are
arranged in groups by hundreds.  The format is bi-columnar, only
the names of the hundreds appearing on the left, the manors and
their assessments appearing on the right.  Aside from the hundredal
arrangement, the list looks very much like the Reg. P assessment
list.  Douglas maintained that this Abingdon list too was extracted
from D.B., and with better reason than in the case of RTD since it
is entitled:  "De hundredis et de hidis ecclesie Abbendonensis in
Berchescire sicut scriptura thesauri regis continet per hund[reta]
singula dispositis."[46]  The order of manors is identical with the
Domesday order except for the inversion of Appleford and Middleton
in Sutton Hundred.  The place-name forms are similar.  The hidation
figures correspond to the T.R.E. figures in Domesday in every case.
As was true for many manors in Kent, spectacular reductions in
assessment between T.R.E. and modo were common among Abingdon's
Berkshire estates, and no case of an increase is recorded.  Wherever
the "survey" gives a description or explanation in the form of a
full sentence, the same text can be found verbatim in D.B.:

| Abingdon "survey" | D.B. |
|---|---|
| Et Bernerus ii hidas in Boxore. Has tenuerunt Brichtwinus et Aluricus et quidam prepositus de abbatia nec potuerunt recedere. | ...Et Bernerius ii hidas in Bovsore. Has tenuerunt Bricstuinus et Alfricus et quidam prepositus de abbate nec potuerunt recedere. (fo. 58b,ii) |
| Winekefelt pro x hidis. De has terra sunt iiii hide in foresta. | ...Wenesfelle...T.R.E. se defendit pro x hidis...De hac terra sunt iii hide in foresta regis.... (fo. 59a,ii) |

Whereas Domesday records numerous sub-tenancies, the Abingdon list includes only one, a large ten-hide holding within the huge fifty-hide manor of "Waliford." There are no omissions or additions of manors; where place-names are omitted, both texts reveal the same deficiencies.

The general impression left by the "survey," therefore, is one of overwhelming similarity to the Domesday text for the Abingdon fief in Berkshire. In light of RTD's relationship to the Exchequer Domesday, it may be asked whether the Abingdon "survey" might not stem from a source which, like the original of RTD, antedated the Domesday Inquest. Douglas himself admitted that the distinction made between the scriptura thesauri regis in the title of the first "survey" and the alio libro thesauri regis in the title of the second "survey" was "hard to elucidate." He suggested, however, that the scriptura might refer to the "returns of hides taken hundred by hundred" which he believed "were stored for some time in the treasury alongside of Domesday itself."[47] Since the whole theory of hundredal returns has been radically modified, if not destroyed, by the Galbraith school, the reference of this term scriptura needs to be explained. Could it not be that the royal treasury possessed a geld-roll for Berkshire similar to RTD for Kent from which the Abingdon "survey" could have been derived, and which itself served as a source for the Berkshire Domesday account of the Abingdon fief? Furthermore, Douglas pointed out a difficulty in his own interpretation of the title to the second "survey." Although maintaining that alio libro thesauri regis must refer to D.B. itself, and describing the Abingdon "survey" as "a shortened version of the full Domesday returns,"[48] he notes that "it contains a few important variations, and in one case a complete entry which could not have been derived from the completed Domesday since it does not appear in that record."[49] Once again it must be asked what precisely was the nature of the "full Domesday returns" from which the Abingdon "survey" was allegedly derived?  Could not the second Abingdon "survey" represent a copy of a preliminary draft for the Berkshire Domesday account of the Abingdon fief, a text which was in turn based on a geld record analogous to RTD?

As for Kent, the experience of the Pennenden Heath trial and subsequent litigation led to the compilation of written records which proved the usefulness of the survey technique.  One such record took the form preserved in RTD, in which information on the tenurial status of individual manors was combined with assessment statistics, and entries in feudal form were arranged under the names of the principal landholders.[50]  This practice may have been extended to geld-records for other counties even before a survey for the whole of England was contemplated.  When the wheels of the Domesday Inquest were set in motion, administrative practice of the immediate past provided a model for the arrangement of the information collected.  Domesday Book, though incomparably more elaborate and comprehensive than any previous Anglo-Norman administrative instrument, was not the result of some diabolical plan conjured up full-blown in the mind of an efficiency expert on William's staff; it was rather the culmination of Norman administrative procedures developed over a twenty-year period in the struggle to organize post-Conquest England.[51]

The picture of the Domesday Inquest and D.B. that emerges from this analysis is considerably less heroic than it has often been portrayed.[52]  Without question Domesday represents a palpable administrative achievement; legitimate doubts can be entertained as to the ability of Harold's officialdom to carry out an assignment as formidable as the Great Inquest.  Nevertheless, it must be remembered that the Anglo-Norman administration had been at work for two decades under English conditions, and that inquest procedure was well-known to both English and Normans by 1086, having been employed frequently by the conquerors since 1066.  It is fair to say that Domesday was unique in magnitude, but certainly not in conception. It was solidly rooted in previous experience, which included both the English geld-collection system, with its series of records stretching back far beyond the Conquest, and newer judicial techniques developed in the Duchy of Normandy before the Conquest.[53] It was a combination of such English and Norman administrative precedents that suggested the idea of a survey on the scale of the entire kingdom in the first place, and offered models for the arrangement of the information. The basic structure of Domesday Book was already "traditional" by 1086.

In his undergraduate lectures on English Constitutional History, Professor Joseph R. Strayer was fond of characterizing the Anglo-Norman government of the late eleventh century as a product of the superimposition of a logical, centralizing Norman feudalism on a highly developed Anglo-Saxon tradition of local institutions, an accident of history that put England a century ahead of the Continent in political development. The Domesday Survey in its use of existing Anglo-Saxon administrative instruments to produce a monumental record of the Norman feudal structure in England stands as the most prominent symbol of the amalgam which Professor Strayer understood and described so clearly.

Chapter 2

Cluniac Administration and Administrators
in the Twelfth Century

Giles Constable

The myth of the administrative centralization of the Cluniac
order dies hard. Seventy years ago, Dom Besse in his pioneering
articles on the government of the order of Cluny, said that the
abbey and the order lived under a monarchical régime. "The abbot
of Cluny was invested with a legislative, judicial, and administrative power over his monastery and over the entire order. The order
was for him only an extension of the abbey."[1] This opinion has
been uncritically echoed and generalized by countless later writers,
until the view that the Cluniac order was highly centralized--"a
great seigneurie developing toward a monarchy," as Claude put it,
under the "quasi-sovereign jurisdiction" of the abbot[2]--has become
almost a truism for many historians.[3] Like many generalizations,
it is not without a measure of truth, but it must be interpreted
in different ways at different times in the history of the order:
in one way, for instance, at its beginnings, when the abbot exercised a high degree of personal control and when Adalbero of Laon
satirized, perhaps not entirely unjustly, the "king" Odilo leading
his Cluniac "soldiers";[4] and in a different way in the late Middle
Ages, when the abbot exercised his authority through an elaborate
administrative hierarchy.[5] It has very little truth at all, however, for the late eleventh and twelfth centuries, the period of
Cluny's greatest prestige and influence.

The lack of effective central control by Abbot Hugh has been
stressed by several recent scholars. "The predominant characteristic of the congregation during Hugh's abbacy" was "formlessness,"
wrote Noreen Hunt, commenting later that "the image of Cluny as a
highly organized, strictly centralized system is manifestly false."[6]
Cowdrey attributed this situation at least in part to Hugh's own
long life, during which the order expanded without any corresponding

administrative development. "Under Abbot Hugh the Cluniac body
became too vast and unwieldly to be ruled by a single man."[7] The
very nature of the order came into question with its rapid growth;
even contemporaries were in doubt over who was and who was not a
Cluniac, and used the term loosely. The number of houses said to
belong to the order varies from two thousand, which includes not
only every priory and cell but any house which was at any time influenced by Cluny, down to the modest number of monasteries listed in
the papal bulls.[8] In the second half of the eleventh century the
constitution became increasingly complicated both because of the
grant to Cluny of a number of abbeys which retained a degree of
jurisdictional autonomy, while still being subject to the abbot of
Cluny,[9] and because of the establishment by some of Cluny's own
greatest priories, such as La-Charité-sur-Loire and St.-Martin-des-
Champs, of their own priories over which they maintained control.[10]
Factors like these, plus the growing hostility of many bishops to
the privileges of Cluny, were responsible, according to some recent
historians, for the constitutional crisis after Hugh's death and
were the underlying factors in the resignation and attempted
restoration of Abbot Pontius and the confusion of the early years
of the abbacy of Peter the Venerable.[11]

   The continued expansion of the order during this period, especially
into regions far from Cluny itself, increased the problems of effective administration. In both his letters and his statutes Peter
complained of the impossibility of supervising all the monasteries
under his control. The anguished doubts expressed at the beginning
of Letter 161, upbraiding the priors and subpriors of Cluniac
houses for behaving like laymen, clearly show his inability to
enforce even some of the most basic rules of monastic life,[12] and
in the causa to Statute 61 he accepted that his statutes would not
all be observed, remarking in the words of Gregory the Great, "that
if I cannot bring back many sheaves from the field of the Lord, I
shall bring back at least a few, at least two, at least one."[13] A
similar picture emerges from the Dialogus duorum monachorum,
written by the monk Idungus soon after he became a Cistercian in
1154/5 (shortly before, that is, the death of Peter the Venerable),

in which the Cistercian criticized the excessive authority among the Cluniacs of custom, "since it does what it wants and omits what it wants," and contrasted the unity of his own order, controlled by the annual chapter-general, with the confusion of the Cluniacs. "Since your abbots are without a head," he said, "like acephali with no master over themselves, everyone in his own monastery does what he wants and omits what he wants. This is the reason that the religious life (religio) in your monasteries is not durable."[14]

In interpreting this passage, allowance must be made both for Idungus' own prejudices and for the relatively loose organization of Cluniac monasticism in Germany. This looseness can be accounted for not only by the distance from Cluny and the introduction of Cluniac customs at a time when the effective power of the abbot was weakening, but also by the special circumstances of monasticism in the Empire, such as its individualistic character, as proposed by Hauck, the comparatively limited development of the system of dependent cells (Molitor), the tradition of monastic independence fostered by Gorze (Hallinger), and the survival of lay--both royal and noble-- and episcopal proprietary rights, which hindered the development of effective monastic centralization (Semmler).[15] The association with Cluny of monasteries in Germany therefore tended to be based on common rules and customs and on associations by prayers rather than on jurisdictional union,[16] as it was in the older areas of Cluniac expansion.

There was no really effective administrative control from Cluny itself, however, even in France, where the system of juridically dependent priories and cells was well established and the independence of Cluny from both lay and episcopal authority was widely accepted.[17] "Up to the middle of the twelfth century," said Berlière, "the administration of the order remained of great simplicity: the abbot of Cluny was the soul of this body; everything depended on his direct action."[18] Peter's complaints must be understood in this light, since the responsibility for directing not only Cluny itself but also the entire order rested on his shoulders, and the task was manifestly too big for one man. He grappled with the problems of administration all his life, therefore, though not

perhaps as consciously and clearly as he did with those of Cluniac
finance, and the purpose of this paper is to look at some of the
techniques he used.  The traditional method of visitation was out
of the question as a means of regular inspection and control.
Though Peter travelled extensively in France, went to Italy several
times, Spain at least once and perhaps three times, England twice,
and Germany once,[19] he cannot have visited, even once, more than
a fraction of all the monasteries nominally under his control.
Effective administration by written documents was also very difficult, though he kept up a large correspondence, much of it concerned
with the affairs of the order.  Business followed him even when he
was on a retreat in the woods near Cluny, according to his companion
Gilbert, who complained, "In addition to the great crowd which
gathers in throngs from the country around in order to gain respite
from legal proceedings, or settlements, or judicial actions, so many
messengers come to us both from across the sea to the East and from
across the Alps [Pyrenees] to the West that the greatest court of a
mighty king could hardly reply."[20]

   In addition to these customary administrative techniques, the
beginnings of several new ones appeared during Peter's abbacy.  The
most important of these was the chapter-general, which met at least
four times, first in 1132, when two hundred priors, according to
Ordericus Vitalis, met at Cluny to discuss Peter's proposed reforms,[21]
and again in 1140, 1144, and 1150, though nothing is known about
these meetings except that a spiritual association between the
Cluniacs and the Premonstratensians was arranged "at Cluny when the
chapter-general was sitting" in 1140.[22]  At the beginning of the
thirteenth century, under Abbot Hugh V, the chapter-general became
a regular part of Cluniac organization, together with the council
of elders, for which there is also some evidence under Peter the
Venerable, and the definatores.[23]  Peter was also the first abbot
to gather his statutes into a body of generalized abbatial legislation, approved by the chapter-general, applying for the most part
to the entire order.  His predecessors had of course issued statutes,
but most of these had been incorporated into the Cluniac customaries.

The break between the age of custom and the age of statute at Cluny came at the end of the eleventh century, and in the twelfth abbatial legislation increasingly replaced the customaries as the basic law of the order.[24]  Although there is no sign of any provincial organi- zation under Peter the Venerable, there seems to have been some uncon- scious movement toward administrative decentralization by making greater use of the superiors of major priories, with dependencies of their own, like La Charité and St.-Martin-des-Champs.[25]

The most effective means by which the abbot of Cluny could exercise his authority in the twelfth century, however, and that with which this paper is principally concerned, was through his control over the personnel of the order.  Since all the monks in Cluniac houses were blessed by him,[26] exactly like the monks at Cluny itself, they could be used in various capacities and moved from house to house without any theoretical breach of stability.  Even under Abbot Hugh, said Noreen Hunt, "The fact that by virtue of profession at Cluny all monks were considered to be members of the community of Cluny led to a considerable movement of monks, especially talented men qualified to hold office,"[27] and she remarked on the number of monks from both Cluniac and independent houses who came to Cluny to learn the ordo and of priors at Cluny who went out as heads of dependent houses. "This was all contrary to the desires of Hugh," she said, who "tried to resist the tendency."[28]  It apparently became an accepted practice under Peter the Venerable, however, who referred as a matter of course in his Statute 46 to the transfer of priors from one priory to another, and it contributed to the tendency at Cluny, remarked upon by De Valous, for a prior "to become a functionary of the abbot, responsible to him alone and consequently seeking to please him alone, even at the cost of his priory."[29]  Combined with the practice of appointing men, especially those of noble birth, to high office at an early age, which according to Morey and Brooke was an "established tradition in an exceptional degree" at Cluny,[30] this system provided the order with a body of trained administrators whose principal loyalty was to Cluny and its abbot rather than to a local house.

Peter the Venerable himself is a good example.  Born at Montboissier in the Auvergne in 1092/4, he spent his youth at the nearby Cluniac

priory of Sauxillanges and received his monastic benediction from
Abbot Hugh shortly before his death in 1109.  Soon after Peter was
at Cluny, where he met Hugh of Amiens, the future archbishop of Rouen,
and from about 1115/6 to 1120 he was seniorum doctor and subprior
(custos ordinis) at Vézelay.  He then became prior of Domène, near
Grenoble, until 1122, and was elected abbot of Cluny when he was not
over thirty years of age.[31]  The careers of two of Peter's brothers
show the same pattern.  Pontius, who spent some years of his youth
with Peter either at Sauxillanges, Cluny, or Vézelay, was a monk at
La Chiusa in northern Italy, an independent abbey which had been
founded by his great-grandfather in the tenth century, and became
abbot of Vézelay in 1138.[32]  Armannus, after serving perhaps as prior
of Sauxillanges and as sacristan (1144) and then prior (1149/52) of
Cluny, became abbot of Manglieu, near his home in the Auvergne.[33]

Similar careers can be traced in the recently published volume on
the heads of religious houses in England and Wales from 940 to 1216.[34]
A monk of Bromholm named Osbert became almoner of Much Wenlock and
then prior of Daventry.[35]  Adam, a monk at Monk Bretton, was successively prior of Pontefract and of Monk Bretton.[36]  A monk of La
Charité named Josbert or Joybert was said by Roger of Wendover to
have served as prior of Daventry (before 1198), Much Wenlock (by
1198), Coventry (1198-1216), and Bermondsey (?1210-?1216), the last
three apparently at the same time.  Such a combination of offices
seems unlikely, but the authors of the volume point out that "The
three Cluniac houses [Daventry, Much Wenlock, and Bermondsey] were
all dependent on La Charité--her only daughter houses, apart from
Northampton, still acknowledging any relationship at this date.  It
is therefore intelligible that he should have oversight of this
group of houses."[37]

On the continent it was common for rising young Cluniacs, like
Peter the Venerable and his brothers, to spend some time at Cluny
itself.  The cursus honorum of Abbot Peter II of St. Martial at
Limoges (a Cluniac abbey) included stages as a monk and chevecier at
St. Martial, prior of Cluny, prior of St. Eutropius at Saintes, and
provost of St. Vaury.[38]  Abbot William of Moissac was prior of Cluny
before his abbacy and returned there, both as chamberlain and as

prior, afterward.  He may also have been the G. adjutor Cluniacensis
ordinis whom Peter sent to transact some business with Abbot Suger of
St. Denis in 1147/9.[39]  Gerald Vert, or Le Vert, to whom Peter devoted
an entire chapter of the De miraculis and to whose recent death he
referred in Letter 58, written in 1133, made himself useful, Peter
said, "in the administration of many priories and subjects and was
esteemed by all who knew him.... I tested his constancy in this
virtue that, when I often imposed on him grave burdens which I would
hardly have dared impose on others, he received them with eagerness
and carried them out with greater eagerness."  He is known to have
been procurator of Marcigny under Geoffrey of Semur-en-Brionnais (who
was prior there from about 1110 to 1123), spent a period at the
Cluniac cell of Beaumont in the diocese of Chalon-sur-Saône, been
prior of St. Stephen at Nevers, gone on a mission to Rome in 1130,
when he was captured and imprisoned by Conrad of Hohenstaufen, and
finally retired to a hermitage on a high mountain near Cluny.  He
may also have been the "Gerald of pious memory chamberlain of Cluny"
who is recorded in the necrology of Marcigny.[40]

Gerald was clearly a man who performed well in a variety of positions and duties, but not all appointments were so successful.  Odo
of St.-Martin-des-Champs, for instance, who appeared as both sacristan
and subprior at St. Martin between 1133 and 1140/1, was apparently a
failure both as abbot of the independent abbey of Marchiennes, where
he lasted less than two years, and subsequently as prior of St. Martin,
since he was deposed by Peter the Venerable in 1150.[41]  A more spectacular failure, both in and out of the Cluniac order, was Henry of
St.-Jean-d'Angély, whose extraordinary career is described in the
Anglo-Saxon Chronicle and has recently been skilfully unravelled by
Cecily Clark.  Of a noble Burgundian family, and related to both the
king of England and the count of Poitou, Henry was bishop of Soissons
from 1087 to 1092.  He then became successively, according to the
Chronicle, monk and prior of Cluny and prior of Souvigny, though his
priorate at Souvigny in fact probably preceded that at Cluny.  In
1104, owing to the influence of the count of Poitou, he became abbot
of the important Cluniac abbey of St.-Jean-d'Angély.

Then, through his great trickery, he obtained the archbishopric

of Besançon and kept it for three days; and then most justly he
forfeited it, since he had previously obtained it unjustly.
Then he obtained the bishopric of Saintes, which was five miles
from his abbey; this he kept for nearly a week; then the abbot
of Cluny removed him from there, just as he had previously done
from Besançon.

In 1123 he was said to have served as papal legate in England, and in
1127 he was made abbot of Peterborough by his kinsman King Henry I.
Five years later, however, in 1132, he was deposed and returned to
St.-Jean-d'Angély, which he had continued to hold as abbot until 1131,
when he was replaced; he died soon afterward.[42]  In this case the
system of shifting positions was obviously exploited by a plausible
and well-connected rascal, but it involves all the elements--noble
birth, high rank at an early age, rapid movement and promotion, a
stint at Cluny itself--that characterized more orthodox Cluniac
careers.

The reputation of Cluniacs as experienced administrators--as well
as the high spiritual prestige of Cluny--was doubtless one of the
reasons why they were in demand as heads of independent houses.  Many
examples can again be found for England and Wales in The Heads of
Religious Houses, where the authors, commenting on the relatively
short terms of office of Cluniac priors, said:

> In some cases, this was because the abbot of Cluny, or some
> mediate superior, replaced the priors from time to time; it was
> also because the leading Cluniac houses, Bermondsey and Lewes
> in particular, were favourite recruiting grounds from which
> abbots were taken to Reading, Faversham, Evesham, Glastonbury,
> and even further afield.[43]

A total of nineteen Cluniacs became superiors in the twelfth century
of Abingdon, Canterbury, Coventry, Evesham, Faversham, Glastonbury,
Gloucester, Malmesbury, Peterborough (the notorious Henry of St.-
Jean-d'Angély!), Ramsey, St. Benet of Hulme, Selby, Sherborne,
Winchecombe, and both the cathedral and New Minster (Hyde) at
Winchester.  Reading shared with Ramsey, among English abbeys, the
honor of supplying an abbot to Cluny itself.[44]  Seven of these nineteen are known to have been monks at Cluny, but all except Peter of
Malmesbury, who came directly from St. Urban near Joinville,[45] had
served in one or more Cluniac houses in England before moving to
independent abbeys there.

A similar situation existed on the continent, though it is more
difficult to document systematically.  Prior Gelduin of Lurcy-le-
Bourg was chosen abbot of Our Lady of Jehosaphat on a visit to the
Holy Land in 1120, probably as a result of his relationship to the
king of Jerusalem, and was later instrumental in securing for Cluny
some relics of St. Stephen the Protomartyr.[46]  The writer Peter of
Celle was a monk and perhaps subprior of St.-Martin-des-Champs before
he became abbot first of Montier-la-Celle and then of St. Remi at
Rheims and, at the very end of his life, bishop of Chartres.[47]  Gerald
of Duras was a monk at Cluny and prior of Bertrée in the Hesbaye (to
an important family of which region he belonged) before being chosen
abbot of St. Trond in 1145.  After ten years, however, he retired
to St. Peter at Ghent but then became prior of Bertrée for a second
time and finally returned to St. Trond, where he died in 1174.[48]
Prior Basil of La Chartreuse (1151-1173/4) was a former monk at
Cluny and a loyal friend to his _alma mater_ and its abbot,[49] as was
Abbot Rainald of Breme, on whose behalf Peter the Venerable wrote
to the pope in 1152, "I received him as a boy, I reared him [and]
have now for many years tested his good behavior both at Cluny and
outside."[50]  Prior Theobald of Cluny became abbot of Molesme in 1166,[51]
and so on.

   From the point of view of Cluniac administration, these appointments outside the order represented a loss, but indirectly they were
a gain because they placed friends in influential positions and provided a pool for future appointments within the order, as the examples
of William of Ramsey and Hugh of Reading show.  More often, indeed,
the shoe was on the other foot, and the monks of the independent
house feared that a Cluniac superior would introduce Cluniac customs.
This must have been the case at Fleury, for instance, when Cardinal
Alberic of Ostia, himself a former Cluniac, appointed as abbot his
nephew Macharius, who had been prior of the Cluniac house of
Longpont before becoming abbot of Morigny in succession to Thomas,
who was forced to resign in 1140 and retired to St.-Martin-des-
Champs.  In a frantic letter to Bernard of Clairvaux ex-Abbot
Thomas objected not only to Alberic's appointment at Morigny of
another nephew, Lancelinus, but also to Alberic's "unheard-of

agreement" at Fleury that Macharius "should not introduce the order
of Cluny there nor send any of the monks to any place subject to
Cluny."[52]

No less important to Cluny than its monks who became superiors of
independent houses were those who took positions as cardinals, archbishops, and bishops in the secular church.  There were six known
Cluniac cardinals during the abbacy of Peter the Venerable, of whom
three require special mention here:  Matthew of Albano (1127-1135),
former prior of St.-Martin-des-Champs and Peter's right-hand man in
the troubles with ex-Abbot Pontius; Alberic of Ostia (1138-1147),
former abbot of Vézelay; and Imar of Tusculum (1142-1161/2), who is
said in the Chronicle of Cluny to have been a monk at St.-Martin-
des-Champs, subprior of Cluny, prior of La Charité, and abbot of
Montierneuf at Poitiers and may also, according to other sources,
have been prior of Crépy.[53]  Among the many Cluniac archbishops and
bishops may be cited Rainald of Lyons (1129-1131), former abbot of
Vézelay, and his successor Peter (1131-1139), who had been a monk at
Cluny, and Theobald of Paris (1144-1158), former prior of St.-Martin-
des-Champs.[54]  Three of the most important bishops in the Anglo-Norman
kingdom were also Cluniacs:  Henry of Winchester (1129-1171), the
brother of King Stephen, whose mother Adela was a nun at Marcigny
and who was raised at Cluny and may have been prior of Montacute
before he became abbot of Glastonbury and bishop of Winchester;[55]
Hugh of Rouen (1130-1164), who was a friend of Peter the Venerable
at Cluny before 1115 and successively prior of St. Martial, prior of
Lewes, and abbot of Reading;[56] and Gilbert Foliot of Hereford (1148-
1163) and London (1163-1187), who was a monk at Cluny and prior both
there and at Abbeville in the 1130's, when he accompanied Peter the
Venerable to Rome and heard the case between Stephen and Mathilda
discussed, and who became abbot of Gloucester in 1139.[57]  It might
be thought that after their elevations these great prelates would
have had little time to spare for Cluny, but such was not the case,
and Henry and Hugh in particular are noted for their loyalty to
Cluny.  Writing to Henry at Cluny in 1157/8, indeed, John of Salisbury,
in the name of Archbishop Theobald, urged him to return to England:
      You surely do not doubt that you are far more strongly bound to

the churches of Winchester and Glastonbury than to that of Cluny.
Indeed, you were given your release by the Cluniacs when you
undertook the rule of those two churches. Why then did you
leave them for Cluny? Is it just that when they are hungry,
Cluny should feed on their bread? This is the complaint, not
merely of our lord the king, but of almost everyone.[58]

Since the essence of this system was the selection and promotion of
loyal and able administrators, something should also be said here
about the process of recruitment, especially of likely candidates from
outside the order. The efforts of Peter the Venerable, in particular,
to attract to Cluny men of experience and proven ability have been
remarked upon unfavorably by historians, one of whom described him
as "an unashamed tuft-hunter, pleading with the great to remember
their souls' health and to end their days at Cluny."[59]  It is true
that many great men retired to Cluny, often with Peter's encouragement.  Especially in four letters to the archbishops of Narbonne and
Bordeaux and the bishops of Winchester and Amiens, apparently written
in 1143, Peter reminded them of Cluny, asked their help, and in at
least one frankly suggested that Cluny would be a suitable place for
retirement, "since it has received many men not only of lower order
but also of yours, who have humbled themselves for Christ."[60]  Stephen
of Baugé retired to Cluny after thirty-six years as bishop of Autun
in 1138/9; Guarinus of Amiens in 1144, perhaps as a result of Peter's
letter, mentioned above, of the previous year; and Peter's old friend
Hato of Troyes in 1145/6.[61]  These three were indeed probably too old
to take any active part in the affairs of Cluny after they became
monks there; but at least two of them are known as bishops who were
generous benefactors of Cluny, and Peter may well have continued to
consult them after their retirement.

In other cases, however, more active service was clearly expected.
Robert de Sigillo, for example, who acted as chancellor for Henry I
from 1133-1135 and whom, after he became a monk, Peter tried in
Letter 77 to attract to Cluny from Reading, was in the prime of life
and later served as bishop of London (1141-1150).[62]  On this occasion
Peter failed, but he was more successful with Louis VII's chancellor
Abbot Natalis of Rebais, who resigned his abbey and came to Cluny
in 1141/2 and was almost immediately sent on a mission to Pope

Innocent II.[63] Even Abelard made himself useful writing and teaching after he became a Cluniac,[64] and Guichard III of Beaujeu, according to Walter Map, not only returned briefly to secular life in order to recover the lands lost by his son but also wrote verses and a sermon in French.[65] Countless other members of the Burgundian nobility who became monks at Cluny after careers in the world also put their experience and connections at the service of the abbey.

A good example of an able administrator recruited by Peter is Durand of Selby, who was a monk of St. Mary at York before he became abbot of Selby in about 1125 and of whom there is a remarkable character sketch in the late twelfth century History of Selby:

> This Durand was very prudent in external affairs but much more negligent than he should have been in internal affairs, with regard to both himself and others. He was endowed with many talents: sufficiently learned in the liberal arts, well trained in the wisdom of the courts, skilled in eloquence, sharp in character, generous in handing out, handsome in appearance, noble in expenditure, outstanding in nobility; but a corrupting fault brought a ferment of deviance to his great stock of virtues, that is, his excessive familiarity with suspect women.

After many warnings, and consultation with Archbishop Thurstan of York, Durand was forced to resign in 1134/5 and went, according to the History, to Cluny, "where he began to behave honestly under the profession of religion and the order, wherefore he later obtained by grant of the abbot of Cluny a noble and excellent priory in England."[66] He crops up again--almost certainly the same Durand-- in two letters of Peter the Venerable to Henry of Winchester, one recommending "brother Durand and all his affairs, whom we are sending to England at present because we hear that he has found grace in your eyes,"[67] and the other asking again that Henry grant "those things for which I asked through brother Durand, that you should choose for your body a place in that place [Cluny] to which you have devoted your spirit more devoutly than to others."[68] He appeared as sacristan of Cluny in 1144-1145[69] and soon after became prior of Montacute, "the noble and excellent priory in England" mentioned in the History of Selby.[70]

The case of Durand shows the risks as well as the advantages of Peter the Venerable's practice and underlines that it was motivated

not by concern for the prestige of Cluny, let alone by snobbery, but
by the need for able administrators.  Durand, as a notorious philan-
derer, was obviously a risk, and by using him for a delicate diplomatic mission so soon after his deposition as abbot of Selby Peter
put his own reputation as a judge of men on the line.  It seems to
have been correct this time, since Durand went on to an honorable
and responsible career in Cluniac service.  Peter was not unaware of
other risks in the system, however, and in Statute 46, where he
accepted in principle the movement of priors from one house to
another, he forbade them to take along any servant, giving as his
reason that the movement of servants from place to place had given
rise to "the evil suspicion, and even the certainty, of unmention-
able things."[71]  More seriously, the movement of priors, as Egger
and De Valous emphasized, though theoretically permissible because
they were all Cluniac monks, in practice was at odds with the principle of stability and the individuality of monasteries.[72]  It implied
a network of faceless bureaucrats performing their tasks efficiently
but having no real knowledge of or responsibility to the communities
they controlled.  It was therefore abolished at the beginning of the
thirteenth century by Abbot Hugh V:  "Wishing to avoid the damage
arising from the frequent change of priors, we decree that conventual
priors ... should not be replaced, and this by judgment of the
definatores in the chapter-general, unless there is some manifest
cause for which the abbot is compelled to remove him."[73]

By this time the new administrative system of the chapter-general
and definatores, referred to by Hugh, was functioning, and the days
of direct, personal control by the abbot of Cluny over the entire
order had vanished in all but theory.  Legally, as Besse said, he
remained as powerful as ever, the sole center of legislative, judicial, and administrative power, but in practice he was hedged in by
new bodies and officials who watched over and controlled his authority.  Not only in everyday affairs but also in long-range administration his hands were increasingly tied, as by the agreement made
by Abbot Hugh V with the earl of Warenne in 1201 that the prior of
Lewes would be chosen by the earl's representatives out of two candidates nominated by the abbot of Cluny "with the council of his

abbey."[74]

   In the administration of Cluny, therefore, as of other ecclesiastical and secular institutions, the twelfth century was an age of transition and experiment.[75] The policy of Peter the Venerable himself
looked partly backward, with his extensive travels and correspondence;
partly forward, with his collection of statutes, the first meetings
of the chapter-general, and the increasing role of the council of
monks; and partly toward his own time, with his active recruitment
of able administrators and personal control over his agents and
appointees.[76] While Cluny was moving spiritually into the rearguard
of monasticism, therefore, together with other old Benedictine houses,
organizationally and administratively it moved with the times, and in
some respects still ahead of them, showing the way to other institutions.[77]

Chapter 3

The Friars and the Delineation of State Boundaries
in the Thirteenth Century

John B. Freed

During the course of the thirteenth century, as Professor Strayer
has shown,[1] medieval lawyers advanced the theory that the authority
of the dominant government in any territory extended without diminu-
tion to a definite frontier.  The formulation of this theory of
limited sovereignty within fixed boundaries was a crucial step in
the evolution of the modern state.  In the early middle ages a _regnum_
had been composed of those peoples who recognized, wherever they happened to live, a specific dynasty as their royal family.  The lawyers'
theory helped to establish the political community in a distinct territorial space.  While the new English and French states coincided
with older _regna_, the German and Italian principalities were fragments
of larger cultural and linguistic units.  But it would have been virtually impossible in 1300, as Professor Strayer has also indicated,[2]
to delineate with precision the boundaries of any European state.
The nascent state consisted of a core region, where the ruler's
authority was readily acknowledged, and fringe areas, such as Wales
or Flanders, whose connection with the nucleus was uncertain.  It
required centuries of warfare to draw the present-day map of Europe.

The Dominicans' and Franciscans' role in helping to define the
boundaries of the new European states should not be overlooked.  The
friars' mission of popular preaching made them peculiarly sensitive
to the linguistic and ethnic composition of the continent.  At the
same time thirteenth-century rulers were increasingly aware of the
significance which could be attached to the provincial assignments
of the mendicant convents in laying claim to disputed border areas,
and they exerted considerable pressure on the friars to adjust their
provincial frontiers to correspond to the princes' political ambitions.
The provinces of the mendicant orders thus corresponded in varying
degrees to the basic political and cultural entities in thirteenth-

century Europe, i.e., to Professor Strayer's core regions.  This
article will examine the friars' role in delineating the French-
German, German-Polish, and Austrian boundaries.  Although the evidence
in each instance is extremely fragmentary, at times merely tantalizing
tidbits, the changes in the provincial assignments of the individual
houses become comprehensible when it is realized that these altera-
tions were part of an over-all European pattern of boundary revision.

  After 1250 much of the Carolingian Middle Kingdom, though nominally
part of the Empire, fell into the French sphere of interest; and
French royal officials were claiming that the Rhine, rather than the
Scheldt and Meuse, was the natural eastern frontier of France.[3]  The
boundaries between the German and French mendicant provinces in the
fourteenth century reflected this political reality.  The Dominicans,
according to the provincial lists drawn up by the inquisitor Bernard
Gui in 1301,[4] had assigned the priories in Flanders, Hainault, the
principality of Liège, and Lorraine to the province of France, and
the convents in Brabant, Luxembourg, and Alsace to Teutonia.  The
Franciscan provinces of Cologne and Strasbourg had similar western
borders in the fourteenth century.[5]

  These were not, however, the original boundaries between the German
and French provinces.  The Dominican houses in Ghent and Bruges,
although located in French Flanders, were assigned after their foundation in 1228 and 1234 to the province of Teutonia.  After his long
captivity in the Louvre, Ferrand of Portugal (d. 1233), the husband
of Countess Joan of Flanders (1206-1244), apparently wished to lessen
French influence in the county by placing the new priories under
German control.  In 1259 Joan's sister and successor, Countess Margaret
(1244-1280), annoyed by the German Dominicans' previous support of her
enemy, William of Holland, and dependent upon French assistance against
her son, John of Avesnes, procured the transfer of the two houses to
the French province.[6]  The Dominican convent in Liège seems also to
have belonged at first to Teutonia.  John, the bishop-elect of Liège
(1229-1238) and an imperial vassal, asked the German provincial prior,
Conrad of Höxter, in 1229 to establish a priory in his episcopal
see.[7]  There is no indication when and under what circumstances Liège
was placed under French supervision.  The Franciscan friaries in

Flanders and the principality of Liège apparently always belonged to the French province.  John of Piancarpino, the minister of the undivided Franciscan province of Germany, on the other hand, received the convent in Metz and initiated Franciscan activity in Lorraine sometime between 1228 and 1230.[8]  Again, there is no evidence when the Franciscan houses in Lorraine were transferred to France.  The Dominican priories in Metz, Verdun, and Toul, which belonged to the metropolitan province of Trier, were affiliated from their foundation with the French province.[9]  Thus by the fourteenth century the French mendicant provinces included most of the fringe areas claimed, though not necessarily yet gained, by the Capetians.

While imperial influence was declining in the Low Countries and in Lorraine, German colonists were pushing steadily eastward into Slavic territory.  In the thirteenth century, the high point in the medieval Drang nach Osten, Germans settled in eastern Mecklenburg, Pomerania, Brandenburg, Lusatia, Silesia, and the Neumark, and conquered Prussia and the Baltic States.[10]  The German Dominicans accompanied the settlers in their occupation of the sparsely populated territory between the Elbe-Saale and the Oder-Neisse, roughly present-day East Germany. By 1250 the province of Teutonia had received priories in Neuruppin, Leipzig, and Freiberg.[11]  The Slavic friars, in the meantime, had established a Polish-Bohemian province in eastern Europe, which by 1228 included convents in Cracow, Prague, Sandomierz, Breslau, and Cammin.[12]  The delineation of the boundary between the German and Polish provinces became in the second half of the century a major source of conflict between the Germans and the Poles.

Margrave John I of Brandenburg (1220-1266) triggered the dispute over provincial boundaries in eastern Europe when he asked the Dominican general chapter and the province of Teutonia in the early 1260's to establish a convent in Prenzlau in the Uckermark, the territory to the west of the Oder sandwiched between Hither Pomerania and Brandenburg (see Map One).[13]  The Uckermark was itself a disputed territory.  It had originally belonged to Pomerania, whose rulers had accepted Polish suzerainty at the beginning of the twelfth century. In 1231 Frederick II had enfeoffed Margraves John I and his brother Otto III (1220-1267) with Pomerania, and Duke Warcislaw III of

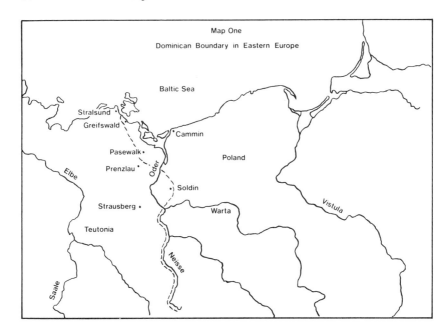

Pomerania-Demmin (1220-1264) had formally recognized the margraves
in 1236 as his feudal lords.  Duke Barnim I of Pomerania-Stettin
(1220-1278) had finally ceded the Uckermark to the margraves in
March 1250.[14]  John's request thus raised once more, in an altered
form, the thorny question whether the Uckermark was in fact German
or Polish territory.  The proposed priory was situated, moreover,
near the poorly defined boundary between the two Dominican provinces.
The house in Strausberg, south of Prenzlau in eastern Brandenburg,
had been received in 1254 by Teutonia; the convent in Greifswald,
northwest of Prenzlau in Hither Pomerania, had been assigned in the
same year to Poland.[15]  The provincial affiliation of the new house
was far from clear.

The Polish Dominicans in Cammin accordingly claimed the proposed
foundation for their own province.  Margrave John insisted in a
letter written to the Dominican general chapter that he would accept
only a house assigned to the province of Teutonia:

> We want you to know that we are neither willing nor able to sup-
> port them (the Polish Dominicans) within that territory if, God
> forbid, you do not grant us a house which belongs to the prov-
> ince of Teutonia.  The Polish princes might otherwise use this

provincial assignment as a pretext to challenge our descendants'
right to this land which we possess by full right from the
Empire.[16]

The provincial assignment of a mendicant convent had become the poten-

tial basis for a territorial or feudal claim to a disputed border

region.

In his reply to the margrave's request, the Dominican master general,

John of Vercelli (1264-1283), promised to send some friars as quickly

as possible to the mark and expressed the pious wish that the Polish

and German Dominicans could compete with one another in the service

of God under the protection of a devout prince.[17]  But relations be-

tween the German and Polish friars steadily worsened.  In 1267, for

instance, the general chapter punished the priors of the two neigh-

boring convents in Hither Pomerania, Stralsund in Teutonia and

Greifswald in Poland, for quarreling violently over the quest for

alms.[18]  A decade passed before a priory was actually founded in

Prenzlau in what appears to have been a compromise solution of the

imbroglio.  A Dominican convent was apparently established in 1272

by Margrave John II (1266-1281), the son of John I, in Pasewalk,

another town in the Uckermark, and assigned to Poland.[19]  In exchange

the province of Teutonia was allowed to receive in 1275 the convent

in Prenzlau[20] and an additional house in Soldin in the Neumark, the

territory north of the Warta and east of the Oder, which had been

acquired by the Ascanians in 1252/53.[21]  Neither the Germans nor the

Poles could use the provincial affiliations of the Dominican priories

in the Uckermark as the basis for a territorial claim.

As a result of this compromise, the boundary between the Dominican

provinces of Teutonia and Poland was somewhat erratic.  The province

of Poland possessed two houses west of the lower Oder, Greifswald

and Pasewalk, and the province of Teutonia had one priory east of

the Oder, Soldin.  Farther south the Neisse formed the border between

the two provinces.  The Dominican houses in Farther Pomerania, Prussia,

and Silesia, as well as Greifswald and Pasewalk, thus belonged to

Poland.  It is highly questionable whether this boundary corresponded

with the ethnic composition of the Pomeranian, Prussian, and Silesian

towns in the second half of the thirteenth century.  The Dominican

general chapter accordingly considered between 1279 and 1282 a number
of resolutions to transfer Greifswald, Pasewalk, and Cammin to Germany,
and Soldin to Poland.[22]  None of these proposals obtained the mandatory
three consecutive approbations by the general chapter, and the Oder-
Neisse continued to be, except for the convents in Greifswald,
Pasewalk, and Soldin, the frontier between the German and Polish
Dominican provinces.

The Ascanians' territorial ambitions apparently precipitated in the
1260's a similar controversy over provincial boundaries within the
Franciscan Order (see Map Two).  John of Piancarpino, the minister of
Saxony in the 1230's, had sent the first Franciscans to eastern
Europe,[23] where a separate Bohemian-Polish province had been organized
in 1239.[24]  The Oder-Neisse seems to have been for most of its length
the original border between the Saxon and Bohemian provinces.[25]  In
1262 Margrave Otto III of Brandenburg, John I's brother, was permanently enfeoffed with Upper Lusatia, which King Wenceslaus I of Bohemia
(1230-1253) had previously mortgaged to him.[26]  The next year the Pisa
general chapter, presumably at Otto's request, transferred the custody
of Goldberg, which included the convents in Upper Lusatia and Lower
Silesia (Bautzen, Crossen, Görlitz, Goldberg, Lauban, Liegnitz, Löbau,
Löwenberg, Sagan, Sorau, and Zittau),[27] from the province of Bohemia
to Saxony and also placed the custody of Moravia under the jurisdiction of the Austrian province.  At its next meeting in Paris in 1266,
the general chapter revoked these decisions.  After considerable
internal dissension among the Polish, German, and Czech friars who
composed the Bohemian province, the Assisi general chapter in 1269
once more assigned Goldberg to Saxony.  In 1272 the custody of Breslau,
which embraced most of the remaining Silesian houses (Breslau, Brieg,
Münsterberg, Namslau, Neisse, Neumarkt, Schweidnitz, and Strehlen),[28]
was likewise added to the German province.[29]  Saxony also annexed
sometime between 1258 and 1284 the custody of Prussia (Braunsberg,
Culm, Neuenburg, and Thorn).[30]  By the early 1280's at the latest,
therefore, the Franciscan convents in Pomerania, Prussia, Lusatia,
and most of Silesia were under German control.  The new eastern
boundary of the Franciscan province of Saxony bore a striking resemblance to the pre-World War I German frontier.

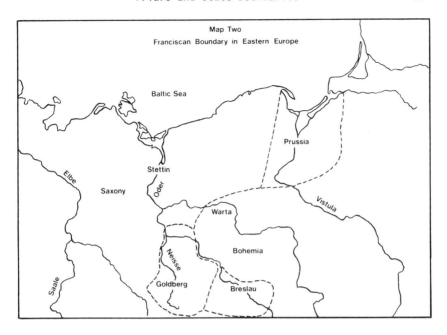

Map Two
Franciscan Boundary in Eastern Europe

The Bohemian court was bitterly opposed to these boundary revisions.
Sometime between 1268 and 1278 Queen Kunigunde of Bohemia rebuked
Abbess Agnes of Trebnitz, the daughter of Duke Henry II of Silesia
and Anna of Bohemia, for favoring the German rather than the Polish
and Czech friars, whom she and her husband Ottokar II were supporting,
and complained to an unnamed cardinal that the German Franciscans had
prohibited the Polish brothers from conducting divine services, had
expelled them from their convents, and had prevented the Czech and
Polish friars from electing their own officials.[31]  It is not difficult to find an explanation for this Bohemian displeasure.  King
Ottokar II (1253-1278), who exerted considerable influence among his
perpetually squabbling cousins, the Silesian Piasts,[32] was attempting
to create a central European state under Bohemian control and independent of the Reich.  He utilized the political chaos during the
Interregnum to unite a number of disparate territories which foreshadowed the later Danubian Monarchy:  his hereditary domains of
Bohemia and Moravia, the duchies of Austria, Styria, and Carinthia,
and the margraviate of Carniola.[33]  The transfer of the Lusatian and
Silesian convents, which were located in fringe areas of the envisioned

Premyslid state, as well as the attempt in the 1260's to reassign the
Moravian custody to Austria, were thus directly opposed to Ottokar's
own state-building activities.

The friars had been forced to choose between the rival ambitions of
the Ascanians, Piasts, and Premyslids in drawing their provincial
boundaries in eastern Europe. In the process the Franciscans and
Dominicans devised different borders for their provinces, which coincided to a striking degree with those of the German state which was
only destined to be formed after the passage of another six centuries--
the frontiers of 1871 and 1945. In the interim it was the eastern
frontiers of Germany's constituent principalities, most notably
Brandenburg and Austria, which separated the German and Slavic
worlds.[34]

The Franciscans helped not only to define the borders of Austria,
but also to develop the concept of an Austrian state in southeastern
Germany.[35] The Latin word Austria, which was first used around
1140,[36] originally referred only to the Bavarian march, which the
Emperor Frederick I elevated in 1156 to the status of a duchy.
Barbarossa's Privilegium minus, which specified the rights of his
Babenberg relatives in the new duchy, can with hindsight be called
the foundation charter of the Austrian state.[37] During the next two
centuries the Babenbergs and their successors the Habsburgs added to
this core area several contiguous territories: Styria (1192),
Carniola (1232, 1282, definitively 1335), Carinthia (1335), and the
Tirol (1363/64). There was a growing awareness in the thirteenth
century that these Alpine lands formed a single political unit.
Duke Frederick the Quarrelsome (1230-1246), the last male Babenberg,
tried, for example, during the papal-Hohenstaufen conflict in the
1240's to obtain from Pope Innocent IV a separate ecclesiastical
hierarchy for his domains and to procure from the Emperor Frederick
II the elevation of Austria and Styria to the rank of a kingdom with
Carniola as a dependent principality.[38] After the extinction of the
Babenberg dynasty, the Hohenstaufen, Premyslids, Árpáds, and Habsburgs
fought for the possession of the vacant fiefs. In the fourteenth century the phrase dominium Austriae was used on occasion to refer col-
lectively to the various territories the Habsburgs had amassed.[39]

The Franciscans had in fact already started in the thirteenth century to apply the name Austria to this complex of Alpine and Danubian
lands.  The province of Austria, which is mentioned for the first time
in a document in 1235,[40] eventually consisted of twenty-five friaries
located in Austria, Carinthia, Carniola, Styria, and the Tirol.[41]  The
friars and their ecclesiastical superiors were at first extremely
conscious that Austria was only the name of a single duchy.  In 1241
the provincial minister styled himself "frater Joannes, minister
Austriae, Stiriae et Carinthiae";[42] in 1245 Innocent IV carefully
instructed the provincial minister to collect funds for the benefit
of the Latin Empire of Constantinople "in Austria et aliis locis,
per quae tua administratio se extendit."[43]  But it was obviously
easier to refer to the entire province simply as Austria.  The papal
curia customarily addressed the provincial minister with slight variations as "ministro provinciali fratrum Minorum in Austria,"[44] even
when a convent outside the duchy was involved.  The nunneries of the
Poor Clares in Judenburg in Styria and in Brixen in the Tirol were described in the 1250's, for example, as being under the jurisdiction of
the Austrian province and minister.[45]  It seems likely, therefore,
that when Innocent IV commanded the Franciscans in 1250 to preach a
crusade against Frederick II and his adherents "per Austriam," he did
not intend that the friars' agitation be limited to the duchy.[46]
Another document gives added credence to this interpretation.  In
1257 Pope Alexander IV ordered the archbishops, bishops, and other
prelates "per Austriam constitutis" not to extort money from the
friars who lived in their lands.[47]  Since the entire duchy was under
the ecclesiastical jurisdiction of the bishop of Passau, in this context the pope could only have meant by Austria the province.  The
Franciscans were thus apparently the first to designate the bloc of
Alpine and Danubian lands in southeastern Germany as Austria.  Although
it is impossible to assert categorically that this Franciscan conception of Austria influenced the thinking of Rudolph of Habsburg and
his successors, it is at least worth mentioning that the Franciscans
Henry Knoderer and Conrad Probus were among the king's foremost
advisers[48] and that Rudolph's descendants were among the friars' most
enthusiastic benefactors.[49]  The modern boundaries of the European

nation states are the product of a long and often bloody evolutionary development, yet the borders of the mendicant provinces in the thirteenth century already anticipate them in a striking and intriguing way.

Chapter 4

The Administrators of the Aids in Normandy,
1360-1380

Charles M. Radding

For a long time historians have known that the ransom of John II
the Good marked a major turning-point in the history of French royal
taxation.[1] The revenues from the sales taxes collected initially
for the ransom were soon diverted to military and other uses, reliev-
ing the government of the constant need to discover new sources of
income for the first time since the end of the thirteenth century.
The position of the crown was further strengthened in 1363 when an
assembly granted a hearth tax to pay the wages of the royal army.
No term was fixed for this grant. Together with the sales tax (converted after the resumption of hostilities with England in 1369 into
a subsidy for the war), the hearth tax was collected until 1380, when
regular taxation was cancelled after the death of Charles V. By then,
however, royal taxation had assumed many characteristics which were
to endure until the end of the Old Regime itself, and subsequent
experiments in taxation were firmly based on the achievements of the
period between 1360 and 1380.[2]

Though much has been done in recent years to illuminate the financial policies of the crown in the reigns of John II (1350-1364) and
Charles V (1364-1380), and some--though too little--to describe the
personalities of the men around the king who formulated those policies,[3] little is known about the men who collected the royal taxes
in the provinces. Despite the fact that as individuals they were
rarely important, as a group they deserve our careful consideration.
Like other minor local officials, they were the royal agents most
frequently in contact with the great mass of the population. Their
efficiency and honesty largely determined the thoroughness with
which the royal taxes were exploited and the attitude of most people
toward the royal government.[4] If they ignored the prerogatives of
seigneurs and towns, or permitted peasants and merchants to be unfairly

abused by tax collectors, the government might have its revenues cut
off by the opposition of local authorities or by popular revolt. On
the other hand, by respecting the rights of landlords and municipal
officials and providing fair administration of the taxes to persons
of every station they could help gain the acquiescence of the population to taxes that still lacked the justification of long usage.

In this paper I propose to examine the administrators of the aids
in Normandy between 1360 and 1380. Although Normandy is a province
so evidently exceptional that it may not be possible to extend the
conclusions drawn here to the rest of France,[5] its selection has
much to recommend it. Normandy's size and wealth alone made it important to French royal finances, and many other provinces seemed to
look to it for leadership during the crises of the middle of the
fourteenth century.[6] This is not surprising, because before 1360
Normandy had a stronger tradition of autonomy in fiscal matters, and
in the use of assemblies to levy royal taxes, than was found elsewhere in Languedoïl.[7] The reasons for Normandy's acceptance of royal
leadership therefore deserve careful study.

Only those officers whose duties centered on Normandy will be discussed here, but this is not to imply that they were the only agents
of the administration of aids (as both the hearth tax and the sales
tax were known in this period) who ever came to Normandy. The
councillors-general of the aids frequently visited the duchy to
inspect the accounts of the local receivers, and commissaires were
occasionally appointed to inquire into the local administration. But
both councillors-general and commissaires were oriented toward the
central administration--many were members of the royal council and
held other offices of trust--and their personal histories are too
closely tied to the political history of the kingdom to warrant
detailed discussion here.[8]

There are two distinct levels of the administration of the aids to
consider. First, there were the élus-general and receivers-general,
whose mandates gave them authority in large areas of Normandy.
Second, there were the receivers and élus who handled the details of
local tax collection, usually within a diocese but sometimes in a
smaller area.

The élus-general and receivers-general had a wide range of responsibilities in the early years of the aids.  One of the most important
duties was the supervision of local officials, and they were expected
to see that the king's instructions were carried out.[9]  They also had
significant judicial responsibilities:  they were often called upon
by the councillors-general of the aids to arrange inquiries into local
disputes,[10] and élus were encouraged to refer difficult cases to the
élus-general for decision.[11]  While the administrative structure was
still incomplete, the élus-general frequently acted on their own
initiative to arrange the leasing of farms[12] or the assessing of
hearths, and the élu-general for the "aid for defense" (the hearth
tax) also arranged compositions with towns.[13]  Even when in the 1370's
their regular duties no longer required such strenuous trouble-shooting
for an immature bureaucracy, they were still consulted about Norman
military and political affairs, especially when a local tax was to be
raised.

The example of Raoul Campion illustrates the activities and career
pattern of an élu-general or receiver-general.  After having served as
a receiver of Caen from 1362, Raoul, a bourgeois of Caen, became
receiver-general of Lower Normandy in 1371, remaining in office until
1375.[14]  While receiver-general he assisted in the collection of the
subsidy for Thury[15] and was receiver-general of the subsidies for
Saint-Sauveur.[16]  He was intermittently active after his retirement
as receiver-general, always in positions of importance.  After 1375
he drew wages of 375 l.t. a year as élu-general and "visitor" of the
aids in Lower Normandy,[17] but little is known of his duties.  In 1376
he was described as a "king's councillor";[18] he assessed the subsidy
of 1379 (for Cherbourg, taken over by the English after the confiscation of the lands of Charles of Navarre in 1378) in the territories
owned by Pierre, count of Alençon;[19] in 1382 he was named a governor-
general of the subsidy granted by the Norman estates in April, 1382.[20]
His wages and the title of "king's councillor" suggest that his standing in the royal administration was comparable to that of a bailli.[21]

Given the importance and varied nature of the responsibilities of
the receivers-general and élus-general, it is not surprising that
the government sought men of proven ability to fill these offices.

Of those who held these offices between 1360 and 1380, nine men are known[22]--fourteen if we include the _élus_ of the diocese of Rouen of the early 1360's, when the _élus_ of Rouen were responsible for the dioceses of Evreux and Lisieux as well as the receipts of the diocese of Rouen.[23]   Most, like Raoul, had other experience in government. Guillaume le Grant, the _élu_-general of Lower Normandy in the early 1360's for fifteen years was the viscount of Caen (1363-1378).[24] Étienne du Moustier had been vice-admiral of France, stationed at Harfleur, for at least ten years before he became _élu_-general of the hearth tax in Lower Normandy.[25]   Five of the fourteen had assisted in the collection of the royal subsidies raised between 1356 and 1360.[26]   Six of the fourteen were certainly known to Charles V while he was still duke of Normandy,[27] and six bore the title of "king's councillor" at some time in their careers.[28]   Three of the fourteen were eventually appointed to the central administration:  Jean d'Orléans, who by 1370 had become a councillor-general of the aids and a treasurer of France,[29] Étienne du Moustier, who became a royal councillor in the 1380's,[30] and Berthaut Aladent, who became a receiver-general of the aids in the 1380's.[31]

Something is known about the social origins of nine of the fourteen. Eight were certainly Norman,[32] and only one, Berthaut Aladent, a bourgeois of Chartres,[33] can be proven to have come from another part of the kingdom.  In addition to Berthaut and Raoul, three other _élus_-general or receivers-general were of bourgeois origin, two being citizens of Rouen and one of Bayeux.[34]  Perhaps more significant, many of these bourgeois were men of high social standing in their home towns.  Jean Vauchis or his son was one of the bourgeois of Bayeux called to settle a dispute about the town's government in the 1380's;[35] Jean d'Orléans and Jacques du Chastel were former mayors of Rouen;[36] and the sister of Gilles de Maudestour, canon and _élu_ of Rouen, was the wife of another mayor of Rouen.[37]   One _élu_ of Rouen, Raoul d'Estouteville, was a member of an important noble Norman family.  Two canons of Rouen served as _élus_ of Rouen--Jean de Pontoise, the chancellor of the cathedral,[38] and Gilles de Maudestour.[39]

If the receivers-general and _élus_-general were similar in status to _baillis_, the local receivers and _élus_ resembled the viscounts of the

domainal administration in importance. An élu's wages, 100 l.t. a year
and 1 l.t. a day for travel expenses, were roughly equivalent to the
compensations of a viscount.[40] The élus and receivers had duties somewhat less broad than a viscount's since they divided between them the
judicial and financial aspects of administration. The élus were
charged with leasing the taxes to farmers, setting hearth tax assessments, and trying complaints arising from the taxes, but they had
nothing to do with the collection of the taxes, for which the receivers
alone were accountable. The methods used by both officials were quite
similar to those applied to the domain, however, and the experience
of being a viscount would have been good preparation for being an élu
or receiver.

The most important study to date of the local officials of the aids
is that of Dupont-Ferrier. He concluded that most élus and receivers
of the aids were men of moderate ability who paid little attention to
the performance of their duties. Many won their appointments by royal
favor rather than by proven merit, and they often engaged in pluralism
to multiply their salaries, hiring substitutes to attend to the responsibilities of their offices.[41] Most historians have accepted his conclusions for the fifteenth century,[42] but they cannot be applied
uncritically to the period discussed here since Dupont-Ferrier worked
primarily from sources of a later date.

The only person who has studied the aids in the fourteenth century
in detail is Maurice Rey. Like Dupont-Ferrier's, his comments about
the administrators of the aids are largely negative. He finds that
the whole administrative system was "too improvised" to be effective;
he suggests, for example, that the lack of congruence between geographical divisions of the receipts of the aids and the traditional
administration must have meant that there was little cooperation between the two. He concludes that:

Surtout, on manque de personnel qualifiée.... [E]n l'absence de
tout mode de recrutement qui eût pu exiger des candidats des
capacités minima, force était de recourir à la cooptation, sys-
tème qui entraîne forcement des abus, mais qui permit cependant
à la monarchie de recruter des serviteurs déjà entraînés à leur
tâche, sinon capables de la comprendre vite et bien. Quant aux
officiers ainsi choisis, leur esprit était loin d'être formé
aux théories juridiques qui leur auraient rappelé les exigences

d'un service public:  c'étaient encore des gens d'affaires et ils
organisaient au mieux de leurs intérêts leurs circonscriptions,
aidés de leur clercs qui n'étaient que leur fondés de pouvoir,
rien de plus.[43]

Rey thinks that the character of the élus and receivers who administered the aids went a long way toward explaining the general discontent with the taxes which broke out in the riots of the first years
of Charles VI's reign.  The officers were, he says, "avide d'épices
et peu scrupuleux sur les moyens," and their regime "devint vite tyran-
nique à l'égard des populations."[44]

The names are known of 121 men who were local collectors of the aids
in Normandy between 1360 and 1380.  Of these, sixty were receivers,
thirty-two were élus, and ten were at different times both receivers
and élus.  The remainder includes seven who performed the functions of
élus but did not describe themselves by that title, and twelve who
were either receivers only of the wine tax or of the hearth tax in
one or more deaneries of a diocese.  That they served in these capacities is all that is known about many of these officers; it is often
impossible even to guess at their terms of office, since the gaps in
surviving records mean that there are many years for which there is
no information about the holders of certain offices.  The fact that a
man can be shown to have been a receiver or élu for two years, or even
one day, does not preclude the possibility that his actual service was
much longer.  But enough information survives to permit us to make
some estimate of the social origins and careers in royal service of
many of them, and this sample is large enough to warrant drawing
general conclusions.

The social origins of forty-five men can be described with some
confidence, including slightly over a third of the receivers and just
under half of the élus.  Only one can be proven to have come from outside of Normandy,[45] and it is probably safe to conclude that most were
of Norman origin.  Twelve of the receivers were of bourgeois origin,
six were clerks, and one a noble; four of the lesser receivers were
also bourgeois, as were two of the ten men who were both receivers
and élus.[46]  Considering the financial nature of the receivership,
the dominance of townsmen is not surprising.  The proportions were
rather different for élus:  three were bourgeois, five were clerks,

and six were of noble origin.  Of those who functioned as élus without claiming the title, three were clerks and two were nobles.[47]

A surprising number of the administrators of the aids are known to
have been influential in Norman politics.  Of the nobles, three were
substantial lords or had powerful family connections:  Fouque Paynel,
sire of Aigeau, Raoul d'Estouteville (already mentioned as one of the
early élus-general), and Jean du Bois, sire of l'Espinay.  Two other
nobles may have been connected with the political elite, but this
identification is not certain.[48]  Six of the bourgeois belonged to
the ruling classes of their home towns, including four members of the
mayoral families of Rouen, one mayor of Falaise, and an alderman of
Caen.[49]  Another three bourgeois held lesser municipal offices.[50]
Four of the clerks were members of the hierarchy:  Henry de Rappelay,
archdeacon of Bayeux, a doctor in laws; Richard le Cappelier, archdeacon of Bayeux (nominated for the position of élu by his bishop);[51]
Richard de Harcourt, dean of the cathedral of Lisieux and probably
related to the Harcourt family of comptal rank; and Jean de Pontoise,
chancellor of the cathedral of Rouen, another early élu-general, who
later returned to be élu of Rouen.  Three more men were canons of
cathedrals.[52]  Altogether thirteen of the fifty men whose social class
we can identify--ten percent of the original sample of 121--can be
identified as members of the Norman elite, and another eight had some
lesser influence which we cannot accurately judge.

The participation of these men in the administration of the aids
is an important clue to the attitudes of the Norman ruling classes
of this period.  They did not feel threatened by royal taxation, and
seem to have been anxious for the taxes to succeed.  This becomes
especially obvious when the dates of service of these individuals are
taken into account.  There were two periods in the twenty years under
consideration when the government especially needed local support to
prevent failure of the taxes.  First, when the taxes were instituted,
between 1361 and 1363 for the sales tax and 1364 and 1366 for the
hearth tax, and, second, immediately after Charles V had tried and
failed to replace the hearth tax with a levy on milled grain in
1369.[53]  The dates of service of all thirteen men whose political
importance has been demonstrated, and of seven of the eight who

probably were members of the elite, fall into one of these two periods.
This was not a matter of chance.  If we look only at the period immediately following the restoration of the hearth tax in December, 1369,
eight of the thirteen were in office, and seven of them seem to have
been enlisted especially to deal with the emergency:  Raoul de Bray,
former alderman of Caen; Jean du Bois; Richard le Cappelier; Richard
de Harcourt; Robert Aupois, to be mayor of Falaise in 1375; Jean de
Pontoise; and Raoul d'Estouteville.  Still surviving are royal letters
of December, 1369, naming Raoul de Bray, Jean du Bois, Richard le
Cappelier, Jean de Pontoise, and Raoul d'Estouteville to office.[54]

   The role of powerful Normans in the administration of the aids
should not be exaggerated.  When they served it was rarely for longer
than one or two years, and few of them seem to have held administrative office in normal times.  Their careers are an important indica-
tor that a close relationship between the royal court and the leaders
of Normandy smoothed the way for royal taxation to be effective, but
it would be wrong to think of them as typical administrators.

   The majority of the officers of the administration of the aids presumably were chosen for their administrative ability, but it is difficult to make a judgment about their professional competence.  To
begin with, two qualities are involved, honesty and efficiency, which
are by no means always present or absent together.  The man who pleases
his superiors may not please his subordinates or the population under
his jurisdiction.  The example of Jean Loton, receiver of the aids at
Dieppe who pleaded guilty to a variety of extortions in 1374 but was
back in royal service by 1376[55] should be a reminder of that fact.
Since the records of the courts of the aids for the period before 1398
have been lost, it will probably be impossible ever to be sure whether
Jean Loton's extortions were practiced by many of his colleagues.

   It is possible to make some judgment of the administrative ability
of these officers.  Two criteria seem especially useful:  experience
in other branches of royal government and length of tenure of office.
The first permits an estimate of the extent to which standards for
officers of the aids were consistent with those demanded in the royal
administration as a whole.  The second gives some idea of whether the
performance of the officers of the aids satisfied their superiors.

For our purposes it seems reasonable to take a term of office lasting
five years or more, or two separate terms of office, as an indication
that the overseers of the aids were generally content with the performance of a given official.

Forty-three of the 121 officials of the aids had some experience in
other branches of the royal administration, and fifty also served long
terms as administrators of the aids. Allowing for those counted twice,
seventy-one officials of the aids seem to have met contemporary standards for royal administrators. This in itself suggests that by fourteenth-century standards the administrators of the aids were not as
a group exceptionally corrupt or incompetent, though this matter
deserves detailed consideration.

Let us look first at those forty-three receivers and _élus_ who at
some time in their careers held office in other royal administrations.
The office most frequently held was that of viscount: eighteen of
these men were viscounts, and sixteen of them were viscounts before
or during their tenure as officials of the aids.[56] Since no one was
simultaneously viscount and official of the aids except in cases where
the viscounty coincided with the administrative center of the receipt
of the aids, this pluralism probably did not adversely affect the performance of duties. It is possible that their familiarity with local
conditions and contacts with other royal agents may even have been an
asset. In any case, we can be fairly sure that these sixteen men came
to their jobs with appropriate administrative experience.

Two of them won promotions to bailliages before or during their term
as officials of the aids; this may be a sign that their superiors
thought highly of their abilities.[57] Another official, Aymar Revout,
who seems to have begun his career in royal service as receiver of
the aids in the diocese of Coutances, was also appointed bailli of
the Cotentin.[58] Three other administrators of the aids served baillis
as lieutenants at some time in their careers.[59]

The next-largest group consists of seven men who had experience
with other subsidies before becoming administrators of the aids. Of
these, six had collected royal subsidies in the late 1350's.[60] It
has already been mentioned that five élus-general and receivers-general
also administered subsidies during those years. Since the Norman taxes

of that period are usually described by historians as failures,[61] it
is somewhat surprising to find so much administrative continuity
between them and the more successful experiments of the 1360's.

   Thirteen men had experience in still other branches of the royal
administration.  Two were _procureurs du roi_ in _bailliages_;[62] one, Huet
de Saint-Erme, receiver of Evreux, was a _huissier_ of the Parlement
before he became receiver.[63]  Three had some political experience:
Nicole de Chacegne, _élu_ of Avranches, had been commissioner to the
Norman estates of 1365;[64]  Jean du Mesnil, _élu_ of Lisieux, had served
Charles V on missions to the dukes of Anjou and Lorraine;[65]  Raoul de
Bray, receiver of Bayeux, had in the 1360's been an adviser to the
king's lieutenant in Lower Normandy, Guillaume du Merle.[66]  The administration terms of Roger Dany, who leased the taxes in the viscounty
of Pontorson in 1367, and Ferran de Saint-Germain, _élu_ of Coutances
were but interludes in their military careers.[67]  On the other hand,
Richard du Til, receiver of Rouen and _élu_ of Evreux, first appears as
captain of the fortress of Sainte-Catherine near Rouen and then became
a professional administrator of the aids.[68]  Richard de Cormeilles was
_panetier_ to the dauphin and then Charles V; after 1370 he was charged
with provisioning the armed forces stationed at the mouth of the Seine;
by 1377 he was viscount of Montivilliers and in 1380 appears as _élu_
of Rouen.[69]  Another early retainer of Charles V was Jean de Cerisy.
Receiver for the dauphin's lands in Melun-en-Brie and Champagne in
1361, he became receiver of Caudebec in 1375.[70]  Jean Cornevalois was
master of the mint of Rouen before becoming receiver of the aids in
Caudebec and Montivilliers.[71]  Perhaps the humblest origins were those
of Guillaume du Hasay, who first appears as a sergeant and jailor of
Vernon but who became an _élu_ of Evreux and eventually receiver of the
important district of Rouen under Charles VI.[72]

   The example of the administration of the aids in Normandy therefore
offers no support to Cazelles' suggestion that after 1350 administrative rigidity began to prevent the movement of bureaucrats from one
branch of royal service to another.[73]  It may even be that in the
area of promotions the French government was opening new possibilities for mobility and advancement.  Examples of promotion to higher
offices within Normandy have already been mentioned.[74]  This follows

earlier practices.  In the thirteenth century viscounts could become
baillis, but they could move no further, and the same was true in the
reign of Philip of Valois.[75]  It seems to be an innovation of this
period of the fourteenth century that men who began in relatively
minor local offices could achieve advancement to the central administration.  Guy Chrestien first appears as viscount of Bayeux in 1369;
in 1372 he was bailli of the Cotentin and élu in the diocese of Bayeux.
In 1375 he became bailli of Rouen and Gisors, a position he held until
1383.  In 1384 he was a "king's councillor" and master of requests.
A master of accounts in 1386, in 1390 he was treasurer of France and
a councillor-general of the aids, and he still held high office in
1407.[76]  Less meteoric was the career of Robert Assire.  He was viscount of Falaise between 1359 and 1368, then viscount of Pontautou
and the Auge.  He was also an élu of Lisieux at this time.  In 1374
he accompanied Jean le Mercier on a mission to Brittany, and in 1377
he appears for the first time as a master and enquêteur of the king's
forests and waters.  In 1387 he was a treasurer of France.[77]  By
demonstrating that there was a chain of advancement from bottom to
top, the promotions of men like Guy Chrestien and Robert Assire must
have heightened the sense, already evident a century before, of belonging to a civil service.

 Guy Chrestien and Robert Assire may properly be described as professional civil servants, and there were many other professional
civil servants who worked in the administration of the aids.  They
can easily be recognized by their frequent shifts from one region to
another, a mobility which must have precluded any territorial loyalty
stronger than their attachment to the king's government.  But many
officers of the aids whose long terms of office suggest that they
gave satisfactory service spent most or all of their careers in one
place.  Typical of these are Jean de la Fresnaye, receiver of Avranches
for eight years,[78] and Nicolas le Prestrel, receiver of Coutances for
eight years;[79] neither man seems to have held any other royal offices.
Jean Vauchis, bourgeois of Bayeux, held the receivership of Bayeux
for almost eleven of the twelve years between 1364 and 1375; the remaining year he spent as receiver-general of Lower Normandy.[80]  Pierre
le Hursin served as receiver of the diocese of Sées for about fifteen

of the twenty-three years between 1366 and 1389.[81]  Yvon Huart, a
native of Caen, was employed as receiver of Bayeux or Caen twenty-two
of the twenty-eight years between 1370 and 1398; some of the remaining
years were spent as receiver of Le Mans and receiver of Sées, but this
does not negate the essentially local character of his career.[82]

Other men who spent time as _élus_ or receivers held many different
offices in the same locality.  Guillaume le Grant, viscount of Caen
between 1363 and 1378, was an _élu_ of Bayeux between 1364 and 1376;
for much of that time he also served as _élu_-general of Lower
Normandy.[83]  Jean le Gey is known to have been receiver, viscount,
and _élu_ of Avranches and viscount of Mortain at different times in a
career lasting over twenty years.[84]  Jean Orenge, receiver of Vire
between 1372 and 1375, and later _élu_ of the lands of Charles of
Navarre beyond the Dyne, became king's advocate and councillor in the
viscounty of Vire between 1386 and 1423.[85]

It is likely that these men were natives of the regions they administered, but the government evidently felt it could trust them as
administrators and was satisfied with their performance.  One ordinance even suggests that local men were preferred over professionals,
since they were exempted from some of the provisions of the administrative review conducted in 1379.[86]  This may be a sign that the
government was relying less than before upon officials of proven
loyalty and more on winning the cooperation of local communities.

The receivers and _élus_ seem to have had few assistants who were
not already employed in other branches of the royal administration.
The receivers were frequently assisted by the clerks regularly
assigned to the viscounties.  When these clerks witnessed quittances
they were probably paid by the persons desiring the quittance, but
when they attended the leasing of the taxes or prepared rolls for the
use of the receiver they received a small salary, about 12 l.t. a
year.  The receiver also hired a clerk to prepare his accounts, whom
he paid about 10 l.t. a year,[87] but this clerk does not seem to have
had independent importance.  Local sergeants who did not receive any
additional wages from the receiver cried the farms and assisted with
the assessment and collection of the hearth tax.[88]  This may have
given them increased opportunity for graft and extortion--at least

one sergeant helped collect the taxes for a dishonest farmer who later absconded with the receipts[89]--and since the sergeants were traditionally unpopular their activities may have been the source of much of the contemporary criticism of the taxes.[90]

In general, however, it does not seem justified to take contemporary complaints about the administrators of the aids as reliable evidence of their incompetence, dishonesty, or rapacity. The _élus_ and receivers of the aids seem to have been very much like royal personnel in other bureaucracies, as their ability to move in and out of other branches of the government testifies, and they seem to have met the standards set for them by their superiors and by the professional ethics of their time. As long as the taxes themselves were resented--and it is the nature of general taxes to affect the lives of many people--those who administered them were likely to get their share of abuse regardless of how well they actually performed their duties.[91]

Chapter 5

Italian Diplomatic History:
A Case for the Smaller Commune[1]

William M. Bowsky

In recent decades much historical research has been devoted to communal Italy in the Middle Ages and early Renaissance. Most has concentrated upon socio-economic, socio-political, or demographic issues,
with a few examinations of cultural history.[2] Except for the discussion of the crucial role of foreign relations in Hans Baron's extremely
valuable thesis on the concept of civic humanism[3] diplomacy and foreign
policy have almost been relegated to the dustbin of Italian communal
history. And were it not for the occasional incursions of Holy Roman
Emperors into the Italian peninsula we might almost wonder whether
foreign affairs has been left largely as the preserve of civic-minded
antiquarians and local history enthusiasts. This is explicable when
we recall the overemphasis on old-fashioned political and diplomatic
history common to many nineteenth-century studies, and the excitement
aroused by the rapid development and increasing sophistication of new
fields of inquiry.

The little research concerning foreign policy has been restricted
largely to the major powers of the peninsula.[4] It seems generally to
be assumed that the smaller towns are not worth studying--either that
they are carbon copies of the few major communes or that they simply
had no independent foreign policies of their own but, willynilly,
danced to the tunes played by their stronger neighbors.

We must question these assumptions. Most people lived in smaller
towns and in the regions they controlled. A Milan that dominated much
of the western Po valley and a Florence with its Tuscan hegemony were
the exceptions and not the rule. The majority of the population lived
in or were subject to many weaker towns, but towns that nonetheless
were relatively autonomous political units. Examination of the
nature and role of foreign policy in those communes may produce new
understanding of the realities of political life and issues in communal Italy.

I suggest that we must study the foreign policies of the lesser communes. This conclusion derives from my preliminary examination of one such town, the Tuscan commune of Siena when it was ruled by the mercantile-banking oligarchy of nobles and bourgeoisie known as the Nine Governors and Defenders of the Commune of Siena--that is, from the closing decades of the thirteenth century until the regime's violent overthrow in 1355. During this period Siena did develop and conscientiously pursue a consistent and successful foreign policy that allowed it to maintain its independence and to attain clearly perceived goals. How then did this come about, and what were the principles on which those who guided the town's destinies acted?

Until recently a single event was viewed as the watershed of Sienese foreign policy, indeed of Sienese history. It marked the culmination of the glories of the Ghibelline commune, whose bankers enjoyed a near-monopoly at the papal court and whose merchants cut a broad swath throughout western Europe. That event was the decisive victory of Sienese forces over Florence and her Tuscan Guelf allies at Montaperti in 1260, "the carnage and great slaughter that dyed the Arbia red," wrote Dante Alighieri.[5] The battle was preceded by grand acts of civic patriotism--one Salimbeni noble single-handedly provided over one hundred thousand gold florins needed to pay imperial troops for their participation. The conflict marked the city's dedication to its new sovereign protectress, the Virgin Mary.[6]

Yet, so the story goes, the Ghibelline victory was short-lived. Twelve sixty-six saw Ghibelline hopes dashed at Benevento with the defeat and death of Manfred, natural son and heir of the Hohenstaufen Emperor Frederick II. The Angevin victory at Tagliacozzo in 1268 was followed by the execution of the young Conradin, last of the "breed of vipers." In 1269 Siena itself bowed to Florence at Colle di Valdelsa.

The Ghibelline epoch drew to a close. Aided by papal policies, Guelf merchants gradually assumed control of Siena. The ruling oligarchy consolidated its power and initiated the regime of the Nine. For nearly three-quarters of a century a humbled Siena was to be but a client state of Florence, the Guelf commune par excellence. Robert Langton Douglas tells how Sienese "citizens devoted themselves more and more exclusively to the acquisition of wealth. The military spirit died out amongst them. They became incapable of conducting warfare. They ceased to value the prestige of the State. All that they desired was peace, peace at any price."[7]

Thus the traditional view. Seen in this light it is no wonder that the years after Montaperti appear as an epilogue to the glories of Siena, and that post-Montaperti foreign policy and the diplomacy of Guelf Siena generally have been passed over in scorn, when not in silence.

Were this picture accurate the problem might perhaps be laid to rest. But the Guelf commune did not receive its continued independence as a gift from its benevolent Arno neighbor, nor did it simply muddle through, preserving autonomy through a series of fortunate but never understood happenstances.

Sienese foreign policies and ambitions were circumscribed by the city's very location, by the assets and disadvantages inherent in its natural resources and geography. This hill town lay some thirty miles south of Florence on a spur of the Chiana mountain range. The limitations placed on its industrial capabilities by its distance from a major river and the lack of an adequate water supply more than offset commercial advantages derived from straddling the principal route to Rome, the Via Francigena. By the mid-thirteenth century its sphere of action was severely limited by its more populous, powerful, and fortunate neighbor to the north. Already Florence was emerging as the strongest commune in Tuscany, rendering all the more serious Siena's lack of natural defenses toward the north. To the east and west Arezzo and Volterra hampered the commune's freedom of action.

The area most open to Sienese expansion lay to the south, southeast, and west--toward the unsettled lands of Montamiata and into the Maremma. This was a rugged and underpopulated zone, rich in minerals and livestock. Here Siena confronted the relatively weak towns of Grosseto and Massa Marittima and the holdings of a host of feudal lords. Here, throughout the thirteenth century, Siena had been pushing toward the Tuscan littoral, consolidating control over

its contado and greatly expanding its area.  It was Siena's misfortune
that the lands most open to its expansion were more distant from the
core of Tuscany and the vital center of that province's connection with
the rest of Europe than was the Arno basin, where Florence grew and
flourished.  It was Siena's good fortune that the newly established
government of the Nine quickly recognized these natural limitations
and that the regime devised a foreign policy that could capitalize on
their assets without courting disaster by overstepping the bounds of
the possible.  This is not the least of its achievements.

Yet the maintenance of independence and a successful foreign policy
called for more.  The Nine had to solve problems posed by the existence
of Florence.  By the early fourteenth century Florence had a population roughly double that of Siena, and Florentine bankers had replaced
their rivals in the lucrative business of the papal court.  The more
richly endowed commune held the hegemony of Tuscany and utilized her
leadership of Tuscan Guelf Leagues to further an ambitious foreign
policy.

The current scholarly estimate of the relationship between Florence
and Siena throughout the regime of the Nine still in essence is that
expressed in 1909 by Ferdinand Schevill.  The Florentines, he wrote,
"manipulated the Guelph League for their own purposes, practically
dictating Sienese foreign policy and disposing of the Sienese military
forces as if they were their own."[8]  The Nine, he continued, never
swerved

> from their allegiance to their city's dearest foe.  In every ex-
> pedition which Florence organized, naturally after loud beating
> of the Guelph drums, a Sienese troop took part and was duly
> butchered pour les beaux yeux of her Arno neighbor.  Of course
> some small returns the Nine could reasonably ask for such exem-
> plary devotion, and some, too, they received not only in the
> form of the support of the Guelph League against internal foes,
> but also in the privilege, certainly not inconsiderable, of con-
> solidating and even extending their power in the Sienese con-
> tado.[9]

Even if we set aside Schevill's failure to consider the realistic
alternatives, if any, open to Siena, or his own assertion that even
by 1270 Siena had lost her contest with Florence "under a decree of
fate," how well does his assessment square with the evidence?[10]

Let us first see how Florence viewed Siena.  Florence operated

within an international rather than a local or regional framework, at
least throughout the first four decades of the fourteenth century.
The major components of Florentine policy took into account the papacy,
the Angevin kingdom of Naples (the Regno), to some extent France, later
Milan, and on occasion the Holy Roman Empire.  Until the death of
Robert the Wise of Naples in 1343 Florence tried to work within a papal
and Angevin alliance to keep other powers out of Tuscany and to expand
her own holdings and increase her hegemony within that province.  She
pushed westwards toward the Tyrhennian Sea and the Tuscan end of the
Via Francigena, toward Lucca and Pisa.  She tried to recruit support
from friendly and satellite communities by frequently renewing and
attempting to dominate so-called Guelf Leagues, leagues through which
she held at bay or tried to cripple rival neighbors (not strangely,
labelled Ghibelline), most particularly Pisa to the west and Arezzo
to the southeast.

   Peter Partner is probably correct in maintaining that although from
about 1313 to 1332 Florence was an "auxiliary in an international
struggle in which the papacy, the French monarchy and the Angevin
kingdom played decisive roles.... Thereafter French and German
intervention in Italian politics, which had held the stage for about
twenty-five years, now finally broke down and left the political field
in Italy comparatively clear for the operation of regional and local
forces."[11]

   Both Partner and Gene Brucker see a downgrading and localization
of Florentine objectives in the mid-1340's or at the end of that
decade--a narrowing of focus and limitation of aims produced by
Florentine weakness.[12]  But this shift marked no major change in the
Florentine view of Siena.

   Florence saw Siena as a weak partner and an ally located along her
southern frontier.  This ally, together with Perugia, maintained a
"relatively satisfactory balance"[13] along a key section of Florence's
Appenine frontier.  While Florence tried to win Sienese support for
the Arno commune's newer goals after the 1340's, Siena's role remained
the same--and it was not the role of a satellite or dependent.

   Florence, moreover, respected Sienese interests.  No longer did
she try to subvert or acquire dominion over such townships as

Montalcino or Montepulciano that Siena was laboring to subdue or retain.  If there was a rivalry, generally it was confined to the northern and western Sienese border, and focused on places that by
tradition and geography were more within the Florentine than the
Sienese sphere of influence.  Both communes walked gingerly in such
places.  Such rivalry as existed was conducted within a strictly
limited range of actions that both governments apparently understood
and accepted.  Thus, for example, merchants of both towns tried to
attain economic control of San Gimignano by becoming the major creditors of that town and its merchants, and the rivals' changing fortunes
were reflected in the shifting selection of podestas and other foreign
officials of San Gimignano, now Sienese, now Florentine.[14]  More indicative of relations in the Sienese-Florentine borderlands is a pact
of 1350 by which the two cities agreed to appoint a common official
to suppress highwaymen.[15]

   The one glaring exception is itself instructive.  In 1333 Florence
tried to fish in the troubled waters of the Maremma.  For at least a
century Siena had striven to dominate Massa Marittima.[16]  At every
possible opportunity Massa had sought to escape from the pacts that it
had been compelled to make with Siena.  Following the Peace of
Montopoli in 1329 between Pisa and the Tuscan Guelf cities, Massa had
drawn increasingly close to the Ghibelline commune.  By 1333 Massa was
the focal point of a war between Pisa and Siena.  Robert of Naples,
Florence, and the other Tuscan Guelf towns, apparently concerned that
the conflict might provide King John of Bohemia with a pretext for
intervening in Tuscany as he had in Lombardy,[17] requested Pope John
XXII to end the conflict.  The pope delegated Francesco Salvestri,
Bishop of Florence, as arbiter.  In July 1333 the bishop ordered that
Massa and all disputed lands be placed in Florentine custody until a
final agreement was concluded.  Two months later the definitive settlement provided that Massa be ruled for three years in the name of the
Florentine bishop, and appointed Florentines as podesta and judge of
the contested commune.  Hiding behind its bishop, and in the guise
of a peacemaker, Florence had thrust deeply into an area long ear-
marked by Siena for its own expansion and control.  But even here
Florence did not push the Sienese to a point where they were forced

openly to recognize Florentine intervention or intentions.  Less than
two years later, in August 1335, when a pro-Sienese party gained the
upper hand in Massa, Florence withdrew swiftly and without protest
and allowed events to take their natural course.  When Florence saw
that a ripe fruit was not about to drop into her lap of its own accord
she left the orchard gracefully.

Our principal indications of Florentine interference in Sienese
affairs relates to dealings with individual Sienese magnate families--
clans involved in banking and commerce, possessed of large contado
holdings, and influential in the Sienese government.  Thus in 1327
and 1328 Florence sought to win favor with the Salimbeni, probably
Siena's richest consorteria, by making a good settlement with them
of the inheritance of the Count of Mangona.[18]  Especially important
was Florentine traffic with the Tolomei, a clan that produced the most
dangerous of the noble Sienese rebels,[19] but one that also contained
some of the staunchest supporters of the Nine.  In October 1353 we
find Tolomei impetrating the cancellation of a Florentine sentence
against a Florentine citizen.[20]  Earlier in the same year Florence
had beseeched some Tolomei to request others of their brethren to
stop harassing certain lands in Florentine custody.[21]

The only way in which Florence may have tried to interfere seriously
in internal Sienese affairs was through the unpredictable Tolomei
clan.  Yet at the time when Deo Tolomei was in open rebellion and
ravaging Sienese territories with a large armed band there are
Florentine records of arrangements to pay Florentine troops for
military service for Siena against those rebels.[22]

Siena, moreover, reciprocated in kind.  In 1303, for example, she
interceded successfully for the Florentine Cavalcanti family with
its own government.[23]  In 1317 she obtained the cancellation of
Florentine sentences against Sienese Cerretani nobles.[24]  That we
have less evidence of Sienese dealings with Florentine families than
vice-versa depends in part on the lack of Sienese sources comparable
to the Florentine Missive, and, I suspect, in part on the differing
social composition of the Sienese and Florentine governing groups.
In Florence magnate clans had been contained more successfully--they
were less powerful and influential than their Sienese counterparts.

And how did Siena view Florence? The rival of the first half of
the thirteenth century was seen differently during the regime of the
Nine. For Siena Florence became a strong ally and a buffer for her
northern frontier. And as against the one occasion when Florence
threatened to interfere seriously with Sienese ambitions (the episode
of Massa Marittima), on many others the Arno city furthered Sienese
goals.

The Sienese government successfully called upon Florence for support in maintaining order following uprisings that threatened the
regime. In May 1322 Florence sent Siena 200 cavalry and 500 infantry
for reasons of internal security, when the city was disturbed by
violent feuding between the Tolomei and Salimbeni clans.[25] Later
that same summer Siena sent precisely that same number of its troops
as its contribution toward the formation of an army totaling some
2,500 cavalry and 10,000 infantry--an army that, as it turned out, did
not need to be utilized.[26] On several occasions Florence served as a
peacemaker, bringing a halt to inter-clan warfare that threatened the
order and well-being of the Sienese state.[27]

Florentine military contingents served Siena in both limited expeditions and major wars. In 1318 Florence lent Siena a hundred cavalry
for a campaign against Massa Marittima and the castle of Gerfalco.[28]
One-hundred fifteen Florentine infantry fought in the Sienese army at
the siege of Arcidosso in 1331,[29] and a Florentine document of 1344
shows still other Florentines in Sienese service.[30] The seven-month
campaign against Montemassi in 1328 is one of the most famous in
Sienese history because of its immortalization by Simone Martini in
the fresco in the Communal Palace depicting the war captain,
Guidoriccio dei Fogliani of Reggio. On that occasion Florence contributed at least 200--possibly 400--cavalry to the Sienese cause.[31]

Siena in turn aided Florence militarily, but that aid could not
always be counted upon. Large commitments were ordinarily made only
when Sienese interests were at stake. Thus in the second half of
the 1280's Siena contributed heavily to two wars waged against Arezzo
by the Tuscan Guelf League under Florentine leadership. Sienese were
in the forefront of the five-month siege of Poggio Santa Cecilia in
1285.[32] Following an unsuccessful siege of Arezzo a large Sienese

force was ambushed and badly mauled at Pieve al Toppo (June 26, 1288),
after, we should note, the Sienese had ignored Florentine advice to
take another, shorter, route home to Siena.[33]   A contingent of 120
Sienese horsemen served in a large Tuscan Guelf force that defeated
the Aretines at the battle of Campaldino in 1289.   But Florence herself
supplied at least 1,600 and possibly 2,000 cavalry for that battle,
together with 10,000 infantry.   (Lucca provided 150 cavalry, Prato and
Volterra 40 each, and Pistoia a combined force of 60 cavalry and
infantry.)   The Sienese contribution, then, was quite small in comparison with the Florentine.   And from that small contribution Siena
acquired numerous lands lying toward Arezzo, including the communities
of Trequanda, Sinalunga, Fabbrica, Montisi, and the long-contested
town of Lucignano in the Valdichiana.[34]   Rivalry with Arezzo was more
vital to Sienese than to Florentine interests, and was more ancient
and more bitter.   Segments of the Sienese contado had been carved out
of the Aretine diocese.   The controversy dated back at least to the
mid-seventh century; the early eighth century had seen the beginning
of a lawsuit over the burial place of the Sienese Saint, Sant'Ansano,
that lasted a full half-millennium (ca. 714-1224).[35]

Unfortunately we do not have reliable figures for the two instances
in which Siena may have been hurt badly and suffered sizable losses--
not surprisingly, the two greatest defeats suffered by Tuscan Guelf
armies during the first half of the fourteenth century.   The first of
these was the battle of Montecatini on August 29, 1315, when Uguccione
della Faggiuola, formerly vicar of Genoa for Emperor Henry VII and now
lord of Pisa, commanding a force of some thousand Lowland cavalry and
aided by the Visconti of Milan, the Bonacolsi of Mantua, and the
bishop of Arezzo, defeated a Tuscan Guelf army that boasted such
worthies as the brother and the nephew of King Robert the Wise of
Naples--Philip of Taranto and his son Charles of Acaia.   Siena itself
would have been imperiled had the Ghibelline heirs of Henry VII burst
through the Florentine shield and threatened Tuscany; and the Sienese
commune contributed some 400 cavalry and 3,000 infantry to an ill-
fated Guelf army that totalled 3,200 horse and 30,000 to 60,000 foot
soldiers.   The Sienese lost about 100 cavalry and 400 infantry; another
400 of its warriors fell prisoner.   But these numbers are dwarfed by

Florentine casualties that may have included 2,000 dead--among them
at least 200 Florentine, not mercenary, horsemen.  Florence had not
committed her allies to pulling her own chestnuts out of the fire.[36]

A similar picture emerges from the second disaster, when at
Altopascio on September 23, 1325, in the course of his wars with the
Guelf League, Castruccio Castracani degli Antelminelli of Lucca inflicted a staggering defeat on his enemies.[37]  Siena had committed
some 500 cavalry, including one hundred from magnate families, and a
thousand infantry from the city and contado.  But her losses and
those of Florence cannot be calculated (and it is of little value to
note that chronicles name some thirty-six prominent Florentines and
only nine Sienese as either dead or carted off to Luccan prisons).
We should, however, note that Castruccio tried to ravage Sienese
lands and that he aided rebellions throughout the Sienese state.  He
presented a real threat to Siena.  And let us recall, too, that these
losses at Montecatini and Altopascio were exceptional, and that, great
though they were, they were far smaller than those of Florence, even
when we take into account the relative size and strength of the two
states.  These losses, moreover, were not the rule.  Siena was not
often badly burned, either within or outside of the structure of the
Guelf League.

It was, though, within the context of the Tuscan Leagues, Guelf
Leagues, or _taglie_, that Siena conducted many of her diplomatic relations with Florence and with a shifting complex of neighboring communes and lords, among them Prato, Pistoia, San Gimignano, Volterra,
Lucca (when that town was not subject to Castruccio), and certain
non-Tuscan communes that adhered to one or another league--Bologna
and Perugia in particular.

These leagues merit scholarly study such as they have not yet
received.  The most striking thing that I have noticed about them
simply is their frequency and durability.  Nothing in the works of
secondary scholarship led me to expect to find that there were very
few years in which Siena was not a member of a league, large or
small, of greater or lesser duration, but nonetheless a league.  A
_taglia_ in 1287 included Siena, Florence, Colle di Valdelsa, Poggibonsi,
Prato, San Gimignano, and Volterra.[38]  Another existed in 1293.[39]  A

ten-year taglia was created in 1295.[40]  In 1304 and 1306 agreements
were concluded for the creation of other taglie--still in existence
in 1307.[41]  On the news of the arrival in Italy of Henry VII in 1310
a five-year taglia was made.[42]  According to another, created in 1315,
Siena was to maintain 200 French cavalry, Florence 600.[43]  Throughout
the 1320's, during the wars with Castruccio, Siena belonged to taglie.[44]  In one of 1324, composed of 1,000 cavalry, Florence provided
314, Siena 200.[45]  The objective, Città di Castello, was of greater
concern to Siena than to Florence.  Siena still was leagued with
Florence in 1330.[46]  In 1335 Siena entered into a ten-year pact.[47]
Documents concerning a five-year Tuscan taglia of 1347 note that
Florence was obligated for 8¼ eighteenths of the payment, Perugia for
4¾, Siena for 4, and Arezzo for one eighteenth.[48]  The year 1351
saw representatives of Florence, Perugia, and Siena meet in Siena to
form a league against the Visconti of Milan.[49]  In 1354 arrangements
were made for a three-year league, with Florence to maintain 1,040
foreign cavalry, Perugia 585, and Siena 375.[50]

   Siena's commitments to the leagues did not exceed her proportional
strength or her ability to pay, and they were commensurate with her
expectations.  These alliances protected her northern flanks and the
peripheral zone of her interests.  When aimed eastward they helped
to keep an ancient enemy at bay, and permitted Siena to increase her
control over portions of the Valdichiana and the Aretine border area.

   Sienese involvements with the taglie were practical and pragmatic,
not ideological, for in Siena Guelfism did not contain the political
magic that it did in Florence.  The Florentine Guelf tradition was
stronger and more ancient, and coincided with communal glories and
successes.  Ghibelline power had been crushed in the Arno commune by
the fourteenth century, and the Ghibelline name tainted with a permanent stigma.  If Peter Partner is correct in emphasizing the conscious
Florentine use of Guelfism in order to win support for her own policies, or can write that "Guelfism was not an 'ideology' but a state of
regional and factional alignments, which produced a particular state
of mind,"[51] I would only emphasize that it did indeed produce that
state of mind.  If Florentine Guelfism was a historical myth it was
a myth upon which men acted.  As Gene Brucker tells us, "Of the

corporate entities in the city, the most powerful and influential, in a political sense, was the Parte Guelfa."[52]

Sienese Guelfism was of more recent vintage and more dubious heritage. Siena's glories dated from an epoch of Ghibelline rule. Most of her leading houses had been Ghibelline, among them the Piccolomini, the immensely wealthy Salimbeni, and even the turbulent Tolomei. Some magnate clans still were Ghibelline. It is no surprise, then, that in Siena the Guelf Party was of little importance and is very sparsely documented, or that Guelfism was not a major issue. On the whole the government trod lightly in this area, and thus was unlikely to be stampeded into foolish courses of action "after loud beating of the Guelph drums," or to send huge contingents into the _taglie_ for purely ideological considerations.

The _taglie_ were more than war leagues for Siena and her allies, and served a variety of functions. In 1308, for example, Volterra and San Gimignano composed their serious disputes over border raids, boundaries, and exiles in their three major allies, Florence, Lucca, and Siena.[53]  And we have already noted the clause in the three-year league of 1354, which provided that in all civil and criminal cases in which judges of a member city tried citizens or residents of another member city, those foreigners were to be treated as though they were citizens and inhabitants of the city in which the case was being tried.[54]  This was a step toward the creation of a common citizenship, and is worth further examination in a separate context.

More usual was the role of the _taglia_ in economic policy, and in particular its relation to the law of reprisals. Especially in later years, league agreements often contained a clause providing for the suspension of reprisals. Thus the five-year _taglia_ of 1347 provided that no member city grant reprisals against another or its citizens and that any reprisals already in existence be suspended for the duration of the league. Even when this general clause was lacking, the towns within the _taglia_ frequently suspended reprisals already granted against allied communes. Such instances can easily be found, for example, in the _Provvisioni_ in the Florentine state archives.[55]

Siena, like other communes, tried to limit the damaging effects of reprisals outside of the _taglie_ as well as within them. She arranged

conventions for mutual suspensions, sent embassies to other towns to
mitigate their reprisals against Sienese, and tried to settle such disputes by compromise.  She established a complex set of procedures that
prevented her residents from utilizing reprisals quickly and without
giving the commune and the Merchant Guild (Mercanzia) a chance to
avoid them.[56]  An especially troublesome reprisal, granted against
King Robert of Naples because one of his naval captains had seized
Sienese goods off the Gulf of Piombino, necessitated a continuous
embassy of over 200 days in Naples in order to negotiate a settle-
ment--and even then the matter dragged on for over seven years.[57]
Despite this solicitude, I suspect that Siena was not a leader in
proposing sweeping general legislation to lessen the evil effects of
reprisals among large groups of cities such as I have found passed
in both Florence and Bologna.

Siena's relations with neighbors other than Florence were conducted
with the same practicality and with a clear recognition of the limitations of the possible.  As with Florence, she did not press them so
hard or long as to provoke serious breaches of peace.  She became
involved in major conflicts only with Pisa over territories essential
to Siena, with Arezzo when strongly supported by her Tuscan Guelf
allies, and with weaker towns such as Massa Marittima and Grosseto
which she was in the process of absorbing.  Relatively cordial or
temperate relations with Perugia and Bologna protected her flanks,
and her dealings with her weaker western and generally Guelf neighbor
of Volterra were neither frequent nor intense--in part because of a
veiled Florentine protectorate over that city.

The main field of Sienese endeavors lay in lands lying in the form
of a crescent, slightly to the west and to the south and east of the
city, including the Montagnola, the zone of Montamiata, and much of
the southern Maremma.  Siena tried to increase the size of her contado.  Efforts to control the mining district of Montieri involved
her in disputes with the bishop of Volterra and with Massa Marittima.[58]
She also tried to complete her absorption of the Aldobrandine lands,
including areas that had been carved out of the Orvietan district in
the mid-thirteenth century--especially in the Valdorcia.[59]

Viewed over the entire time span of their rule, the Nine were rather

successful. They crushed the Aldobrandeschi counts, once a major
factor in the Maremma. At the turn of the fourteenth century Siena
took advantage of the Countess Margherita's difficulties with Orvieto
and with the scheming Gaetani pope, Boniface VIII, to wage a war
against the Aldobrandeschi--a war from which Siena emerged with
numerous southern Maremma towns. After the death of Henry VII in
1313 Siena punished the counts and other feudal lords for their adherence to the imperial cause and stripped them of many holdings.
About 1330 she again warred against the Aldobrandeschi and won the
city of Arcidosso. By 1345 Count Jacomo of Santa Fiora was compelled
to make Siena his universal heir, and his five sons were forced to
accept Sienese citizenship and to submit many holdings to Siena,
including Santa Fiora itself.[60]  Massa Marittima fell definitively
to Siena in 1335. Grosseto, originally an Aldobrandeschi fief which
had repeatedly rebelled against Siena,[61] fell to her in 1336 and remained subject until the overthrow of the Nine.

On only one occasion can Siena perhaps be accused of dealing in
Siena attained her successes by long-range planning, by defining her
goals and adhering to them, and through practical politics and diplomacy. As with the Aldobrandeschi war of 1300, the Sienese recognized
unexpected opportunities and capitalized upon them. Keeping their
goals in mind and not shifting them arbitrarily, the Sienese did not
dissipate their limited means, following now this wisp, now that.
They kept their opponents under pressure, relaxed or increased as
external conditions dictated,[62] and used threats when they were
likely to be effective, and made purchases when possible.

On only one occasion can Siena perhaps be accused of dealing in
fantasies. And accused she was, by no less a critic than Dante,
who characterized the Sienese as "those vain people who place their
hopes in Talamone, and there will lose more hopes than in finding
the Diana...."[63] That final reference is not to a goddess of the
hunt but to Sienese efforts to rectify their lack of an adequate
water supply by doggedly hunting for a fabled stream that was supposed to run beneath the city. The poet linked this chimerical
solution of a real problem to the Sienese attempt to gain and develop
a viable seaport on the southern coast of the Maremma. They saw their
chance in 1303 when the monks of Montamiata, hard pressed by the

Aldobrandeschi, sold their questionable rights in Talamone to Siena
in return for a guarantee of Sienese protection for the monastery's
other holdings.

This project was not chimerical. Nor did Dante's own commune and
its merchants believe it so. In 1311, 1344, and 1356 Florence tried
to negotiate with Siena for the use of Talamone,[64] and when in 1347
Florentine merchants petitioned their government to find less expensive
and dangerous trade routes the Florentines once more turned to
Talamone.[65] Success at Talamone would have allowed Siena to free herself from dependence on the upper Via Francigena, a highway often
blocked by Pisa and made unsafe by long Luccan wars.

The Sienese idea was a good one and the commune put herculean efforts into the project. But the scheme was over-ambitious. Talamone
was too far from Siena, was not connected with it by good, safe roads,
and the intervening area was not sufficiently secure. Siena could not
protect the port from attackers--Ghibelline exiles in 1312, Genoese
exiles in 1320, an army of Robert of Naples in 1326, and other enemies
in 1326 and 1328. As with its attempt to build the largest cathedral
in Christendom, here too Siena overreached herself. She simply did
not have the resources with which to implement so ambitious a project.
But Siena made only two such major miscalculations during the regime
of the Nine, of which Talamone was that in the field of foreign policy.

Such great leaps and projects were exceptional. In treating wider
issues and more far-flung affairs, the Nine showed the same practicality, lack of ideological impetus, and dogged attention to detail
with an eye to the possible that they did in dealing with Florence
and other neighboring communes. Again Siena's aims were limited,
her goals modest.

Like Florence, Siena functioned within an Angevin, French, and
papal alliance. This alliance, and those with other predominantly
Guelf cities and lords, helped protect Siena against would-be signori
who threatened to expand their holdings throughout Tuscany (such as
Uguccione della Faggiuola and Castruccio Castracani), and against
emperors whose presence might encourage militant exiles and whose victories could endanger the communal regime. But even in opposing an
emperor Siena was not carried away by the spirit of party. When it

was likely to be advantageous she sent out overtures.  She procras-
tinated in sending troops and money to her allies when she could not
see an immediate return, and committed a large portion of her own
forces only when her own lands and the city itself were menaced.  And
if the Nine fell due to conditions in the city made possible by the
visit of the Emperor Charles IV, we might recall that Florence too
had temporized and toyed with the idea of inviting him within the circuit of her walls.  In dealing with the Angevins of Naples, Siena long
refused to aid Charles II against his Aragonese foes unless he participated personally in an invasion of Sicily.[66]

Sienese relations with the papacy generally were cordial, but even
here the city did not lose sight of her own interests.  When papal
inquisitors or auditors seemed to threaten the economic well-being of
the commune or of powerful segments of Sienese society they were
resisted, to the point of withstanding a papal interdict imposed as
part of a papal attempt to seek funds from members of the defunct
Bonsignori Company and their heirs in the fifth decade of the fourteenth century.[67]  Nor did the imperious diplomacy of Boniface VIII
sweep the government away in a wave of pro-papal enthusiasm.  When
Siena joined the pope against the Aldobrandeschi it was for the commune's advantage.  When she gained the desired prizes, Siena made a
separate peace without notifying the pope and against his outraged
protests.  Sienese support of the Gaetani's campaign against the
Colonna was limited and cautious--and in 1306 the commune very nearly
hedged its bets by helping the Colonna rebuild Palestrina.[68]

If Sienese aims were modest they also were largely attainable.  But
they had not always been so.  It is to the credit of the Nine that
they liquidated the free-wheeling policy of the pre-Montaperti years.
They tried to keep peace, and when possible to achieve their aims
through diplomacy and purchase.  After the Aretine wars of the late
1280's, the 1290's saw a decade of relative peace and of great prosperity.  The commitment to the Aldobrandine wars of 1300-1301 allowed
Siena to take advantage of a sudden opportunity to achieve old goals
and weaken an ancient foe.  During the next decade the Sienese contributions to the _taglie_ brought security and the possibility of for-
warding the commune's Maremma policy.  The Nine became belligerent

only when compelled to do so, as with the threat of Henry VII, or
when they saw an immediate advantage in bellicosity. Even then commitments were commensurate with risks and possible gains.

The degree of success that the government of the Nine attained in
foreign policy depended in large part on the methods by which policies
were formulated and then effected. The ruling oligarchy quickly recognized that it had to involve all the most powerful and well-organized
elements of society in the decision-making processes so as to arrive
at positions that would have broadly based support and to avoid unde-
sired surprises and setbacks.[69] Theoretically the Nine were the commune's ruling signory. Membership on the Nine allegedly was denied
physicians, judges and notaries, and members of the casati--specifi-
cally listed magnate houses. In this context we must note that the
Nine included some families just as noble as those listed among the
casati. These noble clans admitted to the Nine differed from the
casati essentially in their life style and in their lesser wealth or
power. This distinction is similar to that found for Pisa by Emilio
Cristiani in his analysis of anti-magnate legislation,[70] and to some
extent that of Niccola Ottokar for Florence.[71]

In actual fact the Nine did not act alone. Ordinarily they discussed important problems with the other so-called "Orders" of the
city, and often too with the chief magistrates of the Gabella--a
key financial magistracy. Those other orders comprised eleven men:
the four Consuls of the Merchant Guild, the four Provveditori of the
Biccherna (Siena's leading financial magistracy), and the three Consuls of the Knights, or Captains of the Party (meaning the Guelf
Party). And from a careful study of the extant documentation I have
found that not only did the Captains include members of the casati,
but so too did the other Orders and the Gabella; while judges, some
of them from the casati, appeared among the Orders of the city.

After the Nine, the other Orders, and the three Executors of the
Gabella held preliminary discussions, if an issue was very important
it was debated by a secret council selected by the Nine or by all
the Orders. This group might contain from about fifty to 200 citizens
chosen from the three Terzi of the city. (The councils were secret
in that those attending them were bound not to reveal their proceedings

outside the meetings.)  The secret councils were broadly based, usually including a wide sampling from among the middling and upper economic and social strata of the citizen body, even if a good number
came from the mercantile and industrial occupations common among the
Nine themselves.  Only after matters were debated and voted upon in
those secret councils did the podesta present their proposals to the
larger City Council (the General Council or Council of the Bell)--a
council that before the Black Death of 1348 included 300 citizens plus
another 150 "de radota" or in addition.  Foreign embassies that were
permitted to testify or whose letters were read aloud in City Council
sessions frequently were heard first at the smaller secret council
meetings.

These processes and the composition of the various participatory
bodies help account for the extremely high record of success obtained
by proposals proffered on behalf of the Nine in City Council sessions.
When they were overruled the Nine rarely pressed the issue.  They
tried to compromise or to wear down resistance by resubmitting a
slightly modified proposal somewhat later.  When opposition was too
strong or too emotionally charged the matter was dropped, at least
long enough to allow for a sufficient cooling-off period.[72]

It is indicative of the regime's security and its success in inte-
grating magnates into the formation of policy that the Nine could use
and trust "excluded" magnates, not only in decision-making but in the
execution of policy--execution that could easily have been thwarted
had the participants so desired.  Magnates were castellans of key
fortresses and towns, and served as leaders of Sienese troops.  Together with nobles drawn from the ranks of the Nine, members of
casati served on delicate diplomatic missions.  Had they wished, for
example, the factious Tolomei could have undermined communal diplomacy and policy in countless ways.  Their connections with Florence
were but one of their strengths.  Tolomei served in political offices
in the Romagna.[73]  Tavenozzo dei Tolomei captained a Sienese contingent of 250 cavalry lent to Florence in 1341 in its attempt to capture
Lucca.[74]  Guccio Tolomei was a member of an embassy sent to the Emperor
Charles IV in Pisa in 1354.[75]  The Nine, then, did not fear having
their policies sabotaged or destroyed by the casati.

Siena did have a foreign policy and a consistent one. It did not
just muddle through from occasion to occasion or crisis to crisis.
That policy had positive aims based upon realistic evaluations of the
possibilities and limitations of Sienese diplomacy. This practical
and non-ideological policy was maintained, and achieved significant
success, in part because the ruling oligarchy recognized that it had
to win the agreement or at worst the neutrality of the more powerful
elements of Sienese society. This it did by involving them both in
decision-making and in the executive processes. It recognized too
that a policy of limited goals should not consume all the city's
energies and resources. It expended great efforts and attention on
the administration and improvement of the state and of its economy.
It was dissimilar from a first-rank Italian power such as Florence,
which threw all of its resources into the long and frustrating Luccan
wars--with the resultant financial disaster and the ill-fated signory
of Walter of Brienne.

Siena's rulers guided the fortunes of a second-rate political power,
and they recognized this. That recognition conditioned Sienese foreign
policy and its limited role in the commune's political life, and helps
to account for its successes. Eschewing the luxuries of blind attachment to ideology or of being swayed by grand passions and grandiose
designs, the Sienese developed and pursued pragmatic and limited foreign policy aims. Over some seven decades they achieved considerable
successes, avoided many pitfalls--and the serious risk of losing communal autonomy. One small commune maintained its independence and
pursued its goals successfully. But it did so by finding its own way,
and that could not be the way of a Florence or a Milan.

This brief survey can be only a beginning. We must look at other
small powers, discover how they operated and why. I suspect that we
may find that they were not always simply tools of major states or
their blind emulators, that they were not always on the defensive or
playing the same games as were the greater powers. A lesser state
could develop its own policy and come to an understanding of the role
of foreign policy in the overall political life of a small, relatively
weak, yet autonomous commune. A study of the extent and the ways in
which this was, and was not, the case in other small towns should

increase our knowledge of how a majority of Italians lived and thought.

Part II

Finance:  Money and Prices

Chapter 6

The Significance of the "Feudal Period"
in the Monetary History of Europe

Philippe Wolff

The so-called feudal period of monetary history does not enjoy a
high reputation among French historians.  To begin with, Charlemagne,
it would seem, deserves the greatest praise for his actions.  He restored the regalian monopoly over coinage (although, to be sure, he
followed the example of Pippin the Short); he strictly limited the
activities and profits of the moneyers; he made supervision easier
by reducing the number of mints until, by his order, all coinage was
to be struck at the Palace; and he issued "heavy" deniers (1 gr. 7)
of pure silver, carefully designed, whose type and inscription con-
formed to a precise pattern regulated by the central government.

From his grandsons on, all the characteristics of this "good coinage"
progressively waned.  The Capitularia had entrusted the counts with
the task of controlling coinage.  But the counts soon became hereditary, and more and more independent of central government.  Moreover,
on their own, the kings had frequently granted the jus monetae:  at
first, this was simply a working license, theoretically subject to
the rules set out for imperial coinage, but the new issuers soon
ignored these rules and began to consider the mint their own property,
until finally their minting was no longer done in the name of the king.
There were also numerous feudatories who usurped the right of coinage,
with (or without) the help of a forged charter of royal grant.  Thus,
together with the regalian monopoly of coinage, monetary unity was
also broken into pieces--two developments anathema to historians of
coinage, who quite naturally appreciate such rules of monopoly and
unity.  As early as the late ninth century, various monetary systems
were referred to in the documents, and by the early tenth century each
coinage was known by its own name:  we have the denarii of Reims, of
Le Mans, of Brioude, of Cahors, of Melgueil, and so on.  Hundreds of
mints issued their coins, which clearly differed in type as well as
in weight and silver content.  But this disorderly variety must be

considered against a general background--namely, the debasement of
the currencies.  Since the possession of a mint was considered a
revenue, and since it was possible to increase that revenue through
debasing the coins, it would be tempting to explain the general trend
toward debasement as a result of the cupidity of the feudatories, some
of whom can be praised for indulging less in this expedient.

A non-feudal coinage, truly corresponding to the rights and duties
inherent in the title of king, was to reappear under Louis VII and
Philip Augustus.  By then the _denier_ _parisis_ was tending toward a
stable uniformity, and was being adopted more and more inside the
royal domain.  In 1205 Philip Augustus took over the mint of the
abbey of Saint-Martin at Tours.  _Deniers_ _parisis_ and _tournois_ would
soon circulate in the whole kingdom.  This royal currency was uniform
and stable, and the design and striking of the coins were again undertaken with care.  Louis IX would be able to decree that only royal
coinage could circulate in the whole kingdom.  There is a certain
symmetrical correspondence between the "bonne monnaie" of Saint Louis,
of which there is such frequent mention during the fourteenth century,
and that of Charlemagne.  But, for the history of coinage, the intervening period is a parenthesis, whose opening cannot be too much regretted, nor whose closing too much praised.

Though there are of course many valid elements in this interpretation[1] it suffers from being incomplete.  Historians of coinage are
mainly concerned with the striking of the coins.  Was it done with
care?  Did it conform to official patterns?  Did its exercise reflect
the authority of the kings and a true state policy?  But coinage is
not currency.  Currency ought to be considered first in terms of its
use by the public.  What use did the public make of the coins issued
by the authorities?  How much did the coins respond to real needs?
These are questions to which precise answers are assuredly difficult,
but they have not been asked enough.  On the other hand, French historians usually limit their investigation too narrowly to French history.  Of course, this is not a unique instance, for there is a natural
tendency among historians to deal mainly with facts that they know
best, those pertaining to their own country.  Yet a general survey,
considering the whole of Europe (or, at least, of Western Europe),

would be much more fruitful, provided it were carried on with sufficient care.

This paper, which I gladly dedicate to a much-esteemed colleague,
Professor Joseph R. Strayer, will endeavor to be the first draft of
such a survey. On the way, I shall ask questions, risk hypotheses, and
point out gaps, rather than make positive statements. Time permitting,
I hope to be able to investigate the matter in a more fundamental and
precise way. I am fully aware that this paper is written only in broad
terms. Yet the true significance of the "feudal period" should emerge
from it, in a way which I offer for general consideration.

That reality did not exactly match the monetary ambitions of
Charlemagne and his successors is obvious. Minting never was as concentrated as Charlemagne wished. Moreover, it is doubtful that the
palace (when he reserved the exclusive right of minting for it in 805)
was well enough equipped to issue currency for the whole of the Empire,
even if we admit that circulation was not very active. This is precisely our main point.

Chapter 5 of the Council of Frankfurt (794) is well known: any free
man refusing the new denarii was liable to a heavy fine of 15 solidi,
whereas unfree people were sentenced to flogging. As these new denarii
were heavier than the earlier ones, the reluctance in using them would
have been for paying debts, and not for accepting payments. Moreover
this measure was not unique in Carolingian legislation. Mrs. Renée
Doehaerd rightly points to this as a sign that "La méfiance incriminée
ne peut viser que l'habitude d'examiner, de peser la monnaie, habitude
invétérée dans la société franque et qui ne se laissait pas vaincre
aisément par le monogramme royal." Thus the coins were considered more
as bullion than as currency--and she adds: "Si le denier carolingien
ne s'imposa qu'avec peine au IXe siècle à l'est du Rhin, c'est qu'ici
la notion de 'monnaie', pièce dont l'Etat out le souverain se porte
garant, n'avait jamais existé."[2]

Arguing along the same line that Mrs. Doehaerd does is Dr. Philip
Grierson. In concluding an article, "Money and Coinage under
Charlemagne," he wrote: "One must also ask--though the question is
not one to which a simple answer can be given--how completely the use

of coin in everyday life was normal in Gaul?  Anyone who has handled
Carolingian coins will have been struck by the excellent state of
preservation in which they are usually found.... It remains true that
Carolingian coins seem to have circulated surprisingly little; their
use in commerce was in fact of a marginal character.  They provided
a standard of value and a means of storing wealth, but they did not
yet play anything like the same role as a medium of exchange that
coins were to do in the later middle ages...."[3]

The evidence that we have for the Carolingian era throws some light
on the circumstances in which the currency had to be used.  As we
know, monetary references are not altogether absent from the polyptychons, yet they are not abundant; mostly they record dues of a public
nature, or taxes paid for the use of common forests and wastes.  Thus
some coins flowed into the treasures of the great landowners, who were
most apt to spend them.  Nonetheless the peasants sometimes had to pay
cash, and the coins necessary for this could be obtained only through
working for wages or selling agricultural products.  Thanks to some
equivalences, the polyptychons enable us to get some idea of how much
they might hope to gain in this way.  Thus, according to the polypty-
chon of Prüm, the price of a pig was somewhere between 20 denarii and
5 solidi.[4]  From what he produced--and everything points to his having
produced very little indeed--the peasant was thus able to derive enough
to pay his dues.  That he may have been tempted to do more (in order
to buy what?), even that he could do it, is not obvious at all.  Furthermore the regions accounted for in the polyptychons are likely to
have been the most progressive ones, those which had the most mone-
tarily active economy.  Doubtless we would learn a great deal from a
systematic inquiry into the monetary references in Carolingian documents.  We may already wonder whether the peasants, who by far were
the enormous majority (too silent, alas) in the populations of the
Empire, had many opportunities to use the currency.  They had some
opportunities of course, or Charlemagne would not have taken the
coercive measures mentioned above; nor do I deny the existence of
some trade in the Carolingian Empire.  But we should not go too far
in assuming that the coinage was of much use.  The conclusions drawn
from the documents concur with those of the numismatists.

It will now be possible to evaluate what was really new during the period between the late ninth and the late twelfth centuries, and this, indeed, for the whole of western Europe.[5]

To begin with, the number of mints grew extraordinarily. This fact is well known in France, where it has been considered a sign that central power was declining (a conclusion, moreover, which is beyond doubt). But the case of Germany is even more striking: the Ottos were successful enough in maintaining the Carolingian principle of monetary unity, and only after the death of Otto III did royal authority very gradually wane because of the contest with the Papacy. Now, in the Carolingian period, there were very few mints east of the Rhine; the emperors were thus led to create new ones: some they kept under their direct supervision, others they granted away, mostly to ecclesiastical princes, who soon ceased complying with the rules set out by the emperor. As silver ore was abundant, especially in the Harz, it was easy to supply these mints with precious metal. A somewhat similar development can be noticed in northern and central Italy, where the few Imperial mints were, from the late eleventh century, rivalled by urban ones whose legitimacy was admitted by Frederick Barbarossa one century later. In England, this development took place at a much earlier date, and in no way corresponded to any decline in royal power: Alfred and his successors were responsible for creating numerous mints outside Kent and East Anglia, where they had been more or less confined until then. To be sure, this is only a broad, general description, and it would be necessary to scrutinize this development in some detail. Nor should we imagine that the abundance of the currency was proportional to the number of mints. Yet we may be certain that it grew considerably.

It is usually argued that the cupidity of the owners of mints accounts for these many creations, but any increase in profits they might have hoped for from such creations would still have to be explained. It is also alleged that, because of unfavorable conditions of circulation, the populations needed a nearby mint--and indeed this idea is expressed in many documents. But might this not have been equally (or almost as) true for the Carolingian period? What was new was doubtless the fact that the need for currency had enormously increased since then.

This is only natural.  The growth of populations, resulting in an
increase in the number of tenants (and accordingly in the many dues
they had to pay) as well as in widespread migration to towns, where
the use of money was necessarily common, required a much more abundant
currency.  But historians of rural economy and of the "seigneurie"[6]
make it clear that precisely during the tenth, eleventh, and twelfth
centuries, this "seigneurie" was both more strictly organized and
expanded throughout western Europe, and that currency had an increasingly fundamental function within it:  there were many more dues;
numerous labor services and rents in kind were commuted; and tallage
developed.  George Duby even suggests that seigneurial pressure was
one of the factors that led peasants to increase agricultural production.  Whatever the case, production was greatly increased, partly
as a result of improved yields, of which we are as well-informed as
scarce documentation permits.  The rise of exchanges is even more
certain:  lords and peasants alike found it easy to sell their agricultural surpluses in urban markets, where they could also purchase
the industrial items that they desired and could pay for.  How would
this rise of exchanges have been possible without a more abundant
supply of money, whose use had become quite common by then?

 We must now ask:  where did this more abundant supply of money
come from?  No doubt, the treasures hoarded by the great landowners
(most ecclesiastical) in the form of silver-plate and bullion were
used for monetary purposes, but it will always be impossible to
measure this phenomenon.  Also, the extraction of silver ore was
greatly increased--chiefly, but not uniquely, in Germany during the
tenth, eleventh, and twelfth centuries.  But the evidence does not
allow us to scrutinize this question as much as we would like:  it
would be all the more necessary to read through the documents carefully and take note of every mention of silver ore in order to get
at least some broad idea of this development.  No history of money
can be written without an informative description of the extraction
of precious metals.  So far, this has not been done enough.  It is
also very probable that trade provided Europe with precious metals
coming from other continents, a fact, it would appear, better established in relation to gold.

Finally, it was necessary to debase the coins.  Such debasements
can always be explained by the cupidity of the mint-owners, for in
debasing their currencies, they may have been conscious only of their
increasing needs.  But this sum of individual explanations does not
suffice, in my opinion, to account for such a wide and general development.  Moreover, we should notice that the most debased currencies
were not always the least sought after by customers.  Studying feudal
currencies in Languedoc, Mrs. M. Castaing-Sicard was able to demonstrate that the success of various currencies had less to do either
with their intrinsic values or with the effective power of the issuing
authorities, than with economic demand.[7]  If the lords profited from
repeated debasements, it is because they were economically necessary,
and we must bring this aspect to the fore.

In any case, the destiny of the denier is a very striking one.  In
the early thirteenth century, the denier of Lucca and that of Pisa
(which were among the best in Italy) included about 0 gr. 25 of pure
silver, against 0.35 for the denier tournois.  Yet the new denier of
Charlemagne had contained as much as 1 gr. 7.  Of course, it would be
necessary to compare the purchasing powers of all these coins--a task
that would be, at the very least, difficult.  But the fact remains
that there was less pure silver in the Italian coins while Italy was
so active economically.  However at the same time the denier sterling
weighed as much as 1 gr. 46, 925/1000 fine, which equals approximately
1 gr. 33 of pure silver.  The contrast with continental coins is
striking.  It leads us to a separate treatment of the English development.


Again, Philip Grierson has pointed to the exceptional historical
interest offered by early Anglo-Saxon coinage.  As a result of the
time gap which separated Roman rule from the Angle and Saxon settlements, it is possible to consider this coinage as pure, so to speak,
from any Roman contamination.  Therefore, Anglo-Saxon society is an
excellent example of one in which the use of currency was only marginal.  Silver coinage emerged in England only in the late seventh
century, and its expansion was very slow.  "L'usage de la monnaie à

travers tout le pays ne se généralisa pas avant le X$^e$ siècle, non
plus qu'en Germanie.  Le fait que ces peuples aient pu se passer si
longtemps de l'argent monnayé constitue pour les numismates une
salutaire lecon, en les obligéant à ne pas accorder á leurs études
une importance exagérée."[8]  This, I think, throws a good deal of light
on the slow pace of development in Frankish Europe as I described it
above.

   "How large was the Anglo-Saxon coinage?" Dr. D. M. Metcalf wonders
in dealing with a later period--up until the eleventh century.[9]  His
questions are indeed extremely relevant.  "Was the institution of
mints by Edward the Elder in his new burhs accompanied by an increase
in the total output of currency?... What proportion of the country's
stock of bullion was involved in warding off the threats of the
Normans?..."  In order to reach a numerical estimate of the quantity
of currency that came out of the mints, he has had recourse to the
number of original dies as revealed by a statistical analysis of the
surviving coins.  Actually some serious difficulties, which he explains at length, make the use of this method rather tentative and
uneasy.  In any case, his conclusion is no less suggestive:  "long
before the Conquest, the monetary sector of the economy was of an
extent that the ordinary historical sources fail to reveal."

   Although continental historians--wrongly, to be sure--usually consider tenth- and eleventh-century England an economically backward
country, the existence of a very abundant coinage there is indisput-
able.  Many caches of hoarded treasures found in England, and even
more in the Scandinavian countries, make this quite clear.  They
also offer us the opportunity to establish a list of the dies used
for such minting.  This fact emerges from an excellent article written
by Professor P. H. Sawyer.[10]  Difficult though it is to know exactly
what proportion of this stock of money was sent to the Scandinavian
countries as tribute (a question asked by Dr. Metcalf) and what proportion was reserved for domestic and strictly monetary uses, these
factors seem to have been at least noticeable.  Thus the plenitude
of bullion in England would itself have resulted in a familiarity with
the everyday use of money more rapidly and more completely than could
have been possible on the Continent.  Most puzzling of all is the

question of where this stock originated. From the output of domestic silver mines? Or, rather, as Professor Sawyer suggests, from the import of German ore, itself brought in by the complementary export of wool, needed for the expanding cloth industry in Flanders and Brabant? Whatever the answer, England was likely to possess a stock of silver bullion infinitely larger, in proportion to the number of inhabitants, than any continental country's. This, as well as the early familiarity of the Anglo-Saxons with a monetary economy, may account for the fact that it was unnecessary later on to debase the silver coins to an extent comparable to what was done on the Continent.

England would thus emerge as a counter-example to the picture I have tried to paint in this paper. We should also notice that English feudalism, as is well known, was peculiar and that, except during the reigns of Henry I and Stephen (and then only to a very limited degree), it had nothing comparable to the feudal dissemination of coinage privileges so general on the Continent. And this is important enough so that, in any monetary history of medieval Europe, England would deserve a treatment of its own.[11]


The difference between the numismatist and the economic historian of currency has often been outlined. The former is concerned mainly with the striking of coins, the latter with their practical use. The standard visitor to a numismatic collection may be unfavorably impressed by the "feudal" coins of the tenth and eleventh centuries, as compared with the more careful products of earlier and later periods. Yet--and this has been the main purpose of this paper--it would be wrong to adhere to that impression, for the monetary significance of the so-called feudal period is highly positive. This is the period in which coins truly became a means of exchange.

Chapter 7

Credit, Prices and Agrarian Production
in Catalonia:  a Templar Account
(1180-1188)

Thomas N. Bisson

On October 8, 1180 the Templars of Palau-solità,[1] in the Vallès
north of Barcelona, lent Guillèm de Torre and his wife Estefania 120
morabetins, for what purpose we do not know.  The debtors pledged
revenues from their lands in the vicinity of Palau toward repayment,
making allowance for a deduction in grain to compensate the Templars
for their labor, and in associated acts of piety Guillèm willed his
body, horse, and arms to Palau and donated his tithe on their local
demesne to the brothers of that house.[2]  The written evidence of these
events would hardly call for comment were it not for the survival of
a much more singular text:  a record of receipts on the de Torres'
pledge for the years 1181 to 1188.[3]  This document is illuminating in
form as well as in content.  It was drawn up and preserved in ways
that enable us to characterize the accounting in relation to general
tendencies in Catalan fiscal administration.  And it records yields
and prices for a short run of consecutive years with an exactitude
that is exceptional in extant texts relating to agrarian management
in the age of the reviving economy.

1.  Accounting

The text appears to be the work of a single scribe who divided the
accounts for 1181, 1182, 1183, 1184, 1185, and 1186 into as many
clearly marked paragraphs.  But his script is so even and continuous
that it cannot have been done sporadically or annually as the collections were made.  It must rather have been done all, or mostly, at
once; and the state of the final entries is such as to suggest that
the record was substantially a summary of the accounts drafted in
1186 in preparation for a final settlement with Guillèm de Torre.
The entry for 1185 is followed by information about seeding of a kind

that had become irrelevant to the preceding paragraphs, or had been
forgotten, but that might have been useful to the brothers in 1186 as
evidence supporting their reports of yields.  Next comes an account
of proceeds and marketing[4] for 1186 which can safely be assigned to
the later months of that year (but prior to December 14), and it was
then, I imagine, that the greater part of the parchment was inscribed.
The final lines, beginning with a reference to a meeting of the debtor
and his creditors on December 14, 1186, are visibly an addition to the
preceding script, probably in the same hand, cast in the descriptive
terms of a third party (possibly the echo or copy of a separate charter?), and lacking the indications of paragraphs characteristic of the
bulk of the text.  Whatever the expectation in 1186, some 30 morabetins remained on account a year or more later, and at that point
our record ends.  There is no reason to doubt that a debt so steadily
and speedily reduced was soon discharged,[5] but when and how it was
discharged cannot be determined.

   Why, then, is our record of the debt incomplete?  The most likely
answer is that the scribe ran out of space, for in fact the text runs
almost to the bottom of the parchment.  The final transactions, if
not left unwritten, could well have been noted on another parchment
(but they do not appear on the extant instrument of pledge).  For it
is very clear that the text, which bears neither marks of cancellation
nor the marginal lettering of a chirograph, was intended to have the
diplomatic character of a memorandum or brief; its opening words--
"this is a commemoration of debt..."--place it unmistakably in the
category of inventories or notices (commemorationes, brevia),
Carolingian in ancestry, of which innumerable Catalonian examples
survive.[6]  But the commemoration of proceeds from a pledge, unlike
inventories of domain, became useless once the debt was liquidated.
It is much easier to understand why most such vestiges perished than
why one should have survived.

   In fact, this one seems to have survived only by chance.  It had
presumably been cast aside when its blank dorse was used to inscribe
a charter of pious donation by which members of the Montreal family
entered into confraternity with the Templars of Palau on March 5,
1189.  But this explanation encounters a curious difficulty.  The

charter, unlike the account, was a chirograph cut off from its mate
through lettering at the top; since both sides of the parchment were
inscribed in the same direction, this must mean that the record of
account which concerns us was originally written on the lower portion
of a long strip of parchment.  It is hard to see why the scribe would
have begun his record on the lower part of such a strip if the upper
part were still blank.  The reasonable inference must be that our
text began where it did because the space above was already filled.
Filled with what?  With other administrative memoranda, or with draft
material?  Quite conceivably, but another possibility suggests itself.
Apparently the space above the text of the account was approximately
equal to the space in which it was written, because the chirograph on
the reverse, which occupies almost exactly the same space as the
account on the obverse, begins on the same line as the account.  This
suggests that the account might have been undertaken as a chirograph,
that our text might have been the duplicate of an upper copy that
vanished with the archives of the house of Montreal.  Such a project
would understandably have been abandoned when the scribe realized
that he had underestimated the space he needed.

These are not idle speculations.  In the very years when the
brothers of Palau were collecting on their pledge, royal administrators with strong associations in the society around Palau were recording local receipts in forms and sessions that bear significant analogy
to procedures of account for debt.[7]  In some cases, Templars themselves
had effectively become, or replaced, royal bailiffs when the king
assigned domanial revenues in pledge for repayment of money borrowed
from the Temple.[8]  To maintain his credit with the Templars if not
also to benefit from their fiscal wisdom, Alphonse I employed Brothers
Ponç Azemar from 1184 to 1191 and Guerau de Caercí, a former preceptor
of Palau, from 1191 to 1194 as associate auditors of royal accounts.[9]
Now, for the king's purposes, it became the practice in the 1180's to
summarize local receipts--year by year, as a rule, but sometimes after
two or more years--in authentic chirographs.  These summae computorum
were normally more condensed than the account of Palau, and the reckoning of marketable produce was only one element of their contents; yet
in one respect they resemble our record.  They invariably refer to

sessions of review such as was indicated at Palau in 1186, and do so
in quite similar descriptive language.  This consideration lends support to the possibility that the commemoration of Palau was intended
to be completed as a chirograph proving repayments as well as the
final settlement of the debt.[10]  In that case, there were two records
(if not certainly two sets of chirographs), for the Templars' copy of
the written statement of debt has survived; but here again the analogy
holds, for the royal bailiffs commonly held chirographs stating the
terms on which they exploited the domain.[11]

Nevertheless, in the absence of conclusive evidence, this hypothesis
remains doubtful.  The document of Palau was begun as a memorandum,
it survived as such, and for all of its external peculiarities, that
could have been its only purpose.  Commemorations, although they often
took the form of charters, were not normally chirographs, and there
survives at least one other account associated with Palau that appears
not to have been duplicated by cutting.[12]  The computations required
of men handling five different measures and at least four denominations
of money cannot have been simple.    There was real need of annotation
and recopying as financial work became more exacting in the later
twelfth century, and the Templars--with their reserves in cash and
their capability of accepting agrarian produce in vif-gage--may have
been instrumental in devising forms of accounting appropriate to marketing.  Their summaries of exchange in the vicinity of Palau, remarkably clear and regular, are not alone in suggesting this.  A very
similar notation appears on the dorse of a statement of account for
the royal bailiwick of Tarragona in 1184:  the sale of grain left on
account was ordered, it says, by the Templar Ponç Azemar.[13]

The calculations of the accountants of Palau present difficulties
independent of the form of the record (see Tables).  With one excep-
tion--the evaluation of the somada at (apparently) 18d. in 1184--
their prices were all expressed in terms of the quarter (quartera),
a dry measure that was demonstrably the eighth part of the sestar
(sextarius).[14]  The quartana mentioned in 1186 must have been the
fourth part of the quarter, for on that supposition the computation
for that year can be verified with an error of only one denier.[15]
But for the punera, evidently some other small portion of the quarter,

we are left in the dark, probably because of a mistake in the reckoning for 1185.[16]  It is likewise the resistance of certain calculations
to verification that prevents us from certifying the exact ratio of
the _medala_ and the _obolus_ to the _denarius_ and to each other.  Probably
the two former were identical.  The entry for 1181 affords some warrant
for assessing the _medala_ at half of the denier.[17]

   That the accounting was measured down to these fractional coins is
a mark of the thoroughness with which the work was done.  But the
statements for three, possibly four, of the seven years cannot be
precisely verified.  An error of 3s. 4d. appears in the receipts
reported for 1182; this is compounded by a miscalculation of the
balance for 1183; and so forth.  These errors can neither be reconciled nor explained away.  They cannot be attributed to hidden interest charges, for several of the statements are correct as they stand;
moreover, the tendency of the discrepancy is generally in favor of the
debtor.  Nor is it possible to determine where all the mistakes lie,
for the information needed to reconstruct the account is not quite
complete.  The price of millet in 1184 was omitted, although it can
be deduced with fair probability, and it is not altogether certain
that the price of milled grain that year was identical with that of
other harvested grain.  What is more serious, the ratio of the _punera_
is neither given nor deducible from the stated receipts, nor is the
price of the morabetin indicated for 1185 and 1186.  The receipts
stated in both sous and morabetins for 1186 can only be reconciled
(approximately) on the assumption that the morabetin had fallen to
6s. 2d. or 3d.; yet on that assumption one arrives at a final balance
almost 10s. lower than that stated.  If I am not mistaken, it proves
useless to emend the stated figures selectively.[18]  But if the receipts
and balances are recalculated, with estimates as needed, it becomes
evident that the final balance cannot have been at variance with the
given figure by more than a few deniers or, at most, a few sous.  The
accounting, after all, was almost as accurate as it was precise.


   2.  Economic Conditions
Guillèm de Torre's holding, or so much of it as was pledged, comprised fields directly exploited (_laboratio_) and proceeds from a mill

and from a tithe.  Of peasants on these lands the mention of tithe
alone affords a hint; the Templars controlled the "working" closely
and doubtless shared in it.  The planting was chiefly in grain,[19]
with the coarse winter crops by far the most important.  There was a
good market for feed-grains in this region of mounted knights and
royal servants.  Whether oats (avena) was among the grains designated
by the term cibaria, as it certainly was in the Conflent a generation
before and perhaps quite generally in Catalonia,[20] cannot be affirmed,
but it is not unlikely.  The reference of cibaria (or civada) to animal food, and specifically to fodder for horses, is well attested in
Catalonian sources.[21]   From the allusion to the mill at Parets,[22] just
east of Palau, it can be inferred that some of the fields in barley
or spelt were located between two main roads leading north.  Of wine
(or grapes) we hear only of 27 deniers' worth in 1184,[23] of millet only
a half quarter, for which no price is given, in the same year, and of
pigs and poultry, amply indicated in other records of the Vallès,[24]
nothing at all.  So in spite of the indication that laboratio, mill,
and tithe produced virtually the same crops, we cannot be sure that
Guillèm's cultivation was perfectly representative of the regional
economy.  The produce de minuturis (1184), which cannot be identified,
undoubtedly figured in the tithe, as it did at nearby Terrassa.[25]

  The changing states of the economy are summarized in Tables 1 and 2.
We find, for example, that in 1181 the brothers of Palau harvested 11
sestars 1½ quarters of grain, half in barley and half in spelt, according to the measure of Sabadell, the market-town close by; that
the sale of barley and spelt fetched respectively 2½s. (or 30d.) and
20d. per quarter in that year; and that counting a payment by Bernat
de Plegamans[26] of 6 mo. at the time of reckoning and with the price
of the morabetin then at 7s., the Templars recovered 32 mo. 4s. 5d.
1 medaia, leaving a balance in the debt of 88 mo. less 4s. 5d. 1m.

  Eleven eighty-one proved to be a good year for these farmers.  Although the total accounted harvest of 89½ quarters of grain was only
one percent larger than that of 1182, the next best year, the sales
of that grain brought in nearly twice as much money.  The difference,
of course, lay in the prices:  2½s. per quarter of barley in 1181,
16d. in 1182; 20d. per quarter of spelt (or cibaria) in 1181, 12d. in

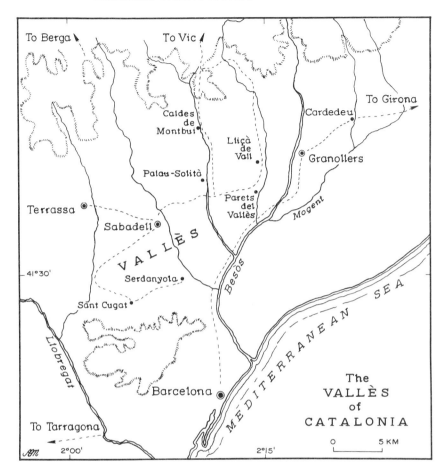

The
VALLÈS
of
CATALONIA

0        5 KM

1182. Although the rates in 1181 seem to have been abnormally high, the pronounced fluctuation in the prices of marketable crops is the most salient economic fact revealed by the accounts (Figure 1). The price of barley varied from a maximum of 30d. in 1181 to a minimum of 10d. in 1188, and averaged around 16d. for the other four years. Feed-grain (<u>cibaria</u>, identified with spelt in 1181) ranged from 20d. per quarter in 1181 to 12d. (1182-1183), and the finer wheats (<u>frumentum</u>, <u>triticum</u>), which were not mentioned in 1181, fluctuated from 2 to 3s. per quarter. Leguminous crops (lentils, <u>de leguminis</u>) varied from 22d. (1184) to 15d. (1185).

These movements of agricultural prices conform to a tendency widely

Table 1

| Year | Crop | Seed Sown | Total Receipts in Crops | Specific Receipts in Crops | Price of Crops per Qt. |
|---|---|---|---|---|---|
| 1181 | Barley<br>Spelt (or cibaria) | | 11 sestars, 1 1/2 quarters grain (89 1/2qts.) | 44 3/4qts.<br>44 3/4qts. | 2 1/2s.<br>20d. |
| 1182 | Barley<br>Cibaria<br>Wheat (frumentum) | | 88qts. | 44qts.<br>41qts.<br>3qts. | 16d.<br>12d.<br>3s. |
| 1183 | Barley<br>Lentils<br>Cibaria | | 50qts. 1 punera | 3sests.<br>2qts.1pun.<br>3sests. | 18d.<br>(?18d.)<br>12d. |
| 1184 | Tithe {<br>Barley<br>Lentils<br>Cibaria<br>Wheat (triticum)<br>De minuturis (3s. 7d.m.) | | 66 1/4qts.<br>1 1/2 somada | 13qts.<br>4qts.<br>5qts.<br>1qt.<br>? | 18d.<br>22d.<br>13d.<br>3s. |
| | Barley<br>Cibaria } mill | | | 11qts.<br>19qts. | (18d.)<br>(13d.) |
| | Barley<br>Wheat (frumentum)<br>Millet<br>De uindemia | | | 8 1/4qts.<br>4 1/2qts.<br>1/2qt.<br>1 1/2 somada | (18d.)<br>(3s.)<br>13d.<br>18d. (per somada?) |
| 1185 | Wheat (triticum) | | 55qts. 1 1/2pun. | 7qts. less 1/2 pun.<br>16qts. 2pun. | 28d. |
| | De leguminis | | | 14 1/2qts. | 15d. |
| | Barley<br>Cibaria } mill | | | 17 1/2qts. | 13d.<br>9d. |
| 1186 | Wheat (triticum)<br>Peses | 6 1/2qts.<br>2 1/2qts. | 17 1/2qts. | 11qts. 1 quartana<br>6qts. 1 quartana | 2s. 2d.<br>17d. |
| 1187–1188 | Barley | | 4sests. (32qts.) | 4sests. | 10d. |

Table 2

| | Price of Morabetin | Stated Recovery in Money | Calculated Recovery, Money | Calculated Balance | Stated Balance |
|---|---|---|---|---|---|
| 1181 | 7s. | 32mo. 4s. 5d.m. | 32mo. 4s. 5d.m. | (120mo.) 87mo. 2s. 6d.m. | (120mo.) 87mo. 2s. 6d.m. |
| 1182 | 7s. | 16mo. | 15mo. 3s. 8d. | 71mo. 5s. 10d.m. | 71mo. 2s. 11d. |
| 1183 | 7s. | 9mo. | 9mo. | 62mo. 5s. 10d.m. | 61mo. 4s. 10d.m. |
| 1184 | 7s. | 104s. 7d.m. (including 3s. 7d.m. de minuturis) said to equal 15mo. 2s. 7d. | 104s. 1d. (including 3s. 7d.m. de minuturis) plus ? [?104s. 7d.m.] equals [14mo. 6s. 7d.m.] | 47mo. 6s. 3d. | 46mo. 4s. 3d. |
| 1185 | (?7s.) / :?6s. 6d.) / :?6s. 2d.) / :(?7s.) / ......... / (?6s. 6d.) | 68s. 6d.m. said to equal 10mo. 3s. 6d. less 3m. | [65s. 2d.] pun. or [9mo. 2s. 2d.] dis-regard-ed; [10mo. 2d.]; [10mo. 3s. 11d.]; [65s. 7d.] pun. or [9mo. 2s. 7d.] 1/3qt.; [65s. 4d.] pun. or [9mo. 2s. 4d.] 1/5qt.; [10mo. 7d. (pun. 1/3qt.)]; [10mo. 5d. (pun. 1/5qt.)] | [38mo. 4s. 1d.]; [37mo. 6s. 1d.]; [37mo. 2s. 4d.]; [38mo. 3s. 8d.]; [38mo. 3s. 11d.]; [37mo. 5s. 8d.]; [37mo. 5s. 10d.] | 37mo. less 22d.m. |
| 1186 | ? | 33s. 3ob. | 33s. 2d.m. | ?(see notes 16,18) | 33mo. 3s.m. |
| 1187–1188 | 8s. | 26s. 8d. | 26s. 8d. | ?(see notes 16,18) | 30mo. 1d. |

apparent in the medieval West.[27]  Local demand was relatively steady,
local supply very variable.  Communications and trade could not altogether compensate for the vagaries of weather and soil.  Barley sold
for 16d. and wheat for 2s. per quarter around Tarragona in 1184 when
the same crops were at respectively 18d. and 3s. per quarter in the
Vallès.[28]  Whether the prices indicated by the account of Palau were
affected by fluctuations in the coinages is more difficult to say.
The deniers of Barcelona seem to have been circulating in issues of
slightly different weight toward 1184-1185,[29] but the sou of account
stood at 7 in terms of the morabetin for 1181 to 1184 and possibly
till 1186.  Its slippage from 7 to 8 in 1187 or 1188 looks like a
local aberration, for other records show the sou of Barcelona holding
firm at 7 to the morabetin (and 44 to the marc) down into the 1190's.[30]

If the account is not misleading in this respect, the planting in
grain may have been over-intense.  The production of barley, spelt
(or cibaria), and wheat totalled 89½ quarters in 1181, 88 in 1182,
fell to 48 in 1183, rose to nearly 62 in 1184, but then dropped to 38
(1185), 11 (1186), and 32 (1187-1188).  Moreover, as the proceeds in
cash continued to plummet in 1183, there appeared traces of a more
varied cultivation:  the 2-plus quarters of lentils harvested in 1183
rose to 4 quarters in 1184, when millet, wine, and other items unspecified were also marketed or credited, and to 16 quarters 2 punerae
in 1185.  In 1186 the brothers tried peas.[31]  But in none of these
years did the revenues from vegetables significantly reward these
efforts, remaining below, generally much below, one quarter of the
declining overall income from the pledge.

Our sense of the difficulties in exploiting the pledged lands would
be confirmed if the remarkable indication of yields from seed in 1186
could be accepted as stated.  In that year the Templars are said to
have sown 2½ quarters of peas and harvested 6¼ quarters; and to have
sown 6½ quarters of wheat (triticum) and harvested 11¼ quarters.
These returns--less than 3:1 for peas, and not even 2:1 for wheat--
are not very impressive.  So far as we know, peas had not been sown
in the years preceding; moreover, if the one half "of all blad" reserved for the Templars in the contract of debt may be taken strictly,
the figures for peas would appear to be gross.  On the other hand, the

## Deniers per Quarter

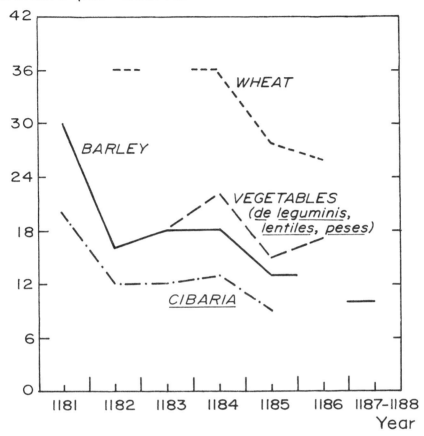

receipts in <u>triticum</u> (a form of <u>bladum</u>) were probably understated by
a factor approaching one-half, according to the stipulation, so that
the true yield of wheat in 1186 may have been around 3½:1.  But even
that figure, perhaps comparable to prevailing yields on some domains
of Cluny toward 1150 although considerably poorer than what was thought
reasonable in northern Europe in the next century,[32] could help to
explain why wheat remained a minor item in the cultivation of the
pledged honor, justified only by its relatively high price.  No doubt
the yields for all these crops were somewhat variable.  Of rotation
or fallow, there is no direct evidence; but it may be significant that

the production of wheat rose slightly from 1184 to 1185 while that
of barley and <u>cibaria</u> fell sharply, that in 1186 wheat was the only
grain crop reported, and that in 1187-1188 we hear only of barley.

 It was a reluctant, poorly fertilized soil that the Templars of
Palau had to work and they seem to have pressed it hard, perhaps a
little too hard. If the 6 mo. paid by Bernat de Plegamans in 1181
had continued forthcoming, the entire debt might have been erased in
six years. It is true that the brothers were dependent on market
conditions not--or certainly not entirely--in their control, yet it
may be that their account conceals speculative operations in their
favor. Although the harvests were evaluated annually for credit
toward repayment, it is by no means clear that the receipts so credited
were realized from sales. Marketing must have been the normal recourse, at least in the good years, but there was nothing to prevent
such a well-endowed community from withholding extraordinary receipts
in dry produce[33] in hopes of the higher prices that would enable them
to realize their interest on the loan.

 The account of Guillèm de Torre's pledge thus provides useful
glimpses of early fiscal accounting and of local economic conditions
in the days when the Templars were establishing their reputation in
finance.[34] Settled in a mature agrarian society[35] increasingly remote
from Saracen dangers, the brothers of Palau moved as easily in their
little fields and markets as on the highways that linked them with
Barcelona and the wider horizons of church and state. They were in
the business of farming, among other enterprises, and their capital
wealth as well as their acceptance of farmlands in pledge point to
their success in that business. Their role in the royal administration of the <u>Corona de Aragón</u>, and probably that of their Order in
general, was firmly rooted in local experience.

## Text

1181--1187-1188.  (Palau-solità.)

Accounts by the Templars of Palau-solità for receipts
   from land given in pledge for the repayment
   of 120 morabetins loaned to Guillèm de Torre.

ACA (Barcelona), Cancelleria, pergamins
Alfons I, 508.  Parchment.  430 x 188 mm.
Script effaced in several places.[1]

Hec est commemoratio de debito quod G. de Torra[2] debet domui milicie,[3] scilicet .c.xx. mobetinos de quibus in primo anno .m̊.c̊.lxx̊x.ı̊.
recepimus de pignore ipsius .xi. sextarios et una quartera et media
de blato medium ordeum et medium espelta ad mensuram Sabbatelli,[4] et
erat precium ordei unius cuiusque quartera .ii. solidos et medium et
de cibaria .xx. denarios.  Et sic sumus paccati de iamdicto debito de
.xxx.ii. mobetinos et .iiii. solidos et .v. denarios et medaia cum
illis .vi. mobetinis quos Bern. de Plicamanibus[5] ei dimisit in tempore
redimendi, et erat precium mobetinum in hoc anno .vii. solidos.  Et
sic restat de iamdicto debito ad huc .lxxxviii. mobetinos minime .iiii.
solidos et .v. d. et medaia.

Et in secundo anno recepimus de ipso pignore Guillelmi de Torra
.xliiii. quarteras ordei et de cibaria .xl. una quartera et de frumento
.iii. quarteras ad iamdictam mensuram Sabbatelli, et erat precium
ordei .xvi. denarios et de cibaria .xii. denarios de unaquaque quartera
et de frumento .iii. solidos de unaquaque quartera.  Et sic sumus
paccati in hoc anno de .xvi. mobetinos de iamdicto debito, et erat
precium mobetinum in hoc anno .vii. solidos.  Et restat sic de iamdicto
debito ad huc .lxx.ii. mobetinos minime .iiii. solidos et .ii.[a]
medales.

[Et] in tercio anno .m.c.lxxx.iii. recepimus de ipso pignore G. de
Turre .iii. sextarios ordei [et] .ii. quarteras et una punera de
lentiles, et erat precium .xviii. denarios de unaquaque quartera et
de cibari[a] .iii. sextarios, et erat precium .xii. denarios.  Et sic
sumus paccati de iamdicto debito in hoc anno de .x. mobetinos, et
erat precium mobetinos .vii. solidos.  Et sic restat de iamdicto

debito ad huc .lx.ii. mobetinos minime .ii. solid<u>os</u> et .iii. medales.

Anno .m̊.c̊.lxx̊x.iiii. recepimus de ipso pignore G̅. de Turre in quarto
anno de decimo .xiii. quarteras ordei et de lentiles .iiii. quarteras
et de cibaria .v. quarteras et de tritico una quartera et de minuturis
.iii. solid<u>os</u> et .vii. denari<u>os</u> et medala, et de molendino in hoc anno
recepimus .xi. quarteras ordei et de cibaria .xviiii. quarteras, et
de laboracione .viii. quarteras ordei et quartam partem unius quartere
et de frumento .iiii. quarteras et media et de mil media quartera et
de uindemia .i. somada et media quam se uendidit .xviii. denari<u>os</u>, et
in hoc anno erat precium ordei uniuscuiusque quartera .xviii. denari<u>os</u>
et de tritico .iii. solid<u>os</u> et de cibaria .xiii. denari<u>os</u> et de legu-
mina .xxii. denari<u>os</u>. Et sic sumus paccati in hoc anno inter omnibus
rebus de .c.iiii. solid<u>os</u> et de .vii. denari<u>os</u> et medala, et erat precium mobetin<u>us</u> .vii solid<u>os</u>. Et sic sumus paccati de .xv. mobetinos
et .ii. solid<u>os</u> et ix. denari<u>os</u>, et sic restat de debito .xlvii.
mobetinos minime .ii. solid<u>os</u> et .ix. denari<u>os</u>.

Anno .m̊.c̊.lxx̊x̊v. recepimus de pignore G. de Turre de laboracione
.vii. quarteras tritici minime media punera et de leguminis .xvi.
quarteras et puneras .ii. et de molendino de Parietes[6] recepimus
.xiiii. quarteras ordei et media et de cibaria .xvii. quarteras et
media, et precium erat de tritici unius cuiusque quartera .ii. solid<u>os</u>
et .iiii. denari<u>os</u> et de leguminis .xv. denari<u>os</u> et de ordei .xiii.
denari<u>os</u> et de cibarie .ix. denari<u>os</u>. Et sic sumus paccati in hoc
anno de .lx.viii.[b] solid<u>os</u> et .vi. denari<u>os</u> et medala, quod faciunt
.x. mobetinos et .iii. solid<u>os</u> et .vi. denari<u>os</u> minus .iii. medales.
Et sic restat de debito ad huc .xxx.vii. mobetinos minime .xxii.
denari<u>os</u> et medala.

In hoc anno seminauimus in honore G. de Turre .ii. quarteras et
media de peses. In isto anno .vi. quarteras et media de tritici
seminauimus. In anno incarnacionis Domini .m̊.c̊.lxx̊x̊vi. recepimus
de ipsa laboratione G. de Turre quam propter pignus laboramus .xi.
quarteras tritici et una quartana, et est precium .ii. solid<u>os</u> et
.ii. denari<u>os</u>, et recepimus de peses .vi. quarters et .i. quaratana,
et est precium .xvii. denari<u>os</u> de uniuscuiusque quartere. Suma
istorum numorum est .xxx.iii. solid<u>os</u> et .iii. oboles, et ad huc
restat de debito .xxxiii. mobetinos et .iii. solid<u>os</u> et .iii. denari<u>os</u>.

Anno ab incarnacione Domini .m̊.c̊.lxxx̊.v̊i., xviiii. kalendas Ianuarii, conuenit G. de Turre domui milicie Templi et fratri G. de Cerdanola[7] ceterisque fratribus in domo Palacii[8] manentibus iiii. sextarios ordei ad mensuram legitimam Sabatelli ad terminum primo ueniente festo Sancti Felicis Ierunde[9] pro debito quod eidem domui debet, scilicet .xxx.iii. mo. et .iii. solid<u>os</u> et .iii. denari<u>os</u>. Supradictos .iiii. sextarios ordei debent accipere in paga computando ut melius uendider- [it]<sup>c</sup> inter festum Sancti Michaelis et Omnium Sanctorum,[10] unde est fideiussor Arnallus sacerdos Sancte Marie Palacii salatani.<sup>d,11</sup>  Et in .viii. ann recepit domus Palacii .iiii. sextarios ordei, et est precium .x. denarios uniuscuiusque quartere.  Suma istorum numorum est .xx.vii. solid<u>os</u> minus quatuor denari<u>os</u>, et erat precium mobetini .viii. solid<u>os</u>, et ad huc restat de debito .xxx. mobetinos et .i. denari<u>um</u>.

---

<sup>a</sup>Possibly et .iii.; <u>one stroke effaced</u>.  <sup>b</sup>.lx.viii., <u>final stroke possibly added</u>.  <sup>c</sup><u>Doubtful reading</u>.  <sup>d</sup><u>salatani, final two letters in superscript</u>.

---

<sup>1</sup>Dorse:  inscribed as indicated above, p. 88.  In the transcription of the account I have consistently extended the abbreviations sol. and d. in the (incorrect) accusative forms that seem to betray the habits of common speech.  There is ample justification for this in the text itself, where, on the other hand, no nominative or ablative forms for these terms are indicated where required.  My extensions are italicized only for such words and letters as could be thought doubtful.  To avoid confusion I have not italicized (other) vernacu- lar, or possibly vernacular, forms:  <u>medales</u>, <u>oboles</u>, <u>peses</u> (?), <u>quarters</u>, <u>ann</u> (for <u>anno</u>?).

<sup>2</sup>Guillèm de Torre; see above, p. 87, note 2.

<sup>3</sup>I.e, of Palau-solità, today Palau de Plegamans (part. jud. Sabadell; pr. Barcelona); see above, p. 87, note 1.

<sup>4</sup>Sabadell (com. Vallès Occidental; pr. Barcelona).

<sup>5</sup>Bernat de Plegamans; above, p. 92, note 26.

<sup>6</sup>Parets del Vallès (part. jud. Granollers; pr. Barcelona).

<sup>7</sup>Guillèm de Serdanyola, preceptor of Palau from 1181 to 1199.

<sup>8</sup>Palau; see note 3 to text.

<sup>9</sup>1 August 1187.

[10]Between 29 September and 1 November 1187.

[11]On Arnau the priest of Santa Maria of Palau, see above, p. 98, note 35.

Chapter 8

Royal Finance and the Crisis of 1297

Richard W. Kaeuper

In his sweeping analysis of English constitutional development,
Bishop Stubbs accorded the crisis of 1297 a place of special honor
and importance.[1] It was, in his view, a critical turning-point in
the slow evolution of the characteristic English political order
based on a limited monarchy watched over by a popular parliament.
Edward I's work brought to completion the interaction between popular and royal forces which could be followed back in time to the
efforts of Simon de Montfort, to the Magna Carta barons, to the solid
achievements of Henry I and Henry II, and even to the necessarily
harsh Norman disciplining of the Anglo-Saxons' racial urge for liberty.
The great Edward in his wisdom consolidated the emerging English
nation in parliament, completing its long education in self-government.
In the late years of his reign, however, Edward played the tyrant,
forced into this role by the unprecedented magnitude of his difficulties: war with Philip IV over Gascony; rebellion in Wales; war in
Scotland. The nation he had patiently schooled in self-government
taught its teacher a lesson in constitutionalism: Edward was forced
to agree to the confirmation of the Charters in 1297. Parliamentary
government was assured.

Stubbs' grand constitutional vision and his particular reading of
the motivation of Edward I have long ceased to command belief as
historical dogma,[2] yet most historians continue to see the reign of
Edward I as a pivotal period of English history. The great crisis
of his reign thus retains its interest.[3] Two decades of successful
rule--the years which brought the conquest of Wales, the great series
of statutes, the continental diplomacy, the apparent resolution of
the Scottish succession--were followed by the crisis which, as
Rothwell has shown,[4] lasted throughout the last decade of Edward's
life. Financial explanations have often figured prominently in
analyses of the causes of Edward's troubles, and one of these deserves
close attention.

In a classic article published in 1946,[5] J. G. Edwards thoroughly
examined the impressive series of eight castles (five integrated with
fortified towns) built by Edward I in mid-Wales and North Wales to
insure the permanence of his conquest.  Builth, Aberystwyth, Flint,
and Rhuddlan arose after the campaign of 1277; Conway, Caernarvon,
and Harlech were begun after the conquest in 1282-1283; and Beaumaris,
on the island of Anglesey, was started after the rebellion of 1292-
1295.  Rather than writing another familiar military or architectural
analysis, Edwards was concerned to present the castle-building as the
"medieval state-enterprise" of a king "wielding in his iron hand the
whole resources of the most compactly centralized dominion of that
day."[6]  In answer to the four basic questions he posed, Edwards
showed that (1) except at Caernarvon and Beaumaris, where work dragged
on for decades, the castles were constructed in five to seven building
"seasons" (the period roughly from April to November), with three or
four of them going up simultaneously in and after 1277 and again in
and after 1283; (2) the large work force required may have numbered
as many as 4,000 men in 1283 and 1284, and it was collected by "tapping
the labour-market over the greater part of England";[7] (3) recorded
costs of the enterprise are hardly complete but "we may almost certainly take £80,000 as a safe notional figure for the total sum....";[8]
(4) these funds came primarily from the king's wardrobe, with Irish
revenue a second major source.

    In their essentials these conclusions still stand.  Just as
Edwards corrected earlier authors' views,[9] his own particulars have
been somewhat revised and expanded by R. Allen Brown, H. M. Colvin,
and A. J. Taylor, the authors of the massive study of royal building,
The History of the King's Works, the first two volumes of which deal
with the Middle Ages.[10]  But what has received less attention is the
important conclusion which Edwards suggests must follow from expenditure of this magnitude:  he posits the closest link between the
castle-building and the great crisis of the reign.  "Now this crisis,"
he writes, "was not altogether of sudden growth:  for although it had
been hastened since 1294 by the coincidence of almost simultaneous
wars with French and Welsh and Scots, it was largely the slow product
of the costly enterprises of Edward's reign as a whole.  Among these

enterprises, none had more steadily devoured his treasure than his castle-building in Wales."[11] These contentions have often been accepted[12] and deserve closer examination. Was Edward falling ever more deeply into debt, with the castles acting as the great millstone? Was there a direct connection between castle-building and the crisis of 1297?

Medieval state finance is a notoriously imprecise study, but we can find one of the clearest indicators of the condition of royal finance in late thirteenth-century England in the king's credit system--that is, in his working relationship with the great Italian societates, the merchant-banking companies drawn to England by papal finance and the wool trade. Throughout the first half of his reign, in 1272-1294, the Riccardi Company of Lucca[13] (Societas Riccardorum de Luka) acted as the king's bankers and virtually as a branch of royal government; they received major royal revenues, such as the wool custom and the proceeds of taxation, and they provided substantial loans for almost any royal need. Riccardi loans were always useful and often essential for the great royal enterprises of the period, such as the campaigns in Wales, the king's stay in Gascony in 1286-1289, the costly process of diplomacy and political marriage, and the still more persistent charges for the king's works both in England and Wales. But Riccardi money also flowed in a small and constant stream to pay for household provisions, officials' fees and the like. The steady stream of mandates for their payments kept the king's debt to the societas at about £18,500 a year on the average, a sum nearly equivalent to half the annual average receipt of the wardrobe, the chief agency of government finance, in this same period. Edward's total obligation to the company no doubt exceeded £410,000.

English historians long assumed the baneful influence of this use of foreigners. William Stubbs complained that "from the very day of his accession Edward was financially in the hands of the Lombard bankers," and he attributed the king's problems with London to this Italian connection. His pressing financial need "forced him to the invention or development of a great system of customs duties in the collection of which he had to employ foreign agents."[15] T. F. Tout was no less plainly displeased with the reliance on Italians and

spoke of Edward being "compelled to make special terms with the
Riccardi"; he was also distressed that the customs revenues were
"directly paid over to Edward's Italian creditors, who in practice
farmed them, just as the modern creditors of a corrupt Oriental despot,
or a bankrupt South American republic endeavour to collect part of the
revenues of the debtor states into their own hands."[16]  Yet far from
revealing a rash and progressive plunge into debt or an unwise dependence on aliens, these astronomical figures are signs of a sensible
and creative use of Italian expertise and credit resources by a king
whose income was substantial but slow and irregular.  The Riccardi
were indeed expensive, apparently collecting a high rate of interest
in addition to favors of a great variety; but the financial flexibility their ready cash allowed justified a cost which was in fact
kept at a reasonable level.  In 1279 Edward owed his financiers
£23,000;[17] in 1294 the debt was £18,924.[18]  In each case the sum was
certainly less than the ordinary revenue collected by his government
each year.  Lending and repayment were going on constantly and simultaneously in a sophisticated system that allowed Edward to anticipate
his income and to act accordingly.  The English government was har-
nessing some of the power of the "commercial revolution" which was so
actively at work in thirteenth-century Europe.

The very existence of such a financial system raises serious objections to a view of cumulative indebtedness leading finally to the
crisis of 1297.  Quite to the contrary, the first half of the reign
must be viewed as a resounding financial success.  Riccardi cash,
ultimately backed by the wealth of a prosperous country, tapped efficiently by an administration which still commanded a good deal of
respect and confidence,[19] paid for a significant part of the great
enterprises Edward undertook, including the castles in Wales.  It
would be difficult to maintain that before the fall of the Riccardi
in the summer of 1294 Edward's finances were in serious disarray.
Though his projects had been ambitious, the king had found sufficient
resources to pay for them and had arranged the credit financing necessary to insure operating cash in any reasonable amount.[20]

Thus, in order for the castles to be viewed as a critical factor
in the crisis, a major portion of their expense must have occurred

after 1294. But this is plainly not the case. Evidence tabulated by
Edwards himself, with the additions of Brown, Colvin, and Taylor,
shows a recorded expenditure of approximately £60,900 before 1294,
and only an additional £17,371 in 1294-1304.[21] This means that nearly
80 percent of the castle expenses which could conceivably be linked
with the outbreak of the great crisis of the reign had been met during
the period of high financial success when the Riccardi were king's
bankers.

In understanding the financial dimensions of the crisis of 1297
there is no need to posit a backlog of debt from the first half of
the reign; events in 1294 and following years provide more than enough
evidence for crippling financial problems. Caught in the vise-like
grip of foreign and domestic crises, Edward overreached his resources
disastrously. Moreover, this overextension came at a time when his
credit structure built upon the Riccardi Company had collapsed utterly.
Recent works have shown the degree of royal extension in quantitative
terms. Edmund B. Fryde[22] estimates that Edward spent more than
£200,000 in the first seventeen months of the wars with the French
and Welsh. The overall estimate of Michael Prestwich is an astounding
outlay of £750,000 on war between 1294 and early 1298.[23] The size of
this figure takes on meaning when it is compared to his estimate for
the total amount of coined money currently circulating in the England
of Edward I; Prestwich suggests that it did not exceed £1,000,000 and
was probably nearer to £800,000.[24] Edward's wars with the French, the
Scots, and the Welsh may thus have consumed a treasure nearly equivalent to the stock of circulating coin in his realm.

Historians have long had some sense of Edward's serious overextension,[25] but his difficulties were vastly complicated by the fact that
he incurred these enormous expenditures at the one period in his reign
when he lacked a working financial relationship with an Italian
societas. The Riccardi slide into bankruptcy began precisely when
Edward most needed them.[26] In fact, their difficulties must have
become known to the king shortly after he learned of the duplicity
of Philip the Fair over Gascony; war with France began officially
with Edward's renunciation of homage to the French king on June 18,
1294,[27] and on July 29 the king's bankers lost control of the wool

customs, the chief prop of their lending and the seal of their understanding with the crown throughout the first half of the reign.[28]   In
the years of greatest challenge the credit system which had served him
in all his plans for the past twenty-two years was in ruin.   The
Riccardi were neither easily nor quickly replaced.[29]   Both the shock
the king felt on the Riccardi collapse and the unwillingness of
another Italian _societas_ to play the Riccardi role delayed the reconstitution of a financial scheme based on the Italians.   The Frescobaldi
of Florence would begin to fill the Riccardi role on a limited scale
only in 1299, and their lending approached the grand Riccardi scale
only from about 1304.   Thus, during the five critical years 1294-1299
Edward lacked a banker altogether; for the following five years, 1299-
1304, Frescobaldi lending was regular, but never rose to Riccardi
levels.   An effective credit system required a new base; the 1274 wool
custom on which the Riccardi system had been built was overcharged
with debts during the years of great crisis.   Only after the negotiation of the new custom with foreign merchants in 1303 was the reconstruction of an Italian relationship similar to that with the
Riccardi really possible.

   How much relief could his bankers have given him in view of the
scale of royal war expenditure in the crisis years?   Would the survival of the Riccardi or the earlier significant engagement of the
Frescobaldi have changed the financial picture considerably and
eased the crisis?   Any really satisfying answers are, of course,
impossible since the effort brings us into the shadow world of what
might have been.   But we do know the aid actually supplied by the
Riccardi and Frescobaldi at other times in the reign, and this gives
us some measure of the loss inflicted by the absence of a banker.
Over the first twenty-two years of the reign Riccardi loans, as we
have seen, averaged about £18,500 annually (probably including
interest), and in 1302-1310 Frescobaldi loans produced a royal debt
of more than £15,300 annually.[30]   But in times of stress Italian support could provide considerably larger sums.   During 1282-1284, years
which brought Edward's second campaign in Wales and the financial
recovery period which followed, the merchants from Lucca advanced
roughly £72,600.[31]   Shortly thereafter, in the three-year period

1286-1289, during which Edward was on the continent and the rebellion of Rhys ap Maredudd broke out in newly conquered Wales, their total was more than £112,000.[32] In the little more than two and one-half years from late November of 1304 to July of 1307 Frescobaldi loans totaling £82,000 were charged on customs revenue alone.[33] Support on this scale would have considerably eased the financial strains of the crisis years, especially since the Italian loans represented ready cash free from immediate political repercussions. Credit of, say, £115,000 or £125,000 would have exceeded the combined proceeds of several of the war taxes on movable property. Even if a _societas_ could have provided only a portion of the funds needed, perhaps only 15 to 20 percent of the suggested total of £750,000 in 1294-1298, the high-handed nature of the king's actions could have been mitigated, and certain famous and stormy scenes might have been played different- ly. It is tempting to argue that if we wish to find a critical finan- cial factor in the crisis of Edward's reign we should look not to the raising of great Welsh fortresses, but rather to the fall of an ob- scure group of Lucchese merchant-bankers.

But although a functioning relationship with some Italian company would undoubtedly have eased the financial pressure, it cannot be argued that such a banker could have spun open the jaws of the vise. In fact, in these years of crisis Edward had gone beyond the limita- tions inherent in his credit system. For projects in reasonable consonance with his revenues the Italians could anticipate his sound income in handsome fashion; but expenditure ran off the scale in the mid-1290's. "Thus tamely and ingloriously," Tout suggested, "the great king's reign came to an end with broken-down finances." In one sense this is not true. Edward had re-established his credit struc- ture and in the last few years of his life it worked once again smoothly and on a most helpful scale.[35] But Frescobaldi lending to Edward I and to Edward II (until they were expelled in the upheaval of 1311) could hardly mend the damage of that decade 1294-1304 when this structure was totally or partially in ruin, and when war expendi- ture had soared so disastrously high. This combination of royal over- extension and Italian failure would darken the last years of the grim and determined old king, leaving its mark in the adverse wardrobe

balances, the snarls and deficiencies of wardrobe records which Tout
knew so thoroughly;[36] and this combination would work its effects as
well on the reign of the second and less capable Edward.

Chapter 9

The Accounts of Cepperello da Prato for the
Tax on Nouveaux Acquêts in the Bailliage of Troyes[1]

John F. Benton

In the opening novella of the Decameron Boccaccio tells in colorful detail of the hypocritical deathbed confession of Ser Cepperello da Prato, known in France as Ser Ciapelletto. According to the tale, an unscrupulous Italian notary--a trusted agent of the Florentine banker Musciatto Guidi--died in Burgundy after making a false confession which created an illusion of sanctity.[2] Research in the nineteenth century confirmed the existence of an Italian financial agent in France named Cepperello da Prato, though not the story itself. In 1885 the Florentine historian and archivist Cesare Paoli published four documents which show that Cepperello acted as royal receiver in Auvergne in 1288-1290 and collected taxes in the bailliage of Troyes in 1295.[3] In 1295 he also acted as procurator for Musciatto (Mouche) and Albizzo (Biche) Guidi, the heads of the Franzesi banking firm, in collecting the forced loan levied in the bailliage of Chaumont.[4] And somewhere about this time, perhaps in 1295, perhaps a few years later, he held the important position of treasurer of the Comtat-Venaissin, again working in connection with the Guidi brothers.[5]

Boccaccio di Chellino spent years in Paris during the reign of Philip the Fair, so that his son Giovanni had access to reliable information from his father about Italians in France during this period. The author may even have been accurately informed about the character of Cepperello da Prato. Although our dry administrative documents are silent about the shameless immorality which is the point of the novella, they do show that Cepperello worked with the notorious Noffo Dei, the Italian notary who conducted the perjured investigation of Bishop Guichard of Troyes.[6] But whatever Boccaccio's justification for pinning on Cepperello the tale of an Italian rascal dying among strangers far from the Tuscan hills, other documents show that the story as given is false.

Information about Cepperello appears not only in the evidence of
his French service, but also in the records of Prato itself.  Moved
by a pious zeal to clear his countryman's name from defamation, Giulio
Giani worked through the municipal archives of Prato and wrote a small
book to show that Cepperello, son of Ser Diotaiuti, of the Porta di
Travaglio section of Prato, served his native city honorably from 1300
to the end of his life and died in the fall of 1304, to all appearances
at Prato.  Far from finding his last resting-place in a Burgundian
friary, the real Cepperello was probably buried with other members of
his family beside the steps of the Pievi di Burgo, which was then the
cathedral.[7]  Historical documents give no basis for thinking that
Cepperello was forced by travel or other reasons to make a fraudulent
deathbed confession.  As might have been expected, diligent research
has demonstrated that Boccaccio mixed imagination with history in his
opening tale.

The purpose of this article is not to add to the biographical dossier
of Cepperello da Prato.  It makes no attempt to deal with the use
Philip the Fair made of Italian bankers and administrators, or the
weighty problem recently posed by Professor Strayer of why Philip did
not squeeze more advantage from his Italians.[8]  Its goal is much more
limited, to re-edit one of the documents published by Paoli and to
comment briefly on its significance.

The survival of Cepperello's accounts is a matter of good luck.
Although one of the documents, written in Italian, is a set of
Cepperello's personal financial records,[9] the other three have a
certain public character.  One is a general account rendered by Jean
de Trie as bailli of Auvergne for the All Saints' term of 1288, the
second records the amounts Cepperello received from collectors of the
clerical tenth in Auvergne in 1288,[10] and the third is the first membrane of the roll from the bailliage of Troyes--which will be discussed
in detail.  None of these accounts is mentioned in the inventory of
royal accounts which Robert Mignon compiled in the 1320's.  Most of
the documents of the Chambre des Comptes have been destroyed,[11] but
since Cepperello either prudently or carelessly took these records of
his royal service back to Italy, they still exist today.  Perhaps
through some accident of inheritance, they became part of the papers

of the Regnadori family and were given to the Florentine archives with a batch of other documents by Vincenzo Gondi in 1883.[12]  There Paoli transcribed them, and there in 1972, luckily untouched by the ravages of the flood of 1966, they were still available for study.

Whatever the truth of Boccaccio's story, it is fortunate for French administrative historians that he mentioned Cepperello, for if he had not, it is unlikely that Paoli would have singled out these foreign records for publication.  Even though they have been in print for almost ninety years, little use has been made of these French historical documents in an Italian literary journal.  The indefatigable Colonel Borrelli de Serres noted them, of course, and historians interested in Italian relations with France have taken account of them.[13]  They did not, however, find their proper place in the Comptes royaux edited by Robert Fawtier.[14]  Paoli made numerous errors of transcription and did not have available the reference books necessary for proper identification of place-names.[15]  Before the accounts from Champagne could be used critically, a new edition had to be prepared.

What most interested Paoli in these rolls was Cepperello's relationship to the Decameron and his use of Italian.  The accounts from the bailliage of Troyes have a different importance, however, both for the study of thirteenth-century French institutions and for the local history of Champagne.  The rest of this article will be concerned with these aspects of the document edited in the appendix.

The money Cepperello collected in 1295 was owed because of the alienation of feudal property to ecclesiastics and non-noble persons incapable of performing feudal service.  For centuries, when a vassal sold or donated property held in feudal tenure to a church or anyone else who could not continue the full spectrum of dues and services (including mainmorte), the normal procedure was for him or the recipient to seek a charter of authorization, called a grant of amortization, from the feudal superior.  At that time, if the lord was unwilling to approve a grant by an additional act of charity, he could exact payment before issuing his confirmation or forbid the transfer entirely.  During the course of the thirteenth century it became more and more common for vassals, including royal vassals, to alienate property without seeking approval or paying for it.  In 1275 Philip III issued

an ordinance setting the terms on which feudal property which had
been alienated without permission could be held:  churches could have
a clear title by paying from one to three years' income from the
property, and non-nobles who would not fulfill all feudal obligations
had to pay two to four years' income.[16]

Philip III's compensatory penalty soon became a revenue-producing
tax.  As Philip IV reached for more and more ways to increase the
royal revenues, he began in 1292 to send commissioners throughout his
domains to seek out churches and non-nobles who owed payments for their
nouveaux acquêts.  The accounts of some of these officials have survived, but no full-scale investigation of the tax and its collection
has been published.[17]  More study of what was in a quite precise sense
a tax on ending feudalism would be desirable.  Systematic research
could show something of where feudal property was being alienated
most extensively, who was doing the purchasing, and perhaps even at
what rate.

When such a study is made the detailed accounts of Cepperello da
Prato should be included.  At present, however, the information we
have on nouveaux acquêts in the bailliage of Troyes is incomplete and
lacks the illumination which comparisons could supply.  We are not
certain how long a period was covered by this survey, or what percentage of alienated property had already been authorized by charters
of amortization, so the scale of the operations accounted for here can
be calculated only approximately.  As we are uncertain of the rates
applied to different classes of transfers, it is hard to make satisfactory contrasts between ecclesiastical and lay purchasers.[18]  Over
35 percent of the revenue which Cepperello collected in the bailliage
came from the castellany of Troyes, but the fragmentary nature of the
accounts prevents further conclusions about the areas of most intensive economic activity.

The most critical question about the roll printed here is the significance of its total and its relationship to other accounts for the
same tax.  The inventory of Robert Mignon lists three accounts for the
collection of the tax on nouveaux acquêts under the heading of the
bailliage of Troyes-Meaux.  The first of these was rendered by
Guillaume de Nointeau, canon of Tours, on January 8, 1294.  A second

was rendered by the same Guillaume and Guillaume de Mantes on the
feast of St. Barnabas (June 11) in 1295. The third, which Mignon
listed second, was rendered by Guillaume de Nointeau in March 1296
(n.s.).[19] Of the accounts with which we are most directly concerned,
rendered by Cepperello along with the royal clerks Pierre de Condé
and Jean de Dammartin on June 6, 1295, Mignon was unaware.

References to the accounts of 1294 and 1295 appear in a list of the
debts of the county of Champagne prepared by Jean Clersens. We learn
from this statement that the tax on the alienation of fiefs was turned
over to Biche Guidi for collection. The account of January 1294 produced 2154 l. 12s. 6d., while that of June 11, 1295 came to a total of
5810 l. 18s. 2d. Of that second total, 3894 l. 7s. 4d. was accounted
for by Biche.[20] From these figures we can see the relationship of
Cepperello's roll to that rendered by Guillaume de Nointeau and
Guillaume de Mantes in the following week, for Cepperello noted (item
141) that he shipped off 3898 l. Since minor expenses could easily
explain the difference from the figure given for Biche's collection,
it follows that Cepperello's roll is an accounting of the collection
he made for Biche when the Florentine banker was working for the two
French administrators. The large amount still uncollected on June 11,
1295 is probably explained by a comment on the dorse of that account
that the bishop of Troyes, the chapters of Saint-Pierre and Saint-
Etienne, and the abbot of Montier-la-Celle still had to make payment
for lands on which they claimed high justice.[21] The roll of March
1296, of which we have no further record, may have settled the matter.
If the two accounts of 1294 and 1295 turned up most of the debts owed
the crown, the paper total for this tax was in the neighborhood of
8000 l., reduced somewhat by expenses and uncollected debts.

Eight thousand pounds was worth collecting, of course, for a government at war and eager to tap every possible source of income, though
the work involved in tracking down the transfers of land and collecting
the money must have made other expedients seem more attractive.[22] In
contrast, the forced loan from the non-nobles of the bailliage of
Troyes in 1295 produced over 12,600 l.[23]

What we do not know, and in the present state of our knowledge cannot determine precisely, is the relationship of the alienations

accounted for in the rolls of 1294 and 1295 to the total amount of
feudal property in the bailliage.  If the tax assessed by the agents
of Philip the Fair was collected at the same rates established by his
father in 1275, then those rates varied from a low (for donations to
churches) of one year's income to a high (for non-nobles who transformed all feudal payments into cens) of four years' income.  If we
then assume for the purpose of making a very rough calculation that
the average rate was two years' income (since acquisitions by churches
seem to have outweighed those of the laity), the total annual value
of the property alienated would be 4000 l.  But I am unaware of any
evidence stating the rates charged by Philip the Fair.  They may well
have been higher than those of 1275; in 1328 the highest rate charged
by Philip VI was eight years' income.[24]  This possibility makes the
4000 l. just calculated appear to be a maximum figure perhaps far
higher than it should be.  Under these circumstances, an estimate of
3000 l. annual income might well be justified.

We are equally unsure of the period covered by this assessment.
The full survey presumably applied to all the time Philip the Fair
had governed the county--that is, about ten years--but it was probably
also intended to be assessed on lands alienated during the time of
Philip's predecessors, and perhaps went as far back as thirty years.
If 3000 l. is divided by these minimum and maximum periods, we come
up with an annual alienation taxed in this survey of land worth from
100 to 300 l. a year.

Philip's assessors in 1310 were instructed to levy the tax on
nouveaux acquêts on fiefs, rear-fiefs, and even allods.[25]  We have as
yet no calculation of the value of all feudal property in the bailliage
of Troyes, though the work currently being conducted by Dr. Theodore
Evergates may establish such a figure.  In 1252 the value of 239 fiefs
in the bailliage was 6400 l., so that the total value of an estimated
432 fiefs in the bailliage of Troyes would have been about 11,500.
In addition, Dr. Evergates calculates the value of the rear-fiefs in
the bailliage at about 7500 l., giving a total of about 19,000 l.
annual income for all fiefs and rear-fiefs in the bailliage at the
middle of the thirteenth century.[26]  I know of no way to estimate the
value of allods, but it was probably not large.  The total annual value

of all property held by the noble class in the bailliage was no doubt
something over 20,000 1.  This figure, uncertain as it is, is large
enough so that we may conclude that the lessening of feudal relations
through the acquisition of feudal property by churches and non-nobles
was probably not a major problem in the bailliage in the later years
of the thirteenth century.

In making his collection Cepperello had the help not only of two
royal clerks but also of the local prévôts.  The prévôt was the official most likely to be familiar with such petty transactions as the
acquisition by a parish church of land worth a few sous a year.[27]  The
roll is arranged by castellanies (which in Champagne were synonymous
with prévôtés), and this division gives it a special value for local
history.  For obvious reasons, ecclesiastical records, including
pouillés and accounts of the collection of the ecclesiastical tenth,
were recorded by diocese.[28]  On the other hand, such secular records
as the late Capetian hearth tax which is the basis of so many demographic estimates, the extenta of income and property belonging to
the count or king, and the precious estimate of ecclesiastical revenues in the bailliage of Troyes made by royal agents around 1300 were
all based on the bailliage or its subdivisions, the castellanies.[29]
In order to make proper comparisons between the two classes of records,
it is necessary to know which parishes or villages were in which castellany and bailliage.  The bailliage of Troyes has presented special
problems:  one text of the État des paroisses et des feux credits it
with 274 parishes, the other with 374.[30]  The latter number is probably
the correct one, but uncertainty over the boundaries of the bailliage
have made it difficult to establish a map which would permit a count
of the parishes and a determination of which ecclesiastical houses
named in the estimate of ecclesiastical revenues were inside the
bailliage and which were not.  The eastern border of the bailliage,
including the castellany of Troyes, has been particularly difficult
to map.[31]  Fortunately, Cepperello's accounts provide a basis for a
reasonably accurate map of the castellany of Troyes in 1295, although
absolute certainty is not possible.[32]

The greatest problem for any editor of Ceperello's roll is the
transcription of proper nouns.  Unfamiliar with the place-names of a

foreign territory, Paoli made numerous errors,[33] some of which, however, may have been the responsibility of the scribe.  A few of the
more difficult words give the impression of deliberate fudging.
Where I have been quite uncertain as to what the scribe meant to
write (as in the differentiation of n and u/v or t and c), I have
given what I think he should have written when I had a basis for such
a judgment, and have otherwise included a warning question mark.

Our fragmentary information about the alienation of feudal property
in the bailliage of Troyes and about its geography would be greatly
increased if we had more than one membrane of a roll which was probably composed of at least five.  Although this one fragment has been
separated from its continuation since its donation to the Florentine
archives in 1883, it is possible that the other pieces still exist
in some unsorted collection of documents and will one day be properly
identified.[34]  Cepperello da Prato was a minor functionary who owes
his fame to the use Boccaccio made of his name rather than to his own
achievements in France.  He made his greatest contribution to history by preserving the souvenirs of his foreign service.  The few
remnants of those records which have come down to us can only make
us wish that he and his associates had stuffed more documents in
their saddlebags.  Until the riches of Italian private archives have
been fully explored we cannot be sure how much French documentation
was taken home by the Italian notaries and financiers who contributed
to the toughness and the skill of the administration of Philip the
Fair.

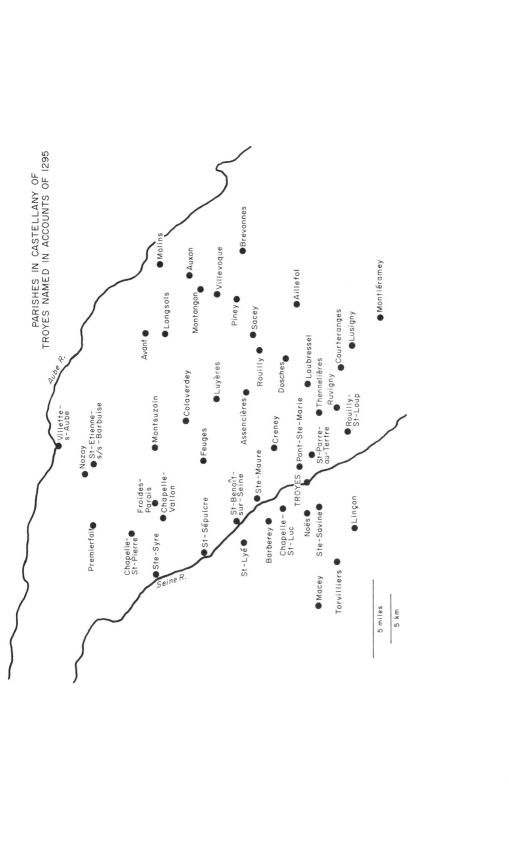

PARISHES IN CASTELLANY OF
TROYES NAMED IN ACCOUNTS OF 1295

Aube R.

Seine R.

Villette-s-Aube

Nozay

St-Etienne-s/s-Barbuise

Molins

Longsols

Avant

Auxon

Montangon

Villevoque

Brevonnes

Piney

Sacey

Aillefol

Montiéramey

Premierfait

Chapelle-St-Pierre

Froides-Parois

Montsuzain

Colaverdey

Luyères

Rouilly

Dosches

Laubressel

Courteranges

Lusigny

Ste-Syre

Chapelle-Vallon

Feuges

Assencières

Creney

Thennelières

Ruvigny

St-Sépulcre

St-Benoît-sur-Seine

Ste-Maure

Pont-Ste-Marie

St-Parre-au-Tertre

Rouilly-St-Loup

St-Lyé

TROYES

Noës

Linçon

Barberey

Chapelle-St-Luc

Ste-Savine

Macey

Torvilliers

5 miles

5 km

Appendix

Accounts of Cepperello da Prato for the collection of the tax on the alienation of feudal property in the bailliage of Troyes, 6 June 1295.

A.  Florence, Archivio di Stato, Dono Gondi (1883), no. 4.  Parchment, 72 x 25 cm.  Dry ruling, 2 cols. on face, 1 on dorse.  The first membrane of a longer roll; holes from sewing at bottom.

a.  Ed. Cesare Paoli, "Documenti di ser Ciappelletto," Giornale storico della letteratura italiana, V (1885), 365-369.

Compotus Chiperelli Dextahit factus in baillivia Trecensi et dotis seu dotalicii illustrissime domine Blance, Dei gratia regine Navarre, super rebus immobilibus acquisitis [ab ecclesiasticis][1] et ignobilibus personis in castellanis sequentibus baillivie supradicte [cum vener][2] abilibus viris magistris P. de Condeto, archidiancono Suessionensi, et Johanne de Donno Martino, illustrissimi regis Francie clericis, anno Domini M°.CC°. nonagesimo quinto, die lune ante festum beati Barnabe apostoli.

[left column]

In castellania Trecensi ab ecclesiasticis personis:

[1]  Curatus ecclesie Sancti Nissecii Trecensis: 9s.
[2]  Curatus Sanctorum Andree et Egidii Trecensis: 20s.
[3]  Prior Sancti Bernardi de Trecis: 19 l. 15s.
[4]  Stephanus de Creni, qui optinet in ecclesia Sancti Petri Trencensis altare fundatum in honore Omnium Sanctorum: 6 l.
[5]  Guillelmus de Carcassone, presbyter beneficiatus ad altare beati Leonardi in ecclesia predicta: 9 l.
[6]  Henricus de Chacenayo, beneficiatus in ecclesia predicta ad altare sancti Augustini: 12 l.
[7]  Humbertus de Meldis et Johannes Allerii, beneficiati in eadem ecclesia ad altaria sanctorum Trinitatis et Bartholomei: 49s.
[8]  Curatus ecclesie Sancti Dyonisii de Trecis: 14s.
[9]  Curatus Sancti Johannis de Foro Trecensi: 10 l. 16s.
[10]  Domus Hospitalis Sancti Johannis Jherosolimitani de Trecis: 17 l.
[11]  Curatus ecclesie de Sancto Sepulcro: 19s.
[12]  Prior eiusdem loci: 29s.
[13]  Prior curatus ecclesie de Sancta Mora: 15s. 6d.
[14]  Curatus ecclesie de Capella Valon: 5s.
[15]  Curatus ecclesie de Sancta Syra: 8s.
[16]  Curatus de Monte Suzano: 73s. 6d.
[17]  Curatus Sancti Benedicti supra Secanam: 13s.
[18]  Curatus ecclesie Pontis sancte Marie: 20s. 11d.
[19]  Curatus ecclesie Sancti Stephani super Barbuise: 10s. 6d.
[20]  Curatus ecclesie de Villete: 38s.
[21]  Curatus ecclesie de Noeroy: 4s.
[22]  Curatus ecclesie de Primo Facto: 12s.

[23]  Curatus ecclesie de Faiges: 10s.
[24]  Curatus ecclesie de Lujeres: 30s.
[25]  Curatus ecclesie de Brevgione:3 9s. 10d.
[26]  Curatus ecclesie de Ruilly:   39s.
[27]  Curatus ecclesie de Saciaco: 108s. 3d.
[28]  Curatus ecclesie d'Aubrissel: 19s.
[29]  Curatus ecclesie de Dosche: 57s.
[30]  Curatus ecclesie de Sancto Patrolo: 100s.
[31]  Prior curatus ecclesie de Lonsolt: 46s.
[32]  Prior curatus d'Auson: 64s.
[33]  Curatus ecclesie de Courlaverdey: 40s.
[34]  Marricularii eiusdem ecclesie: 20s.
[35]  Prior curatus de Lusigny: 24s.
[36]  Curatus ecclesie de Tenillieres: 16s.
[37]  Curatus ecclesie des Noes: 10s. 6d.
[38]  Curatus ecclesie de Sancto Leone: 26s.
[39]  Curatus ecclesie Monasterii Arramerensis: 15s.
[40]  Curatus ecclesie de Ruvigniaco: 32s.
[41]  Curatus ecclesie de Courtrangis: 3s.
[42]  Curatus ecclesie d'Avens: 3s. 6d.
[43]  Marricularii dicte ecclesie: 3s.
[44]  Curatus ecclesie de Molins: 28s. 11d.
[45]  Marricularii de Molins: 8s. 9d.
[46]  Curatus ecclesie de Lincon: 37s.
[47]  Curatus ecclesie d'Aillefo: 105s.
[48]  Curatus ecclesie de Borbere sancti Supplicii: 32s.
[49]  Curatus ecclesie de Torviller: 6s. 3d.
[50]  Curatus ecclesie de Mace: 2s. 9d.
[51]  Curatus ecclesie d'Acensieris: 38s. 6d.
[52]  Abbas Sancti Luppi Trecensis: 73 l. 12s.
[53]  Girardinus, vicarius in ecclesia Sancti Urbani: 24 l.
[54]  Abbas Sancti Martini de Areis: 9 l.
[55]  Magister Domus Dei Sancti Spiritus Trecensis: 40s.
[56]  Abbas monasterii de Arripatorio: 69 l.
[57]  Rector domus Templi Trecensis: 6 l. 16s.
[58]  Prior de Claro Loco: 4 l.
[59]  Capitulum Sancti Stephani Trecensis: 123 l.
[60]  Capitulum Sancti Petri Trecensis: 203 l. 14s.
[61]  Abbas et conventus Monasterii Arramerensis: 126 l. 6s.
[62]  Fratres Trinitatis Trecensis: 37 l. 8s.
[63]  Johannes li Mangineus et Jacobus li Flamens, beneficiati ad
altare beati Andree apostoli subtus crucifixum in ecclesia Sancti
Stephani: 6 l. 15s.
[64]  Dominus Petrus le Sauvage, capellanus in dicta ecclesia ad
altare sancti Petri: 60s.
[65]  Capellani altaris sancti Thome martyris: 20s.
[66]  Dominus Nicholaus de Montigny, capellanus altaris sancti
Johannis Evangeliste in dicta ecclesia: 60s. 4d.
[67]  Martinus de Montaulain, cappellanus altaris sancti Martini in
dicta ecclesia: 6 l.
[68]  Guillelmus de Sancta Margareta, capellanus altaris sancti
Pauli: 50s.
[69]  Dominus Stephanus de Sublanis, capellanus altaris sancti

Dyonisii: 100s.

[right column]

Ab ignobilibus personis dicte castellanie Trecensis:

[70]  Bricius de Champiguion, civis Trecensis: 40s.
[71]  Provencel, corretarius equorum, de Trecis: 9 1.
[72]  Dyonisius de Primo Facto, civis Trecensis: 20 1.
[73]  Gibertus de Chastillon, de Trecis: 36s.
[74]  Theobaldus li Lorgnes, de Trecis: 10 1. 10s.
[75]  Phelisetus Marescalli, de Trecis: 12s.
[76]  Sebilla, filia Ade capellarii Monasterii Cellensis: 8s.
[77]  Perrotus Bachelait, de Lanis Barrosis: 8s.
[78]  Thiericus, Johannes l'Orge [or Lorge], Gorgete, Miletus filius
Mariete, et Maria la Sourde, de Lanis: 32s.
[79]  Johannes Matons, clericus, gener Mathe de Auberville, et
Johannes Burserii, de Trecis: 48s.
[80]  Jacobus la Belle, de Trecis: 12s.
[81]  Bertholotus Muete et eius gener, Trecenses: 12s.
[82]  Garnerus de Villarcel et Perrotus, eius filius: 12 1. 15s.
[83]  Heredes Oberti de Villelous, de Trecis: 30 1.
[84]  Johannes Berthier, de Trecis: 15 1.
[85]  Relicte dicti Guion et Johannes Carbonnellus, parrochie de
Sancta Maura: 12 1.
[86]  Girardus d'Espinci, parrochie de Savieres: 50s.
[87]  Dictus Belliers, de Capella sancti Petri: 7s. 6d.
[88]  Agnes la Goullere, de Trecis: 50s.
[89]  Liberi defuncti Renaudi de Vitriaco et liberi defuncti Galteri
Comitis, parrochie de Creny: 60s.
[90]  Galterus, frater Colardis maioris de Crony: 50s.
[91]  Heredes Bartholomie dou Doches, parrochie de Pigny: 60s.
[92]  Dictus Thierryez, de Pigny:  100s.
[93]  Jaquins et Johannes, filii Christiane d'Aubrussel: 3s.
[94]  Johannes Garneri minor, civis Trecensis:  14 1.
[95]  Johannes Pinons et Michael Pissionarius, parrochie Sancti
Remigii de Trecis: 4 1. 4s.
[96]  Johannes de Lonsolt, parrochie de Lonsolt: 30s.
[97]  Rogerus Generi, de Lonsolt: 3s.
[98]  Galterus de Latre, parrochie de Lonsolt: 10s.
[99]  Jaqueta la Beresse, parrochie de Montaingone: 6s.
[100]  Oudardus, eiusdem parrochie: 6s.
[101]  Johannes Notay, de Villevesque: 5s.
[102]  Jaquetus Renart, de Trecis: 10 1.
[103]  Robinetus Renart, de Trecis: 100s.
[104]  Ogerus de Poilli, de Trecis: 15s.
[105]  Clemens de Sancto Anthonio, de Trecis: 4 1. 10s.
[106]  Galterus le Cornu, parrochie de Capella beati Luce: 30s.
[107]  Johannes Normannus, parrochie d'Avens: 9 1.
[108]  Katherina la Roiere, de Trecis: 60s.
[109]  Flos, relicta Theoberti Lavener.[?], de Trecis: 21s.
[110]  Symon Coci, de Barbere: 60s.
[111]  Johannes Prepositi, de Barbere: 60s.

[112]  Johannes Billons, de Barbere: 40s.
[113]  Johannes Margueus, de Barbere: 30s.
[114]  Guillelmus Malrex, de Barbere: 12s.
[115]  Felisetus Chapon et Alisia dicta la Guillote, de Barbere: 20s.
[116]  Johannes li Bouvars, de Barbere: 10s.
[117]  Decanus de Villa Mauri:⁴ 30s.
[118]  Johannes li Reus, civis Trecensis: 20 1. 5s.
[119]  Felisotus Mumerus [?], parrochie de Mace: 6s.
[120]  Laurentius Durars, eiusdem parrochie: 2s.
[121]  Margareta, relicta Petri Durart: 2s.
[122]  Johannes Durars: 2s.
[123]  Jaquetus Clericus, eiusdem parrochie: 2s.
[124]  Radulphus dictus Conchemeille, eiusdem parrochie: 3s.
[125]  Jaquardus Conchemaille: 5s.
[126]  Perrardus Conchemaille: 4s.
[127]  Felisetus Conchemaille: 5s.
[128]  Michael, gener Jaqueti Clerici de Mace: 6s.
[129]  Giletus Aubert, parrochie Sancte Savine, Robinus filius Au
Caoussin, et dictus Riceus du Mesnil, parrochie de Assencieris: 24 1.
[130]  Giletus de Crassi, Guillelminus, Juliana, Jaquenetus, Colinetus,
et Johannes Garnerii minor: 40 1.
[131]  Liberi le Monnoier, parrochie de Mace: 7 1. 10s.
[132]  Radulphus Cressart: 6 1.
[133]  Dictus Johers, Jaquins Boisseres [?], Felisia uxor dicti
Folfais, et Jaquenus Bayars: 40s.
[134]  Robinus, filius Au Caoursin, de Mesnilio prope Seellieres: 100s.
[135]  Petrus de Marnay: 30s.
[136]  Stephanus de Lardilli, de parrochie de Ruilly: 18 1.
[137]  Heredes Johannis Nicholay: 9 1.
[138]  Johannes Quarrez, de Trecis: 60 1.
[139]  Guillelmus de Castelleto: 200 1.

[on dorsal side]

Expense et missiones facte per Chipperellum Diextahit pro financia.

[140]  Primo pro expensis servientum et pro nunciis missis: 4 1. 18s. 6d.
[141]  Item pro portagio trium milium octies centum quatuor viginti
decem et octo librorum tur., cordis, sacellis,⁵ stalaticis,⁶ et aliis
minutis expensis: 4 1. 15s.
[142]  Item pro scriptura rotulorum et aliarum litterarum et cedularum:
53s.
[143]  Item pro restauro unius equi: 7 1.

Summa:  19 1. 6s. 6d.

Hec sunt nomina illorum qui non solvunt de financia.

Troyes

[144]  Curatus beate Marie: 6 1. 5s.

[145] Curatus de Sancto Aventino: 30s.  Nihil habet.
[146] Curatus de Froiz Parez: 26s.

Laici

[147] Guillelmus de Castelleto:  100 l.

Summa:  319 l. 3s.[7]

Apud Insulas

[148] Petrus le Charnigues, de Montalvain: 40s.

Summa: 2 l.

Apud Meriacum supra Secanam

[149] Curatus de Meriaco: 12 l.[8]
[150] Capellanus Sancti Laurentii de Plansiaco:[9] 10 l.
[151] Liberi dicti Clerici de Mesnilio, de parrochia de Claelles:
7 l.[10]
[152] Perrinus de Nemore: 4 l. 10s.

Summa: 33 l.

A Hervy

[153] Matricularii de Flogniaco: 5s. 6d.
[154] Curatus de Montefuoil: 5s.
[155] Reginaldus capellanus de Donne Marime:[11] 25 l.
[156] Guiotus et Henrycus Lumbart:  40 l.[12]
[157] Bernart de Jannoy, baillivus de Tonnerre: 6 l.

Summa: 272 l. 14s. 6d.[13]

Apud Sanctum Florentinum

[158] Curatus de Sancto Florentino: 15 l. 13s. 6d.[14]
[159] Prior monasterii de Leuz: 60s.
[160] Fratres minores de Trecis: 45 l.[15]
[161] Capellanus de Vriennon:[16] 36 l.
[162] Curatus de Chanlot: 20 l. 5s.
[163] Archiepiscopus Senonensis: 60 l.
[164] Curatus de Soumentrion: 11s. 6d.
[165] Monachi de Bello Prato: 15 l. 10s.[17]
[166] Abbas Sancti Germani de Autissiodoro: 65 l.
[167] Prior Sancti Nicholai de Ruvillon in dyocesi Nivernensi:[18] 15s.
[168] Abbas Sancti Marienni de Autissiodoro: 15s.
[169] Capellanus Beate Marie de Autissiodoro: 12 l.
[170] Prior curatus de Venousse: 13 l. 8s. 10d.

Laici

[171]  Reginaldus de Chichi: 18 1.
[172]  Heredes Guillelmi Renardi: 6 1.
[173]  Johannes Viarius et eius mater: 15 1.
[174]  Heredes Domenchi Bordos: 16 1.
[175]  Gauvarius de Ferray, lombardus: 181 1.
[176]  Bergeon la Marcheande: 30s.
[177]  Johannes Erart de Wlpiliers et Guillelmus de Coudrayo: 6 1. 18s.
[178]  Oudinus de Ceretollaz [?]:[19] 26s.

Index personarum

Adam, capellarius Monasterii Cellensis: 76
Agnes la Goullere, of Troyes: 88
Alisia la Guillote, of Barberey-Saint-Sulpice: 115
Bartholomeus dou Doches, his heirs, of Piney: 91
Belliers, of Chapelle-Saint-Pierre: 87
Bergeon la Marcheande: 176
Bernart de Jannoy, baillivus de Tonnerre: 157
Bertholetus Muete, of Troyes: 81
Bricius de Champiguion, of Troyes: 70
Chipperellus Diextahit: pp. 121, 124
Christiana d'Aubrussel, her sons: 93
Clericus de Mesnilio, his children, of Claelles: 151
Colinetus: 130
Decanus de Villa Mauri: 117
Domenchus Bordos, his heirs: 174
Dyonisius de Primo Facto, of Troyes: 72
Felisetus Chapon, of Barberey-Saint-Sulpice: 115
Felisetus Conchemaille: 127
Felisetus Marescalli, of Troyes: 75
Felisia, uxor Folfais: 133
Felisotus Mumerus [?], of Macey: 119
Flos, relicta Theoberti Lavener. [?], of Troyes: 109
Galterus, frater Colardus maioris, of Creney: 90
Galterus Comes, his children, of Creney: 89
Galterus le Cornu, of Chapelle-Saint-Luc: 106
Galterus de Latre, of Longsols: 98
Garnerus de Villarcel: 82
Gauvarius de Ferray, Lombard: 175
Gibertus de Chastillon, of Troyes: 73
Giletus Aubert, of Sainte-Savine: 129
Giletus de Crassi: 130
Girardinus, vicarius Sancti Urbani Trecensis: 53
Girardus d'Espinci, of Savières: 86
Gorgete, of Laines-Bourreuses: 78
Guillelminus: 130
Guillelmus de Carcassone, of Troyes: 5
Guillelmus de Castelleto: 139, 147
Guillelmus de Coudrayo: 177
Guillelmus Malrex, of Barberey-Saint-Sulpice: 114
Guillelmus Renardi, his heirs: 172
Guillelmus de Sancta Margareta: 68
Guion, his widow, of Sainte-Maure: 85
Guiotus [Lumbart?]: 156
Henricus de Chacenayo, of Troyes: 6
Henrycus Lumbart: 156
Humbertus de Meldis, of Troyes: 7
Jacobus, doyen de chrétienté of Villemaur [?]: 117
Jacobus la Belle, of Troyes: 80
Jacobus li Flamens, of Troyes: 63
Jaquardus Conchemaille: 125

Petrus de Marney: 135
Petrus le Sauvage: 64
Phelisetus Marescalli, of Troyes: 75
Provencel, corretarius equorum, of Troyes: 71
Radulphus Conchemeille, of Macey: 124
Radulphus Cressart: 132
Reginaldus de Chichi: 171
Reginaldus capellanus de Donne Marime [?]: 155
Renaudus de Vitriaco, his children, of Creney: 89
Riceus du Mesnil, of Assencières: 129
Robinetus Renart, of Troyes: 102
Robinus, filius Au Caoursin, of Mesnil-Seillières: 129, 134
Rogerus Generi, of Longsols: 97
Sebilla, filia Ade capellarii Monasterii Cellensis: 76
Stephanus de Creni, of Troyes: 4
Stephanus de Lardilli, of Rouilly-Saint-Loup: 136
Stephanus de Sublanis, of Troyes: 69
Symon Coci, of Barberey-Saint-Sulpice: 110
Theolbaldus li Lorgnes, of Troyes: 74
Thiericus, of Laines-Bourreuses: 78
Thierryez, of Piney: 92

Index Locorum

[Note:  When no department is given, Aube is understood.]

Clairlieu (ar. Nogent-sur-Seine, can. Marcilly-le-Hayer, com. Pâlis),
  prior (Cist.): 58
Clarus Locus, see Clairlieu
Clesles (Marne, ar. Epernay, can. Anglure), residents: 151
Colaverday, now Charmont-sur-Barbuise (ar. Troyes, can. Arcis-sur-Aube),
  parish church: 33, 34
Condé-sur-Aisne (Aisne, ar. Soissons, can. Vailly-sur-Aisne), see
  Petrus de Condeto
Courleverday, see Colaverday
Courteranges (ar. Troyes, can. Lusigny-sur-Barse), parish church: 41
Creney-près-Troyes (ar. and can. Troyes), residents: 89, 90; see
  Stephanus de Creni
Donne Marime [?], unidentified, possibly a distorted reading for
  Sainte-Marine, see Reginaldus capellanus de Donne Marime
Dosches (ar. Troyes, can. Piney), parish church: 29; see Bartholomeus
  dou Doches
Ervy-le-Châtel (ar. Troyes, ch.-l. can.), castellany: 153-157
Espincey (ar. Nogent-sur-Seine, can. Méry-sur-Seine, com. Savières),
  see Girardus d'Espinci
Faiges, see Feuges
Feuges (ar. Troyes, can. Arcis-sur-Aube), parish church: 23
Flogny (Yonne, ar. Avallon, ch.-l. can.), parish church: 153
Froides-Parois (ar. Nogent-sur-Seine, can. Méry-sur-Seine, com.
  Chapelle-Vallon), parish church: 146
Hervy, see Ervy-le-Châtel
Insulae, see Isle-Aumont
Isle-Aumont (ar. Troyes, can. Bouilly), castellany: 148
Jannoy or Jaunoy, unidentified, see Bernart de Jannoy
Laines-Bourreuses (ar. and can. Troyes, com. Rosières-près-Troyes),
  residents: 77, 78
Larrivour (ar. Troyes, can. and com. Lusigny-sur-Barse), abbey (Cist.):
  56
Laubressel (ar. Troyes, can. Lusigny-sur-Barse), parish church: 28;
  see Christiana d'Aubrussel
Leuz, see Montlhéu
Linçon (ar. and can. Troyes, com. Saint-Germain), parish church: 46
Longsols (ar. Troyes, can. Ramerupt), priory (O.S.A.)-parish church:
  31; residents: 96-98; see Johannes de Lonsolt
Lujeres, see Luyères
Lusigny-sur-Barse (ar. Troyes, ch.-l. can.), priory (O.S.A.)-parish
  church: 35
Luyères (ar. Troyes, can. Piney), parish church: 24
Macey (ar. and can. Troyes), parish church: 50; residents: 119-128,
  131
Margerie (Marne, ar. Vitry-le-François, can. Saint-Rémy-en-Bouzemont),
  see Guillelmus de Sancta Margareta
Marney (ar. and can. Troyes, com. Sainte-Maure), see Petrus de Marnay
Meaux (Seine-et-Marne, ch.-l. ar.), see Humbertus de Meldis
Meldis, see Meaux
Méry-sur-Seine (ar. Nogent-sur-Seine, ch.-l. can.), castellany: 149-
  152; parish church: 149
Mesnil (Marne, ar. Epernay, can. Anglure, com. Clesles), see Clericus
  de Mesnilio

Mesnil-Seillières (ar. Troyes, can. Piney), residents: 129, 134; see
  Riceus du Mesnil
Molins-sur-Aube (ar. Bar-sur-Aube, can. Brienne-le-Château), parish
  church: 44, 45
Monasterium Arremarense, see Montiéramey
Monasterium Cellense, see Troyes
Monasterium de Leuz, see Montlhéu
Mons Suzanus, see Montsuzain
Montaingone, see Montangon
Montalvain, Montaulanus, see Montaulin
Montangon (ar. Troyes, can. Piney), residents: 99, 100
Montaulin (ar. Troyes, can. Lusigny-sur-Barse), resident: 148; see
  Martinus de Montaulain
Montefuoil, see Montfey
Montfey (ar. Troyes, can. Ervy-le-Châtel), parish church: 154
Montiéramey (ar. Troyes, can. Lusigny-sur-Barse), abbey (O.S.G.): 61;
  parish church: 39
Montigny-les-Monts (ar. Troyes, can. Ervy-le-Châtel), see Nicholaus
  de Montigny
Montlhéu (Yonne, ar. Auxerre, can. and com. Saint-Florentin), priory
  of Saint-Denis (O.S.B.): 159
Montsuzain (ar. Troyes, can. Arcis-sur-Aube), parish church: 16
Noeroy, see Nozay
Noës-près-Troyes (ar. and can. Troyes), parish church: 37
Nozay (ar. Troyes, can. Arcis-sur-Aube), parish church: 21
Piney (ar. Troyes, ch.-l. can.), residents: 91, 92
Plancy (ar. Nogent-sur-Seine, can. Méry-sur-Seine), collegiate church:
  of Saint-Laurent: 150
Pont-Sainte-Marie (ar. and can. Troyes), parish church: 18
Pouilly, hamlet (ar., can. and Com. Troyes), see Ogerus de Poilli
Premierfait (ar. Nogent-sur-Seine, can. Méry-sur-Seine), parish church:
  22; see Dyonisius de Primo Facto
Rouilly, now Rouilly-Sacey (ar. Troyes, can. Piney), parish church:
  40
Ruvigny (ar. Troyes, can. Lusigny-sur-Barse), parish church: 40
Sacey, now Rouilly-Sacey (ar. Troyes, can. Piney), parish church: 27
Saint-Antoine, commandery in the parish of Saint-Martin-ès-Vignes of
  Troyes, see Clemens de Sancto Anthonio
Saint-Aventin (ar. Troyes, can. Lusigny-sur-Barse, com. Verrières),
  parish church: 145
Saint-Benôit-sur-Seine (ar. and can. Troyes), parish church: 17
Sainte-Maure (ar. and can. Troyes), priory (O.S.A.)-parish church:
  13; residents: 85
Saint-Etienne-sous-Barbuise (ar. Troyes, can. Arcis-sur-Aube), parish
  church: 19
Saint-Florentin (Yonne, ar. Auxerre, ch.-l. can.), castellany: 158-
  170; parish church: 158; prévôt: 158 note
Saint Lyé (ar. and can. Troyes), parish church: 38
Saint-Parre-au-Tertre (ar. and can. Troyes), parish church: 30
Saint-Sépulcre, now Villacerf (ar. and can. Troyes), parish church:
  11; Cluniac priory: 12
Sainte-Syre, now Rilly-Saint-Syre (ar. Nogent-sur-Seine, can. Méry-
  sur-Seine), parish church: 15

Part III

Medieval Trade and Urban Life

Chapter 10

Northern European Sea Power and the
Straits of Gibraltar, 1031-1350 A.D.

Archibald R. Lewis

One of the more important developments of the later Middle Ages
took place between 1250 and 1350 when Genoese, Venetian, and Catalan
galleys, joined some decades later by those of Florence, began to
sail directly, on regular schedules, from the Mediterranean to northern European ports like Southampton and Bruges, thus linking Northern
Atlantic waters with those of the Mediterranean.  In doing so they not
only helped to bring about the demise of the Fairs of Champagne but
also played a part in increasing that widespread Italian domination
of western European commerce and business which was such a feature
of the later Middle Ages.  And since these Italians, in particular,
became so intimately connected with and integrated into Portuguese
and Castilian maritime and business enterprise, this interconnection
also helped to form the basis of an Iberian mastery of the waters of
the Atlantic and western Mediterranean which was to last until the
seventeenth century.

There remains an important question, however, which has not yet
received sufficient attention from historians.  Why didn't this movement proceed in the other direction?  Why was northern Europe, which
possessed considerable sea-power, not able to open up the Straits of
Gibraltar for its own ships instead of allowing the Italians and
Catalans to do so?  Why was it not until the last years of the fifteenth century before English and other Northern European commercial
shipping entered the Mediterranean and shared in the profits which
had so long poured into Italian and Iberian coffers as a result of
Mediterranean-Atlantic voyages?  To understand the failure of the
maritime peoples of northern Europe to play a decisive role in establishing regular communication by sea between these two bodies of
water, we need to examine in some detail the crucial centuries between
the fall of the Caliphate of Cordova in 1031 A.D. and 1350 A.D. when

Italian-Iberian control over the Straits of Gibraltar was at last assured.

Perhaps we should begin by emphasizing some important aspects of physical geography which dictated the difficulties attendant upon the use of the Straits as a means of regular sea communication. A double current links these two bodies of water. The upper one flows from the Atlantic into the Mediterranean, averaging four to six knots. And there is a corresponding lower countercurrent which carries the heavier, more saline Mediterranean water into the Atlantic and runs under the upper one. At the same time the prevailing westerlies which generally blow into the Mediterranean mean that although it is easy to sail directly into the Middle Sea from the west it is difficult for a sailing vessel to reach the Atlantic against a strong current often combined with adverse winds. As late as the mid-nineteenth century there were times when sailing ships had to lay up in Mediterranean ports near the Straits for as long as three months before east winds made it possible for them to proceed westward.[1]  For ordinary sailing vessels, then, passage past Gibraltar from west to east presented few problems, but the return trip could prove extremely difficult. This tended to be the case unless such ships carried oars or had available nearby Mediterranean holding ports along Spanish shores from the Balearics to Algeciras, or along African coasts as far west as Ceuta, where they could safely anchor and wait for the infrequent eastern winds which would allow them to beat their way west against the current.

In addition to all this, ships emerging from the Straits into the Atlantic against the current, and often against prevailing winds as well, could easily be intercepted by fleets from Cadiz, Seville, or the Algarve or even by flotillas based upon Atlantic Moroccan ports like Salé, though it was more difficult for such fleets to operate against vessels sailing relatively freely from the Atlantic into the Mediterranean, since these latter generally did so with favorable winds at their back and a favorable current as well. Hence the importance, for those who hoped to use the Straits, of having friendly sea-power in control of the Southern Atlantic shores of the Iberian peninsula from Alcácer do Sal and Cape Saint Vincent to Gibraltar, if

they expected to pass safely from the Mediterranean out into the
Atlantic on a return voyage.

The Caliphate of Cordova seems to have understood all this, for by
the tenth century or even earlier its rulers appear to have organized
their naval forces with these facts in mind, especially after ninth-
and tenth-century Viking attacks convinced them that they were vulner-
able from the sea. Their major naval base at Almería and their sub-
sidiary ones at Ibiza in the Balearics, at Alicante, and at Algeciras,
as well as their dominion over Ceuta, assured them control of the
major ports which dominated the exit into the Atlantic. And in addition to this, their bases at Seville, Silves, and Alcácer do Sal, and
their power over the western shores of Morocco made certain that they
controlled the Atlantic side as well. As long as their naval establishment remained intact and their flotillas were well-manned they
could make it difficult for Atlantic ships to enter the Mediterranean
or, for those that did so, could make it all but impossible for them
to make it back without suffering heavy losses.

A new era began with the end of the Omayyad Caliphate in 1031 and
the break-up of its imperium in Spain and Morocco into a number of
small, warring states, which in Spain were known as taifas. This
state of affairs continued until the first decades of the twelfth
century, when the second Almoravid ruler, Ali (1106-1142), united all
Andalusia with Morocco and Algeria, organized effective fleets from
his twin capitals of Marrakesh and Seville, and reestablished Islamic
control over both the Straits and nearby Mediterranean and Atlantic
waters, even advancing his frontiers as far north as Coimbra in
Portugal as he did so.

During the century which separated the fall of the Caliphate of
Cordova and the rise of a new Almoravid empire, it appears that few
western European Mediterranean ships entered these waters. This is
so in spite of the advances by land, of Leonese, Castilian, Aragonese,
and Catalan forces at the expense of the Moors, which forced taifas
to pay heavy tribute and to give up considerable territory, including
Valencia, which fell to the Cid in 1094 and remained in the hands of
his heirs until 1102. Instead, Italian and Norman fleets concentrated
their efforts exclusively in the central Mediterranean, where the

Guiscards took Sicily and then Malta with Italian naval assistance,
and where the Pisans and Genoese cleared Sardinia of Moslem flotillas
and captured Bone and Madiya on the North African coast in great expeditions.  Once this conquest had been accomplished the Normans of
the Two Sicilies turned east and attacked the Byzantine Empire and
sent crusading contingents east as well to join Pisan, Genoese, and
Venetian fleets which were helping establish crusading principalities
along the shores of Syria and Palestine.  All this explains, no doubt,
why no Italian naval forces arrived to help the Cid's heirs hold
Valencia when it fell to the Almoravids in 1102.

It is true that within two decades the Aragonese king, Alfonso the
Battler, was able to take much of the Ebro Valley from the Moors,
including important cities like Saragossa, Tudela, Tarragona, and
Borja.  It is also true that Count Raymond-Berenger III of Barcelona,
assisted by Guillem V of Montpellier and the Viscount of Narbonne and
a Pisan fleet, was able to capture Majorca and Ibiza in the Balearics
and hold them for a brief time in 1114-1115.  Their efforts, however,
ended in failure, since an Almoravid fleet regained these islands
almost at once and Almoravid naval forces kept Tortosa from falling
into Christian hands even after the great Aragonese land victory at
Calatayud.  As for the Genoese, except for a few raids the only evidence of their interest in these waters during these same years is
provided by a trade treaty which they negotiated with the Count of
Toulouse in 1109.  And even this agreement seems more a by-product
of their assistance to him in establishing a Syrian county of Tripoli
than the result of a positive Genoese concern with the far-western
Mediterranean.

Once this brief flurry of Christian activity had ended, the
Almoravids were able to consolidate their hold upon Moslem Iberia and
along the shores of North Africa as far east as Tunis.  It would probably be wisest to ascribe inactivity on the Christian side to internal
preoccupations which made it impossible for them to take action against
Islamic enemies.  In southern Italy and Sicily, for instance, we find
a number of rival princes struggling for control until Roger II tri-
umphed over his opponents, reunited Norman holdings, and in 1130 forced
Pope Innocent II to accept him as king of the Two Sicilies.  While he

was thus busy consolidating his power, the Almoravids were able to
send fleets to attack Sicily and intervene in Tunisia. Nor was Norman
sea-power unique in its impotence, for the years 1118-1133 saw Genoa
and Pisa so busy fighting each other in central Mediterranean waters
that they were not able to oppose Almoravid fleets effectively either.

A similar concern with other matters distracted the Christian rulers
of the Iberian peninsula. At first Count Raymond-Berenger III of
Barcelona was occupied in absorbing Besalú in 1111, Cerdanya in 1117,
and in extending his hold over much of Languedoc and Provence after
his marriage to Douce of Provence in 1112 had made him a power in the
Midi. And then in 1137 the marriage of his son Raymond-Berenger IV
to Petronilla, the heiress of Aragon, involved the Barcelona house in
Aragonese affairs. The fact that the Count of Barcelona was not able
to gain complete control of Aragon as king until 1150 explains why he
made little attempt to advance his frontiers along Mediterranean shores
at the expense of his Islamic neighbors.

Turning to the central and western areas of the Iberian peninsula,
we find a similar state of affairs, as new Burgundian dynasties took
over in Portugal and Leon-Castile amidst disorder and civil war.
Not until 1128 was Afonso Henriques, Count of Portugal, able to free
his frontier principality from Leonese-Castilian forces, and not until
about the same time was Alfonso VII of Castile able to gain complete
control of his realm and then, in 1135, to assume the title of Emperor of
the Christian states of the Iberian peninsula. Until this time, however, the Almoravids did not need to worry about Christian princes'
intervening in the affairs of Islamic Iberia. In Spain, as in Italy
and Sicily, no concerted effort was possible against the Moslems, who
continued to control both sides of the Straits of Gibraltar.

Interestingly enough, it was during the century when Christian
flotillas, based upon Mediterranean ports, failed to operate in either
Meditteranean or Atlantic waters close to the Straits--for reasons
outlined above--that northern European mariners sailed into the
Mediterranean from the Atlantic for the first time since ninth- and
tenth-century Viking raids. Though some northern ships may have
passed through the Straits as early as the 1050's or 1060's, our
first clear evidence of such a voyage concerns the pilgrimage of

Count Robert the Frisian of Flanders, who certainly sailed past
Gibraltar about 1089 or 1090 on his way to the eastern Mediterranean.
Others may soon have followed his lead, for we know of English ships
and pirates, active in Byzantine waters about the time of the First
Crusade, who must have reached there by this same route.

Later, a considerable flotilla, composed of Danish, Frisian, and
Flemish vessels and commanded by a certain Guynemer, sailed directly
from Boulogne to Cilicia and Syria, where it operated with considerable success in 1098-1099. And, finally, we know of a large fleet
which King Sigurd mustered in Norway and which in 1107 sailed directly
into the Mediterranean, where it helped the king of Jerusalem capture
Moslem ports along the Syrian coast as late as 1110. Thus, between
1090 and 1110 northern European ships proved that it was possible to
sail directly through a Moslem-controlled Straits of Gibraltar into
the Mediterranean.

A few points about these expeditions, however, seem worth emphasizing. In the first place they all had a strong Scandinavian flavor.
Robert the Frisian had a Danish wife and was allied to the King of
Denmark. Guynemer of Boulogne's fleet included a number of Danish
vessels. And Sigurd of Norway's fleet was entirely Scandinavian.
All these facts suggest that these expeditions relied upon Scandinavian
expertise and traditions in sailing south into the Mediterranean as
the Vikings had done a century earlier.

Second, the nature of these expeditions makes it clear that the
mariners who took part in them did so with no commercial purposes in
mind, except in a few instances raiding along their routes. In the
third place, they had a further characteristic in common. They seem
to have been one-way affairs, for no single ship which took part in
them returned to home port by the route whereby it had reached the
Middle Sea. Instead, those who took part in these voyages and who
returned afterward appear to have abandoned their vessels in the
Mediterranean and returned overland.

We have every reason to believe that most of those ships which
passed through the Straits of Gibraltar between 1090 and 1110--perhaps
all of them--were of the Viking type and carried oars. Their crews
could thus have rowed them back into the Atlantic when they reached

the Straits.  But none of them did so.  We can only assume, then,
that their captains were aware of the difficulties such a passage
entailed--even in the face of a disorganized Moslem naval establish-
ment--and chose not to attempt it.  And once well-organized Almoravid
fleets had been established on both sides of the Straits after 1107,
even one-way passages from the Atlantic into the Mediterranean seem to
have been abandoned as impractical for the next few decades.

As hostilities between Pisa and Genoa came to an end, a new era
dawned in the western Mediterranean which was to last some four dec-
ades--until 1172--and which was to affect passage through the Straits
of Gibraltar.  It began with Pisa's negotiating a trade treaty with
the Almoravids in 1133, with Genoa following suit some five years
later.  Meanwhile, these two maritime cities showed their teeth by
sending a joint fleet to seize Bone in 1136, a move which was preceded by a Genoese attack on Bougie in 1134 and followed by a Pisan
raid on Tabarka in 1140.  During the same period Roger II of the Two
Sicilies also began offensive naval operations along African shores
by occupying Gerba and the Kerkenes Islands off the coast of Southern
Tunisia.

These renewed naval attacks by the Pisans, Genoese, and Normans
coincided with a weakening of Almoravid power in North Africa caused
by the rise of the Almohads.  During the reign of the second Almohad
ruler, 'Abd al-Mu'min (1130-1163), these Berbers from the Atlas
Mountains gradually conquered the western Maghreb, taking Marrakesh
in 1147, and drove the Almoravids into Andalusia.  These latter, however, were not able to hang onto Andalusia very long, and Moslem
Iberia broke up into a number of small, unstable states, some controlled by Almoravids, some by other kinglets.  These principalities
were only very gradually absorbed by the Almohads, who crossed the
Straits, took Algeciras and Tarifa in 1147, and then slowly moved
north to absorb the rest of Andalusia.  This chain of events gave the
Latin Christian powers of the Mediterranean, already on the offensive,
even more opportunities, for while Almoravid power was declining and
Almohad authority was slowly being extended over both the Maghreb
and Andalusia, no effective Islamic resistance to Christian advances
was possible.  So the Christians were able to use a combination of

sea-power and land forces to dominate briefly the waters of the western Mediterranean and to open up the Straits of Gibraltar to their
ships.

One aspect of this advance occurred when between 1140 and 1152
Roger II used his considerable fleet, which had already occupied
islands off southern Tunis, to capture every important port from
Tripoli to Bougie--ports which were to remain in Norman hands until
1160, some six years after Roger's death.  During this same period,
which coincides with the years of the Second Crusade, the Genoese,
Pisans, and Christian Spaniards renewed their offensive also.  Thus
in 1147 a joint Pisan-Genoese fleet, joined by Raymond-Berenger III
of Barcelona and Alfonso VII of Castile, captured the great port of
Almería, which remained in the hands of allies of the Christian powers
for a decade until it fell to the Almohads.  And on the way back from
Almería the Genoese and Catalan forces, joined by Guillem VI of
Montpellier, also took the port of Tortosa, which was then divided
among the victorious allies.  These successful expeditions were followed by a treaty negotiated in 1151, between the kings of Aragon
and Castile, which set up spheres of influence and in anticipation
divided Islamic Spain between the two kingdoms.  According to this
treaty Moslem Murcia, Valencia, and the Balearics were to be Aragonese,
the rest Castilian.  Thus as early as 1151 Almería and Mediterranean
shores near the Straits were recognized as being under Castilian control or influence--an important precedent.  And at about the same
time, in 1152, the Genoese negotiated a trade treaty with Bougie following its conquest by the Normans, and in 1160 one with Ceuta, which
was at least officially under Almohad control.  Now the Genoese, with
Almería in friendly hands, and treaties with Bougie and Ceuta, had
holding ports on both sides of the Straits which could be used by the
ships that wished to proceed westward to Atlantic Moroccan and
Andalusian ports.  The Straits had at last been opened to Christian
Mediterranean trading vessels.

The Genoese almost at once took advantage of this state of affairs,
for by 1146 they had established trading enclaves or _fonduks_ in both
Leon and Castile, and a few years later between 1154 and 1164, notarial documents show, they sent ships to Atlantic Moroccan ports as

well.  These ports were at this time the principal northern termini
of Sudanese gold arriving via Sigilmasa or over sea routes.  The
Genoese were particularly interested in procuring it because they
needed gold to pay for the eastern wares they were purchasing in
Byzantium and Eastern Mediterranean Arab lands.  As long as the Arab
bedouins of the Beni Hilal were blocking Saharan caravan routes with
termini in the Central Maghreb, and gold could find its way only to
Atlantic Morocco, that coast attracted Genoese merchants, although it
is true that Morocco also produced other desirable trade commodities,
such as hides, grain, and fish.  We also know that this heavy reliance
upon Sudanese gold to balance accounts in the east did not last long
beyond this period, for after 1150 the Genoese increasingly began to
act as purveyors of fine northern European woolen cloth to Eastern
Mediterranean lands, cloth which they first procured at the fair of
Saint Gilles and later on at the fairs of Champagne and which was in
great demand in the east.

It is worth noting that the Genoese and others from the Mediterranean
who could now use the Straits of Gibraltar had managed during this
period to do so under the best of conditions.  Holding ports in friendly hands were now to be found all the way from Tortosa to Almería,
controlled either by Christian Spanish princes or by Moslem rulers who
were friendly because they feared the Almohads.  In the same way Norman
control of the eastern Maghreb littoral and trade treaties with Bougie
and Bone assured the Genoese and other Christian Mediterranean mariners
of holding ports on the African side as well.  Beyond the Straits,
arrangements with Castile and Leon and with Moroccan ports going back
to as early as 1133 or 1138 also assured peaceful conditions which
facilitated commerce.  And finally, although the nef seems to have
been the trading ship for excellence during this period, both the
Genoese and Pisans also possessed galleys which were propelled by
oars and were thus especially useful when passing through the Straits
from east to west in the face of unfavorable winds and the strong
current.

As the Genoese, Pisans, Normans, Catalans, Provencals, and
Castilians won a commanding position in the western Mediterranean,
northern Europeans also began to play a role in these waters for the

first time in almost four decades.  This started when Afonso Henriques, Count of Portugal, defeated the Moslems at Ourique in 1139 and then advanced south to recapture Coimbra and some neighboring fortresses. These successes led to his being proclaimed king in 1143 by the Cortes of his principality and a recognition of his independence by Alfonso VII of Leon-Castile in the treaty of Zamora.  Subsequently, Afonso continued his advance and in 1147 took advantage of a crusading fleet, composed of Flemings, English, and Germans, to capture Lisbon.  Some years thereafter in 1158, again aided by English and Flemings, he took Alcácer do Sal, briefly seized Badajôz in 1169, though he could not hold it, and a few years later sent a fleet to attack Seville.  At about the same time he was finally recognized as king and a vassal of the papacy by Pope Alexander III.

This Portuguese expansion seems to have had two special features. First of all, it was successful because Portugal's ruler was assisted by both the Flemish and English in capturing ports like Lisbon and Alcacer do Sal.  In the case of the Flemish this assistance seems in part to be based upon a formal alliance, since Afonso Henriques' son was married to a daughter of Count Tierry of Flanders.  The English, however, also had a political connection with this part of Iberia, since Henry II's eldest daughter, Eleanor, in 1170 had married the king of Castile.  Even more important, however, is the fact that, following the conquest of Lisbon, English, Flemish, and other northern European merchants settled in Portuguese ports and a lively trade began to develop between the north and this part of the Iberian penin- sula.  This, of course, represents a sharp contrast with that earlier northern European maritime presence along these shores represented by fleets of pilgrims and Crusaders on their way to the eastern Mediterranean.  Now a solid base of northern European commercial interest had been planted along the Atlantic shores of Iberia not far from the Straits of Gibraltar.

There remains the question whether or not northern European ships actually passed through the Straits and sailed into the Mediterranean between 1133 and 1172.  There is a certain amount of indirect evidence that they did.  Idrisi, who wrote about 1150 in Sicily, for instance, shows in both his text and maps a surprising knowledge of northern

European waters which can best be explained by the fact that he had
direct contacts with northern European seamen.[2]  There was also a
series of institutional links between Sicily and Britain dating from
these years that suggest direct connections, perhaps by sea, contacts
that finally resulted in the marriage of the English Angevin Princess
Joan to King William II of Sicily in 1176.

In addition to all this, we know that the writings of an English
chronicler of about 1200 A.D. contain a set of sailing directions for
the entire Mediterranean from Gibraltar east to Syria.  And since some
of these sailing directions mention that four Moslem dynasties controlled Moslem Iberia, they must reflect a situation which dates from
the period when this was the case.[3]  And, finally, Genoese notarial
documents dating from the late twelfth century show us that English
and Flemish merchants were carrying their woolens to Genoa.  It has
always been assumed, perhaps rightly so, that they did so by following
overland routes.  On the other hand, they may also have done so by sea,
via the Straits of Gibraltar, during this period.

However we assess the importance of the opening of the Straits to
Mediterranean shipping and perhaps to that of northern Europe as well
during the decades of the mid-twelfth century, such a situation did
not long prevail, thanks to the Almohads.  They occupied Malaga in
1153, Granada in 1154, and Almería in 1157, thus establishing a solid
base in Andalusia.  Then in 1160 they turned their attention to the
Maghreb, where they over-ran all of eastern Algeria and Tunis, in the
process expelling the Normans from their coastal ports and driving
the Beni Hilal bedouins out of southern Tunisia.  With these African
areas secure, they returned to the offensive in Iberia and occupied
the rest of Andalusia, took over Murcia and Valencia from independent
Moslem rulers, and drove the Portuguese from some of their conquests
south of the Tagus.  By 1172 all Islamic Spain except the Balearics
was under their dominion.

This counteroffensive of the Almohads seems to have been the main
reason for the establishment of a number of crusading orders in the
Iberian peninsula:  Calatrava (1158), Alcantará (1176), Santiago
(1176), Evora (Avis) (1166-1176) in Portugal, Leon, and Castile and
somewhat similar orders, including an active branch of the Templars,

in Aragon.  These orders stubbornly resisted the Moorish advance along
the Portuguese and Castilian frontiers, though they were less effective to the east, where the king of Aragon was so busy in operations
against the Count of Toulouse in the Midi that he tended to neglect
his Muslim borders and even found it necessary in 1179 to revise his
earlier treaty with Castile and to allot Murcia, once to have been
his, to the Castilian sphere.

The Almohad advance, however, was slowed down by more than the
resistance of Christian Spanish princes and crusading orders, for
other factors were at work.  One of these was a successful attack upon
Almohad-held Tunisia by the Almoravid ruler of the Balearics which
drew troops from the Iberian peninsula to the Maghreb for a number
of years.  And a second was help given the Portuguese by northern
European forces on their way to the east during the period of the
Third Crusade.  In 1189 one such force of English, Germans, and
Flemings helped the King of Portugal take Silves, and a little later
when Richard the Lionhearted's main flotilla passed these shores it
helped regain Silves again and capture Alcácer do Sal as well.  Thus
despite the fact that the Genoese and Pisans between 1162 and 1189
were engaged in chronic hostilities and thus giving the Christian
Spanish little assistance, the Almohads were not without their problems either.  Not until the 1190's were they able to send sufficient
naval forces and troops across the Straits to clear the Portuguese
from all territory they held south of the Tagus and to win the great
battle of Alarcos from the Castilians in 1195.  And not until 1203
were they able to capture the Balearics from the Almoravids and expel
them from Tunis as well.  In short, it was not before the first decades of the thirteenth century that an Almohad naval empire ruled,
without rivals, from the Tagus to Valencia and from the Balearics to
Tripoli, and had firm control over both sides of the Straits of
Gibraltar.

During these decades of Almohad advance, it seems possible that
Genoese ships continued to trade with Atlantic Moroccan shores and
perhaps with Andalusia as well.  The fact that they had a trade treaty
with Ceuta in 1160 makes this a reasonable possibility.  But it also
seems certain that such commerce was less vital to them than it had

been earlier, for now that the entire Maghreb had become Almohad, all
western caravan routes to the Sudan had reopened.  It was now possible
for the Genoese and Pisans to tap gold supplies arriving in central
North African ports via Gadames and Ouargla instead of having to proceed west to Safi and Salé to do so.  In short, although the Genoese
probably traded beyond the Straits after 1160 on a small scale, their
need to do so was not so imperative as it had been earlier.

As for northern European shipping, we have already noted that certain large armed crusading fleets in 1189 and 1190 found it possible
to pass the Straits on their way to Syria and Palestine.  So, too,
did some fifty Flemish ships which the Countess of Flanders took
through these same Straits on their way to the Fourth Crusade in 1202,
and which had some difficulties near Ceuta on their way east.  But all
these expeditions were large ones.  In no case do we find a record of
any individual merchant ships from the north following this route into
the Mediterranean.

A further point is worth noting.  Though these northern expeditions
managed to sail successfully into the Mediterranean, we have no record
of a single ship's having sailed out again.  Instead, as was the case
during the period between 1090 and 1110, those who returned home, as
Richard the Lionhearted did, did so using overland routes.  Perhaps
one special reason for this lies in the nature of the ships--most of
which were cogs or busses, which carried no oars.  Such ships would
have had great difficulty in negotiating an east-west passage through
the Straits against current and wind.  But it also seems probable
that the commanders of these expeditions recognized the danger of
attempting such a passage in the face of strong Almohad flotillas on
the Atlantic side.  So these expeditions had no long-range effect on
opening up the Straits to western European commercial traffic.

Nevertheless, despite the limited success of shipping through the
Straits, these years were important in the development of both northern
and Mediterranean European maritime power--and were to make its eventual success against the Moslems in this part of the world all but
inevitable.  Throughout these decades both Genoa and Pisa, for
example, became increasingly prosperous and more than doubled the
maritime shipping at their disposal.  To this Italian maritime estab-

lishment we should add new shipping which developed along the coasts
of Catalonia and the French Midi as Barcelona, Montpellier, and
Marseilles began to become commercial centers, rivalling in importance
seaports in Italy.  It is significant in this regard that French and
English contingents of the Third Crusade which did not arrive via the
Atlantic sailed to Syria and Palestine from Mediterranean ports instead
of reaching there by overland routes, as their predecessors had done
during the First and Second Crusades.  Obviously, Mediterranean Europe
now had the shipping to make this possible.

Exactly the same kind of development was taking place in Atlantic
Europe, too, where these decades saw the Portuguese and Cantabrian
Spanish take to the sea, witnessed a maritime revival along the shores
of western France from Bayonne to the Loire, and saw English, Flemish,
and German merchants carry an increasing volume of commerce along maritime routes.  By the early thirteenth century northern and Atlantic
Europe were almost as advanced in a maritime sense as the Mediterranean.
And all of this was happening when the Islamic maritime world of
Andalusia and the Maghreb, despite its prosperity and gold maraboutin
dinars had reached the limits of its possible development and could
expect no further growth.

Thus, once the effects of the Almohads' maritime success and their
victory at Alarcos had worn off, Christian Europe returned to the
offensive with renewed vigor.  It has generally been emphasized that
it was the subsequent great land victory of Las Navas de Tolosa in
1212 which broke the power of the Almohads and allowed the Reconquesta
to proceed to a victorious conclusion.  There is some truth in this
contention, for this battle did open up Andalusia to the advancing
armies of Castile.  On the other hand, it is worth emphasizing also
that this victory had no immediate consequences, since the Christian
Spanish princes who won it were in no position to follow it up.  Pedro
II of Aragon was killed at Muret in 1213; his son Jaime, to whom he
left his domains, was a minor; and Alfonso VIII of Castile died in
1214.  It was not until the latter's grandson Ferdinand III had succeeded to the throne, come of age, and added Leon to his realm in 1230,
that he was able to move south either.  Even in Portugal the reigns
of Afonso II (1211-1223) and his son, Sancho II (1223-1245), saw royal

authority limited indeed.  Thus, the Almohads were little disturbed
during the reign of the Caliph Al-Mustansir (1213-1224), except for
the loss of Alcácer do Sal again in 1217 to a Portuguese force aided
by a flotilla of northern European ships on its way to take part in
the Fifth Crusade.

All this ended when Al-Mustansir died.  Immediately, the Balearics
revolted and the Hafsids of Tunis threw off the Almohad yoke.  And
then great revolts and civil wars swept Andalusia and the Maghreb, as
the Almohad empire began to disintegrate, a process which was to continue until it was finally extinguished by the Merinids in 1260.  And
as it fell to pieces, so too did its naval forces which had so long
held the Christian Europeans at bay.  Now from the Mediterranean and
Atlantic the armies and seamen of western Europe moved south to make
the waters about the Straits of Gibraltar their own.

Perhaps the most dramatic advances were those of Jaime the Conqueror
of Aragon, who in 1229 sent a Catalan fleet to begin the conquest of
the Balearics.  Majorca fell in that year, Minorca in 1231, and Ibiza
in 1235, though Minorca continued to be ruled by a vassal Moslem king-
let until it was annexed in 1287.  Even before the conquest of the
Balearics had been completed, though, Jaime attacked Valencia, which
finally fell to his Catalan-Aragonese forces in 1245 after a series
of campaigns.  And as he reached the borders of Murcia he came to an
agreement with his fellow-conqueror Ferdinand of Leon-Castile, with
whom in 1244 he signed the treaty of Almegra, which repeated the provision of the earlier treaty of Cazorla (1179) and allotted Murcia
to Castile.

As Jaime of Aragon moved south, so too did Ferdinand.  In 1236
Ferdinand's forces were deep in Andalusia and had conquered Cordova.
By 1243 they had reached the Mediterranean and Murcia had submitted
to them.  But his most important conquest took place in 1249 when
Seville, the largest Islamic city in Spain, fell into his hands,
thanks to the assistance his armies received from Castilian ships
from the north and some important Genoese and Aragonese naval contingents as well.

Five years later, in 1253, the Moslem dockyards had been rebuilt
and began to turn out <u>galleys</u> and <u>nefs</u> for a new Castilian fleet.

These were ships of Mediterranean type built by a mixed group of ship-
wrights from Bayonne, Bordeaux, Catalonia, and Italy (mainly Genoa).
This new Castilian fleet was at first commanded, at least nominally,
by a court official, Ruy López de Mendoza, and in 1260 was used to
attack Salé and in 1262 to capture Cadiz.  Since the most effective
contingents of this fleet, however, were Genoese vessels commanded by
the Genoese Ugo Venta, Venta soon became admiral of the entire fleet
in 1264, a post he and a number of his gifted compatriots were to hold
for a number of years thereafter.  By 1266, after a serious Moslem
revolt in Murcia had been put down with Aragonese assistance, a new
Castilian naval establishment had appeared on both the Mediterranean
and Atlantic sides of the Straits--one, however, which was clearly
dependent upon a close alliance with Genoa and friendly cooperation
with Aragon to maintain itself.  And since nearby Granada, under a
new Nasrid dynasty which had been established in 1238, was a vassal
of Castile, the Castilian writ now ran from the borders of Valencia
to the Algarve.  Even though Alfonso X's effort to take Salé in 1270
failed, an effort which seems clearly to have been timed to take advantage of the fall of Marrakesh to the Merinids in 1269, the Straits
of Gibraltar were now in western European hands.

   There remains the matter of Portuguese expansion, which was less
dramatic than that of Castile and Aragon because Portugal's monarchs
were so at odds with their church and nobility that they could not
act decisively.  At last Afonso III, the brother of Sancho II, became
king in 1245 after Sancho had been deposed.  Before coming to the
throne Afonso had been a count of Boulogne, a fact that shows that
his house still maintained Flemish connections.  By 1253 he had
managed to complete the conquest of the Algarve and make peace with
Castile.  To cement this peace he married Beatrix, the daughter of
Alfonso X of Castile (1252-1284) and thus became part of that network
of alliances which knit together the Iberian Christian states.  His
reign, which lasted until 1279, was to see considerable economic
progress, with Lisbon and Oporto gaining charters of liberty; money
becoming more abundant; fairs established; and the navy reorganized.
Portugal, maintaining close ties with England and Flanders, had already joined Aragon and Castile as a maritime power of some importance.

During these years a number of changes were also taking place in
the central Mediterranean which had some effect upon the Straits of
Gibraltar.  One of the more important was the end of independent sea-
power exercised by the Kingdom of the Two Sicilies.  At first, after
a late twelfth-century decline, Sicily's fleet was rebuilt by the
Emperor Frederic II (1215-1250) and was powerful enough so that the
Hafsids of Tunis felt it wise to pay Sicily regular tribute.  After
Frederic's death this state of affairs continued under his son Manfred,
until in 1266 he was killed and his kingdom was taken over by Charles
of Anjou, who was backed by the Papacy, France, and Florence.  This
event ushered in two decades of wars.  When they had ended Pisa had
been eliminated as a trading power, the Kingdom of the Two Sicilies
was divided into Neapolitan and Sicilian kingdoms, and two maritime
groupings had appeared in the western Mediterranean.  One was composed of France, the Angevins of Naples and Provence, and Genoa; the
other of a loose association of Aragonese, Catalans, Majorcans,
Valencians, and Sicilians ruled by various members of the house of
Aragon.  Both these maritime groupings had Provençal connections and
both were firmly established on the Atlantic and Mediterranean sides
of the Straits of Gibraltar.  They were both also prepared to make
use of their considerable financial, technological, and political
advantages to move north by sea and firmly link northern Atlantic
Europe with the waters of the Mediterranean.

We can best understand the nature of these advantages by briefly
noting the economic changes which had taken place in Genoa since 1164.
Starting in the later years of the twelfth century, in place of a
small group of great merchants a larger and growing number of capi-
talists had appeared, who used commenda contracts and bills of exchange on a large scale and borrowed for commercial ventures from
bankers who charged 10 percent interest.  Shipbuilding on shares,
known as locas, was extremely active and vessels built in this way
returned those who invested in them a 100 percent profit if the ships
made a single successful round-trip voyage.  Genoese commerce had
tripled or quadrupled in value during the thirteenth century--produc-
ing profits in which most Genoese shared, thanks to their wide involvement in maritime enterprises of various sorts.

Though the Catalans and Provençals had been less well advanced than the Genoese and Pisans, by the late thirteenth century their economic development was precocious and flourishing also. Commendas had become the normal way of pooling maritime venture capital and were used, especially at Majorca, to link the investment and business interests of Catalan and non-Catalan merchants alike--including a number of Jewish and Moslem traders. By this same time some of these commendas had become more permanent and had developed into joint-stock companies, as happened in Genoa, companies which over a period of years specialized in sending ships carrying special types of cargo to various ports of the Maghreb and elsewhere.

The Catalans and Provençals possessed a rudimentary banking system, but it was the Italians who were the pioneers in this regard. By the mid-thirteenth century they had already managed to establish a network of Lombard and Tuscan financiers throughout northern Europe--at the fairs of Champagne and in northern France, in the Low Countries and in Britain, and after 1230 in southern Germany as well. They also were serving as bankers to the Papacy, transferring Papal revenues to Rome from the north. Thus, when the Genoese galleys reached England and Flanders for the first time in 1277-1278, they found large groups of powerful Italian financiers awaiting them, who could assure them help in handling their cargoes or making other business arrangements.

Equally important were certain technological changes which began to affect the maritime enterprise of the Italians, Catalans, and Provençals in the western Mediterranean. One of these was the development of the boxed compass and portolan charts dependent upon it. These began to be extensively used late in the century by the mariners of Pisa, Amalfi, and Genoa, and were swiftly adopted by the Catalans. They revolutionized Mediterranean navigation in two ways. First, they encouraged more direct voyages out of sight of land instead of coastal ones, thus cutting down shipping times and increasing profits. And second, by making possible accurate navigation when skies were overcast, they permitted two round-trip convoys a year to the eastern Mediterranean instead of one, thus again greatly increasing profits. And as Italian and Catalan mariners began to establish themselves in Seville and other Atlantic ports, they brought with them their

compasses and portolan charts, which could be adapted to Atlantic
conditions as well.

At the same time these years also saw a number of changes in the
ships used in the western Mediterranean.  The cog had been known in
these waters since the time of the Third Crusade, when it was introduced by northern European mariners.  Now it began to be used by
Mediterranean sailors, who found it in some ways superior to their
sailing nefs and tauridas.  Even more important, the large square sail
and rudder of the cog were now used to propel and steer Mediterranean
craft.  Equally important were improvements in galleys, which were
enlarged, changed from biremes to triremes, and now were able to carry
considerable cargoes.  It was such galleys, no doubt, which were constructed in Seville's dockyards and were specially adapted to Atlantic
navigation by the Italians and Catalans.  And, of course, such oared
galleys were particularly useful in negotiating the east-west run past
Gibraltar.

Finally, these years saw the culmination of special politico-economic
privileges won by Italian and Catalan merchants and mariners on both
sides of the Straits.  We have already alluded to such privileges embodied in trade treaties negotiated by the Genoese and Pisans in the
course of the twelfth century and continuing into the thirteenth.
Especially important were those given the Genoese and other Italians
in Seville and other southern Castilian seaport centers.  What is even
more remarkable, however, is the evidence of even more extensive privileges won by Catalan, Majorcan, and other merchants from Aragonese
realms in North African ports on both sides of the Straits and at
Seville as well.  Such privileges not only assured Catalan and Italian
mariners the necessary Mediterranean holding ports, but meant that the
duties they paid on the merchandise they handled were considerably
lower than those charged their competitors trading with the same
centers.

Northern merchants and mariners lacked all the above advantages--
except for those from northern Castilian ports, who were especially
well treated at Seville and in Murcia.  It is true that by 1270 such
merchants were to be found in considerable numbers at Seville and
continued to carry on a lucrative commerce with Portuguese ports and

those of Galicia and Cantabria.  We even know that some northern <u>cogs</u>
made their way past Gibraltar to join Saint Louis at Damietta during
the Sixth Crusade, and that as late as 1267 another north Atlantic
crusading flotilla sailed east through the Straits on its way to Syria.
But there were no resident northern European merchants and financiers
in western Mediterranean ports to welcome northern merchants and sailors.  Nor did these latter have at their disposal a knowledge of the
use of credit, partnerships, contracts, and banking equal to that of
their Italian, Catalan, or Provençal rivals.  What they had been able
to develop along these lines, and it was considerable, tended to be
almost exclusively confined to the business and trade of the northern
seas of Europe and could be adapted to distant markets only with great
difficulty.

It is also important to note that in some respects northern Europeans
lagged behind Mediterranean seamen in the field of marine technology.
Though they had known the compass since 1187, they do not appear to
have made use of it in its boxed form or to have employed portolan
charts as early as the Italians and Catalans did.  Nor do they appear
to have used galleys, necessary for the Straits, except along the
English Channel and North Sea coasts.  Indeed, the special craft they
used during these years, the <u>cogs</u>, the <u>hulks</u>, and the <u>keels</u>, being
without oars, were simply not very useful in the narrow seas contiguous with the Straits of Gibraltar.

Finally, northern merchants had no way of being able to assure themselves of favorable treatment in Mediterranean or Atlantic Moslem
centers such as that enjoyed by Italian, Catalan, and Provençal merchants.  This meant not only that they could not be assured of safe
holding ports in which to await a favorable wind near the Straits,
but that beyond Portugal the duties they paid on their merchandise
were appreciably higher than those charged their Mediterranean competitors.  Wherever they turned, then, they found themselves at a
serious disadvantage.

The results of all this were soon apparent.  The Genoese were first
to exploit the possibilities of Atlantic trade.  Proceeding beyond
Seville, where one of their captains was serving as the admiral of
the Castilian navy, in 1277-1278 they sent galleys to England and to

Bruges, which by 1298 they had done on a regular annual basis.  And,
although they took no part in the great wine trade of Gascony, which
remained an English preserve, they helped the French king, Philip the
Fair, set up an arsenal at Rouen and commanded some of the flotillas
in his new Atlantic navy.  By the 1320's Genoese were also serving as
hereditary admirals of a thriving Portugal and furnishing King Dinis
with galleys, which they could use in times of peace to trade on their
own account.

At the same time, they continued a lucrative trade along the coasts
of Atlantic Morocco, and in 1291 two Genoese, the Vivaldi brothers,
sailed south into the Atlantic to pioneer the routes Prince Henry the
Navigator was to explore more than a century later.  The Vivaldis were
never heard from again, but other Genoese captains seem to have discovered or rediscovered the Madeiras and Canaries before 1350.  In
short, the entire Atlantic from the Channel to Cape Bojador became an
area open to Genoese enterprise and commerce.

The Catalans were hardly less active.  They, too, proceeded to sail
beyond a Seville in which they had special privileges to the northern
seas of Europe, using galleys, though on a less regular schedule than
the Genoese.  Despite periodic troubles with Castile, which interfered
with their use of Seville as an entrepot, they, too, began to trade
in galleys or cogs with the north.  By 1303 a Catalan merchant at
Dordrecht was trading with London, and in 1340 Edward III was asked
by Flemish towns to place the ships and merchants of Majorca, Barcelona,
and Spain under his special protection.  By 1353 Bruges had a large
Catalan colony, and we know that Catalan merchants were buying wool,
cloth, hides, and tin in England.

Much the same thing happened in more southerly Atlantic waters.
Traders from Aragonese domains were particularly active in Moroccan
ports, where they had extensive privileges, and by 1278 were trading
in barcas as far south as Safi.  Later on they joined the Genoese in
exploration and in 1346, according to the Catalan atlas for 1375, one
of their sailing-ships was off the Guinea coast of West Africa--long
before the Portuguese arrived there.

So profitable did this Atlantic trade become that it attracted the
attention of Venice, which heretofore had not been much interested in

the commerce of the extreme western Mediterranean, leaving it to their
Genoese rivals and Catalan allies.  In the early fourteenth century,
however, they changed their minds and in 1320 launched a regular gal-
ley service to English and Flemish ports.  These galleys, like those
of Genoa and the Catalans, seem to have made a specialty of carrying
Mediterranean alum and a variety of spices and other wares to Atlantic
ports and to have returned with tin, wool, fine cloth, and various
metals, thus firmly linking the maritime world of the English Channel
and North Sea with the Mediterranean and, in the process, by 1350,
involving Atlantic Spanish coasts, Morocco, and Portugal in their
network of commerce.

During these years the Straits of Gibraltar remained generally open
to European commercial shipping, although Castilian weakness encouraged
periodic forays ∟cross the Straits by either the Merinids of Morocco
or the Nasrids of Granada.  Such efforts could not amount to much so
long as the Maghreb and Granada were ruled by four rival dynasties
constantly at war with one another.  On the other hand, divisions and
civil wars that took place in Aragonese domains and in Castile following the deaths of Jaime the Conqueror and Alfonso X also prevented
Castile and Aragon from carrying out their 1291 agreement to divide
up the Maghreb, with Morocco going to Castile and Algeria and Tunis
to Aragon.  The situation of 1270 changed little during the next five
decades.

For a brief period in the 1330's and 1340's, however, we find a
changed picture.  At that time ambitious Merinid rulers briefly united
the entire Maghreb under their rule, destroyed the Castilian fleet
which controlled the Straits, and sent a large army into Andalusia.
This effort, however, proved vain.  The Portuguese fleet moved south
to protect Seville and a joint Castilian-Portuguese army with some
northern assistance defeated the Merinids in 1340 at the Rio Salado.
This was followed up by a Genoese naval victory which destroyed the
Merinid fleet, and an occupation of Algeciras by Castile which was
to prove permanent.  By 1350, when the Merinid African Empire had come
apart, the Straits were again in European hands and were to remain so
in the years to come.

All this leaves us with a final question.  Why did not northern

Europeans make use of the Straits of Gibraltar as Italian and Catalan
merchants were doing after 1270?  Why was it that only a few northern
Spanish and Biscayan vessels sailed into the Mediterranean, and other
northern merchants and mariners did not trade beyond Seville and
Portuguese ports down to 1350?  In addition to all the reasons given
earlier, we need to note one further fact--the way in which the overall European alliance system operated after 1270.  During this period
two rivals faced each other in the Northern Seas, an English-Flemish-
Gascon combination opposed by France, which increasingly was tied to
Mediterranean Genoa and Castile.  Throughout the reigns of Edward I
and Edward II and the early years of Edward III, the English-Flemish-
Gascon combination, which was based economically on wine and wool,
held firm and kept Flanders and Gascony from becoming French.  As
late as the battle of Sluys the English fleet was even able to destroy
French-Castilian-Genoese flotillas that threatened its control of the
English Channel.  But despite these successes, the hostility of Castile
proved fatal to English ships which had to stop in Iberian ports if
they wished to enter the Mediterranean.  It even weakened English relations with a Portugal where the Genoese became increasingly powerful.  By 1350, then, English commercial interests and those of a
Flanders linked with England became increasingly less important along
Atlantic routes beyond Bayonne and were in no position to exploit the
opening of the Straits of Gibraltar.

It seems probable that the English were aware of this situation and
tried to counter the Genoese-French-Castilian combination by allying
themselves with the Venetians and Catalans, Genoa's Mediterranean
rivals.  All this effort accomplished, however, was to assure that
Venetian and Aragonese merchants and galleys were warmly welcomed in
Bruges and England without gaining any reciprocal advantage for northern European merchants in the Mediterranean.  This welcome did
nothing to open up Gibraltar to northern European shipping or even
to the Portuguese, who had stood by Castile in her hour of trial in
1340.

One final English effort was made, however, just after 1350, to remedy
this state of affairs.  After the victories of Crécy and Poitiers had
destroyed French resistance, and English fleets had defeated Castilian-

French fleets in the Channel, the English intervened in Spain in support of Pedro the Cruel. Had they been successful in this enterprise, they could have broken the Franco-Castilian alliance, opened up Castilian ports to their merchants, and proceeded into the Mediterranean. As it was, although they won the battle of Najera in 1369, Pedro the Cruel was assassinated, Henry of Trastamara became king, and Castile returned to her Genoese-French alliance. Worse was to follow, for in 1373 a Castilian flotilla destroyed the English fleet off La Rochelle and England lost control of the narrow seas about her. Although John of Gaunt was able to salvage something in a Portuguese-English alliance, all hope that northern European merchants and shipping might use the Straits of Gibraltar was gone and remained so until the late fifteenth century. Then, at last, Henry VII's alliance with the new united Spain of Ferdinand and Isabella, coupled with Juana's Burgundian marriage, allowed northern merchants access to a Mediterranean which they had done much to help open up to Atlantic commerce between 1031 and 1350, but which they had not been able to use profitably.

General Bibliography


Limitation of space has made impossible full notes with this article, but some general bibliographical information seems very necessary. The best overall economic treatment of both northern and Mediterranean Europe during this period is R. Bautier, The Economic Development of Medieval Europe, trans. H. Karolyi (London, 1971), which should be supplemented with two excellent surveys by R. Lopez, The Birth of Europe (New York, 1967) and The Commercial Revolution of the Middle Ages, 950-1350 (Englewood Cliffs, N. J., 1971), as well as The Cambridge Economic History of Europe, vols. I and II (Cambridge, 1952 and 1961). Also worth examination are R. Doehaerd (ed.), Les relations commerciales entre Gênes, la Belgique et l'Outremont d'après les archives notariales génoises aux XIIIe et XIVe siècles, 3 vols. (Brussels, 1941); L. Liagre-DeSturler, Les relations commerciales entre Gênes, la Belgique et l'Outremont d'après les archives notariales génoises, 1320-1400 (Brussels, 1969); C. Dufourcq, L'Espagne catalane et le Maghrib aux XIIIe et XIVe siècles (Paris, 1966); B. Diffie, Prelude to Empire:  Portugal Overseas before Henry the Navigator (Lincoln, Nebraska, 1960); and a collection of important articles on Genoese expansion into the Atlantic by C. Verlinden, The Beginnings of Modern Colonization, trans. Y. Freccaro (Ithaca, 1970).

More detailed treatment of Genoese expansion in the Mediterranean and Atlantic are to be found in a number of articles and monographs by Lopez, some of which are soon to be available in book form, and in H. Krueger "Genoese Trade with Northwest Africa" in Speculum, VIII (1933).  For Venice's activities see F. Lane, Venice and History (Baltimore, 1966) and Venice, a Maritime Republic (Baltimore, 1973). For Seville see F. Pérez-Embid, "Navigation et commerce dans le port de Séville au bas moyen-âge," in Le Moyen âge, LXXV (1969).  No good recent treatment exists of early English commerce with the Iberian peninsula, although for late in this period see E. Carus-Wilson and O. Coleman, England's Export Trade, 1275-1547 (Oxford, 1963).  A similar lacuna exists in regard to recent treatment of southern French commerce in the western Mediterranean or that of the Norman Kingdom of the Two Sicilies.

On the Islamic side considerable pertinent information can be gleaned from S. Goitein, A Mediterranean Society, Vol. I (Berkeley, 1967); C. Verlinden, L'esclavage dans l'Europe médiévale, Vol. I:  Peninsule ibérique. France (Bruges, 1955); le comte de Mas Latrie, Traites de paix et de commerce et documents divers concernant les relations des chrétiens avec les Arabs de l'Afrique septentrionale au moyen âge (Paris, 1866-1872); H. Idris, La Berbérie orientale sous les Zirides, Xe-XIIe siècles (Paris, 1962); H. Terrasse, Islam d'Espagne (Paris, 1958); A. Miranda, Historia política del imperio almohade (Tetuan, 1956-1957); R. Le Tourneau, The Almohad Movement in North Africa in the Twelfth and Thirteenth Centuries (Princeton, 1969), R. Brunschvig, La Berbérie orientale sous les Hafsids, 2 vols. (Paris, 1940-1947), R. Burns, The Crusader Kingdom of Valencia, 2 vols. (Cambridge, Mass., 1967) and J. Devisse, "Routes de commerce et échanges en Afrique occidentale en relation avec la Meditérranée," in Revue d'histoire économique et sociale, L (1972).

For northern European Crusading expeditions into the Mediterranean from Scandinavia see Count P.-E.-D. Riant, Expéditions et pélerinages des Scandinaves en Terre Sainte au temps des Croisades (Paris, 1865). See also L. Machade, Expedições normandes no occidente da Hispania (Coimbra, 1931). For early English Crusading expeditions, see C. David, Robert Curthose (Cambridge, Mass., 1920), and De Expugnatione Lyxbonensi, ed. and trans. C. David (New York, 1936), as well as T. Archer, The Crusade of Richard I (London, 1912). For Flemish Crusades see R. Doehaerd (op. cit.). Overall treatment is to be found in C. de la Roncière, Histoire de la marine française I, 2nd ed. (Paris, 1909).

Two books give a generally adequate overview of European shipping during these years; B. Landström, The Ship (New York, 1961), and G. Bass (ed.), A History of Seafaring (London, 1972). Although the works of Dufourcq, Lane, Lopez, and others present much information concerning Mediterranean European ship construction, naval tactics, and navigational skills, there is a need to revise in some detail the classic accounts of Jal, Manfroni, and de la Roncière dealing with this period. For instance, the only semi-satisfactory account of the Norman fleets of the Two Sicilies is to be found in E. Jamison, Admiral Eugenius of Sicily, His Life and Work (London, 1957).

The same thing is true of Atlantic Europe despite the works of A. Brøgger and H. Shetelig, The Viking Ships, 2nd ed. (Oslo, 1971), of F. Brooks, The King's Ships (London, 1931), and of J. Tinniswood, "English Galleys, 1272-1377" in Mariners' Mirror, XXXV (1949), which give us a good idea of English naval and maritime shipping. Two other works that shed considerable light on navigational skills developed by Europeans in the Atlantic and Mediterranean are F. Lane, "The Economic Meaning of the Invention of the Compass" in American Historical Review, LXVIII (1963) and D. Waters, The Rutters of the Sea (New Haven, 1967).

Spanish medieval historians like Vicens Vives and Soldevila for Catalonia or Sánchez-Albornoz, Valdeavellano, and Ballesteros for Castile have been almost exclusively land-oriented in dealing with the Reconquista. For what little has been produced recently by Spanish maritime historians of this period see F. Pérez-Embid and F. Padrón, Bibliografía española de historia marítima (1932-1962) (Seville, 1970). On the other hand, Portuguese medieval historians have been very maritime-minded. See Diffie (op. cit.), A. Oliveira Marques, History of Portugal, I (New York, 1972); A. Sampaio, Estudos históricos e económicos, 2 vols. (Oporto, 1923); and V. Godhino, Les Grandes découvertes (Coimbra, 1953). For Moslem maritime developments affecting Iberia during this period little exists. See, however, the pictures of Islamic flotillas from the Cantigas of Alfonso el Sabio in R. Burns, "Christian-Islamic Confrontation in the West: the Thirteenth-Century Dream of Conversion," in the American Historical Review, LXXVI (1971).

Chapter 11

Supplying Aigues-Mortes for the Crusade of 1248:
The Problem of Restructuring Trade

William C. Jordan

All medieval villages and their lords made charges for the privilege of entering or selling goods in their marketplaces; often there
were additional levies on transported goods, personnel, and capital.
Whether these charges--hallowed by custom--are called tolls, sales
taxes, or péages, they were an omnipresent condition of medieval commerce. When, in preparation for the crusade of 1248, Louis IX (Saint
Louis) decided to promote the development of the Mediterranean port
of Aigues-Mortes as an embarkation point for his army,[1] he was faced
with an entrenched system of customary obligations and financial
requirements which nearly frustrated his intention. To put it bluntly,
the usefulness of Aigues-Mortes as a port was so intimately connected
with the quantity of goods which could profitably be moved there that
the king found it necessary to authorize the suppression of tolls on
all possible routes leading to it.[2] The methods employed to this end
were often devious, but usually successful.

Perhaps in response to a petition of the townsmen of Aigues-Mortes,[3]
goods belonging to them which passed through the king's land or through
royal towns and which were specifically destined for Aigues-Mortes were
exempted by its charter from all tolls, imposts, exactions, and péages
previously levied in royal territory.[4] In other areas of the south,
outside the jurisdiction of Louis IX, more cautious methods were employed in suppressing tolls. Montpellier, the port city nearest
Aigues-Mortes, was, ironically, the town from which Aigues-Mortes was
principally supplied. In order to placate and, more importantly,
enlist the aid of Montpellier in the creation of this rival port town,
the king was obliged to grant concessions to the great men (syndics,
consuls[5]) of Montpellier.[6] This does not seem to have gone so far as
to include James, king of Aragon, the partial overlord of the town.[7]
However, the bishop of Maguelonne, the other lord of Montpellier, was

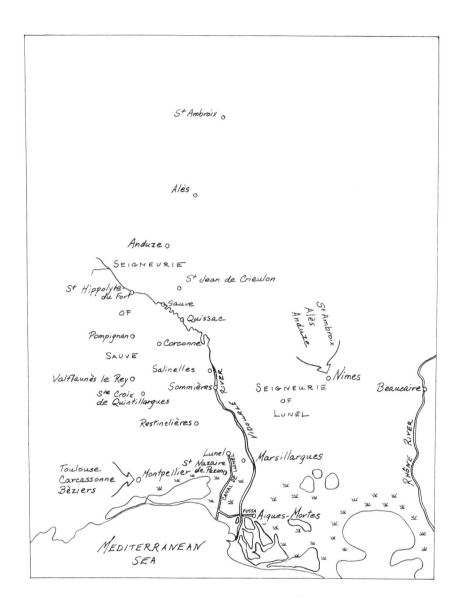

The original route would traverse St Ambroix, Alès, Anduze, St Croix de Quintillargues to Montpellier. The proposed diversion would traverse St Ambroix, Alès, Anduze, Sommières, Restinclières to Montpellier.

persuaded by a series of concessions--ostensibly involving Louis'
protection of his see against the jurisdictional encroachments of the
king of Aragon[8]--to allow a restructuring of trade which eliminated
one of his own péages on royal goods destined for Aigues-Mortes.[9]
Likewise, this restructuring of a trade route in the Cevennes,[10] the
semi-mountainous region directly bordering the Mediterranean littoral,
was undertaken to limit the tolls on goods going to Aigues-Mortes.
In part for this reason Louis IX kept in his hands the lands temporarily confiscated from the sire of that region,[11] Bermond de Sauve,
who had participated in a baronial rebellion against him in 1241-
1242.[12]  Louis' temporary control of the important towns of this
region allowed him to suppress baronial levies (or to collect them
for himself).  Part of the purpose of his outright purchase of the
town of Sommières, one of the chief mercantile centers of Bermond's
lands, was the diversion of goods to it so that they might be economically directed to Aigues-Mortes.[13]  He also purchased Lord Bermond's
rights on the Vidourle river,[14] which ran through the town and on
which there was a set of encumbering péages.[15]

The consuls of Montpellier were given authorizations both by Louis
IX and, after he left on crusade, by the regent not to pay péages
levied by the sire of Lunel on goods bound for Montpellier.[16]  The
sire of Lunel, Raymund de Gaucelin, like Bermond de Sauve, had been
an active rebel in 1241-1242, and the privilege of military victory
gave Louis temporary control over his estates.[17]  These lands bordered
Aigues-Mortes and, therefore, were of immediate interest to the king
not merely as a place from which a possible concessionary gesture
might be made to Montpellier, but also as a hindrance (because of the
tolls there) to the direct vitality of Aigues-Mortes.  For this reason,
the sire of Lunel's péage on the Radelle (Fossa), a canal leading to
Aigues-Mortes from the salt-storage complexes of the seignurie of
Lunel, was suppressed.[18]  The specific intention, surely, was to make
salt more easily and cheaply available to Aigues-Mortes, for even
though Aigues-Mortes was built on étangs, the lagoons were not
suitable for extracting salt, and because the canals (graux) of the
étangs were constantly silting up, there was no convenient access
from the town to the Mediterranean itself.  At any rate, this is the

gist of a complaint the Aigues-Mortes population lodged with the king
on the necessity of importing salt from Lunel.[19]  The charter of
Aigues-Mortes itself speaks of eliminating all salt taxes pertaining
to the town and about which the king had a say.[20]  Moreover, the
initial toll imposed on Lunel salt, at Saint Nazaire (see map), as
it began its export travels, was also suppressed by the king in the
exercise of temporary control over the sire of Lunel's lands.[21]

Finally,[22] Louis successfully surrounded his accomplishment here
with the aura of papal approbation, for Pope Innocent IV (August 16,
1249) issued a bull aligning the papacy with royal opposition to any
new péages in the Mediterranean littoral.[23]

While discussing péages, we referred to the restructuring of trade
around Aigues-Mortes.  Since existing trade routes almost completely
ignored his town, Louis tried to create new routes or, more properly,
to divert existing routes to his advantage.  The central concern here,
as far as I know, was a trade route in the Cevennes.

The king's agents in Aigues-Mortes (sénéchal of Beaucaire-Nîmes,
royal chamberlain, and perhaps governor[24]) probably informed Louis
when he arrived in August 1248 that there was a supply problem at the
port.  In the first place, even with an aggressive policy designed
to limit the impact of péages, direct overland transportation to
Aigues-Mortes was impossible from Montpellier, which had been chosen
for the supply point.  Intervening between the two towns was a large
expanse of marshland which necessitated travelling in an arc from
Montpellier to the town of Lunel and down from there via Marsillargues
to Aigues-Mortes (see map).[25]  In the second place, because of Aigues-
Mortes' harbor, supplying the town by sea from Montpellier was equally
difficult.[26]

Therefore, Louis was in the awkward position of buying goods at
Montpellier, transporting them 25 kilometers or so northeast to Lunel
(in order to avoid the swamps) and then transporting the same goods
another 25 kilometers to Aigues-Mortes.  An alternate route from
Lunel was to travel to Marsillargues, load goods on barges on the
Vidourle river near Marsillargues, follow the river down toward
Aigues-Mortes, unload as near the town as possible (the river is
shallow), and finish the trip (i.e., in good weather, for rain flooded

the accesses to Aigues-Mortes) with a few kilometers of overland transportation.  With other natural hazards ignored, it is still clear that
the use of Montpellier as a supply point for Aigues-Mortes, theoretically of immense value, actually increased costs and time considerably.
Some alternative was essential.

Being about the same distance from Aigues-Mortes, Nîmes was the
only obvious alternative.  But Nîmes was a less important commercial
center since it was not a port.[27]  Aigues-Mortes might still be partly
supplied from there, but, again, no direct route between these two
towns was in existence in 1248.  The type of marshy wasteland separat-
ing Aigues-Mortes and Montpellier was less of an obstacle in the
stretch of land between Nîmes and Louis' embarkation point (see map),
but certain political problems with Nîmes (stemming from its role in
anti-royal activities)[28] were also a negative factor.  More significantly, however, all these conditions were aggravated by the king's
péage policy in the Nîmes region.  Either because Louis IX wished to
destroy Nîmes' commerce in deference to Montpellier (although
Montpellier and Nîmes had a vigorous trading relationship based on a
direct trade route through Lunel--see map) or because he found it
necessary to offset losses in péage revenue in the Montpellier-Aigues-
Mortes region, in 1247 he ordered very specifically that péages around
Nîmes be farmed out to the highest bidders.[29]  For better or worse,
therefore, in the royal opinion, Montpellier was preferable to Nîmes
as a supply point for Aigues-Mortes in the early history of the town.[30]
But the problem of double costs remained.

A radically different solution to this problem was apparently proposed in 1248.  If merchants who travelled along an existing trade
route from Saint-Ambroix, Alès, and Anduze to Montpellier[31] could be
induced to divert their itinerary temporarily from Montpellier to a
town on the line between Anduze and Aigues-Mortes, then Louis' agents
could procure the king's goods at that town before the merchants re-
sumed their journey to Montpellier.  Thus, the king could save tre-
mendously on transportation costs for raw goods, especially timber,
shipped from the north (see map).[32]  The geographically logical town
to select for the end-point of the diversion was Lunel, for at Lunel
the traders could pick up their former itinerary and veer southwest

toward Montpellier along the Nîmes-Montpellier trade route (see map). In fact, political considerations prevented Lunel's selection: most important, it was the seigneurial base of a rebel family which controlled a great deal of the region between Nîmes and Montpellier. Although the scion of that family, Raymund de Gaucelin, was a vassal of Louis IX, it was unwise to choose a seat of baronial power for so important a royal function. Understandably, some other town approximating the geographical advantages of Lunel ought to be selected.

Geographically, either Marsillargues or Sommières would suffice (see map), but Sommières (since Marsillargues was also under the suzerainty of the Gaucelins[33]) was the more attractive alternative. In addition, the choice of Sommières was less unfavorable to the merchants themselves. It required less travelling on their part, and there was a good road from Sommières to Montpellier, their original destination.[34] It is true that the town had formerly been in the hands of another rebel, Bermond de Sauve, but he had temporarily lost possession of it in 1243; the Gaucelins had not been dispossessed of Lunel. Moreover, the king had intended to make the dispossession permanent and to acquire the town for himself. This is quite clear because, as early as 1246, Louis had agreed to give the abbot of Psalmody property in Sommières in exchange for the abbot's cession of the land on which Aigues-Mortes was built.[35]

To accomplish the reconstitution of the trade route, the king gave important concessions to the Montpellierans, for whom diverted goods meant lost revenues, including exemption for her merchants from royal péages, suppression of some baronial péages, royal action against abusive economic activity by the Italians, etc.[36] These concessions were interconnected with Louis' original policy of suppressing péages to reconcile Montpellier to the very creation of the rival town of Aigues-Mortes. The bishop of Maguelonne reserved his péage affecting goods on the diverted route,[37] but it was to be levied at the town of Restinclières (see map),[38] which is to say that the levy would be imposed after the king's agents had purchased their goods at Sommières. In effect, therefore, the king's goods went untaxed. Sommières, itself, was relieved of its temporary dispossession from Bermond de Sauve and was secured outright by the king from the baron.[39] One

half of it (not including the <u>strata</u> or fortifications) was ceded to
the abbot of Psalmody as had originally been planned,[40] but the rest
fell to the king, and thereby he insured that no financial exactions
were levied on his goods.[41]  In 1249, when the technical preparations
were complete, the merchants themselves were ordered to follow the
new route.

> Blanche, by the grace of God queen of the Franks, to all who
> will see these present letters, greeting.
>    Know that it is our wish that the trade route (<u>strata publica</u>)
> from Alès, Anduze and Saint-Ambroix which passed through Sainte-
> Croix to Montpellier be diverted through Sommières as long as it
> pleases our beloved son and us....[42]

The most important commodity transported along the new route was
wood, for the Mediterranean littoral lacked well-forested regions.[43]
The present-day chestnut forests are modern implantations; the natural
plant life is low scrub vegetation.[44]  Although the littoral, westward
toward the Pyrenees, was somewhat better wooded, it was in the control
of Spanish kings and counts.[45]

If we accept the figure of 5,000 as a minimum estimate of that part
of Louis' army which was prepared to embark from Aigues-Mortes in
August 1248,[46] we must understand the implications of that figure.
A sedentary feudal army of 5,000 would require extraordinary amounts
of wood.  First of all, shelters had to be constructed for the troops,
most of whom were attended by camp women, servants, grooms, or families.[47]  These shelters were constantly augmented and reinforced because of tardy arrivals to the port.  Similarly, firewood in huge
quantities was essential for the camp.  Stores of firewood were also
needed for the ships since a large amount of the supplies already
contracted for the navy had been consumed, because of a delay in the
original date of departure, 1247.[48]  Finally, shelters had to be constructed for the hundreds of horses eventually present in the town.[49]
The need for wood coupled with the lack of indigenous forests helps
to explain some of the oddities in forest policy during this period.

The preponderance of the royal forests were in and around the Seine
valley, the seat of the royal domain, and in the nearer upper-Loire
valley,[50] but the distance from both these regions to Aigues-Mortes
was great.  It is possible, of course, that purchases of wood were

made in the north for supplying Aigues-Mortes.[51]  Even so, in order
to meet the really heavy requirements (such as providing the great
timbers for the earliest ramparts of the town) the nearer, more hostile local lords of the wooded Cevennes were solicited.  Bermond de
Sauve supplied practically all the timbers for the original ramparts
from a heavily forested region near Sommières and Sauve (see map).
It may be true that Louis paid nothing for these trees, for in 1255
royal officers made restitution to the local notables of the region
for over 1,000 trees--many oak but most willow--cut for the fortification of Aigues-Mortes.[52]  Moreover, the abbey of Psalmody received
restitution in 1255 for 5,000 sea pines (probably used for pitch for
ship repairs, fortifications, and firewood).[53]  How this massive
project was accomplished we can only guess, but the fact of restitutions in 1255 points up the doubtful propriety of the original requisitions.  And after these requisitions, we should recall that the
timber was transported to Aigues-Mortes <u>over a route cleared of tolls</u>
<u>and redirected at the king's pleasure</u>.  When wood got to Aigues-
Mortes, it was worked and fitted by expert carpenters who had been
conscripted for that purpose from Alès, where the trees were originally
cut.  And five years later (in 1253) young couples in Alès still could
not burn wood in torchlight parades to celebrate their weddings.[54]

 By cajolery, concessions, and force, Louis IX succeeded in outfitting
the largest military crusade of the great age of the crusades.[55]  He
was determined that nothing should stand in his way in meeting his holy
obligation.  Our description, of course, has merely focused on one
illustration of his activities, but this same determination is repeated
with striking regularity throughout his preparations for the crusade.[56]
That the crusade, even after these massive preparations, still failed
was, as it turned out, of momentous consequence, for the great failure
of 1250 was to change fundamentally the attitudes and policies of royal
government.[57]  But "Saint" Louis is a post-crusade phenomenon; the king
whose policy we have just described might perhaps better have been
called Louis the Bold in 1248.

Chapter 12

Castilian Merchants in England, 1248-1350

Teofilo F. Ruiz

The history of the commercial relations between Castile and England
in the thirteenth and early fourteenth centuries has not received sufficient study. Although general works on the history of trade and
economic histories of England and Castile point to these relations,
they do not examine them in detail.[1] For example, L. F. Salzman's
English Trade in the Middle Ages includes a substantial number of
references which show Castilian merchants actively trading in
England,[2] but his book fails to clarify how important this commercial
activity was.

In addition to the secondary works mentioned above, we must consider
the wealth of information available in English public records. The
considerable data present in the published materials, above all in the
Calendars of the Patent, Close, and Fine Rolls, deserve to be brought
to the attention of English and Castilian historians. This paper,
using the Calendars as its main source, will examine these data and
relate them to similar Castilian material, the bulk of which remains
unpublished.[3] The purpose of the following pages is to encourage
further study of some of the issues and problems, rather than to
essay an exhaustive study of Castilian-English trade.

Questions should be raised as to the nature of these commercial
relations, who was involved in the trade, and the role of Castilian
merchants in the overall pattern of English trade during the years
between 1248 and 1350.

Why these two dates? The chronological limits chosen are marked
by major historical events which ushered in great changes in both
societies. The capture of Seville in 1248 brought about a radical
transformation of Castile's political, economic, and social structure.
The Christian advance into Andalusia led to the final and complete
opening of the Straits of Gibraltar to the trade between northern
Europe and the Mediterranean. It also signaled the beginnings of an
uneasy peace between Castile and Al-Ándalus which lasted for almost

the next hundred years.[4] With the end of the campaign, the maritime
towns of the Bay of Biscay, which had been active in the siege of
Seville, turned their energy to trade.[5] At the other extreme of the
chronological boundary, the mid-fourteenth century witnessed the
crowning of a new king, Peter I, the plague, and renewed economic
and political upheaval.[6] Moreover, the rise of the Castilian wool
trade after 1350 radically altered the pattern of trade with England
and the rest of western Europe.[7]

In England, the mid-thirteenth century marked the end of the Anglo-
French conflict with the conclusion of the treaty of Paris in 1259.
Prince Edward's marriage to Eleanor, Alfonso X's sister, at Las Huelgas
(Burgos) in 1255 initiated a period of fairly good relations between
Castile and England. The mid-fourteenth century found England at war
with France, in the midst of the plague, and still bound to Castile
by dynastic ties.[8]

The century between the conquest of Seville and the coming of the
plague was not a single epoch in the history of trade. Between these
dates there were events and changes which were critical in shaping
the relations between the two kingdoms. The Anglo-French war of 1294-
1303 was such an event.[9] Sancho IV and Philip the Fair had signed a
peace agreement at Bayonne in 1290 which held the promise of an understanding on the claims of the Infantes de la Cerda.[10] With Sancho
IV's death in 1295, the peace between Castile and France came to an
end; prince Henry (Enrique), regent for the child king Ferdinand IV,
sided with England in the conflict against France.[11] This new Anglo-
Castilian alliance opened new opportunities for trade between the two
countries. It is not a coincidence that grants to Castilian merchants
increased dramatically after 1300.

Though the chronological framework spans a little over a hundred
years, the period between 1248 and the last years of the thirteenth
century has to be considered as a preparatory stage. The events of
1248 did not bring about an immediate increase in the volume of trade.
Castilian merchants had visited northern markets before, but the number
of their visits did not rise to significant levels until the end of
the century. By then, the events and changes mentioned above, as well
as the favorable policies of Edward I toward foreign merchants and his

marriage with Eleanor, lured Castilian merchants to England in ever-
increasing numbers.  Even if trade between the two kingdoms did not
reach important proportions in the late thirteenth century, the
foundations for a greater volume of exchange were laid during those
years.

As the volume of trade rose, it was not evenly distributed throughout the Castilian kingdom.  The greater part of the Castilian goods
exported to England were shipped from the ports of the Bay of Biscay.
There are some mentions of Galician merchants in English records (there
was a regular maritime route to the ports of El Ferrol and La Corunna
for the pilgrims to Compostela)[12] and of merchants from Seville,[13] but
both areas did not constitute, in my own rough estimate, even five
percent of those entries in the Calendar of the Patent, Close, and
Fine Rolls dealing with Castilian merchants or trade.  Most of the
Castilian merchants visiting and trading in England came from the
towns of the Bay of Biscay and the interior cities of Burgos, Medina
del Pumar, Vitoria, and Tolosa.  This area of northern Castile formed
a commercial and geographical unit, with Burgos as distribution center
for the north-south trade.[14]  The region also had ties which went beyond geography and commerce.  In times of trouble, the Bay of Biscay
towns joined with the interior cities in defensive leagues or brother-
hoods (Hermandades) designed to protect their economic and political
well-being.[15]

The main towns trading with and providing ships in which to carry
goods to England were Santander, Bermeo, San Sebastián, Lequeitio,
Guetaria, Portugalete, Laredo, Bilbao (after 1300), Plencia,
Fuenterrabía, Castro Urdiales, and the interior cities already mentioned.[16]

It is only by drawing attention to the commercial relations between
Castile and Flanders that we can properly understand the nature of
Castilian trade with England and other countries.  England was not
the main trading partner of Castile during most of the period under
study or afterward.  That position was reserved for Flanders, which
supplied most of the finished goods, mainly fine cloth, bought in
great quantities by the spendthrift Castilian nobility.  In one year
alone, 1293-1294, Castile imported close to one million maravedises

worth of cloth from Flanders and smaller quantities from Brabant and
northern France,[17] and cloth was not the only item imported.  A varied
assortment of finished goods such as buttons, fish hooks, hats, mir-
rors, religious articles, rings, vases, dice, needles, bone combs,
and toothpicks found their way to Castile from Flanders and other
foreign markets.[18]

Castilian trade with England can be seen as a triangular trade.
England became a stopping-point for Castilian merchants on their way
to northern markets, who could sell their goods in England or exchange
them for English merchandise.[19]  If their cargo could not be sold, the
merchants proceeded to other markets with the authorization of the
English crown.  In 1337, for example, Sanceius Ferandi de Frias (Sancho
Fernández de Frías) brought "fifteen tuns of honey, one thousand salt
hides of Seville, dry and salted, and eight pipes of grain to Sandwich."
Because he could not sell his goods, he was given permission to take
his cargo to Brabant or Hainault in a ship of Zeeland or Spain.[20]  The
same year Domingo Pérez and Peter Nicholas of Spain came to England
in the "ship of St Mary of Santander in Spain with a cargo of honey,
hides, fells, cinnamon and fat."  Unable to sell their goods, they
were granted leave to depart for Brabant and Zeeland.[21]  These examples
are but a few of the many instances in which Castilian merchants
reached markets in the Low Countries by way of England.[22]

England was not only a convenient station on the way to Flanders,
Brabant, and northern France, but also a market for Castilian goods.
Though as a market it could not compare with Flanders or Champagne,
it attracted a fair number of Castilian merchants, considering that
trade relations between the two countries were often hampered by
many incidents of piracy and attacks on the high seas.  Sailors from
Castro Urdiales, Santander, and other ports on the Bay of Biscay were
particularly active pirates throughout the period under study, but
with the increase in the volume of trade and good relations between
the two kingdoms, reports of piracy and complaints against Castilian
seamen decreased.[23]  Let us now consider the amount and nature of
these commercial relations.

Between 1248 and 1350 there was rarely a year in which Castilian
merchants did not visit England.  A glance at the Calendars of the

Patent, Close, and Fine Rolls will attest to their continuous presence
in England, to which they came under two different types of royal safe-
guards.  First, they were included in general privileges granted to
foreign merchants by the English kings.  In 1309, 1311, 1316, 1322,
1338, 1340, and 1341 the English crown confirmed and expanded the
policies of the Statute of Merchants of 1283 and the Carta Mercatoria
of 1303.[24]  Obviously, Castilian merchants also profited from the
three Edwards' desire to attract and protect foreign merchants.

Second, after 1300 the crown frequently granted privileges of safeguard directly to Castilian merchants.  For example, in 1315 Edward
II wrote to Alfonso XI, king of Castile and Leon, promising that all
the merchants from Castile "will be protected from demands of Arnold
of Sanct Martino, citizen of Bayonne."[25]  Merchants from San Sebastian
received safe-conducts for one year to trade in England in 1337.[26]
The same year Edward III promised Alfonso XI that he would give preference to Castilian merchants if they avoided going to Flanders,
renewing his offer the following year.[27]  In 1345 the English king
issued two additional charters protecting Castilian merchants.[28]

But these general privileges were not so important as the individual
safe-conducts granted by the English kings.  Between 1248 and 1350
they reached into the hundreds, the majority of them coming after
1300.  These safe-conducts to individuals or small groups of three
or four merchants guaranteed protection for periods ranging from a
few months to five years.[29]  They covered merchants selling their
goods at port-side, traveling throughout the land to sell their wares,
and visiting the fairs of St. Giles and St. Ives.[30]  Royal justice
also protected them, if not always successfully, from attacks by the
local population.[31]  Let us consider now some of the most important
Castilian merchants trading in England.

Andrew Peres de Castro Xeriz (Andrés Pérez de Castrogeriz), merchant
of Burgos, was the most prominent of the Castilian traders doing business in England between 1248 and 1350.  Born in Castrogeriz (38 kilometers west of Burgos), he settled in Burgos and achieved a high
social and economic position in the city.[32]  His first recorded voyage
to England apparently occurred in 1299, when a royal privilege gave
protection for two years to Peter Peres (Pedro Pérez) and Andrés Pérez

de Castrogeriz, merchants of Burgos.  They came with their men and
merchandise in English ships, and by royal grant they were exempted
from an "arrest called 'la Mark' which the king lately granted to be
made for the men of the duchy of Aquitaine."[33]  Their safe-conduct
was renewed for two years in 1301 and 1303 at the request of Edward,
the king's son.[34]

   After 1303 Andrés Pérez de Castrogeriz's name appeared alone in
royal grants, as Pedro Pérez ceased to trade in England.[35]  Andrés
received further safe-conducts in 1308, 1312, and 1314, each privilege extending for two years.[36]  In 1315, 1317, 1321, and 1323 the
privileges covered periods of three years, allowing the Burgalese
merchant "to come within the realm with his men and wares to trade."[37]
By 1325 Andrés had gained special protection from Edward II.  One of
his men, John de la Pays, went to Gascony "on the business of the
king's merchant Andrew Peres de Castro Soryz of Burgos in Spain."[38]

   While an active merchant in England, he also served the Castilian
crown as envoy and representative in the negotiations for the wedding
of Alfonso XI and Eleanor.[39]  As merchant of Burgos, the unofficial
capital of Castile, Andrés' ties with the Castilian court and his
long residence in England made him an ideal envoy for matters involving
both courts.  While employed by his native Castile, he also worked
for his adopted land, and even though it might have proved difficult
to serve two masters at the same time, at least Andrés served Edward
well.  In 1325, prior to his participation in the negotiations for
the royal wedding, Andrés Pérez received a procuration from the king
of England to arrange a loan in Spain or "neighbouring places."  The
loan was for six thousand pounds, and Andrés was "to pledge the king's
goods" as security and make provisions for its repayment within the
realm.[40]

   The engagement of foreign merchants in missions of this sort was
rather common, and many Castilian merchants performed such duties
for the English crown.  In 1336 Andrés traveled to Castile accompanied
by Gunsalvus Goderitz (Gonzalo Gutiérrez ?) and carried one thousand
marks sterling of Edward's money to buy destrier-horses and bring them
back to England.[41]  He never completed his task, dying in Spain while
on business of the king of England.  Edward II demanded restitution

of his thousand silver marks from Alfonso XI, the concejo (municipal council) of Burgos, the executors of Andrés' will, and Gunsalvus Goderitz. His claims seemed to have been successful, because the next year Arnald Garcia of Saint John, another Castilian serving Edward II, returned to England with the horses.[42]

Another important Castilian merchant was Ferrand Mangoun (Mangeon). Ferrand and Peter Loupez (López) Mangeon, probably a relative, accompanied Peter de Galiciano abroad on the affairs of the English king.[43] In 1331 Ferrand Mangeon and John de Sagassola (Zaragoza), "merchants of Spain, put in their places Peter Gardeche to prosecute the execution of a recognisance for sixty pounds made to them in chancery by John Peche, knight, and Nicholas his son."[44] The courts failed to provide a swift decision, and three years later the two merchants were still pleading their case.[45] In 1337 Ferrand and an English merchant, Richard Lacer, gave security to the authorities of London "that they will not take elsewhere than to Middleburgh in Seland (Zeeland) lasts and ox hides which they had a royal licence to export there."[46]

The following year Ferrand Mangeon received protection and safe-conduct for one year for himself, his men, and his servants while trading in the counties of Warwick and Leicester, and elsewhere in the kingdom.[47] By then, Ferrand must have been well on his way to settling permanently in England and had probably married an English-woman. As much can be inferred from a donation by John de Harewell, who in 1338 alienated in mortmain "67 s. 2¾ d. of rent in Heule to a chaplain to celebrate divine service daily in the chapel of St Mary the Virgin...in honor of the said Virgin" for the good health of Ferrand Mangeon and his wife Margaret (not a Castilian name) and for their souls after death.[48] Late that year Ferrand Mangeon, "citizen of London," lent £50 to the prior and convent of Andover, diocese of Winchester.[49]

Lupus Johannis (Lope Juánez), a merchant of Bermeo in Biscay and master of the ship St. Saviour of Bermeo, received protection and safe-conduct from the king of England in 1345 while going to Spain to trade with English goods.[50] In 1346 he was carrying "fish and other things" from Spain to Flanders when his ship was attacked and robbed by English subjects. Lope, under the protection and safeguard of the

king, brought his complaints to the English courts.[51] A document shows
that a few months later he had obtained a license "at the request of
the king's daughter Joan" to buy and export one thousand quarters of
wheat to Spain.[52]

Other Castilian merchants also made good use of royal favor. In
1276 Peter de Mundenard received a grant for five years at the instance of Eleanor, the king's consort, exempting his goods from litigation which did not directly involve him. The privilege allowed him
to remain in the kingdom and trade there under the protection of the
king.[53] Queen Eleanor had been brought up at Burgos, and she sought
goods imported by Castilian merchants from her native land.[54]

Finally, let us consider the members of the Frías family. Politically and economically one of the most influential families of Burgos,
they traded in England between 1309 and 1346.[55] Their commercial
activities were not restricted to England but also included Flanders
and northern France.[56]

The first member of the family mentioned in English documents was
Fernando Gonsalvi (Fernán González) de Frías. In 1309 he carried a
letter from Edward II to Ferdinand IV in which the English king complained of the many acts of piracy committed by men from the Bay of
Biscay. Fernán, a citizen of Burgos, was a member of the brotherhood
of Our Lady of Gamonal in Burgos. This religious fraternity counted
among its members all the municipal officials, important urban knights,
and merchants of the city.[57] His membership in the oligarchy of
Burgos did not seem to interfere with his service to the English
crown.

In 1312 Diego González de Frías and his son, John González de Frías,
received protection for one year while "coming into the realm with
their wares." The elder de Frías returned again "with his men and
wares" in 1320. Both merchants were influential citizens of Burgos
and members of the brotherhood of Our Lady of Gamonal.[58]

Another member of the family, Andrew (Andrés) Pérez de Frías, went
to England with his men and wares in 1315, receiving royal protection
while trading throughout the realm. On leaving England, Andrés commissioned Benedict de Gounceales (González) to act as his attorney
for one year.[59] Andrés, like other Castilian merchants, left

unfinished business or ongoing commercial operations while he continued his voyages to and from other markets in Flanders, Brabant, and northern France.

In 1337 Sanctius Ferrandi (Sancho Fernández) de Frías was granted a licence to take fifteen tuns of honey, one thousand salt hides of Seville, and eight pipes of corn to Brabant.[60] His relative, Ferrandi Martínez de Frías, merchant of Burgos, received protection and safe-conduct to trade in England until Whitsunday of 1337;[61] his safe-conduct and those of other Burgalese merchants were extended soon after until Easter, 1338.[62] That same year John Ruiz de Frías carried hides from England to Brabant, and in 1346 John Fernández de Frías transported in a Castilian ship six hundred quarters of English wheat for Edward's armies operating in Gascony in 1346.[63]

The next problem concerns the type of goods traded between the two countries. This is a question which Salzman has partially answered, but some aspects of the nature of this trade require elaboration.

Among the items England imported from Castile, two had strategic importance--horses and iron. The first of these two items presents difficulties because the trade of horses from the Iberian peninsula has not been fully investigated.[64] Castilian horses played an important role in medieval warfare and were highly valued in countries north of the Pyrenees; therefore the Castilian crown was careful to keep this important commodity under strict supervision. To this end long-standing royal decrees and ordinances of the Cortes forbade the export of horses throughout most of the thirteenth and fourteenth centuries.[65] Added to their military value, there was an economic factor, as the price of horses rose to almost prohibitive levels by the late 1330's.[66] Since Castilian merchants seldom enjoyed the right to export good horses out of Castile,[67] they served as mediators between the courts of England and Castile. Negotiations for the purchase of horses were carried out by envoys of the English crown, usually Castilian merchants in the service of England, sent directly to Castile or other countries.

On at least thirteen occasions during the period under study, Castilian merchants or English envoys traveled to Castile to buy

horses for the English kings.  Some examples will illustrate the
importance of this trade.  In 1282 Edward I assigned one thousand
pounds tournois to acquire an undetermined number of horses in
Aragon and Spain (Castile).[68]  William de Tholosa (Tolosa in Biscay),
merchant and envoy of the king of England, visited Castile to purchase horses in 1309, 1312, 1313 and 1314.[69]  As we have already seen,
Andrés Pérez de Castrogeriz and Gonzalo Gutiérrez performed similar
service for England in 1331.

   Iron was another strategic item of trade.  Most of the Castilian
iron came from the area of Bilbao in Biscay, one of the "two main
European sources of high quality iron."[70]  Salzman has already pointed
out the importance and volume of this trade, offering revealing
examples.  Other instances of iron exported to England from the Bay
of Biscay can be cited.[71]  In sheer quantity, iron was the main
Castilian export until the rise of the wool trade.[72]

   Other goods imported by England from Castile during the thirteenth
and early fourteenth centuries were tallow, rice, quicksilver, alum,
honey, almonds, figs, dates, other types of fruit, liquorice, leather,
skins, dishes, fells, cumin, armours, and, of course, wine--mainly
sweet wines, which were the third most important item among those
exported by Castile.[73]  There are also a few references to wheat,
but it seems to have been imported to England only during the 1317
famine when the country was forced to import grain.[74]

   Trade means exchange, and this leads to the question, what did
England export to Castile?  This is a puzzling problem, and the correct answer is nothing or close to nothing.  Indeed, the few entries
in English records indicating permission to export and actual export-
ing of grain to Castile cluster around the mid-fourteenth century, a
period of agricultural crisis and famine in Castile.[75]  Even fewer
entries show export of wool to Seville.  Castile did not need wool,
and most of the importing was done by Genoese merchants based in
Seville.  The final destination of this wool was probably Italy.[76]

   If the Castilian merchants did not take back English goods to Spain,
what then was the nature of their commercial relations?  It is evident
from the entries in the Patent and Close Rolls that Castilian merchants carried English goods to Flanders, Brabant, Hainault, French

ports, Gascony, and Italy. These goods they exchanged for cloth or
other merchandise in northern ports to take back to Castile. More
important in terms of the overall pattern of English trade with
Flanders, Brabant, France, and Gascony, they served as carriers of
English goods to those ports. Although there are numerous examples
of Castilian merchants engaged in this carrying trade throughout the
period under study,[77] the evidence is overwhelming for the year 1337
and the early part of 1338. With the outbreak of the war between
England and France, Flanders sided with the French. Edward III, tied
to Castile by dynastic and military alliances, made every effort to
attract Castilian merchants to England while barring them from their
traditional Flemish markets, and was successful.

At the beginning of hostilities, with the English ships engaged in
the watch on the Channel, Castilian merchants and ships, almost all
from the Bay of Biscay or northern Castile, increased their participation in English trade. They continued to bring Castilian products
to England while carrying a greater share of English goods to Brabant,
Hainault, Zeeland, Gascony, and Italy. Their presence in England
reached record numbers in 1337 and early 1338. More than one hundred
Castilian merchants and forty of their ships visited England in less
than fifteen months, and these figures do not totally reflect the
real volume of trade during that time-span.[78]

Above all, their role as carriers of at least part of the English
wool exports to Italy deserves a closer look. Diagus Lopes de Arbo
Lanchia, Lopes Sanches de Bassurco, and their fellow merchants of
Bilbao received protection for one year in 1337 to "trade in Gascony,
Brabant, Ireland and other lands friendly to England, and passing to
and from Lombardy and their own ports."[79] The same day Sebastian of
Nordyncho of San Sebastian, master of la Seint John, and other merchants of San Sebastian received the same protection. Two days
afterward, on November 20, 1337, Sebastian of Nordyncho hired his
ship to merchants of the Bardi society who were sending six hundred
sacks of wool to Lombardy. La Seint Johan carried three hundred
sacks, and Martin Inaignes de Fraro's ship la Seinte Marie de Bermeo
took the rest.[80] The Bardi also exported another three hundred sacks
of English wool to Lombardy in two Castilian ships, la Seinte Marie

and <u>la Seinte Katerine</u>;[81] the same year merchants of the Peruzzi
society hired John Amour of Santander and his ship <u>la Katerine of</u>
<u>Spain</u> to carry wool from Southampton to Lombardy.[82]

Castile also served as a stopping-point or base for Italian merchants. Several royal privileges of protection were granted to
Italian merchants in 1338 to trade in England, Gascony, Brabant,
Ireland, and other lands friendly to the king and to return "to Spain
and their own parts."[83]   One of these royal grants gave safe-conduct
for one year to John Bussyns, merchant of Piacenza "going to Wynchelse
and other places to recover goods and merchandise lately put on board
a ship of Spain which have been carried away by men of Wynchelse."[84]

Castilian contributions to Anglo-Italian trade were not limited to
1337 and 1338. In 1353 a Castilian ship with a Genoese merchant as
its master received protection from the king of England to take Genoese
goods from Seville to Flanders.[85]   The same year, Martín de Laparada
of Santander hired his ship to Genoese merchants taking English wool
to Genoa, and Ferrandus Sanchos de Arrieta, master of the <u>Seinte Marie</u>
<u>la Rose</u> of Castro Urdiales carried goods of Genoese merchants from
Seville to Flanders under an English safe-conduct.[86]

Why did the Castilian ships take on this role in 1337? Several
reasons should be considered. The war between England and France
decreased England's ability to supply its markets while augmenting
the need for Castilian ships--after all, a friendly ally. The war
itself affected the overland route through Gascony, making the voyage
through the Straits of Gibraltar a more acceptable option.[87]   Finally,
the growth of an Anglo-Castilian-Italian trade was determined largely
by the increased influence of Italian merchants in Seville.[88]   It must
be stressed, nevertheless, that, in addition to these economic considerations, the structure of Anglo-Castilian trade was shaped by the
political and dynastic alliances of the two kingdoms. Castile's
economic interests lay in Flanders and not in England. With the rise
of the Trastamaras in Castile in 1368, Henry II, who had captured the
crown with French support, abandoned the long-lived alliance with
England.

To summarize, Castilian trade with England, although not so important
as Castilian trade with Flanders, was important enough to influence

English commercial life.  Above all, the part played by Castilian traders in the first years of the Hundred Years' War, as carriers of English goods to foreign markets--especially to Italy--deserves further study, for the promise of the Bay of Biscay ports as a center of international trade was never realized.

Chapter 13

Proxy in Medieval Trade

Robert S. Lopez

"No one may contract an obligation through another free person unless that person is subject to his authority or is his bona-fide servant,"
says the Digest (XLV, 1). "Any one may do on behalf of another anything that he may do on his own behalf," says the Corpus Juris Canonici
(VI, 5, 12). Between these diametrically opposite statements lies the
evolution of one of the most important legal innovations of the Middle
Ages: representation or agency, of which proxy (procuratio) was the
foundation stone. Its uses have been so many--not only in the judicial process, but in every kind of economic, religious, and political
affairs--that it takes an effort to understand how the ancient Romans,
for all their juridical genius, were satisfied to get along without it.
   The emergence of representation in the course of the Middle Ages has
been linked to a variety of contributing factors, all of which must
have played a certain role: the fuller working out of concepts already
implicit in Roman law, such as that of the negotiorum gestor; the
Christian emphasis on the sanctity of all promises and the duty of
all men to help one another; the barbarian feeling of solidarity between members of an extended family or of a brotherhood of warriors;
the influence on the West of Muslim and Byzantine traditions of mutual
trust and support in commercial ventures. Every seed, however, needs
a favorable climate to become a plant and branch out; representation
came forth in the late Middle Ages, I believe, above all because that
was the season of associations, not a new phenomenon, of course, but
more vigorous then than at any prior time. More pronounced in Western
Europe than elsewhere, but visible in certain sectors of Muslim and
even Chinese and Japanese life, the "associative spirit" tended to
make collective or joint action an effective middle course between
anarchic individualism and submission to the leader. The appointment
of representatives, bound to instructions of their constituents but
entrusted with a certain latitude within the limits of a proxy, was

an effective means to achieve that aim.

No matter to what association or institution it was applied, the concept of representation stemmed from the same mental attitude; applications, however, differed sharply according to local conditions. The Islamic world made room for agency or proxy (wakāla) in commercial law as early as the eighth century, but discouraged representative forms in all other fields, probably because it recognized no intermediate religious community or body politic between the entire commonwealth of the faithful (umma) and the individual or, at most, the extended family. The Christian church introduced representative forms in the West pretty early, through the practice of monasteries to appoint procuratores with full powers to bind them, but found its own hierarchic structure and growing papal absolutism an insurmountable obstacle against representative government. The barbarians echoed Justinian's strictures, stating that "no one may stand in a suit for another" (Ratchis, 11; Capitulary of Charlemagne, year 802) while introducing a curious counterpart of the Roman negotiorum gestor (the professional champion fighting a judiciary duel in the place of incapable persons). Yet it was the solidarity of the feudal and urban classes against the heirs of barbarian monarchs that produced the first seedlings of political representation in Spain, in England, and elsewhere in the West. In Italy an implicit notion of representation may be postulated as early as 977, when a committee of citizens of Atrani (near Amalfi) contracted an obligation toward their bishop "both for themselves and for all others who are away at sea" (Codex Diplomaticus Cavensis, II, 296 and 299); but representative assemblies did not thrive, not so much because there was greater awareness of what a late municipal statute called "the subtilities of Roman Law," but above all because Italian city-states were both independent and small enough for direct democracy. On the other hand, Italy was the leader in the development of representation in commercial law.[1]

It is not my purpose to describe here the more complex contracts, but merely to call attention to the primordial importance and flexibility of proxy, the simplest. As Sarakhsi, an eighth-century Muslim writer of the Hanafite school, points out, "proxy is the necessary basis of contractual partnership, in the sense that each partner is

his colleague's agent in making purchases with the capital specified
in the contract." In Italy and the West, too, there were almost no
business associations and not many transactions that did not involve
powers of attorney for some or all of the parties. Whether these
powers were extended through separate contracts or merely mentioned
in contracts designed for other purposes, procuratio was the bonne à
tout faire of medieval business. In spite of its ubiquity, however,
it has never been adequately studied in its own right. This neglect
is not altogether unjustifiable: though innumerable examples of proxy
survive, most of them are depressingly vague and discouragingly alike.
They consist chiefly of standardized, generalizing formulae, none of
which really tells what is the business at hand. Hence scholars usually skip them as mere preliminaries or accessories to the more complex
and specific contracts.

Procuratio, however, was not only and not always a handmaiden of
other transactions; it sometimes played a role of its own in the
organization of commercial and banking enterprises. From the great
mass of Genoese notarial records of the thirteenth century we can
single out at least three aspects of its independent functions. One
of them may be dismissed here with a brief mention, because it has
received more than perfunctory attention in scholarly works on business techniques: procuratio paved the way for the emergence of nego-
tiable instruments of credit. By inserting in an order of payment
the formula "pay to X or to his certified messenger (certo misso or
certo nuncio)" one could make the payment easily transferable to anyone who could show a general or ad hoc instrument of proxy. This
special clause, already used in the earliest extant commercial records
(second half of the twelfth century), did not lose its popularity
after the practice of endorsement introduced a simpler way to transfer a payment. (Simpler, but less sure; still today, an endorsed
check is not readily honored unless the endorsement is guaranteed or
the endorser well known.)[2]

Another special clause inserted in proxies aimed at putting a ceil-
ing over the engagements a partner or an agent of a compagnia (the
most important partnership of land trade and banking) was entitled to
contract on behalf of the compagnia. Such restriction was the only

remedy one could contrive for the enormous risks incurred by the other
partners on account of the joint and unlimited liability that medieval
and early modern law imposed on all members of a partnership.  In the
earliest example we have encountered, a proxy drawn in Genoa, in 1259,
for two Florentine brothers, Bene Gualtierotti and Grazia Gualtierotti,
the former gives the latter full powers of attorney "to buy in my name
and behalf, in Mantua, Cremona and wherever else he wishes, gold and
silver, sterling, marks, cloth, wool and whatever other commodities he
wishes, and to accept and contract loans, and to buy coins of Provins,
Tours and any other currency, and to contract and buy exchange instruments from whomever he wishes, and to promise the price of those commodities and moneys, and to contract debts...but all this he may do
only up to the sum of £500 Genoese...and up to that amount he may
obligate me and my goods." This did not suspend the law of joint and
unlimited liability, of course, but gave each partner a chance that
his liability in case of default by another would be kept within
reasonable bounds by the fact that the commitment of the other did
not exceed the specified amount.[3]

Restrictive clauses of the same kind continued to appear off and on
in proxies, but never attained the popularity of the clause "or to his
certified messenger."  It could have paved the way for the emergence
of limited liability only if the courts had recognized a difference
between authorized and non-authorized commitments of a partner or
agent.  They did not; no matter who or what caused a partnership to
fall into debt, the law held every partner unlimitedly and jointly
liable for all debts of all partners, and indiscriminately sent to
jail partners and agents of an insolvent partnership until and unless
third parties had recovered all that was owed to them or agreed to
settle for partial payment.  The only remedy provided by the restrictive clause against a partner or agent who overstepped it was to sue
him for damages before he went too far.  The restrictive clause could
also serve as a warning to third parties who took care of inspecting
the proxy document, not to trust a partner for more than he was
authorized to promise.  We find no record, however, that either remedy
was actually used; with its numerous personnel and its involved business, the compagnia partnership was both the most powerful and the

most precarious capitalistic organization of medieval land trade and
banking.  Since it was normally contracted for a term of several
years renewable at the end, and bringing together the partners under
the strictest solidarity, a compagnia lent itself to the most diversified activities.  Unlimited liability gave third parties an impression of great reliability enabling the compagnia to attract capital
and multiply investments with considerable speed; some investments
were bound to be poor, and unlimited liability could cause the compagnia to crumble because of a single error or a rush of creditors.[4]

Sea trade, with its extraordinary risks of total loss through ship-
wreck or piracy, could not afford unlimited liability and long-term
investments; nor did it need them, for most operations did not drag
on for years but were brought to a natural conclusion by the safe
arrival of a ship (or its total loss).  Hence compagnia partnerships
were seldom used.  Businessmen normally got together by short-term
contracts of commenda, sea loans, commissions and the like, whose
common characteristics were that they involved no joint and unlimited
liability, expired at the completion of a single voyage (one-way or
round-trip) or of a single sale of goods (in return for cash or for
other salable goods), and were not renewed in the same form and with
the same associates.  It has been generally assumed that under those
circumstances international sea trade lacked the continuity of land
trade, and could not build capitalistic structures as powerful and
diversified as could overland trade.  To some extent, this is true.
Yet if sea merchants were reluctant to tie their capital and their
liability to others over long periods, we usually see that each of
them tended to contract limited engagements again and again with the
same people, seldom on the same terms and for the same amounts, but
with almost the same regularity as if he were bound to those people
by a compagnia partnership.  Without forming oversized business firms
such as the Arcelli, Bonsignori, or Bardi partnerships of merchant-
bankers of Piacenza, Siena, or Florence, many powerful maritime
traders, such as Riniero Zeno of Venice and Benedetto Zaccaria of
Genoa invested large capitals in a great variety of enterprises requiring the employment of many collaborators for many years.  Obviously the unstructured, flexible business practices of sea trade were not

incompatible with a tight organization, but the secret of that organization is not easily found.

A close examination of Benedetto Zaccaria's extant contracts (several
hundreds survive) has convinced me that, in his case at least, proxies
served as the thin threads sewing together the whole.  Before describing this highly important special function of procuratio, let us recall
briefly the highlights of his remarkable career.  One of ten children
of a fairly affluent merchant, he not only was a merchant, but on
various occasions commanded fleets of Genoa, Castile, France, and the
Byzantine Empire.  In the course of his naval operations he scored
smashing victories over the Pisans and the Moroccans, blockaded the
port of Bruges, and fought with variable fortune against the Venetians,
the Egyptians, the Turks, and the English.  He played a significant
role in the diplomatic preparation of the Aragonese decisive intervention in Sicily against Charles of Anjou, in two unsuccessful attempts
to rescue a shred of the Kingdom of Jerusalem from Muslim conquest,
and in the opening of a direct route for commercial navigation from
the Mediterranean to the North Sea.  He discovered or reactivated the
rich alum mines of Phocaea in Asia Minor, made himself the ruler of
Phocaea and of the nearby island of Chios (both of which were inherited
by his descendants after his death in 1307), and for a short time held
in fief Puerto Santa Maria, the seaport of Seville.[5]

Above all, Zaccaria was a sea merchant, always on the move, ever
ready to sail, seldom in Genoa for more than a few months at a time.
His trade extended from Egypt, Armenia, and South Russia to Spain,
Flanders, and England; it included a complete control of mastic gum
production and commerce, a quasi-monopoly on high-grade alum, and a
variable participation in a wide range of other commodities.  His
capital and revenue compared favorably with those of all but two or
three of the greatest compagnia partnerships of land trade.  So did
the number of his collaborators and dependents, which was swollen by
the administrative and mining personnel in Phocaea and Chios as well
as by officers and crews in the ships owned or chartered by him.
Yet, so far as we can tell from the contracts, none of those collaborators and dependents was bound to him by an agreement other than proxy
exceeding the duration of one round-trip voyage or, at most, one year.

None was designated expressly as his partner (socius)--not even
Manuele, one of his brothers, who shared with him the government of
Phocaea and underwrote jointly with him almost one-half of his con-
tracts.

It is clear, in conclusion, that the joint ventures of Benedetto
and Manuele Zaccaria were based on no more formal agreements than a
mutual proxy, first drawn in 1262 without mention of time limits, and
renewed at irregular, long intervals (in 1272 and in 1284). The formula, identical in the documents that each brother delivered to the
other, was so brief and generic that it gives no inkling of its being
the beginning of an extraordinarily close and durable collaboration:

> In the name of God, amen. I...make, constitute and order you...,
> my brother [here] present and receiving, my certified messenger
> and procurator in my place to demand, collect, and receive in my
> name and behalf anything I am to get, demand, and receive from
> any person for any reason; and to make compromises and composi-
> tions and defend me against any person in any lawsuit; and to
> deal with and carry out other business of mine; and in conclu-
> sion to do all that may be needed in this and for this, and that
> I could do if I were present, promising...that I will keep and
> hold as settled and firm whatever will be done by the said pro-
> curator....[6]

A very large number of proxies made out to others, by Benedetto alone
or Benedetto and Manuele, complete the roster of Zaccaria's collaborators. These men pooled capital with him or gave him their labor, or
a combination of both, usually for an indefinite term and an indefinite number of affairs (but sometimes for a more limited period or
purpose), while using the ordinary short-term commenda and sea loan
contracts in various connections. The collaboration did not necessarily last for a long time: one agent, allegedly because he had
"badly carried out and governed the affairs, business, and proxy of
the Zaccaria brothers," was dismissed before he could come back to
Genoa and give a full account of his administration; other agents
severed their ties after a single venture. More often than not, however, each procurator was sent out again and again, as soon as he had
completed a mission and settled its accounting with Benedetto and
Manuele. Of that accounting, which we know was ordinarily made in
writing, almost no record has remained, because it was not done through
notaries; but the essential points of the mission were generally

mentioned in the notarized proxies, which, curiously enough, were more
specific and detailed when the collaboration was circumscribed than
when it was broad.

On the other hand, the same generalizing formulae of proxy were
included for men of different responsibilities and stature.  One procurator was Nicolino Zaccaria, a younger brother of Benedetto (but
Vinciguerra, another brother, does not appear ever to have joined him
in business); another was Paolino D'Oria, a son-in-law of Benedetto,
entrusted with conspicuous sums; another was entitled to a share in
all revenues from the fief of Phocaea; still another apparently was
a standing second-in-command to Benedetto in business and at war; but
other agents were hardly more than non-commissioned officers and
employees of a humbler rank.  No matter; there was a proxy for each
of them, regularly renewed as long as a business connection lasted.
As time went by and the organization became more complex, however,
restrictive or declarative clauses were added to the standard formula
of proxy.  An agent may commit the Zaccaria brothers or Benedetto alone
only up to a certain sum, or should act particularly in some regions
or concerning some merchandise.  This man is to take care of business
in the Byzantine territory, the Black Sea and the Levant; that other,
in Provence, Spain, and North Africa.  This procurator will deliver a
sum to other agents in Phocaea and carry French cloth for sale in
Constantinople, that procurator will take charge of a ship and do
business in Sardinia.... Altogether, the documents show that in the
international trade of the Zaccaria brothers proxy is both the alpha
and the omega, the underlying agreement of the smallest as well as
the largest transactions, and the tie that holds together one of the
most powerful capitalistic structures of the Middle Ages.

Chapter 14

The Fairs of Nîmes: Evidence on Their
Function, Importance, and Demise

Raphael R. DeSoignie

The fairs of Nîmes in the early fourteenth century have not attracted
scholarly attention since Ménard published some of the basic sources
for them in his history of Nîmes.[1] This neglect is understandable,
since the fairs were of brief duration, and since Nîmes never was a
major commercial center. There is, however, useful information to be
gained from a study of the legal process by which the consuls of Nîmes
sought to revoke the grant of a fair to the town of Montagnac, which
competed with that of Nîmes. It is the purpose of this paper to examine a document which has not yet been fully exploited.[2] It consists
of an extract of the legal process at the seneschal's court in Nîmes
which resulted in a ruling by the seneschal on May 8, 1332, favorable
to the consuls of Nîmes.

Up to now, knowledge of the fairs of Nîmes has been limited to what
is contained in the documents published by Ménard concerning this fair.
Chief among them are the granting of the fair by Charles IV (July,
1322);[3] the letter of Philip VI to the seneschal of Beaucaire ordering him to determine whether the newly established fairs at Montagnac
were harmful to those of Nîmes and to suppress them if they were
(March 5, 1331); the sentence of the seneschal abolishing the fairs
of Montagnac (May 8, 1332);[4] and subsequent documents showing that
the case was appealed by the consuls of Montagnac and ended up in
the Parlement of Paris.[5] The date for the definitive sentence in
this long process is to this day unknown, but the final outcome is
beyond question--Montagnac kept its fair and that of Nîmes vanished.[6]

The unpublished document to be examined here records the process
which opened on March 14, 1332, at Nîmes and lasted until May 8. In
it, the consuls of Nîmes presented a case which may be summarized as
follows: the king granted Nîmes a fair to be held yearly for eight
days beginning on Monday before mid-Lent; the fairs were in fact held

at Nîmes after that time; the consuls of Montagnac, without mentioning
the fairs of Nîmes, "surreptitiously" obtained from the king, in April,
1330, the right to hold a yearly fair starting just three days before
the fair of Nîmes, thus rendering the Nîmes fair useless; the ruin of
the fairs of Nîmes was causing the king a loss of over 1000 l. in
revenues each year, and the citizens of Nîmes a loss of over 2000 l.;
the seneschal was empowered by royal letters to abolish the fairs of
Montagnac if he found the above to be true.[7] The chief interest in
this document lies in the testimony of sixty-five witnesses presented
by the consuls of Nîmes to support their case. An analysis of this
testimony will lead to a clearer understanding of two important aspects of the commercial history of late medieval Languedoc. The first
of these is the export trade generated by the development of an important textile industry in Languedoc. The other is the role played by
Italian merchants in this trade, a role whose obvious importance led
Ménard to comment on it at some length.[8] The various types of useful
information contained in this testimony will now be discussed in turn.

From the testimony of the witnesses a clear view emerges of the
types of places from which merchants went to Nîmes to trade at its
fairs. Several distinct groups are easily discerned. There was first
of all frequent mention of towns from which woolen cloths were transported to Nîmes to be sold at the fairs. These were, predictably,
cloth-producing towns of western Languedoc: Toulouse, Fanjeaux,
Limoux, Montolieu, Carcassonne, Narbonne, Béziers, Lodève, Saint-
Thibéry, and Montagnac. With the exception of Saint-Thibéry, each
of these towns was mentioned several times by the witnesses.[9] A
second large group of towns in this trading area consisted of the
Provençal towns across the Rhône from Nîmes. Nearby Avignon, with
its newly established Papal court, was prominent among these. Also
frequently mentioned were Marseille, Arles, Tarascon, Salon-de-
Provence, and Carpentras.[10] It is not clear to what extent the merchants coming from these Provençal towns were natives and to what
extent they were Italians established in the towns. Certainly both
types were involved.[11] There was frequent reference to Italian merchants coming from Avignon and, to a lesser extent, from Arles.[12]

As would be expected, many of the merchants who traded at these fairs were members of the large Italian mercantile community of Nîmes.[13] Other Italian merchants were mentioned as coming from Italian towns. The Genoese appear to have constituted the largest single group of these; Italians were frequently lumped together as "Januenses et Ytalici" by the witnesses.[14]  Pisa, Lucca, Milan, Pistoia, Savona, Asti, and Piacenza were also mentioned.[15]  A final category of towns is that which the witnesses described as "nearby," or "in the seneschalsy," or "in the hills." These were mostly smaller towns not far from Nîmes: Lunel, Sommières, Aimargues, Beaucaire, Sauve, Anduze, Alès, Vézénobres, Uzès, Bagnols-sur-Cèze, Pont-Saint-Esprit.[16] Frequently mentioned with these, however, was distant Le Puy-en-Vélay.[17]

The inclusion of Le Puy in this trading area points out the importance of communications, by both land and sea, in attracting trade to the fairs of Nîmes. As will be seen below, the port of Aigues Mortes was an integral part of the trade structure of these fairs. Roads were no less important. Le Puy was connected directly to Nîmes by the Via Rigordiana, one of the chief arteries of north-south communication in France.[18]  The work of Bautier on the medieval roads of southern France shows that all the towns of Languedoc mentioned above lay along the network of medieval roads and had fairly direct communications with Nîmes.[19]

The kind of goods traded is the next type of information to be considered here. The witnesses almost unanimously indicated that woolen cloths were the chief item traded at these fairs. As has been seen above, this cloth was manufactured in towns of western Languedoc. It appears that cloth merchants (pareurs) from these regions had the cloth transported to Nîmes and sold it there themselves or through agents. There is evidence of arrangements made by the consuls of Nîmes with the cloth dealers of Fanjeaux for setting up booths at the Nîmes market for sale of their cloths.[20] Arrangements like this were evidently made with the cloth dealers of other towns, for one of our witnesses mentioned that each cloth-producing town had booths in Nîmes with a sign displaying the origin of the cloths.[21]

Many witnesses also stated that livestock was brought to these fairs.

Horses were most frequently mentioned, but all other types were indicated as well--hogs, sheep, cattle, mules.[22]  This livestock was evidently brought in from nearby regions.[23]  Meats and furs were also for
sale.[24]  One witness, a local furrier, indicated that fur dealers
from Provence brought unfinished furs to the fairs and acquired finished ones.[25]  Iron tools, feathers, the miscellaneous items known as
merseria, gold cloth, and a varied assortment of imported wares complete the list of goods traded.[26]

   Several witnesses mentioned specifically what items were imported
from overseas and sold at these fairs.  Pepper and ginger, spices in
general, alum, leather, and wax were most frequently mentioned.[27]
Some quantities of linens, sugar, and olive oil were also imported.[28]
It is in the import-export aspect of these fairs that the Italian
predominance makes itself most apparent.  Imports were brought in
exclusively by Italians through the port of Aigues Mortes expressly
for the purpose of being sold or traded at the fairs of Nîmes.  At
Nîmes, the Italians sold these items and bought cloths with the proceeds; they also frequently traded these items directly for cloth.[29]
This was the predominant activity carried out at the fairs of Nîmes--
the exchange of woolen cloths from western Languedoc for finer items
imported through Aigues Mortes.  The cloths acquired by the Italians
were in turn exported through Aigues Mortes, some bound for Italy
and others for unspecified "other parts."[30]  We know from Pegolotti's
Pratica della Mercatura, which reflects the author's experiences during this same period, that cloths from Languedoc were sold throughout
the Mediterranean region.[31]  It is therefore probable that the cloths
traded at Nîmes were, after export, distributed throughout a wide
region.  This may help to explain the puzzling frequency with which
Pegolotti mentioned the correspondence of Nîmes' weights and measures
with those of far more important commercial centers.[32]  In any event,
the Italians who controlled this trade seem to have been to a large
extent merchants established in Nîmes who had connections with other
merchants in Italy.  Many of the witnesses indicated that these
Italians at Nîmes would order shiploads of goods to be brought in
from Italy in order to be traded at the fairs of Nîmes.[33]  There was
also frequent mention, however, of merchants who came from various

Italian towns to sell their imported wares and to acquire cloths at
these fairs.[34]  Compared to this import-export trade, the other functions of these fairs were more modest.  Cloths were purchased by
traders from across the Rhône and from towns in the seneschalsy.  It
is clear from the testimony that it was chiefly cloth which attracted
merchants from these areas, although they also acquired the items imported by the Italians.[35]  The map shows the geographic extent of the
cloth trade associated with the fairs of Nîmes.[36]

A third type of information to be obtained from the testimony is
provided by the attempts of these witnesses to demonstrate that the
fairs were important and that their loss would be a serious financial
setback for the king.  In considering this evidence, we must exercise
the usual wariness of medieval carelessness with numbers, as well as
a degree of skepticism over the witnesses' motives.  They were all
asked to estimate what the king's loss would be if the fairs ended.
A few scrupulously honest ones said they could not tell.  Most of the
others, however, said just what the consuls of Nîmes hoped they would--
that the king would lose more than 1000 l. each year and the people of
Nîmes 2000.  These have the appearance of purely arbitrary figures.
Some of the witnesses, however, gave more specific information, and
it is their testimony that is of interest here, for it can give a
good idea of the volume and value of the trade carried out at these
fairs.

A number of them gave specific facts about sales of cloth based on
their own experience.  Petrus Aloci, a Genoese broker residing in
Nîmes, stated that he once sold 5000 pounds of cloth "in one throw"
at the fair.[37]  It is not immediately apparent whether "pounds"
(libre) here refer to weight or to monetary value, but since cloths
were sold not by weight, but rather by the piece or by length, in
all probability his figure refers to pounds tournois.  Another broker,
a local named Durantus de Montiliis, said that he at times saw a certain Italian merchant buy 6000 pieces of cloth at a time.[38]  This
figure seems beyond belief; we know from Sapori's work on the company
of the del Bene that this medium-sized Calimala company bought a total
of only 1043 pieces of cloth, all in Flanders and northern France,

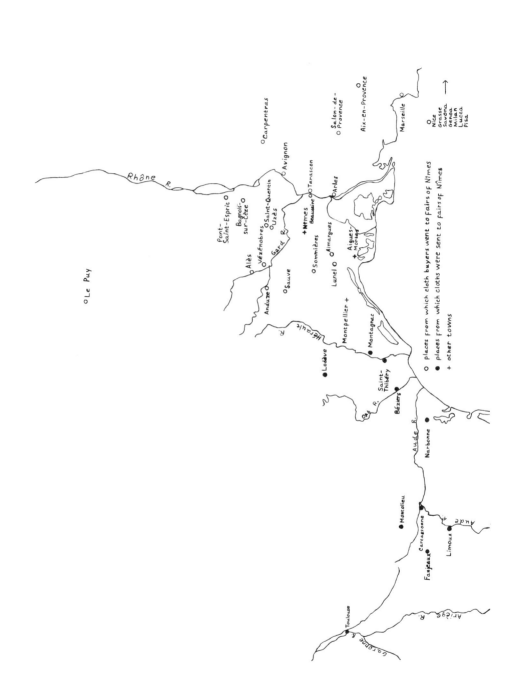

Le Puy

Rhône R.

Pont-Saint-Esprit
Bagnols-sur-Cèze
Saint-Quentin
Uzès
Vézénobres
Alès
Anduze
Sauve
Carpentras
Avignon
Tarascon
Beaucaire
Arles
Nîmes
Aimargues
Aigues-Mortes
Sommières
Lunel
Salon-de-Provence
Aix-en-Provence
Marseille
Montpellier
Lodève
Montagnac
Saint-Thibéry
Béziers
Narbonne
Moncalieu
Carcassonne
Fanjeaux
Limoux
Toulouse

Nice
Grasse
Savona
Genoa
Milan
Lucca
Pisa

Gard R.
Hérault R.
Orb R.
Aude R.
Garonne R.
Ariège R.

○ places from which cloth buyers went to fairs of Nîmes
● places from which cloths were sent to fairs of Nîmes
+ other towns

between September 12, 1318, and April 5, 1322.[39]  If we assume this
witness' candor, the most that we may safely accept from his testimony
is that he saw large quantities of cloth being bought at one time.
More credible is the testimony of Guigo Bertache, a Florentine who
seems to have fulfilled in Nîmes the function of "host" for other
Italian merchants.[40]  He testified that one year he saw Italian merchants buy 1000 pieces of cloth in his house in Nîmes; evidently his
house was used as a depository for cloths brought to Nîmes.  Fredericus
de Monelia, a bourgeois of Nîmes, but of Genoese origin, testified on
his own purchases of cloth.  He bought at times 500 pounds of cloth
and at times 1000.[41]  For the reason stated above, these figures probably refer to monetary value.  It is difficult to estimate how many
pieces of cloth such purchases represented, since the type of cloth
is not mentioned.  The records of the del Bene company mentioned above
show that the cloths they bought cost an average of 34 1. 4s. 10d. a
fiorini (about 18 1. 4s.t.), but these were northern cloths, much finer
than the product of western Languedoc.[42]  The testimony of Bernardus
de Fontibus, a Nîmois, indicates that important Italian companies were
active in the Nîmes fairs.  He testified that on the first year of the
fairs nine hundred pieces of cloth deposited in his house were bought
by a single company of Italians.[43]  If this information is accurate,
the company that bought these cloths must have been a large one, for
such a purchase would have run into thousands of pounds tournois.  A
Nîmes bourgeois of Genoese origin, Johannes de Nigra, said that in
one year he bought a good two hundred pieces of cloth.[44]  Information
of a different sort was provided by Betus de Portu, a Lucchese merchant
established in Nîmes.  From the "penny that is given for God," he
determined that on the first year of these fairs the Genoese bought
7000 pieces of cloth.[45]  This is a difficult statement to interpret.
The denarius dei appears elsewhere as one gros tournois paid on each
transaction regardless of value,[46] but this witness' statement makes
sense only if it was paid on the basis of number of cloths purchased.
A penny per piece of cloth was in fact paid on each transaction, as
is shown by the testimony of four other witnesses,[47] and this was
evidently what this witness had in mind.  A local smith, Raymundus
Fanardi, provided two facts of interest.  He heard certain merchants

from Savona say that they used to bring six galleys laden with wares to
Aigues Mortes expressly for the purpose of being traded at the fairs
of Nîmes.[48] The same witness, in trying to show that Nîmes was a
better market for cloths than Montagnac, stated that he heard certain
merchants from Carcassonne say that they took three hundred pieces of
cloth to Montagnac and were unable to sell ten of them;[49] presumably,
comparable amounts of cloth could be taken to the fairs of Nîmes by
merchants from that region. The testimony of all these witnesses
taken together leaves little doubt that the Nîmes fairs were an important market of woolen cloths. Although individual figures may be
viewed with skepticism, the thrust of the testimony shows that the
fairs attracted purchasers for important Italian companies and generated a major movement of cloths from western Languedoc.[50] To balance this cloth trade, large shipments of fine items were imported
through Aigues Mortes to be sold or traded at the fairs.

Another type of information which gives an idea of the importance
of these fairs is specific mention of amounts of taxes and duties
collected there. Four of our witnesses claimed knowledge of the
amounts collected for the droit de rève, a 4 d./l. duty on the purchase of items destined for export.[51] Bartholomeus Scatisse, a
Lucchese merchant established at Nîmes, testified that on the first
year of these fairs he had received (habuit) this tax to the amount
of 800 l. t., whereas now that these fairs were ruined this tax was
worth no more than 100 l. t.[52] This statement presents problems, for
the fairs of Nîmes were granted in July, 1322, and the first one ought
therefore to have taken place on mid-Lent of 1323; the droit de rève,
however, was not imposed until December, 1324.[53] Several of the witnesses said they saw these fairs held at Nîmes for eight years prior
to 1331, which indicates that the fairs did in fact begin in 1323.[54]
This witness, however, saw these fairs for only seven years and thus
could not have been a tax collector at the very first one.[55] Allowing
for the failings of memory, it can be assumed that some time in the
early years of this fair this witness collected some 800 l. t. for
the droit de rève, presumably from transactions carried out at the
fair itself. Another receiver (recollector) of this tax, Bonetus

Bonifilii, a notary from Lucca, testified that on the second year of
the fair he collected 600 l. t.[56] The same problem of dating presents
itself here, and no precise date can be safely assigned to this collection. Still a third witness, Uguathius Ebriaci, a notary, testified that he had been the collector (accepit et levavit) of this tax
in Nîmes. "Eight years ago or thereabouts" he had collected 1200 l.
t. for one year, and he heard from the collectors of subsequent years
that they too had collected large amounts, some more than he, and
some less.[57] It appears that whereas the two previous witnesses had
collected this tax at the fairs only, this witness collected it for
a whole year, hence the large difference in sums collected. One
final witness testified on the droit de rève. Puchinus Esbarra, a
Lucchese living in Nîmes, stated that he collected (tenuit et levavit)
this tax for four unspecified years during the time of the fairs and
asserted that from the fairs this tax yielded each year 800 l. t.,
but this year it was worth only 200 l. t. because of the cessation of
the fairs.[58] Although the testimony of these four witnesses is not
altogether clear, it is safe to conclude from it that the fairs of
Nîmes yielded about 800 l. t. per year to the collectors of the droit
de rève. Since this was a tax of 4 d./l., or ⅙₀ , it would in principle mean that the sale of goods intended for export, mostly cloths,
amounted to 48,000 l. t. for the eight days of the fair each year.
In practice, however, tax collection was never that neat, and such
calculations are unsound. These figures, nevertheless, do give some
idea of the value of trade at these fairs.

Testimony was offered on a different tax by Andreas Guirardi, a
Florentine residing in Nîmes. He testified that he saw the receipts
of his uncle Hugo Beti, receiver of the "penny per pound," and they
showed "that just for the fairs of the year in which they were held
it was worth a good 4000 l. t. and more, and this year it was worth
only 2000 or so for the whole year, because there were no fairs."[59]
Here again there are problems of interpretation. The tax to which
this witness is referring appears to be the boîte aux Lombards, a 1
d./l. sales tax paid by all Italian merchants in certain areas where
they enjoyed special privileges, including Nîmes. The text above
seems to indicate that at the fairs of Nîmes alone the revenues from

this tax amounted to 4000 l. t., which would in principle represent
transactions totaling 960,000 l. t. by the Italians attending the
fairs. Assuming that this witness was not deliberately lying, we
must conclude that he misread his uncle's books. In 1330 the boîte
aux Lombards for the whole kingdom, which by this time was levied at
the higher rate of 1 d. ob./l., was farmed for 12,500 l. t. per year.[60]
The proceeds from this tax from the fairs of Nîmes alone could therefore not have amounted to anything close to 4000 l. t. per year. It
is possible that this witness read 4000 for 400. The latter sum would
be perfectly in line with what we know of the droit de rêve; since the
boîte aux Lombards was assessed at one-fourth the rate of the droit de
rêve, but, unlike the latter, affected both sales and purchases by
Italians, its proceeds should have amounted to roughly half as much,
given the fact that most of what the Italians bought was intended for
export. The evidence presented by these witnesses tends to confirm
the view expressed above that the fairs of Nîmes were, if not "colos-
sal" as Piton characterized them,[61] then at least of considerable
importance.

It will be interesting here to compare the figures that have been
presented with the revenues generated by the fairs of Champagne at
the height of their prosperity. Bourquelot was able to ascertain the
revenues from all six fairs for the year 1296; these were as follows:
Troyes (Saint John's)--1375 l. 18s. 1d.; Troyes (Saint Remy's)--1386 l.
8s. 4d.; Provins (Saint Ayoul's)--1554 l.; Provins (May)--1925 l. 12s.
1d.; Lagny--1813 l. 7s. 6d.; Bar-sur-Aube--2140 l. 13s. 4d.[62] If, as
the figures we have cited indicate, the king derived about 1200 l. t.
in revenues each year at the fairs of Nîmes from just the two taxes
on which we have presented evidence, we can at least conclude that
these fairs were not much less important than any one of the six
Champagne fairs at its height. Needless to say, the fairs of Nîmes
are dwarfed if compared with the full cycle of fairs of Champagne.

Finally, the information contained in this testimony is also of use
in trying to explain the failure of the fairs of Nîmes to take permanent hold, and, by extension, the ultimate failure in the attempt
to make Nîmes a major commercial center. It is well known that from

the time of the royal conventions with the Italian merchants in 1278,
it had been royal policy to concentrate Italian commercial activity
in the south around Nîmes and Aigues Mortes.[63]  The fairs of Nîmes for
a time functioned precisely along the lines envisioned by royal policy.
Imports and exports on a large scale entered and left the kingdom
through Aigues Mortes on the way to or from Nîmes, the place designated
by the crown for their marketing.  The royal port and the royal administrative center functioned as an "economic couple," as Bautier put
it,[64] where commerce was entirely under royal control and easily
supervised.

The arrangement, however, was fragile and was brought to grief by
new developments coupled with its innate artificiality.  At this very
time the fairs of Champagne were declining rapidly as a result of the
increase in direct shipping between Italy and the markets of Bruges
and London.[65]  Thus, although one of the principal routes from the
fairs of Champagne to the Mediterranean passed through Nîmes, the
city now found itself being bypassed by the north-south trade.[66]  Although English wool was still carried overland from the Atlantic to
Aigues Mortes, it went through Montpellier, bypassing Nîmes altogether.[67]  The fairs of Nîmes kept trade alive in the city for a few
years by tapping a source of intense commercial activity--the export
of woolen cloths from western Languedoc.  This too failed when a rival
market appeared, for Nîmes and its surrounding area had nothing locally
produced to offer to the international market.  The testimony here
discussed has shown that the lifeblood of these fairs had been cloth
from distant towns in western Languedoc, but once a rival market closer
to the source of this product appeared at the same time of the year,
the fairs of Nîmes lost all attraction for the cloth merchants.[68]
Once the flow of cloths stopped, the fairs of Nîmes died out, for
then there was little else that could attract major trade to Nîmes.[69]
Its impracticality as a major trade center became fully evident.  This
occurred at the very time that the port of Aigues Mortes was becoming
increasingly land-locked.  Thus a series of seemingly unconnected
developments combined to frustrate royal policy.

## Chapter 15

## The Government of Calais in 1363

### Robert L. Baker

The organizational development of the staple of wool remains one of
the unsolved problems of English medieval history.  The staple system
for marketing England's prime export commodity can be traced back to
the thirteenth century, but its formal sanction by an English king
dated from 1313.[1]  In a charter of that year Edward II empowered "the
mayor and commonalty" of English merchants to select a port in the
Low Countries to which all wool destined for Flanders, Brabant, or
Artois was to be shipped for sale.[2]  Changes in the pattern of the
staple took place during the fourteenth century.  In the last year
of Edward II's reign and under Edward III and Richard II certain
English towns rather than an overseas port served as centers where
wool for export was to be sold.[3]  In time, there emerged chief officials responsible for the oversight of staple affairs, a mayor and
two constables.  When the staple towns were in England, the mayor and
constables in each were elected annually "by both native and alien
merchants."[4]  In the case of an overseas staple the king often appointed the officials, but he frequently granted the right of selection to "the commonalty of the merchants of the staple."[5]  After 1353
domestic staples had become a permanent addition to the system.
Affairs in the staple were ruled by the mayor and constables, who
received the authority to supervise all staple transactions and exercise full jurisdiction in all mercantile disputes.  These powers of the
staple officials, granted by both the English king and the prince in
whose lands the overseas staple was located, were deemed by the merchants trading in staple goods as their "franchises" or "privileges,"
guarantees of freedom from outside interference.

The principal problem is if (and if so, when) in the fourteenth
century there emerged a Company of the Staple, a corporate body, so
that the term "merchant of the staple" ceased to mean simply any merchant handling wool and referred to a member of this company.  The

purpose of this paper is to evaluate the role of one group of men,
put forward as being such a company, and determine the validity of
accepting them as founders of a corporate body of staple merchants.
These men, twenty-six in number, were English merchants who, on March 1,
1363, obtained from Edward III a charter assigning to them governance
of the town of Calais.[6] The charter named two of the twenty-six,
John Wroth and John de Wesenham, as mayors and the remainder as aldermen, and by its terms mayors were to be elected annually by those named
in the charter. Because this grant came less than a month after the
establishment of Calais as the overseas staple for English wool,[7] historians have adopted the thesis that the rule of the town had now
fallen under the control of a Company of the Staple.[8] It seems a
plausible theory. Most of the merchants of the new governing body
traded in wool, and half of them had sufficient importance to be among
those summoned by the king to assemblies of merchants that met in 1353
and 1356.[9] Moreover, those who lived in or close to English staple
towns (except four of the seven from London) had been or would become
officials in these domestic staples. In view of their undoubted stature as wool merchants,[10] it has seemed reasonable to consider them
as "the Company of Merchants of the Staple."[11] However, documents
found in the Public Record Office prove this common assumption to be
incorrect. This group of twenty-six merchants were simply what the
charter made them, governors of Calais. Their interference in the
wool trade was looked upon as an infringement of the rights of staple
merchants.

Complaints about the new government came very soon. A Commons
Petition in the October Parliament at Westminster referred to losses
that were being suffered by merchants because of actions taken by
"the new Company of Merchants dwelling now at Calais."[12] The petition stated that town officials were imposing a 40d. duty on each
sack of wool coming to Calais and were, also, setting wool prices
according to their pleasure. As a result "great quantities [of wool]
remain there in the hands of Merchants who are not of the company."[13]
Two months later, on December 20, the king commissioned the resident
governor of the Calais lordship, Henry le Scrope, and its treasurer,
Thomas Brantingham, to discover the reason for disputes between the

mayors and aldermen and other merchants, and ordain whatever seemed
necessary for the safety and security of the town.[14]  Then, in mid-
February, a royal commission appointed six Justices, including the
governor and treasurer and three merchants, to conduct a thorough
investigation into all aspects of the government in Calais.[15]  Their
general task was "to survey the condition and governance" of Calais,
and the commission detailed thirteen specific matters that were to be
considered in the course of the inquiry.  The reason for this inquisition, the commission reveals, was the complaints of prelates, lords,
and Commons.  These were the wool producers, who, as the October petition of the Commons had shown, were worried lest conditions in Calais
result in depressed prices for domestic wool.  Although mercantile
quarrels between the merchants and the mayors and aldermen were not
the prime cause for this investigation, they quickly assumed importance during the inquiry that began on March 1, 1364.  The records of
this investigation, hitherto unused, refute the thesis that a Company
of the Staple ruled in Calais.[16]

Three kinds of witnesses appeared before the Justices:  all the
aldermen,[17] representatives of the burgesses, and representatives of
merchants of the staple.  The Justices held six general inquests,
during which testimony was taken from groups of varying composition.
The first group included aldermen, burgesses, and merchants of the
staple; the second, aldermen and burgesses; the third, aldermen and
merchants of the staple; the fourth, burgesses and staple merchants;
the fifth, staplers alone; and what was apparently the sixth, burgesses alone.[18]  In addition, the Justices queried aldermen, burgesses,
and merchants individually as to what they believed were the principal causes for the defects in the government.[19]  The fifth inquest,
in which only staple merchants testified, contains the most complete
statement of wool dealers against the twenty-six.  The merchants
asserted that for their personal gain the mayors and aldermen fixed
wool prices, interfered with the entry of wool into the town, cor-
rupted wool brokers and haulers of wool, located the house for weigh-
ing wool in an inconvenient place, denied to merchants suitable buildings at reasonable rates to house their goods, and refused to grant
them toutes maneres des franchises et priuileges busoignables.[20]

Refusal to grant to staple merchants their "franchises and privileges," the customary management of the wool trade by its own officials, was undoubtedly the chief grievance of those importing wool
into Calais. Yet, if this was the Company of the Staple, such a charge
is incomprehensible. A Company of the Staple by its very nature would
rightfully assume control over all aspects of the wool trade. The
fact was that the staple merchants considered the mayors and the aldermen as constituting that outside interference from which their own
officials should protect them. They were not alone in this view.
Charges that such liberties were denied to the staple merchants were
made in two of the other inquests. In addition, aldermen mentioned
this refusal in their individual answers concerning the government's
shortcomings. According to many of the witnesses, it was John Wroth
who was most obdurate in his unwillingness to allow to merchants of
the staple their freedom from control by the town government. It was
noted by four complainants that the other mayor, John de Wesenham,
wanted to grant to the merchants of the staple their franchises, but
John Wroth would not allow this. The accusation of refusal to accord
to staple merchants the liberties they enjoyed in English and foreign
staples is manifest evidence that the company of twenty-six was not
a Company of the Staple.

Transformation of the governmental arrangements at Calais followed
soon after these inquests of March, 1364.[21] In July, the treasurer,
Brantingham, assumed supervision of the collection and disbursement
of the town revenues, replacing the mayors and alderman as overseers.[22]
According to the treasurer's account the system of dual mayors had
been abolished, and a single mayor held office.[23] Since the new mayor,
William de Spaigne, was a former alderman, he may have been chosen
according to the charter regulations that empowered the twenty-six to
elect mayors. The account also reveals that the aldermanic body had
been refashioned. Only five of those named in the charter still held
office. Now associated with them as aldermen were five burgesses of
Calais and a merchant of the staple. Formal recognition of this re-
organization, with some additions, came on June 1, 1365, with the
publication of an ordinance establishing the new government in
Calais.[24] Jurisdiction in the town was to be divided between the

mayor of the town and a mayor of the staple.  This did not mark a
return to the old system of two mayors, for the mayor of the staple
was also to be one of the town's aldermen, but it did assure that
through him and his subordinates, two constables, the franchises of
the staples would be upheld.  The other eleven aldermen were to be
the marshal of the town, the bailiff of the water, five merchants of
"good repute," and four burgesses of Calais.  The ordinance also enumerated the remaining positions to be filled in Calais and set fees
for all officials.  The king and his council appointed the more important of the office-holders.  For the moment, full control over
Calais, burgesses and merchants[25] alike, had reverted to Westminster--
with provision now for the special interests of the merchants of the
staple.

## Appendix

La quinte enqueste prise des Marchants de lestapel auantdite, Cest-
assauoir par le serement de Johan de Allerton, William de Kirketon,
Thomas de Euesham, Thomas Bernak, William Warin, Johan de Benyngton,
Johan Skye, Wauter Sistern, Robert Baker, Alisaundre Clerc, Robert
Holand, et Henry Penshurst qi diont par lour serement...
...qe les ditz Meirs et Aldremans, poi apres qils auoient la gouer-
naille de la dite ville, des Marchantz, et de lour marchandises illeoqes, sans lassent des communes Marchantz mistrent vn pris des
leins de chescun pais Dengleterre nient due ne couenable, et firent
assembler les Marchantz adonqes illeoqes et les monstrerent le pris
issint par eux assis, enioinantz eux del tenir, et les ditz communes
Marchantz, pur doute des outrageouses damages et perdes qe de reson
deussent auenir de ceste ordenance, ne oserunt a ce assentir, et
surce les ditz Meirs et Aldremans, voillantz lour volentez estre
parfaitz en celle partie, deffenderent la monstre des leins par vn
iour de monstre, a quele iour y feurent plusours Marchantz estranges
en la ville pur achater leins qe ne feurent vnqes puis en cea a vn
foitz, des queux Marchantz estranges la greindre partie se departerent
hors de la ville sans denier emploier par cause diceste ordenance.
Et puis apres dedeinz brief les ditz Meirs et Aldremans firent assembler les communealte des Marchantz et les constreinderent deslire
sys Marchantz del commune pur estre assis oue sis des Aldremans pur
ordeigner vn pris des leins, quele chose les communes Marchantz
firent encontre lour gree, a tresoutrageouse damage au Roi et sa
terre Dengleterre, et a grant deffesance des Marchantz et destrese
de vent des leins pluis qils ne sauont dire.
Item, ils diont qe les ditz Meirs et Aldremans ont ordenez sanz
commune assent des Marchantz qe apres ce qe les leins et autres
marchandises sont venuz in saluete dedeinz la hauene de Calais et
mises a terre, ils ne poent entrer la dite ville sanz bille des
ditz Meirs et Aldremans directe as Baillifs del eawe, a grant
damage et destourbance des Marchantz et grant peril empeirement
de lour biens....
Item, ils diont qe les Correcters, Portours, et autres laborers, qi
de droit et aunciene custume deussent estre attendantz si auant as
meindres des Marchantz de la compaignie come as grantz pur lour
deuoir faire, par cause qils ont manacez destre ousteez de lour
offices par ascuns des Meirs et Aldremans sils nesploitent lour
busoignes a lour volentes, lessantz les busoignes des communes
Marchantz, ils nosent droiturelement faire ce qappartient a lour
office as toutez les communes, a grant damage de tote la commune.
Item, ils diont qe le meson de pois est ordene en lieu nient couenable, a grante diseise et damages des communes Marchantz, sibien as
estranges come as autres, et pur singuler profit des Meirs et
Aldremans qont lour hosteux et autres tenementz ioust et enuiron
la dite meson de pois
Item, ils diont qe puis le temps qe les ditz Meirs et Aldremans ont eu
la gouernaills de la dite ville, les communes Marchantz ont fait grant
pursuit et clamour pur auoir les mesons couenables pur lour marchandises, mises a resonable ferme, sicome ils ont este en altres lieus la

ou les estaples ont este, sibien en Engleterre, Bruges, et Flandres
come aillours.  Et les ditz Meirs et ascuns des Aldremans, qont pur-
chasez en fee et a ferme plusours tenementz deinz la dite ville pur
lour singuler profit, destourbent qe ceste chose ne poet duement estre
fait, a outrageouse damage des Marchantz et lour marchandises.
Item, il (sic) diont qe pur nulle requeste ne clamour des Marchantz,
ne pur nulle suggestion des greuances et meschiefs qont este suffertz
en temps passe et vncore sont suffertz, les communes Marchantz ne
purroient auoir grante des ditz Meirs et Aldremans de nulle point
de franchise ne priuilege qe lour purroit auoir tourne au profit
et a ease de eux et de lour marchandises illeoqes, einz toutes
maneres des franchises et priuilegies busoignables lour ont [este]
retretz pur singuler profit des Meirs et Aldremans suisditz.  Et
diont qe ceste chose est issint contredit soueraignement par Johan
Wroth, Esmon Stapelgate, Piers de Grymesby, William de Spaigne,
Johan de Gisburne, Thomas Frost, et Philipe de Neuton, a plus outrageouses damages qils ne sauont dire a notre seignur le Roi, ces
roialmes Dengleterre, Gales, et Irland, et descrees de toutz les
communes Marchantz et marchandises repeirantz a la dite ville, et
diont qe les ditz Johan, Esmon, William, Piers, Johan, Thomas, et
Philipe sont principals destourbours de droit et del commune profit
des Marchantz

K.R. Various Accounts, Bdle. 101, No. 2, mm. 1-2

Chapter 16

Investigating Urban Uprisings with Examples from
Hanseatic Towns, 1374-1416

Rhiman A. Rotz

The fourteenth and early fifteenth centuries in Western Europe are
now generally viewed as a period of crisis.[1]  A small but unavoidable
and knotty problem in our understanding of the nature of that crisis
is proper evaluation of the many uprisings in the towns of that period.
The range of historical opinion on the subject, however, is at least
as wide as positions on the crisis itself.[2]  Are these uprisings ex-
pressions of mass discontent at a wholly repressive social structure?[3]
Efforts of the lesser bourgeoisie to "democratize" town government?[4]
Symptoms of a deep economic depression?[5]  Inevitable "growing pains"
accompanying a change in the economic structure which would lead toward
capitalism?[6]  Or are they simply protests against heavy taxation,[7] or
even squabbles within the elite over a suitable distribution of political power,[8] such as one might find in any age?  As Joseph R. Strayer
noted in his Presidential Address to the American Historical Association, at stake ultimately in our answers to such questions is the depth
of the crisis itself and the extent of its effects on men's lives and
feelings toward their institutions.  Were economic and social conditions so severe that they spawned widespread popular despair or a
desire for radical transformation of society and government?  Professor
Strayer, on the contrary, finds in them a surprising amount of faith
in the concept that existing institutions could be reformed, and thus
further evidence that in these hard times, unlike those of the later
Roman Empire, men had not yet lost hope or faith in their traditions.[9]
This essay will discuss the state of the problem and show how Professor
Strayer's insights, both in method of research and in interpretation,
can bring us to a better understanding of the true nature of urban
unrest in the fourteenth and early fifteenth centuries.

Even the most cursory inspection of the problem indicates that if
we are to interpret these events correctly we must begin with a

reasonably accurate estimate of the social and economic status of the
urban opposition forces.  This necessity would of course be true if
not a word had ever been written about uprisings, but it has been
made critical by the trends in recent literature.[10]  The fourteenth
century is now usually described as an era of economic depression,
and particularly of agricultural crisis.[11]  Several attempts to tie
the uprisings to this economic depression have been made by showing
how one particular urban class suffered from it more than others.
Obviously, such an economic explanation will work only if that class
was in fact principally responsible for the uprisings.  At one time
or another, however, every class, from the poorest to the richest,
has been judged the prime culprit.

  Among the many changes often associated with the depression, for
example, is intensification of emigration from rural areas to towns.
While agricultural earnings, particularly grain prices, plummeted,
wages and earnings from manufacture rose; this tended to drive peasants
off the land and into towns, where most became wage-workers.[12]  The
temptation to assign primary responsibility for urban unrest to such
a dislodged, dependent "mass" is great, and not only because it would
fit neatly with existing analysis of the economy.  Some authors, notably Marxists anxious to show the existence of class struggle and the
"power of the masses to shape history" in a "feudal" period, see in
this group an embryonic "plebian" or "pre-proletarian" revolutionary
force which provided the spark for social upheaval.[13]  Others, particularly descendants of or self-appointed defenders of the aristocratic urban regimes, find it easier to dismiss this contemporary
criticism of those governments if only "rabble" were involved.[14]
The great difficulty in this approach is finding any trace of significant participation by property-less wage-workers in the uprisings
themselves.  Even in the Ciompi revolt in Florence and the urban con-
frontations in Flanders the effective presence of truly property-less
"plebians" in the opposition forces, i.e., proposing or supporting
some kind of program (as opposed to a few hours of mob action), has
been questioned; elsewhere it is virtually impossible to establish
from documents.[15]  The openly ideological works are easily criticized
on this basis; nevertheless they have left a considerable and unfor-

tunate legacy to other scholars in the form of a tendency to assume,
if not "proletarian," at least low status for any urban opposition.

Traditionally the consensus has been that artisans bore the responsibility for most of these uprisings. Work done in the nineteenth
and early twentieth centuries generally assigned them the motive of
desire for greater political participation, i.e., either representation on the town council or some other device such as consultation
with guild aldermen before the making of major decisions. More recently,
however, research has tended to connect the uprisings with artisan
economic discontent stemming from the depression. If the property-
less immigrants did not themselves start the uprising, they could have
severely undercut the economic position of artisans who did, by offering the same products at lower cost. In most towns, councils had the
power to authorize production outside guilds or to change guild regulations in such a way as to force them to accept additional members.
Of course, not all trades would have been affected; those requiring
a large initial outlay of capital for tools, machinery, or raw materi-
als--such as goldsmiths, smiths, brewers, and armorers--were presumably out of the reach of peasant immigrants. Textile workers, butchers, and others engaged in skills familiar to the peasant would have
suffered the most from such competition--and precisely these guilds,
according to these authors, were the principals in a number of uprisings.[16]

The problem with this approach lies not in establishing artisan
participation, which seems certain, but in verifying the mechanism
of competition from immigrants which transmitted economic pressure
to the craftsman, for if that did not happen the economic changes of
the period should have improved artisan incomes. Grain prices fell,
while prices for animal and industrial products temporarily rose,
leveling off well above their former index to grain. Thus most
artisans should have enjoyed greater purchasing power, at least relative to staples like bread and beer; one historian has labelled the
fourteenth and fifteenth centuries "the Golden Age of the craftsman."[17]

Further questioning of this interpretation has come from scholars
who found that in several towns artisans were far from alone in the
urban opposition. Beside them stood a number of wealthy merchants,

and at times even a few members of the town's recognized elite.  In
most of these cases it would seem that these "middle-rank merchants,"
not the artisans, provided much of the impetus for revolt, served in
a leadership capacity, and were the key factor in any success.[18]
Explanations of the presence of the merchants vary, but many believe
that they were men economically on their way up, who had been thwarted
in their attempts to secure political power and higher status.  These
"new men," either self-made nouveaux riches or men who stemmed from
successful families elsewhere but were new to this particular town,
could well have turned to revolt to achieve their goals.[19]  Others
suggest that, although perhaps less wealthy than the members of the
existing patriciate, these men were in fact more active commercially.
The tradition in most commercial towns, especially in the Hanseatic
area, was rule by the town's leading merchants; after the mid-fourteenth century, however, according to this school of thought, descendants of these old merchant families turned increasingly to more secure
investments in land, annuities, or urban property, while nevertheless
keeping their grip on town government.[20]  Since commerce was the lifeblood of these towns, this transfer of capital eventually led to an
estrangement of the town elite and its government from the large segment of the population that still lived primarily from merchant activity; the latter group (including "pure merchants," mercers, drapers,
and some guildsmen with commercial interests such as goldsmiths,
brewers for export, and so on) sought political power in part to force
a return to a more commercially oriented government.[21]

  By placing the burden of responsibility on those apparently upwardly
mobile and interested in commerce, these interpretations, whichever
variation one prefers, have clearly moved uprisings yet another step
away from the economic crisis.  Certainly the depressed economy, particularly after the outbreak of plague in mid-century, created an
environment in which some surprising individual cases of economic
success or failure could occur.[22]  Also, since the crisis affected
the agricultural sphere with particular severity, it seems likely
that rural land, at least, was available at attractive prices;[23] this
could well have helped to persuade some members of the old mercantile
elite to move into property investments.  Nevertheless the history of

towns even in earlier and more prosperous times is dotted with success
and failure stories and with merchants' efforts to find in property
some security for a portion of their capital;[24] the new economic conditions could at most have widened and accelerated these tendencies
in urban life.  Thus, though social and economic factors were not
absent, these interpretations describe somewhat less a social movement and more a political one.

Finally, other interpretations make urban unrest even more political in character; that is, the key factors were struggles over personalities in government or the policies of the government.  In some
cases patricians themselves, or more properly certain patricians, were
the initial force; a split within the ruling class led some of its
members to search for allies outside their class and open the door for
revolt.[25]  In most uprisings, certainly, the opposition forces, whatever their composition, perceived their efforts as attempts to correct
policies they found offensive.  At the top of the list in an overwhelming number of cases was excessive taxation; most frequently that
taxation was seen as a direct result of expensive feuds and wars and/
or corruption and self-interest in the regime.[26]  In addition, some
scholars detect a tendency of the patriciate to "close up" at precisely
this time, to draw members of the government from a diminishing circle
of families.[27]  Such problems need not, of course, be seen as totally
isolated from the economy.  A town's financial position, particularly,
was likely to deteriorate in part from difficulties spawned by depression and plague.[28]  Nevertheless the major factor in this heavy taxation was usually the high cost of war, and the major factor in wars
was a town's foreign policy.  Certainly by far the greatest number of
urban uprisings in Europe appeared in the territory of the Holy Roman
Empire, where central government was weakest, and thus where towns were
most frequently obliged to pursue an independent foreign policy; also,
uprisings frequently came during or on the heels of wars.[29]  High taxation and war policies were issues which affected all taxpayers and
citizens, and could quite conceivably have united artisans, merchants,
and even some members of the elite in opposition to the government.
In short, it is possible to explain a number of uprisings almost entirely by political and financial factors.

In summary, then, it is necessary to admit that in recent literature, scholars who have treated the problem of urban uprisings do not seem to be talking about the same events.  Some see a response to declining economic conditions on the part of either destitute proletarians or artisans caught in a buyers' market; others see an essentially politi- cal quarrel--over persons in power and how that power should be used-- led by mercantile elements, perhaps even by members of the elite it- self.  One possible explanation for this is that in fact most are not looking at precisely the same events; the nature of most research on this topic has been individual studies of individual uprisings widely separated in both time and place.  The studies have then been tied together more by assumption than by investigation.  A few authors have simply assumed that where violence is, there the poor must be also, and have taken them together with little further thought on the matter. More importantly, however, a great many authors have begun by assuming, implicitly or explicitly, that since unrest occurred with such fre- quency in the fourteenth and early fifteenth centuries, it must have expressed discontent with conditions common to all in that period, perhaps even indicating an embryonic "social movement."  Evidence and conclusions from one uprising are then applied to all.  This assumption has not been the property of any one ideological position; Marxist, "bourgeois," and apparently non-committed historians have embraced it with equal willingness.[30]

Perhaps we will eventually find the key that will enable us to con- sider all uprising as part of a single phenomenon; it seems useful, however, to suggest that to start with this assumption may not be the most productive way to develop accurate investigations.  The uprisings themselves varied from what we would now call wholly non-violent demonstrations--a small group delivering a formal list of suggestions to the town council, such as at Hamburg in 1376--to the burning of palaces at Florence and the execution of councilmen at Brunswick. Contemporary chroniclers saw them all as frightening breaches of peace and order, but that does not require modern scholars to place them all in the same classification nor to assume that great violence must im- ply great mass participation.  It is at least possible that some were urged on by lower classes and some were not, that some can be tied to the economic crisis and some cannot, that some were part of "movements" and some were not.[31]  If one takes this position, then investigation of any urban uprising must begin by assuming as little as possible, and this obviously includes not assuming the social and economic composition of the parties to it without a full investigation.

The overriding difficulty in the way of such investigation is that the usual literary sources, such as chronicles, simply cannot be reliably used for judgments on the social and economic standing of participants in uprisings.  This can be illustrated with examples from Hanseatic towns.  Even a fairly accurate and thorough chronicle describing an uprising is likely to give only some of the groups involved or at best a few leaders with guild or professional labels.  Such labels can be translated into useful socioeconomic information only with great difficulty.  Towns of the period varied considerably in economic function and in social structure; one must know the precise local circumstances in order to estimate the true position of many common professions in any one town.[32]  For example, a cooper in a Hanseatic seaport town was usually a particularly prosperous artisan because of the great demand for his barrels at the Scania herring fisheries.[33]  Further, each town developed its own system of labels which did not always correspond to usage elsewhere; for example, the term "guild" in some localities often included not only craftsmen but some merchant associations as well.  On the other hand, the term "citizen" in many towns referred not to the average man but to men of considerable wealth standing just below the patriciate.[34]  A draper was originally a textile merchant who also retailed pieces from his bolts of cloth, but several authors are convinced that in some towns the term lost all connection with both cloth and retailing and was used for a class of wholesalers; in one town it seems quite possible that "merchant" did not mean merchant at all, but rentier, and in another that "brewers" referred to the great merchants (who were, of course, not brewers).[35]

Even within the same town and within the same profession scholars have found considerable extremes of wealth; economic equality may have been an expressed ideal within a guild but it rarely corresponded with reality.  Thus while some members of a craft guild stood near the

poverty level, an exceptional member or two might have ranked just
below the town's elite.[36] This may reflect unusual success in a particular profession; it may also stem from the often-overlooked fact
that people in fourteenth- and fifteenth-century towns were not necessarily specialists. Wholesalers engaged in retail, retailers engaged
in wholesale, and even craftsmen engaged in commerce. The most common
example is the craft which developed a particularly fine product; as
it acquired a regional reputation its makers would in effect follow
it into export. Successful weavers who became cloth merchants are
often cited, but this occurred in a wide range of trades, for example
brewers at Hamburg and makers of metal bowls at Brunswick. Other
craftsmen might have been drawn into commerce initially through a
search for new materials for their product, as in the makers of amber
rosaries at Lubeck.[37] There need not have been a logical connection,
however; individuals might have made a transition from craftsman to
merchant, or engaged in both kinds of activity, from any trade. Thus
a great many terms as used by chroniclers which would seem to hold
socioeconomic meaning can lose that meaning on closer inspection. A
phrase such as "the uprising was led by the guilds, particularly the
weavers and metal-workers" could conceivably refer to any or all levels
from poor manual laborers to fairly wealthy merchants, depending on
local conditions and individual circumstances.

To the above risks inherent in an accurate chronicle must be added
the danger that a literary source may intentionally not be accurate.
Chronicles of towns or short reports on events in them, with only very
rare exceptions, were written by the elite for the elite. Their
authors were normally clerics from the patriciate or clerical civil
servants employed by the council; on occasion councilmen would directly
commission the writing of a chronicle. Councilmen and patricians constituted their chief audience. Therefore, not surprisingly, these
chronicles and reports display a pro-council, pro-patrician political
orientation and a conspicuous lack of concern for precision when re-
porting the activities of those beneath them. Moreover, town chronicles of the fourteenth and fifteenth centuries are infrequently general histories; usually they were written for a purpose, and that
purpose was closely tied to town events at the time of writing. Often

those events were uprisings; councils saw that their legal and political authority was being challenged and wrote histories to justify
themselves.[38]   The chronicle of Lubeck by the Franciscan Detmar illustrates this.  It was commissioned by two Lubeck councilmen in 1385,
immediately following the uprising of 1384.  In Detmar's treatment of
that event, which was a planned conspiracy rather than a spontaneous
uprising, blame was assigned not only to the conspirators but to artisans in general; guilds were painted as potential threats to peace at
all times.  Such a picture of craftsmen would have served to justify
their continued exclusion from the council.[39]

A somewhat different and more unusual example of a misleading literary source is the introduction to a special accounting of the town of
Brunswick issued in 1406.  It refers to the Brunswick uprising of 1374
as a time of "great unwisdom, debt, and damage" and to the victims and
exiles of that unrest as "pitiable" and "without guilt," blaming the
uprising for most of the town's financial problems.  It fails to give
any information on those who supported the uprising, and clearly allows
the reader to assume that the upheaval had been completely put down and
was best forgotten.  In fact, however, the government of Brunswick at
that point was dominated by supporters of the uprising who presumably
well knew that the expensive territorial defense policies of those
victims and exiles had wrecked the town's finances, and who had successfully engineered a settlement and new constitution which left only
severely limited political power to supporters of the old regime.
Their willingness to forgo their proper place in town history in an
official document presumably reflected their part of a new bargain
which made possible a merger of old and new council families into a
wider elite.[40]   At any rate, even in a town where the patrician
monopoly of government had been broken, a patrician bias prevailed
in literary sources; by the sixteenth century a chronicler had reduced
these highly creative and successful politicians to "tanners, arro-
gant men" whose influence on Brunswick history had been totally negative.[41]   Literary sources, then, do not necessarily offer a satisfactory picture of the parties in an uprising.

Joseph R. Strayer has often suggested prosopography as a research
method which can provide a solution to this and similar dilemmas

facing scholars of the later Middle Ages.  This approach has been used
for certain defined occupational or clerical groups--for example,
lawyers and nuns--to write "a sort of collective biography...by assembling hundreds of scraps of evidence."[42]  We can learn in this way
if certain features were common to most members of the group, such as
a particular geographic origin or descent from a particular social
classification.  The same method, however, can also be used for a
defined political group, such as the participants in an urban uprising;
"if local records are good we can determine the occupation, social
standing, and often the wealth of many of the individuals involved."[43]
One may find common social or economic characteristics in the urban
opposition using this approach.  However, in this case, if one fails
to find such common characteristics, that is equally significant,
since it would indicate an opposition drawn from not one but many
social and economic levels.

   Obviously this method cannot be used for every uprising; one must
first be able to determine the names of as many of the participants
as possible.  This tends to limit one to particularly successful or
particularly unsuccessful uprisings:  on one hand, those which managed
to establish their own council or governing body, or at least a semi-
permanent consultative committee, for which a list of names survives
or can be reconstructed from documents it issued; on the other, those
which suffered sharp repression, and thus for which records of imprisonment or execution survive.  Also, this method is not without
its potential pitfalls; names were far from fixed in this period, so
that one individual can appear under two or more different names, and
on the other hand even two closely related individuals may appear
under identical names.[44]  In addition, of course, documentation of
such individuals is never as full and complete as one would like,
and invariably a few men will seem to have appeared in history only
for the uprising and then disappeared again without a trace.  None
of these, however, are valid reasons for not using prosopography in
those uprisings where a number of names are known.  In the past, as
mentioned previously, historians have assumed all too quickly that
individuals who took part in uprisings were of low social and economic
worth; this has led to the further assumption that documentary mention

of them would be sparse or nonexistent.  In fact, however, useful information can usually be found for most of them.  This information
admittedly will rarely be sufficient for statistical handling; ultimately it must be interpreted subjectively.[45]  Nevertheless one can
establish through this method a much broader base, founded on more
solid documentation, for general conclusions about the social and
economic composition of parties than is available in literary sources.
This is true even in towns where the survival of documentation has
not been particularly outstanding, as the following studies from
Hanseatic towns will illustrate.[46]

The Lubeck "butchers' rising" of 1384 has been examined using this
method, and would seem to fit the conception of revolt brought on by
downwardly mobile artisans.[47]  Sixty to 65 conspirators planned to
seize the town hall during a council meeting and take the councilmen
prisoners.  They intended to put one of their own houses to the torch
at the same time, to signal a group of local knights who would then
enter the town in support.  The fire also was expected to draw a crowd
of citizens who would then support the coup--or so the conspirators
hoped.  None of this ever occurred, however; the council learned of
the plan a day in advance, possibly through one of the nobles, and
began arresting the conspirators, although some were able to flee.
The names of 47 of them survive, largely through a "book of traitors"
compiled at the time, others through judicial records.  Most of them
can be traced in documents.  The leaders and presumably organizers
of the conspiracy included a merchant, two furriers, two bakers, and
two butchers.  Overall, however, it would seem that the uprising was
aptly named; at least 27 of the 47 were butchers.  The remainder included three merchants, none of them particularly successful, and 11
other artisans.  All were probably citizens; at least 34 held property
in the town and nine others were members of a guild.  There were presumably no true "plebians" here, and certainly no members of the elite.
Interestingly, however, some 15 of them seem to have been in financial difficulty, having run up several unpaid debts; this could well
have been true of others.  Also, they probably all knew each other
before joining the conspiracy; 30 can be documented as neighbors and
either business partners or relatives of other conspirators.  What

they hoped to accomplish by their rising is not known, but since guilds
had made demands for lower taxes and greater participation in policy-
making in 1376 and 1380 with little success, this uprising may represent an attempt to achieve those goals by less open means.  The council responded by executing 19 of them and slashing both the size and
the privileges of the butchers' guild.  The "butchers' rising" in
Lubeck, then, might well have been a symptom of the economic crisis;
certainly it also could have included an element of social protest
against the low political and economic power of craftsmen in a seaport
town.

   This picture, however, does not fit every uprising, as work done
with this method in Brunswick indicates.[48]  A glance at literary
sources alone would give the impression of an artisan-patrician conflict:  in 1374 a crowd stormed the town hall and the homes of councilmen, eight of whom were executed; over 50 patricians left town.  After
12 difficult years a new constitution fixed guild representation on
the town council.  Nevertheless further investigation shows that the
Brunswick opposition cannot be characterized as from any single class;
this can be determined by investigating the 68 known men who served
the new regime as councilmen or ambassadors.  Those who can be identified include patricians, wealthy merchants, drapers, prosperous artisans engaged in commerce, butchers, tanners, and so on--representatives
of every level, it would seem, except the poorest.  At least 24 of
them held rural land; nine of those, plus two others, can be established
from documents as engaging in merchant activity.  These figures are
surprisingly comparable to those obtained for the 60 known victims
and exiles of the uprising, presumably patricians, from the same documentary base:  some 26 held rural land, albeit in larger quantities;
four of those, plus one other, left traces of commercial activity in
documents.  Thus the Brunswick opposition, regarded from a social and
economic viewpoint, certainly represented nothing lower than a cross-
section of the entire citizen community and probably ranked quite a
bit higher than that.[49]

   Uprisings, even quite violent ones, were no monopoly of the poor.
One must therefore doubt that artisan presence on the council was the
central issue in this struggle--a doubt that is further confirmed by

evidence which indicates that craftsmen also sat on the pre-1374 council and thus at most broadened their participation.  The opposition's
complaints cited high taxes, unnecessary debts, and mismanagement as
their reasons for revolt, complaints at least partly justified.  The
funds raised by the taxes had gone largely to support a policy of territorial acquisition, defended by extensive holdings of castles and by
feuds with the nobility, which had probably been inspired in part by
the councilmen's own rural property interests; this policy was openly
abandoned after the settlement.  In short, the Brunswick uprising of
1374 can scarcely be given the character of a struggle of one class
against another and apparently bore little relationship to economic
conditions; one would hesitate to say that it had no social implications, but local policy issues seem paramount.

Similar conclusions emerge if we return to the seaport towns to
investigate the chain of uprisings beginning there in 1408, a complicated series of events which can only be summarized briefly here.[50]
Discontent over high taxes in Lubeck had led to the establishment of
a citizens' Committee of Sixty in 1405 with the council's permission;
this body made a tax increase conditional on an inspection of town
books and the placing of two citizen "assistants" in each of the four
major administrative offices of the council.  The council agreed, but
then in 1407 announced that this experiment had been so successful
that it could now be discontinued.  The citizens responded that its
success was rather an excellent reason for making the arrangement
permanent, perhaps even giving the Sixty a voice in the selection of
new councilmen.  After a year of increasing hostility on both sides,
culminating in a stormy meeting with an angry crowd milling outside,
some two-thirds of the council left town, probably out of fear, but
of their own volition.  Negotiations with the remnant broke down and
the citizens decided to establish a new constitution.  No physical
harm came to any councilman; some property was later confiscated from
the exiles, and many annuities were rewritten on terms more favorable
to the council, both in an effort to reduce town debt.  Both sides
spent the next eight years seeking allies outside town walls.  Citizen
committees appeared in Rostock and Wismar in 1409 and in Hamburg in
1410, following which these towns declared themselves for Lubeck; the

exiles however managed to have Lubeck placed under the ban of the
empire and excluded from meetings of the Hanseatic League.  Finally
in 1416, just when it appeared that Lubeck would be able to bribe the
new emperor Sigismund into lifting the ban, the exiles turned to
King Eric of Denmark, who began imprisoning Lubeck merchants at Scania
precisely at the time of the herring run.  At this point the new regime
capitulated, and under Hanse arbitration a compromise was reached by
which five members of the 1408-16 council would join a restored council of 27.  By 1417 the Hanse had forced the citizen committees in
the other three towns to disband as well.

Several sources make it possible to investigate this opposition.
One undated list of members of the Sixty survives.[51]  In addition we
have two lists of the Sixteen, a special finance committee, from 1408
and 1415, a list of a delegation which met with the remnant of the old
council and the electors which chose the new one, both in 1408, and
the signers of a "secret document" of 1415.[52]  Various documents issued
by the new council between 1408 and 1416 allow a reconstitution of the
bulk of its membership,[53] and a few letters and chronicles yield a few
more names.[54]  Although many individuals served in several of these
capacities, these sources still yield 102 different names for investigation.[55]  Of these, 94 can be identified with some information useful
in determining their social and economic standing.[56]

Once again we find an opposition that cannot be described as representing a single social or economic class.  The group included one
sitting councilman, the brother of another, the sons of former councilmen, and fourteen members of Lubeck's elite Circle Society.[57]  At
least 52 of the 94 are known to have engaged in commercial activity.
On the other hand, at least 25 artisans are also represented; however,
it is worth noting that a large portion of these artisans came from
trades which presumably felt little effect from any competition from
immigrants (five brewers, four goldsmiths, two amber-workers, two
smiths, one armorer).  This was clearly a very different group from
those who led the "butchers' rising" of 1384.

In the interests of brevity a full treatment of all 94 profiles
will be omitted, but a look at the five men singled out by a chronicler as leaders of the opposition in 1407-08 will illustrate its

diversity. Hermen van Alen was the brother-in-law of a councilman
exiled by the uprising. A merchant to Cologne and Reval, he held the
right of advowson over two benefices in local churches. Borcherd van
Hildessem, a merchant both to Flanders and in the Baltic, was also a
banker and the son-in-law of a councilman. He held one manor in pawn
and shared ownership of three others, and served as an arbitrator in
the case of an inheritance disputed by local nobles. Johan Lange was
the son of a councilman and was married to the daughter of a burgomaster and Circle Society member; his ties to the elite are further
indicated by a later judgment which allowed his widow and children
to inherit funds paid as damages to an exiled councilman. A merchant,
at least in his early years, he eventually purchased several manors
and established a benefice. Hinrich Schonenberch, a successful brewer,
owned part of a woods near Lubeck and twice arbitrated disputes between
owners of a paper mill. Eler Stange, the armorer mentioned above, was
prosperous enough to own a grain storehouse and to marry the niece of
a councilman.[58]

Overall, enough information is available to establish some categories
for analysis. These categories are not intended necessarily to correspond to or imply any individual's membership in any coherent social
class; they are designed simply to facilitate analysis of the data in
somewhat more meaningful social, economic, and political terms, based
not on ideal classifications but rather using distinctions which can
be made from the available evidence.

The first group includes only those who meet one or more of the
following qualifications: 1) was a councilman in years other than
those of the uprising (before 1408 or after 1416); 2) was a member
of the Circle Society; 3) was related by blood or marriage to such a
councilman or member of the Circle Society; or 4) apparently possessed
great wealth, as indicated by such evidence as a large bequest or
extensive land investment.[59] Thus this group should consist of men
with apparent political or social prestige and/or major personal fortunes. Some 38 individuals, or just over 40 percent of those identified, can be placed in this group, most of them satisfying more than
one of these requirements.[60] Such extensive representation of men of
prominence in the uprising, together with the fact that one-third of

the council remained in town under the new regime, strongly suggests
that a split within the town's elite was a factor in the unrest.

The second group includes those who were excluded from the first
but who show evidence of one or more of the following: 1) merchant
activity; 2) some investment in land; 3) practice of an artisan trade
which in Lubeck often engaged in commerce (brewers, goldsmiths, amber-
workers). This of course is a varied group; nevertheless, given the
lack of specialization of the time, without other or repeated evidence,
one cannot be certain from isolated entries in poundage books or claims
for lost goods that an individual was primarily a merchant. Also, it
is probably unwise to try to make precise distinctions between some
less active merchants and some very active commercial artisans who
might well have stood at an equal or even superior economic level.
Defined in this way, the group should include all those with commercial interests, and some not in commerce who nevertheless shared their
economic rank. Overall, 40 individuals, or 42.5 percent of those
identified, fit this category. Of them, 23 would appear to have been
merchants, with 14 probable commercial artisans and three uncertain.[61]

This process of classification leaves only 16 participants, or 17
percent of those identified, for the third group, those without any
known interest in commerce, ties to the elite, or land investment.
Most of these can be identified as noncommercial artisans, although a
few may of course have fallen into this group for lack of evidence
rather than lack of wealth. All seem to have been at least at the
citizen level, with some economic independence and/or possession of
some property.[62]

These are broad groups, and one should not make too much of this
analytic device. Nevertheless, even allowing for possible error in
classification and for the eight unidentified participants, it is
impossible not to conclude that the opposition which created the
Lubeck uprising of 1408 was drawn from relatively high, not low, social
and economic groups, particularly commercial groups. There is no
generally agreed-upon definition of the terms "patrician" or "elite"
for Hanseatic towns; certainly, however, many if not most of these
in the first group were either part of the town's elite or on its
fringes. Work using less narrow classifications has been done, and

indicates that those with interests in commerce (or their descendants
with comparable incomes from property) constituted roughly the top 20
to 25 percent of the taxable population of a Hanseatic seaport town.[63]
This includes the elite, all but the most unsuccessful merchants, most
brewers, and many other commercial artisans such as goldsmiths and
amber-workers--a definition roughly comparable to those included in
both Group I and Group II in this analysis. With the understanding
that none of the figures used here should be taken to imply the kind
of precision possible with more modern sources of data, one may safely
conclude that probably at least three-quarters of the Lubeck opposition came from the top one-quarter of the town's taxable population.

For comparison it is possible to take a similar, if less precise,
look at the opposition in Hamburg. A list of its Committee of Sixty,
probably from 1410, survives in Adam Tratziger's chronicle, and a few
members were identified by the editor of that chronicle.[64] Others can
be checked against poundage books and treasury records.[65] Over half
of the members of this committee, 31, were probably merchants, and six
of this group later joined the Hamburg council.[66] In addition, five
others were certainly from commercial or propertied families, since
they also later served as councilmen.[67] Seven others must have been
men of some standing, as indicated by their appearance as parish
jurors.[68] The Hamburg Sixty also included two coopers, a cobbler,
a goldsmith, and a tinker.[69] An additional four men can at least be
identified as citizens,[70] leaving eight unidentified. Here again
artisans were present but far outweighed by merchants, and men of
recognized status, such as future councilmen, supported the uprising.

The revolts of the early fifteenth century in the seaport towns
drew their support not from the masses and only partly from those who
worked with their hands; merchants and other leading citizens were
the mainstays of these movements. In Lubeck the issues which brought
them out, in their own words, were high taxation, unnecessary expenses
of war, mismanagement of town resources, and failure, in their opinion, properly to protect the economic interests of merchants and
artisans.[71] Successful for several years, they were defeated by pressure on commerce--not surprisingly, since that was a body blow to
the livelihood of most of them--but in defeat preserved something of

a compromise.  Whatever social tensions these events reflect, clearly
these men attacked neither an entire class (many of them were themselves members of the leading group) nor entire institutions (their
first action once in power was to set up a town council).  The logical
conclusion for Lubeck is that the movement arose in an effort to im-
prove government and took power in 1408 to preserve institutional reforms which citizens found valuable.

Any summary of these results must begin by noting how little can be
found which was common to all four uprisings; the one salient point
is the lack of "mass" participation in all of them.  Only the abortive
coup of 1384 in Lubeck will fit into a scheme of unrest caused primarily by economic distress and an impulse for social protest, and
even in that case such an interpretation rests in part on speculation.
Otherwise one finds movements in which artisans possibly under economic pressure played very little part.  Although the uprisings of
Brunswick in 1374, Lubeck in 1408, and Hamburg in 1410 occurred in
an environment of economic crisis, it would be difficult to consider
that crisis as the whole or even a primary cause of unrest.  A desire
for increased participation in government by upwardly mobile groups
which felt excluded from that government either by council restriction
or by their lack of income from property remains a real possibility;
such an interpretation, however, in no way implies loss of faith in
society or institutions on the part of the opposition, but rather a
wish to make them better.  A further possibility is simply to see here
a series of revolts against suspected corruption, expensive wars, and
above all high taxes by those who fought the wars and paid the taxes.[72]
The Hanseatic town of the fourteenth and fifteenth centuries lacked any
device other than persuasion for the peaceful changing of town policy;
if the council remained adamant an uprising was the only alternative.
That citizens felt a right to say and do something to their "council
lords" about government may well be significant in the social as well
as the political history of these towns, but such an attitude scarcely
reflects loss of hope, even less loss of interest.

Finally, if unrest within such a small area as Brunswick-Hamburg-
Lubeck, and within a time span of less than four decades, can show
such variation, then caution toward attempts to explain all such

unrest by a single cause would seem advisable.  We need not more
generalization but more investigation; wherever possible, that investigation should be based on identification of the participants.  Use
of that method already indicates that one need not see in clusters of
urban uprisings the despair of the proletariat or radical social protest.  Some, at least, were clearly attempts to alleviate grievances
by reforming and improving existing institutions; the hard times had
not robbed men of such desires.  For both that methodology and that
perspective on urban unrest we are greatly indebted to Joseph R.
Strayer.

Part IV

The Social Order

Chapter 17

The Counts of Mortain and the Origins of the
Norman Congregation of Savigny[1]

Bennett D. Hill

"Les généalogies ont ouvert une perspective d'histoire régionale
nouvelle pour nous.  Et nous avons acquis la conviction que la force
la plus puissante et la plus stable du XIIe et du XIIIe siècle était
la famille, plus puissante même que l'Église et la coutume."  So wrote
the distinguished scholar of early Capetian history, William Mendel
Newman, in the Introduction to his recent study of the nobility of
Picardy.[2]  What was true of Picardy was also characteristic of
Normandy, and the study of monastic history there reveals the strong
and intimate connection between religious houses and the great baronial families.  In fact, wherever we turn in the politics of the eleventh and twelfth centuries--whether feudal or ecclesiastical--the
issues seem to dissolve into family history.  A particular monastery
could not come into existence, whatever the sanctity, imagination,
or charisma of a religious leader, without the endowment of laymen,
which meant landed lords.  Monastic history is not only the study of
a remarkable individual's piety, reformist goals, and breadth of vision;
nor is it the study of spiritual movements disassociated from the
larger secular society from which they sprung, though it has usually
been written that way.  Monastic history must include the study of
genealogy and family history.  This paper is a study of the family
which established the Norman abbey of Savigny, the chief and mother-
house of a religious institute which in the twelfth and later centuries
was to have vast economic interests and no little political power, but
slight religious prestige.  The Congregation of Savigny in the first
half-century of its history was inextricably tied up with the counts
of Mortain.

The county of Mortain, in the far southwestern corner of Normandy,
was carved out of ducal territories by Duke Richard II (996-1026) as
a portion for his younger brother Mauger.[3]  The location of the fief

on the barbarous and poorly defended fringes of Normandy and Brittany, and the fact that it was given to a member of the duke's own family, suggest that it was intended to be a sort of marcher appanage.  It was undoubtedly created for purposes of defense, and the pattern estab-lished by Duke Richard was followed by all of his direct and collateral descendants until the conquest of Normandy by Philip Augustus in 1204. The central fact in the history of Mortain, then, is that the dukes always reserved it for members of their own families.[4]  From Mauger the fief passed to William Werlenc, who was either his son or his grandson.  For reasons which remain obscure, but which probably in-volved real or suspected treachery, Duke William (1035-1087) summarily stripped William Werlenc of Mortain in 1055 and gave it to his own half-brother, Robert.[5]  Count Robert I was throughout his long life-time a close advisor of the duke and is portrayed on the Bayeux Tapes-try sitting at his left hand in council.  Robert fought for the Con-queror at Hastings, took an active part in the subjugation of the new island kingdom, and for his services and loyalty was granted vast, if characteristically scattered, estates throughout England.[6]  William the Conqueror's original confidence in Robert was fully justified: he never engaged in an act of treachery, unlike their other brother, Bishop Odo of Bayeux (1050-1097), and for his undivided fidelity, Count Robert I was a legend in his own time.[7]  Upon his death in 1091, the county of Mortain passed to his eldest son, William.  This man, the fourth count of Mortain, supported Duke Robert in opposition to King Henry I, and as the consequence of Henry's victory at the battle of Tinchebrai in 1106 was deprived of the fief.  Henry gave it to William de Vitre, the nephew, through his sister Agnes, of Count Robert I.[8]  It was with the family, household, and feudal dependents of the counts of Mortain that Vital, the founder of the monastery of Savigny, was intimately connected.

   Vital was born about 1050 at Tierceville in the canton of Ryes about nine kilometers from Bayeux.  He was one of nine children.[9] His parents Reinfroy and Roharde apparently were not members of the nobility, but they were sufficiently well-off to make large donations to the poor of the neighborhood and to make such a sizable benefaction to Duke William's new monastic foundation of St. Etienne at Caen that

they were listed among that abbey's great patrons.[10]  How Reinfroy
accumulated his money, no source deigns to suggest, but twelfth-century
chroniclers and hagiographers did resist the common tendency to fabri-
cate for the youth who was to become a distinguished monastic founder
an aristocratic ancestry; from what little we know, it is possible,
at the risk of anachronism, to call the family middle-class.  Reinfroy
and Roharde gave their son Vital, who was by all later reports intel-
lectually inclined from childhood, an excellent education by the
standards of the times.  He was well instructed in Scripture, theology,
and canon law, probably at one of the nearby monasteries.[11]  Vital's
intelligence, industry, and learning brought him to the attention of
his bishop, the powerful and influential Odo of Bayeux, who sent him
away to study.[12]  Vital's later biographers do not specify where this
phase of his education occurred, but a hint is provided by Ordericus
Vitalis who, describing Bishop Odo, says:  "He also sent young clerks
to Liège and other places where he knew that the study of philosophy
flourished most, making them liberal allowances for their maintenance,
that they might, uninterruptedly and for a long period, employ themselves in the pursuit of learning."[13]

The interest and support of Bishop Odo was the most auspicious event
in Vital's early life; in fact, it launched his career.  On returning
to Normandy, Vital was singled out by Count Robert I of Mortain, who
appointed him his private chaplain.  Was this simply fortuitous, the
result of the count's recognition of the young man's learning and considerable personal charm, as Vital's biographers and the surviving
sources would have us believe?[14]  Or could Bishop Odo have ordained
Vital to the priesthood and have introduced him to his brother of
Mortain for the position of chaplain, as the nineteenth-century scholar
Louis du Bois flatly asserts, without, however, offering any documentation.[15]  Given the otherworldly cast of mind of medieval biographers,
combined with their tendency to stress the virtues of their subjects
and to ignore their vices, I am inclined to accept the suggestion of
du Bois.  Ordination and some form of ecclesiastical appointment frequently followed the completion of formal education, and Vital is
called by all the sources Vital of Mortain, which was neither the place
of his birth nor the scene of his subsequent monastic activities.

Certain aspects of Vital's early life parallel the career patterns
of many Anglo-Norman clerics in the late eleventh and the twelfth centuries:  the clever and industrious youth of "middle-class" background,
who is early recognized by a powerful benefactor, sent abroad to study,
lands an appointment in the household of a great lord or ecclesiastic,
and through contacts made there rises in episcopal, monastic, or even
royal circles:  one thinks of Ralph Flambard, John of Salisbury, even
Thomas Becket.  Vital, however, was to take a different turn in his
career from those royal and papal servants.

Vital became very much a part of Robert of Mortain's household.  The
chaplain in a royal or noble family was responsible for the chapel,
the performance of all religious services, spiritual ministration to
members of the establishment, often too the fundamental education of
the children of the family, and preaching on occasion.  It was in the
last-mentioned area that Vital distinguished himself and built his
reputation, for several contemporary authorities emphasize his preaching.[16]  But Vital interpreted his duties as involving much more than
strictly spiritual consolations.  The vita reports that on at least
one occasion he interfered in a domestic squabble between the count
and his wife.  The story goes that one day Vital came upon the Countess
Matilda, a daughter of the count of Montgomery, crying because her
husband had insulted her and physically abused her.  Vital vigorously
reproached Count Robert, threatened to leave the household if he did
not mend his ways, and required that Robert submit to a severe lashing
on his bare shoulders as penance.[17]  If this tale is true, it suggests
that Vital saw himself as a spiritual father with the obligation of
correcting and chastising, and that he was accepted as such by the
count of Mortain.  If the tale is apocryphal, the fabrication of a
hagiographer who wanted to moralize on the power of his subject over
a member of the nobility, nevertheless it claims an unusual degree
of influence and familiarity between a baron of royal blood and his
chaplain, one of his servants.  During Vital's tenure, Robert decided
to rebuild the church in the town of Mortain, dedicating it to St.
Evroul, the sixth-century missionary who had introduced Christianity
into Mortain.  This was established as a collegiate church and endowed
with the sizable number of sixty canons (the college); a collegiate

church, like a cathedral, is situated in an urban center and has canons
or prebendaries attached, but unlike a cathedral it was not the seat
of a bishop.  Such a religious establishment in Mortain, and with such
a large number of canons, reflects Count Robert's considerable wealth
and great social status.  The church was blessed by the archbishop of
Rouen and three other Norman bishops in 1082, and in the same year
William the Conqueror raised it to the dignity of a royal chapel.[18]
Vital was appointed one of the canons of the new collegiate church,
living a communal life there and sharing in the income of the foundation.  He continued at the same time to serve as chaplain in the comital household, and over the years he must have been in contact with
his former mentor, Odo of Bayeux, and may well have had occasional
dealings with King William I and his sons William Rufus and Henry.

Vital remained in his positions as chaplain and as canon of St.
Evroul for twelve more years, until about 1094.  Then, desiring a
more solitary life, he withdrew from Mortain and built for himself a
hermitage in the nearby forest of Dompierre.[19]  Whether this withdrawal
was prompted by some personal inner need, the expression or result of
a spiritual crisis, or whether Vital was inspired by the rumor and
reputation of others who had already gone into the same place, we
shall never know.  For the last decade of the eleventh century witnessed, in the remote, isolated, and heavily forested area that connected Brittany, Normandy, and Maine, a widespread eremitical movement
with which the names of Robert d'Arbrissel, Bernard of Tiron, and
Ralph de la Futaye are associated.  The significance of their operations, both for the monastic institutes which eventually emerged from
them and for the history of western France in the late eleventh and
twelfth centuries, deserves more attention than space here permits.
It may suffice to say, for the present, that this movement was a response to the wretched moral conditions in the monasteries and local
churches of Brittany and represented the introduction into that territory of the ideals of the international reform movement which modern
students have named after Pope Gregory VII.[20]

Vital's retreat from the court of Robert of Mortain was only a partial one.  He continued, from time to time, to advise Count Robert,
and he travelled widely in the lands of the Anglo-Norman monarchs.

He preached at the London Council of 1102, where he supported the aims of the papal reformers.[21]  These journeys gained him a great reputation as a preacher and spiritual leader, and they attracted to his forest hermitage a large number of followers in the decade between 1094 and 1104.  The circumstance of a large number of men, living an austere eremitical life under the personal tutelage of a locally well-known spiritual leader and in conscious imitation of the ancient desert fathers of the East, but living without an officially approved set of constitutions or a Rule, has many precedents in western monastic history.  To none of these movements has the organization-conscious Roman Church been especially sympathetic.  Hence, it would be interesting to know whether the impetus for a structured and communal life under papally approved regulations for his followers came from Vital of Mortain, or whether there was pressure from the hierarchy.  In any case, sometime in 1104 or 1105 Vital decided to establish a monastery.[22]

In the logical course of events Vital would have turned for support to his long-time friend and patron, Count Robert of Mortain.  He, however, had died in 1091 and the fief had descended to his only son William.  This posed no difficulty whatsoever.  Vital may have known William, the fourth Count of Mortain, since he was mewling and puking in his nurse's arms, perhaps twenty-five years before.  He had instructed him as a child, heard his youthful confessions, and, since he had been chaplain and about the new count's household as he had his father's, advised and counseled him.  The years 1104-1105 were fortunate for Vital; had his desire to establish a monastery come a year later, the idea probably would not have been realized.  In 1106 the conflict between Duke Robert of Normandy and his youngest brother King Henry I of England was approaching a crisis, and creating turbulence throughout the entire duchy, and Count William elected to throw his support behind the eldest of his uncles, Duke Robert.  When, on the 28th of September 1106, the fortieth anniversary of Hastings, King Henry scored a great victory over Robert at Tinchebrai, William of Mortain was captured and imprisoned for life.  The county of Mortain was forfeited and handed over to Robert de Vitre.[23]  The grant of land to Vital to establish a monastery was made before Count William was deprived of his fief.  In the meantime, the violent conditions of the times had prompted Vital to remove his hermitage and his followers into the forest of Savigny, which happened to be situated on the lands of the lords of Fougères.

The word <u>Savigniacum</u> is a combination of the Latin name <u>Savinus</u> or <u>Sabinus</u> and the common suffix -<u>acum</u>. Savinus suggests the Umbrian origin of the first recorded inhabitants of this area of northwestern France.[24] The French termination <u>gny</u> means a habitation near water, and Savigny was located near two bodies of water, the Combe River, which separates Normandy from Brittany, and the stream Chambesnet. These waterways formed the borders of the forest in which the monastery of Savigny was to be founded. In the early twelfth century this territory was held of the counts of Mortain by the lords of Fougères. They were minor lords of the area, related distantly by blood to the Breton counts of Rennes, and holding fiefs of the Norman counts of Mortain. The house of Fougères was founded in the late tenth century when the first count of Mortain, Mauger, endowed Méen I[25] (<u>ca</u>. 972-1020), a younger son of Count Juhell of Rennes, with lands at the bottom of the valley of Nancon, some forty kilometers northeast of Rennes. On the rocks high above the valley, and surrounded by marshes, bogs, and bracken, Méen constructed a castle, and both the castle and the town which grew up around it took their names from the word fougères (bracken) which describes the physical atmosphere of the place.[26] Méen I had at least one son, Alfred (1020-1048), who inherited the fief and who, as a mark of his social standing, built both a chapel of canons in his castle and the Benedictine abbey of Rilley near Fougères. Alfred's heir was his son, Méen II, whose son Ralph succeeded to the fief in 1091.[27]

It was to Ralph of Fougères, then, that Vital had first to go to request land in the forest of Savigny and permission to begin a monastic settlement on it. Ralph consulted his family, and after what was apparently some opposition from his youngest son, who may have feared the loss of his inheritance, gave his entire forest of Savigny to God and Vital and the hermits over whom he presided.[28] The approval of Count William of Mortain was then secured. Land, of course, even waste or forest land, was a most valuable possession in Norman society, the source of food, fuel, material for construction, and manpower,

since the number of vassals a lord enfeoffed and could call upon was
the criterion of his power and social status. Why then did Ralph of
Fougères and the count of Mortain make this grant? Ralph of Fougères
was known to his contemporaries first and foremost as a vassal of the
count of Mortain. He is known to history because of his endowment of
the monastery of Savigny. The second fact is necessarily the result
of the first. As a vassal of the counts of Mortain Ralph could have
been no stranger to Vital and must have known him in the count's household. Earlier lords of Fougères had founded monasteries; why should
Ralph not follow the example of his ancestors in a world where custom
was so strong? There is no way of knowing whether Vital had the prior
support of Count William before approaching Ralph of Fougères, but
certainly without comital support the project had little possibility
of success.

How do we account for the count's endowment? Vital's long and intimate association with the counts of Mortain and their households
has already been described. This is certainly the most significant
explanation, and it accounts for the earlier grant to Vital. In the
words of the chronicler: "Because he was extremely learned, he was
made a canon of the collegiate church of St. Evroul of Mortain and a
chaplain of the count, by whom he was so highly valued that Count
William gave him a charitable income at Mortain in honor of the Most
Holy Trinity; this Vital afterwards gave, with the consent of King
Henry I, to the abbot of Caen."[29] This leaves little doubt of Count
William's regard for Vital. Significantly, the abbey of Savigny (and
all her daughter houses) was dedicated to the Holy Trinity. Family
clearly determined the individual and the religious house to be supported. There were other reasons for this endowment. The Count of
Mortain was one of the greatest barons of Normandy and England, and
several generations of his family had established and endowed religious
houses. The patronage of the Church was a mark of their expected
largesse and an expression of their social status. Why should Count
William not seek some of the prestige that his father had gained by
his foundation of St. Evroul, that his uncle Duke William had gained
by his two well-known monastic foundations in Caen, and that came to
Count William's other uncle, Bishop Odo of Bayeux, through his many

benefactions? A third reason for the foundation of Savigny is what
contemporaries would call the desire for the prayers of the monks,
for spiritual help, what modern writers might bluntly describe as
blood money. What was, for the nobility, the pomp and circumstance
of glorious war meant for the peasantry and the clergy chronic violence,
bringing savage and barbaric crimes. These evoked strong feelings of
guilt in the nobility, which they sought to overcome, or compensate
for with charitable benefactions to religious communities. The great
number of monasteries which dot the map of medieval France and Europe
are evidence of a powerful fear of retribution on the part of the
nobility.

As the twelfth century went its course, the lords of Fougères and
the counts of Mortain continued to endow and support the abbey of
Savigny. It received a large number and a wide variety of gifts from
its old patrons and from new ones. Lands and messuages, mills and
granaries, vineyards and toll roads, oil for lamps and wine for the
sacramental use of the Mass, churches and tithes poured in upon the
monastery, probably for the same reasons as those behind the initial
endowment.[30] Most of these gifts seem to have been small, probably
because the donors, who are often obscure and unidentifiable, had
little to give. In the aggregate, of course, offerings received over
several decades amounted to a great deal, and the monastery wanted
episcopal, royal, and papal protection of them. Grants were customarily formalized and protected in a charter.[31] Consequently, Simon,
the eleventh abbot of Savigny (1179-1186) sought from his bishop a
general confirmation of all his possessions and rights. Bishop Richard
of Avranches (1171-1182) responded with a charter in 1179, one very
similar to other episcopal confirmations of possessions issued in the
same period to Savigny.[32] It enumerates the abbey's possessions in
the diocese of Avranches with the names of the donor of each particular gift; states that the benefactions were made and are held in perpetual alms, which was intended to protect the monastery from later
demands for feudal services; and places all properties and rights
under the protection of the church of Avranches, threatening ecclesiastical punishment to violators. None of these aspects is in any way
unique. What is striking in the Avranches charter is the frequency

with which the names of members of the Fougères family and the Counts
of Mortain appear as patrons of Savigny.[33]

From its beginnings through the twelfth century, then, the history
and fortunes of the abbey of Savigny were inextricably tied up with
the families of Fougères and Mortain.

COUNTS OF MORTAIN

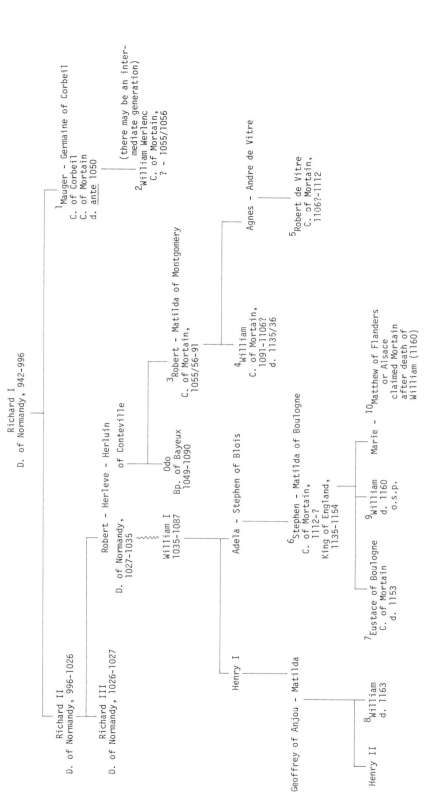

## Appendix

<u>Archives National</u> L 967, no. 103.  Confirmation of Richard, Bishop
of Avranches of Savigny's possessions in the diocese of Avranches
dated 23 October, 1179.

Richardus Dei gratia Abrincensis ecclesie minister humilis, dilecto
filio Simoni abbati Savigneii suisque successoribus et toti conventui
eiusdem loci in perpetuum.

Cum ad nostrum spectet officium ecclesiasticas personas per diocesim
nostram protegere et eorum bona tueri; eis precipe quos in Dei servitio
videmus assidue mancipatos tanto diligentius tutele debemus et protec-
tionis opem prebere, quanto vigilantius eos laboribus et servitio
divino novimus insudare.  Ea propter dilecti in domino filii omnia
beneficia vestra que nobis a fidelibus collata sunt in episcopata
Sancti Andree in perpetuam elemosinam quiete et integre vobis habere
concedimus et confirmavimus.  In quibus et hec duximus experimenda
vocabulis.

Ex dono Radulfi et Henrici et concessione regum Anglie et comitis
Moretonii, Savigneii sicut cingitur tribus aquis chamba et chambesna
atque nigra aqua, cum pertinentiis suis.

Ex dono Henrici regis antiquioris vineam et nemus de Campo Botri
cum pertinentiis suis.

Ex dono predecessorum nostrorum episcoporum bone memorie Richardi,
Herberti, Achardi:  totam decimam eiusdem vinee.

Ex dono Durandi de Groleio et concessione Henrici de Filgeriis
totam terram que est inter vineam de Campo Botri et vetus stannum de
Verdun, et inter Groleium et viam de Ponte Avbaudi et viam de
Abrincensis.

Ex dono Hugonis filii Ansketis totam terram suam de Verdun et iuxta
eandem terram ex dono Rainaldi Camerarii de Abrincis, et concessione
Durandi de Groleio terram quandam et pratum.

Item iuxta eandem terram:  ex dono Rogerii Rufi et Vitalis cognati
eius et concessione Gisleberti presbyteri dominici eorum virgultum
quodam et terram iuxta virgultum.

Ex dono Estormi de Verdun duas acras terre.

Ex dono Bertranni de Verdun terram quandam iuxta grangiam de Campo
Botri.

Ex dono Galteri Alori et Guillelmi Goion et concessione Ranulfi
Grimaut:  vii acras terre iuxta Abrincas.

Ex dono Roberti filii Martini et Maltildae uxoris eius, et

concessione Henrici regis et Richardi comitis Cestria et Stephani
comitis Moretonii, terram de Venioris cum molendino et molta eiusdem
ville et aliis pertinentiis suis.

Ex dono Radulfi de Filgeriis totum dominicum suum de Maretis Maidreii,
et totum dominicum suum de Verdun, excepto molendino.

Ex dono Radulfi de Filgeriis et Henrici filii eius et concessione
Henrici regis et Stephani comitis Moretonii dimidum molendinum de
Romaigneio cum masura, et terra molendinarii et aliis pertinentis suis.

Item ex dono Henrici de Filgeriis, et concessione heredum Alelmi
Calvi in Romaigneio, totam terram que fuit Alelmi Calvi cum capella
Sancti Johannis de Filgeriis que in eadem sita est, et terra Joselini
molendinarum et aliis pertinentis suis.

Item ex dono Henrici de Filgeriis et Radulfi in parrochia de Savigneio terram que appellata masura Bernerii et Coumailleriae cum pertinentiis suis.

Ex dono Roberti Filii Girondi, et concessione Henrici de Filgeriis,
in molinis terciam partem molendini de Ossibus cum pertinentiis suis.

Ex dono Juhelli de Savigneio et Guillelmi Bastart, et concessione
Henrici de Filgeriis, totum rivagnium aque chambe contra terram de
habitu Alberti cum pertinentiis suis.

Ex dono Hasculfi de Soligneio terram de Vacuavalle.

Ex dono Maleffant in Martigneio masuram quernam viii scilicet acras
terre.

Ex dono Guillelmi de Kernet et Odeline uxoris eius, et concessione
Petri de Sancto Hylario, terram de Montelaigneio.

Ex dono Martini Pichart, et concessione Petri de Sancto Hylario in
Marotin, terram inter viam Sancti Jacobi et coglarum et Montelaigneium.

Ex dono Garini Tirel et concessione Guillermi Avenel:  acras terre
in Pasbran.

Ex dono Oliveri filii Alani et Marie uxoris eius masuram quandam
terre apud Pasbran et dimidium molendinum eiusdem ville.

Ex dono Radulfi Moles dimidum Torcular et dimidiam viniam suam,
cuius dimidiam partem habent sancti moniales Moretonii.

Ex dono Vitalis Vacce vineam quandam cum modica terre ei adiacente.

Ex dono Petri de Sancto Hilario vinum ad missas, singula scilicet
sextaria singulis septimanis reddenda in villa Sancti Hilarii, et tres
quartarios frumenti ad hostias de redditu suo apud Sanctum Quintinum
reddendos singulis annis.

Ex dono Petri Chaucon, concedentibus filiis suis domum unam apud Abrincas.

Ex dono Guillelmi comitis Moretonii et hominum suorum elemosinas de Surda Valle.

Item ex dono eiusdem comitis novum vicum Moretonii, et extra vicum: duas carracatas terre.

Ex dono Stephani comitis Moretonii dimidium stannum de Moreta, et terram de Haia ei adiacentem.

Ex dono Alveredi Piscis, concedente Guillermo nepote eius, domum unam in Castro Moretonii.

Ex dono Gaufridi de Ferrerus et hominum suorum terram de Brildoet. Ex dono Hugonis de Houme, concedente Ruellone filio sius, unam acram terre in ville de Houme.

Ex dono Roberti de Helceio et Guillelmi filii eius terram de Sparchons.

Ex dono Rainaldi Canis, et concessione Guillelmi de Sancto Johanne, terram de Groleio.

Ex dono Guillelmi de Plaissitio et hominum suorum et concessione Petri de Sancto Hilario, terram de Castanis.

Ex dono Roberto filii Roberti filii Guillelmi de Bresceio terram suam de Bresce, excepta masura filiorum Galteri.

Ex dono Ruellonis de Mille masuram unam terre in villa de Calido loco.

Ex dono Rogerii de Mille masuram alteram in Calido loco.

Ex dono Roberti Gislaut septem acras terre et dimidiam iuxta forestam Savigneii.

Ex dono Mathei de Praerus et Roberti fratris eius et concessione Rainulfi comitis Cestrie, terram de Monchabot in Venions cum pertinentiis suis.

Ex dono Pagani de Sancto Bricio et Gervasie uxoris eius, et filiorum suorum, iuxta forestam Savigneii totam terram que Melion dicitur, et masuram que vocatur Aurineria, et campum qui dicitur Guernunusle, et masuram Aucherrii, et in parrochia Maidreii terram de Martigneio et pratum quoddam, et totum dominicum suum de Maretis Maidreii, et duas acras terre iuxta Cimiterium Vireu.

Ex dono Marie filie Ruellonis Bastardi et Richardi patrui eius, in parrochia Savigneii totum feodum Guillermi Bastart.

Ex dono Richardi Iuhelli totum feodum suum de Savigneio et donationem quam fecit Alanus frater eiusdem Richardi.

Ex dono Achardi episcopi predecessoris nostri et concessione heredum Savigneii ecclesiam eiusdem ville.

Ex dono Eudonis Babilonie et Johannis filii eius et Guidonis fratris eiusdem in Logis quandam terram que Rohardet vocatur, cum duabus partibus decime eiusdem terre.

In predictis quoque Logis ex dono Rogerii de Vireio et fratrum suorum landam Gaufriduli cum duabus partibus decime eiusdem terre.

Ex dono Radulfi de Vireio et generorum eius Guillelmi et Oliveri et hominum ipsorum, et concessione Jordani filii Adam et Alani filii eius, elemosinas de terre Guasta cum pertinentiis sius.

Ex dono Gaufridi filii Guimundi et filiorum eius Alani, Juhelli, Sequaiti, in terra Guasta dimidiam partem terre Calumpniis.

Ex dono Pagani de Ceresel et Guillelmi filii eius et Radulfi Rohais et Guiborgis uxoris eius:  alteram medietatem eiusdem terre de Calumpniis, quas donationes concesserunt Oliverus de Ardene et Radulfus Brito ad quorum feodum terra ipsa pertinebat.

Ex dono predecessorum nostrorum episcoporum bone memorie Turgii, Achardi, et concessione Roberti de Appenticio et filiorum suorum, ecclesiam de Appenticio cum pertinentiis suis.

Ex dono eorundem episcoporum ecclesiam Sancti Hilarii de novo burgo Moretonii.

Ex dono <u>Visi</u> de Logis et Roberti filii eius et Guillelmi Coisler nepotis eorum, et concessione predecessoris nostri Achardi episcopi, concedente etiam Hasculfi de Sancto Hilario, ecclesiam de Logis cum pertinentiis suis.

Ex dono Durandi et Roberti et Andree de Groleio, concedente Graalendo de Tania domino eorum, clousum ante portam grangie de Campo Botri.

Ex dono Roberti Guarrel, concedente Hugone Letroisne, masuram de Puizceauis.

Ex dono predecessorum nostrorum bone memorie, Turgii, Richardi, Herberti, Achardi, et concessione Rannulfi de Vireio et Guillelmi et Rogerii Fratrum eius, ad quorum feodum ius patronatus sub scriptarum ecclesiarum pertinebat:  ecclesiam Sancti Gervasii et Prothasii de Vireio ex integre et decimas totius parrochie exceptis duabus partibus de masura Lame; et ecclesiam Sancti Martini de Bresceio ex integro; et ecclesiam de Maidreio, excepta tercia parta decime quam inde habent sancti moniales de Redonensi cenobio; Ecclesiam etiam de Molinis ex integro cum pertinentiis suis.

Quin etiam concedo et confirmo donum quod fecit Guillermus de Duxeio ecclesiam videlicet Sancti Martini de Guasto, et ecclesiam de Champcervor, et unam planteam in Vico de Duxeio, et medietariam de Tessues cum pertinentiis suis.

Nos autem quod Romani pontifices ex autoritate sua vobis concesserunt, scilicet presentationem capellanorum et liberam dispositionem in ecclesiis vestris, vos habere concedimus, salvo iure Abrincensis ecclesie.

Hec omnia et quecunque Deo propitio iustis modis adquirere poteritis sub nostra et Abrincensis ecclesie protectione incipimus; statuentes ne quis super his vos temerarie perturbare aut inquietare presumat. Quod si quis presumere attemptavent; ecclesiastici rigoris vindictam, et districti indicis ultionem se noverit insursurum.

Ut ergo vobis omnia in perpetuum firme et stabiliter conserventur, presentis pagine inscriptione, et sigilli nostri et sigilli capituli Sancte Andree impressione et episcopali autoritate concedimus et confirmamus.

Testibus his:  Rogero cantore; Guillermo thesaurio; Gisleberto et Guillermo archidiaconis; Ricardo Capellano; Georgio canonico; Magistro Ricardo; Ricardo de Spineto, Johanne Gruel, monachis; Luca de Vein, et aliis quampluribus.

Facta et autem his nostra concessio atque confirmatio anno ab incarnatione Domini millesimo centesimo septuagesimo nono, nono kalendas Novenbris, in domo nostra apud Abrincas.  Regnatite Domino nostro Jesu Christo.

## Chapter 18

The Castles of the Trencavels:
A Preliminary Aerial Survey[1]

Fredric Cheyette

August 1209. Carcassonne has fallen. The young Raimond Roger
Trencavel, viscount of Beziers, is prisoner. The barons of the siege
meet to elect a new ruler for the conquered land, just as--so they
know from chronicles and songs--their predecessors over a century before had elected a king for the newly conquered Jerusalem. The count
of Nevers is their first choice; the duke of Burgundy their second.
But both refuse, for they have other plans: they and their followers
"with a strong hand and an outstretched arm" have done their service,
have won remission for their sins. Summer is over. It is time to go
home. Though delegates of the army soon agree to offer the Trencavel
inheritance to Simon of Montfort, there may soon be little army left
to support him. Beziers is destroyed, Carcassonne in the hands of the
northerners, but the crusaders are still in hostile territory. "Stay
awhile," the abbot of Cîteaux pleads with the two princely leaders,
"for there are still many well fortified heretic strongholds to capture. Three of them--Minerve, Termes, and Cabaret--are impregnable,
not to speak of innumerable others."[2]

The good abbot was pleading a special cause and might understandably
have enlarged upon the present danger. But "innumerable" was no
exaggeration. Even the harried modern tourist hurrying to the beach-
front of the Costa Brava cannot help but notice the watch tower of
Tautavel and the frowning ruins of Opoul where the last southern
thrust of the Corbières crowds the coastal road toward the sea. The
more leisurely wanderer in the interior discovers many more--even
Minerve, Termes, and Cabaret, if he is willing to make the special
trip--though not so many as once dominated the land. What the passing
tourist now notices are the rural castles standing lonely in the
midst of vineyards or garrigue; in the Middle Ages almost every village was itself a castle, ringed with walls, and often possessed--at

the high point of the hillock, or on an isolated, well defended spur
of rock--of its own tower and moated palisade.  With good reason
Peter of Vaux-de-Cernay spoke of the inhabitants of the <u>castles</u> between Beziers and Carcassonne who took to the hills on hearing that
the crusaders had sacked Beziers.[3]  To men used to the open villages
of the north, these castle-villages must indeed have seemed innumerable.

How many such fortified villages were there in fact in twelfth-
century Languedoc?

The <u>répertoires archéologiques</u> and the always handy <u>Guides Bleus</u>
provide the beginnings of a list of those where the visitor may discover some significant physical remains.  To this we can add by
searching through the pages of Mahul's <u>Cartulaire de Carcassonne</u> and
the various nineteenth-century descriptions of the southern depart-
ments.  This procedure, however, would repay the searcher's labors
with fragments, at best.  For some village walls were rebuilt in the
thirteenth and fourteenth centuries; many undoubtedly were destroyed
by English raids; and Richelieu later systematically dismantled whatever might have induced "overmighty" sentiments in the king's southern
subjects.  What these rebuilders and destroyers allowed to remain
standing, nineteenth-century villagers quarried, transformed, or razed
to the ground, leaving only an occasional tower or fragment of wall
as testimony to what once secured their ancestors' lives and property.

At the same time, however, this destruction and rebuilding left
engraved on the village landscape--in the alignment of house walls
and the patterns of streets and field roads--the shape and size of
the medieval village now submerged.  On the ground the narrow streets,
broad boulevards, and winding lanes seem random and arbitrary.  From
the air, however, the defensive plan they outline can be clearly read.
The aerial survey, furthermore, allows us to inspect these villages
one by one, and occasionally to discover in the open fields as well
the trace of a moat long since filled or a bailey long since leveled.

### The Use of Aerial Photography as Evidence

The basic techniques for using aerial photographs to rediscover
the medieval landscape are identical to those developed over the last

several decades for classical and pre-historic archeology.[4] Essentially, these techniques require the observer to read back in time,
to peel away the recent accretions to the landscape in order to reveal
the patterns of an earlier age.  Since the medievalist has fewer centuries to peel away than does the classical archeologist, his task is
much easier.  In Languedoc this task is further simplified by the fact
that no major upheavals have destroyed those patterns in the last five
hundred years.  The plague decimated the population, war burned villages and leveled castles, the economic expansions of the sixteenth
and eighteenth centuries reopened old lands and cleared new, but until the nineteenth century--despite the disappearance of some villages
and the depopulation and repopulation of others--the basic skeleton
of the landscape remained virtually untouched.  And despite the massive turn to wine production in the nineteenth century, despite the
construction of railroads and newly planned paved highways, changes
have been so slow that much that predates the nineteenth century
still shapes the ground.  The reasons why this should be so are easy
enough to list.  The reader, however, would probably first prefer to
be shown that it is in fact so.

Figure I is an aerial photograph of Olonzac, a village in the
Herault, and a graphic analysis of that photograph.[5]  Olonzac is a
particularly useful village territory on which to demonstrate the
reading of aerial photographs, for it includes a number of roughly
datable objects:  a segment of Roman road (R-R), the Canal du Midi
(built 1666-1681), and the route N. 610 (built in the nineteenth
century).  In the Middle Ages the village occupied a strategic position on the roads between Carcassonne and Beziers.  Just to the east
was a narrow passage between two sharp escarpments.  Through this
passage (known, significantly, as la Pierre plantée [G. Z. 6354
1085][5]--an indication of the highway's antiquity) ran the more southern of the two main roads along the left bank of the Aude.  Here,
where the river turned southward toward Narbonne, the road continued
directly towards Beziers.  Olonzac and its lands lay athwart the connecting roads between this east-west road and its companion that
skirted the Minervois hills to the north.  One of these connectors
is the identified Roman road.  Another ran directly through the village

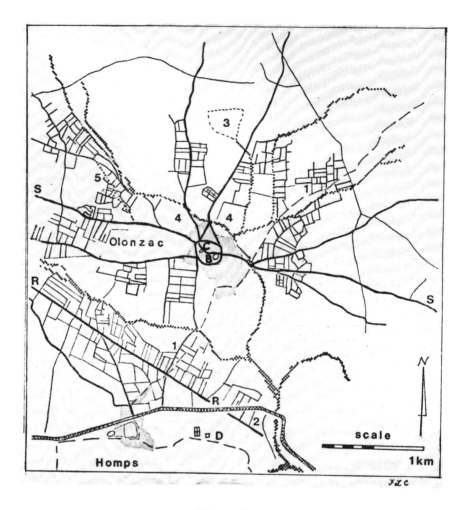

Figure I.

(R-R)--Roman road. (S-S)--Connecting road. (B)--Probable site of medieval fortification. (C)--Market. (D)--Probable site of Hospitaler house. (1)--Modern highway superimposed on pre-existent field patterns. (2)--Canal crossing pre-existent field patterns oriented on Roman road. (3)--Drained marsh. (4)--Modern redivision of fields. (5)--Field road crossing pre-existent field divisions; the original road probably passed slightly to the east, along the edge of the brook.

Figure I A.

Photograph courtesy of the Institut National Géographique.

(S-S). The two roads that ran directly north from the village (T, T)
met again at the intersection of the northern east-west road with the
road to Minerve.[7]

With the aid of a map we can easily identify the major features of
this landscape. But what historical evidence does it provide? It
is a photograph of the present. Can we nevertheless date its features,
at least approximately? Without archival documents, we must admit at
the beginning, absolute dating is impossible: for this purpose the
medievalist would require dated documents in the same way the archeologist requires coins, datable pots, or strata. It is possible, however,
for us to reconstruct a relative chronology of the landscape from the
photograph alone, much like an archeologist whose trench uncovers a
succession of overlapping walls with different orientations. Since
optical resolution does not allow us a precisely detailed view of
objects in the landscape (I was able to recognize objects down to
about ten feet in diameter with the equipment available) we must depend for our information on the relationship of features to each other,
rather than the shape of each one taken individually.

Let us begin peeling off the layers, starting with the nineteenth-
century highway (identified on the map by a broken line) running
roughly from south to northeast. In the immediate vicinity of the
village, fields and house-lots have been reoriented parallel or per-
pendicular to this road; elsewhere along its trajectory, most visibly
at the points marked (1), field boundaries seem to ignore it. Since
we cannot imagine a peasant laying out a field to abut on a tiny track
if a macadamized road were available, especially if this would mean
continuing a field line across the highway and creating a truly minis-
cule and irregularly shaped parcel on the other side, we can only conclude that the field boundaries predate the road and have remained
undisturbed by its construction.

The Canal du Midi disturbed field patterns in its vicinity much
more. Dikes had to be built, brooks rechanneled. At Homps (at the
bottom of the photograph), the combination of the canal and the highway have destroyed all traces of preceding patterns. Nevertheless,
at (2) the continuation of the Roman road is clearly visible; northeast of that segment a field pattern runs continuously to the other

side of the canal, ending at a field boundary roughly parallel to the road.  Although this evident superposition of the canal over field patterns is much less common than with recent highways, it does occur here and there along the waterway, enough to show the durability of field boundaries in this region and the possibility of their survival untouched since the reign of Louis XIII.

What formed the skeleton of this field system?  The Roman road on the southwest (which here forms not only the boundary between the two communes of Olonzac and Homps but also that between the two depart- ments of Aude and Herault); the two streams--the Ognon and the Espère-- and their tributary brooks; and the set of field roads that radiates out from the center of the village.  Some of these field roads have been paved and now serve as departmental or vicinal roads.  Others are nothing but dirt tracks.  One way or the other, the field bounda- ries abut perpendicularly, or nearly so, to these roads and to the brooks, and run back to other boundaries roughly parallel to the basic skeletal elements.  Rarely do field boundaries cross a stream or field road and continue in the same line on the other side (as they do with the modern highway and the canal).  Normally only the tracks that mark quarter boundaries are continuous across the radial field roads, and then the road or brook often marks a change in direction.

We can therefore conclude that the field roads and the field bounda- ries came into being at the same time, or--more likely--that the field roads predated the fields.  Fields, old field roads, and natural water courses visibly form a single integrated system.

The village is the core of this radial pattern.  But not the entire village.  With the exception of (S-S), none of the field roads run all the way through the settled area.  They run instead to a somewhat ovoid street, forming at the northwest and southwest "corners" what the French picturesquely term "goose feet."  This curving street must have been a major boundary, permeable at only a few points:  that is, a wall with three gates.  As it happens, a fragment of this wall can still be seen at Olonzac.  But even had it been destroyed, or (as is so often the case) absorbed into the walls of the village houses, the street and field road pattern would demonstrate its past existence.

By reading the field pattern toward the center, we have thus found

a fortified village whose walls must have predated the field roads,
or at least have been originally thrown up at the same time the fields
around the town were laid out.

The photograph suggests one further hypothesis about the history of
this village. At (B) a circular pattern of house walls probably marks
the location of a medieval motte and tower. At (C), a widening and
sharp bend in (S-S) as it goes through the village, is the village market, now a modern hexagonal building, but undoubtedly on the spot where
the medieval market once stood. We are perhaps here in the presence
of a village that grew up around a market and guard post on this
major connecting link in the regional road system.

Despite the obvious fact that the photograph presents only what is
currently visible, it is nevertheless a historical document that can
be read backward into the Middle Ages. Although an archeological dig
might be able to date the origins of the wall absolutely, there would
be no way to do so with field roads and boundaries. A relative dating
of most of the features is probably the best that can be done, for
these features have been constantly used through the centuries and
thus constantly rebuilt to meet the demands of each succeeding age.
And this relative dating, as we have seen, is possible with the photograph and a stereoscopic viewer.

Why did village road and field patterns remain stable over so long
a time? The answer is found in those hundreds of mundane sales, donations, and mortgages that fill Languedocian cartularies. The field
roads were more than just passageways: they were, to use a twentieth-
century expression, "affected with the public interest." Viae publicae,
strata publica, the scribes and notaries called them. And that public
quality was enforced not only by the communal interest in the roads
and tracks that gave each villager access to his fields, to the neighboring villages, and to the highways that led to cities and market
towns, but by every person's interest in his own property. Streets,
like neighboring fields, were definitions of property boundaries.
Throughout the Middle Ages they travelled with the village fields as
those fields were passed from hand to hand and from generation to
generation. Even before the first compoix and the first mapped surveys of village holdings, there were thus public (though not

centralized) records of the basic skeleton of village fields and a
public interest in maintaining that skeleton intact.

Field boundaries were fixed on the land by stone walls and on parchment in scribal ink.  Their chances of longevity were increased by the
practice of partible inheritance--the creation of those thirds, quarters, and eighths of fields and vineyards that formed the subject of
many petty contracts--which made it increasingly difficult for anyone
without substantial resources, time, and local power, to reassemble
adjoining fields and redivide them in a regular pattern.  (One such
modern redivision can be found in the immediate vicinity of Olonzac,
at [4], where the regularity of the checkerboard bespeaks the sur-
veyor's tools.)  It may indeed be the case that the tiniest, most
fragmented fields represent medieval subdivisions.  For, throughout
the region, the swamps drained since the sixteenth century, even those
put to the plow before the survey for the Cassini map (1747-1789),
appear from the air as a distinct type of field pattern, both larger
and more regular.  (One appears north of Olonzac at [3], in a rural
quarter still called "l'Etang"; since it does not appear on the Cassini
map, it must have been drained by the mid-eighteenth century.)

## Villages, Castles, and Roads

Figure II is a sketch-map of the principal medieval roads north and
south of the Aude River between Beziers, Narbonne, and Carcassonne.
On this map I have indicated all the fortified villages and rural
fortifications revealed by aerial photographs.  The roads were first
located on the aerial photographs by the methods I have just described,
then transcribed as an overlay on 1:50,000 scale maps.  Their trace,
in general, is easy to follow.  Here and there, to be sure, they dis-
appear; but that disappearance is itself a proof of their antiquity,
since the cause is either the shifting bed of a torrent bringing
alluvial mud down from the mountains, or, less often, a modern reallot-
ment of land.  Without fail, the road reappears, usually within a
kilometer, and always with the proper alignment.  The longest section
without a visible trace is the road through Homps, where the construction of the canal and highway, together with reallotments, has eliminated all trace for several kilometers.  This road is easily followed,

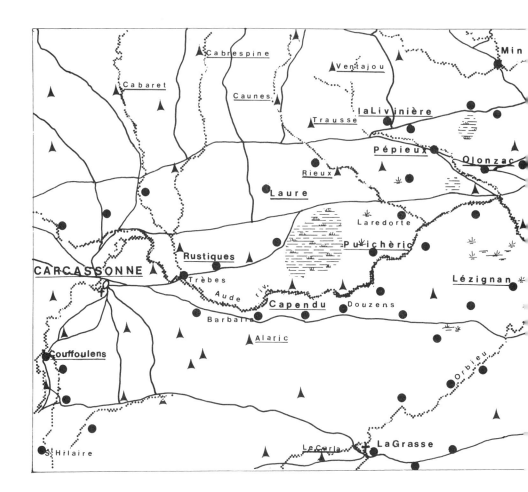

Cabrespine

Ventajou

Min

Cabaret

Caunes.

laLivinière

Trausse

Pépieux

Olonzac

Rieux

Laure

Laredorte

Pu ichèric

Rustiques

CARCASSONNE

Trèbes

Aude    riv.

Lézignan

Capendu

Douzens

Barbaira

Alaric

Couffoulens

Orbieu

St Hilaire

LeCurla

LaGrasse

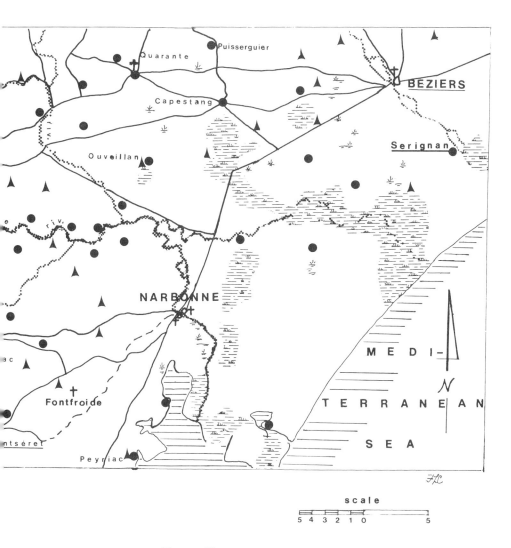

Figure II.

Legend

—  Principal roads

●  Walled villages

▲  Other fortifications

**Laure**  Fortifications for which oaths of security were
rendered to the Trencavels, 1000-1200

however, west of the pond of Jouarres (drained in the nineteenth century) and east of Olonzac.  Wherever possible I have sought confirmation for the trace in reports of archeological discoveries, indications
of old, disused roads and bridges in Mahul's Cartulaire de Carcassonne,
and indications of Roman roads on I.G.N. maps.[8]

This was the heartland of the Trencavel domains in the twelfth century:  after the loss of Nîmes to the counts of Toulouse around 1185,
Beziers and Carcassonne were the family's major city strongholds.  It
was also one of the most densely populated areas under their rule.
Even today, village centers in some parts of this alluvial plain are
barely three kilometers apart.  And in the twelfth century some places
that now are only mas or châteaux de vigneron were peasant villages.[9]
A few of these villages, furthermore, were substantial:  the walls of
Capestang enclosed about the same area as did the medieval walls of
Beziers.  Yet Trencavel family records--quite substantial where castles
are concerned--record claims to power over very few of these fortifications.[10]

Why so few?  The answer, ultimately, must rest on an analysis of
the mechanisms of Trencavel political control.  For the moment I can
only offer a hypothesis and outline the preliminary data suggesting
that this hypothesis is true.

It is striking that the few castles for which such oaths were given
were of major strategic importance for guarding the two east-west
roads on the left bank of the Aude and the only road on the right bank.
The Trencavel, so it would seem, considered castles to be centers for
controlling traffic--both military and commercial--rather than for
controlling population.  In 1209 these castles were overwhelmed; but
Languedoc had probably not seen since the days of the Frankish recon-
quest an army as large as that of the crusaders.  The principal purpose of these fortifications, furthermore, may have been relatively
peaceful:  to extract tolls and dues for "safe conduct" from the merchants carrying their wares from the Mediterranean to Toulouse,
Bordeaux, and beyond.

Such a theory, at least, is strongly suggested by a third piece of
aerial evidence (Figure III).  The ancient Via Domitia, the Roman
road from the Rhône to Spain, can be traced almost without a break

from Nîmes to the Corbières.[11] The trace has disappeared near Courson,
when the Aude changed its course in the fourteenth century, breaking
through the marshy coast to gain direct egress to the sea. Curiously,
it has also disappeared further to the east where it crossed a small
hill called "Puech Monier" between the villages of Poussan and Loupian.
The terrain here offered no obstacles. The land, once intensively
worked (the stone field walls are still clearly visible on the photograph), is only now returning to garrigue. To the west, the trace of
the Roman road coming from the bridge at St.Thibéry runs straight
across the countryside. To the east, at a slightly different angle,
it runs directly northeast toward Castelnau-de-Montpellier. Yet between Loupian and Poussan it has disappeared. Why?

Local road names provide a first hint. The Via Domitia east of St.
Thibéry is called "Chemin de la Reine Juliette." Another road that
angles off to the south, eventually branching toward Mèze and Loupian,
is called "Chemin des Romains."[12] We are undoubtedly faced here with
the transfer of a name as travelers changed their path from one road
to another. The highway that was deserted and allowed to degenerate
was still striking enough in its physical appearance to be given a
mythical name. To the new long-distance road was attached the name
of Rome.[13] But why did travelers at this point change their path?
The answer is to be found in the role of Loupian and Poussan as fortified villages.

At St. Thibéry the Via Domitia crossed the Herault River on a monumental Roman bridge. Here it intersected the road north from Agde
to Lodève.[14] By the late tenth century the counts of Carcassonne
were already in control of this strategic passage, encircling it with
well placed fortifications: Florensac, Mèze, Villevayrac, Poussan,
and the castellum and abbey of St. Thibéry itself. Up the river
Pezenas and St. Pons de Mauchiens gave them control of the roads on
both banks.[15] Poussan was still important enough to be mentioned
along with Florensac and St. Thibéry in the division of family lands
between William and Peter, the sons of Count Raimond Roger of
Carcassonne and Viscountess Garsendis of Beziers.[16] By the beginning
of the twelfth century the castle had passed out of the family's immediate possession, but by then the neighboring village of Loupian

Figure III. (Photo mosaic)

The Via Domitia is indicated by the parallel broken lines. The
"Chemin des Romains" is indicated by the solid white line. The vil-
lage of Loupian is on the left (to the southwest), the village of
Poussan on the right (to the northeast).

had been fortified and was already, or soon afterward became, one of
the two principal toll stations in the region of Agde (the other being
Agde itself).[17]  Apparently these two fortified villages (the walls
and gates of Poussan still exist) acted as a magnet on the road, pulling merchants, pilgrims, and soldiers aside from the Roman highway
to pay tolls before passing on.

The Trencavel family laid claim to control over more than one hundred
such castles during the twelfth century, some of them--like Balaguier,
Hautpoul, or the four castles of Cabaret--strongholds in the midst of
the countryside, others--like those we have just seen--fortified villages.  A preliminary mapping of many of them suggests that what we
have seen between Beziers and Carcassonne and along the Via Domitia
was true elsewhere in their lands as well.[18]  Where population was
densest--in the rolling hills southwest of Albi, in the lower lands
drained by the Orb and the Herault, and along the coastal plain--
their castles were few.  They tended rather to cluster on the edge of
mountainous terrain:  over a dozen ringed the Montagne Noire north of
Carcassonne.  Or they were used to guard the roads through the barren
and wild country north of the Monts de Lacaune.  On the western frontier of the Trencavel lands, facing the counts of Foix and Toulouse,
they likewise clustered at strategic points:  Montaigu, Brens, Gaillac,
Cadalen, and Lagrave guarded the approach up the Tarn towards Albi;
Mirepoix, Belpech, Molandier, and Montaut formed a northern defense
toward the Ariège valley; Queille, Laroque, Pareille, Montferrier,
Chercorb, and Balaguier formed one to the south.  Merchants or warriors
crossing the Pyrenees through the Cerdagne would be stopped in their
descent through the upper valley of the Aude by one block of castles
in the Pays de Sault, another farther north near the fortress of
Rennes, and a third near the abbey of Saint Polycarpe.  In all these
cases, strategic or commercial considerations appear to have been
uppermost.  Castles, it would seem, were not mechanisms for day-to-
day political control.  Had they been so, their distribution across
the vast Trencavel lands, from the valley of the Tarn to Nîmes in the
east and the foothills of the Pyrenees in the south, would have been
far different.

If the hypothesis is true that the Trencavel viscounts placed their

castles with an eye to the strategic necessities of warfare in mountainous terrain or to taxing the passing merchants, of what significance would it be for our understanding of the political and social
organization of their lands?  Two problems come immediately to mind.
The first is the vexing question of southern oaths of fealty.  The
second concerns the castellans who held these castles.

We possess copies of over three hundred oaths of fealty rendered to
the Trencavel viscounts from the late eleventh to the end of the
twelfth century.  A few of these are appended to, and apparent confirmation of, important convenientiae:  treaties, family divisions,
marriage agreements.  The overwhelming majority, however, refer to the
holding of castles:  indeed, they are our primary means for discovering which castles the Trencavel laid claim to.  Their form was extremely rigid, was already fixed when the first evidence for them
appears in the mid-tenth century, and tells us almost nothing of the
oath's political or social function.  It assured the person to whom
the oath was given that the oath-taker would not harm him in his body,
would not betray him, and would not deprive him of the specific castle
or castles named in the oath.[19]  Madame Magnou-Nortier, in her recent
analysis of these oaths of fealty, has shown how difficult it is to
assimilate them to oaths of homage and fealty on the northern model.
Mentions of homage are late and extremely rare.  The fief remains
totally foreign to them.[20]  The geographical distribution of the
castles for which these oaths were rendered leads toward the same
conclusion:  these oaths of fealty could not have functioned in the
south as oaths of homage did in the north.  Fealty for castles, given
the locations of those castles, could not have served to organize the
aristocracy of the Trencavel domains.  To argue otherwise would first
require that we ignore the geographical specificity of the oaths themselves.

Discussion of castles and oaths leads naturally to the men who took
those oaths:  the castellans.

It has recently been argued that the spread of castles in tenth- and
eleventh-century Languedoc is evidence for a "new militarism"; that
these castles became the center of new territories, requiring new dues
and services, and dispensing a "new justice"; that "they gave to their

possessors a practical independence which made it difficult for a ruler...to deal with them."[21]  The argument appears plausible if we count the castles mentioned in surviving documents, especially when we consider the experience of certain areas in northern Europe.  But once again, the distribution of castles over which the Trencavel viscounts claimed authority, the way they clustered around certain points, their scarcity in areas of denser population, make this argument difficult to sustain.  That kind of independence, the carving out of territorial blocks, would appear to require both wealth and a certain degree of isolation.  But where castles were truly isolated (as was, for example, Arifat, southeast of Albi)[22] their possessors could not, by the nature of the terrain, have commanded much wealth.  And where castles were in the midst of rich farmlands there were other castles and castellans close by:  obvious rivals should they feel stirred to excessive independence or thirst for new "customs" on neighboring peasants.

Furthermore, the castles mentioned in surviving documents were but few of the fortifications whose existence is revealed from the air. The essential political problem for the Trencavel viscounts would seem to have been to control the lords (seniores or domini, the documents unfailingly call them) of the fortified villages in which most of the population lived, and where most of the wealth was produced.  This, rather than enforcing oaths of fealty, would appear to have been the substance of day-to-day politics.

Such questions are too vast for this article even to begin to explore. It has been my purpose here only to raise some questions and to suggest that the reconstruction of the medieval countryside through the systematic exploitation of aerial photographs and maps may clarify those questions--and perhaps eventually enable us to answer them.

Chapter 19

Ennoblement by the Crown and Social
Stratification in France 1285-1322:
A Prosopographical Survey

Jan Rogozinski

   Philip the Fair, in granting the first charter or patent of nobility
between 1285 and 1290,[1] introduced a practice that in later centuries
provided many thousands with entry into the ranks of the second estate.[2]  In this as in so many ways, his reign and the subsequent half-
century witnessed the creation of social and governmental forms that
characterized the French nation until the Revolution and after.  The
fecundity of the later Middle Ages in governmental institutions is
immediately apparent, and the most recent guide to French institutional
history can confidently ascribe the creation of virtually all organs
of the state to the 1300's.[3]  Although it was again the fourteenth
century that first outlined the legal rules for the class structure
of the ancien régime,[4] we know much less about the evolution of social
institutions or about the process of social change at the local and
regional levels than we do about accounting techniques in Paris.  Marc
Bloch called for an enquiry into the earliest letters of nobility over
thirty-five years ago,[5] and advances in prosopographical methods make
it possible to identify almost all their recipients.[6]  But Bloch's recommendation has been ignored:  The sole explanation of this remarkable
innovation remains that sketched by Anatole Barthélemy more than a
century ago.[7]
   Recent predilections have helped to deter enquiry into the nature
of nobility and ennoblement even though the fourteenth and fifteenth
centuries represent a significant turning-point in French history.
The creation of new institutions during the fourteenth century had
as one consequence a dramatic increase in the volume of written records[8] that has, ironically, discouraged rather than encouraged historical research.  Medievalists avoid the later period, finding far
too much data for any one historian to handle in traditional ways.

At the same time, historians of the _ancien régime_ eschew the fifteenth
and sixteenth centuries because the techniques of the social sciences
cannot be applied; above all, since medieval records are normally dis-
continuous, statistical quantification is not possible.  While understanding of the social order in other periods has greatly increased
since World War II, there has been little concern for the governing
classes of later medieval France.[9]

Medieval élites continue to be treated for this reason as if they
comprised fixed and unvarying classes; we write, for example, of the
rise (or decline) of the Nobility or the Patriciate during any given
century as if their memberships were not constantly changing.  Had
not, however, many new families continuously joined those calling
themselves noble the normal accidents of genealogy would inevitably
have led to the rapid extinction of the entire class.[10]  More important, _noble_ itself had no fixed signification and connotations--or
none that historians have been able to get at.[11]  The nobility was
set apart from other élite groups through the enjoyment of legal
privileges, a special style of life, and the exercise of certain functions.  The crown never, however, attempted to codify noble privileges;
it allowed them to be defined by the many courts in each province.  A
historian who wished to impose more precision than contemporaries
then thought desirable would need several lifetimes simply to collate
the decisions in cases appealed to the _parlements_ or the _chambres des
aides_.[12]  Literary and artistic portrayals of the noble life-style
are more accessible, but they present ideal types whose characteristics, fixed by centuries of tradition, are often contrary to what is
known of everyday habits.[13]  Evidence so tenuous is liable to disparate
interpretation, and there is no agreement as to the nature of the relationship between nobility and knighthood or between nobility and the
practice of arms.[14]  Some men called noble performed military functions; others, also called noble, carried out the tasks of priests,
judges, burghers, or merchants.[15]

The letters of nobility issued by Philip the Fair and his sons provide objective evidence not obtainable from other sources.  They give
us, as Marc Bloch foresaw, fresh insights into the interaction between
the actual nature of social stratification during the later Middle Ages

and contemporary conceptions of social status.  A complete biography
of any one of their recipients is not feasible; a composite picture
can be sketched of the kinds of circumstances that led men to seek out
ennoblement as well as those that induced the crown to accede to their
requests.  No fixed rules or policy as yet bound the king and his ministers.  Only a small number of letters were given out, and the initiative in each case lay with the individual or family concerned.  The
fortunes of those who wished to acquire nobility in this manner thus
reflect the ways in which the boundaries were being drawn between
social classes in different provinces in conformance with deeply felt
beliefs about the correct order of society.

If letters of nobility were never numerous in later-medieval France,
Philip the Fair and his son Louis X granted them with an especially
sparing hand.  Systematic and continuous recording of royal acts began
in September 1307 when Guillaume de Nogaret became Guard of the Seal.[16]
During the seven years between 1307 and the king's death, the chancery
registered ten charters of ennoblement, a little more than one a year.
Chance has preserved two earlier grants, and tradition insists that
Nogaret was himself so honored.[17]  A few others may have been lost
but certainly not many.[18]

The ennoblement of Gilles de Concevreux between 1285 and 1290[19]
and of Jean de Taillefontaine in 1295[20] expressly arose out of their
desire to circumvent northern French custom requiring nobility of
both parents as a prerequisite to knighthood.[21]  These first letters
did not radically transform their recipients' social standing but
rather confirmed a status socially accepted but juridically ambiguous.
In allowing them to retain their titles and fiefs, the crown exercised a "gracious justice" made necessary by the increasing rigidity
of laws governing social etiquette.  Jean de Corrobert, ennobled in
1311, also had some right to the privilege sought.  Legally a serf
through his mother, Jean had been styled knight as early as 1297 when
he held a royal commission to raise taxes for the Flemish campaign.
The letter on his behalf is the only one under the Capetians that
specifically mentions payment, and the enormous fine indicated must
represent taxes he had failed to pass along to the government and not
a charge for ennoblement.[22]

Three of the twelve extant letters of ennoblement went to residents
of northern France.  Nine benefited men who made their homes in the
south--eight in Languedoc and the ninth in the Limousin, not yet separated from Languedoc administratively and sharing with it a common
culture and law.[23]  The southern recipients had small right to nobility
by the custom of Paris; they did have claims upon the throne through
their own services or through highly placed patrons the king wished
to conciliate by small favors.  Pope Clement V secured the ennoblement
of Pierre de Bordes and Élie Géraud,[24] both of whom had brothers among
his intimate advisors.  Bertrand de Bordes held the most powerful post
at the papal court and often guarded for Clement letters he would not
wish divulged;[25] Hugues Géraud also enjoyed the full confidence of the
Pope as referendary and confidential ambassador to the courts of
Germany and France.[26]  Both wanted ennoblement for their brothers in
order to remove legal and financial impediments to the creation of
landed estates.[27]  The de Bordes family had its roots in the Agenais
and had been counsellors to the English administration; Bertrand de
Bordes began to assemble an extensive lordship in the Toulousain while
Bishop of Albi, and the letter for Pierre makes clear his desire to
obtain from the crown high justice and other "noble" rights.[28]  Nor
is it coincidental that Élie Géraud's ennoblement immediately followed
his brother's appointment to the bishopric of Cahors supplemented by
a papal gift of ten thousand gold florins.[29]  Only the church provides
so munificently for its servants.  Less striking aggrandizement lay
behind the ennoblement of two other southerners.  Jacques de Jean,
like Hugues Géraud a citizen of Cahors, had recourse to the king's
brother, Charles of Valois.[30]  Simon de la Chassagne of Limoges
profited from the intercession of Bernard de l'Isle-Jourdain, who
drew upon his influence as head of a clan allied to the most powerful families of Languedoc[31] and distinguished among the southern
aristocracy for its loyalty to the crown[32] in order to sell a fief
isolated from his main holdings.[33]

The desire to exploit recently acquired estates, although present,
did not provide the primary motivation of the third group of men ennobled by Philip the Fair.  All five, almost half of those so honored,
were connected to the governing council of the sénéchaussée of

Beaucaire-Nîmes.  Jean Marc and Hugues de la Porte gained nobility
at their own request.  Citizens of Montpellier, as was Guillaume de
Conques, they had helped to increase royal control over that wealthy
and semi-autonomous commune.  Honoré Firmin and Raimond Barrian owed
their ennoblement to Guillaume de Plaisians and Guillaume de Nogaret,
royal officers in Nîmes before they earned power and fame in Paris.[34]
All had performed services of value to the crown or to their patrons
that did not endear them to their neighbors in southern France.

   If it was highly unusual for a provincial judge to receive nobility,[35] the story of Jean Marc is exceptional in many ways.  Members
of the faculties of law at Montpellier and Toulouse often held judgeships for a brief time or assisted the seneschals at the assizes and
meetings of their council, but few made a career in the royal administration.  An eminent jurist could earn more through private practice,
and bribery or peculation were dangerous and unpopular.[36]  For about
fifteen years, Jean Marc followed a path proper to his patrician
origins as legal adviser to the city government and as judge of the
municipal court.[37]  Although he became a royal judge in 1307,[38] he
retained the trust of his fellow citizens and was sent to Paris three
years later on a very delicate mission:  in return for a municipal
grant of fifteen thousand pounds, Marc was to obtain from the crown
confirmation of various municipal privileges despite the objections
of the king of Majorca, nominal lord of Montpellier, to the recognition of royal authority implicit in such a transaction.  The resulting
negotiations were profitable both to the crown, which significantly
enhanced its rights, and to Marc, who took advantage of his presence
in Paris to register the patent of nobility.[39]  They had less happy
consequences for the town, since Marc apparently led the royal council
to believe that no conditions had been attached to the promised grant.
Such infidelity could not remain undiscovered:  Jean Marc ended his
days exiled to neighboring Toulouse after being removed in November
1317 as major judge of Beaucaire-Nîmes at the outraged and express
request of the consuls of Montpellier.[40]  The acquisition of
Montpellier was a cherished goal of French policy, and it is likely
that Jean Marc had a hand in the ennoblement of Hugues de la Porte
and Guillaume de Conques, with whom he had long been associated in

private and municipal affairs and in the governance of the <u>sénéchaus-</u>
<u>sée</u>.  As royal proctor, Hugues sedulously advanced royal interests as
well as his own; but he did no more than many other officials who were
not ennobled.[41]

Honoré Firmin and Raimond Barrian, who received letters of nobility
in 1308 and 1309,[42] never held royal office; they were fully occupied
with the personal concerns of Guillaume de Plaisians and Guillaume de
Nogaret.  Both Plaisians and Nogaret maintained strong ties to their
native province by acquiring large estates from which they sought
maximum return and by marrying their children into the landed aristocracy.[43]  The ennoblement of their representatives was advantageous
whenever the latter had dealings with tenants and vassals or with
neighboring lords.[44]  In 1308 Raymond Barrian was involved, moreover,
with the marriage between the eldest son of the lord of Clermont-
l'Hérault and Nogaret's daughter; the prospective bride brought as
dowry a royal promise to deny forever that town's requests for self-
government.[45]

Most of the men ennobled prior to 1314 had little regard for the
rules of professional and personal ethics.  Their circumstances and
the small number of letters issued provide corroboration, nevertheless, for the thesis that Philip the Fair was a "constitutional king"
anxious to observe the letter, if not always the spirit, of the laws
and customs of his realm.[46]  Royal officers did not benefit as a
class; with the possible exception of Nogaret, even officials of the
highest rank in Paris kept the status of their birth.  Each letter
responded to a specific request that was not entirely without justification.  The first recipients had lived as nobles but could not
meet the increasingly rigid rules of northern French custom, and
their ennoblement can be considered a legitimate exercise of gracious
justice similar to the legitimizing of bastards.  The eight letters
to residents of southern France also had grounds in equity.  Jean
Marc and the others connected to the royal court in Nîmes had been
especially useful to the king or his councillors.  Earlier kings had
granted knighthood for valor in war.  Now that written law governed
social status, why not confer written letters of nobility on royal
lawyers who showed unusual courage in legal battle?  The extension

of the practice on behalf of the powerful lord of Isle-Jourdain and the pope had appeal as a tool of diplomacy and as reciprocity for benefices granted at the royal request.

Louis X was as parsimonious with letters of nobility as Philip the Fair. Only six were granted during the thirty months of his reign, all during his first months on the throne. The Count of Eu was favored by the ennoblement of Guillaume de Coldesson, a member of his staff.[47] Jean Bérenger, a royal sergeant at arms resident in the Toulousain,[48] was sponsored by the king's brother Philip for whom he was acting in Poitou.[49] Jean had, moreover, previously been royal seneschal in the Limousin, an office largely military in scope and normally reserved to knights.[50] His ennoblement can be considered a confirmation of ambiguous status, and the letters for Pons and Guillaume Rey, who had rights of lordship in several fiefs near Nîmes, can be placed in the same category.[51] Pierre and Jean de Mussy of Champagne were already noble in law since the status of their father, Guillaume de Mussy, had been affirmed by the Parlement when it investigated his status in 1312.[52]

Philip V, who became regent in June 1316 and succeeded to the throne the following January, gave out letters of nobility much more generously than his brother or father: the chancery recorded forty-five separate grants during the fifty-four months of his reign,[53] a striking increase over the eighteen known from the two preceding decades. At the same time, the new king largely followed precedents established earlier. The majority of letters benefited royal officials who lived in southern France; several had some claim in law or custom to the privilege, as did almost all the northern recipients. A greater innovation lay in the ennoblement of ten members of the royal household in Paris through which Philip sought to single out and honor branches of the government severely attacked in recent years. Because of the larger number of families raised to the nobility, regional variations in social etiquette and patronage stand out more clearly than in earlier reigns. They are most marked when the north is compared to Lower Languedoc, whereas Upper Languedoc drew upon the forms of both northern and southern France.

Letters of nobility continued to serve as an inexpensive way of expressing royal favor toward the beneficiary or his patron. The

five inhabitants of northern France ennobled during the first years of
the new reign had performed well in administrative and military posts.
Each could also draw on the recommendation of members of the great
families of the realm.  Raoul de Macart and Jacques de La Noë held
important offices in Champagne[54] where there was serious opposition
to the succession of Philip V and his disposal of the claims of Louis
X's widow; they enjoyed, moreover, the patronage of Gaucher de
Châtillon and Anseau de Joinville who had strongly supported Philip
during the interregnum.[55]  Jacquin de Nogent, as guardian of the affairs of Marguerite de Blâmont, worked to increase French influence
in the border province of Lorraine.[56]  André Roualt of Picardie had
the assistance of Jean L'Archevesque, cadet of the famous house of
Montfort and allied by marriage to the equally powerful Clermont-
Nesle.[57]  The letters for Guillaume Gobe can be considered a confirmation of ambiguous status:  the son of a noble mother, Guillaume
held fiefs of the crown and had presented himself before the constable
to perform the military duties of a noble.  But his defense of Mahaut
of Artois and royal authority when Robert of Artois attempted to overthrow his aunt undoubtedly speeded up the successful outcome of an
inquest into his standing.[58]

   The royal power of ennoblement was also used to strengthen the ties
of friendship that united Philip V and Pope John XXII.  Philip had
been present in Lyons during the convocation that brought John to the
papacy and openly backed his candidacy; the pope had in turn intervened
against the leagues hostile to Philip and prevented his predecessor's
widow from joining their party.[59]  The first ennoblement Philip V con-
ferred thus went to the pope's brother, Pierre Duèse, together with
large grants of money and land.[60]  An additional and more striking
example of John's influence is provided by the case of his protégé
Raoul de Préaux.  Only two months after he was raised to nobility,
Préaux incurred the wrath of the queen and was accused of high crimes;
although dismissed from office when the charges proved true, he was
saved from punishment by the pope's friendship and lived out his days
as a wealthy country gentleman.[61]

   The twenty Occitanians granted nobility by Philip the Long also had
friends at court; because of their different style of life, however,

they were more likely to seek the help of ecclesiastical rather than
lay lords.  The new nobles from northern France already "lived nobly"
in the sense that phrase acquired in later centuries.[62]  They were
clients of the landed aristocracy and continued to prefer military and
administrative posts when they worked for the royal government; none
had commercial interests or was legally bourgeois as an enrolled member
of a municipal corporation.  They differed from other gentry only in
enjoying an opportunity to approach the crown.  In contrast, the seven
families resident in Lower Languedoc owned extensive urban property
and were deeply involved in the machinations of municipal politics.
Their first concern was power within their own community, and they
took office under its lord mainly to acquire influence that might
prove useful at home.

The councillors of the seneschal of Nîmes ennobled in the spring
of 1320 knew of the letters issued to Jean Marc ten years earlier
since members of their families had taken part in council meetings
while Marc was major judge.  Whereas Marc had himself earned royal
gratitude, however, they drew upon past services by their families
to gain whatever advantages nobility might bring in struggles with
other factions within the urban patriciate.[63]  Bernard de Godols became
in subsequent years one of the most active and influential among the
seneschal's councillors.  In June 1320 he was at the beginning of his
career,[64] and noble rank recognized not only his personal merits but
also the standing of a family, the wealthiest in Nîmes, that for more
than two centuries had helped to shape the policies of the city and
its successive lords.[65]  The title and its perquisites became desirable
after the sons of Bertrand Imbert were ennobled a month earlier because
the two families were traditional rivals.[66]  Like Bernard de Godols,
Pierre de Thome was legum doctor and carried on a family tradition of
royal office; but the de Thome were of lesser stature in Nîmes than
the de Godols or the Imbert and possibly obtained nobility as parti-
sans of one of the two rival factions.[67]

The internal politics of southern cities were normally of little
concern to the government in Paris.  Through participation in the
council of the sénéchaussée, however, the de Godols had allies of high
rank in the Bishops of Mende and Montpellier, prelates of great power[68]

notable for zeal in advancing clients,[69] while Pierre de Thome turned
to Cardinal Pierre d'Arrabloy, a trusted royal councillor whose father
had been seneschal in Nîmes a decade earlier.[70]  By the reign of Philip
V, an advanced degree in Roman law was virtually a prerequisite for
royal office and membership in provincial governing bodies.[71]  Families
without such influence in the seneschal's councils had to go farther
afield for patrons.  The Enguillebert of Beaucaire, where legal training was not as common as in Nîmes or Montpellier, hence looked to the
prestigious house of de Baux in neighboring Provence.[72]  Bérenger de
l'Église was not himself active in government, but he shared the lordship of Clarensac[73] with Raymond de Nogaret who had a large say in
local affairs although he lacked the larger ambitions of his more
famous father.[74]

The patterns of patronage found in Nîmes prevailed as well in
Carcassonne and Toulouse.  Although of sufficient standing as landowners to be invited to the assizes of the seneschal of Carcassonne,
the Tardieu had to approach the crown through the household of the
Queen.[75]  Like the de Godols of Nîmes, Géraud de Lignan of Béziers
was helped by the bishop of Mende.[76]  Pierre Roche did not need to
go outside Carcassonne for advocates since he was related to both
the major judge and the royal treasurer.[77]  So large an accumulation
of provincial offices in one family provided opportunities for profit
as well as advancement:  when Roche was hanged two years later for
extortion and counterfeiting, the bishop of Alet paid the very substantial sum of eleven thousand pounds for his property.[78]

The mountains of Upper Languedoc and the Auvergne present a geographical barrier but also routes of communication along which ideas
and institutions as well as goods were transmitted; and the region
thus mixed the social and legal forms of northern France and Languedoc
proper.  Although the merchants of Cahors were second to none in the
techniques of banking, cities in Upper Languedoc were generally smaller
and poorer than those on the coast of the Mediterranean, and their
citizens enjoyed less autonomy and smaller influence in provincial
affairs.  Local custom used the procedures of Roman law, but it took
longer to develop an organized hierarchy of governmental offices.[79]
The privileges and immunities of the church were fewer, those of

secular lords greater.

The backgrounds of those who acquired letters of nobility and the
ways through which they gained them typify this mingling of regional
practices.  Several came from administrative and military backgrounds.
Eustache Fabri was bailiff of the Auvergne,[80] Arnaud Petit bailiff of
Saintonge,[81] and Arnaud du Portal had charge of the customs service
for the four sénéchaussées of Toulouse, Quercy, Beaucaire-Nîmes, and
Lyons.[82]   Like Jean Bérenger, who had been ennobled by Louis X, Fabri
and Arnaud du Portal were royal sergeants at arms, and the same title
was also used by Guillaume du Vernet.  Vernet's letter confirmed his
prior ennoblement by the late count of the Auvergne, under whom he
had fought in the Flemish campaign of 1299;[83] he may also have enjoyed
ecclesiastical patronage since the count's son assiduously cooperated
with the last Capetians as bishop of Tournai and archbishop of Cambrai.
The friends of Eustache Fabri were also well-placed:  twice removed
as bailiff for favoritism and injustice, he was restored to office
coincidentally with his ennoblement[85] and later given an equally important post as viguier of Béziers.[86]

While new forms of social etiquette evolved at the end of the Middle
Ages, we have seen that the extended family, with its tight network of
relationships through both the male and female lines, continued to
have first place in men's emotions.[87]   For this reason, laws limiting
nobility to the male line could not be applied to families able to
reach the crown.  Bernard de l'Isle-Jourdain used his association with
the king's favorite[88] on behalf of his maternal cousin Pierre Grimoard,
lord of Villebrumier;[89] although their relationship was distant, he
probably also solicited the letter for Arnaud and Guillaume Daniel of
Saint Léonard de Noblat in the Limousin.[90]   Nicholas and Jean de
Moulins, citizens of the bourg of Noblat, were similarly ennobled
because they had married into the family de Châtelus.[91]   All held
fiefs, as did Pierre Mancip of the Rouergue,[92] and Guillaume Daniel
was briefly bailiff of the Limousin.[93]   But the standing of their
parents and patrons determined their status as much as personal wealth
or office.  The Saumade were patricians of Villeneuve in Rouergue
without seigneurial or "feudal" rights; following a pattern more common in Lower Languedoc, they had taken to the law and were now rewarded

when Gaillard Saumade became bishop of Arles and councillor of Philip
of Tarente, cousin to the king.[94]  In the same way, Guillaume de Breuil
of Figeac, author of the Stilus curie parlamenti, received his grant
as partial payment for legal services on behalf of the count of
Comminges.[95]

Some three-fourths of the families brought into the nobility by
Philip V lived in provinces distant from Paris--in Champagne, Lorraine,
the Auvergne, or Languedoc.  The record shows that they secured the
royal grant through the intercession of great lords, both lay and
ecclesiastical, to increase their political weight in relation to
other élite families in the locality.  Like the fief-rente, the first
letters of nobility were one of the devices used during the later
Middle Ages to forgo a chain of clientage between crown and magnates
as well as between magnates and gentry.  In this sense, the larger
number of letters during this reign reflects no conscious effort to
enlarge the role of the crown in the regulation of social stratification; indeed, such letters might enhance the influence and power of
the patrons who obtained them, to the detriment of national unity.

Philip V broke with tradition by granting nobility for the first
time to members of the royal household in Paris.  No precedent was
set, however, for the later creation of the noblesse de la robe.
Almost all were fiscal and not judicial officials; as in the provinces,
their ennoblement largely resulted from the rivalry between families
connected to the royal court.  Three years elapsed before the first
of these letters was granted in July 1319 to the royal treasurer Jean
Billouart.[96]  They began to flow out of the chancery in great numbers
in October 1319 when Géraud Gayte, at the height of his influence in
financial affairs, arranged the ennoblement of himself, his two brothers, and Géraud and Raoul Chauchat to whom he was related by marriage;
the sons of Géraud Chauchat received separate grants, a superfluous
act suggesting that the whole procedure was thought to be of dubious
validity.[97]  Martin des Essarts, another master in the chambre des
comptes, procured letters for his son-in-law and, in August of the
next year, for his brother Pierre des Essarts.[98]  August 1320 also
witnessed the ennoblement of the two remaining treasurers, Guarin de
Senlis and Guillaume du Bois (father-in-law to Pierre des Essarts),

and the royal _argentier_, Geoffroi de Fleury.[99]  A few days later, the
privilege was extended to two lawyers, Philippe de Villepreux, who
was head of the _requêtes de l'hôtel_ and chancellor of the queen,[100]
and Jacques de Vertus, advisor and familiar of the king's brother.[101]
In July 1321, letters of nobility were even given to Jean Haudry,
merchant of cloth to the royal household.[102]

The ennoblement of these royal servants established new precedents
destined to have important consequences during the _ancien régime_.  With
the possible exception of Guillaume du Bois,[103] there could be no am-
biguity about their legal status or way of life.  Philippe de
Villepreux was a converted Jew enriched by accumulating benefices he
never saw,[104] and the others were merchants and bankers who lent their
talents as manipulators of money to the royal government.  Most were
legally enrolled citizens and officials of northern French communes;[105]
unlike the southern French judges or _rentiers_ ennobled earlier, moreover, they remained active in trade and styled themselves _bourgeois_
long after they received the royal grant.[106]  Since they preferred
the latter status for personal and business use, it is the administrative careers of these financial advisors that explains their ennoblement.  They had been actively involved under Philip the Fair in the
creation of an independent fiscal bureaucracy following the suppression of the Templars; they thus fell prey after 1314 to the widespread
hatred of Philip's councillors.  Several were jailed and feared for
their lives, the more fortunate demoted to lesser tasks.  Having returned to power with Philip V, they saw in nobility increased prestige
as well as justification and protection for the great riches acquired
in public office.[107]  When the king's decision to go along with their
request is balanced against the grants to clients of provincial magnates, the much larger number of letters of nobility emanating from
the chancery can be seen not as weakness but as consistent with the
general willingness to experiment that has been found to mark his
reign.[108]

Although Philip V firmly established ennoblement as a legitimate
and recognized way of gaining a new status in law, the addition of
some forty families to the nobility can not significantly have affected
the nature of social stratification in a nation of millions.  One

conclusion to be drawn from a study of ennoblement between 1280 and
1322 is thus negative:  the royal patent was not a normal or common
way of acquiring noble rank.  The princes of the realm issued similar
letters from the reign of Philip VI (or earlier) and continued to do
so throughout the fifteenth century;[109] even taken together, however,
royal and princely grants were never very numerous during the later
Middle Ages.[110]  The majority of families calling themselves noble
thought it unnecessary to get written proof from their sovereign;
they were content to have their social standing recognized by the other
members of their community.

   The conclusion that social status remained a matter of local acceptance and not royal regulation is supported by the motives of those
who did turn to the crown.  Although financial gain was the proximate
cause of some letters, recent laws against the acquisition of fiefs
by non-nobles were as effectively evaded through a simple grant of
dispensation,[111] and nobility in itself did not bring exemption from
royal or communal taxes.[112]  Present in every case was the desire for
a title their peers would not allow them because of the rules of custom and political factionalism or the unpopularity attendant on blatant
unscrupulousness.  Jean Marc and Pierre Roche were removed from office
at the request of those they judged, and Roche, together with Eustache
Fabri and Jean de Corrobert, was also convicted by higher courts.  If
judges rarely hang for their misdeeds, it is even more unusual for a
bishop such as Hugues Géraud to suffer the final penalty.  Officials
in the financial administration more frequently went to jail, not always with just cause; but documentary evidence supports the guilt of
Raoul de Préaux, Philippe de Villepreux, Géraud Gayte, and Pierre des
Essarts.  Even those who escaped punishment--such as Martin des Essarts,
Guillaume Gobe, and Guillaume de Breuil--were barred by their oppro-
brium from favorable acceptance in local tribunals.

   In deciding the membership of the nobility, élite families in each
region gave meaning to the title of noble.  The seventy men studied
went outside the usual channels; nevertheless, their styles of life
and the patrons available to them provide clues to the various ways
in which different regions drew the boundaries of social class.  It
is not surprising that the first letters of nobility to men unques-

tionably bourgeois responded to the initiative of lawyers in Nîmes.
Municipal constitutions in southern France allowed nobles to enroll
in the urban corporation and assigned them an important role in the
governance of the city.[113] Southern practice also saw no contradiction between nobility and the bar; indeed, local custom considered
the doctorate in law equal to knighthood for purposes of precedence.[114]
Royal intervention in the process of ennoblement may have offended
regional sensibilities, but it did not violate the established order.

The larger number of letters granted by Philip V allows divergent
conceptions of nobility to stand out more clearly.  The families so
honored were of high rank in the community and able to obtain the
patronage of the lay or ecclesiastical lords who were the intermedi-
aries between the provinces and the national government.  Nobility
everywhere carries connotations of authoritative and legitimate command, but Raoul de Macart in Champagne and Bernard de Godols in Nîmes
participated in the exercise of power within the context of different
traditions.  Feudal forms such as vassalage had never been essential
to the maintenance of public order in Languedoc.  Most conflicts were
not resolved by seigneurial courts; they were arbitrated by the regional assemblies of all landowners, noble and non-noble, that provided the model for the executive councils governing each sénéchaussée.[115] The rentier families that were represented at these assemblies and councils over the centuries now formed a class of minis-
teriales equivalent in standing to the lesser nobility in a region
like Champagne.

These different ways of exercising power expressed deeply felt convictions about the correct ordering of society.  All élite groups in
France were more urban than rural by the fourteenth century.  Where
southern custom placed great stress, however, on the unity of the
urban corporation as one mystical body of citizens contributing to
the welfare of the whole through different offices, northern laws
emphasized less strongly the unity of the town as a legal corporation
and allowed a relatively greater degree of immunity from communal
obligations.  Northern France thus came in the thirteenth century to
entrust the main burden of police and military service to the nobility
and to require nobility as a prerequisite of knighthood, while the

south obligated all citizens of wealth and allowed knighthood to <u>bour-geois</u> as well as to noble.[116]

Whatever the titles signaling their greater worth and prestige, the notable families in any region needed no royal letters to confirm their duties and rights. Even in southern France, indeed, royal letters did not suffice to confer noble status in the absence of community recognition.[117] The nobility was evolving toward the estate of the <u>ancien régime</u>, and the letters of nobility issued by the last Capetians indicate the limits of royal power in the creation of class privileges. The crown did not control the course of social change. The nobility created itself as the expression of a class consciousness that drew upon regional traditions deeply implanted in historical realities of power and deference.

## Index Personarum

(The numbers refer to the footnotes.)

Chapter 20

Obligations of the Church in English Society:
Military Arrays of the Clergy, 1369-1418

Bruce McNab

It has been said concerning the division of labor in the Middle Ages
that knights fought, clergy prayed, and peasants worked. Like other
such generalizations, this one is not altogether accurate. Certainly
both knights and peasants could and did pray, and at least some clerks
labored in the fields. But it was against the laws of the church and
the traditions of society that a churchman, particularly one in major
orders, should fight. A cleric was strictly forbidden under canon law
to bear arms or to shed blood, although one who incurred canonical
penalties by defending himself against an assault on his person might
readily find dispensation.

There had been a time in Europe when at least fighting prelates were
not unknown. Odo, bishop of Bayeux and brother of William the Conqueror, is supposed to have fought at Hastings with a mace designed to
maim but not to shed blood. (He is shown with this _baculum_ in the
Bayeux Tapestry.) There were also northern prelates who aided the
German kings in their frequent Italian campaigns during the eleventh
and twelfth centuries, sometimes leading armies in person and participating actively in the fighting.[1] But by the thirteenth century
such adventurous bishops appear to have become uncommon, and it was
everywhere understood that churchmen should fulfill their feudal
military obligations by proxy, and if present on a field of battle
should comport themselves as noncombatants.[2] The fourth canon of
the legatine council held at London in 1268 by Cardinal Ottobuoni
Fieschi specified that any member of the clerical order who bore arms
or otherwise violated the canon would _ipso facto_ incur excommunication.
If such a one did not submit himself to the judgment of his bishop by
a certain time, he would also be deprived of all his benefices within
the realm. If he by chance held no benefices, then he would be dis-
abled from obtaining any for a period of five years thereafter.[3]

There is evidence that scattered violations of this prohibition continued, despite the legatine constitution issued to reinforce the
similar canons which were already a part of the ius commune of the
church.

Philippe Contamine has observed that in fourteenth-century France
it was deemed normal for a clerk or a religious to defend his church
or monastery, but he also provides evidence that French churchmen
sometimes took up arms in other, less holy, causes as well.[4]  In 1356
Pope Innocent VI, addressing himself to the kings of France and England,
denounced the participation of ecclesiastical persons in warfare.[5]
The papal strictures, however, seem to have been widely disregarded,
for as late as the early fifteenth century members of the military
orders, generally the Hospitallers, are to be found among the armies
of France, and even less likely ecclesiastical warriors than these
seem to have been summoned for service in England.[6]

English evidence of military activity on the part of the clergy in
the late fourteenth and early fifteenth centuries consists of royal
writs of array and bishops' returns to these writs, now in the Public
Record Office, as well as muster-lists, entries in episcopal registers,
chronicle accounts, and royal notifications of exemptions from array.
Among the most interesting of these bits of evidence are the royal
writs of array and the bishops' returns to Chancery issued in execution of them.  The first such writ of array was issued by Edward III
on July 6, 1368, and subsequent similar writs were issued by him in
1372 and 1373, by Richard II in 1377, 1391, 1385 and 1386, by Henry
IV in 1400 and 1402, and by Henry V in 1415 and 1418.[7]  There may
have been other such writs issued, but a careful search of the
Calendars of the Close and Patent Rolls and the Syllabus to Rymer's
Foedera has disclosed no published record of any others, either before
1369 or after 1418.  The language of the writs is much the same in
each instance, but there are some minor changes in the later ones and
only the last two require the bishops to return certificates of execution to Chancery.[8]  The writs are addressed to the diocesans in
each case (and in 1400 also to the Abbot of St. Albans for his exempt
jurisdiction), except in 1418 when they are addressed to the two archbishops, each for his province.  The writs inevitably begin by stating

the threat to the realm which exists from the French or Scots and
their allies, who are variously said to be threatening to invade or
already to have invaded, to wreak havoc and upset the church and the
king's dominion.  The writs sometimes note how well-known it is that
the archbishops and bishops and other prelates and clergy "are bound
to lay to their hand" with the other lieges of the king and help to
resist the malice of the enemies.  The writ of 1369 and all the others
except those of 1415 and 1418, which use a somewhat different formula,
and that of 1386, which is unique, order the bishop to

> cause all abbots, priors and men of religion and other ecclesias-
> tical persons of your diocese whatsoever to be armed and arrayed,
> furnished with arms every man between the ages aforesaid [16 and
> 60] according to his estate and means (iuxta statum et facultates),
> and put in thousands, hundreds and twenties, so that they shall
> be ready with other the king's lieges to march against the said
> enemies within the realm, with God's help to overcome and destroy
> them, defeating and crushing their insolence and malice.[9]

These arrays were ordered only when the king and his council felt
that the realm was threatened by invasion from across the Channel or
from across the northern border, or both.  The clergy were to be armed
as a home-guard force or militia, no doubt intended to be a last-ditch
defense.  Arrays of the clergy were usually ordered at about the same
time that commissions were appointed to array the laity, and as the
quotation from the writ of array given above indicates, the procedures
ordered for the clergy are similar to those followed at arrays of the
laity, i.e., all eligible males between sixteen and sixty were included; they were formed into companies of thousands, hundreds, and
twenties; and each man was armed according to his "estate and means."[10]
The clergy, however, were armed and arrayed separately from the laity
and were formed into distinct units of their own.  There is some evidence that clergymen were at least occasionally included among the
commissioners appointed to array the laity, as in the Isle of Thanet
in 1372; and sometimes laymen were included as commissioners to supervise the array of the clergy, as in Derbyshire in 1381.[11]  Neither
practice ever seems to have become common, however.  Bishops must have
preferred that the clerical contingents also be led in the field by
churchmen, for in 1373 when Edward III ordered William Wykeham, bishop
of Winchester (1367-1404), to array his clergy "in the county of

Southampton [sic]," the king threatened the bishop that if he were
"lukewarm or remiss in the said array of the clergy," the king "would
make them to be arrayed and led by laymen."[12]

The only scholarly attempt to evaluate and understand these arrays
of the clergy in any detail was made in 1908 by The Reverend William
Hudson, who contributed an essay on the subject to the Sussex Archaeological Collections number for that year.[13] Hudson was drawn to the
problem by a document which he encountered in the register of Robert
Rede, O.P., bishop of Chichester (1396-1415), under the date February
10, 1400.[14] This document is an order from the bishop directing two
of his clergy to execute within their respective deaneries the writ
of array issued by Henry IV on January 27, 1400.[15] In his essay,
Hudson asked two important questions concerning the arrays of the
clergy: (1) was the practice of arming and arraying the clergy something new, introduced by Edward III? and (2) was this practice some
form of imposition upon the clergy of the requirements of the Assize
of Arms (1181) and the Statute of Winchester (1285)? Hudson determined that the first question should be answered affirmatively, because
it is clear from the Parliament Roll for that year that Edward III
specifically asked the bishops and other prelates in parliament if
they would, in defense of the church and realm, if his adversary of
France should wish to enter the kingdom to destroy and subvert it,
give their aid and array their subjects "as well themselves and all
[men] of religion, as Parsons, Vicars, and other men (gentz) of Holy
Church of every kind to rebut the malice of his enemies, if perchance
they wished to enter the kingdom."[16] The prelates present agreed that
they would do as the king requested, in aid and defense of the realm
and holy church, and they subsequently authorized the use of canonical
penalties against clergy who refused to be armed and arrayed as the
king commanded. Edward III alluded to the bishops' concession in his
writ of July 6, 1369. If such arrays of the clergy had been ordered
previously under the Statute of Winchester, the king would scarcely
have needed to make a special request of the prelates to allow the
clergy to perform what was their legal duty. No subsequent similar
appeals by the king to parliament for its consent, or to the prelates
separately, either in parliament or provincial councils, for their

consent are to be found for any of the later arrays of the clergy.
The initial experience of 1369 seems to have established a formal
precedent for these procedures, and no further consents were deemed
necessary in order for the king to call the clergy of the realm to
arms to repel invaders.[17]

By essentially the same argument, that is, the novelty of Edward
III's request to the prelates in 1369, Hudson denied that the arrays
of the clergy were an attempt to impose upon them the provisions of
the Assize of Arms and Statute of Winchester, laws which regulated
the local, non-feudal militia, the military force historically continuous with the ancient Anglo-Saxon _fyrd_.  He noted that the Assize
of Arms spells out which weapons were to be held ready for use by
"any free layman" (_quicunque liber laicus_), and although the Statute
of Winchester, c. 6, simply says "every man" (_chescun home_), that
statute referred to the standards established by the "ancient assize,"
meaning the Assize of Arms, which was directed only to laymen.[18]  None
of the writs of array speak of the Assize of Arms or of the Statute
of Winchester, nor are they mentioned in the records of Edward III's
request to the prelates in parliament in 1369.

It is important to note that the writs of array of the clergy were
not feudal summonses.  The arrays included clergy of every grade, from
the adolescent clerk with first tonsure up to the most senior bishop.
They were not restricted only to that class of the clergy who also held
lands "in lay fee" subject to the same burdens as estates held on similar tenures by laymen, including the payment of lay subsidies and the
performance of military service.  Those clerical lords who held their
lands by military tenures (i.e., knight service or military serjeanty)
were supposed to render their due service when summoned, as they were
on June 4, 1385, when Richard II ordered both archbishops and all the
bishops of England, as well as fifteen abbots and one prior, to meet
him at Newcastle-upon-Tyne on July 14 with all the military service
each vassal prelate owed him.[19]  Institutionally speaking, the arrays
of the clergy were parallel to the ordinary arrays of the laity, ordered under the provisions of the Statute of Winchester and designed
to call forth the local militia, supposedly a different body of fighting men from that summoned to the feudal host.  This may be illustrated

by the writ of array issued by Richard II to Bishop Wykeham of
Winchester only four days after his letter summoning the bishops and
abbots to the royal standard at Newcastle.  In this writ, Richard II
ordered the bishop "to arm and array all abbots, priors, men of religion and other ecclesiastical persons of his diocese" and put them
in the customary companies of thousands, hundreds, and twenties in
order to defend the Isle of Wight against invasion by the French.[20]
The army assembled by Richard at Newcastle was gathered not to repel
invaders, but rather to march across the frontier into Scotland.  The
writ of array of the clergy directed at the same time to Bishop Wykeham
anticipated an invasion of the southern coast, particularly of the
Isle of Wight, by the French, gauged to coincide with the time of the
king's expedition in the north, a time when the enemy might expect the
south to be stripped of trained and experienced fighting men.  The
clergy of the diocese of Winchester were to muster as a defense force
to withstand the expected invasion from across the narrow seas.  Since
the bishop had also received the king's summons to the feudal host, he
was bound--at least in theory--to send to Richard at Newcastle his
regular levy of knights for service against the Scots.[21]  This would
leave only his clergy and local armed retainers for the home defense
forces.  Wykeham presumably sent a force to join the king in the north,
but he himself remained in his diocese, perhaps to attend in person
to the defense of the coast and of the Isle of Wight.

Defense of the southern coast against frequently threatened (and
sometimes realized) French invasions was a regular obligation of the
ecclesiastical magnates of the region, particularly the greater abbots,
at least from the latter part of the reign of Edward II.  Sometimes
this defense appears to have been undertaken solely by the churchman
and his military retainers, perhaps as a part of his customary obligation to the Crown.  At other times, when the danger was very great,
the prelate would be authorized to array the clergy of his particular
jurisdiction to assist him and his armed retainers in the defense of
the coast.[22]  In the summer of 1377, taking advantage of the death
of Edward III and the accession of a minor to the English throne, the
French and their Castilian allies surprised and sacked the towns of
Rye, Dartmouth, Portsmouth, Plymouth, and Hastings, and generally

ravaged the Isle of Wight.[23]  To meet the invasion, the council of
the boy king ordered the archbishops and bishops to arm and array all
their clergy, secular and religious, and they appointed commissioners
to array all the fencible laymen in every county.  The bishops were
ordered to hold their clergy, arrayed and marshalled in the customary
companies, in readiness "to march with other the king's lieges" for the
defense of the realm.[24]  According to at least three chronicles, monastic prelates and the forces under their charge took an active part in
the fighting along the southern coasts during that summer of French
raids.  According to William Thorne's chronicle of the abbey of St.
Augustine, Canterbury, the abbot there, Michael Pecham, "who, although
a religious, was laudably active in the defense of his country," led
"a strong body of his own men and other valiant men he had specially
kept with him" and gave battle to the invaders at Folkestone and later
at Dover, forcing the enemy to retreat in both engagements.[25]  Thomas
Walsingham records that the prior of Lewes, armed, together with some
knights, was captured by the French that summer as he and his compatriots were defending the village of Rottingdon, not far from the
abbey of Lewes.[26]  The seventeenth-century chronicle of Richard Baker
agrees and adds that shortly before the French raiders captured the
prior of Lewes and his associates, they had been compelled by the
abbot of Battle and forces under his command to withdraw from an assault on Winchelsea.[27]

Invasion from Scotland was also to be feared, and on a number of
occasions incursions from beyond the northern border gave cause for
an array of the clergy in the affected dioceses.  In the troubled
year of 1381 the king ordered the archbishop of York to array the
clergy of his diocese so that they might "be ready to march with the
archbishop for the defense of the realm when danger threatens by invasion of the king's enemies, which it is said they are preparing,"
and, in a unique departure from the customary military objectives of
the clergy in arms, they were to be "also ready to put down any lieges
of those parts who shall rise in unlawful assemblies or levies contrary to the peace."[28]

It is only from the northern dioceses that records show any evidence
of hostility on the part of churchmen to the practice of arraying the

clergy.  The grant of a half-tenth of ecclesiastical goods and benefices, and of temporalities annexed to spiritualities (with noted
exceptions), made by the prelates and clergy of the York convocation
on April 21, 1385, was made contingent upon the king's going in person against the Scots or the French, and "on the understanding that
the prelates and clergy should not be compelled to labour, either
personally or by their men, for the warding off or expulsion of any
enemies within the realm."[29]  And another such grant by the York convocation on February 16, 1389, was made on the condition, among others,
"that the clergy should not be constrained to arm or array themselves,
or to find men-at-arms or any other men for the war, except only those
who by reason of their temporalities were wont and are bound to find
such men in the king's presence."[30]

The best evidence we have for the thoroughness with which the royal
writs of array were executed comes from the later period, from documents relating to the last three general arrays, those of 1400, 1415,
and 1418.  The procedures ordered in each diocese in 1418 were exactly
what they had been in 1415.  Each bishop was instructed to certify to
Chancery by a certain date the number and armament of his arrayed
clergy.  The bishops complied, and a number of these returns are found
yet among the Ancient Correspondence of Chancery in the Public Record
Office, London.[31]  Procedures in 1400 were similar, except that no
returns to Chancery were required.

The precise methods the bishops followed in carrying out the arrays
of the clergy varied slightly from one diocese to another because each
bishop was left free to execute the array in the fashion he thought
best.  The similarity of procedure from one diocese to another shown
in the records of the 1415 and 1418 arrays testifies to the fact that
by that time the routine best to be followed had become familiar everywhere.  Most likely it was based as closely as possible on the procedures followed at arrays of the laity.[32]  There has come to light only
one description, given by the supervisor of an array, of what was done
at an array of the clergy.  This is the certificate of the abbot of
St. Osythe to Bishop Robert Braybrooke of London (1381-1404), in which
he recites his acts as the bishop's commissary for the array of the
clergy of the archdeaconry of Colchester, held at Colchester on the

Thursday after Michaelmas, 1386. On September 26, the bishop had
ordered the archdeacon of Colchester to cite and strictly enjoin all
abbots, priors, and their convents and chapters, exempt and non-exempt,
and all rectors, vicars, priests, and all other ecclesiastical persons
whatsoever of his archdeaconry to gather in person (personaliter) "in
any spacious place at Colchester before us or our commissary," with
competent arms and array, horsemen as well as infantry (tam equestres
quam pedestres), according to their status, ability, and fitness
(secundum status sui possibilitatem et congruenciam).[33]   On October 5,
the abbot certified to the bishop that he had, on the preceding day,
held the ordered array, at which he had called all the abbots, priors,
convents, rectors, vicars, etc. by name and had pronounced the absent
contumacious, reserving punishment to the bishop. Those whom the abbot
found to be sufficiently armed and arrayed according to their status,
ability, and fitness, he listed by name on a schedule annexed to the
certificate (but not copied into the register). Those whom he found
not to have competent arms or array he admonished three times, in
virtue of the obedience they owed to the bishop, and enjoined upon
them that they provide themselves with good and sufficient arms and
array within fifteen days. Then he put those who were armed and
arrayed on oath that the arms they bore were their own, and warned
them by the bishop's authority, and in his place, that according to
the holy obedience they owed the bishop and under pain of the penalties described in the bishop's mandate, they guard those arms and that
array which they had and neither diminish nor alienate them, but rather
acquire more (iniunximus eisdem quatinus armatura et arraiamenta sua
huiusmodus penes se custodiant et ea non minuant neque alienent set
pocius plura sibi adquirant), so that when they were called or "pre-
monished" by the bishop for the defense of the lord king and his realm,
they would be always found fitted-out and ready.[34]
    The most common difference of procedure between dioceses was in the
number of arrays held in each diocese and in the persons who supervised them in each case. In the diocese of Chichester in 1400, the
bishop ordered arrays to be held by deaneries, although two deaneries
may have been arrayed jointly at a single time and place which the
clerks appointed to superintend the arrays in each deanery were free

to choose for themselves.[35]   In the diocese of Durham in 1400, five
distinguished men of the diocese (one of whom, the constable of Durham,
was surely a layman) were named to array the clergy of the archdeaconry
of Durham.  A muster-list from this array is extant and was published
by James Raine in 1839.[36]  Although no record of it remains, we may
assume that a similar array was held at the same time in Northumberland,
the other archdeaconry of the diocese of Durham, just as arrays had
been held in each archdeaconry of the diocese of London in 1386.

   In his diocese of Canterbury in 1415, archbishop Henry Chichele
(1414-1443) named four clerks to array the clergy.  His mandate to
the arrayers says nothing about how many arrays should be held in the
diocese or when, but it does order that they furnish to him a certificate of the number of clergy arrayed and their furnishings by no later
than July 8, in order that he might return his own certificate to
Chancery by the specified date of July 16.[37]  At the same time in the
diocese of Bath and Wells, the vicar-general of Bishop Nicholas Bubwith
(1407-1424), who was then absent from his see, ordered no fewer than
eight arrays to be held within that diocese.[38]  He required that the
arrayers in each instance send to him the full names of those who were
arrayed and of those who refused to be arrayed by not later than July
7.  The Bath and Wells return for 1415 unfortunately lacks the list of
names the vicar-general called for, but the certificate in the Public
Record Office does include the totals of armed men, hobelars, and
archers arrayed there.[39]  On the same occasion in his diocese of
Lincoln, Bishop Philip Repingdon (1405-1419) ordered two arrays.  One
was restricted to the clergy of the cathedral and city of Lincoln and
was to be held there by the sub-dean of the cathedral.  The other was
to include all the other clergy of the diocese and was to be held before the bishop's commissaries at Leicester on July 1.[40]  Master Henry
Welles, archdeacon of Lincoln, was directed to cite the diocesan clergy
to appear at Leicester on the appointed day.  This worthy was associated with the notorious John Macworth, dean of Lincoln, in a reprimand
issued to them jointly about this time by Henry V.  Writing from
Portchester castle on August 7, immediately prior to his departure
for France, the king strictly enjoined these two to betake themselves
to Lincoln cathedral, put themselves in array, and remain there until

he returned from France, in order forcibly to resist the malice of the king's enemies, should the need arise, "et ce in nulle Manere ne lessez sur le Peril Garrant."[41]  This is the only instance which has so far come to light of anything like a royal reprimand being issued, and it may suggest the degree of seriousness with which the king regarded the arrays of the clergy.

At least two bishops, Rochester and Llandaff, appear to have supervised in person the arrays of their clergy in 1415.  According to his certificate dated July 12, 1415, Richard Young, bishop of Rochester (1404-1418), ordered the official of the archdeacon of Rochester to cite the clergy of the diocese to arm and array themselves and to appear before him or his commissaries on the first and third days of July, in the cemetery of St. Edmund near Dartford, there to show themselves to be sufficiently armed and arrayed and prepared to serve as the king required.  On the said days the bishop himself and the prior of Rochester were present to supervise the array.  Attached to the certificate which Young returned to Chancery on this occasion is a schedule containing the names and equipment of the Rochester clergy who were mustered then.[42]

In his 1415 return to Chancery, John de la Zouch, O.F.M., the scholarly bishop of Llandaff (1407-1423) in war-torn Wales, begged the king's mercy on account of the bad conditions and poverty of the benefices in his diocese which made it difficult for him to muster a large array of clergy.  He stated that he held three arrays in person at three places in his diocese, Cardiff, Usk, and Magor.[43]

Except for minor differences, all of the certificates returned by bishops for the arrays of 1415 and 1418 are quite similar.  Twenty-three of these returns survive among the Public Records, eleven for 1415 and twelve for 1418.[44]  Certificates from Lincoln, Ely, Rochester, Winchester, Bath and Wells, Exeter, and Hereford exist for both years; Llandaff, St. Davids, Salisbury, and York only for 1415; and St. Asaph, Coventry and Lichfield, Chichester, Worcester, and Norwich only for 1418.

The certificates normally give the number of men arrayed in each diocese according to the weapons with which they were furnished. Since each bishop was free to conduct his own arrays as he saw fit,

the descriptions of the arrayed clergy may be more or less complete
from one diocese to another.  Nevertheless, they fall roughly into
three categories:  (1) well-armed men (usually designated as viri
competenter armati or else simply as homines armati), who generally
appear to have been armed with lances and were probably mounted;[45]
(2) hobelars, a kind of light cavalry, who rode horses unprotected by
armor; and (3) archers.[46]  There is a fourth category included in
some returns, comprising all those who were arrayed with an assortment of arms, such as some combination of basinets, glaives, shields,
poleaxes, battle-axes, and gisarmes.

   Hobelars appear as a distinct category in only six of the certificates:  Bath and Wells, 1415 and 1418; Winchester, 1415 and 1418;
Norwich, 1418; and Worcester, 1418.  In the Winchester return for
1415, there is no number of "well-armed men" given, only numbers of
hobelars and archers.  The other five returns list all three categories separately.  That from Norwich, 1418, lists "armed men, all
appearing with lances," "hobelars," and "archers arrayed with hauberks,
bows and arrows, swords, shields and daggers."[47]  The Worcester, 1418,
return includes summa hoblariorum arraiatum cum loricis et palettes
ac curtis lanceis vel pollaxis.[48]  The two returns from Bath and Wells
refer to fighting men of the second category as mixti seu neutri,
vulgariter dicti hoblarii.[49]  (There is no satisfactory explanation
at hand for this extraordinary description.)  There are two other
returns which mention hobelars, but in them the hobelars are either
grouped with the well-armed men (i.e., Lincoln, 1418, which describes
them as alia que arriate vulgo dicunt hoblers)[50] or else are named
in a total figure of all clergy mustered, not broken up into sub-
totals for each category (i.e., Rochester, 1418).[51]

   The returns from the diocese of Lincoln for both 1415 and 1418 dif-
fer from all the others in that the totals of each category of fighting men arrayed are divided into persone de cleri seculari; de
religiosis exemptis et non exemptis, non mendicantibus; and de
religiosis mendicantibus.[52]  The bishop adds in the 1418 return that
the Lincoln convent of Friars Minor expressly refused to be arrayed.
The convent must have experienced some form of the royal displeasure
for its recusancy, but we have no evidence of it, nor is there evidence

that canonical coercion was applied, even though its use was authorized
in cases where the clergy refused to comply with the order to arm and
array themselves.

As mentioned above, the 1415 return for the diocese of Rochester
is unique among the similar returns now collected in the Public Record
Office in that it has a muster-list of the clergy arrayed, appended to
the bishop's certificate.  The muster-list is on a separate piece of
parchment from the certificate which serves as a covering letter for
it.  The covering letter is in all other respects a typical 1415 certificate to Chancery, except that it gives no totals of the clergy
arrayed according to their type of armament, referring instead to the
cedula huic annexa.[53]  The muster-list, which is written upon both
sides of a single sheet, is in very deteriorated condition and most
of the lower portion of it is either missing or completely illegible.
Nevertheless, enough of it remains to excite our interest.  Written
at the top, recto, in the same hand, apparently, as the bishop's certificate, are these words:

Tenor dicte cedule de qua superius sit mencio [de personis (?)]
una cum armis ipsis personis ecclesiasticis per officialem nostrum Roffen' iuxta antique Registra [sic] expresse impositus
talis est.

This introduction poses a problem.  What are the "old registers"
(antiqua Registra) to which it refers?  The 1418 Rochester return,
which does not include a muster-list, does include this enigmatic expression in the body of the certificate:

...bene et sufficienter armatos et munitos iuxta eorum status et
ordinaciones antiquas registrorum vestrum.[54]

None of the twenty-one other extant certificates makes any reference
to old registers or royal ordinances, nor are such things mentioned
in any of the writs of array.  There is, however, evidence from other
sources which suggests that there was a scale established in each
diocese which determined the arms with which each clerk was to be
furnished and with which he was to appear at the array, according to
the annual value of his benefice.  Thomas de Brantyngham, bishop of
Exeter (1370-1394), in response to the writ of Edward III dated
June 16, 1372, ordered two arrays within his diocese, and he spelled
out for the six clerks who would superintend the musters precisely

with what arms the clergy should be arrayed, according to whether they
were religious or seculars and according to the annual value of their
benefices, if they held any.  For example, the prior of St. Michael's
Mount was to have at the array three armed men, and the priors of
Tywardreath, Bodmin, Launceston, and St. Germans six armed men and
six archers each.[55]  Secular churchmen and religious who held benefices
were to be armed and arrayed as follows:  rectors or vicars who held
benefices of an annual value of 10 marks should be armed and arrayed
in the manner of an archer, with bow and arrows (sit armaturus vel ad
modum sagittarii cum arcu et sagittis arraiatus); those with benefices
worth £10 should be armed (sit armatus), presumably as a "well-armed-
man" of the sort referred to in the 1415 and 1418 returns; those with
benefices worth £20 should be armed and appear with two archers (sit
armatus cum duobus sagittariis); those with benefices worth £40 should
have two armed men and two archers (habeat duos armatos et duos sagittarios); those with benefices worth 100 marks should have three armed
men and four archers (iii armatos habeat et iiii$^{or}$ sagittarios); and
those beneficed with £100, five armed men and six archers (v homines
armatos et vi sagittarios).[56]  Further, the canons of the collegiate
church of Penryn residing or not residing but having farm in that
church should have one armed man and one archer, and the dean and
prebendaries of the collegiate church of Crantock the same.  Stipendiary priests should have a bow and sheaf of arrows.[57]

  There is a similar entry in the register of Archbishop William
Courtenay of Canterbury (1381-1396), dated August 29, 1386.  This is
a mandate from the archbishop to his commissary of Canterbury ordering
an array of all the clergy of the diocese to defend against an invasion from France, and asserting that it is needful to move the clergy
of the city and the diocese both to pour out prayers to God and to
prepare themselves with various kinds of arms, since "it is attested
by the page of both laws, divine and human, that all, both clerks
and laymen, ought to see to the defense of their own country and as
men to repel the invasion of enemies."[59]  Rectors and vicars are
warned that they must provide necessary and competent arms "for themselves and theirs" (pro se et suis), as follows, according to the
value of their ecclesiastical benefices:  those with benefices worth

100 marks annually and above are to be well and competently armed
themselves (<u>sint bene armati in se</u>) and each is to have with him one
man competently armed and two archers; those with benefices worth £40
and above are to be well-armed themselves or by a proxy (<u>sint in se</u>
<u>vel per alium bene armati</u>) and each is to have with him two archers;
those with benefices worth £20 are to be well-armed themselves or by
proxy (as above) and each is to have with him an archer; others who
hold only minor benefices are to be well-armed themselves or by proxy.
Stipendiary chaplains are to be armed with chain-mail, breastplates,
and basinets with aventails, if they be supplied with such armor;
otherwise, they are to have bows and arrows or other kinds of arms
with which to serve, "the better to guard and defend themselves and
their country."[60]  A simple comparison of this scale of assessments
of arms in Canterbury diocese with that required in Exeter diocese
fourteen years before shows that considerably more was expected in
Exeter from beneficed clerks whose benefices were worth £20 and more
per year in 1372 than from their counterparts in Canterbury in 1386.
If more such entries in episcopal registers were known--and surely
they must exist--it would perhaps be possible to ascertain whether
the scale of assessments varied radically among different dioceses
at the time of any given array or whether the same scale was imposed
everywhere at any one time but might be altered from the time of one
general array to another.  On the basis of the known writs of array
and returns to Chancery, it seems plausible that each bishop established the scale of assessment for his diocese as it seemed proper
to him at any given time.  The references in the Rochester 1415 and
1418 returns, however, are to armaments as imposed by "your" (i.e.,
the king's) "registers" and "ordinances."[61]  The only royal ordinances
which would seem to fit this reference are those which relate to the
assessments of arms expected to be borne by laymen when they were
arrayed under the provisions of the Statute of Winchester and subsequent confirming statutes.  The royal response to a petition of the
Commons in the parliament of 1404 concerning commissions of array is
particularly illuminating with respect to procedures that were followed at the time an array of the laity was held.[62]  According to this
royal response, the commissioners of array in each shire were

responsible for determining what arms would be borne by each man, according, presumably, to the criteria set down in the Statute of Winchester relating to his possessions and ability to arm himself. If this principle were applied to the arrays of the clergy, clearly each bishop, as the recipient of the royal writ of array for his diocese, would be in a position corresponding with that of the lay commissioners of array in each shire, and he would therefore determine with what arms each clerk should be arrayed according to his estate and means (iuxta status et facultates).

The two muster-lists which have been preserved, that of the array for the archdeaconry of Durham in 1400 and that of the array for the diocese of Rochester in 1415, provide some evidence of the composition of the forces which were turned out. Only the Rochester list includes any monastic clergy, the prior of Bermondsey and the abbot of Boxley, both of whom were required to participate in the Rochester muster because of the benefices they held in the deanery of Rochester. (There may have been other monastics included in the list, but its decayed state is such that only the names for the deanery of Rochester are legible; those for the deaneries of Dartford and Malling are discernible only in fragments.) Certainly the prior and abbot "found" men to be arrayed and did not appear in person, and others must have done likewise. The muster-list, in fact, records that "the prior of Bermondsey, for his church in the deanery will find (inveniet) two armed men."[63] The archdeacon of Rochester, whose name heads the list, is recorded as "appears by proxy and will find one armed man."[64] Half of the Rochester muster-list is made up of stipendiary chaplains, non-beneficed clergy, each listed by name and by the church where he celebrates. Although the beneficed clergy are listed by title, not name, and are shown to have been arrayed with various different arms, every stipendiary chaplain is described with the words comparet ut archienus, "appears as an archer."[65] It is possible that all the beneficed clergy appeared by proxy, since the muster-list, except for the first two entries, simply names the clerk by title and says, for example, "one archer with bows and arrows." However, if the muster-list is to be taken at face falue, all the stipendiary chaplains appeared in person, prepared to serve as archers.

The muster-list for the Durham array fifteen years earlier is somewhat different in form.[66]  It includes no monastics, and it lists only
the beneficed clergy who were arrayed, usually only by title but sometimes by name as well.  The list indicates that each clerk appeared
with some other fighting men, e.g., Rector de Stanhop cum una Lancea,
et uno Hobler et tribus Sagittis comparet.  It also names some clergy
and gives their assessment and notes that they did not appear, e.g.,
Rector de Gaynforth cum i Lanc. et ii. Sagitt. non comparet.[67]

One entry in the Durham muster-list would appear to be at variance
with the scheme of assessing arms and service due from each clerk on
the basis of the annual value of his benefice.  This is the entry for
the vicar of Gaynforth, who is listed as appearing at the array with
one lance, one hobelar, and three archers (literally "arrows," sagittis).  It so happens that the rector of Gaynforth is also listed, as
are two other pairs of rectors and vicars, and although the rector of
Gaynforth is noted as non comparet, his assessment is given as one
lance and two archers, considerably less than the assessment of the
vicar, whose share of the income from the living would presumably be
less than the rector's.  (It should be noted, however, that this is
not the state of affairs with the other two pairs of rectors and
vicars; therefore, the Gaynforth information could be a scribal error
reversing the assessments from their proper order.)  Further question
is raised by the entry for Master William Hull, who is not arrayed for
his prebend at Darlington because he was otherwise arrayed as rector
of Stanhope (oneratur in alia parte quia rector de Stanhop sufficienter).  Would this indicate that in Durham in 1400 a clerk was assessed
for service at an array on the basis of his income from only one of
his livings, if he were a pluralist?  And, if this were true, which
living was chosen as the basis for his assessment?  This question
cannot be entirely resolved without the discovery of new evidence.

It seems clear that although in some cases a clerk was not arrayed
in person but instead provided the arms assessed against his benefice
and found someone else to use them,[68] in other cases the clergy themselves bore arms and participated in combat.  There exists among the
Public Records a certificate of Archbishop Alexander Neville of York
(1374-1388), dated November 1, 1386, and endorsed to the king in

Chancery, which states that Master Robert Manfeld, provost of the
church of Beverly; William Monkton, rector of the church of
Kirtlington; John Seggefeld, rector of the church of Catton; together
with some thirteen other rectors, vicars and prebendaries were arrayed
by the archbishop for the expulsion of the king's enemies from the
realm and, armed, were in the king's army _in toto viagio vestro in
regnum Scotiae_. They were apparently seeking exemption from payment
of a clerical tenth because they had marched with the king against
the Scots.[69]  The previous summer, Richard II had addressed a letter
to Archbishop Neville instructing him not to suffer Brother Thomas
Sees, prior of the alien priory of Brustalle, "by reason of his priory
or benefices thereto belonging, to find any men at arms, armed men,
hobelars or archers to march with the clergy to Scotland," because
the priory was presently too heavily burdened at the Exchequer to
bear any other charges.[70]  The evidence of these documents is supported by another, a letter sent by Henry IV to the arrayers of the
clergy in the diocese of Chichester in 1400; the king orders them

> not to meddle in arraying of Thomas Anlaby, clerk, parson of
> Petworth, by color of any command or commission of the king so
> long as he shall stand in service of the king; as he has marched
> toward Scotland in company of Henry de Percy, lord of
> Northumberland, there to abide for a set time on that service,
> as the king has true information.[71]

Not long after this, two clerks received papal dispensation for having
taken up arms in the service of Henry IV against Henry de Percy.[72]
The petition of one of them, Robert Bawe, _alias_ Gough, of the diocese
of Lincoln, asserts that "the said priest who, on account of his office,
was following the king, in defense of himself, the king and the realm,
with his bow shot manfully a number of arrows against the assailants,
but whether they mutilated, wounded or killed anybody he does not
know."[73]

These documents confirm at least two things:  first, some clergy
did undertake military service in person; second, monastic foundations
could "find" armed men to be arrayed with the secular clergy, the
numbers and equipment of such men most likely being determined by the
value of the monastery and its appropriated benefices.  The second
point explains why the prior of Bermondsey, for the church in the
deanery of Rochester appropriated by his house, found two armed men

in 1415.  A monk could fight in person, just as secular clerks did.
We have seen the evidence of the martial activities of the abbot of
St. Augustine's, Canterbury, the abbot of Battle, and the prior of Lewes
at the time of the French invasions in 1377.  (Certainly an abbot or
prior who was accustomed to horses and weapons as used in the hunt must
not have felt very ill at ease with sword or lance in hand.)  As,
however, medieval ecclesiastics were accustomed to delegating many of
their official duties and to conducting much of their business through
proctors, it would be quite logical to assume that most abbots and
priors (and probably cathedral deans and archdeacons as well) provided
others to be arrayed in their places.  This is not to say that they
provided laymen to take their places, although conceivably they might
have done so.  If laymen were customarily proxies for large numbers
of clergy at the arrays, there would have been little excuse for holding the arrays of the clergy quite separately from those of the laity
and for marshalling the clergy into separate units.  By the same token,
if lay proxies customarily served for the higher clergy at arrays,
there would have been little for Bishop Wykeham to dread from Edward
III's threat in 1373 to make his clergy to be arrayed and led by laymen if the bishop were deficient in executing the array himself.
Other facts also militate against a theory that laymen served widely
as proxies for clergy in the arrays.  For example, most arrays of the
clergy were held at the same time as arrays of the laity in each of
the counties affected.  Fencible laymen were all required to muster
with their fellows and there would most likely have been few of them
left unarrayed to serve as substitutes for any great number of churchmen in the arrays of the clergy.  Nothing is to be found in any of
the certificates returned to Chancery in 1415 and 1418 which suggests
that laymen substituted for clergymen as a matter of course.  In fact,
the involvement of others than clergy in the arrays of the clergy seems
to have been carefully noted when it occurred.  There are instances
in the returns to Chancery and elsewhere which indicate that along
with the clergy arrayed, who provided the main body of men, there
were also some familiares, perhaps tenants of church lands, who came
to assist and who were enumerated separately in the musters of the
clergy.  For example, the return for the diocese of Llandaff in 1415

lists "230 ecclesiastical persons, competently armed, with <u>familiaribus</u> <u>assistentibus</u>, and 24 others competently armed, mostly archers."[74]
The return from Hereford diocese for the same occasion lists as the numbers arrayed there "68 sufficiently armed men, 487 archers with hauberks, swords, bows and arrows...and 540 <u>personas familiares</u> with hauberks, swords, axes, etc."[75]

Since not all the returns to Chancery are equally legible, and since not all of them apply exactly the same criteria in categorizing the armaments of the clergy arrayed, it is not possible to get a wholly accurate count of the total number of clergy arrayed in either 1415 or 1418. The grand totals for each occasion, which for the reasons given are only approximate, are 11,769 arrayed in 1415, and 15,487 in 1418. These figures only represent eleven dioceses in 1415 and twelve in 1418, therefore the real total for each year must have been significantly larger.[76] Such information as is available, however, indicates that there were sufficient clergy in each diocese in 1415 and 1418 for all the numbers given in the returns to Chancery to have been composed exclusively of clergy, without any need for laymen to be added in order to swell the numbers to meet some arbitrary quota.[77]

Although many aspects of the arrays of the clergy in England still remain unclear--particularly regarding the involvement of clerks in minor orders and of ordinary monks, neither of which groups is represented in either of the known muster-lists--we are now in a position to propose some conclusions and to ask some new questions. The evidence seems clearly to indicate that despite canonical and traditional prohibitions on bearing arms and shedding blood by persons in holy orders, in England during the late fourteenth and early fifteenth century the ecclesiastical authorities were willing to commit the entire body of the clergy, religious as well as secular, to the defense of the realm <u>and</u> of the <u>Church</u> of England, as each writ of array significantly adds. The only recorded protests against the practice seem to have been the conditions attached to clerical subsidies by York convocation in 1385 and 1389, and these seem to have had little influence on Richard II.[78] Not only did bishops agree that the arraying of the clergy take place, but they actively supported the practice by agreeing to impose canonical penalties to compel recalcitrant clergy to arm themselves.[79]  It further seems to have been the case that, at least in this period, each clerk was expected to maintain the arms specified by his bishop for a churchman of his status and benefices, in much the same way as laymen were required to do by the Statute of Winchester.  Beneficed clerks with good livings were expected to have "competent arms" for fighting from horseback.  Stipendiary chaplains were expected to possess at least bows and arrows and lighter arms. This may explain why some wills of well-to-do clerks of the time include among bequests such un-ecclesiastical items as suits of armor, swords and bows.[80]

Willing acquiescence of the hierarchy in royal demands for military service from the clergy, ca. 1369-1418, indicates yet another degree to which the church in England had become subjected to the crown by the late Middle Ages.  But why did the practice terminate in 1418? It would be enlightening to know what were the reactions of canon lawyers to these activities.  How did pluralists render their service? Were the arrays of the clergy, restricted as they are to this half-century, simply the phenomenon of a particularly "nationalistic" period, a time during which heightened anti-French and anti-Scottish sentiment among every class of the population served to justify any policy which might promote English arms in the field?  Is there any relationship between the willingness of the prelates to have clergy under arms and the outbreak and spread of Lollardy which is a feature of this period?  Wyclif opposed the involvement of clerics in warfare, saying that fighting priests were unfit either to preach or to pray or to administer the sacraments.[81]  Perhaps he had the arrays of the clergy, or something like them, in his mind when he wrote those words, but elsewhere he allowed that it was meritorious (presumably for lay-men) to fight in defense of the ecclesia, with the infidels for example, in order that the faith be defended or that the infidels be converted through forceful means.[82]  Is there any connection between Wyclif's political theories and the requirement of the crown that clergy of the realm serve in arms against the invading representatives of the "heretical" anti-pope?  Answers to these questions must await further research.

## Manuscript Sources Cited

London,

  Guildhall Library,
    MS. 9531/3, Register of Robert Braybrooke, bishop of London,
    1381-1404.
  Lambeth Palace Library,
    MS. Register of William Courtenay, archbishop of Canterbury,
    1381-1396.
  Public Record Office,
    Ancient Correspondence of Chancery, S.C. 1/57.
    Miscellanea of the Chancery, C. 47/2/49
        "    "   "    "   , C. 47/18/19
        "    "   "    "   , C. 270/13

NOTE: Since the research was completed for this essay, the Chancery Miscellanea documents in classification C.47 have been redistributed and are now to be found under various new class numbers in the Public Record Office.

Part V

Personality and Ethics:
The Spirit of Man in the Middle Ages

Chapter 21

The Personal Development of Peter Damian

Lester K. Little

Peter Damian (c. 1007-1072) holds one of the pivotal positions in
the spiritual history of the Latin West.  That he was a major figure
in the Gregorian reform needs no repeating, but attention should be
given to his long-range influence, because his basic views on the
preaching and penitential ministry of the priesthood, as well as on
the relationship of material poverty to preaching, bore fruit a century and a half after his death in the reform program of the Fourth
Lateran Council and in the actual accomplishments of the Franciscan
and Dominican friars.  Seen in the still wider perspective of the
development of religion in Europe between the eleventh and sixteenth
centuries, from the superficial, liturgical, and expiatory religion
of the monks to the intensely personal, internalized, and deeply moral
religion of the laity, Peter Damian emerges as an astonishingly perceptive critic and capable reformer.  Even so, no historian in modern
times has written a biography of Peter.  Portraits of the mature Damian
have been traced--one could hardly imagine improving on the one by
Leclercq[1]--but, for all their complexity and richness of texture, these
inevitably retain a somewhat static quality.  A proper biography must
above all be dynamic:  it must both document the evolution of its subject and explain as fully as possible the processes of change involved.
In the case of Peter Damian, only the most fragmentary evidence relating to the chronology of his early years can be found; furthermore,
though the extant body of his writings is large by any standard, his
autobiographical reflections were minimal.  These are serious obstacles, but even with the material at hand a clearer chronology of the
young Damian can be established, and the writings of the mature Damian
can be made to yield more evidence concerning his personal development.

I

From the time he was named cardinal-bishop of Ostia in 1057 until
his death at Faenza in 1072, Peter combined with his cherished eremitic

solitude the career of a busy and influential public figure.  Given
such public importance, this final phase of his life, a decade and a
half long, received careful notice at the time.  The problem of chronology seems best approached by proceeding from this solidly based later
period back to the relatively obscure earlier period.  As early as the
winter of 1058, when he was seeking to be relieved of his prelacy, he
complained of the discomforts of declining health and advanced age.[2]
Peter did not of course spring from utter solitude to the prominence
of the papal court in 1057; the very reason for which he was well
enough known to be named a cardinal was his participation, by writing
tracts, in the reform activities that had started nearly a decade
earlier, with the accession of Leo IX in 1049.[3]  And even earlier than
that he was writing letters to prelates on the urgent needs for clerical reform, for example to Gregory VI in 1045,[4] or to the archbishop
of Ravenna in 1043,[5] the very year in which he became prior of the
hermitage at Fonte Avellana.[6]  The complex task of establishing a
chronology of Peter's writings has yielded evidence of a steady literary production spread over three decades, the earliest work being
The Life of St. Romuald, usually dated 1042.[7]  Thus some thirty years
of the maturity of Peter Damian have been well established.

   Before that time, however, nothing whatever is known of his life from
strictly contemporary sources.  All that is known of the earlier, for-
mative period is indicated by sources from this later, mature period
or even, in the case of at least one other writer, from after Peter's
death.  The two most important of these indications concern the dates
of his conversion and of his birth.  In a letter to the Empress Agnes,
dated 1067 according to a complicated but convincing argument by
Wilmart, Peter mentioned the period of thirty-two years that had passed
since his entry into the hermitage; thus the conversion is placed in
1035.[8]  As for his birth, Peter wrote, this time in a work dated by
Neukirch as between ca. 1049 and 1063, that Otto III had died scarcely
five years before he, Peter, was born; as Otto died on January 23,
1002, Peter's birth is placed in 1007.[9]  On the basis of this latter
indication, Peter's age at various stages of his life is usually com-
puted in the following way:  he was twenty-eight when he became a
hermit, thirty-six when he became prior of Fonte Avellana, fifty when

he wrote that complaint about old age, and sixty-five when he died.

The weak point in this apparently solid scheme becomes evident when
we try to establish some facts about the period right before 1035,
the period that covers the transition from Peter's being a student to
his being a hermit.  His formidable erudition offers the best proof
of his having been a student, for his writings, in addition to being
expressed in forceful rhetoric, show a mastery of history, sacred and
profane literature, theology, and both civil and canon law.[10]  Peter
referred once to having studied at Faenza and once also to having
studied at Parma.[11]  The reference to Parma contains a chronological
clue, for Peter there said that he recalled from his student days in
Parma that a certain cleric (clericus quidam) lived openly with a
woman next to where he himself lived, and that they lived together
thus for about twenty-five years (per quinque fere annorum lustra)
until they perished together in a fire that destroyed the same city.
Working with a belief that had been current from at least as far back
as the mid-eighteenth century, that Parma burned in 1058, and trans-
lating the passage to mean that the couple died in a fire separate from
and a year earlier than the one that destroyed Parma, Wilmart placed
the death of the couple in 1057 and placed Peter as a student at Parma,
by an odd arithmetic, in 1034.[12]  But Peter had written to Agnes saying
that thirty-two years had passed since he changed his clerical robe
(clericalem cycladem) for his monk's habit, and Wilmart, though admitting that clericalem cycladem could mean a teacher's gown, said that
in this case it must have meant that of a student.  He noted that
Peter had said he was greatly disturbed by that couple at the time
and then afterward when he went to the hermitage.  For this reason,
Wilmart surmised that the conversion period was brief; he concluded
that Peter observed the priest living with the woman at Parma in 1034
and that within a year Peter had entered the hermitage.  This became
the standard argument after Wilmart published his study in 1932,[13]
yet there remains at least one problem.  Peter's account of the couple
at Parma specifically states that he was there studying the liberal
arts and that he was in the flower of adolescence, when new puberty
makes its impact.[14]  Similarly in the reference to Faenza he says he
was an adolescent and was studying letters there.[15]  If we accept the

date of his birth as 1007, then he would have had to be in the flower
of adolescence at age twenty-seven, in 1034.

Our initial reaction may be to say that at least the date of birth
is certain because it is precise and because it comes from a text by
Peter Damian himself. Yet this reaction could well be misleading.
Is not Peter's recollection of being an adolescent at Parma really
more trustworthy than his assertion about the year of his birth? How
could he have known when he was born? How could anyone at the time
know the date of his own birth? The problem for Peter was perhaps all
the more difficult because both of his parents died when he was still
an infant. This Peter Damian was, after all, the same one who wrote
that St. Romuald lived to be one hundred twenty years old, an estimate
that was inaccurate by some fifty years.[16] When Peter was writing
about his days in Parma, how could he not have been correct in recalling that he had then been an adolescent? He did not confuse sexual
urge with adolescence; he would know such urges again when he was,
beyond any dispute, a mature man.[17] Without knowing precisely the
years when he had been a student, he was surely capable of associating
a particular stage of his life with a particular place and episode.
The slightly vague reference to his adolescence in Parma has greater
scientific validity than his seemingly precise statement about the
year of his birth.

But although prudence suggests in any case that the birth-date of
1007 should not be accepted at full face value, there remains still
some flexibility with the timing of Peter's student experience. The
date of the fire at Parma has been set back three years from when it
was previously thought to have occurred, i.e., to 1055.[18] The scholar
most fully engaged in this problem of chronology, though accepting the
date 1055 for the burning of Parma, gives an odd variation of Wilmart's
interpretation of the passage by Peter, saying that Peter was claiming
to be writing in the year after the fire.[19] This interpretation is
needlessly complicated, for the text states that the couple lived
together for about twenty-five years before the year when the city
went up in flames and they were found destroyed by fire in the same
house.[20] In any case the notion of "about twenty-five years" is itself very rough, especially in contrast to that of thirty-two years

that had passed between his entry to the hermitage and the year 1067. Peter knew perfectly well when this central event in his mature life, his becoming a hermit, had taken place. So, though keeping the date for his conversion in 1035, we are now fully justified in placing Peter in Parma at least as far back as 1030. Moreover, why need we insist that Peter was at Parma for one year only, instead of two or three or four? Such a period, in addition, could as easily have been ending as beginning in 1030. And from what we know of schooling at that time, do we really expect anybody to have been engaged in the arts course much beyond the age of twenty?[21] If we look still again at Peter's reference to Parma, we find that he said merely that afterward he was to be troubled by the memory of the cleric and the woman when he was a hermit.[22]

This does not mean that he passed directly from being a student at Parma to being a hermit. There is no need to posit a short time for the retention of this memory; after all, he was still clearly impressed by the event and by the memory of it when writing on the subject in the late 1050's. Consider the context of this recollection: he was writing to a priest in Milan about clerical immorality and its punishment. He had been traumatized by the Parma experience when an adolescent; the memory haunted him when he was a hermit; and his recollection of both the event itself and of the troubles the memory of it later caused him remained vivid for him still later when he was engaged in the reformation of the Milanese church. As for his saying he exchanged a cleric's robe for a monk's habit, this is a manner of saying that he changed from one order to another, but it carries no implication that this change took place rapidly. Moreover, there remains the possibility that he meant to say he gave up being a teacher, rather than being a student, to become a hermit. If Peter did indeed have a career as a teacher, then we could accept the birth date of 1007--but always as being approximate--and we could see him as a student at Faenza and Parma in the decade of the 1020's, i.e., from the onset of puberty until his early twenties. And by the same schedule we could picture him as a teacher for perhaps three or four or even five years before his entry into the hermitage. One source, the biography by John of Lodi, specifically states that after his

studies and before becoming a hermit, Peter Damian was a teacher; but
Wilmart, and others since, have rejected this testimony.[23]

John of Lodi was a well-educated priest who became a hermit at Fonte
Avellana in the mid-1060's.  He became the close personal companion
of Peter Damian, both at the hermitage and on the road.  Following
Peter's death, John wrote a biography of Peter, served as prior of
Fonte Avellana, and, in his final years, was bishop of Gubbio.[24]  The
details of Peter's early life as given by John need only a brief synop-
sis here.  When Peter was born, one of the older brothers in the
family had an argument with the mother, scolding her for thus further
dividing the family wealth by having this child, when they were already
so numerous.  She reacted furiously to this scolding and then refused
not only to nurse the infant but even to hold or touch him.  He grew
pallid and weak, so that his shivering body could voice no stronger
protest than a whisper.  The wife of a priest, herself a former servant
in the household of Peter's father, came to lecture the mother on her
proper duty to the infant; then this woman took the infant and nursed
him.  The mother later felt remorse, so she took her infant back and
cared for him with deep affection until, at about the time he was
weaned, she died.  It was around then, also, that Peter's father died.
The child subsequently came under the care of one of his brothers and
of that brother's wife; the two of them imposed hardship, indignity,
and severe cruelty on their young charge.  There follows a story of
Peter as a little boy finding some money and giving it to a priest,
asking that a mass be said for his father.  Eventually Peter's fortunes improved; he came under the capable and affectionate care of
another brother, Damiano, who would later be an archpriest of Ravenna.
This brother saw to Peter's getting a good education.  Peter flourished
as a student, continued to flourish as a teacher, then became greatly
troubled by his worldly life, and settled the problem by becoming a
hermit.[25]  For this account, John of Lodi's principal source must
have been Peter himself.[26]  Surely we are justified in picturing the
elder statesman of the eremitic life reminiscing about his early years
with a younger disciple; Peter's few written autobiographical fragments date from those same final years that correspond to the friendship with John of Lodi.

Peter's childhood, as related by John, was truly disastrous, and
indeed many modern readers have been troubled by it. The discovery
by Wilmart of Peter's letter of 1067 to the Empress Agnes offered
those readers a way of discrediting John of Lodi's account. In that
letter, Peter tells of going to the deathbed of his eldest sister, a
saintly person who had been as a mother to him.[27]  Wilmart, thus armed
with an authentic statement from Peter Damian himself, was able to
announce, with some relief, that John of Lodi need no longer be believed and that Peter Damian was in fact neither an orphan nor a child
martyr.[28]  We will return to criticize this announcement by Wilmart,
but let us note right away that such a statement by Peter confirms
rather solidly that he was an orphan. Among the scholarly consequences
of this discovery by Wilmart have been the dropping of the story of
the cruel brother, the affirmation of a "happy childhood," and the
elimination of any mention of Peter's teaching career.[29]  By this line
of argument, the John of Lodi biography is not dropped altogether, but
the early part of it (dealing with events that took place several
decades before John even met Peter) is explained as extravagant exaggeration typical of saints' lives. John himself supplies a theme for
this argument in saying that the future saint was going to have to
suffer all sorts of adversities, i.e., he would be severely tested by
God. John compared Peter to a martyr and to a soldier being tried
in battle.[30]

Here indeed is a traditional theme of saints' lives, and we do well
to be warned against the exaggeration of the author, whose goal was
to praise his subject and to edify his audience. But beyond such
general caution, what specific episode are we to eliminate? Criticism
based on comparison of the work with others of its genre and leading
to a discrediting of certain episodes demands identification of specific commonplaces, such as a pregnant mother's miraculous dream fore-
telling her progeny's saintly career. We cannot simply eliminate the
whole John of Lodi account, for some of its main points can be cor-
roborated (there was a brother named Damiano;[31] Peter had been a student when he was a young man, etc.). So we must be aware of the possibility of exaggeration, e.g., the detail that Peter was for a while
nursed by the wife of a priest. Although it is difficult to see how

he could have known about that, it is easy to see how a biographer
might have added this ironic touch to the life of one who became a
leading proponent of clerical celibacy.  And we can acknowledge that
John of Lodi was weak on the chronology of this early period, just as
his source, Peter Damian, was also weak.  Two serious problems remain:
Peter's upbringing and his conversion.

Was Peter raised by a cruel brother or by a saintly sister?  John
of Lodi's biography and Peter's letter to Agnes seem to be directly
contradictory on this point, but perhaps they can be reconciled.
Scholars have been right to examine this biography in the light of
the traditional genre of saints' lives and of the particular context
in which John of Lodi was writing.  Let us do the same with the letter.
The Empress Agnes, wife of Henry III and mother of Henry IV, a widow
since 1056, unhappy and bitterly opposed regent, came to Rome in the
early 1060's to live as a nun.  Peter Damian met her there in 1063
and received a general confession from her at St. Peter's.[32]  Thereafter he sent spiritual advice to her in writing.  Agnes meanwhile
retained considerable political influence in Germany, a point that
did not escape the papal court.  Four times she returned to Germany
on political missions.  When she stayed through the latter part of
1066 and on through the winter of 1067, Peter became troubled that she
might regain her taste for court life, abandoning her recently acquired
one for the religious life.  He wrote a brief note in March of 1067
urging her to return to Rome, the capital of the world, where her
spiritual example was so urgently needed.[33]  Later in the spring he
wrote her a longer letter, the one that was found and published by
Wilmart.[34]  Peter expressed regret at having approved of her going
away.  He urged her to return.  He confided his own temptation to return home, but tells how he had avoided giving in to it.[35]  Once at
night in Ravenna he did walk in the street where his home was, and
just once he crossed the threshold of that house, to visit the sickbed
of his dear sister, a person of holy life, who had been like a mother
to him.  Even then, such a cloud of timidity hung over his eyes that
he saw practically nothing of the household.  And thus again, now by
his personal example, Peter urged Agnes to return to Rome and not
linger any more in the environment of the life she had vowed to abandon.

That is all Peter said about his sister.  And what could have been
more natural?  The episode was poignant and it spoke to the point.
The coherence of the letter was maintained, even strengthened, rather
than dissipated in personal reminiscence.  He did not stop to tell the
story of his childhood.  Any mention of an unhappy period of his childhood with one or more of his brothers would have been entirely out of
place.  On the other hand, whereas John of Lodi did stress the theme
of childhood unhappiness and did not talk at all of this sister, his
account was not one of unrelieved misery.  John, after all, tells of
Damiano's compassionate care for his little brother.  If Peter's sister lived in the household at the time he was maltreated by one brother
and nicely cared for by another, and if she were sympathetic toward
Peter, then he could perfectly well state later on that she had been
like a mother to him, without in any way impairing the veracity of
John of Lodi's account.  The two accounts are still different, but
they are not mutually exclusive; given the utterly different contexts
in which they were written, they appear instead to be plausibly complementary.[36]

Was Peter a teacher before he became a hermit?  John not only states
that Peter went directly into teaching from being a student, but adds
that he attracted many students and received an abundance of money
(divitiarum copia).[37]  Those scholars who have sought to discredit
John's biography have seized on this last point.  The argument goes
like this:  Peter Damian never said he was a teacher; it is absurd to
think that one could amass a fortune teaching in a city school in
northern Italy early in the eleventh century; therefore, he was not
a teacher at all.[38]  Such an argument leaves us without a clue as to
why Peter became a hermit.  Let us note in any case what else John of
Lodi had to say about this period.  He indicates that Peter was soon
very disturbed by his worldly success; he agonized over the guilt he
felt, for example over being able to eat elegantly.  He tried to impose some austerities on himself but this inner discipline was insuf-
ficient to calm his anxieties; it did not provide a fundamental re-
scheduling of his values.

Then one day he encountered two hermits from Fonte Avellana.  He
was favorably impressed by them and wished to send a heavy silver vase

back with them to their abbot as a mark of his esteem. They refused
the gift and Peter was astonished. This was the critical moment of
his life: rather than take offense at their refusal, he seemed to
understand right away that these men were "truly free and truly happy"
(vere liberos vereque beatos), and the events leading to his entry to
Fonte Avellana were thus placed in motion.[39] Even this story has not
been given much importance in the standard accounts, and yet it forms
an essential part of a consistent and very serious theme being developed by John of Lodi. The tremendous personal crisis suffered by Peter
Damian in his early to mid-twenties, rooted in a level too deep for us
to explore, developed--on a manifest level, relatively easy to observe--
over the specific cultural-historical problem of being paid for teaching. No generality such as "disdain for the things of this world"
(contemptus mundi) would be of help here; each age has its own excesses
and its own austerities.

    As with so many other critical issues of the newly developing commer-
cial society in Europe, we see in Peter Damian one of the earliest
cases, perhaps the earliest case, of an awareness that will grow to
major proportions in the following two centuries. Teaching for pay
in a city school was radically different from being an elder monk
charged with imparting a traditional literary corpus to novices and
younger monks.[40] There existed no ethical justification for paying
money to teachers. This was to be a major problem for Abelard and his
contemporaries.[41] And though the moral theologians and the lawyers
would catch up with the problem by the late twelfth century, the practical solution for many scholars even in the thirteenth century would
be to combine teaching in city schools with a religious life based on
poverty, i.e., to join one of the mendicant orders.[42] Although the
date of Peter's ordination to the priesthood has usually been placed
after his entry into the hermitage, a recent study argues that it came
before; if this latter view is correct, not only might the clericalem
cycladem have been a priestly garment but Peter's clerical status
might have exacerbated this crisis over receiving payment for teaching.[43] As for Peter's "abundance of money," anyone who lives as a
student and then teaches would regard his first payments as large,
especially since he has the feeling of merely continuing to do what

he had been doing all along, though without having been paid for it.
More significantly, from the perspective of Fonte Avellana several
decades later, where material poverty was truly observed and the use
of money practically non-existent, any sum that Peter would have recalled earning earlier would at that later time have seemed embarras-
singly excessive.  For clues to his earlier period, we need to pay
attention not only to what Peter said in his later period, but also
to what he then did.  People who change their identities do not lose
their former skills; they put their same old skills at the service of
the new person.  The new person, as we have said unceasingly, was a
hermit.

But what did this hermit do?  Almost right away he began instructing
the other hermits at Fonte Avellana; then he received, and accepted,
an invitation to teach at Pomposa, where he stayed for two years.
Such an invitation to Pomposa, it has been pointed out, would have
been plausible if Peter had established a strong reputation as a
teacher at nearby Ravenna, but less so if he had been an unknown student who passed directly to distant and remote Fonte Avellana.[44]
Shortly after returning to Fonte Avellana he again went away to teach
in a Benedictine abbey, this time to St. Vincent, near Urbino.  Later
in his life, Peter acknowledged that he was not proficient at manual
labor.[45]  Obviously he was good at studying and liked it, but as a
scholar he seems never to have been engaged solely in the pursuit of
truth.  He was a rhetorician of the first rank; everything he wrote
had a didactic purpose; he was, by trade, a teacher.  His earliest
writings show him to have been already a mature teacher and scholar.
The crisis of the young Peter Damian was resolved--at least on the
manifest level we have been discussing--by his abandoning a secular
teaching career for the hermitage, where he continued to pursue, in
its essence, his chosen work, free of the external, compromising elements that had so tormented him previously.

Building on this more flexible but more internally consistent chronological framework for Peter's childhood, youth, and early manhood, and
keeping the essentials of John of Lodi's moving and purposeful biography, we are able to give a more appreciative reading to Peter's occasional remarks about himself and to those parts of John's biography

that have long troubled scholars. Among the topics worthy of recon-
sideration in this light are Peter's family ties, his conversion, his
reaction to money, and his attitude toward sex.

## II

Peter experienced a cruelly unfortunate family life. He passed
through most of his childhood deprived of maternal affection. Since
he would later refer to his sister as having been like a mother to
him, he probably enjoyed the affectionate protection of this older
sister during a part, at least, of his boyhood. As with his mother,
Peter barely could have known his own father. John of Lodi's story
of Peter's finding a piece of money one day when he was a boy speaks
to this critical point. In the first moments of his good fortune,
Peter's mind was flooded with thoughts of immediately gratifying delights he could purchase with the money. But as these thoughts re-
ceded, the idea grew in him of giving the money to a priest to have
a mass said for his departed father, and that is precisely what he
did. We make a grave error if we follow those many commentators who
have pointed to Peter's pious, self-denying, generous character in this
story, as if he had given up something he really wanted for something
that was, from a selfish point of view, undesirable. On the contrary,
he seems to have eliminated the initial, frivolous ideas that passed
through his mind, until he hit upon the very thing he was searching
for and desired most in life, a major element missing from his existence, i.e., his father. As for brothers, there was that cruel one
who, with his wife, looked after Peter for a while, reducing him to
a slave-like status, keeping him ill-fed and ill-clothed, assigning
him all the most onerous tasks, and in general subjecting him to hostile and cruel treatment. The other older brother, Damiano, was the
good one, who gave him his start in the schools of Ravenna. If it is
true that Peter chose to add the latter's name to the name he had already, we may again be witnessing Peter in search of his father.
Damiano seems in any case to have served for a while in a fatherly
role toward Peter; thus we should not be surprised if Peter would
have sought to associate a surrogate father's name with his own given
name. Did this quest for a father continue? After leaving Damiano's

care and going away to study, Peter might have encountered other men
whom he could emulate, such as his teachers, but there is no direct
evidence. The probability is high since he was an earnest student and
subsequently became a teacher. When those two hermits from Fonte
Avellana appeared, however, they held out to him the inspiring model
of a great and accomplished, even if deceased, father: St. Romuald.
At a key moment in his spiritual crisis, Peter found the man he had
all along been looking for in Romuald of Ravenna. This spiritual
father had been the principal instigator of the eremitic renaissance
in Italy, and Peter was to become its principal theologian and propa-
gandist. Peter was giving instructions about the eremitic life even
at the very time he was being initiated into it himself. He gathered
the still vivid oral tradition at Fonte Avellana concerning Romuald,
injected into it a heavy dose of his own ideas about the eremitic
life, and produced a biography of his new, spiritual father.

Though the object of the present essay is to study a unique case,
the resulting view of Peter's family relationships gains corroboration
from the structural analysis of kinship and sexuality in early European
history. Such analysis, still a fresh form of inquiry, suggests that
we should not be startled by a dispute among siblings or between children and parents over the family's wealth, by infanticide as a solution
to the problem of an unwanted child, by the harsh treatment of a child
by a father or an older brother, or by the continuing presence in the
household of an unmarried older sister who mothers her younger, or-
phaned siblings.[46]

But did Peter retain a happy memory of his childhood home? Some
have thought so, even though he made no direct remark on this point.
Recall that he did say that when he went to the deathbed of his sister
such a cloud of timidity hung over his eyes that he saw practically
nothing of the household. To some this may appear to be modesty
proper to his religious vocation;[47] although it could indeed still be
that on one level, could it not also be, on another, deeper level,
the convenient repression of disturbing childhood memories? That he
chose not to write about such memories is understandable. That he
chose to relate them personally, when he was old, to his young disciple
John, is equally understandable.

Turning to Peter's conversion experience, we need to see if his
writings reveal some personal views about conversion. Without citing
examples from his own experience, he did write generally about the
significance of the act of embracing the monastic life. He saw this
act as unavoidably radical and momentous. Every monk, according to
Peter, is a convert. Secular life is fundamentally different from the
religious life, so any passage from one to the other involves a complete reorientation for the person making the change. There may be
no projection of personal experience into this formula, but it seems
unlikely that the general formula he was stating would have been in
contradiction with his own experience. The strongest expression he
found for conveying the totality of a conversion was to refer to the
monastic life as a second baptism. He justified the analogy by explaining baptism as the sacrament that, initially and radically,
washes away sins in preparation for a new life. The monastic life
has a similarly regenerative character; it provides the sinful man
with a genuine opportunity to come back into direct community with
God.[48] Along with this statement of principle, there may be a personal message from Peter Damian, telling us that the whole course of his
life changed sharply at the time of his conversion, that he had then
become a new man, that he had then started a new life.

Peter's conversion, so efficacious in resolving his personal, familial problems, turned on an immediate, cultural issue, as we have noted,
namely that of monetary payment for teachers. In what other ways
might money have been important in the formation of Peter's spirituality? Money had been the immediate issue in provoking the argument
between Peter's mother and one of his brothers at the time he was
born. While he could not of course have known about it at the time,
he could well have heard reverberations of this argument later on
during his childhood. Recall also the money he found as a child,
the money he earned as a teacher, and the gift of silver he offered
to the two hermits from Fonte Avellana. The life Peter adopted did
not so much resolve the problem of money for him as it allowed him
to avoid the problem, i.e., it kept him free from money. In the
earliest extant letter written by Peter, addressed to the archbishop
of Ravenna in 1043, he listed the most serious abuses in the church

at that time, and at the head of the list he placed avarice, the excessive love of money.[49]  More than two decades later, he argued that
the leading problem in contemporary monastic life was the love of
money.  For the individual monk the question was how best to preserve
his treasure, which was Jesus Christ.  And the answer prescribed by
Peter began as follows:

> First of all, get rid of money, for Christ and money do not go
> well together in the same place.  If you were to close both of
> them in at the same time, you would find yourself the possessor
> of the one without the other, for the more abundant your supply
> of the worthless lucre of this world, the more miserably lacking
> you are in true riches.  Thus if you have any money around, let
> it go somewhere else immediately, so that Christ may find vacant
> the cell of your heart.[50]

He stated this principle forcefully, but the truth of the assertion
that he avoided the problem for himself more than he resolved it is
shown by the terrible confusion and inner conflict he suffered when
once he was offered a gift of silver.  Not long after his trip to
Milan in 1059, he reported that an abbot there had sent him a silver
vase.  Peter was horrified by this act but proceeded to inquire tact-
fully why the abbot had done it, pointing out that representatives
of the apostolic see while on mission could not possibly accept any
gifts from someone who might have a case pending before them.  On the
other hand, where no interests were involved, the custom was that such
representatives would accept gifts.  The abbot assured Peter that he
had no interests involved, either of his own or of his monastery, and
that the gift was just an expression of friendship.  Peter suggested
that between religious brothers gifts in the manner of lay people
were not needed.  But the abbot insisted and so Peter kept the gift.
Over the next days he began to be disturbed about this matter, becoming especially troubled when he recited some of the Psalms at night-
time.  Just as he tried and failed to purchase the affection of his
departed father and, later, that of the two hermits from Fonte Avellana,
he feared this attempt by someone else to purchase his affection.
Again Peter protested to the donor but again the donor prevailed, this
time by suggesting that the silver be used to support certain monastic
communities that Peter was then trying to establish.  Once he had returned to the hermitage, Peter began to suffer all over again, and

even worse than he had previously, to the point where he felt a great
dizziness in the head and the sensation of a swarm of worms eating away
at his intestines.  That one gift could cause Peter such a severe depression in the head and abdomen is perhaps an indication of the strain
caused by trying to be both a cardinal-legate and a hermit; it also
signifies his failure to work out a clear set of values for guiding
him through a situation such as this one at Milan.  To resolve this
conflict for all time, he returned the gift and vowed never again to
accept any gift whatever, never again to risk an affective response
to someone who was reaching out to him.[51]

In writing on the common life of canons to the priests at Fano,
Peter criticized the Rule of Aix for allowing the individual canon to
hold possessions.  Once canons are engaged in the fatal cycle of possessing some things and desiring yet more, the love of money will cost
them a loss of liberty (by making them dependent on laymen) and will
disqualify them from the apostolic task of preaching (since the Apostles held all their goods in common).[52]  Many of Peter's utterances
against money and avarice are couched in especially strong and hostile
language.  He wrote an entire tract on avarice (between 1063 and 1068),
arguing that there is nothing whatever worse than avarice and resorting
to anal imagery to denounce it.[53]  There are many such passages in
Peter's writings and they must not be taken as casual observations
about wealth in general or material goods; they deal specifically and
consistently with money, the characteristic instrument of the commercial economy, a type of economy barely yet known in most of Europe but
flourishing already in the Po Valley.  Peter was among the first to
be sensitive to the dangers of a newly awakened avarice.  His succinct
warning said:  "Charity fosters communion; avarice, division."[54]

If we ever are to have a developmental biography of Peter Damian,
considerable attention will have to be given to a subject almost
totally excluded from previous studies--sex.  This is not merely a
matter of general principle for all biographies, but one of specific
and central importance here, for sex formed one of the major themes
of Peter's writings and of his career as a reformer.  With regard to
his personal experience, there is no explicit proof of his having had
sexual contact with a female.  The torment he endured on account of

the couple at Parma, both at the time and in his subsequent memory of
them, could signify a lack of any happy experience, i.e., either that
he had suffered a significantly unhappy experience or simply had had
no experience at all.  This torment could also signify, alone or in
conjunction with these other possibilities, guilt engendered by indulgence in his own fantasies.  While Leclercq argues that Peter did not
write abstractly about women, but rather of concrete persons and situations, it remains that the close feminine associations Peter developed
were always with sexually inaccessible women.[55]  His correspondence
with them contained specific sexual imagery, for example in proposing
to the Empress Agnes the ideal of an intimate and amorous union with
her true king, Jesus Christ.[56]  In writing to a young, attractive
woman, he said that seeing an old woman had no effect on him, but that
the mere sight of a pretty young woman impressed his mind more dis-
tinctly than a hundred readings of the evangelical mysteries; he pre-
sumed in this case that he could, without danger, at least write a
letter.[57]

Turning to the question of any possible sexual contact with males,
we must confront the problem of his having written the Liber Gomorrhianus.[58]  The problem stems from the unique character of this book; we
cannot be satisfied with a simple assertion that this is a forthright
statement of existing conditions in need of reform.  Peter Damian was
a leader among the reformers; he, like the rest of them, wrote extensively on simony and clerical concubinage, but none of his fellow
reformers apparently thought masturbation and homosexuality to be the
central problems that he made them out to be.  The law codes and the
penitentials indicate a concern about such behavior both before and
during the eleventh century, but without suggesting that it became
more prevalent in the eleventh century.[59]  Clerical marriage and
clerical concubinage in the Western church probably attained their
highest levels in the eleventh century, a fact that could have affected the incidence of homosexuality, yet the same period marked the
high point in the practice of admitting young boys, from about age
seven, into monasteries.  Perhaps what we are really witnessing here
was a newly awakened awareness.  Still, with respect to the Lateran
synod of 1059, the canons that issued from that meeting conform very

closely with the reform program of Peter Damian, but with the notable
exception of the subject he treats in the Liber Gomorrhianus.[60] Leo
IX, to whom the tract was addressed, acknowledged its receipt and expressed discreet gratitude.[61] Anselm of Baggio, with whom Peter served
on the mission to Milan, held views on reform generally consistent
with Peter's but diverged from him on this one issue. Peter considered
homosexuality a cancer eating into the body of the church.[62] Anselm,
even if he agreed about the nature of the problem, apparently thought
the propagation of this book an inappropriate way to deal with it.
Once Anselm had become Pope Alexander II, he asked for a copy of the
book, ostensibly to have it copied, and then had it locked up instead,
to Peter's great annoyance.[63] Thus, at least on this one subject,
Peter was evidently isolated from his fellow reformers; hence the
question of why he wrote this book focuses on him personally. The
Liber Gomorrhianus is startlingly frank; the law codes, to be sure,
are specific in distinguishing among different forms of homosexual
activity, as indeed they had to be. Peter, moreover, was well-versed
in contemporary law, but his use of graphic detail, even if the reform
he had in mind involved changes in the law, went beyond the needs of
an advisory memorandum to the pope. He appears to have filled some
needs of his own by spelling out the very acts he found so repugnant.

Writing in general, not just the writing of this particular book,
served an intensely felt need in Peter Damian. For him, writing was
an avowed pleasure; he sometimes wrote out of duty, but not against
his will. As Leclercq has shown, he did without those formal apolo-
gies so familiar in some other writers who claim to have taken up the
pen only after continued supplications from over-insistent friends.[64]
He liked to write. In the midst of some carefully controlled writing,
for example on clerical celibacy, he would occasionally let loose with
a sudden burst of emotion.[65] In the book called Dominus vobiscum, a
work with a clear argument and an orderly plan, he came to his praise
of the hermitage and there suddenly lost all sense of proportion.[66]
The chapter is inordinately long; it is swollen with a flood of language. Figures from every imaginable phase of existence are invoked
in a fascinating, poetic, richly indulgent statement. And he was
aware of this indulgence, for in the concluding chapter he said: "I

could have said what I have to say more briefly, but I must admit
that it gave me pleasure to prolong my speaking to your sweet self
while I had the opportunity [the work is addressed to Pope Leo IX].
We are happy to spend a long time in pounding spices, especially when
he in whose service they are to be used has himself so sweet a fra-
grance."[67]  In his literary testament, he wrote more generally about
the matter of his own writing.  There he explained that he wrote not
in order to add anything to the laws of the church, which he said
would have been presumptuous, but to fight off the inactivity and
boredom of the solitary cell.  As he could not do manual labor very
effectively, he found that the best way to drive off sloth and bad
thoughts was to write.  With admirable self-understanding, Peter pursued writing for its therapeutic value.[68]

In another flash of self-revelation and analysis, he wrote of his
irritable nature.  He described how anger would boil up and expand
within him, but also how he would resist letting it explode, exerting
rigid control until the crisis had passed.[69]  Then, almost as an after-
thought to this discussion about controlling anger, he said that the
same pattern was repeated with respect to sexual temptation.  Again
he was remarkably specific in describing the symptoms of this temptation.  As with anger so with sexual temptation, he could not eradicate
nature but he could exert his reason and will against it.[70]  Even the
act of writing this tract on the control of anger might have been
helping him give vent to an inner problem since, by his own admission
elsewhere, his self-control was not so effective as his tract on the
subject might imply.  In a summary statement of his sins, written
during the final years of his life, he listed so complete an inventory
of sins that it would seem impossible to identify any of them as particularly important in his life.  But then he picked out the one that,
for him, was the worst of all, scurrility, which he had always known
beyond measure and which, he said, even with his conversion never left
him completely.[71]  He thus admitted being deeply concerned over his
continuing predilection for coarse and ludicrous talk, a type of
language, however, that only rarely found a place in his writings,
as for example when he was denouncing the antipope Cadalus.[72]  The
solitude of the hermitage gave him at least temporary relief from

this predilection: "You, hermitage," he wrote, "cause light-minded men to be serious and jesters to stop mouthing scurrilities."[73]

Speaking occasionally with an acerbic tongue and writing often with great verve and control, Peter appears to have been a lonely man, lacking close friends, filled with an obsessively controlled anger and sexual drive, with few efficacious means of expression readily available. We do not describe or explain his spirituality sufficiently by merely recalling his career as a hermit and his role as a propagator of the eremitic life. Eremitism was a general, though of course new, social movement of his time; when we try to perceive within it some personal or unique approach of Peter Damian, we see his tendency toward a spirituality of solitude, or even of self-sufficiency. In arguing that in certain liturgical passages even a lone individual should use the standard plural forms, he put forth the principle that the church is both one in its plurality and whole within each individual.[74] In the Vita Romauldi he has Romuald remove to "delightful solitude."[75] And in describing the good monk he said: "The workshops where the brothers talk to each other and the monastic cloister are like public marketplaces to him. He seeks and delights in remote and lonely places, avoiding all human contact as much as possible, so that he may the more easily stand in the presence of the Creator."[76] The hermitage he called "an escape from the persecuting world,...a comforter of the sorrowful, a cool refuge from the world's heat, the rejection of sin and the freedom of souls."[77]

The hermitage was a place where he sought freedom, but not even there was Peter's quest for liberation an easy matter. He took up the contemporary practice of voluntary flagellation and gave it a purpose, a theology, a set of coherent limits, and a more general currency.[78] Thus not alone by solitude or by rigid control or by words, spoken or written, did Peter Damian achieve inner peace and strength, but with self-inflicted physical abuse in addition to all of these. Flagellation had the multiple purpose of expiating sins, of imitating Christ and the martyrs, and of checking what Peter considered the body's natural inclination to evil. But it was in arrogating to himself the divine functions of judging and punishing that Peter, the self-reliant orphan, brought his spirituality to a level of self-sufficiency.  In the De laude flagellorum he wrote:

> What a joy, what an extraordinary sight it will be when the celes-
> tial judge looks from heaven and man is hurting himself on account
> of his transgressions.  There the accused, presiding over a tri-
> bunal within himself, holds a three-fold office:  in his heart
> he makes himself the judge, in his body the defendant, while with
> his hands he rejoices to assume the role of executioner.  It is
> as though the holy penitent were to say to God:  "Lord, you need
> not command your official to punish me, nor is it worthwhile to
> threaten me with the vengeance of a lawful trial.  I have laid
> hands upon myself; I have taken revenge upon myself; and I have
> offered myself in place of my sins."[79]

With the hopeful but shaky optimism of a child who dreads some punishment, Peter thus assures God that though he has, of course, sinned,
he has also taken care of the punishment, so God need no longer consider the matter.  Peter's deepest concern as a hermit was his submission to the will of God, his love for God, and his striving for a
mystical union with God; yet at the same time he was here displaying
his old ambivalence in this dread of any direct encounter or contact.

### III

From these disparate but related observations, the main lines of the
personal development of our subject begin to take shape.  Peter Damian
had a seriously disturbed personality, yet he was able to coordinate
his abilities into serving a creative and influential career.  The
question of how he functioned as well as he did can be dealt with by
summarizing these observations.

As a newborn infant, Peter suffered the shock of rejection by his
mother.  The family atmosphere was poisoned both by the mother's
argument with one of her sons and by the animosity between the mother
and the priest's wife.  The latter saved Peter's life (and saved his
mother from a charge of infanticide), but then he was taken away from
his rescuer by a now deeply remorseful mother, who pampered him until,
all at about the same time, he was weaned, she died, and his father
died.  For the rest of his childhood, he remained under the care of
one or another of his siblings.

The initial maternal rejection could not have lasted for much more
than a day, or else the infant would have expired.  Similarly he could
not have remained long under the care of the priest's wife--at the

most a few weeks--or his mother would not have been able to nurse him
when she took him back.  We are given no clues about when the child
was weaned, but a pioneering study in the history of childhood during
this period would lead us to estimate that it took place when he was
about one and one-half or two years old.[80]   The next chronological
reference point occurs with Damiano's getting Peter started on his
formal studies; in no case would this have been earlier than the age
of seven and in Peter's case it might have been as late as twelve.[81]

   The earliest infancy of Peter Damian was therefore not entirely so
frightful as John of Lodi's account might at first have made it seem.
Peter would have been unaware of many of the hostile goings-on about
him.  He was able to develop some degree, at least, of confidence or
basic trust, which would continue to sustain him throughout his life.
Yet even this early time was not wholly untroubled, and he must have
been partly blocked in developing a fully adequate capacity to sustain
anxiety.  Then, in his second or third year, separated forever from
his parents, he suffered the simultaneous loss of affection, trust,
and guidance.  In the hostile environment supplied by the unfriendly
brother, Peter had to make his initial attempts at exerting control
and exercising choice on his own, and this he had to do without encouragement for doing well or protection against failure and its concomitant humiliation.  When he should have been building up his own
initiative and industriousness, he was instead sinking further into
the morass of anxiety and guilt, which individuals seek to counter
with obsessional mechanisms and attempts at reparation.  Little wonder
that the one incident John of Lodi relates for this whole period is
that in which Peter tries to bring back, or restore, his father.
Probably the most successful period of Peter's life followed, when
Damiano took him in and gave him even better than a father's love.
With Damiano's help he began his schooling, which was to serve all
through adolescence as the main avenue for his intellectual and psychic
energies, each new success nourishing newer initiatives.  Outside that
one avenue he was lost, however, for we see him painfully and permanently traumatized by having to live close by the indiscreet unmarried lovers.  Freed from the protective discipline of formal study,
he held firmly to his well-earned erudition and began his career of

teaching.  The teaching itself was apparently both successful and ful-
filling, but the absence of other supports made his life as a city
schoolteacher unbearable.  The decision to become a hermit resolved
this problem:  he sacrificed nothing that he wanted; he kept everything that he needed and wanted.[82]

Peter Damian, if we have understood him at all correctly, was largely
deprived of the most critical affection and assurance of infancy,
failed to develop a strong sexual identity as a boy and adolescent,
found the lonely pursuit of his studies the only activity suitable
and rewarding for his energy and ability, could not bear the uncertainties and independence of a secular schoolmaster's career, and resolved this personal crisis of young manhood by immersing himself
totally in a promising new socio-religious movement, namely eremitism.
The hermitage did not supply a solution for every problem he had.  He
would remain, for example, obsessed with money and sex, and with his
own sinfulness.  Neither did conversion make it any easier for him to
give or receive affection.  He continued always to be confronted with
a problem of control, a conflict between the wish to hold on and the
wish to let go.  Should he keep the gift of silver from the Milanese
abbot?  Should he go back to his family home in Ravenna?  Should he
give vent to his anger?  Should he restrain his urge for sexual release?  Should he employ the full extent of his erudition?  Should
he give free rein to his scurrilous tongue?  Should he express his
thoughts and feelings freely and completely in writing?  Should he
discipline himself by auto-flagellation?  These were real issues for
Peter, posed in concrete situations in the present tense, some just
one time, others again and again through the years.

His responses varied.  His tormented vacillation over the gift of
silver led to the extreme conclusion that he would never again accept
a gift.  He went to his family home only because his sister was dying,
but he built up such formidable defenses against that place and the
memories he associated with it that his sensory perceptions were, for
the duration of the visit, effectively blocked.  He faced the question
of the extent to which learning could be brought to bear on theology,
a question that would perturb scholars during the next two centuries;
he had clear ideas on this subject (which did not seem to engage his

emotions significantly) and he was generally successful in adhering
to them himself.  Still, his saying that Christ was his grammar ("mea
grammatica Christus est") displayed a fundamental, lingering doubt
about the value of his own learning.[83]  He probably engaged in no
activity with greater abandon than he did in writing.  He acknowledged
that he liked to write; he was successful at it; he said it rescued
him from boredom; and indeed he indulged himself in it.  He was particularly self-assured with regard to his desire--and to the right-
ness of his desire--to curb both his anger and his sexual urges.  He
was sure that they were both dangers that needed to be suppressed, and
he felt sure that he dealt with them adequately.

The path Peter chose was most efficacious, and his having taken it
is a sign not of weakness or resignation but rather of strength and
initiative.  The foundation of this inner strength had been laid in
earliest infancy when his mother was still alive and caring for him.
Peter entered upon a form of life that permitted him to marshall his
talents and exploit them constructively and fully.  By assuming the
spiritually exalted role of hermit he placed himself at a social and
physical distance from the people and things he had had difficulty in
coping with directly.  From such a distance he could better control
his contacts with that world, determining when and how and in what
form those contacts would take place.  The means usually chosen was
writing, a means in which distance was maintained and in which, as
we have observed, he was particularly unrestrained.  He sought self-
control partly through flagellation, which, while it served him as he
wished, at the same time gave him erotic pleasure and relieved him
from some of the pressures of guilt.  His isolation and judicious
balancing of his own forces reduced to a minimum any dissipation of
energies, gathering them instead into a prodigious and accomplished
creativity.  He had withdrawn into a hermit's cell, which he made the
center of his world, beautifying and ennobling it by both deeds and
words.  He was never free of suffering, but as we recall the intensity
of that suffering, which he never wanted to discuss fully but which
he nonetheless failed to hide completely from our view, we stand in
greater awe of his restraint, discretion, self-awareness, and
charity.[84]

The Peter Damian we have hitherto known is flat, two-dimensional, bloodless, frankly rather boring, and not altogether believable.  He is like some Byzantine icon, and the context in which he has been set is as imaginary as a field of glittering gold.  Our historical sophistication permits us to appreciate the beauty and significance of icons, but that does not make them a suitable means of expression for us, living and trying to understand life in the final quarter of the twentieth century.  Materials sufficient for bringing Peter Damian back to life may not exist, but with the texts we have, we begin to see, if only as through a morning mist, the solid form of a man:  he breathes, he has blood in his veins, he is acquainted with grief (and to a lesser extent joy), he grows--steadily--older.

Chapter 22

## An "Angel of Philadelphia" in the Reign of Philip the Fair: The Case of Guiard of Cressonessart

Robert E. Lerner

Which of the following great nineteenth-century historians would have developed an interest in a medieval religious zealot who called himself "the Angel of Philadelphia": Henry Charles Lea, Charles-Victor Langlois, or Heinrich Seuse Denifle? The correct answer is none of the above, for as disparate as the proclivities of these three great scholars were, they all had in common an indifference to, if not an outright impatience with, the seemingly more bizarre varieties of religious experience. Lea and Langlois agreed that anyone who called himself an Angel of Philadelphia must have been mad, and Denifle ignored the case even though he should have been aware of it. It would be a renewed intolerance to take nineteenth-century historiography to task for not having the interests that some of us have now, but the indifference of these three medievalists to the case of the Angel of Philadelphia led them into dereliction of duties in their own chosen fields--the history of the medieval Inquisition, the French monarchy under Philip the Fair, and the personnel of the University of Paris--because the documents that tell of the Angel of Philadelphia cast light on all three topics. As for the history of heterodoxy which neither Lea, Langlois, nor Denifle cared about, the Angel of Philadelphia was noteworthy for being an unlicensed exponent of the apostolic life who--hardly like a madman--espoused historical views that were in the tradition of such sophisticated thinkers as Joachim of Fiore and Saint Bonaventura.[1]

Henry Charles Lea at least first called the Angel's case to scholarly attention. Lea, the rich private American scholar, never so much as set foot in Europe, let alone the Archives Nationales in Paris, where the documents concerning the Angel of Philadelphia are located.[2] He simply hired copyists (who very well may have considered _him_ to have been an angel of Philadelphia) to do his archival work for him,

and it is remarkable that he found and published as many new documents
as he did by this method of remote control.  Through his helpers, Lea
became aware of documents in a layette of the Trésor des Chartes pertaining to the case of a woman named Marguerite Porete, who was burned
for heresy in 1310 in Paris, and of related documents concerning a
man tried for heresy at the same time:  the Angel of Philadelphia,
whose real name was Guiard of Cressonessart.  But in an appendix to
his History of the Inquisition of the Middle Ages Lea published only
the documents he considered to be the most important, thereby pre-
senting only a partial dossier on Marguerite Porete and neglecting
entirely the documents concerning Guiard of Cressonessart.  Lea did
treat the latter briefly in his text in a way which shows that he had
read the relevant documents, but he made no mention of the documents
in his footnotes and showed his lack of interest in the Angel's ideas
by concluding that "his brain seems to have turned."[3]

Much more surprising was the negligence of Charles-Victor Langlois,
"érudit impeccable" and the most respected authority of his day on the
reign of Philip the Fair.[4]  In 1894 Langlois published a short article
on Marguerite Porete in which he edited a piece concerning her condemnation from the Trésor des Chartes left unpublished by Lea, and
also a record of the examination of Guiard of Cressonessart from the
same layette.[5]  The latter is the surest guide extant concerning
Guiard's ideas, but all Langlois had to say in commenting on it was
the observation--probably borrowed from Lea--that "ce pauvre homme...,
sans doute, avait la tête un peu dérangée."  Ironically, this same
Langlois, who in his Introduction aux études historiques stressed the
importance of gathering all the available documents on a particular
subject,[6] did not even mention that there were still more documents
concerning "ce pauvre homme," as well as one more concerning the trial
of Marguerite Porete in the same layette used by Lea and himself.
Yet no one since has detected the omission.  Shortly after Langlois'
article appeared either the notoriously censorious H. S. Denifle or
his aide E. Chatelain called attention to some of Langlois' editorial
mistakes in their Chartularium universitatis Parisiensis but omitted
any mention of the documents ignored by Langlois, even though they all
certainly belonged in the Chartularium.[7]  Nor has there since been

anything more than passing reference to the trial or ideas of the
"Angel of Philadelphia," despite the fact that the related case of
Marguerite Porete has attracted great interest in the last decades.[8]

Given this history of omissions, it seems best to begin with a list
of all the relevant documents in that seemingly bottomless layette
(J. 428), a carton described in the published inventory as containing
documents pertaining only to the "Albigeois, 1225-1310."[9] There are
in fact documents concerning the Albigensians in layette J. 428, long
since edited.[10] Remaining are six documents pertaining to the cases
of Marguerite Porete and Guiard of Cressonessart.[11] The first, J. 428,
#15, is the only original document. It is a notarial instrument that
begins with a judgment of theologians of the University of Paris,
dated April 11, 1310 (new style--as are all following dates), declaring
extracts from a book written by Marguerite Porete--now identified as
the extant Mirror of Simple Souls--to be heretical. Then it proceeds
to the formal condemnation of Marguerite by the papal Inquisitor
William of Paris, dated Sunday, May 31, 1310, and concludes with the
formal condemnation of Guiard, issued on the same date. Characteristically, Marguerite Porete's condemnation was edited by Lea, who said
nothing about the other parts of the document, and the judgment of
the theologians was edited by Langlois, who said nothing about the
condemnation of Guiard of Cressonessart.

The second relevant document, J. 428 #16, has hitherto been entirely
unknown. It is a copy notarized on October 4, 1310 of a notarial
instrument containing a judgment by canon lawyers of April 3, 1310
on the case of Guiard of Cressonessart. J. 428 #17, also never mentioned by Lea or Langlois, is an unofficial copy of the central text
of #16, probably made from the now missing original. J. 428 #18 is
an unofficial copy of a second judgment on Guiard's case, dated
April 9, 1310, made by most of the same canon lawyers who issued the
first judgment. Most of this text was published by Langlois, who,
however, did not indicate that he omitted the beginning and the end.
J. 428 #19 is the most remarkable omission by Lea and Langlois because
it pertains solely to Marguerite Porete. It is an unofficial copy of
a judgment of the same canon lawyers who dealt with Guiard's case with
substantially similar wording as #17 and issued on the same date,

April 3, 1310. Finally, J. 428 #19<u>bis</u> is the only document of all
those in the dossier which has been fully edited (by Lea). It is a
copy of the judgment of the canon lawyers (now to be seen as the
second one) concerning Marguerite Porete, dated May 9, 1310. Although
Lea did edit this completely, he dated it falsely.[12]

The sum of these documents allows us now to reconstruct most of the
judicial proceedings concerning Guiard in order to see how the
Inquisitor William wrestled with an "Angel" and, incidentally, to add
some details concerning Marguerite Porete. Guiard, from Cressonessart
in the diocese of Beauvais, was arrested late in 1308 in Paris by order
of the papal Inquisitor William of Paris for "aiding and defending"
Marguerite Porete. Guiard was probably arrested at the same time as
Marguerite because the judgments of canon lawyers of April 3, 1310,
refer to both of them as having already been imprisoned for almost a
year and a half. We can only speculate about what "aiding and defending" Marguerite really meant: Guiard, in his subsequent testimony
of 1310, said that he "exposed himself" at Paris for her sake, but it
is unclear whether this was by word or deed. In any event, having
tried to intervene for Marguerite, who was "vehemently" suspected of
heresy, he became suspect himself, and, exactly like her, for almost
a year and a half refused to take the oath necessary for his examination. Finally, in March of 1310 the Inquisitor William called together a collection of Parisian theologians and canon lawyers for
advice about both cases.[13] This resulted on April 3 in judgments of
the canon lawyers which in similar terms declared that Guiard and
Marguerite had already been so contumacious that they should be condemned as heretical and turned over to the secular arm. Apparently
these judgments were brought as an ultimate threat in the succeeding
days to Guiard and Marguerite, who reacted very differently. For
Guiard, the threat of death had the desired effect: he suddenly decided to cooperate and on April 9 the canon lawyers were able to issue
another judgment based on his sworn examination. Thereafter he recanted and was saved from the stake.[14] But Marguerite remained steadfast and the Inquisitor could only present extracts from her book to
theologians from the University of Paris who declared them heretical
on April 11. On May 9 the canon lawyers pronounced her to be a

relapsed heretic and on May 31 she and Guiard were formally sentenced, he to life imprisonment and she to be handed over to the secular arm, which saw to her burning the next day.[15]

The concurrent arrest, trial, and condemnation of Guiard and Marguerite suggests that they must have been intimate partners in alleged heresy.  Lea, indeed, went so far as to call Guiard a "disciple of Marguerite."[16]  But there are indications that they may have met only in Paris at the eleventh hour.  Marguerite came from Hainaut and before 1308 had twice been apprehended:  once in Valenciennes and again in the same region, within territory under the jurisdiction of the Bishop of Cambrai.  Guiard, on the other hand, came from the diocese of Beauvais--Cressonessart is today Cressonsacq, a small town four-teen kilometers northeast of Clermont-en-Beauvaisis--and referred in his testimony to having been previously in Paris and Reims.  Since both Marguerite and Guiard were wanderers, it is possible that they had met each other before 1308, but our present evidence makes it seem more likely that they wandered in different territories.  Chances are either that Marguerite had fled to Paris as a fugitive from inquisi-torial prosecution and that Guiard first met and aided her there, or that she was escorted to Paris under inquisitorial custody and that Guiard impetuously tried to intervene for her.

Whether they knew each other before 1308 or not, it is false to assume that because they were tried together they held the same be-liefs.  Marguerite was a "Free Spirit."  That is to say that she taught a daring version of the doctrine that the individual soul can become united with God this side of paradise and can thereby reach a state of extreme "annihilation" or passivity.  Almost none of this, however, is to be found in the testimony of Guiard.[17]  He, rather, was set in the conviction that he was called to be an apostle of a new dispensation in history.  Far from insanely thinking himself to be a real angel, he explained that the term "angel" was the name of his office and that "Philadelphia" meant for him "saving the adherence to the Lord."[18]  As this and other parts of his testimony indicate, he considered himself to be a minister and defender of a special group of faithful individuals who "adhered to the Lord."  The term "Angel of Philadelphia" comes from the Book of Revelation (3:7-13) and Guiard's testimony reveals that he had given much thought to this text as well as to certain current interpretations of it.

Asked who "sent" him to be Angel of Philadelphia, Guiard replied that he was sent by "him who has the key of David," meaning, as he explained, Christ. The purpose of this choice of words becomes clear on viewing the third chapter of Revelation where John is commanded to write to the Angel (i.e., minister) of the Church of Philadelphia that "he that hath the key of David" knows the Angel's "works" and has set before the Angel "an open door." Guiard too felt that Christ had set before him an "open door," which for him was the opening of the meaning of Scripture. He felt that this special illumination and calling as Angel of Philadelphia had been granted to him more than four years earlier in a moment when he was in the lower royal chapel in Paris (i.e., the Sainte Chapelle), but he also said that he reckoned that the office of Angel of Philadelphia had been granted to him twenty years before his illumination.[19] Asked whether anyone else had been "sent" in the same manner, he responded decisively in the negative: Angels of Philadelphia could be sent only one at a time and there could be no other until he was gone.

The Inquisitor was most anxious to know whether Guiard believed in the existence of more than one Church, and here he came to the central part of Guiard's understanding of Church history. Asked what he understood by the seven churches of the Apocalypse, Guiard replied that there was always only one Church but that this Church went through different "states." At different times the Church would shine forth more in one "state" than another and would take its name from that preferred "state." Thus the Church of Philadelphia represented a state that was embodied by those "runners" (meaning wanderers?) who give "everything away, wishing to hold to evangelical rigor."[20] Guiard, moved in his hearing by the fear of death, insisted that the members of the Church of Philadelphia acted without offense to divine dispensations or those of the (Roman) Church, adding that all who adhered to Christ (i.e., all the members of the Church at large) were able to be saved. Nonetheless, the members of the Church of Philadelphia--the "adherents of the Lord"--were most likely to be saved.

It was as their "angel" that Guiard felt his special calling. This
involved no small risk since it meant not merely ministering to the
"adherents of the Lord" but actively defending them. Thus, even
though Guiard was at the end of his life and of "little strength"--
another phrase from Revelation 3--he had "exposed himself" for such
"adherents" against the Dominicans and Franciscans at Reims after the
Franciscans there had preached against them. Similarly, he had "exposed himself" at Paris for the sake of Marguerite Porete. Indeed,
he stressed that the authority of his office, granted to him specially,
was to stand against all who impugned "adherence to the Lord" when
those who had the office in the Church for so doing were silent.

The Inquisitor's last set of recorded questions concerned Guiard's
coreligionaries. Asked whether others knew of his calling, Guiard
replied in the affirmative, indicating that others who knew of it
wore "the habit of Christ" that he himself wore. He had warned them,
he said, not to wear this "habit of a new order" on their own authority,
clearly a reference to the prohibition of new orders in 1274 by the
Second Council of Lyons. Rather, they were to wear it only on having
received the authority to do so from Christ. Asked whether those who
wore "tabards" were of his society, he said that not all of them were,
but only those who wore in addition "a long tunic and a leathern waistband." The waistband in particular was the "essence of the habit"
(i.e., Guiard's "habit of Christ") but he also considered those who
wore tabards alone to be "adherents of the Lord." In other words,
Guiard distinguished first between members of the Church at large
and "adherents of the Lord," and then between "adherents" at large--
who wore tabards--and members of his own "society"--who wore tabards,
long tunics, and leathern waistbands.

Who were the people, prima facie suspicious to the Inquisitor, who
wore tabards? Undoubtedly they were those semi-religious known as
beghards, who in Guiard's day were coming under increasing clerical
fire.[21]  In 1310, just when Guiard's examination was taking place in
Paris, a provincial council of Trier--a province that bordered on
that of Reims where Guiard had been active--issued a decree against
beghards who wore "tabards, long tunics, and long hoods."[22]  Since
the full dossier on Guiard's trial has never been studied carefully,

it has escaped notice that the first judgment of the canon lawyers
refers to Guiard himself as beguinus, the French-Latin term for beghard.  Similarly, the second judgment calls him pseudo religiosus,
another expression with the same meaning.  Complications arise from
the fact that Guiard's condemnation specifies that he be deprived of
all clerical privileges and stripped of his clerical insignia, imply-
ing that he had once been ordained.  Perhaps this clause was just a
precaution taken against someone who had been assuming some clerical
functions in the ignorance of whether he was truly in orders or not.
But even if Guiard really had at one time been ordained, at the time
of his arrest he was certainly acting like a beghard.

   Guiard's society of those who wore tabards, long tunics, and leathern
belts must be understood as a particular group of beghards who were
not united in any formal way to other similar groups.  The importance
Guiard attached to the particular habit and belt is indicated by the
only first-hand chronicle report we have.  According to this, he said
that he would not remove the belt or the habit even at the order of
the pope, indeed, if the pope so ordered it would be sinful.  Only
in the end, when faced with death, did Guiard remove the offending
garments.[23]  To understand his vehemence it must be remembered that
he was aware of the papal prohibition of new orders and habits but
had told his followers that they could wear their special habit (the
"habit of Christ") on the authority of Christ.  No doubt he regarded
the habit as having been granted miraculously.

   It was just this habit and belt, however, that were causes of particular offense.  Not only were new habits prohibited in 1274 but the
habit bound by a belt must have made Guiard and his followers look
like Augustinian or Franciscan friars.  The Augustinians wore a habit
bound by a zona pellicea, the same term used to describe Guiard's most
distinctive item of clothing.[24]  Guiard must therefore have looked
more like them than the Franciscans, who wore not leathern belts but
cords.[25]  As we will see later, Guiard no doubt chose the zona pellicea
not to imitate the Augustinians but on biblical and eschatological
grounds.  Yet in wearing any cincture at the waist at all and profes-
sing a life of evangelical rigor he and his followers must have appeared to be rivals of both Augustinians and Franciscans.  This

circumstance may help to explain the Franciscan hostility revealed in
Guiard's statement that he had "exposed himself" on behalf of "adherents of the Lord" at Reims against the Dominicans and Franciscans
after the Franciscans had preached against them.

It was not only Guiard's conduct and dress that were related to and
thus in conflict with that of contemporary Franciscans; so was his
thought, which was descended ultimately from that of Joachim of Fiore.
More than a century before Guiard, Joachim too felt that he had received a special insight into the meaning of Scripture in general and
the Book of Revelation in particular.  Joachim reported that he had
once been struggling with the meaning of Revelation for a year but a
certain passage had stood in his way like a great stone at the entrance
of a sepulchre.  Then suddenly at Easter, at the hour of the Resurrec-
tion, the stone was moved aside and in a dazzling moment of truth he
was allowed entrance into the meaning of the particular passage as
well as the whole Bible.[26]  Guiard's moment of truth in the Sainte
Chapelle had much in common with this, indeed, Guiard, just like
Joachim, felt "an opening of the entrance"--an image that both took
from Revelation 3:7-8.  Both Joachim and Guiard also attached great
importance to Christ's possession of the "key of David" mentioned in
the Apocalyptic message to the Angel of Philadelphia as a symbol for
the divine dispensation over spiritual truth:  Joachim placed the
words "key of David" in one of his most important "figures" in relation to a symbol for the deepest understanding of Scripture,[27] and
Guiard played on Christ's disposition over the "key of David" or "key
of excellence" in contradiction to the pope's disposition over the
mere "key of office" (i.e., key of St. Peter).

Above all, Guiard's conception of the role of the Angel and Church
of Philadelphia was ultimately Joachite in inspiration.  For Joachim
a basic means for understanding the hidden truth of Scripture was the
concordance he saw between the twelve Old Testament tribes and twelve
New Testament churches.  Joachim found in Joshua (18:2) that the twelve
tribes were divided into groups of five and seven:  five who received
their inheritance first and seven who received it later.  For him
there were also five "principal churches" (Jerusalem, Antioch,
Alexandria, Constantinople, and Rome--not all to be found literally

in the New Testament, but no matter) and seven churches "remaining,"
that is to say, the Apocalyptic seven churches of Asia.  The first
five of each set symbolized the five Augustinian ages of the world
from Adam to Christ and the "remaining" seven the seven "times" (<u>tem-</u>
<u>pora</u>) of Church history from the advent of Christ to the end of time.[28]

   Calculated from there, the Church of Philadelphia, the sixth of the
seven last churches, represented the sixth "time" of the Church and
one that for Joachim was most propitious.  This sixth time was to be
one of transition to the seventh or ultimate time of earthly Church
history which was identical to Joachim's famous third "status" of the
Holy Spirit.[29]  In Joachim's words:  "from the sixth time of the
second status must begin the third status and new order which is created in the image of the Holy Spirit."[30]  In this sixth time divine
truth was to begin to become clearer, for the Angel of the Church of
Philadelphia "has been given to know in spirit the hidden sacraments."[31]
Joachim also wrote that the Church of Philadelphia and the last Church
of Laodicea symbolized two new orders that would bridge the second
and third "states" and be more "spiritual" than all the earlier
orders.[32]  Here Joachim clearly foreshadowed Guiard of Cressonessart's
view that the Church of Philadelphia represented a special new class
of the godly.

   Of course Joachim's and Guiard's schemes were not identical.  Joachim,
needless to say, did not envisage himself as the Angel of Philadelphia.
In fact, he did not even believe that the time of the Church of
Philadelphia, or sixth time of the Church, had yet come, although he
saw it as imminent.[33]  Also, although he conceived of this time as
one of growing spiritual insight, he never equated it, as Guiard did,
with a new dispensation of evangelical poverty.  Guiard most likely
never read Joachim and may not even have heard of him, for without
doubt his particular kind of Joachism was the sort transmitted by
thirteenth-century Franciscans.

   In the past it was generally assumed that the only Franciscans who
were attracted to Joachism were the zealots or "spirituals," but it
is now clear that even that greatest of "moderate" Franciscans, Saint
Bonaventura, was appreciably indebted to Joachim in shaping his own
theology of history.  Bonaventura's modified Franciscan Joachism was

more closely related to the testimony of Guiard of Cressonessart than
were Joachim's writings themselves.  For one, he believed that the
sixth period of Church history, betokened by the Angel and Church of
Philadelphia, had already come, even though it had by no means reached
its culmination.[34]  Bonaventura glossed Philadelphia (here following
a medieval exegetical tradition) as meaning "saving" or "conserving
the inheritance."  Likewise, he equated the Angel--who represented
the eleventh New Testament church--with Joseph--who founded the eleventh Old Testament tribe--as one who would store grain for future
famine.[35]  Thus the Angel and Church of Philadelphia, both of which
had a special understanding of Scripture,[36] were preservers of spiritual treasure.  Although they already existed they also foreshadowed the
future marvelous seventh period of Church history which Bonaventura,
like Joachim, expected on earth.

In addition, Bonaventura equated the Angel of Philadelphia with the
Apocalyptic Angel of the Sixth Seal,[37] who for him was a symbol for
Saint Francis, sealed, like this Angel, "with the seal of the living
God."  Therefore the Angel of Philadelphia, by implication, was also
a symbol for Saint Francis, and the Church of Philadelphia represented
the community of 144,000 elect sealed by the sixth Angel.  In
Bonaventura's thought, these elect stood in one sense for the Franciscan order of the present that foreshadowed the eschatological order
of the seventh time of the Church.[38]  Guiard of Cressonessart changed
this only by replacing Saint Francis with himself, and by replacing
the Franciscan order with his own band of beghards.

Viewing Guiard's testimony in the light of Bonaventura's theology
of history also helps to elucidate the significance Guiard attached
to his leathern belt (zona pellicea).  This appears as the garb of
Elijah in the Old Testament (4 Kings 1:8) and of John the Baptist in
the New (Matth. 3:4; Mark 1:6).  For Bonaventura both these figures--
voices crying in the wilderness--were forerunners of Saint Francis.
Elijah was associated with John the Baptist by Christ, who called
John the returned Elijah (Matth. 11:14; Mark 9:12-13; Luke 1:17),
and John was associated with Saint Francis by the fact that Francis'
original name was John.[39]  Moreover, Saint Francis, most notably in
the miracle of the fiery chariot, showed himself to be, like John, a

returned Elijah.  For Bonaventura all three were heralds of a new
dispensation:  Elijah and John of Christ's coming, and Francis of the
coming of the final earthly age.  Once more, it seems that Guiard
merely transposed one of the terms in the equation, making himself the
new composite Elijah and John the Baptist instead of Saint Francis.

Saint Bonaventura delivered his major statement on the course of
history--his Collationes in Hexaemeron--at the University of Paris in
the summer of 1273, about thirteen years before the time Guiard of
Cressonessart first reckoned himself to have been the Angel of
Philadelphia.  Guiard probably had no first-hand knowledge of
Bonaventura's Collationes, but it does seem possible that some of
Bonaventura's theories could have filtered through to him from Franciscan circles.  At the least, Bonaventura's interpretation of Saint
Francis as the Angel of the Sixth Seal and the returned Elijah was
familiar to every Franciscan through Bonaventura's Legenda maior,
obligatory reading for Franciscans.

Another possible influence on Guiard was Peter John Olivi, who was
most active in southern France but did appear in Paris in 1292.
Olivi's Lectura super Apocalypsim, written around then, also identified the seven churches of Asia with seven periods of Church history.[40]  For him, just as carnal Judaism was rejected by the coming
of Christ in the sixth age of the world, so in the sixth age of the
Church (the time of the Church of Philadelphia, in which he thought
he lived) the carnal Church would be rejected by the renewal of the
Christian law, life, and cross personified by Saint Francis.[41]  To
this degree his thought resembled Bonaventura's, but Olivi went further by interpreting the granting of the key of David to the Angel
of Philadelphia as a sign for the opening of a third historical sta-
tus--a Joachite concept eschewed by Bonaventura.[42]  Since Guiard of
Cressonessart said nothing in his testimony about a third status or
any sort of trinitarian division of history, he appears to have been
less a Joachite than Olivi was.

As a further indication of how certain Franciscan-Joachite ideas
were in the air around 1300 it can be pointed out that Guiard was not
the only heterodox thinker of that time who attached special importance
to the Angel of Philadelphia.  In August of 1300 the Italian heretic

Fra Dolcino issued a manifesto in which he referred to the seven
angels of the seven churches of Asia, interpreting those of Ephesus,
Pergamon, Sardis, and Laodicea to be Saint Benedict, Pope Sylvester
I, Saint Francis, and Saint Dominic, respectively.  After them came
representatives of the "apostolic congregation" of the last days:
the Angel of Smyrna, whom Dolcino saw as Gerard Segarelli (the founder
of Dolcino's sect of Apostles); the Angel of Thyatira, whom Dolcino
saw as himself; and finally the Angel of Philadelphia, who was to be
a "holy pope" (papa sanctus) who would come after the death of Pope
Boniface VIII and reign until the coming of Antichrist.[43]  Thus, although Dolcino did not consider himself to be the Angel of Philadelphia,
he placed that Angel at the top of his scale of apostolic and eschatological values.  The exact sources of his ideas cannot be identified
any more precisely than can those of Guiard, but scholars generally
agree that Dolcino too was influenced by Joachism.[44]

  Guiard of Cressonessart can thus be seen as one who, like Dolcino,
linked adherence to a code of apostolic poverty with a theory of progressive historical development, and who may count as a hitherto unnoticed example of the spread of Franciscan Joachite ideas around 1300.
This, of course, did not interest the canon lawyers who judged him.
For them the major issue was his position toward the papacy.  Even
though Guiard explained that there was really only one Church and that
the "adherents of the Lord" acted without offense to it, his testimony
was still hostile to the authority of the pope and the ecclesiastical
hierarchy.  Not only did he maintain that he was "sent" by Christ instead of the pope and imply that those who had the office in the Church
for defending the true adherents of apostolic poverty were neglecting
their duties, but he gloried in his own unauthorized office and, according to the well-informed chronicler, first refused to remove his
illicit habit even if so commanded by the pope.  Thus the canon lawyers
concluded that Guiard proposed a division in the Church and judged him
to be heretical on the grounds of canons that ordered obedience to
papal authority.

  This concern for obedience to the papacy in the Paris of Philip the
Fair may initially appear a bit strange, but in fact it is quite fitting.  To appreciate this we must first see whether Guiard's trial can

be taken as an expression of royal policy. The answer seems to be
that King Philip and his ministers probably did not order the trial
or interfere directly in its proceedings (there is no evidence at all
for the theory that they did), but that the royal presence and the
broad dictates of royal policy must have been felt throughout. How
could it have been otherwise when the director of the case, Brother
William of Paris, O.P., was an intimate of the king of France? William
was chosen to be Philip's confessor about 1305, and in 1307 presided
as Inquisitor over Philip's campaign against the Templars so zealously
that Heinrich Finke has written: "never in the Middle Ages had Inquisition and Crown worked so closely together."[45]  Indeed, even though
Clement V suspended William in his inquisitorial duties, he continued
for a while thereafter to act in them to the king's pleasure. In July
of 1308, only as the result of royal pressure, Clement V restored
William as Inquisitor, despite the fact that the pope felt that "it
went against his honor."[46]  There is no further evidence of William
participating in the case of the Templars after that--perhaps pope
and king made a tacit agreement that he would be restored if he stayed
out of this sensitive case--but we now see how he took up his inquisitorial activities against Marguerite Porete and Guiard of Cressonessart
late in 1308.[47]  From then until his death sometime before November 28,
1314, he remained sufficiently in the king's good graces to be a beneficiary of the royal will of May 17, 1311.[48]

It is impossible to estimate as closely as this the relations to
the king of all the theologians and lawyers involved in the case. In
any event, the role of the theologians was apparently minimal. (Theologians did play a more important role in the case of Marguerite
Porete, but, considering the extracts from her book they saw, it is
hard to see how they could have judged them differently from the way
they did.) As for the lawyers whose judgments were in the event decisive, only one, Hugh of Besançon, was an actor we know much about,
but he was certainly in tune with Capetian policy and adept at gaining
perquisites. Hugh was the son of the chief of the French party in
Besançon during a time when the Franche-Comté was being contested
between French and German interests.[49]  Like his father, Hugh threw
in his lot with France and was appropriately rewarded. Doctor of canon

law at Paris after August, 1302, at the latest, he became a canon of
Notre Dame of Paris sometime before November, 1305.[50]   On October 25,
1307, he witnessed the confession of the Grand Master of the Templars
in Paris, and in August of 1308 he was paid three gold florins by the
pope for unspecified services in the case of the Templars that could
hardly have been displeasing to the French king.[51]   Around this time
Philip the Fair charged Hugh with the instruction of Jeanne, the heiress of the Franche-Comté who was engaged to the king's son Philip
(later Philip V).[52]   Clearly Hugh ingratiated himself with the young
Philip as well, because when the latter became regent of France in
1316 he made Hugh a master of the Grand Chambre of the Parlement of
Paris.[53]   Finally, in 1326 Hugh capped his successful career by becoming bishop of Paris.

   The surest sign of royal interest in the cases of Guiard of
Cressonessart and Marguerite Porete comes from the survival of the
relevant documents in layette J. 428 of the Archives Nationales.  These
belonged to Philip the Fair's ministers William of Nogaret and William
of Plaisians, after whose deaths they were deposited in the Trésor des
Chartes.[54]   Neither Nogaret nor his alter ego Plaisians was on the
scene in Paris in the spring of 1310, but they saw reason to obtain
the documents in question sometime between then and their roughly
contemporaneous deaths in 1313.[55]   The original notarial instrument
containing the condemnation of Guiard and Marguerite came into Nogaret's
hands, as did the notarized copy of the first judgment against Guiard,
for some unstated reason drawn up on October 4, 1310, months after
Guiard had been condemned.[56]   Likewise, the other surviving texts,
unofficial copies including the record of Guiard's interrogation,
turned up in Plaisians' papers.  These copies were probably made from
the originals, because the one containing the text of the first judgment against Guiard has better readings than the official transcript,
with which we can compare it.  Probably all the copies were made on
government order; certainly they were regarded with interest by two
of Philip the Fair's most prominent lawyers.

   Philip and his ministers were no doubt grateful for the occurrence
of two heresy trials in Paris in which no questionable motives could
be found at a time when the crown was pressing controversial proceedings

against the Templars, against Guichard, bishop of Troyes, and against the memory of Boniface VIII.[57]   Joseph R. Strayer has justly maintained that Philip the Fair, for all the questionable actions of his reign, was a man of genuine piety.[58]   No doubt, on grounds of conventional piety, Philip was pleased to see his confessor proceed against two alleged heretics, but he must have been still more pleased to have one of them condemned for disloyalty to the pope just when he wished to show his own loyalty.  Philip's ministers too must have been pleased, and, more, seem to have thought of using the trial documents for royal purposes in the future.  Thus Guiard of Cressonessart, who felt that Christ had set before him an "open door," was locked behind a closed door for life by the confessor of Philip the Fair, and this "angel," who preached a supposedly new historical dispensation of absolute poverty, had his memory preserved by men who represented a really new historical dispensation--the rise of the absolute state.

## Appendices

## The Documents Pertaining to the Trial of
## Guiard of Cressonessart

I.  Archives Nationales J. 428 #15--last section:
Guiard's Condemnation.[a]

Item.  In nomine Patris et Filii et Spiritus Sancti, Amen.  Quia
nobis fratri Guilelmo de Parisiis, Ordinis Predicatorum, inquisitori
heretice pravitatis in regno Francie auctoritate apostolica deputato,
constat legitime te Guiardum de Cressonessart, diocesis Belvacensis,
in fautoriam et defensionem Margarete de Hannonia dicte Porete ex
causis variis probabilibus super labe pravitatis predicte vehementer
suspecte et propter hoc per nos Parisius arrestate notorie incidisse,
et ob hoc et alia quedam de crimine heresis nobis esses suspectus
necnon et ex parte nostra competenter et canonice monitus fueris ne
nobis in nostro inquisicionis officio procedentibus impedimentum pres-
tares nec dicte Margarete sic predicta labe infecte preberes defensionem, auxilium, consilium seu favorem, in quibus te rebellem et contumacem invenimus, quoniam[?][b] pocius coram nobis in iudicio constitutus
pluries exortatus a nobis et requisitus et nichilominus sufficienter
et canonice monitus ut coram nobis iurares ad sancta Dei evangelia
super hiis que ad nostrum predictum officium pertinent tam de te quam
de aliis respondere et dicere plenam, puram et integram veritatem,
in quo effectus es contumax et rebellis respondere et iurare contemp-
nens, pro quibus contumaciis et hoc exigentibus de multorum peritorum
consilio in te sic pertinacem, contumacem et rebellem exigente iusticia
sentenciam excommunicacionis tulimus, et in scriptis quam excommunicacionis sentenciam fere per annum et dimidium in tue salutis dispendium postquam tibi notificata fuerat substinuisti animo pertinaci,
licet tibi pluries obtulerimus nos in forma ecclesie tibi absolucionis
beneficium impensuros, si hoc humiliter postulares, quod usque nunc
petere distulisti, propter que secundum sanctiones[c] canonicas te tanquam confessum et convictum de heresi et ut hereticum condempnare
possumus et debemus.
    Hiis eciam non contentus post omnia predicta coram nobis in iudicio
constitutus et iuramento demum a te prestito te in tantam vesaniam
erexisti ut te esse angelum Filadelphie assereres et constanter[?]
necnon et missum immediate a Christo qui habet clavem excellencie,
non a domino papa qui solum habet clavem ministerii ut dicebas, addens
quod non potest mitti alius a te nisi te deficiente ad salvandum adhesionem Domini vel adherentes Domino; quod et si ad alios ex zelo,
ad te tamen ex officio magis spectat, et quedam alia derogancia summi
pontificis potestati.  Ex quibus manifeste liquet quod divisionem ponis
in ecclesia militante, immo pocius ponis duas ecclesias militantes
ipsumque dominum papam non esse unum caput ecclesie militantis, que
veraciter reputanda sunt heretica et eciam tanquam heretica condemp-
nanda.
    Super quibus omnibus comunicato peritorum multorum tam in theologia

quam in iure canonico et civili deliberato consilio, et concordi de [1]
reverendi patris et domini domini G., Dei gracia Parisiensis Episcopi,
consilio et assensu, Deum et sacrosancta evangelia habentes pre oculis
sic perniciosa, sic erronea, sic derogancia catholice fidei veritati
dissimulare ulterius sana consciencia non valentes te Guiardum predictum ut hereticum finaliter condempnamus, denunciantes te esse privatum
omni privilegio clericali, supplicantes predicto patri reverendo ut
insignia clericalia tibi auferat et confestim, omnibus peractis; et
te ad murum perpetuum finaliter condempnamus, nobis et successoribus
nostris in predicto inquisicionis officio mitigandi, minuendi, mutandi,
aggravandi vel penitus absolvendi prout tua exegerint merita et nobis
et successoribus in predicto officio expedire videbitur potestate
retenta.

   Actum Parisius in Gravia, presente reverendo patre predicto, clero
et populo dicte civitatis, ibidem sollempniter congregatis Dominica
infra octavam Ascencionis, anno Domini M° CCC° decimo [Sunday, May 31,
1310]. Actum ut supra.

   Notarized with sign manual by Jacobus de Virtuto, diocese of Châlons-
sur-Marne, notary public.[2]

## II.  Archives Nationales J. 428 #16 & 17:
### First Judgment of Canon Lawyers concerning Guiard[a]

In Christi nomine, Amen.  Hoc est sumptum seu transcriptum cuiusdam instrumenti publici, cuius tenor de verbo ad verbum sequitur sub hac forma.

In nomine Domini, Amen.  Cum quidam beguinus nomine Guiardus de Cressonessart, dyocesis Belvacensis, in defensione et fautoria Margarete dicte Porete de Hanonia ex causis variis et probabilibus super labe pravitatis heresis suspecte et propter hoc per religiosum virum fratrem Guilelmum de Parisiis, Ordinis Predicatorum, inquisitorem pravitatis[b] eiusdem in regno Francie deputatum auctoritate apostolica arrestate,[b] publice et notorie se haberet et ob hoc et alia quedam de crimine heresis esset suspectus, dictusque inquisitor nolens contra dictum Guiardum super dicto crimine impetuose et indeliberate, immo iuris peritorum consilio mature procedere, magistros in theologie et decretorum facultatibus coram se fecit personaliter evocari eidem super consilium prestiturum anno Domini M° CCC° nono, indictione octava, mense Marcii, pontificatus sanctissimi patris et domini nostri domini Clementis divina providencia pape quinti anno quinto.  Ipsis igitur presente me notario et testibus infrascriptis ad hoc vocatis specialiter et rogatis congregatis magistris dictarum facultatum coram inquisitore predicto, videlicet:  venerabilibus et discretis viris magistris Symone de Gibervilla, decano[1]; Thoma penitentiario[2]; Iohanne de Gandavo, canonicis ecclesie Parisiensis[3]; Petro de Sancto Dyonisio, Ordinis Sancti Benedicti[4]; Gerardo de Sancto Victore[5]; Henrico de Alemannia[6]; Iohanne de Poilliaco[7]; Priore Vallis Scolarium[8]; Iohanne de Monte Sancti Eligii, canonico regulari Ordinis Sancti Augustini[9]; fratre Berengario, Ordinis Predicatorum[10]; fratre Iacobo de Esculo, Ordinis Minorum,[11] magistris in theologia; ac magistris G. dicto Fratre, archidiacono Laudonie in ecclesia Sancti Andree in Scocia, utriusque iuris professore[12]; Iohanne de Tellu[13]; Hugone de Bisuncio, canonico Parisiensis[14]; Henrico de Bethunia[12]; Petro de Valle[12], magistris in decretis, petiit dominus inquisitor a dictis magistris ut super dicto negocio sibi sanum consilium exhiberent.  Quidam magistri in theologia et decretis, deliberacione inter ipsos adinvicem habita pleniori consulendo, eidem inquisitori decreverunt stare consultacioni seu consilio magistrorum in decretis ipsisque tale consilium dederunt prout in litteris sigillis ipsorum sigillatis ut dicebant continetur que tales sunt:

[c]Universis presentes litteras inspecturis, Guilelmus dictus Frater, archidiaconus Laudonie in ecclesia Sancti Andree in Scocia; Hugo de Bisuncio, canonicus Parisiensis; Iohannes de Telluz,[d] canonicus Sancti Quintini in Viromandia; Henricus de Bethunia[e]; Petrus de Vallibus, curatus ecclesie Sancti Germani Autisiodorensis[f] de Parisiis, actu regentes Parisius in decretis, salutem in actore salutis.

Cum quidam beguinus nomine Guiardus de Cressonessart, dyocesis Belvacensis, in defensione et fautoria[g] Margarete[h] dicte Porete de Hanonia[i] ex causis variis probabilibus super labe pravitatis heretice suspecte et propter hoc per religiosum virum fratrem Guilelmum de Parisiis, Ordinis Predicatorum, inquisitorem pravitatis eiusdem in regno Francie deputatum auctoritate apostolica arrestate, publice

probabiliter et notorie se haberet et ob hoc et alia quedam de crimine
heresis esset suspectus, dictus inquisitor ut nobis intimavit in hunc
modum processit.

Ipsum namque Guiardum post moniciones[j] legitimas ex parte dicti inquisitoris canonice sibi factas de non impedjendo ipsum in suo inquisicionis officio procedentem, et non prestando[k] Margarete[h] predicte defensionem, auxilium seu favorem, in quibus inventus est contumax et rebellis, tandem coram se fecit personaliter presentari cui de dicenda
veritate super predictis et[l] aliis ad suum inquisicionis officium pertinentibus[m] ex officii sui debito detulit iuramentum, quod ipse obstin-
atus et pertinax subire seu prestare contumaciter recusavit, quamvis
postea sufficienter informatus ipsum fratrem Guilelmum plene[n] recogno-
sceret esse inquisitorem ac eciam fateretur.  Et propterea idem inquisitor ipsum in sua contumacia persistentem post multas exortaciones
salubres sibi factas ab eo maioris excommunicacionis vinculo innodavit,
quam quidem excommunicacionem fere per annum et dimidium in sue salutis
dispendium animo sustinuit indurato.  Qui prius et postea frequenter
de iurando et respondendo per eundem inquisitorem legitime requisitus
ipsi beneficium absolucionis in forma iuris inpendendum sepius offer-
entem iurare et respondere renuens contumaciter sicut prius absolucion-
em sibi oblatam petere vel recipere suam salutem refugiens non curavit.

Quibus peractis idem inquisitor quasi desperans de correctione Guiar-
di predicti quid ulterius esset agendum de iure in ipso negocio a nobis
licet ad ipsius negocii consummacionem non dubitetur sufficere consilium
in hac parte postulare curavit.  Nos autem tanquam obediencie filii et
fidei catholice zelatores ipsius inquisitoris iuste peticioni[o] annuen-
tes ut tenemur et decet iuxta modulum nostrum sibi sane consulendo
diximus et dicimus facto et processu prelibatis suppositis ulterius
contra dictum Guiardum sic fore iuxta iuris exigenciam procedendum,[p]
videlicet quod cum prefata defensio et fautoria heresis primo in
vehementem et postmodum in violentam presumpcionem transierit[q] suis
contumaciis,[r] rebellionibus et pertinaciis pensatis, et hoc exigentibus
iuris interpretacione, prefatus Guiardus infelix pro heretico est
habendus et diffinitive tanquam hereticus condempnandus relinquendusque
curie seculari debitam ulcionem pro qualitate criminis recepturus, nisi
confestim ante sentenciam vel post penituerit, recurrens[s] sponte ad
fidei catholice unitatem et errorem suum ad arbitrium ipsius inquisitoris[t] publice consenciens abiurare.  Quo[u] casu pro tanti sui excessus
satisfactione subeunda et ne alios forsan infirmos pestiferis doctrinis
inficiat in carcerem perpetuum merito detrudetur.  In cuius rei testimonium ad requisicionem inquisitoris eiusdem sigilla nostra presentibus
duximus apponenda.

Datum Parisius, anno Domini M° CCC° nono, die veneris post Dominicam
qua cantatur letare Ierusalem (Friday, April 3, 1310, n.s.).[v]

Actum in domo fratrum Predicatorum Parisius, anno, indictione, mense,
die et pontificatu predictis, presentibus religiosis viris fratribus
Alexandro de Marcia[15]; Radulpho de Hotot[16]; Iacobo de Dyvione, Cister-
ciensis Ordinis[17]; et Gregorio de Luca, Ordinis Sancti Augustini,[18]
magistris in theologia, qui eciam consilio dictorum magistrorum consen-
serunt et acquiererunt expresse testibus ad hoc vocatis specialiter et
rogatis.

Originally notarized by Evenus Phili de Sancto Nicasio, diocese of
Quimper.[19]

This copy notarized with sign manual by Jacobus de Virtuto[19] in
Paris on October 4, 1310.

III.   Archives Nationales J. 428 #18:   Second Judgment
of Canon Lawyers concerning Guiard[a]

Universis presentes litteras inspecturis, G. dictus Frater, archidiaconus Laudonie in ecclesie Sancti Andree in Scocia; H. de Bisuncio,
canonicus Parisiensis; Iohannes de Theuleu, canonicus Sancti Quintini
in Viromandia; P. de Vallibus curatus ecclesie Sancti Germani Autis-
siodorensis de Parisiis, actu regentes Parisius in decretis, salutem
in actore salutis.
    Cum quidam[b] pseudo religiosus nomine Guiardus oriens ex se et intus
occidens ex variis probabilibus causis super heretica pravitate suspectus haberetur ipsius pravitatis labe necabiliter diffamatus, vir
venerabilis ac devotus, frater G. de Parisiis, Ordinis Predicatorum,
pravitatis heretice inquisitor a sede apostolica in regno Francie
deputatus, prefatum Guiardum sic  suspectum ad presenciam suam fecit
evocari, et tandem post multas contumacias et tergiversaciones varias
ipse Guiardus coram inquisitore predicto personaliter comparuit, qui
de dicenda veritate super sibi impositis et expositis in hac parte
per inquisitorem eundem super infra articulis scriptis et iudicialiter
requisitus deposuit et confessus est in hunc modum, prout nobis dictus
inquisitor intimavit:
    [c]Dicens videlicet se esse angelum Philadelphie, et, exponens verbum,
dicit quod angelus est nomen officii, non nature, et Philadelphia interpretatur salvans adhesionem Domini vel adherentem Domino; et sic reputo
me missum ad salvandum adhesionem Domini vel adherentem Domino in ecclesia Dei.
    Et tunc requisitus a quo missus erat, respondit quod ab illo qui
nabet clavem David, exponens quod per hec[d] intelligit Christum qui
habet clavem excellencie, et quod vicarius eius dominus papa habet
clavem ministerii.  Et addit quod quatuor annis elapsis et ultra percepit illud officium sibi datum fuisse, sed reputat sibi datum fuisse
vinginti annis elapsis cum primo percepit a dictis quatuor annis vel
citra, et hoc Parisius in capella domini regis inferiori, et quod
modus percepcionis vel[e] recepcionis illius officii, et apercionis ostii, fuit in momento per aperturam intellectus scripturarum.
    Item requisitus si sciat quod alter sit missus eodem modo, respondit
quod non, nec potest mitti nisi unus in singulari, nisi ille defecerit,
et tunc potest alter mitti.
    Item requisitus quid intelligit de septem ecclesiis designatis in
Apocalipsi, respondit quod semper est una ecclesia, sed bene sunt et
esse possunt diversi status in ea, et secundum diversa tempora ecclesia
magis relucet in uno statu quam in alio secundum missionem divinam,
et magis se denominat ab illo statu in quo magis se diligit.
    Requisitus cum sit una ecclesia, quid est ecclesia Philadelphie,
respondit quod inter diversos status ecclesie est quidam status currencium qui omnia dimiserunt, volentes tenere rigorem evangelicum,
et pretendere lucem suam per conversacionem extrinsecam, pretendentem
ardorem interiorem, et licite absque iniuria dispensacionis ecclesie
vel divine, et in istis habet principium suum ecclesia Philadelphia,
licet in omnibus Christo adherentibus possit salvari, tamen in istis
precipue, et inter istos ille qui est angelus Philadelphie habet quam-
dam prerogativam secundum donum sibi factum a Domino in speciali

missione et apercione ostii.

Et dixit quod sicut in fine vite sue fuit percussus pro scelere
populi et factus est modice virtutis in corpore ita quod non potuit
baiulare crucem, ita est vel potest esse quod angelus mitteretur et
percuteretur a Domino pro scelere populi in statu innocencie, hoc est
antequam peccaverit mortaliter, et extimat talem angelum missum et
percussum pro scelere populi. Addit eciam quod pro sustinendis et
deffendendis aliquibus personis adherentibus, paratus esset se exponere
usque ad mortem quousque cognovisset ius suum esse vel non, id est
utrum ille esset adherens Domino vel non, et quod ipse Remis se exposuit pro talibus personis contra Predictores et Minores, qui Minores
directe predicabant contra tales, et Parisius eciam se exposuit pro
Marguareta dicta Porret. Dicit eciam qui loquitur quod auctoritas
sui officii, quod est sibi speciale, est insurgere contra omnem hominem
impugnantem adherentem Domino vel adhesionem Domini ubi silerent illi
qui habent officium in ecclesia hoc agendi.

Et tunc requisitus utrum magis spectet ad ipsum quam ad alium,
respondit quod ad alios pertinet ex zelo, et videtur quod magis pertinet ad ipsum ex officio.

Item requisitus si sciant aliqui quod ipse habeat illud donum,
respondit quod sic, quia dixit aliquibus recipientibus habitum Christi
(intelligens de tali habitu qualem ipse defert) aperturam ostii; quibus
dixit quod bene caverent, quia non debebant recipere intencione recipi-
endi habitum nove religionis[l] auctoritate propria, sed habitum auctori-
tatem a Christo. Et addit qui loquitur quod quia non posset[f] habere
patronum in Novo Testamento propter prohibicionem ecclesie, resumit in
Veteri, monicione Salvatoris libertatem dantis et auctorizantis.

Item requisitus si illi qui deferunt tabardos sunt de societate sua,
respondit quod non quantum ad omnia, nisi illi qui tenent et portant
tunicam longam et zonam pelliceam, que zona est de essencia habitus;
tamen reputat illos adherentes Domino, licet habeant formam secularem
in suo habitu.[g]

Quibus diligenter inquisitus, auditis et intellectis idem inquisitor
in tanto negocio absque iuris peritorum consilio ulterius precedere
non presumens, consilium nostrum petiit in premissis. Nos autem[?][h]
obediencie filii et zelatores catholice fidei ipsius inquisitoris iuste
peticioni tam ex debito quam ex congruo devocius inclinantes iuxta
modulum nostrum sibi sane consulendo diximus et dicimus suppositis
facto confessionibus et processu prelibatis quod dictum Guiardum debet
verum hereticum reputare, iudicare ac eciam condempnare, habita cum
racione sui ex misericordia ut non tradatur curie seculari si vel ante
sentenciam vel cito postea penituerit sicut iura docent. Liquet namque
manifeste ex dictis suis et confessionibus prelibatis quod ipse ponit
divisionem in ecclesia militante, immo pocius ponit duas ecclesias
militantes, seipsum unius claves excellentes gerentem et alterius papam
claves ministerii optinentem, et ipsum papam non esse omnino unicum
capud ipsius ecclesie militantis nec posse ipsam omnino ordinare per
se et ministros suos sacrosque canones et statuta sua, quod totum est
hereticum: vide xix. d. c. i.[2]; xxv. q. i. violatores[3]; et q. ii. si
quis dogmata[4]; et Extra, de Summa Trinitate c. i, paragraphus una
vero[5]. In cuius rei testimonium ad requisicionem inquisitoris eiusdem
sigilla nostra presentibus apposuimus.

Datum Parisius, feria quinta post Dominicam qua cantatur iudica me,
anno Domini M° CCC° nono (Thursday, April 9, 1310, n.s.).

Chapter 23

Royal Salvation and Needs of State
in Late Capetian France

Elizabeth A. R. Brown

The more secular impulses of the last Capetians have sometimes received more attention than those acts which are reminiscent of less
sophisticated, more primitive attitudes and practices generally associated with earlier times.[1] Clear it is that Philip the Fair and his
sons could be shrewd, calculating, and opportunistic, particularly in
financial matters. It is equally evident that they invoked interest
of state and fatherland to justify policies whose moral defensibility
was open to question.[2] Still, impatience to see modernity emerge can
lead historians to lay excessive emphasis on this aspect of royal
activities.

The last Capetians may have been realistic and practical, but they
were also sensitive to the traditions and priestly admonitions which
reminded them of their duty as good Christians to search their consciences and to adhere to the highest possible moral standards.[3] Their
own personal salvation was, they believed, at stake, and this invested
the church's teachings with immediate urgency.[4] The impulse to deny
private responsibility for deeds performed for public ends existed,
but, following Augustine, theologians did not hesitate to point out to
rulers their final responsibility for all their acts and their
special obligation as princes and leaders to adhere to the highest
standards of conduct.[5]

The extent to which these principles were accepted varied.[6] Such
a king as Saint Louis might dedicate himself wholeheartedly to reform;[7]
a less pious prince, pressed by circumstances, might permit requirements of state to take precedence over demands of conscience, his
anxieties relieved through rationalization and compartmentalization.[8]
Still, in the last resort the Capetians could not take refuge in any
comforting distinction between public and private morality, and none
of them was immune from the church's pressures. Concern for their
souls led them to perform acts and institute measures which, while

furthering prospects of salvation, also imposed heavy burdens on their
treasuries.  Taxes of dubious legitimacy were cancelled, tangible
amends were made for wrongs done, donations were given to ecclesiastical institutions, religious foundations were established, thus divert-
ing from other uses the funds available to the monarchy.[9]

Anticipation of death understandably stimulated feelings of remorse
and inclinations to appease the Lord by atoning for sins.  Ordinarily,
however, the prospect of distant death did not lead rulers in general
or the Capetians in particular to introduce radical modifications of
policy or to strain their current budgets by making wholesale restitutions or large outright gifts to the church.  There were more attractive means of resolving the conflict between immediate needs and
pleasures, on the one hand, and the soul's final welfare, on the
other, since the ruler could, through wills or pledges left unfulfilled,
make suitable provisions which would become effective only when he had
died.[10]  During his own lifetime, his financial and political effectiveness remained unimpaired, and his worries about salvation were
assuaged.  To find relief through these means required a certain insen-
sitivity, an ability to tolerate the awareness that policies of admitted illegitimacy were not being corrected and that actions which should
be performed were not being done.[11]  For individuals incapable of living with these contradictions or for those who found it possible temporarily to overlook the moral implications of their deeds, deathbed
repentance offered a means of satisfying demands of conscience.  In
all these cases the alms, endowments, and compensatory measures would
be instituted only after the ruler's death.  It was not he but his
successor who would bear the responsibility for carrying them out,
and who might, if the provisions were extensive enough and if they were
in fact implemented, find his income and freedom of action sharply
curtailed.[12]

The situation was, in some sense, no different for rulers and their
realms than it was for lesser families and their estates.  The ecclesiastics whose establishments benefited from wills staunchly insisted
on the obligation of all executors to carry out the wishes of testa-
tors.[13]  Whatever his status, the executor who failed to implement
the testator's instructions was assured that his inaction threatened

the fate not only of the testator's soul but of his own as well.[14]
Still, a distinction must be drawn.  If testamentary benefactions
could, unless limited, undermine the integrity and continuity of private estates and fortunes,[15] rulers who made inordinately sweeping
attempts to guarantee their salvation could jeopardize not only their
heirs' own material prosperity, but also their successors' ability to
marshal resources to administer and defend their lands.[16] And it was
if anything more difficult for a royal heir to contest the provisions
of his predecessor's will or deathbed instructions than it was for a
non-princely heir to take such action.[17]  Because of the number, magnitude, and publicity of a ruler's final dispositions, whether bequests
or policy determinations, failure to fulfill them was likely to attract
widespread notice and blame.

  For a number of reasons the problems raised by this situation were
not resolved.  Neither king nor subjects distinguished between the
needs of king and realm where royal revenues, whether current or anticipated, were concerned.[18]  All royal income was thought to be the
king's to dispose of as he judged best, to support himself and his
family, to advance his spiritual well-being, to benefit his subjects.
During the thirteenth century increasing acceptance was being given
to the principle that rulers, whether living or dying, should not be
able to alienate or divide the endowment and rights associated with
their offices, but in France the doctrine was applied only slowly to
the king and his lands.[19]  In any case, the principle of inalienability
did not resolve the problem of equitable division of income, which
was bound to exist as long as the king was expected to provide for
his private requirements from the same sources which also had to
cover administrative, military, and judicial expenses.  Neither king
nor subjects could have been expected to advocate establishing separate
funds for the needs of king and kingdom.  The monarch's discretion
would thereby have been limited, and subjects would have found it
more difficult to resist demands for contributions to support projects
related primarily to their interests rather than to the king's.  As
long as it was assumed, as it was at the end of the thirteenth century,
that the regal endowment had been assigned to the king for the benefit
of kingdom as well as king, subjects could rightfully insist that the

king exhaust his revenues and drastically limit his own personal expenditures before asking them for any extraordinary grant.[20]  Under
these circumstances, it was crucially important that until the moment
of death each ruler exercised decisive control over all policies of
state, including the disposition of royal revenues, and that successors believed themselves obligated to carry out the decisions and ordinances of their predecessors.

It is easy enough to see, in the abstract, the sorts of difficulties
these circumstances might produce, and such spectacular acts as Philip
the Fair's and Charles V's cancellation of taxes when they were dying
have been studied.[21]  Largely for want of evidence, attention has not
been paid to the effect of less dramatic pronouncements and measures
on royal policy.  That relevant documentation should be scarce is
understandable, for rulers were too discreet, too conventionally
respectful, and too cognizant of their own mortality to comment unfavorably on their predecessors' wills and acts of piety.  Furthermore,
slow payment and calculated delay in implementation generally made it
possible to reduce the immediate impact of such pledges--just as they
make it exceedingly difficult to investigate the process of execution.[22]
Hence the interest of the document published for the first time in
the appendix to this article, an agreement between Louis X, eldest
son and heir of Philip the Fair, and the executors of his father's
will, concluded soon after Philip's death and burial, in December
1314.[23]  In addition to providing indirect evidence about Philip's and
Louis' attitudes to their souls and their realm, the document shows
dramatically that royal testamentary provisions could so affect the
state of the kingdom's finances as to force an heir, however deferen-
tial and however mindful of his own salvation, to modify these provisions to protect his own immediate interests and those of the state
his predecessor had left to his care.

Philip the Fair died an impressively pious death on November 29,
1314, at Fontainebleau, where he had been born.[24]  Eyewitness accounts
and documents issued the day before the king died show how deeply
Philip was concerned about the disposition of property which he knew
would follow his death, and, connected with this, about atoning for
wrongs he felt he had committed and attending to deeds left undone

and worthy projects begun but not completed.[25]

In Philip's case, anxieties about his salvation and the morality of
his acts were activated not solely by the approach of death, for many
of his earlier deeds and declarations testify to his continuing, if
sporadic, interest in these questions. Apparent in the reform charters
he issued, in the statements and policies concerning taxation and
coinage which he made and implemented, in the peace treaties he concluded, in the papal bulls he solicited and obtained, in his zealous
and determined prosecution of those whom he judged sinful,[26] this preoccupation was also evident in each of the three testaments he prepared.[27]

Advancing age and involvement in political enterprises of dubious
defensibility may have increased Philip's scrupulosity and generosity
in almsgiving, but his first will, drawn at Maubuisson[28] in August,
1288, when he was just twenty years old, suggests that even then he
was temperamentally inclined to introspection and seriousness of purpose. Having provided for his burial, the foundation of chaplaincies,
and observance of the anniversary of his death, he commanded that all
his debts be paid and restitution be made for all illicit exactions,
and he specified that 10,000 livres tournois be divided by his executors among property-holders in or near different forests, listed in
the will, who had been harmed by the royal beasts. Bequests to
churches and other charitable gifts totalled more than 20,000 livres
tournois, and he declared that his legacies, debts and restitutions
should be paid from the proceeds of the movables he possessed when he
died, with any deficit being supplied from the sale of royal woods.
Aside from the clause relating to the animals of the royal forests,
Philip's stipulations were conventional.[29] If he bound his heir and
his land, generally, for the payment of his bequests, there was precedent for this as well, and his stipulations were in any case limited
enough so that neither heir nor realm would be crippled by them.[30]

Almost nine years later, in March 1297,[31] Philip prepared another
will, which reflects the trials he had suffered since 1288 and which
indicates that his sensitivity had increased since then. On a personal level, a change in his feelings about his father may be reflected
in his decision to have his heart buried near the tomb of his father's

heart in the Dominican church in Paris, rather than with his own body
at St.-Denis. This modification suggests not only heightened dedication to the Dominican order, demonstrated elsewhere in the will, but
also lingering regret for his abrupt and unpopular decision in 1285
to override his father's express wish and have his father's heart
buried at the Dominican church rather than at St.-Denis.[32] Changes
in alms were few in number and minor in nature, except for the large
bequest to the Dominican nunnery of Poissy, a house which, doubtless
in connection with his efforts to have Louis IX canonized, Philip had
founded at his grandfather's birthplace.[33] Philip decreed that the
house be provided with an endowment sufficient to produce 3000 livres
tournois a year and ordained that if the endowment had not been made
or the house itself not completed by the time of his death, his executors should carry out his wishes. To accomplish these aims and his
other bequests, they were to draw upon the revenues of all Normandy
and of the bailliages of Amiens and Vermandois, revenues which Philip
also assigned to implement the most spectacular and unusual new clause
of the will. After specifying generally, as he had done in his first
will, that his debts should be paid and restitutions made, Philip, evidently troubled then as earlier by the monetary changes his war with
England had necessitated, announced in terms similar to those of a
declaration of May 1295, that full recompense should be made to all
those harmed by the coinage changes affecting weight, alloy, and value
that he had introduced.[34] It was to fund this restitution, which
would evidently seriously burden the treasury, that he gave his executors control not only over the revenues of Normandy--the only source
designated in 1295--but also over the two northern bailliages. Doubtless aware of the controversy this provision could arouse, Philip
stipulated that these revenues should not revert to his heirs and
successors until complete restitution had been made, even if the
executors of his testament were willing to accept a different arrangement.[35]

The clause concerning coinage mutations was omitted from Philip the
Fair's final will, completed on May 17, 1311, at Maubuisson.[36] In
other respects, however, this will attests his continued concern with
restitution and atonement and his continued determination to require

his executors to use specific income from specific areas to fulfill
his bequests.  He now provided explicitly that all revenues of Normandy
should be utilized to pay his debts and restore undue exactions, and
he expressly prohibited his successors from receiving any Norman income until this had been accomplished, even if his executors assented
to some other mode of settlement.  Philip tapped the Norman Exchequer
as well, ordaining that each of its two sessions should furnish 500
livres tournois to complete the buildings at Poissy.[37]  The devotion
to Saint Louis and Poissy seen in the will of 1297 had apparently
increased over the years, for in 1311 Philip decreed that his heart
should be buried at Poissy rather than with his father's in Paris.

  There was a striking general increase in the size of Philip's
bequests to churches and charitable gifts, and since the inflation
resulting from the coinage manipulations of the 1290's had not caused
Philip to change radically the similar provisions in his will of 1297,
it seems improbable that the less dramatic inflation of 1311, which
could only have been beginning when Philip drew his will,[38] was responsible for the modifications he introduced.  The changes were in
any case not uniform,[39] and they are likely to have been prompted by
his own reactions to individual establishments and beneficiaries and
by increased anxieties concerning the welfare of his soul.  Several
new beneficiaries appeared:  particularly notable is the large bequest
of 4000 livres tournois left to the Celestine order, founded by the
predecessor of Philip's enemy Boniface VIII on the papal throne, whom
Boniface was widely rumored to have hounded to his untimely death.[40]
Additional forests were included in the list of areas where compensation would be awarded for damages done by the king's beasts, thus
increasing by 2000 livres tournois the sum set aside for this purpose.
Philip more than doubled the amount of money left to his clerks and
servants, many of whom were mentioned by name in this will, as had
not been true in earlier testaments.  As a result of these increases
and additions, Philip's executors were now specifically instructed
to dispense at least twice as much as they had been in 1288.  The
will of 1311 perhaps indicates that relentless fiscal pressures had
convinced Philip that necessity justified his coinage changes, or that
time, increasing age, and experience had diminished his sensitivity

to their moral implications.  It also shows, however, that earnest and grave as he may have been since his youth, his preoccupation with eternity and salvation had increased as he grew older.

On a copy of the testament of 1311, a clerk of Philip V noted that it was "of no value, since afterwards it was cancelled by the introduction of another, because of some additions and diminutions, as is more fully indicated in the codicil annexed to this duplicate."[41] The clerk's comment is exaggerated.  Still, the codicil and two other documents prepared on November 28, 1314, the day before Philip died, increased the number, scope, and magnitude of the king's testamentary dispositions, as they also limited the resources available to his executors and his heir to implement his will and provide for the needs of his kingdom.  These three acts show that during the last days of his life Philip was intent on providing for the salvation of his soul by manipulating the property and revenues which were still his to control.

On November 26, 1314, Philip had confessed, taken communion, and sunk into his bed.  Discussion of his testament and other matters pertaining to his salvation had followed,[42] but not until November 28 was a final codicil drafted.[43]  Although the codicil contains numerous small bequests and divides Philip's especially cherished treasures, its most detailed clauses deal with religious foundations which had been instituted but not completed--a chapel of the church of Paris, the Celestine establishment of Mont-de-Châtre, the Dominican house of Poissy, and the Franciscan nunnery of Moncel.[44]  Poissy was, as it had long been, the focus of Philip's attention, and Yves de St.-Denis records that shortly before his death Philip specifically admonished his son Louis to complete the work begun at Poissy.[45]  In the codicil the king assigned two pieces of forest property to complete the house's endowment, which was to yield 6000 livres parisis annually.  The house was also to receive an additional 2000 livres parisis, to be realized from the sale of royal woods, as well as several valued objects.[46] Of far greater potential significance for the kingdom's fiscal stability were Philip's provisions for the crusading expedition to which he had committed himself in 1311, since he stated that unless his son Louis set out before the end of the six years within which he himself

had pledged to leave, 100,000 <u>livres tournois</u> would be donated to the
Holy Land, to be spent by the nearest of his survivors who agreed to
fulfill his commitment.[47]

   Another testamentary document was drafted on November 28, probably
after the codicil was completed.[48]  According to the preface, the act
was prepared to prevent dissension among the king's children and to
determine precisely how his debts should be paid, his will implemented,
his unfinished works of piety completed, and his sons' succession
arranged.[49]  To accomplish the first three purposes--and in this connection Philip mentioned especially his unfulfilled benefactions for
Moncel and Mont-de-Châtre--the king allocated to his executors all
revenues of the seneschalsies of Beaucaire, Rouergue, and Carcassonne,
and all ecclesiastical tenths belonging to him except those destined
for the crusade.[50]  There followed stipulations relating to his sons
Philip and Charles, each of whom was to receive property with an annual
value of 18,000 <u>livres tournois</u>.[51]  In addition, Charles was to recover
the 200,000 <u>livres petits tournois</u> due to him as the dowry of his wife,
Blanche of Artois.  The 140,000 <u>livres</u> already paid by Blanche's mother,
Mahaut of Artois, Philip acknowledged having spent,[52] and he decreed
that this money should be paid to Charles from the debt owed by the
Hospitallers because of their succession to the Knights Templars'
rights and obligations.  The remaining 60,000 <u>livres</u> were then being
paid in annual installments of 5000 <u>livres</u> by the town of St.-Omer,
indebted to Mahaut, and three years earlier Mahaut had been given close
oversight over the payments.[53]  With Blanche imprisoned as a result
of the adultery scandal of 1313, however, the situation had radically
changed, and Philip ordered that the 60,000 <u>livres</u>, together with the
remainder of Charles' Artesian fortune, be kept at St.-Martin-des-
Champs rather than in Arras, and that its expenditure--for Charles'
benefit alone[54]--be supervised by Philip's officers, Enguerran de
Marigny and Hugues de Bouville, in consultation with his own brothers,
and with Gui, count of St.-Pol, and Gaucher de Châtillon, count of
Porcien.[55]  Finally, at the end of the act, Philip turned to an issue
which was apparently--and understandably--burdening his conscience,
the execution of the testament of his widow Jeanne, who had died nine
years earlier.[56]  Philip himself had appropriated the funds intended

for its fulfillment, and therefore he ordered that 8000 livres tournois
should be taken annually from the revenues of the bailliage of Auvergne
until all he had taken had been restored; if Auvergne failed to produce
8000 livres in any year, the deficit was to be drawn from the bailliage
of Sens.[57]

A third and much briefer act promised to curtail royal revenue.  In
it Philip informed the duke of Burgundy that because he wished to relieve his subjects from oppression, because he had heard complaints
about his current tax for the Flemish war, and "because he believed
that his wars were over and ended," he had commanded that the war tax
be halted.[58]  Comparison with actions Philip had taken a year earlier
suggests not only that the cancellation of 1314 was made solely because
of the threat of imminent death but also that it was basically a compromise measure.  In 1313 a similar tax had been stopped, but the king
had cancelled it as soon as a truce was concluded, he had declared
collection of the tax illicit, and he had pledged restitution of all
sums paid.  In 1314, in contrast, Philip had continued to collect the
tax after the truce, whatever the implication of the contrived terminology of the act of revocation.  Furthermore, the act did not impugn
the legitimacy of the tax and made no reference to restitution.[59]

The terms of the tax cancellation of 1314 may indicate a reluctant
recognition on the part of Philip or his counsellors of the needs of
his heir and kingdom, but the lavish provisions of his will, codicil,
and testamentary ordinance--as well as the revocation itself--demon-
strate his overriding concern to promote his own salvation through
his final acts.  Implementation of these acts could, of course, be
deferred, and Philip, apparently determined to guard against this,
took peculiarly elaborate precautions to insure that his orders would
be followed.[60]  One report, admittedly based on hearsay evidence,
stated that after completing his will--which, the report noted, "is
said to contain wondrous things"--the king "asked and commanded his
heir to carry out swiftly all things contained in the testament and
all his oral instructions, [saying that] if he did so, he blessed him
with paternal blessing, but [that] otherwise he called his heir to divine
judgment, beseeching God that, in that case, his son should swiftly
follow him."[61]  There is other, perhaps more reliable evidence of

Philip's concern. A final clause of the codicil records that Louis
swore while holding his father's hand to observe and fulfill all his
father's provisions, and the codicil was warranted by the king "and
with the consent of the lord king of Navarre," Louis himself.[62] Louis'
pledge to execute Philip's orders also appeared in the testamentary
ordinance of November 28.[63] To include an heir's pledge in a testamentary document was striking but not unprecedented.[64] More unusual
was the promise made to Philip on November 28 by Gaucher de Châtillon,
count of Porcien and constable of France, "well and loyally to counsel
[Philip's] son the king and diligently to carry out the execution as
it should properly be accomplished."[65]

Philip's apprehensions about his stipulations are understandable,
for their potential effect on the kingdom's finances was immense.
The will and testamentary ordinance set aside for Philip's executors
the revenues of Normandy--which was expected to produce 100,000 livres
tournois in 1314[66]--and of the seneschalsies of Beaucaire, Rouergue,
and Carcassonne, as well as the profits of all ecclesiastical tenths
except those intended for the crusade.[67] And because of the ordinance
of November 28 the treasury would lose, first, 8000 livres tournois
annually from the revenues of Auvergne and Sens; second, the 36,000
livres tournois of annual revenue assigned to the king's sons; and
third, 140,000 livres tournois of the money anticipated from the Hospitallers. In addition, Philip's codicil had disposed of many precious
treasures which might otherwise have been sold. Finally, cancelling
the war tax meant that there would be no more income from this source,
and it also raised the possibility that restitution of all payments
would be demanded from the king's executors and heir.[68] For a realm
whose annual revenues seem to have totalled approximately 600,000
livres tournois,[69] these provisions posed a dilemma.

In the days following Philip's burial[70] considerable thought was
given to the king's dying orders, for Louis and his counselors,
prominent among whom were some of Philip's executors, seem quickly
to have realized the necessity of acting immediately to protect king
and kingdom. Negotiations and deliberations, reflected in a surviving
draft agreement, took place between, on the one hand, Philip's seventeen executors,[71] and, on the other, the king, his brothers, and five

of Louis' chief advisers, including Gaucher de Châtillon, constable
of France, who had promised Philip before he died to see that his will
was executed.[72]

The compromise these men reached was issued by Louis X at Vincennes,
probably toward the end of December 1314,[73] and it placed severe
limitations on the revenues available to the executors.  In the first
place Louis retained control of an impressive amount of his father's
movable property:  the old treasury; the treasury and the jewels of
the Louvre, except for those items left to Poissy; the money collected
and due for the last war tax; the clerical tenths intended for the
Holy Land.[74]  Furthermore, although the executors were assigned all
debts of any sort due to Philip at the time he died, by special arrangement Louis was to receive from them a third of these debts, except for the "debt of England"--doubtless the 33,000 livres tournois
borrowed from Philip by his son-in-law Edward II in connection with
Edward's trip to France in 1313.[75]  If and when paid, this "English
debt" would be the executors' to spend; a third of all other debts
collected would pass to Louis.  Finally, without alluding to the
revenues of Normandy--specifically assigned to the executors in
Philip's will--Louis merely gave them control of the income of the
three seneschalsies mentioned in the testamentary ordinance of
November 28, thus depriving them of 100,000 livres tournois Philip
had expected them to receive.[76]

The executors were well aware of Philip's intention to assign the
Norman income to them,[77] and they must have acquiesced, however re-
luctantly, in Louis' decision neither to acknowledge nor apologize
for retaining these funds.  Still, the executors' concurrence could
not relieve Louis' guilt.  He may not have tampered with the assignment of revenues to execute his mother's will, he may himself have
pledged to pay all annuities established by Philip, but his intervention nonetheless severely restricted the effectiveness of his father's
executors.

Louis' worries about his actions are reflected in the agreement of
December 1314, where, in the preamble, he emphasized his desire to do
everything possible to accomplish what his father "could and should"
have wished him to do, thus suggesting that Philip's orders were not

necessarily to be literally obeyed.  If he mentioned his sense of duty
and his soul--"which," he commented poignantly, "should be of principal concern to us"--he also invoked the interests of his kingdom and
his honor.[78]  Later in the agreement he promised that if God granted
peace and prosperity to the kingdom he would relinquish to the executors the portion of Philip's debts being paid to him, and he left it
to his two uncles, the counts of Valois and Évreux, and to the count
of St.-Pol to decide when such a situation existed.  Finally, by securing their sworn pledges to observe the agreement, he in some sense
made his two brothers and his chief advisers parties to it, and he
also ordained that all present and future officials of the Chamber of
Accounts, royal treasurers, and members of his estroit conseil should
swear to keep the agreement and cooperate with the executors if and
when the executors requested them to take such an oath.

Because of this arrangement, because Louis and his counselors were
able to evade demands for restitution of tax payments,[79] because the
process of executing the will dragged on for years,[80] Philip's testament and last acts did not exercise the dramatic influence on royal
financial policy that might have been expected.  His executors set to
work at once, but if their activities satisfied their own feelings of
obligation to the dead king, they can have done little to allay the
conflicts raised for Louis X by his interference with his father's
arrangements.  Whatever the needs of the realm, Louis' intervention--
and he not only curtailed Philip's executors' funds but also traded
an annuity of 400 livres tournois for the treasures Philip had left
to Poissy[81]--was similar to actions taken by Philip himself after his
own father's death,[82] and, like those actions, it may have been to
some extent a gesture of independence on the part of a son suddenly
released from the control of a domineering father.

Whatever his feelings about his father in 1314, when Louis drafted
his own testament in June 1316 he had severe misgivings about his
failure to carry out his father's final wishes.[83]  Although wills
traditionally began with clauses concerning body, burial, and debts,
Louis' will opened with the declaration that "to accomplish the testament of our dear father, we command and order our father's executors
to execute his testament according to the arrangements we have made

with them."[84]  Louis also commanded that his father's executors should
suffer no hindrance whatsoever and that his own executors should do all
they could to see that his father's wishes were implemented.[85]

  Louis survived his father by less than two years, dying soon after
he had prepared his testament, on June 5, 1316.[86]  The superstitious
might attribute his sudden and unexpected demise to his disobedience
to his father's final wishes and to Philip's deathbed curse, but whatever the causes of his death, the brother who succeeded him to the
throne, Philip V, found himself obliged to implement not only his
father's but also his brother's will.[87]  The financial burden this
involved makes it understandable that when soliciting papal support
in late 1317 Philip emphasized the economic problems caused by his
duty to execute the testaments.[88]  Less ceremoniously, several months
later Philip openly acknowledged that he himself had grant besoing
of the 400 livres parisis left by one of his former clerks for the
express purpose of carrying out his father's bequests.[89]  Philip V's
concern with establishing the principle of inalienability of crown
lands, doubtless prompted by the gifts his father and brother had
made during their lifetimes, may well have been increased by the
drains on royal income caused by their legacies.

  The will of Philip V, drawn on August 26, 1321, shows that, faced
with the necessity of providing for his own requirements, he had
failed to implement his father's and brother's provisions--and that,
as a result, he was suffering pangs of conscience.  Less sensitive,
perhaps, than Louis X, he opened his testament by ordering payment of
his own debts and amendment of his own wrongs and exactions,[90] but
he immediately passed to the chaplaincies established by Philip and
Louis and stated his intention of seeing them established.  Making
his own bequests, he also confirmed his father's orders concerning
the support Poissy and Moncel were to receive from the Exchequer of
Rouen, and concerning damages inflicted by the king's beasts.  Following a provision dealing with crusading which was remarkably similar to his father's, Philip gave specific instructions concerning
repayment of debts he and Louis had incurred, and he commanded the
prompt payment of money owed for prayers for his father, his brother,
and himself, as well as of sums due for customary alms left by his

predecessors.[91]

Within the space of eight years--between 1314 and 1322--three Capetian rulers died, and although the deaths of Philip the Fair, Louis
X, and Philip V have generally seemed most significant because of
their effect on the evolution of the principle of male succession in
France, the cumulative impact of the testamentary provisions made by
those kings cannot be underestimated.  Not only did they drain royal
income at a time when such losses could be ill afforded, not only
were they a source of administrative confusion,[92] but they also produced nagging conflict in the consciences of the rulers who were
responsible for seeing them carried out.  More sophisticated, less
scrupulous princes might have disregarded them completely or, at the
very least, might have learned from them to protect the interests of
the state by preparing less flamboyantly extravagant testaments themselves.  In the case of Philip's sons, this did not happen, and if
their wills differed in detail, they were strikingly similar in their
attention to salvation and repentance.  Louis X may have invoked the
needs of the kingdom of France to justify the compromise he reached
with his father's executors, but the terms of his will forced his
own heirs to confront problems and shoulder burdens far greater than
those with which he had wrestled.  So long as the kings of France
exercised ultimate and absolute control over the present and future
income of the lands they ruled, as well as over the treasures they
amassed and the lands they acquired by utilizing these revenues while
they lived, the financial well-being of the realm could not escape
subjection to the private and unpredictable impulses of mortal men
whose concern for the eternal welfare of their souls inevitably assumed
precedence over the more mundane material interests of their kingdom
and their subjects.

## Appendix

Paris, Archives Nationales, J 403, no. 20.  See n. 23 to the text of
the article.
On the dorse of this act are the following two notations:
Due littere regis Ludouici super conuentionibus habitis inter ipsum
& exequtores testamenti regis Philippi genitoris sui in quibus fit
mencio de assignatione senescalliarum Ruth' Carcass' & Bellicad'
facta dictis exequtoribus.  m ccc xiiii duppl'
Lacort du roy Loys & des exequeuteurs du roy Philippe ouesques lassignation des senechaucies de Roargue de Carcassonne & de Beauquaire.

Loys par la grace de dieu . Roy de france et de Nauarre Sachent tuit
Que nous voulanz & conuoitanz si comme faire le deuons acomplir en
toutes manieres tout ce que Nous sauons qui A la Volente de tres Bone
memoire nostre tres chier seigneur & Pere . Philippe par la grace de
dieu . Roy de france Iadis pouoit & deuoit plaire / et especialment
desirranz meitre entente A lenterin Acomplissement de son testament du
Codicille a celui annexe & de sa derraine volente / Consideranz que
en ce faisant ce Soit le profist de nostre Ame a quoy Nous deuons
principalement entendre Au profist aussi de nostre Royaume / & A
lonneur de Nous Voulons / Loons / Greons / & approuuons le testament
& le codicille dessus diz & toutes les choses contenues en iceuls Et
de nostre auctorite Royal par la teneur de cez presentes lettres con-
fermons . Pour la perfection & lacomplissement des quels testament &
Codicille par commun Acort fait & traictie entre Nous dune part Et
Noz amez & feals Leuesque de Paris / Labbe de saint Denys Labbe de
Royaumont . Challes de Valoys / et Loys deureus Contes nos chiers
oncles / Guy Conte de saint Pol . Mestre denise dean de Sens / Mestre
Philippe le conuers Chanoine de Paris / frere Renaut daubigny prieur
de Poissy de lordre des prescheurs frere Jehan de grant pre de lordre
du Val des escoliers ausmonier / Mestre Guillaume de linays de lausmone
/ & mestre Pierre destampes Chanoine de Sens / Clers / Enguerran seigneur de Marrigny / Pierre seigneur de chambly / Hue seigneur de Bouille
/ Cheualiers / & Chambellanz / Guillaume courteheuse / Cheualier
Martin des essarz familier nres' / executeurs du testament & de la
derraine Volente du dit nostre Seigneur & Pere / dautre part Touz les
meubles que le dit nostre seigneur & Pere auoit ou temps que il trespassa de cest Siecle / tourneront par deuers les diz executeurs /
Excepte lancien tresor / le tresor & les Ioyaus du louure fors tant
comme il en appartient a lesglise des Sereurs de Poissy Pour la reson
du don que nostre chier seigneur & Pere leur fist en son testament /
Les deniers qui sont leuez & deuz pour cause de ceste derreniere
subuention / et exceptez les diziesmes qui peuent apartenir a la
terre saincte / des quieux se len en auoit riens oste / li executeur
seroient tenuz A restablir Les queles choses exceptees nous demourront
/ Tout ce qui est en depos de touz autres diziesmes / exceptez ceuls
qui peuent Apartenir a la terre saincte si comme dessus est dit / et
touz les Arrerages qui sont deuz des diz diziesmes excepte ceuls de
la terre sancte tourneront par deuers les diz executeurs ou Nom de
la dicte execution / & oncore demourront par deuers euls ou Nom dessus
dit toutes les debtes qui au dit nostre seigneur & Pere estoient deues

en quelque maniere que ce fust au Iour & a leure que il trespassa /
fust de Rentes de Reuenues dautres emolumenz ou de Compositions / ouec
quiconques ne comment elles fussent faites / combien que les termes
des paiemenz ne fussent pas cheuz / Des queles debtes toutes Nous
pour certaine cause par Acort fait entre Nous & les diz executeurs
deuons auoir la tierce partie par la main deuls / Exceptee la debte
dengleterre la quele tournera deuers les diz executeurs enterinement
& franchement / sanz ce que Nous hi puissons Riens demander / En tele
maniere touteuois que ou cas ce que diex Nous otroit / paiz Viuroit /
& habundance de Biens Vendroit en nostre Royaume / Nous pour la dicte
tierce partie des dictes debtes que Il nous lessent / exceptee celle
dengleterre qui demeure toute leur si comme dessus est dit / Nous
eslargirions enuers euls pour le dit testament au dit & au regart
des deuant diz nos Oncles / de Valois / & de Eureus & du dessus nomme
Guy de S Pol / Contes / Sauf ce oncore pour les diz executeurs que
Nous deuons & Sommes tenuz a paier du nostre parmi lacort dessus dit /
toutes les Rentes a Vie & a heritage que nostre dit seigneur & pere a
lessiees en ses diz Testament & codicille . Lassignation faite des
Rentes de la Baillie dauuergne / & de la Baillie de Sens / se celles
dauuergne ne soufisoient pour lacomplissement de lexecution de nostre
chiere dame & Mere / Iehane Iadis par la grace de dieu . Royne de
france demourant en sa vertu / & auec toutes les choses dessus dictes
pour lacomplissement du dit testament & du dit Codicille de nostre dit
seigneur & Pere / toutes les Rentes les essues les emolumenz & les
Reuenues des seneschaucies de Biauquaire / de Carcassonne / & de
Roargue / demourront aus diz executeurs / A prendre / leuer / &
Receuoir par euls ou par iceuls qui a ce Seront deputez depar euls
Iusques a tant que toutes les choses & chascune contenues es diz
testament & Codicille soient enterinement paiees & Acomplies / Les
queles Rentes / yssues / emolumenz / & reuenues des dictes seneschaucies / debtes / meubles / diziesmes / excepte celui de la terre saincte
si comme dessus est dit / lancien tresor & le tresor du louure & les
deniers qui sont leuez & deuz de la derreniere Subuention qui nous
doiuent demourer si comme par dessus est escript / Nous delessons des
maintenant en la main des diz executeurs / ou Nom & pour lexecution
dessus dicte / & les meitons hors de nostre main Iusques a la fin de
lacomplissement dicelle . Sauf a Nous la tierce partie des dictes
debtes / sus la condition de leslargissement que nous deuons faire
aus diz executeurs ou cas dabundance & de paiz que diex nous otroit /
Selonc le dit & le Regart des deuant diz Contes / si comme dessus est
escript / La quele tierce partie des dictes debtes exceptee celle
dengleterre qui Sera toute leur nous deuons prendre & Receuoir par
leur Main / Toutes & chascune des choses qui sont contenues ou testament & ou codicille du dit nostre seigneur & Pere / lacort dessus dit
/ & tout ce qui est contenu en cez lettres / Nous en lame de Nous pour
Nous & en nostre Nom de certaine science auons fait Iurer par nostre
tres chier ame & feal frere . Philippe Conte de Poitiers / A tenir /
garder / & Acomplir de point en point enterinement sanz aler A len-
contre / Et Il pour li & en son Nom / Nostre chier frere aussi Challes
Conte de la marche / pour li & en son Nom / de leur pure Volente /
Gauchier de chasteillion / Conte de Porcien / & Connestable de france
Mile Seigneur de Noiers / Guillaume de Harecourt seigneur de la Saucaye
/ Mahy de Trie seigneur de fontenoy & Chambellan de france / Herpin

seigneur derquery / Noz Conseilliers / presenz deuant Nous de nostre
Volente / auctorite / & commandement Iurerent sus sanctes euangiles
que quant a euls apartient Il tendront & garderont de point en point
toutes les choses dessus dictes & Chascune dicelles / & que Il ne
conseillieront ou temps auenir en maniere nulle que elle soit / Nous
ne autre a qui Il puisse apartenir contre le testament / Codicille /
& acort dessus diz / ne contre chose contenue en iceuls / Ne ne feront
ne porchaceront chose nulle estre faite par quoi lexecution du dit
testament & Codicille / & les choses contenues en cez lettres / puis-
sent en aucune maniere / estre empeschiees / ou delaiees / Eincois
donront toute layde le conseil & la faueur que il porront a lacomplissement des choses dessus dictes & de chascune dicelles . Et ce
meismes Volons Nous & commandons expressement par cez lettres / que
Nos Genz des Comptes / Noz tresorriers / & ceuls qui ores sont de
nostre estroit conseil / Iurent sus sainctes euangiles / si tost comme
Il en Seront requis des diz executeurs / ou de ceuls qui A ce Seront
deputez depar euls / & que tuit cil qui des ores en auant seront
retenuz depar Nous es estas dessus diz ou en aucun diceuls facent ce
meisme Serement sus cez choses / Si tost comme Il Seront retenuz / &
en Seront requis des diz executeurs / ou de leur mandement si comme
dessus est dit / Et Derechief / Nous toutes les choses dessus dictes
& chascune dicelles sus nostre Serement dessus dit fait par nostre
dit frere / prometons loialment / & en Bone foy A tenir / garder /
enteriner & Acomplir Bonnement sanz enfraindre / & sanz Venir encontre
/ Et quant ace Obligons aus diz executeurs ou Nom de lexecution dessus
dicte Nous & noz hoirs / & touz noz Successeurs / Et a ce que elles
soient plus Briement faites & acomplies / Nous donnons expressement
en mandement / A noz Genz des Comptes / Noz Tresorriers / Ceuls de
nostre estroit conseil qui ores sont & qui seront pour le temps
auenir / A noz Iusticiers des dictes Seneschaucies / de Biauquaire /
de Carcassonne / & de Roargue / & A touz noz autres Subgiez de nostre
Royaume / que Il & Chascun deuls / aus diz Executeurs / & A leur
Mandement & a ceuls qui seront par leur lettres deputez depar euls es
choses dessus dictes & chascune dicelles / Obeissent & entendent / &
donnent Ayde / Conseil / & faueur A iceuls A lacomplissement des choses
dessus dictes .. En tesmoing de la quele chose Nous Auons fait meittre
Nostre Scel / en cez presentes lettres[1] . Donnees A . Vicennes ou Mois
de Decembre / Lan de Grace . Mil . Troiscenz / et Quatorze / --
.. Per dominum Regem                          . Stamp,
Vobis presentibus                             Collatio facta est

Chapter 24

Queens, Queans, and Kingship:
An Inquiry into Theories of Royal Legitimacy
in Late Medieval England and France[1]

Charles T. Wood

In the spring of 1314 scandal threatened to envelop the court of
France. It was alleged that two of Philip the Fair's daughters-in-
law, Marguerite of Navarre and Blanche of Burgundy, had for three years
been involved in an adulterous relationship with two knights, Philip
and Gautier d'Aunay. The royal reaction was immediate: Marguerite
and Blanche were imprisoned in Chateau Gaillard while their unfortunate
lovers were subjected to a public execution which (depending on which
chronicler we care to believe) may or may not have included such popular delights as emasculation, flaying, drawing, hanging, beheading,
and quartering--all followed by long and open display of the remains.[2]

Scarcely a decade later England was rocked by a similar scandal involving the queen herself, but with quite different consequences. When
Isabella became the mistress of Roger Mortimer, earl of March, the
final outcome was scarcely Mortimer's execution or the queen's imprisonment. On the contrary, in 1326 the two of them raised troops, invaded England, and overthrew the cuckolded Edward II; these events
were, in the following year, to lead to that monarch's forced abdica-
tion and the accession of Isabella's son, Edward III.[3] And even when,
in 1330, Edward III turned against his mother and her paramour, the
charges for which Mortimer was executed related almost exclusively to
his bad rule and complicity in the murder of Edward II. The closest
the government came to raising the question of adultery was in a vague
and ambiguous claim that "the said Roger falsely and maliciously caused
discord between the father of our Lord the King and the Queen his
wife...."[4] A true statement, perhaps, but not very revealing. As
for Isabella, though her role in government came to an end, no charges
were brought. She was permitted freedom of movement and £3000 per
year as a widow's portion. Some found her an unlikely widow, even
though she did end her life a Poor Clare.[5]

Chroniclers contemporaneous with these events serve only to reinforce the sense of difference between them.  In France, every chronicle alludes to the adulteries of 1314 in straightforward detail;[6] in
England, however, even as Stubbs remarked, sources are more circum-
spect.  Most explicit are Thomas Walsingham and the Chronicon of
Lanercost, and they appear hesitant to say much more than:  "Intimacy
was suspected...as public rumor testified."  More typically, Avesbury
argues that "as things more secretly done must not be spoken about,
I shall be silent."[7]

Since so much of medieval political history has been thought of in
national focus, no historian has ever concerned himself with the implications of these striking differences.  Traditionally, the English
have viewed the overthrow of poor benighted Edward II as scarcely
worthy of explanation, and if Edward III chose not to blacken his
mother's name, that too was perfectly understandable.  Similarly, if
the French mention the scandals of 1314 at all, they pass off their
consequences either as proof of the Capetian court's continuing puri-
tanical morality, or as a foreshadowing of difficulties and dissensions to come.

Nevertheless, as Joseph Strayer has taught us, "the full value of
history comes only when knowledge of other countries and other times
is added to that of our own country and period."[8]  Thus, to gain that
full value, we must examine these similar yet different events in
England and France not just for their own sake, but in relationship
to each other, for it is only in that way that we can begin to understand their true significance and the light they shed on the different
constitutional histories of those two lands.

In this regard it seems not unreasonable to focus on the possible
problems these adulteries posed in terms of succession to the throne.
After all, both cases involved women whose progeny would in the normal
course of events have been expected to rule, so one would assume that
uncertainties about legitimacy of birth would inevitably have been
reflected in disputes about the person to whom the crown should pass
after the demise of either cuckolded king.

Such, indeed, appears to have been the case in France, where the
accession of Philip V and the concomitant exclusion of women from

rights of succession cannot fully be understood without reference to
the implications of the adulteries of 1314.[9]  For Louis X's wife,
Marguerite of Navarre, stood convicted of a liaison which was alleged
to have begun a year before the birth of her one child, Jeanne.  And
contemporaries did draw the appropriate conclusions.  As the Chronicle
Attributed to Jean Desnouelles puts it:  "King Louis had two wives:
the first was the daughter of Mahaut, countess of Artois, and this
queen committed misdeeds of the body, for which she was separated from
the king and imprisoned in Chateau Gaillard.  This queen had one
daughter of the king, as she claimed, but for the misdeeds of her
mother she lost her lands."[10]

The issues here are tricky.  At Louis' death in 1316 Jeanne was only
four, and everything suggests that a significant prejudice already
existed against the rights of women.[11]  On the other hand, it is
dangerous to assume that Jeanne's sex alone kept her from the throne.
The chronicle cited above denies that view, and the various agreements
negotiated between the regent, Philip of Poitiers, and the duke of
Burgundy further demonstrate that her rights were far from nugatory.[12]
And when the royal council reviewed the whole question during the
pregnancy of Louis' second wife, the duke continued to maintain his
position firmly, arguing (as John of Saint Victor reports it) that
"King Louis, while alive, recognized her as a legitimate daughter."[13]
Such views, which have to do not with sex, but with paternity, are not
lightly to be disregarded, even if advanced out of self-interest; it
seems likely, therefore, that succession devolved on Philip V largely
because, given Jeanne's possible illegitimacy, he was Louis X's closest
blood heir.

In France, then, doubts about legitimacy played a significant role
in changing the anticipated royal succession.  But what of England?
How should the transfer of power to Edward III be seen?  Here we are
on shakier ground, thanks to the reticence of the available sources,
but the general dimensions of the problem are nonetheless clear.

First, Queen Isabella was an acknowledged adulteress.  Admittedly,
her relationship with Mortimer appears to have developed only around
1324 or 1325,[14] and Edward III had been born in 1312, but the possibility always exists that she had had earlier lovers.  This is

particularly the case when the question of her husband's own sexual
proclivities is raised.  For historians have long speculated (albeit
in discreet and muted tones) about the extent of Edward II's apparent
homosexuality.[15]  And men in the fourteenth century were equally suspicious.  Froissart claims that Hugh Despenser's private parts were
cut off "because he was...guilty of unnatural practices, even with
the king, whose affections he had alienated from the queen by his
wicked suggestions."[16]  Geoffrey le Baker presents Edward's murder
as a symbolic reenactment of sexual perversion,[17] and the Chronica de
Melsa sums it all up with the statement, "Edward especially delighted
in the vice of sodomy."[18]  All in all, then, we have a much more explicit case than chroniclers present with regard to Isabella's adultery, something which in itself has interesting implications.

Now all these charges may not be true; Edward may, in fact, have
been the father of his supposed offspring.  He certainly recognized
them as his, and he was always with Isabella at the appropriate and
necessary times before the birth of each of her children.[19]  Many
homosexuals are bisexual, and in this regard it is possibly significant that even though the queen began complaining to her father,
Philip the Fair, about her husband's friendship with Piers Gaveston
almost immediately following the wedding,[20] Edward III was born only
after the barons had hurried this royal favorite to his final reward.
On the other hand, it is equally plausible that Isabella, who was
twelve at her marriage in 1308, had become fertile only later.

Be that as it may, in the context of the present argument the actual
truth of the matter is largely irrelevant.  What is relevant is the much
simpler question of whether people of consequence in 1326-1327 would
have had reasonable grounds for challenging Edward III's legitimacy.
On that question there is no logical basis for doubt:  an adulterous
queen married to a probably homosexual king leads necessarily to the
thought that the progeny of one may not have been the progeny of the
other.  Honi soit qui mal y pense.

That contemporaries had such doubts is nowhere better illustrated
than in the differences we have noted between French and English
chronicles.  French authors could write openly because their adulterous queen had been punished and her daughter excluded from the

succession.  But in England, where nothing of the kind had happened, to write too explicitly about Isabella's activities was inevitably to bring into question the paternity of her son, the king.  For those with doubts, the only sensible solution was silence, and if chroniclers inadvertently reopened the subject with their treatment of Edward II, that seems entirely understandable:  the deposed king's eccentricities provided both a tempting theme and ample explanation of (not to mention justification for) the events which had brought young Edward III so precipitately early to the throne.  In regard to the problem of succession, the king's sodomy was a relatively safe subject; the queen's adultery was not.

If so, the coup d'état of 1326-1327 becomes vastly more interesting than previous analysts have assumed.  The proposed king was a minor, just fourteen, and his sponsors, Isabella and Mortimer, were hardly popular.[21]  Nevertheless, the lovers were clearly going to rule unless the opposition could devise some means of getting rid of them.

And the opposition did try, as demonstrated by the events surrounding the last days of Edward II.[22]  For everything indicates that initially the new regime had no intention of murdering him, but came to it only after revolts aimed at rescue and restoration began to break out.  That people so opposed Isabella and Mortimer that they were prepared to chance the return of even a hopeless incompetent suggests with what hostility the regnant adulterers were viewed.  But Edward's death cut off this avenue of resistance, and that seems momentarily to have ended the matter; the opposition quieted down, not to reemerge until three years later when Edward III solved the problem by having Mortimer executed.

This chain of events is troubling.  If, as is always assumed, the English throne had become predominantly hereditary, and if there were reasonable grounds for challenging Edward III's legitimacy--at least on the part of those who wanted to be rid of Mortimer and Isabella-- it would seem that the logical solution would have been to deny that legitimacy and to proclaim the next clearly legitimate heir as king, in this case Thomas Brotherton, earl of Norfolk, marshal of England, and the elder of Edward II's two half-brothers born of Edward I's second marriage, to Margaret of France.  In many respects Norfolk was

an ideal candidate.  An early supporter of Isabella's and Mortimer's
invasion and their subsequent coup, he was nevertheless scarcely an
ardent follower of the upstart earl of March:  Rather, it was simply
a question of his disliking Hugh Despenser, the fallen king's favorite,
even more.[23]  If, ten years before, Philip V had seized the crown of
France by taking advantage of the consequences of his sister-in-law's
adultery, what better way for Thomas to solve the governmental crisis
than by imitating Philip's example and claiming the throne himself?

Yet he never tried, and nothing in the surviving evidence remotely
suggests that the idea even occurred to him or to anyone else.  Given
the French precedent, this lack of initiative would appear incomprehensible.  We must ask, therefore, why such similar events in neighboring lands should have had, at roughly the same time, such contrary
results.

Part of the answer may lie in the field of private law, particularly
in those customs governing illegitimacy and rights of inheritance.
At first glance, this hypothesis may appear unlikely because both
countries sought rigorously in theory to deny that bastards had any
rights transmitted from parents.[24]  In practice, however, we find significant differences.  The French appear genuinely to have applied
this principle, whereas the English demonstrated a marked willingness
to adjust theory to circumstance in such a way that children of adulterous relationships could be given some chance of succession.  In
2 Edward II, for example, the king's justices heard a case in which
plaintiff alleged that one Thomas of Boudon was not, as he claimed,
the son of Hervey, but rather that of William of Rusting.  Bereford,
J., replied:

> What you have said as yet will not suffice..., for he says that
> he was holden and acknowledged as Hervey's son all his life and
> he is "in" as heir.  And as to your averment that he is son of
> William of Rusting, how could one try such a matter?... It can-
> not be known who begot him; the only proof of filiation is the
> presumptive proof.[25]

Not content with this denial, Spigurnel, J., then added:

> May be he was begotten and born upon and of one Margery as you
> have said, and that he was acknowledged and holden as son of
> Hervey in his, Hervey's, lifetime.  That lies within the knowl-
> edge of the country.  But as to what you say about his being
> William's son, that cannot be known for the reason already given.

So it is better in this case to be acknowledged and holden as son, albeit you really are not heir, than to be the very heir in blood but not acknowledged and holden as such.[26]

Even more germane to the question of female adultery are the reminiscences of Hengham, J., from the Year Books of 32-33 Edward I:

> I remember a case in which a damsel brought an assize of mort d'ancestor on the death of her father. The tenant said that she was not next heir. The assize came and said that the [alleged] father after that he had married the mother went beyond seas and abode there three years; and then, when he came home, he found the plaintiff who had not been born more than a month before his return. And so the men of the assize said openly that she was not his heir, for she was not his daughter. All the same, the justices awarded that she should recover the land, for the privities of husband and wife are not to be known, and he might have come by night and engendered the plaintiff.[27]

Or, as Metingham, J., put the case under similar circumstances:    "Who so bulleth mine kine, / Ewere [always] is the calf mine."[28]

In the thirteenth and early fourteenth centuries, then, English common law with regard to disputed paternity based itself on two principles:  first, "the privities of husband and wife are not to be known"; and second, "better to be acknowledged and holden as son, albeit you really are not heir, than to be the very heir in blood but not acknowledged and holden as such."  If so, the relevance to the status of Edward III is immediately apparent.  Edward II had consistently recognized him; indeed, he appears to have abdicated only after becoming convinced that this was the one way to insure that his son would reign.[29]  The privities of husband and wife being beyond review, we could argue that even those hotly opposed to the rule of Isabella and Mortimer had no choice but to accept Edward III if they, like their sovereign, were to "keep...the laws and customs given to them by the previous just and god-fearing kings."[30]

Here, however, further questions arise.  To quote from the coronation oath of 1308 is to remind ourselves that succession to the throne involved matters of public, not private, law.  And by the opening of the fourteenth century it was becoming evident that there could be sharp differences between them.  To search out the rules governing the inheritance of private property may not, therefore, be terribly instructive about rights of succession to the monarchy.  To understand them, we must ask, rather, for the prerequisites of kingship, for those

conditions that had to be met before a man could legitimately be considered to have the sanction to rule.

During the earlier Middle Ages, both monarchies appear to have
developed remarkably similar theories of legitimacy, theories in
which the right to the throne depended on three familiar elements:
kin-right or, in other words, a "throne-worthiness" based on some form
of blood membership, even illegitimate, in the ruling dynasty; election, or recognition/acceptance by the community (however defined) of
one's successful candidacy; and, finally, religious coronation, the
most important element of which was unction.[31]  But over time, and
particularly in the course of the eleventh and early twelfth centuries,
these requirements underwent subtle modification.  Again, though, most
scholars have seen these changes as having continued in parallel on
both sides of the Channel.

First, the redefinition of the family in more nuclear terms, a
Europe-wide phenomenon at the time, tended to underline and increase
the inheritance rights of a monarch's own children, and this tendency
was necessarily reinforced by the appearance of the rex-designatus
system in France and a related inclination in England, not quite so
marked, to provide for the succession during an incumbent's lifetime.[32]
Second, the reforms of Gregory VII led to a downgrading of the importance accorded to coronation and unction.  Hitherto, they had not infrequently been viewed as one of the sacraments; they had, as such,
become one of the principal supports of sacral kingship and of a
monarch who was himself directly the vicar of God.  After Gregory,
however, these claims diminished, with the result that the French and
English monarchies seem to have begun the thirteenth century with an
outlook and ambiance much less receptive to religious and sacramental
justifications for kingship than had been the case fifty or one hundred years before.[33]

Moreover, the evidence suggests that these changes had further consequences.  For example, most scholars agree again in citing the
apparent disappearance of election or recognition previous to a candidate's installation as king; by implication, heredity was coming
to the fore, and primogeniture is therefore seen as beginning to over-
shadow all other elements in the king-making process.  As a symbol of

this kind of transformation, many works emphasize the accessions of
Philip III in 1270 and Edward I in 1272, for in both instances the
new kings dated their assumption of royal power from the time of their
fathers' deaths and not, as had previously been the case, from that
of their own coronations.[34]   Since, as Ralph Giesey has pointed out,[35]
coronations are inherently anti-dynastic in principle, at least if
given great weight in creating and legitimating royal power, it is
claimed that these twin events should be taken as the final victory
of hereditary right over those other factors, election and coronation,
which had earlier been equally central to the shaping of monarchy.

The striking feature of these views, one common to most of the literature, is their insistence on the continuing similarity between
theories of kingship in England and France.  By 1300 both monarchies
are judged to have become predominantly hereditary, and if the ruler
of one is found to have had unusual attributes (thaumaturgic powers,
say, or inviolability of person),[36] so, invariably, is the other.
Yet all of this reasoning is highly misleading since, accurate as it
may be within limits, it fails adequately to note significant differences in emphasis already beginning to develop.  And these differences are crucial if we want to understand why, in public law, female
adultery in France should have deprived women of rights to the throne
whereas in England it led to the deposition of the then reigning
monarch and the substitution of his putative son.  Or, to put the
matter more cautiously and the other way around, the very fact that
the two adultery crises had different consequences suggests that dis-
similarity in public law, so seldom stressed in this period, may have
had greater importance than is generally appreciated.

Although measurement of such differences is fraught with difficulty,
it seems safe to say that the tendencies of the French monarchy from
987 were much more in the direction of a legitimate and sanctified
hereditary succession than was the case in England.  Insofar as the
practice of kings designate worked toward this end, we could argue
that a hereditary throne had been the goal from the moment that, only
months after his own accession, Hugh Capet decided to associate his
eldest son in the kingship.  But such thoughts enjoyed little initial
acceptance, and it is not until 1165, when Arnoul of Lisieux wrote

Louis VII to congratulate him on the birth of Philip Augustus--a boy, the bishop said, who would rule by right of birth alone--that we can say with any confidence that blood had begun to supersede election as a prime criterion for elevation to the throne.[37]

To some extent, the Capetians faced difficulties simply because they had come to power a century before new modes of family structure and family rights began clearly to be defined; such changes were largely a by-product of Hildebrandine reform. But even as these new views of the family emerged, that phenomenon posed new problems since the fact of the matter was that the Capetians were usurpers, men who had wrested the throne from the Carolingians, a dynasty whose right to rule the pope had guaranteed under pain of excommunication in 754.

Hugh had claimed that his elevation to the kingship had been the dying wish of the last Carolingian, Louis V, and the first century of Capetian rule had seen a number of royal marriages with women of at least faintly Carolingian descent. Further, Louis VI's adoption of the Oriflamme, the supposed banner of Charlemagne, tended further to associate the new dynasty with the old.[38] Nevertheless, these ties came to be inadequate under the new conditions of the late twelfth and early thirteenth centuries, or so it would appear, for how else are we to explain the profound significance attached to Philip Augustus' Carolingian (albeit maternal) blood, the Carolingian descent of his son Louis VIII, and the decision to abandon the rex-designatus system?[39]

From the time of Philip Augustus, then, hereditary right came to prevail, a right dependent not on Capetian, but Carolingian legitimacy --itself a blood grouping that was carefully linked to Merovingian beginnings.[40] Under Louis VIII "Charles" re-emerged as a family name, and during St. Louis' reign the royal tombs at Saint Denis were re-arranged--Carolingians on one side, Capetians on the other--with Philip Augustus and Louis VIII providing the bridge and union between them.[41] The culmination of these views came in the reign of Philip III with the synthesis, in the Grandes Chroniques, of older myths and legends into the so-called Reditus Regni ad Stirpem Karoli Magni, a piece of royalist propaganda that both legitimized the existing dynasty and justified its territorial ambitions.[42]

·So strong did the claims of hereditary succession become that it
began to be claimed that a king assumed his full powers previous to,
and without legal need for, coronation.[43]  Here, however, a caveat
should be entered, for if blood right became the predominant element
in royal legitimacy, this blood carried with it associations strongly
linking the kingship to religious mission and rites.  The Capetians
traced their immediate origins to Clovis, first baptized among the
Franks, and to Charlemagne, the recently canonized emperor.  Thus it
is scarcely surprising to find them emphasizing the capital importance
of their unction brought by a dove from heaven for that first baptism;
nor is it remarkable that their crusading ardor should have been
rationalized by constant reference to the zeal of the great Charles so
vividly portrayed in the Song of Roland.[44]  All the same, everything--
even these religious elements--depended on blood, for only in its
purity, seminally transmitted,[45] could there be any guarantee that
past greatness would be realized again in times to come.[46]

In short, thirteenth-century France enjoyed a kingship that was increasingly sanctified on the basis of legitimate dynastic descent.
"Royal" and "most holy" became nearly synonymous;[47] unsuccessful attempts to underscore the point with the canonization of Philip Augustus
were finally realized with the elevation of his grandson;[48] and Rigord
could unblushingly, if inaccurately, refer to Louis VIII as regis
Philippi unigenitus, a formula whose credal and christological implications are unmistakable.[49]  Small wonder, then, that Beaumanoir, who
enjoined justice as a duty on all sovereigns, did so "more especially"
in the case of his own lord, Robert of Clermont, "who is a son of the
king of France";[50] or that Matthew Paris, who called Louis IX "the
king of mortal kings," should likewise have agreed with that monarch
in finding it preferable "to be the brother of such a king, whose
lineage of royal blood has exalted him to rulership of the Franks"
than to be mere emperor, "whom voluntary election alone exalts."[51]
As Guillaume of Plaisians put it in attacking Boniface VIII, the
better to defend Philip the Fair:  "Seeking to destroy the faith, he
has long harbored an aversion against the king of France, in hatred
of the faith, because in France there is and ever was the splendor of
the faith, the grand support and example of Christendom...."[52]

Although much more could be said, it is sufficient to note that by
1314 we are already dealing with what Joseph Strayer has called, with
characteristic succinctness, "France: The Holy Land, the Chosen
People, and the Most Christian King."[53] And because these concepts
had become embedded in the fabric of public law, reinforcing blood-
right legitimacy with a sense of awful mystery, it becomes apparent
why the adultery scandals of that year should have provoked a crisis.
Regardless of sex, no product of a possibly adulterous union could
have been allowed to succeed in such a realm, and if Philip V manipulated the situation to his own advantage, he was justified by much
more than personal, private ambition.

Strikingly, as Kantorowicz points out, "...similarly exalted elabora-
tions of mystic endowments of the royal house by grace and by nature
were hardly found in England at that period."[54] Given the difficulties
of precisely defining the complexities of different historical developments, we can never fully explain why they should have occurred, but
in the present instance it seems likely that accident, stimulated by
the reality of trans-Channel possessions, provides as good an explanation as any.

After Hastings William the Conqueror found himself in a position not
dissimilar to that of Hugh Capet a century earlier, and he responded
to it in much the same manner, arguing that the throne had devolved
on him for four reasons. First, Edward the Confessor had promised it
to him and, second, he claimed kin-right, somewhat dubiously citing
the fact that the Confessor's mother Emma had been the daughter of his
own great-grandfather, Richard I of Normandy. Next, God had demonstrated the justice of his cause in battle and, finally, he had been
elected by the Witan of England, and subsequently crowned.[55] Thus all
the elements of traditional kingship were clearly present.

Nevertheless, from this point on, English experience begins to
diverge from the French. As befitted a duke of Normandy, William
selected his first son to succeed in the duchy and only his second
to rule in the kingdom. Moreover, the suspicious displacement of
Rufus by Henry I served further to emphasize the lack of clear rules,
and even though Henry himself attempted to correct this deficiency by
having his own son recognized as rex designatus,[56] the wreck of the

White Ship ended that hope:  Henry's death was to bring in its train
a disputed succession, the elevation of Stephen, and twenty years of
anarchy.

In twelfth-century England, calculation and chance made it impossible
for the principles of election to be harnessed and focused by the practice of designation, a custom which in France had created a fully
hereditary monarchy based on primogeniture.  On the contrary, sons
were lacking or died young;[57] cross-Channel possessions blurred and
fragmented ambitions;[58] and at least four times (Henry I, Stephen,
Henry II, and John) the throne was either seized by force or devolved
on a king whose accession denied the rights of those who might otherwise have been considered the heir or heiress presumptive.  And these
difficulties were compounded by the failure to develop any dynastic
myths comparable to the Reditus Regni ad Stirpem Karoli Magni.  The
Conqueror had claimed kinship with Edward the Confessor, and Henry I
had reinforced the point by marrying back into the Anglo-Saxon royal
line, but these tendencies came early and, like the Carolingian links
established by Hugh Capet and his immediate successors, carried no
dynastic weight.[59]  Unhappily, by the end of the century, when newer
notions of the family could have given increased importance to such
dynasticism, there were neither Anglo-Saxon heiresses surviving for
marriage nor heroic legends about the return of the line of Alfred on
which propagandists could build.

Endowed with no more than a weak principle of hereditary right, the
English monarchy, unlike the French, was forced to rely on coronations
for much of its legitimacy.  When, for example, Henry II's death
brought Richard to the throne, the Chronicle of Benedict of Peterborough
referred to him as count of Poitiers before his investiture in Normandy;
as duke following that ceremony; and as king only after his crowning
in England.[60]  Similarly, Henry III lacked the essential powers of
kingship before his majority and coronation,[61] and even though Gregory
VII and his successors had consistently denied the sacramental efficacy of unction, Robert Grosseteste still found it not improbable that
the full legal prerogatives of office came only with anointing.[62]  We
can understand, then, why coronation oaths and charters had such vastly
greater significance in England than in France;[63] they stood as

testimony to the weakness of the hereditary principle and to the
monarch's need, given the resultant greater strength of election and
crowning, to bind himself with a set of near-contractual obligations
to those whose willingness had made him king.

The confusions of the situation are evident under Edward II. On
the one hand, he would write that he was "ruling in the hereditary
kingdom of England."[64] On the other, he was equally insistent on the
centrality of unction. As the poet Richier had pointed out, only in
France had the coronation oil come from heaven; "In all other places
kings must buy their unction from merchants."[65] In 1318, however,
Edward came into possession of a miraculous oil that the Virgin had
vouchsafed to St. Thomas Becket in a vision, prophesying that the
fifth king after Henry II (i.e., Edward II) would be "a man of integrity and champion of the Church."[66] That Edward, weak and beset by
enemies, immediately sought papal permission for a second coronation
goes without saying; similarly, that he should have sought salvation
through blatant imitation of the French is wholly unremarkable. What
needs to be stressed is the simple fact that his decision to emphasize
the efficacy of renewed unction had the effect of undercutting all his
otherwise hereditary arguments. This was to have long-term consequences.

For the moment, however, Edward's contrary theories served only to
emphasize the confusion then existing in English public law with regard
to the justifications for kingship. Given a common law that chose not
to delve too deeply into questions of paternity; and given a kingship
whose authority depended more on election, anointing, and the coronation oath than it did on legitimate heredity, we can see both why
Isabella and Mortimer were able successfully to depose Edward II and
why Edward III, once crowned, could rule without opposition. There
was nothing in the traditions of English monarchy to prevent it.

Nevertheless, this is but half the story, for if the events of the
twelfth and thirteenth centuries had helped to form quite different
theories of royal legitimacy in England and France, theories that
help to explain the differing results of queenly adultery, it is
equally true that these results themselves--the exclusion of women
from rights of succession and the deposition of a reigning monarch--

were further to intensify the legal and constitutional differences
between the two realms. In France, whereas assemblies had simply
found, on the accessions of Philip V and Charles IV, that "a woman
cannot succeed to the kingdom of France,"[67] by 1328 experts in canon
and civil law were being called upon to present more elaborate justifications, all aimed at demonstrating, contrary to the pretensions of
Edward III, that it was impossible for a female to transmit rights of
hereditary succession that she did not herself possess.[68] In this way
purely hereditary succession was preserved even as France changed
dynasties. Even though these theories failed to reach full flower
until Charles V--or even Charles VII--France was well on her way to
rediscovering the Salic Law.[69] And if coronations retained their importance, it was largely because they came to be viewed as wedding
sacraments, religious ceremonies which served to unite until death
legitimate kings with their bride, the kingdom.[70]

   In England, however, the deposition could only further confound
unsettled principles. A draft coronation, apparently from the 1330's,
cautiously provided that a lay assembly was to elect the king prior
to coronation and that the archbishop could not begin the ceremony
until the people had confirmed this election.[71] Richard II found
parliamentary recognition useful to insure, as he hoped, the succession of his designated heir, Edmund Mortimer,[72] and if this same unfortunate monarch agreed to abdicate the throne, he was equally certain
that he could not renounce its spiritual honor, something that had
been "in-oiled" in him by his unction.[73] We understand why Henry IV,
his hereditary claims rejected by the commission appointed to review
them, should have thought it desirable to buttress his dubious rights
with anointing with that oil, newly rediscovered, that the Virgin had
given to Becket.[74] Last, although in theory the Yorkists based their
claims on principles of strict hereditary legitimacy, in practice each
of them found, like the Lancastrians before them, that if (in the words
of Bagot's case) he "was not merely a usurper," it was because "the
crown was entailed on him by parliament."[75] When England reached this
point, she was well on the way to the wonders of the Tudor constitution, one that would allow Bloody Mary and Elizabeth--bastards both
in the new Protestant world--to succeed to the throne purely by virtue

of parliamentary enactment.

These events may sound suspiciously like a story of Isabella the She-Wolf's revenge, but they do serve to emphasize just how far apart French and English theories of royal legitimacy had drifted by the end of the Middle Ages. And the implications are enormous. We see, for example, why it was so much easier to depose a king in England than in France. The madness of a French Charles VI could lead to civil war, as could the madness of his grandson, the English Henry VI. But although Charles remained secure on his throne for forty years, Henry had the misfortune to be deposed not once, but twice.[76] The difference is instructive.

Little wonder, either, that Charles VII, his royal paternity denied by his adulterous mother ("a great whore," Louis XI called her),[77] should have been subject to so many fits of doubt and crises of leadership. It was to take a Joan of Arc, bringing assurances from heaven that he was truly king and proving it by having him crowned at Reims, to convince him that he alone had the right to rule. For surely God would have struck him dead at his coronation/wedding had his blood been in any way unroyal and tainted.[78]

How different the realm of England! There, kings had to depend on power and ability, not sacredness of blood, and in their coronation oaths they gave witness not to an indissoluable marital bond but more to a contract with the people, their subjects, whose laws they swore to uphold. Thus, if the logical outcome in one kingdom was the preaching of Bossuet, in the other it was the philosophy of John Locke. This is, perhaps, still Isabella's revenge--the contrary consequences of the queanly conduct of queens--but that is the chance one takes in trying to keep up with Professor Strayer, seeking out "the full value of history" with "knowledge of other countries and other times."

Chapter 25

Philosophy and Citizenship in the Thirteenth Century--
Laicisation, the Two Laws and Aristotle[1]

Gaines Post

Always, of course, there has been some ideal of good citizenship,
of active participation in the life of a community for the common
good.  In antiquity the city-state demanded it, and the philosophers
responded with statements of the theory--Plato, Aristotle, and Cicero,
not to mention others, in their separate ways.  Much of the Stoic doctrine is to be found in the Roman jurisconsults.  But Christianity
was marked by a reaction against this secularism in favor of the
Heavenly City.  Nevertheless the Christian church was an organization
on earth, and the administrators had to live in the world in order to
carry on the work of saving souls.  The bishop, indeed, might be
scorned by monks as so worldly that he could not win heaven for himself.  In the early thirteenth century, however, Pope Innocent III in
a left-handed way offered the proper justification of the bishop as a
worldly administrator:  a bishop, he said, who is necessarily in office
to help others save their souls and thus to serve the higher common
welfare, cannot resign without special permission of the pope, in order
to save his own soul.[2]  In this one case, clearly, the common good was
superior to the individual spiritual welfare, whereas normally the
right of a soul was above the collective right or common good or public utility of a community on earth.  Of course the clergy recommended
that laymen serve society by ruling according to law and justice and
defending the church.  The church, therefore, was never completely
other-worldly, and always it carried on some of the tradition of "good-
citizenship" expressed by Cicero, the Stoics and Roman lawyers, St.
Ambrose, and St. Augustine.
  While the older, Christian ideal continued to exist, the secular
ideal gained momentum in the eleventh to thirteenth centuries.  The
revival of learning, the rise of cathedral schools, the flourishing
patronage of learned men by princes, and the development of universities accentuated the training of students for practical citizenship--

for teaching, healing, waging lawsuits, drawing up contracts and other
documents for businessmen, prelates, towns, and kings, and advising
princes and their courts on problems of private and public law.  The
contemporary economic, social, and political revival demanded all
these things--as the world demands them today.

  Newer intellectual appreciations and rationalizations of the active
life in the world accompanied this great revival.  Some were old--re-
statements, that is, of what was read, and now understood in a more
worldly sense, in the Latin classics, as in Cicero.  For example,
Cicero's ideal of active citizenship, rather than his belief in the
value of occasional withdrawal from the world, found favor among
Italian experts on the notarial art, who by the middle of the thirteenth century were in the service of the communes.  More important,
however, was their response to the demand in the communes for men
trained in the practical composition of business letters; and teachers
like Boncompagno, Guido Faba, and Mino de Colle di Val d'Elsa were at
times aware of the public law and common welfare of all in the city-
state.[3]  Further, the revival of the Roman law resulted in a like emphasis on the supremacy of the state.[4]  In fact, in the mid-thirteenth
century, a great legist at Bologna, Odofredo, said that the bonus civis
was bound to defend the rights (iura) of his patria and to serve in
the government.[5]  The new Aristotle, naturally, acquainted scholars
with a similar stress on the worldly problems of the community, and
the Politics and Ethics taught the value of active citizenship for
the common good.  This Aristotelian doctrine became influential in
the second half of the thirteenth century, and one finds the theory
of the common good of the community stated abundantly by Thomas
Aquinas.[6]  It was developed in a still more worldly sense, in relation to the powers of the ruler to act for the common and public welfare, by secular theologians, e.g., Henry of Ghent and Godefroid de
Fontaines.  A man was not truly a man if not a (good) citizen--so said
Remigio de Girolami.[7]

  But in Aristotle the active political life, though good because it
was for the common good and welfare of the state, was not the highest
good, was not the supreme happiness of the citizen.  This happiness
resulted from philosophy, the intellectual life of learning and

contemplation. Yet the philosopher should not withdraw from the world.
He should practice the virtues, private and public, including "good
citizenship." Father F. A. Gauthier has shown this from the "extreme
Aristotelian" commentaries that he has studied.[8] It was emphasized
also by Boethius of Dacia.[9]

Another illustration, which I now present, comes from the incomplete
commentary, Questiones in libros ethicorum, in the Paris, BN, MS. lat.
14698, fols. 130-164$^V$. Father Gauthier has studied the work, and concludes that it belongs to the school of "integral" Aristotelians at
Paris in the later thirteenth century. Gauthier offers a few passages
illustrating the author's justification of the philosopher as a good
citizen, and his doctrines of happiness,[10] but does not reveal his
discussion of the superiority of the contemplative life over that of
administrators of the community for the common good, nor his treatment
of morality in relation to the state. Further, the author's mention
of the bailli and prévot (below, to n.30), suggests that he was at
the University of Paris and was familiar with the royal institutions
of Northern France.

Given the similarity to other commentaries of the period, the
Questiones belong probably to the late thirteenth century, but I am
not so sure as Gauthier is that the works must be dated after 1277
because of the opinions condemned in that year.[11] In one respect it
is true that the author is not an extreme Aristotelian on happiness,
for he says (fol. 137$^V$ c.2): Homo igitur felix ipse beatus est, non
sicut deus aut intelligentia, sed sicut homo in genere humane nature.
Unde qui poneret ultimam perfectionem hominis in hac vita, sicut
perfectionem dei aut intelligentie, ipse errat. Elsewhere, however,
he argues, like the extreme Aristotelians, that felicitas is only indirectly from God as the first cause, but immediately from the human
cause or from man's own efforts (fol. 140 c.1-c.2, Utrum felicitas sit
a deo inmissa). Whether extreme or moderate, his outlook is generally
secular, and his discussion of the philosopher as a citizen bears
little trace of the medieval Weltanschauung that preceeded the revival
of Roman law and Aristotle.

His introduction, as Gauthier observes, is a justification of
philosophers. Alexander, he says, referring probably to Alexander

of Aphrodisias, wrote that philosophers, devoting themselves to study
and contemplation, are naturally virtuous, and do not pursue sensual
pleasures. Yet according to the common opinion of men this is not
true. Many believe, indeed, that philosophers are wicked, without
faith, and disdainful of the law. Wherefore, they say, they should
be expelled from the community. Thus all who give themselves to study
and philosophical contemplation are defamed and suspected.[12]

Many doctors and students withdraw, therefore, from study and from
speculation. This results in serious damage to the knowledge of the
truth, particularly of veritas theorica, for philosophy leads to the
cognitio veritatis de multis entibus secundum viam rationis (fol. 130
c.l). But many say that they can advance themselves more rapidly in
the Faculty of Theology than in others. Since, however, they do not
go into philosophy, they are not capable of appreciating what is true
according to theology.

Now the author defends philosophers. Philosophers, he says, are
virtuous and obey the law. They should not be expelled from the community. For those who devote themselves to study and to philosophical
contemplation are virtuous, since they take delight in intellectual
pleasure. Just as pleasure follows the operation of the senses, so
a certain (higher) pleasure results from the operation of the intellect. Hence philosophy, as it is said in Book X of the Ethics, brings
marvelous pleasures with purity and strength. Intellectual pleasure
is more powerful and excellent than the sensual, just as the intellect
is more powerful and excellent than the senses. Wherefore it is not
likely that philosophers will choose to lose a greater for a lesser
pleasure.[13] The token of this fact is that they are virtuous; and
this is what the Commentator (Averroes?) says on the Prologue to Book
VIII of the Physics, that when men begin to examine the truth in the
philosophers, they spurn every other pleasure.[14] Another token is
that they obey the law.

Philosophers, moreover, should not be driven out of the community,
because those who do good and strive for good in the community ought
to be a pars civitatis, and must not be expelled. Nay, they should
be preferred and honored. Philosophers strive for the good of the
community, and they love the good of the community.[15] Thus they are

a part of the state (civitas) and should not be driven out.

What matter that there are errors in philosophy! Although such errors exist, nonetheless it is useful that errors of the kind be studied and heard, not that men should believe them but that they should know how to combat them according to the way of reason by means of philosophy. It is useful, therefore, that philosophy be studied and that errors be exposed, so that men will reject them.[16]

Philosophers, then, are good citizens, and are interested in the good of the community. But in turn the state should provide law and order, control passions, remove external disturbances, and establish peace in order to assure civil happiness. Felicitas civilis, to be sure, is inferior to the highest happiness, felicitas contemplativa, to which only the few, the philosophers, can attain. Nevertheless, civil happiness is a means to the higher, the contemplative philosophy. Hence civil happiness in the community, peace and quiet, must be achieved in order to assure the superior happiness of philosophers.[17] Again, however, since happiness includes both the good of the soul and the good of the body, or exterior goods as instruments of the good of the soul, the truly happy man is not only a philosopher but a political animal. He must be a good citizen, helping others but also needing others.[18]

Yet it may be argued that the active life in society (vita civilis et activa) and civil happiness are superior to the contemplative life and the happiness of philosophers. For the life of prelates and secular authorities seems to be better, since in them one finds the active life and felicitas civilis. Almost all men abandon the contemplative for the active life. Some become prelates, who withdraw from speculation and contemplation. Since therefore all men (except a very few) accept the active and abandon the contemplative life, it seems that the active life is better and more excellent. Moreover, that activity which rules over other kinds of life is superior. But the civil or active life commands and arranges the contemplative, prescribing what arts must be taught, and usque ad quot tempus debent audiri. Finally, the active life aims at the common good of the whole community; the contemplative aims at the good of one man. What is good for the whole community and state (civitas), therefore, is a higher good than the good of one.[19]

On the contrary, however, as Aristotle says, in Book X of the Ethics, the contemplative life, based on the speculative intellect, is superior. For the contemplative life responds to what is divine in man, the intellect. And that life by which man is above all assimilated to God and the intelligences and is made most pleasing to them, is the more excellent and principal. Such is the speculative life, for through the contemplative life man is assimilated to God.[20]

In conclusion, then, the happiness of the contemplative life is superior to the civil or active life, for its object is God and divine beings, and the man engaged in such a life is pleasing to God and the intelligences. But in the civil life a man's mind is occupied not with the divine, but with practical affairs (agibilia) and inferior things, that is, utilia. There is greater pleasure, however, in the intellectual than in the active or civil life. Nevertheless, felicitas civilis aims at contemplative happiness by preventing disturbances and sufferings, for the sake of tranquillity, speculation, and contemplation. But men who lead only the active, civil life are in truth not superior and more worthy except by reputation (worldly fame). Some men, however, abandon the active for the contemplative life, and they become superior. Nonetheless most men are prone to sensual pleasures and worldly honors, and hence they choose the civil life. Again, the ars civilis or active life does not rule over the content of the speculative sciences, but only over the practice (usus). Speculative science, because it is of the will and is a moral science, rules over the ars civilis. The civil art, or active life, does not determine what geometrici should teach and demonstrate concerning the angle. Finally, what is the good for one man, such as the contemplation of and speculation on truth, is better and more worthy than the good for the whole state, although not more useful.[21] Here our author agrees with St. Thomas Aquinas.[22]

Now comes the question whether riches are necessary for happiness. The answer of Tholomeus is that a man who is a slave to wealth is prevented from engaging in works of virtue, and thus wealth is not needed for happiness. But as Aristotle says, riches are a means to virtue, the intellectual life, and happiness--moderate riches, at any rate. Hence Tholomeus is wrong, for the happy man is the master, not the slave of his wealth.[23]

But if the contemplative happiness is superior to the civil, civil happiness is good, for by it, too, one is made like unto God, because just as God rules over many things, so the man who is happy in civil happiness rules over many.[24] Yet again, through contemplative happiness man is most similar to God, because by it he is made divine and most beloved of God.

Civil happiness, in sum, is a virtue, and the philosopher should participate in the civil life for the common good. Normally such a life must be led according to the moral virtues. But is it not possible that the common good of the state as the higher end may justify certain deeds that are ordinarily bad? Our author asks, in fact, whether homicide, theft, and adultery can ever be justified by reason.[25] On the affirmative side, to kill a thief is good; hence one kind of homicide is just. Besides, licitum est vim vi repellere;[26] killing in self-defense is therefore excusable; and in addition the legislator for the common good of the state decrees that latrones be killed and hanged.[27] But theft itself is licit in cases of necessity.[28] Similarly, it may be argued that adultery is lawful in such a case of necessity as this: let us suppose that a tyrant intends to destroy the community and the common good of the civitas, but his plan is not known. In such a case it seems that it is a good thing for a man to sleep with the tyrant's wife (accedere ad uxorem eius) in order to wrest the tyrant's plans from her. This is adultery; therefore it is sometimes good, it seems, to commit adultery.[29] But on the contrary, adultery is a sin and, as Aristotle shows, cannot be a virtue. But there are some cases in which it is licit to perform such an act. To do it, however, is never good, but evil. But this evil thing is done to escape a greater evil. From this it does not follow that the lesser evil is done rightly, for its very name involves evil.[30]

The final conclusion of the author in this discussion is that it is good to kill a thief only when it is done "by him who has the public power," e.g., a bailli or prévot (hence the author seems to be northern French, and his work done at the University of Paris): then

the act is not homicide.  Killing in self-defense is lawful if it
is unavoidable; it is not good in any case.  It is a lesser evil,
moreover, to steal if one is starving, but it is not good.  Finally,
as for adultery with the wife of the would-be tyrant, it is neither
good nor licit--although if a man finds it necessary to commit adultery
in pluribus et frequenter in order to learn the intentions of the husband from the wife, it is licit.[31]

There are other questions in this commentary dealing with problems
of ethics in public life, e.g., on whether a philosopher should demand
fees, and on justice.  But these are quite frequently treated by commentators and canonists.[32]  I have singled out the questions summarized
in order to show how the revival of Aristotle's Ethics, along with the
Roman law, resulted in an increasingly secular point of view in the
later thirteenth century.  When the common or public good and necessity, as principles of public law and as reasons of state, are used
to excuse immoral acts, even though such acts are called not good but
simply lesser evils, the end of the state justifies the means.  Ragione
di stato is already at hand, even if it is not yet the amoral reason
of state of Machiavelli.  Cicero did not furnish all such ideas of
civic duty to the lawyers and dictatores of the thirteenth century.
Laicisation resulted from the classics (Cicero, Aristotle, and the
Roman law), from the Canon law, and from the practical development
of cities and states.

Footnotes

Chapter 1

[1]Round, *Feudal England* (1895), pp. 6-10.  Not a scrap of these returns has ever been found.

[2]He went so far as to assert that the legal distinctions inherent in Domesday terminology are to be understood primarily with reference to the geld system.  *Domesday Book and Beyond* (1897), pp. 3-6 and *passim*.

[3]F. H. Baring's perceptive article, "The Exeter Domesday," demonstrating that the text of Exon was not derived from the Exchequer Domesday but was in fact the very opposite, a source used by the Exchequer scribe in the compilation of D.B. I (*E.H.R.*, XXVII (1912), pp. 309-318), was completely overlooked until Professor Galbraith recognized its importance.

[4]"Some Early Surveys from the Abbey of Abingdon," *E.H.R.*, XLIV (1929), pp. 618-625; *Feudal Documents from the Abbey of Bury St. Edmunds* (1932); "Odo, Lanfranc, and the Domesday Survey," *Historical Essays in Honour of James Tait* (1933), pp. 47-57; "The Domesday Survey," *History*, XXI (1936-1937), pp. 249-257; *Domesday Monachorum* (1944).

[5]"The Making of Domesday Book," *E.H.R.*, LVII (1942), pp. 161-177.

[6]Galbraith, *Studies in the Public Records* (1948), p. 91.

[7]R. Lennard, "A Neglected Domesday Satellite," *E.H.R.*, LVIII (1943), pp. 38-39.  The Bath Abbey text had been recognized as an important "Domesday satellite" by F. H. Baring (*E.H.R.*, XXVII, pp. 315-316), but it had lain unnoticed until Lennard revived it.  On the question of feudal returns, see C. Stephenson's remark, "Notes on the Composition and Interpretation of Domesday Book," *Speculum*, XXII (1947), p. 8 and n. 39.  See also R. S. Hoyt. "The Terrae Occupatae of Cornwall and the Exeter Domesday," *Traditio*, IX (1953), pp. 155-175, and Galbraith's critique, *The Making of Domesday Book* (1961), pp. 83-84.

[8]P. H. Sawyer, "Evesham A, a Domesday Text," *Worcester Historical Society, Miscellany*, I (1960), p. 8.  Cf. R. R. Darlington, "Aethelwig of Evesham," *E.H.R.*, XLVIII (1933), p. 194:  "There is reason to believe that the compiler of certain 'hundredal lists' preserved in the opening folios of one of the Evesham cartularies had access to the original (i.e. uncodified) returns of the Domesday commissioners...."

[9]Review of Douglas' *Domesday Monachorum*, *E.H.R.*, LXI (1946), pp. 256-257.

[10]Round had already noticed the phenomenon (*V.C.H. Essex*, I, pp. 410-411), but not until Sawyer's article, "The 'Original Returns' and Domesday Book," *E.H.R.*, LXX (1955), pp. 177-197, was the method systematically applied on a scale yielding significant results for the whole of England.

[11] Galbraith, The Making of D.B., p. 161.

[12] Ibid., pp. 160-162, 166-180.

[13] Other important contributions can be found in the works of R. W. Finn: "The Immediate Sources of the Exchequer Domesday," Bulletin of the John Rylands Library, XL (1957-58), pp. 47-78; "The Exeter Domesday and Its Construction," B.J.R.L., XLI (1958-59), pp. 360-387; The Domesday Inquest and the Making of Domesday Book (1961); An Introduction to Domesday Book (1963); Domesday Studies: The Liber Exoniensis (1964); Domesday Studies: The Eastern Counties (1967). The most recent addition to the body of evidence is a record unique among Domesday materials. It is a "business letter" from Lanfranc to a Domesday Commissioner of the East Anglian circuit, answering a query about the tenurial status of some Canterbury estates in Essex and Suffolk; see F. Barlow, "Domesday Book: A Letter of Lanfranc," E.H.R., LXXVIII (1963), pp. 284-289. If direct correspondence between Commissioners and a tenant-in-chief took place in this instance, there is no reason to believe that such a method of collecting information was not used to settle other doubtful points. Once again Galbraith's theory of a complex and highly pragmatic administrative process using a variety of written sources receives unexpected support.

[14] Canterbury Cathedral, Library of the Dean and Chapter, MS. E.28, fos. 5$^v$-7$^r$, which appears on pp. 99-104 of Douglas' D.M. This text will be referred to as "RTD."

[15] E.H.R., LXI (1946), p. 259.

[16] Sawyer, "The 'Original Returns' and Domesday Book," E.H.R., LXX (1955), pp. 177-197, and Hoyt, "A Pre-Domesday Kentish Assessment List," Pipe Roll Society Publications, LXXVI (new series XXXVI) (1960), pp. 189-202, laid the foundation for this view. The basis for this assertion can be found in my unpublished dissertation, "Domesday Monachorum Reconsidered" (Princeton University, 1967).

[17] We are not told which of the Conqueror's councilors played major roles in the "deep speech" at Gloucester in December, 1085, where the Domesday Inquest seems to have been conceived (Anglo-Saxon Chronicle, s.a. 1085). Lanfranc was undoubtedly present, and would have been familiar with any Kentish records as a result of his litigation against Odo of Bayeux. On the identity of the Winchester compiler of vol. I of D.B., see Galbraith, "Notes on the Career of Samson, bishop of Worcester (1096-1112)," E.H.R., LXXXII (1967), pp. 86-97.

[18] Sawyer, pp. 194, 185.

[19] Hoyt, p. 196.

[20] Some cases of this type have been uncovered in connection with attempts to date the geld rolls in Exon Domesday: Manasses Coquus (Galbraith, "The Date of the Geld Rolls in Exon Domesday," E.H.R.,

LXV (1950), p. 14); Serlo de Burci (J. F. A. Mason, "The Date of the Geld Rolls," E.H.R., LXIX (1954), pp. 283-285); and possibly Odin the Chamberlain (Mason, ibid., p. 287). On the other hand, there is substantial evidence that D.B. did not always reflect up-to-the-minute conditions; in many places its information was long out of date by 1086; see R. Lennard, Rural England, pp. 41-43.

[21] The classic statement of the thesis that the Conqueror introduced an arbitrary system of servicia debita is J. H. Round's "The Introduction of Knight Service into England," in Feudal England (1895), pp. 225-314. His ideas were accepted in toto in regard to ecclesiastical fiefs by H. M. Chew, The English Ecclesiastical Tenants-in-Chief and Knight Service (1932), pp. 1-10. Although Round's interpretation of the significance of this Norman innovation for the development of English military institutions has been challenged (see C. W. Hollister, "The Norman Conquest and the Genesis of English Feudalism," Amer. Hist. Rev., LXVI (1960-61), pp. 641-663 for a succinct summary of the literature), nobody seriously questions the early establishment of the servicium debitum except H. G. Richardson and G. O. Sayles, The Governance of Mediaeval England... (1963), pp. 62-91. The date 1070 is based on Matthew Paris, Historia Anglorum, R.S., XLIV, Vol. 1 (1866), p. 13.

[22] C. W. Hollister, The Military Organization of Norman England (1965), pp. 216-260.

[23] Ibid., p. 59 and p. 48, n. 4.

[24] Ibid., pp. 253-254. Hollister offers a fascinating description of the fyrd-service owed by the Peterborough estates in connection with the much-discussed hidage reductions in Northamptonshire (pp. 235-243). Fyrd-service on the Canterbury manors is probably included in the figures of knight's-fees owed by the militibus archiepiscopi in D.M., for the total in the Cartae Baronum of 1166 is substantially lower than the total in D.M. (ibid., pp. 57-60).

[25] D.B., I, fo. 7b, ii; A. Ballard, An Eleventh-Century Inquisition of St. Augustine's Canterbury (1920), p. 2.

[26] "Wicham" (4 sulungs) is listed as one of Odo's demesne manors; "Wycham" (1 sulung) was held of Odo by Adam son of Hubert, and Adeloldus camerarius held "Hledes" (3 sulungs) of Odo (D.M., pp. 100-101). The RTD list of St. Augustine's manors mentions no holding in either Wickham or Leeds.

[27] In 1946 J. Le Patourel concluded that the date of the Pennenden trial could not be determined on the evidence then available, "and is unlikely ever to be determined." ("The Date of the Trial on Penenden Heath," E.H.R., LXI (1946), p. 379). In a subsequent article, the same author made a strong case for the 1072 date, showing that Levison's "official Canterbury record" in D. & C., Cart. Ant. A.42 is the most primitive record that survives ("The Reports of the Trial on Penenden Heath," in Studies in Medieval History presented to

Frederick Maurice Powicke, eds. R. W. Hunt, W. A. Pantin, and R. W. Southern (1948), pp. 15-26). In the light of this exposé of the real nature of the "literary accounts," his speculative rehabilitation of the 1072 date in the first article no longer seems far-fetched. At the time he wrote, Eadmer could inadvertently have added the (to him) familiar title "episcopus de rouecestra" to the name "Ernostus," even though the latter was only a member of Lanfranc's household at the time of Pennenden and not yet bishop. The date cited in the Acta Lanfranci could refer to 1072 as easily as to 1073.

[28]"Odo, Lanfranc, and the Domesday Survey," pp. 47-51.

[29]Ibid., pp. 51-52; see also F. R. H. DuBoulay, The Lordship of Canterbury (1966), pp. 38-41.

[30]Douglas, "Odo, Lanfranc, and the Domesday Survey," pp. 53-54; there seems to be no good reason to pick on these two years rather than any others between Pennenden Heath and the Domesday Inquest.

[31]A certain degree of uniformity in geld-administration over the whole of England must be presupposed; specifically, it will be assumed that extant geld-records from other counties create a presumption that analogous records could have existed for Kent. This is precisely the assumption made by Galbraith in his successful reconstruction of the stages in the compilation and writing of D.B.; in his analysis Exon Domesday and "Little Domesday" are taken as representative of whole classes of similar records which have perished.

[32]Feudal England (1895), p. 148.

[33]Galbraith, The Making of D.B., pp. 96-98; F. Barlow in The Norman Conquest, essays by D. Whitelock, et al. (1966), p. 146; R. W. Finn, Domesday Studies: The Liber Exoniensis, p. 110.

[34]Finn, Domesday Studies, pp. 100-110.

[35]Round proposed 1075 as the terminal possibility by identifying "the lady, the king's wife" as Edith, Edward the Confessor's widow (F.E., p. 148). Later commentaries have tended to favor Matilda, the Conqueror's wife (d. 1083) as the more likely candidate (A. J. Robertson, Anglo-Saxon Charters (1939), pp. 481, 483 n. to p. 232, line 30, and 484 n. to p. 236, line 10; F. M. Stenton, Anglo-Saxon England (1943), p. 636, n. 3). Professor Stenton ventured a series of conjectures that would place the date between 1072 and 1078 (ibid.). Round (F.E., p. 148) furthermore suggested that the document was actually an Old English translation of a Latin original because the English "kynges writere" appeared to him to be a literal rendering of "clericus regis." Robertson, on the other hand, pointed out that "notarius" is the Latin word translated by O.E. "writere" (Anglo-Saxon Charters, p. 482 n. to p. 232, line 4), and indeed the expression "clericus regis" did not come into common usage for a recognized group of royal clerks until much later. It would now seem safer to assume that the Northamptonshire geld-roll was a genuine O.E. document,

written in that language even after the Conquest because it represented the continuation of a tradition reaching back into the past
far beyond 1066.

[36] J. H. Round, "The Domesday Survey," V.C.H. Northamptonshire, I
(1902), pp. 259-260.

[37] Ibid., p. 260.

[38] Ibid., pp. 263-265; see also Round, "The Hidation of Northamptonshire," E.H.R., XXV (1900), pp. 78-86.

[39] Maitland, Domesday Book and Beyond (1897), pp. 457, 469.

[40] R. S. Hoyt, The Royal Demesne in English Constitutional History,
1066-1272 (1950), pp. 39-51.

[41] V.C.H. Northamptonshire, I, pp. 261-263; F. H. Baring, "The
Conqueror's Footprints in Domesday," E.H.R., XIII (1898), pp. 17-25.

[42] "Odo, Lanfranc, and the Domesday Survey," pp. 51-52.

[43] The problem of dating the geld-rolls in Exon Domesday is, of
course, germane to this argument.  Galbraith collected an impressive
array of evidence for his novel contention that the Exon Domesday
geld-rolls were compiled in 1086 (not 1084 as was previously believed),
and that they depended upon the unique procedures of the Domesday
Inquest itself for the mass of detailed information they record ("The
Date of the Geld Rolls...," E.H.R., LXV (1950), pp. 1-17; The Making
of D.B., pp. 87-101).  Without intending to become involved in the
controversy, I wish to point out that all doubts have not been laid
to rest on this score.  Finn has recently stated his reservations on
the 1086 date (Domesday Studies:  The Liber Exoniensis, pp. 114-119).
The principal difficulty in Galbraith's theory is the impossibility
of bringing the hidages recorded in the geld-rolls into harmony with
the Domesday statistics.  Hoyt's suggestion that at least some reas-
sessments may have been "accomplished during the Domesday survey itself" offers a possible explanation (The Royal Demesne..., p. 33).
Galbraith's use of paleographic arguments (E.H.R., LXV, p. 6; The
Making of D.B., p. 94) is unconvincing; surely the same scribes could
have been at work on the various parts of the Exon Domesday in both
1084 and 1086, and their hands would not necessarily be distinguishable
over such a short interval.  Yet even if Galbraith is right, the RTD
form of geld-list presupposes none of the complicated inquisitorial
techniques which must have preceded the compilation of the Exon accounts.  RTD may even be thought of as a transitional stage between
the Northamptonshire and Exon forms.

[44] E.H.R., XLIV (1929), p. 623.

[45] Canterbury Cathedral, Library of the Dean and Chapter, Register
P, fos. 29$^r$-29$^v$; Lambeth Palace MS. 1212, p. 340.  Hoyt published
the text in "A Pre-Domesday Kentish Assessment List"; I have called

this the "Reg. P assessment list."

[46]E.H.R., XLIV (1929); for Douglas' comments, pp. 618-620.

[47]Ibid., p. 620.

[48]Ibid., p. 619.

[49]Ibid., p. 619, n. 2.  I have not had an opportunity to check the
manuscript, and Douglas did not publish the text of the second "survey"; hence this remark must be accepted on faith.  It seems safe to
do so, since the observation is so damaging to Douglas' own cause.

[50]In this connection, it is interesting to consider Finn's reconstruction of the procedure used in the compilation of Exon Domesday
(Domesday Studies:  The Liber Exoniensis, pp. 6-25).  From his intense
scrutiny of that text, Finn concludes that the Exon Domesday "does
seem to be the result of fitting into a skeleton list of manors, a
list which probably included a few of the details required--the information which the authorities of the shire must continually have needed,
e.g. the names by which holdings were known, tenancies, and assess-
ments--the details of manorial equipment which could be furnished only
by the tenants' representatives, and the claims and illegalities
brought before the Commissioners for their consideration" (p. 6).
In casting about for the starting-point of the compilation he suggests
that "possibly we should look for this in the now lost geld accounts
for the latest occasion of its collection before the Inquest" (p. 9).
His line of reasoning in this chapter parallels what I have argued
about the Kentish Domesday.

[51]For an independent argument to a similar conclusion, see S.
Harvey, "Domesday Book and Its Predecessors," E.H.R., LXXXVI (1971),
pp. 753-773.

[52]See, for example, the terms in which F. M. Stenton described
Domesday in William the Conqueror (1908), pp. 457-458.

[53]Pollock & Maitland, History of English Law..., 2nd edit. (1898),
vol. 1, p. 143; C. H. Haskins, Norman Institutions (1918), pp. 47,
56.

Chapter 2

[1] J.-M. Besse, "L'ordre de Cluny et son gouvernement [I]," Revue Mabillon, I (1905), 8. Though far from the first to express this view, Besse was the first to base it on a thorough analysis of the constitution and administration of the order, especially in the late Middle Ages.

[2] Hubert Claude, "Le légat Gérard d'Angoulême et la résistance de l'abbaye de Baigne à la centralisation clunisienne," Mélanges...René Crozet (Poitiers, 1966), I, 515.

[3] There is a parallel tendency to refer to Cluniac policy as if all Cluniacs were dragooned into a single pattern: cf. among recent works H.E.J. Cowdrey, The Cluniacs and the Gregorian Reform (Oxford, 1970), who reacted against the perhaps excessive emphasis by Tellenbach and his circle on regional tendencies in Cluniac monasticism and who stressed the role of the papacy in creating the liberty of Cluny and in confirming its rights over its dependencies.

[4] On the emergence of the Cluniac order, which started as a loose confederation of monasteries--some actually joined to Cluny, some subject to the personal control of its abbot, and some more or less following its customs--and only slowly developed into a juridical union, see the two articles by Patrice Cousin, "L'expansion clunisienne sous l'abbatiat de saint Odilon," and Jacques Hourlier, "Cluny et la notion d'Ordre religieux," in À Cluny: Congrès scientifique...9-11 juillet 1949 (Dijon, 1950), pp. 186-191 and 219-226. Cf. also Cinzio Violante, "Il monachesimo cluniacense di fronte al mondo politico ed ecclesiastico (Secoli X e XI)," Spiritualità cluniacense (Convegni del Centro di Studi sulla spiritualità medioevale, 2; Todi, 1960), pp. 192-194. On Adalbero's attack on the Cluniacs in his Carmen ad Robertum regem, which was probably written in 1016, see Robert T. Coolidge, "Adalbero, Bishop of Laon," Studies in Medieval and Renaissance History, II (1965), 70-75 and, on the date, Jacques Hourlier, Saint Odilon, abbé de Cluny (Bibliothèque de la Revue d'histoire ecclésiastique, 40; Louvain, 1964), pp. 214-216.

[5] See the subsequent articles by Besse in the Revue Mabillon, I (1905), 97-138 and 177-194 and II (1906), 1-22. Suitbert Gammersbach, "Das Abtsbild in Cluny und bei Bernhard von Clairvaux," Cîteaux in de Nederlanden, VII (1956), 85-101 cited contemporary references to the abbot of Cluny as king, prince, ruler, and abbot of abbots, and contrasted this royal view of the abbot with the more patriarchal view of Bernard of Clairvaux.

[6] Noreen Hunt, Cluny under Saint Hugh, 1049-1109 (London, 1967), pp. 161 and 184.

[7] Cowdrey, Cluniacs, p. 254 (and 253-254 generally).

[8] Georg Schreiber, Kurie und Kloster im 12. Jahrhundert

(Kirchenrechtliche Abhandlungen, 65-68; Stuttgart, 1910), II, 303,
who cited 131 houses in the privilege of Paschal II and 140 in that
of Honorius II.

[9]On the question of Cluniac abbeys, of which there were three in
1088, eighteen in the 1120's and eight by the end of the twelfth century, see Philipp Hofmeister, "Cluny und seine Abteien," Studien und
Mitteilungen zur Geschichte des Benediktiner-Ordens und seiner Zweige,
LXXV (1964), 183-239; also Schreiber, Kurie, II, 306-315; Ursmer
Berlière, L'ordre monastique des origines au XIIe siècle, 3rd ed.
(Collection "Pax," 1; Maredsous, 1924), p. 217; and Cowdrey, Cluniacs,
pp. 76-107. These abbeys were not only an anomaly in the order but
also a source of trouble, owing to their resistance to control and
efforts to regain independence.

[10]In the time of Peter the Venerable, indeed, according to Berlière,
Ordre, p. 218, "L''Ordre' clunisien offrait un reflet de la féodalité,
avec ses fiefs et ses arrière-fiefs, dans les abbayes et prieurés qui
lui étaient subordonnés à des titres différents." This question concerning the monarchical or feudal organization of the order is quite
distinct from the vexed question of whether Cluny was pro- or anti-
feudal, which concerns its attitude toward lay society.

[11]See Gerd Tellenbach, "Der Sturz des Abtes Pontius von Cluny und
seine geschichtliche Bedeutung," Quellen und Forschungen aus
italienischen Archiven und Bibliotheken, XLII-XLIII (1963), 13-55,
esp. 32-35 on episcopal opposition to Cluny's privileges; Cowdrey,
Cluniacs, pp. 253-254; and Adriaan Bredero, "Cluny et Cîteaux au
XIIème siècle: Les origines de la controverse," Studi medievali, 3
S., XII (1971), 159-160, who saw Pontius as a reformer and the election of Peter the Venerable as a reaction against Pontius by the
traditionalists.

[12]The Letters of Peter the Venerable, ed. Giles Constable (Harvard
Historical Studies, 78; Cambridge, Mass., 1967), I, 388 (cited hereafter as Letters).

[13]The statutes are cited here by number alone from the new edition
soon to appear in volume VI of the Corpus consuetudinum monasticarum
(Siegburg, 1963 ff.). There are earlier editions in the Bibliotheca
Cluniacensis, ed. Martin Marrier and André Duchesne (Paris, 1614;
rp. Mâcon, 1915), coll. 1353-1376 and in Statuts, chapitres généraux
et visites de l'ordre de Cluny, ed. G. Charvin, I (Paris, 1965), 20-40.

[14]R.B.C. Huygens, "Le moine Idung et ses deux ouvrages: 'Argumentum
super quatuor questionibus' et 'Dialogus duorum monachorum'," Studi
medievali, 3 S., XIII (1972), 437 (Dialogus, II, 62) and 452 (Dialogus,
III, 31).

[15]See in particular Kassius Hallinger, Gorze-Kluny (Studia
Anselmiana, 22-25; Rome, 1950-1951), II, 778-779 and Josef Semmler,
Die Klosterreform von Siegburg (Rheinisches Archiv, 53; Bonn, 1959),
pp. 322-324, both with references to other works. Cf. also Cowdrey,

<u>Cluniacs</u>, pp. 191-213 on the Cluniacs in Germany, stressing the tradition of lay advocacy there (211).

[16]Semmler, <u>Klosterreform</u>, pp. 324-333.

[17]On the constitutional importance of the priory system for extending the power of the abbot of Cluny without breaking the ties with local families, see Georg Schreiber, "Vorfranziskanisches Genossenschaftswesen" (1943/4) reprinted in his <u>Gemeinschaften des Mittelalters</u> (Münster, 1948), pp. 429-431; also Berlière, <u>Ordre</u>, p. 216.

[18]Berlière, <u>Ordre</u>, p. 218.

[19]See the itinerary in <u>Letters</u>, II, 257-269, and D. Van den Eynde, "Les principaux voyages de Pierre le Vénérable," <u>Benedictina</u>, XV (1968), 58-110.

[20]Letter 127 in <u>Letters</u>, I, 324; cf. <u>ibid</u>., II, 14-15, for this and other references on Peter's occupation with worldly affairs.

[21]Ordericus Vitalis, <u>Historia ecclesiastica</u>, XIII, 13, ed. A. Le Prévost and L. Delisle (Société de l'histoire de France; Paris, 1838-1855), V, 29-31.

[22]See the references in <u>Letters</u>, II, 173-174 and 208.

[23]Hugh V, Statutes (1200), 58-61 and (1205/6) 1 and 24-26, in Charvin, <u>Statuts</u>, I, 51-52, 54, and 59-60. The <u>definatores</u> are mentioned in his Statute 40, cited n. 73 below. On the chapter-general at Cluny, see Alexandre Bruel, "Les chapitres généraux de l'ordre de Cluny depuis le XIIIe jusqu'au XVIIIe siècle," Bibliothèque de l'Ecole des Chartes, XXXIV (1873), 542-579, who dated the first reference to the chapter-general in 1200; Besse, in Rev. Mab., I, 97-138; P. Anger, "Chapitres généraux de Cluny," Rev. Mab., VIII (1912-13), 105-147 and 213-252 (126-133 on the definatores); Guy de Valous, Le monachisme clunisien des origines au XVe siècle (Archives de la France monastique, 39-40; Paris, 1935), II, 70-94; Jacques Hourlier, Le chapitre général jusqu'au moment du Grand Schisme (Paris, 1936), pp. 33-41 and 68-78; and Jane Sayers, "The Judicial Activities of the General Chapter," Journal of Ecclesiastical History, XV (1964), 29.

[24]See my paper on "Monastic Legislation at Cluny in the Eleventh and Twelfth Centuries," to appear in the proceedings of the Fourth International Congress of Medieval Canon Law held at Toronto in August, 1972.

[25]In the eleventh century, under Abbot Hugh, there was already a tendency to rely on some of the great regional houses as centers of Cluniac influence, but apparently not of administration: cf. Hansmartin Schwarzmaier, "Das Kloster S. Benedetto di Polirone in seiner cluniacensischen Umwelt," <u>Adel und Kirche: Gerd Tellenbach zum 65. Geburtstag dargebracht von Freunden und Schülern</u>, ed. Josef Fleckenstein and Karl Schmid (Freiburg-Basel-Vienna, 1968), pp. 280-

294. Even in the twelfth century there was no consistent or conscious policy of regional administrative decentralization, such as was later introduced for purposes of visitation.

[26]Peter the Venerable reasserted this principle in Statutes 35 and 38, in the causa of which he complained that some priors out of parsimony delayed sending their novices for blessing at Cluny for up to twenty years. Statute 38 was reissued in 1200 by Hugh V, Statute 11, in Charvin, Statuts, I, 43.

[27]Hunt, Cluny, p. 176.

[28]Ibid., p. 54, cf. 172.

[29]De Valous, Monachisme, I, 191; cf. Bonaventura Egger, Geschichte der Cluniazenser-Klöster in der Westschweiz (Freiburger historische Studien, 3; Freiburg, 1907), pp. 71-73, who commented on the appointment by the abbot of priors in Cluniac houses in western Switzerland and on the numbers of priors.

[30]Adrian Morey and C.N.L. Brooke, Gilbert Foliot and his Letters (Cambridge Studies in Medieval Life and Thought, N.S. 11; Cambridge, 1965), p. 77.

[31]Letters, II, 257-258.

[32]Ibid., II, 243-244.

[33]Ibid., II, 240-241 and 344, to which should be added the reference to him as sacristan on a document in O. Morel, Inventaire sommaire des archives communales de Brénod (Ain) (Bourg, 1932) between pp. 32-33.

[34]David Knowles, C.N.L. Brooke, and Vera London, The Heads of Religious Houses: England and Wales, 940-1216 (Cambridge, 1972) (cited hereafter as Heads).

[35]Ibid., p. 117.

[36]Ibid., pp. 120 and 124.

[37]Ibid., pp. 41, 116, 117, and 126 (quotation on 116). These examples do not include those mentioned below of Cluniacs who moved within the order before becoming superiors of independent houses.

[38]Charles de Lasteyrie, L'abbaye de Saint-Martial de Limoges (Paris, 1901), p. 99.

[39]Peter the Venerable, De miraculis, II, 25, in Bibl. Clun., col. 1324, and other references in Letters, II, 348, to which should be added that in Morel, Inventaire, between pp. 32-33. An Abbot William of Moissac is listed in 1135, between two abbots whose last and first appearances were respectively in 1131 and 1140, in the Gallia christiana, new ed. (Paris, 1715-1865), I, 165.

[40]Peter the Venerable, De miraculis, I, 8, in Bibl. Clun., col. 1259b (quoted passage and mission to Rome, on which see Letters, II, 114-115), 1260cd (Beaumont), 1261d (Nevers), 1262bc (retirement to Altum iugum, which may be Mont St. Romain: see Letters, II, 182); see also Letters, I, 162, and II, 134 and 137 (Marcigny and Cluny). The Index priorum Marciniaci printed in F. Cucherat, Cluny au onzième siècle, 2nd ed. (Autun [1873]), p. 265 adds that Gerald was prior of Villeneuve near Perreux and became dean of Marcigny after serving at Nevers; cf. Le cartulaire de Marcigny-sur-Loire (1045-1144), ed. Jean Richard (Analecta Burgundica; Dijon, 1957), pp. xvii-xviii on the general reliability of the Index, in spite of its relatively late date, and 93, no. 148, 135, n. 2, and 242 for further details on Gerald and his family and identifying him as the Gerald nobilis miles mentioned, with a reference to the De miraculis, in an analysis of a lost charter in the cartulary and said to have entered the religious life at the same time as his wife. This must be another man, since Peter the Venerable referred explicitly to the education of this Gerald at Cluny, to his chastity, and to his reception as a monk by Abbot Hugh as a young man (Bibl. Clun., col. 1258de).

[41]Letters, I, 188.

[42]The Peterborough Chronicle, 1070-1154, ed. Cecily Clark, 2nd ed. (Oxford, 1970), pp. 43 (s.a. 1123), 48-49 (s.a. 1127), 50 (s.a. 1128), and 52-54 (s.a. 1130-1132), and the relevant commentary at the end of the book; cf. Cecily Clark, "'This Ecclesiastical Adventurer': Henry of Saint-Jean d'Angély," English Historical Review, LXXXIV (1969), 548-560, from which the translations from the Chronicle cited here are taken, and Heads, p. 60, accepting Clark's conclusions.

[43]Heads, p. 4.

[44]William I came from Ramsey in 1178 and Hugh V from Reading in 1199: Heads, pp. 62 and 63.

[45]See Letters, II, 298, and Heads, p. 55.

[46]Quomodo reliquiae b. Stephani Protomartyris Cluniacum delatae fuerunt, in Bibl. Clun., col. 565cd; cf. H.-François Delaborde, Chartes de Terre Sainte provenant de l'abbaye de N.-D. de Josaphat (Bibliothèque des Écoles françaises d'Athènes et de Rome, 19; Paris, 1880), p. 18, dating his abbacy 1120-1130, and Letters, II, 291-292.

[47]The Letters of John of Salisbury, ed. W. J. Millor and H. E. Butler, revised by C.N.L. Brooke, I (Medieval Texts; Edinburgh, 1955), p. ix, n. 1.

[48]Jacques Stiennon, "Cluny et Saint-Trond au XIIe siècle," Anciens pays et assemblées d'états, VIII (Louvain, 1955), pp. 73-77, and Letters, II, 159.

[49]Letters, II, 221.

[50]Ibid., I, 437 and II, 222-223.

[51] Chronicon monasterii Molismensis, in Cartulaires de l'abbaye de Molesme, ed. Jacques Laurent (Collection de documents publiés avec le concours de la Commission des antiquités de la Côte-d'Or, 1; Paris, 1907-1911), II, 546.

[52] Patrologia latina, CLXXXII, 682d-685a (quoted passage on 683b); cf. La chronique de Morigny (1095-1152), ed. Léon Mirot, 2nd ed. (Collection de textes pour servir à l'étude et à l'enseignement de l'histoire, 41; Paris, 1912), p. xiii and passim on Abbots Thomas and Macharius. The whole affair is very complicated, but the letter clearly shows that Thomas (who was abbot from 1110/11 until his resignation in 1140) was having second thoughts and regretted his withdrawal to St.-Martin-des-Champs, since he asked Bernard whether he should return either to Morigny, "ubi me juvenis dedi et in communi capitulo me fieri monachum devovi," or to Ste.-Colombe-lès-Sens, "in qua...monachi vestes indui et professionem feci, et cum mitterer ad abbatiam Mauriniacensem, me Columbas rediturum, si eam reliquissem, spopondi." (685a) He was not a Cluniac, but his choice of St.-Martin-des-Champs as a place of retirement, if voluntary, suggests that he had Cluniac sympathies and may account for his outrage at Alberic's agreement at Fleury, which he called simony.

[53] See the appendix on Cluniac cardinals in Letters, II, 293-295, stressing that there is outside evidence only for the abbacy of Montierneuf in Imar's cursus honorum.

[54] Ibid., II, 109, 158, and 187.

[55] Ibid., II, 130-131 and Heads, pp. 51 and 121.

[56] Letters, II, 99-100; Heads, p. 63; cf. also the unpublished Harvard doctoral dissertation (1970) on Hugh by Patricia King.

[57] Morey and Brooke, Gilbert Foliot, pp. 35, 52-53, 73, and 77-79, where they emphasized the youthful appointments and long careers of Cluniacs like Henry, Hugh, and Gilbert; cf. also Letters, II, 252-256 and 346 on his mission to Rome and career at Cluny.

[58] John of Salisbury, Letters, I, 68.

[59] Anonymous reviewer (in fact, R. W. Southern) of Letters in the Times Literary Supplement for March 7, 1968, where the review was headed "Tufthunter of Cluny."

[60] Letter 105 in Letters, I, 268; see also Letters 106-108, ibid., I, 269-271 and II, 169-171. These letters, though they appear together in the collection, may not have been written at the same time. Only those to Arnold of Narbonne and Guarinus of Amiens are recruiting in nature.

[61] Ibid., II, 97-98, 171, and 194.

[62] Ibid., II, 149-150.

[63]Ibid., II, 160 and 168. In 1140 Natalis served with Alvisus of Arras and Hugh of St. Victor as an arbitrator in the disputed election at Morigny (see n. 52 above).

[64]Ibid., I, 307, and II, 178.

[65]Peter the Venerable, De miraculis, I, 27, in Bibl. Clun., col. 1290, and Walter Map, De nugis curialium, I, 13, ed. M. R. James (Anecdota Oxoniensia: Mediaeval and Modern Series, 14; Oxford, 1914), p. 19; cf. Mathieu Méras, Le Beaujolais au Moyen Age (Villefranche-en-Beaujolais, 1956), p. 29, n. 44, defending the authenticity of the sermon, and Letters, II, 214.

[66]Historia Selebiensis monasterii, I, 35, ed. J. T. Fowler, The Coucher Book of Selby, I (Yorkshire Archaeological and Topographical Association: Record Series, 10; Durham, 1891) [28]; cf. Donald Nicholl, Thurstan, Archbishop of York (1114-1140) (York, 1964), pp. 160 and 210, dating his abbacy from 1127 and citing a passage from a letter from Pope Innocent II to Thurstan: "De caetero noverit tua fraternitas, quam, si abbas ille de quo nobis significasti ad nostram praesentiam venerit, quod ad honorem Dei et tuum pertinet superna cooperante clementia sollicite providere curabimus:" in A. W. Haddan and William Stubbs, Councils and Ecclesiastical Documents relating to Great Britain and Ireland (Oxford, 1869-1878), II.1, 29. The immediately following reference to Selby makes it certain that Durand was the abbot in question. He may have contemplated an appeal to Rome but on the way, like Abelard later, stopped and stayed at Cluny. Innocent's letter is dated 1135 by Nicholl and 1136 by Haddan and Stubbs (and Jaffé-Löwenfeld, no. 7767). Cf. also Heads, p. 69, dating his abbacy c. 1125-1134/5.

[67]Letters, I, 190. This is followed immediately by a request for Henry's help in securing permanently the manor of Letcombe Regis, which King Stephen granted to Cluny some time in 1136 in lieu of the pension of a hundred marks granted by Henry I in 1131: see Regesta regum Anglo-Normannorum, III: 1135-1154, ed. H. A. Cronne and R.H.C. Davis (Oxford, 1968), pp. 74-75, no. 204 (cf. Letters, II, 138-139). This seems to date Peter's letter and Durand's mission either in 1136 or soon after, but it is not certain that the manor was the subject of the mission, which seems to have been concerned with, inter alia, Henry's place of burial.

[68]Letters, I, 191.

[69]Ibid., II, 345, to which should be added the reference in Marcigny, p. 102, no. 171 bis.

[70]Heads, p. 122. The identification again is not certain.

[71]Statute 1 of Hugh V in 1205/6 forbade the abbot of Cluny to have a private servant within the monastery (Charvin, Statuts, I, 53), and it stands to reason that what applied to the abbot also applied to the priors.

[72]Cf. Egger, Cluniazenser-Klöster, pp. 72-73, and De Valous, Monachisme, I, 191.

[73]Hugh V (1200) Statute 40, in Charvin, Statuts, I, 47.  He went on with a list of manifest causes for removal, such as damage to their priories, disobedience, rebellion, infamy, and incontinence, and applied the same rule to junior priors.  In Statute 47, issued at the same time, he forbade the movement of monks from place to place, as a cause of irresponsibility and impiety (ibid., 48).

[74]G. F. Duckett, Charters and Records among the Archives of the Ancient Abbey of Cluni (Lewes, 1888), I, 92-93.  The use of two seals, one abbatial and one conventual, which symbolized the consent of the chapter, appeared in the last quarter of the twelfth century among the Cluniacs, somewhat earlier than among other Benedictines, according to Giacomo Bascapè, "Appunti di sfragistica benedettina," Rassegna degli Archivi di Stato, XXI (1961), 158-159.

[75]To what extent Cluny's backing the wrong side in the schism at the beginning of the pontificate of Alexander III undermined its position with the papacy and affected its privileges is a question in need of study:  cf. Schreiber, Kurie, II, 315.

[76]Gammersbach, in Cîteaux, VII, 91, suggested that Peter was a traditionalist in his view of the position of the abbot, calling him "ein echter Repräsentant des monarchischen Geistes von Kluny."

[77]The importance of Cluniac financial administration for the organization of papal finances in the late eleventh century has been studied by several scholars, most recently Jürgen Sydow, "Cluny und die Anfänge der apostolischen Kammer," Studien und Mitteilungen zur Geschichte des Benediktiner-Ordens und seiner Zweige, LXIII (1951), 45-66; but there are still no studies of the influence of other aspects of Cluniac administration, or of Peter the Venerable's financial reforms, on which see Georges Duby, "Un inventaire des profits de la seigneurie clunisienne à la mort de Pierre le Vénérable," Petrus Venerabilis, 1156-1956, ed. G. Constable and J. Kritzeck (Studia Anselmiana, 40; Rome, 1956), pp. 128-140.  Schreiber, Gemeinschaften, p. 432, remarked on possible Cluniac influence on the royal administration in the twelfth century through St. Denis.

Chapter 3

[1] Joseph R. Strayer, "The Laicization of French and English Society in the Thirteenth Century," Medieval Statecraft and the Perspectives of History, eds. John F. Benton and Thomas N. Bisson (Princeton, 1971), pp. 258-262; "Defense of the Realm and Royal Power in France," Statecraft, pp. 291-299; "France:  The Holy Nation, the Chosen People, and the Most Christian King," Statecraft, pp. 300-301; "The Historical Experience of Nation-Building in Europe," Statecraft, pp. 341-348; and On the Medieval Origins of the Modern State (Princeton, 1970), pp. 3-56.  I wish to thank Father Landulf for his assistance in using the Minoritenarchiv in Vienna and my colleagues, Professors Lawrence Walker and Roy Austensen, for their criticism and advice.

[2] Origins, pp. 58-59.

[3] For further information, see Fritz Kern, Die Anfänge der franzö-sischen Ausdehnungspolitik bis zum Jahre 1308 (Tübingen, 1910).  Kern was seemingly unaware that the boundaries between the French and German mendicant provinces had been redrawn as a result of Capetian eastward expansion.

[4] Jacques Quétif and Jacques Echard, Scriptores ordinis Praedicatorum, 2 vols. (Paris, 1719-1721), I, pp. vi and ix; and Paulus von Löe, Statistisches über die Ordensprovinz Teutonia, in Quellen und Forschung-en zur Geschichte des Dominikanerordens in Deutschland, I (Leipzig, 1907), p. 7.

[5] Bartholomew of Pisa, De conformitate vitae beati Francisci ad vitam Domini Iesu, in Analecta Franciscana, IV (Quaracchi, 1906), 548-551.

[6] G. Meersseman, "Les Débuts de l'ordre des frères Prêcheurs dans le comté de Flandre (1224-1280)," Archivum fratrum Praedicatorum, XVII (1947), 9-11 and 29-38.

[7] Corpus documentorum Inquisitionis haereticae pravitatis Neerlandicae, ed. Paul Fredericq, 5 vols. (Ghent and The Hague, 1896-1906), I, no. 75.

[8] Jordan of Giano, Chronica, ed. Heinrich Boehmer, in Collection d'études et de documents sur l'histoire religieuse et littéraire du moyen âge, VI (Paris, 1908), ch. 55.  Although Jordan of Giano gives no date, John could have received the convent in Metz only during his tenure as minister of Teutonia between 1228 and 1230.  As minister of Saxony during the 1230's he lacked the authority to receive a convent in Lorraine.

[9] The Dominican general chapter referred in 1249 to the priory in Metz, located in the province of France.  Acta capitulorum generalium ordinis Praedicatorum, I, ed. Benedictus Maria Reichert, in Monumenta ordinis fratrum Praedicatorum, III (Rome, 1898), 54.

[10]For information about German expansion in eastern Europe, see the books and articles cited by K. Bosl, A. Gieysztor, F. Graus, M. M. Postan, and F. Seibt, Eastern and Western Europe in the Middle Ages, ed. Geoffrey Barraclough (London, 1970), p. 208.

[11]Paulus von Loë, Statistisches über die Ordensprovinz Saxonia, in Quellen und Forschungen zur Geschichte des Dominikanerordens in Deutschland, IV (Leipzig, 1910), pp. 11-12.

[12]Raymond-J. Loenertz, "La Vie de s. Hyacinthe du lecteur Stanislas envisagée comme source historique," Archivum fratrum Praedicatorum, XXVII (1957), 31-37.

[13]Heinrich Finke, Ungedruckte Dominikanerbriefe des 13. Jahrhunderts (Paderborn, 1891), no. 15.

[14]The Cambridge History of Poland, eds. W. F. Reddaway, J. H. Penson, O. Halecki, and R. Dyboski (Cambridge, 1950), I, 46-47; and Johannes Schultze, Die Mark Brandenburg (Berlin, 1961), I, 141-143.

[15]Loë, Saxonia, p. 12; and H. Hoogeweg, Die Stifte und Klöster der Provinz Pommern, 2 vols. (Stettin, 1924-1925), I, 620.

[16]Finke, Dominikanerbriefe, no. 15.

[17]Ibid., no. 16.

[18]Acta capitulorum generalium, I, 139-140.

[19]Hoogeweg, Stifte, II, 229-233.

[20]Finke, Dominikanerbriefe, nos. 63-66.

[21]Loë, Saxonia, p. 12; and Schultze, Brandenburg, I, 154-158.

[22]Acta capitulorum generalium, I, 202, 206, 212-213, and 216.

[23]Jordan of Giano, Chronica, ch. 55.

[24]Leonhard Lemmens, "Annales Minorum Prussicorum," Archivum Franciscanum historicum, VI (1913), 702-704.

[25]The custody of Stettin, which straddled the mouth of the Oder, eventually included four convents east of the lower Oder in Farther Pomerania: Pyritz, Greifenberg, Arnswalde, and Dramburg. Patricius Schlager, "Verzeichnis der Klöster der sächsischen Franziskaner-Provinzen," Franziskanische Studien, I (1914), 236. Since these convents are mentioned for the first time in a document or chronicle in the late thirteenth or early fourteenth centuries, there is no way of determining whether the boundary of the province of Saxony already extended east of the lower Oder before the annexation of the custody of Prussia by Saxony sometime between 1258 and 1284. There is no evidence that the convents west of the lower Oder in the custody of

Stettin were ever assigned to the Bohemian province.

[26]Schultze, Brandenburg, I, 140.

[27]Schlager, "Verzeichnis," 236.  Not all the convents in the custody were actually in existence by the 1260's.

[28]Ibid.

[29]The chief source on these German-Polish provincial reassignments is Jan Kazimierz Biernacki's summary and confused account in the Speculum Minorum (Cracow, 1688), pp. 229-233.  André Callebaut has reconstructed the probable sequence of events in "Le Chapitre général de 1272 célébré à Lyon," Archivum Franciscanum historicum, XIII (1920), 313-314.

[30]Lemmens, "Annales Minorum Prussicorum," 704.

[31]Franz Palacky, Ueber Formelbücher, zunächst in Bezug auf böhmische Geschichte (Prague, 1842), pp. 287-288, nos. 54 and 55.  The letters cannot be precisely dated, but Chrysogonus Reisch, ed. Urkundenbuch der Kustodien Goldberg und Breslau, Part I, in Monumenta Germaniae Franciscana, Part II (Düsseldorf, 1917), p. 8, fn. 2, points out that Agnes was abbess of Trebnitz between 1268 and 1278.

[32]Colmar Grünhagen, Geschichte Schlesiens (Gotha, 1884), I, 94-98.

[33]The best account of Ottokar's reign is still Ottokar Lorenz's Geschichte König Ottokars II. von Böhmen und seiner Zeit (Vienna, 1866).

[34]Hermann Aubin, "Die Ostgrenze des alten deutsches Reiches," Historische Vierteljahrschrift, XXVIII (1933), 252.

[35]The best general accounts of medieval Austrian history can be found in Hugo Hantsch, Die Geschichte Österreichs, 5th ed., 2 vols. (Graz, Vienna, Cologne: 1969), I; and Erich Zöllner, Geschichte Österreichs: Von den Anfängen bis zur Gegenwart, 2nd ed. (Munich, 1961).

[36]Heinrich Fichtenau, Von der Mark zum Herzogtum: Grundlagen und Sinn des "Privilegium Minus" für Österreich, 2nd ed. (Vienna, 1965), pp. 23-24.

[37]Fichtenau, pp. 37-52; Hantsch, Geschichte, I, 70-75; Zöllner, Geschichte, pp. 69-71; and Gerhart B. Ladner, "The Middle Ages in Austrian Tradition: Problems of an Imperial and Paternalistic Ideology," Viator, III (1972), 435.  The newest edition of the Privilegium minus can be found in the Urkundenbuch zur Geschichte der Babenberger in Österreich, ed. Heinrich Fichtenau (Vienna, 1968), IV, no. 803.

[38]Hermann Krabbo, "Die Versuche der Babenberger zur Gründung einer

Landeskirche in Österreich," <u>Archiv für österreichische Geschichte</u>,
XCIII (1905), 30-38; and Oswald Redlich, "Die Pläne einer Erhebung
Österreichs zum Königreich," <u>Zeitschrift des historischen Vereines</u>
<u>für Steiermark</u>, XXVI (1931), 88-92.

[39]Erich Zöllner, "Formen und Wandlungen des Österreichsbegriffes,"
<u>Historica: Studien zum geschichtlichen Denken und Forschen</u>, eds.
Hugo Hantsch, Eric Voegelin, and Franco Valsecchi (Vienna, Freiburg,
Basel: 1965), pp. 67-68.

[40]G. E. Friess, "Geschichte der oesterreichischen Minoritenprovinz,"
<u>Archiv für österreichische Geschichte</u>, LXIV (1882), no. 2.

[41]Bartholomew of Pisa, <u>De conformitate</u>, pp. 552-553. Friess, pp.
100-101 and 106-107, could find no evidence for the existence in the
Middle Ages of the convents in Grein and Zistersdorf, which are mentioned by Bartholomew of Pisa.

[42]Friess, no. 4. In 1253 the papal legate granted the Franciscans
"per Austriam et Stiriam constitutis" permission to preach and to
hear confessions in other churches as well as in their own convents.
Vienna, <u>Minoritenarchiv</u>, no. 7 (Friess, no. 18).

[43]Friess, no. 5. See also nos. 6 and 8 and <u>Minoritenarchiv</u>, no.
22 (Friess, no. 36).

[44]Friess, nos. 2, 3, 5, 6, 8, 10, 14, 15, 32, 34, 35, 36, 40, 45,
and 50.

[45]<u>Ibid</u>., nos. 20 and 25. The text of the latter document is published in its entirety in <u>Facies nascentis et succrescentis provinciae</u>
<u>Seraphico-Austriacae strictioris observantiae</u> (Regensburg, 1743), pp.
35-36.

[46]Friess, no. 15.

[47]<u>Minoritenarchiv</u>, no. 16 (Friess, no. 24).

[48]Konrad Eubel, "Die Minoriten Heinrich Knoderer u. Konrad Probus,"
<u>Historisches Jahrbuch</u>, IX (1888), 393-449 and 650-673.

[49]See, for instance, Marquard Herrgott, <u>Taphographia principum</u>
<u>Austriae</u>, in <u>Monumenta aug. domus Austriacae</u>, IV (Vienna, 1772), Part
2, no. 12.

Chapter 4

[1]The research for this article was done for a thesis under Professor Strayer's supervision. I also wish to acknowledge the valuable criticisms and helpful advice I received from Elizabeth Brown, Bernard Guenée, and John Henneman.

[2]F. Lot and R. Fawtier, Histoire des institutions francaises au moyen âge, II: Institutions royales (Paris, 1958), pp. 256-260; P. S. Lewis, Later Medieval France: The Polity (London, 1968), p. 105. M. Wolfe, however, insists that decisive changes did not take place until the reign of Charles VII. The Fiscal System of Renaissance France (New Haven, 1972).

[3]J. B. Henneman, Jr., Royal Taxation in Fourteenth Century France (Princeton, 1971); "The French Ransom Aids and Two Legal Traditions," Studia Gratiana, XV (1972), pp. 615-629; R. Cazelles, "Les mouvements révolutionaires du milieu du XIVe siècle et le cycle de l'action politique," Revue Historique, CCXXVIII (1962), pp. 279-312; Georges Mouradian, "La rancon de Jean II le Bon," Positions des thèses, École des Chartes, 1970.

[4]Their importance in many ways is analogous to the viscounts'; see J. B. Strayer, "Viscounts and Viguiers under Philip the Fair," Speculum, XXXVIII (1963), p. 242; now reprinted in Medieval Statecraft and the Perspectives of History (Princeton, 1971), p. 213.

[5]This reservation is somewhat mitigated by the fact that Charles V, first as dauphin and later as king, seems to have overseen the creation of the administration of the aids in Normandy; the techniques he developed there may well have been applied deliberately to other regions.

[6]For the role of Normandy as a testing ground of royal policies between 1340 and 1356, see Henneman, Royal Taxation, pp. 228-231, 247-248, 284-287, 292-294, and esp. 307. "It is hard to overestimate the importance of this duchy, which had played a pivotal role in the history of royal finances since its acquisition by the crown. In 1339, 1347, and 1355 the Norman estates granted sizeable taxes and established models which the rest of the kingdom followed." For Normandy as a leader in the crisis of 1380-1382, see L. Mirot, Les insurrections urbaines au début du règne de Charles VI (1380-1383) (Paris, 1905), pp. 39-45, 53-54.

[7]The best general history of Normandy in this period is still A. Coville, Les états de Normandie. Leurs origines et leur développement au XIVe siècle (Paris, 1894).

[8]For a biography of one councillor-general, see H. Moranvillé, "Étude sur la vie de Jean le Mercier" (Paris, 1888), in Mémoires présentées par divers savants à l'Academie des inscriptions et belles-lettres, 2e série, t. 6.

[9] B. N., P. O. 167 Baigneux no. 22.

[10] B. N., ms. fr. 26006 no. 193, ms. fr. 26007 no. 455.

[11] B. N., ms. fr. 26006 no. 1159.

[12] B. N., ms. fr. 26008 no. 745.

[13] B. N., ms. fr. 26006 no. 30, ms. fr. 26007 no. 300.

[14] B. N., ms. fr. 26005 no. 1358, ms. fr. 26010 no. 1156; G. Dupont-Ferrier, Gallia Regia ou état des officiers royaux des bailliages et des sénéchausées de 1328 à 1515 (Paris, 1942-1965) [henceforth to be cited as Gallia Regia] no. 1631; B. N., P. O. 580 Campion no. 22.

[15] B. N., ms. fr. 26010 no. 1179.

[16] B. N., P. O. 580 Campion nos. 16, 23.

[17] A. N., KK 350 ff. 297, 316.

[18] B. N., P. O. 580 Campion no. 24.

[19] B. N., P. O. 1838 Marchant no. 3.

[20] Coville, Les états de Normandie, p. 313.

[21] The Norman baillis of the thirteenth century were paid between 300 and 600 l. t. a year. J. R. Strayer, The Administration of Normandy under St. Louis (Cambridge, Mass., 1932), p. 97. For the status of "king's councillors," see R. Cazelles, La société politique et la crise de la royauté sous Philippe de Valois (Paris, 1958), pp. 305-314.

[22] Jean d'Orléans and Lucas le Courtois, receivers-general of Normandy; Guillaume le Grant, Aymar Revout, Renier le Coutelier, and Étienne du Moustier, élus-general of Lower Normandy; Jean Vauchis, Raoul Campion, Berthaut Aladent, receivers-general of Lower Normandy. Interested scholars may find complete manuscript references supporting this and subsequent lists of officers in Appendix II of my unpublished Ph.D. dissertation, "The Administration of the Aids in Normandy, 1360-1389" (Princeton, 1973).

[23] B. N., ms. fr. 26005 nos. 1445, 1515; P. O. 167 Baigneux no. 22; L. Delisle, ed., Mandements et actes divers de Charles V (1364-1380) (Paris, 1874) [henceforth to be cited as Mand.], no. 48. The élus were Raoul d'Estouteville, Symon de Baigneux, Jean de Pontoise, Jacques du Chastel, Gilles de Maudestour.

[24] Gallia Regia, no. 4500.

[25] Coville, Les états de Normandie, pp. 303-307.

[26]Jean d'Orléans, B. N., ms. fr. 26001 no. 609, P. O. 2169 Orliens no. 24; Raoul d'Estouteville, ms. fr. 26002 no. 738, P. O. 1082 Estouteville no. 6; Gilles de Maudestour, P. O. 1882 Maudestour nos. 3-5; Guillaume le Grant, ms. fr. 26001 no. 640.

[27]Jean d'Orléans, Gilles de Maudestour, Symon de Baigneux, Raoul d'Estouteville, Jean de Pontoise, Jacques du Chastel.

[28]Jean d'Orléans, Jean de Pontoise, Gilles de Maudestour, Jacques du Chastel, Raoul Campion, Etienne du Moustier.

[29]Mand., no. 655.

[30]Coville, Les états de Normandie, pp. 303-307.

[31]B. N., ms. fr. 25705, F. Beaurepaire, Sources médiévales de l'histoire de Normandie dans les Bibliothèques de Bayeux (Saint-Lô, 1966), no. 15.

[32]Jean d'Orléans, Renier le Coustelier, Raoul Campion, Gilles de Maudestour, Symon de Baigneux, Jacques du Chastel, Jean Vauchis, Jean de Pontoise, Raoul d'Estouteville.

[33]P. Timbal, La Guerre de Cent Ans vue à travers les registres du Parlement (Paris, 1961), pp. 226-227.

[34]Jacques du Chastel and Jean d'Orléans, bourgeois of Rouen, Jean Vauchis, bourgeois of Bayeux.

[35]B. N., ms. fr. 26021 no. 116.

[36]A. Chéruel, Histoire de Rouen pendant l'époque communale, 1150-1382 (Rouen, 1843-1844), II, 447.

[37]Coville, Les états de Normandie, pp. 277-278.

[38]B. N., ms. fr. 26006 no. 23, P. O. 2366 Pontoise no. 10.

[39]Coville, Les états de Normandie, pp. 277-278.

[40]Although Dupont-Ferrier found that the salaries of élus and re-ceivers ranged between 60 l.t. and 100 l.t. a year, Études, I, 78, I have seen no evidence that any Norman administrator was paid less than 100 l.t. a year. The receiver of Caen, and perhaps receivers of other wealthy districts, received a bonus of 50 l.t., but this seems to have been intended to offset the losses he incurred adminis-tering his receipt. A. N., KK 350 f. 79. The wages of Norman viscounts in the thirteenth century ranged between 60 and 100 l.t. Strayer, The Administration of Normandy, p. 101.

[41]G. Dupont-Ferrier, Études sur les institutions financières de la France à la fin du moyen âge (Paris, 1930-1932), I, 68-77.

[42]Lewis, Later Medieval France, pp. 141-146; M. Rey, Le Domaine du roi et les finances extraordinaires sous Charles VI, 1388-1413 (Paris, 1965), p. 163.

[43]Ibid., p. 198.

[44]Ibid., p. 165.

[45]Jean Loton, receiver of Arques, who seems to have been a bourgeois of Paris. B. N., P. O. 1756 Loton no. 3.

[46]Thomas de Tilly, bourgeois of Bayeux, receiver of Bayeux; Jean Vauchis, bourgeois of Bayeux, receiver of Bayeux; Raoul de Bray, bourgeois of Caen, receiver of Bayeux; Yvon Huart, resident of Caen, receiver of Bayeux and Caen; Raoul Campion, bourgeois of Caen, receiver of Caen; Raoul Rouillart, bourgeois of Caen, receiver of Caen; Jean de Beuville, bourgeois of Rouen, receiver of Evreux; Richard du Til, bourgeois of Rouen, receiver of Rouen, and élu of Evreux; Martin du Chastel, bourgeois of Rouen, receiver of Rouen, Jacques Filleul, bourgeois of Rouen, receiver of the 13th on wine in Rouen; Robert le Maistre, bourgeois of Rouen, receiver of the 13th on wine in Rouen; Guillaume Godefroy, bourgeois of Rouen, receiver of the 13th on wine in Rouen; Pierre de la Ferriere, bourgeois of Rouen, receiver of the 13th on wine in Rouen; Jean Mareschal, bourgeois of Rouen, receiver of Rouen; Mahieu Maillart, bourgeois of Dieppe, receiver of Dieppe, the viscounty of Arques and the counties of Longueville and Eu; Guillaume Longueil, bourgeois of Dieppe, receiver of Dieppe, the viscounty of Arques and the counties of Longueville and Eu; Jean Loton, bourgeois of Paris, receiver of Dieppe, the viscounty of Arques and the counties of Eu and Longueville; Jacques Mosque, bourgeois of Bayeux, élu and receiver of Bayeux; Gilles de Jumièges, rector of Crestot, receiver of Evreux; Pierre le Caurmer, priest, receiver of Evreux; Jean Gosse, priest, receiver of Lisieux; Guillaume Charet, priest, receiver of Lisieux; Robert Caronges, priest, receiver of Sées; Guillaume Bretel, priest, receiver in the lands of dowager queen Blanche; Étienne Asse, écuyer, receiver of Lisieux.

[47]Robert Aupois, bourgeois of Falaise, élu of Sées; Jean Filleul, bourgeois of Rouen, élu of Rouen; Geoffrey le Gras, bourgeois of Bernay, élu in the lands of Charles of Navarre beyond the Dyne; master Guillaume Laverne, canon of Avranches, sold the leases of the sales taxes in the diocese of Avranches in 1363; Geoffrey Henry, priest, assessed the fouages in the dioceses of Coutances and Avranches in 1366 and 1368; Nicole de Verdun, priest, élu of Avranches; master Henry de Rappelay, doctor in canon law, archdeacon of Bayeux, élu of Bayeux; Richard le Cappelier, archdeacon of Bayeux, élu of Bayeux; Guillaume de la Sautoge, canon of Evreux, commis on the aids for the ransom in the diocese of Evreux in 1361; Richard de Harcourt, arch- deacon of Lisieux, élu of Lisieux; Jean de Pontoise, canon and chancellor of Rouen, élu of Rouen; Roger de Dany, captain of Pontorson, sold the leases to the sales taxes in the diocese of Avranches in 1363; Fouque Paynel, knight, sire of Aigeau, assessed the fouages of

the diocese of Coutances and Avranches in 1366 and 1368; Nicole de
Chascegne, knight, élu of Avranches; Jean du Bois, knight, sire of
l'Espinay, élu of Gisors and Bayeux; Renier le Coustelier, élu of
Bayeux; Cordelier du Mesnil, knight, élu of Lisieux; Jean du Mesnil,
knight, élu of Lisieux; Raoul d'Estouteville, sire of Rames, élu of
Rouen.

[48]Cordelier du Mesnil and Jean du Mesnil, élus of Lisieux, may have
been related to Guillaume du Mesnil, whom Coville listed as having
received a personal summons to the estates of Normandy; Les états de
Normandie, p. 266.

[49]Martin du Chastel, Jacques Filleul, Pierre de la Ferriere, and
Jean Filleul of Rouen; Robert Aupois, mayor of Falaise in 1375; Raoul
de Bray, alderman of Caen in 1360 and 1363.

[50]Jean Vauchis, bourgeois of Bayeux (cf. supra, n. 37); Raoul
Rouillart, bourgeois of Caen, councillor of the keepers of the "tripot
à blé" in 1364; Guillaume Godefroy, bourgeois of Rouen, receiver of
the town's portion of the revenues of the sales taxes in 1373 and 1374.

[51]Mand., no. 668.

[52]Guillaume Laverne, canon of Avranches; Guillaume de Sautoge, canon
of Evreux; Jean Gosse, canon of Evreux.

[53]A. Vuitry, Études sur le régime financier de la France avant la
Révolution de 1789, nouvelle série, II, 126-130.

[54]Mand., nos. 625, 626.

[55]Ordonnances des roys de France de la troisième race, VI, 191;
between 1376 and 1378 he was charged with provisioning the navy at
Honfleu, B. N., P. O. 1756 Loton nos. 4, 10.

[56]Jean Bomant, viscount and receiver of Avranches; Jean le Gey,
receiver of Avranches, later viscount and élu of Avranches and viscount of Mortain; Étienne de la Cervelle, viscount of Vire, later
élu of Avranches; Geoffrey Morice, viscount and receiver of Vire;
Guillaume le Grant, viscount of Caen, élu of Bayeux; Renier le
Coustelier, viscount of Bayeux, later bailli of Caen and élu of
Bayeux; Guy Chrestien, viscount of Bayeux, later élu of Bayeux and
bailli of the Cotentin; Aymar Revout, viscount and receiver of
Coutances, Guillaume Basire, viscount of Montivilliers and the Auge,
later receiver of Evreux and élu of Lisieux; Robert Assire, viscount
of Falaise, later viscount of the Auge and Pontautou and élu of
Lisieux; Symon de Baigneux, viscount of Pont-Audemer, later viscount
and élu of Rouen; Guillaume Longueil, receiver of Dieppe and (if it
is the same man) later viscount of Montivilliers, the Auge, and Pont-
de-l'Arche; Jean le Prevost, viscount of Arques and receiver of the
region of Arques and Dieppe; Symon Maubuisson, viscount and receiver
of Neufchâtel; Jean Ribaut, viscount and receiver of Caudebec, later
viscount of Montivilliers; Robert Hale, viscount of Pont-de-l'Arche,

in 1363 and 1364; Guillaume le Dyacre, viscount of Conches, élu in the lands of Charles of Navarre between the Seine and the Dyne; Richard de Cormeilles, viscount of Montivilliers, later élu of Rouen.

[57]Renier le Coustelier, bailli and élu of Caen; Guy Chrestien, bailli of the Cotentin and élu of Caen.

[58]Aymar Revout, receiver of Coutances, 1363-1370, viscount of Coutances, 1365-1369, bailli of the Cotentin, 1369-1371. B. N., ms. fr. 26005 no. 1407, ms. fr. 26009 no. 902; Gallia Regia, nos. 7377, 7040; L. Delisle, Mémoires sur les baillis du Cotentin (Paris, 1851).

[59]Raoul Paien, receiver of Bayeux, lieutenant of the bailli of Caen; Colin le Roy, receiver of Montivilliers, receiver of Caudebec, élu of Coutances, and later lieutenant of the viscount of Coutances and lieutenant of the bailli of the Cotentin; Geoffrey Herault, élu in the lands of Charles of Navarre beyond the Dyne, later élu of Avranches and lieutenant of the bailli of the Cotentin.

[60]Gilles de Jumièges, receiver of Evreux, was receiver of the subsidies of 1356-1357; Guillaume Longueil and Mahieu Maillart, receivers of Dieppe and the viscounty of Arques, were commis of the élus of Rouen in 1357; Gautier de Tourpes, receiver of Arques, was receiver of a subsid for the renovation of the castle of Pont-Audemer in 1357; Pierre Manneville, receiver of the 13th on wine in Harfleur, was receiver in the viscounty of Montivilliers for the subsidy of 1356; Jean du Bois, élu of Gisors and Bayeux, was a commissioner of the subsidies of 1359 in Gisors; Guillaume de Trussebourc, receiver of Montivilliers in 1361, was receiver of Montivilliers for the subsidy of 1359-1360; for the élus-general and receivers-general, see above, note 28.

[61]See, for example, Henneman, Royal Taxation, pp. 298-301; Coville, Les états de Normandie, p. 84.

[62]Fouquet Tribout, élu of Coutances, was previously procureur in the bailliage of the Cotentin; Jean le Prevost, receiver for the region of Arques and Dieppe, was procureur in the bailliage of Caux before he became viscount of Arques and receiver of the aids.

[63]B. N., P. O. 2748 St. Erme no. 2.

[64]Coville, Les états de Normandie, p. 301.

[65]B. N., P. O. 1947 du Mesnil en Norm. nos. 26, 28.

[66]B. N., Clair. 214 no. 70.

[67]Roger Dany was captain of Pontorson at the time he leased the taxes; B. N., ms. fr. 26007 no. 352. Ferran de St. Germain, knight, inspected the fortresses of the Cotentin in 1371; B. N., P. O. 2743 Saint-Germain no. 8.

[68]Francois de Beaurepaire, "Sources de l'histoire du moyen âge à la bibliothèque de la ville de Rouen," Cahiers Léopold Delisle, t. fasc. 2 (1964), no. 129; B. N., P. O. 2843 Til no. 3.

[69]B. N., P. O. 856 Cormeilles nos. 2, 4, 5, 6, 13, 17, 18, 19, 20.

[70]B. N., P. O. 637 Cerisy no. 14; N. A. Latin 2320 no. 80.

[71]B. N., P. O. 1226 Fournier en Norm. nos. 3, 4.

[72]B. N., P. O. 1489 du Hasay nos. 2, 3.

[73]Cazelles, La société politique, p. 348.

[74]Receivers-general Jean Vauchis and Raoul Campion had previous experience as local receivers; see also nn. 56, 57 above.

[75]Strayer, Administration of Normandy, p. 96; Cazelles, La société politique, pp. 342 ff., surveys the officials of Philip of Valois' government but mentions no high-ranking official who started his career at a post lower than bailli.

[76]Coville, Les états de Normandie, pp. 324-327

[77]Gallia Regia, nos. 19166, 19286, 4538; B. N., ms. fr. 26011 no. 1306, ms. fr. 26102 no. 1590; P. O. 114 Assire nos. 6, 7, 13. Another example is Jacques de Launay, receiver of Montivilliers in the 1370's who became a treasurer of France under Charles VI; B. N., N. A. Latin 2320 no. 74, ms. fr. 20857 no. 56; Rey, Le Domaine, p. 111.

[78]B. N., Clair. 215 no. 49, P. O. 644 Chacegne no. 9, ms. fr. 26015 no. 2292, Gallia Regia, no. 7138.

[79]B. N., P. O. 2580 le Roy en Norm. no. 10, P. O. 580 Campion no. 14, P. O. 19 Aladent no. 6, ms. fr. 25705 no. 14.

[80]He was receiver of the fouage in the town and viscounty of Bayeux from January 1, 1364 until September 2, 1369; in 1368 and 1369 he may have been receiver of the sales tax as well. B. N., ms. fr. 23904 nos. 89-96, ms. fr. 26008 no. 750, Clair. 215 no. 22, Beaurepaire, Bayeux, no. 19. Between September 2, 1369 and December 21, 1370 he was also receiver-general of the aids in the diocese of Sées, Bayeux, Coutances, Avranches, and Lisieux. B. N., P. O. 2940 Vauchis nos. 2, 6, Beaurepaire, Bayeux, nos. 21, 22. He was probably receiver of Bayeux again from January 1, 1371, when Yvon Huart ceased his receivership, until December, 1375. B. N., P. O. 580 Campion nos. 4, 16, P. O. 930, Chrestien no. 3, Mand., no. 754.

[81]Pierre le Hursin was receiver of the fouage in the diocese of Sées for some period after 1366 ending before May 24, 1372 when Matthew Edouard appears as receiver. B. N., P. O. 1362 Gosse en Norm. no. 7, ms. fr. 26008 no. 676, P. O. 580 Campion no. 10. He was again receiver from July, 1375 until the aids were cancelled in 1380. B. N.,

P. O. 1553 Hursin no. 5. He was named receiver of Sées by the
governors-general of the Norman estates in 1381, but was soon afterward replaced. B. N., Clair. 216 no. 89, ms. fr. 26018 no. 243. He
was again receiver by October, 1382, however; he left office sometime
between March, 1388 and October, 1389. B. N., ms. fr. 26019 no. 354,
P. O. 7 d'Acqueville no. 2, P. O. 1947 du Mesnil en Norm. no. 81.

[82]Yvon's accounts for the years between 1370 and 1377 survive as
A. N., KK 350; f. 319 v⁰ mentions that he was subsequently receiver
of Le Mans; in May, 1381 he was appointed receiver of Sées, but held
that office no more than a year, B. N., ms. fr. 26018 no. 243; in 1384
and 1385 he was receiver-general of the diocese of Bayeux; by 1387 he
was again receiver of Caen where he was still receiver in 1398; in
1393 he was receiver-general of a taille in Normandy. B. N., P. O.
1541 Huart en Norm. nos. 8, 9, 13; Beaurepaire, "Rouen," no. 295.

[83]Gallia Regia, no. 4500; B. N., Clair. 214 no. 40, A. N., KK 350
show him active as élu in 1364 and 1370-1376; see also nn. 26, 28.

[84]He was receiver of the aids between March, 1369 and March, 1371
but not later than August, 1371, and élu of Avranches between October,
1373 and January, 1376. B. N., P. O. Chacegne nos. 2, 4, 6, P. O.
1319 le Gey no. 2, ms. fr. 23904 f. 70. He was viscount of Avranches
(1373-1378) and viscount of Mortain (1387-1392). Gallia Regia, nos.
7330, 7405.

[85]B. N., P. O. 580 Campion no. 8, ms. fr. 26012 no. 1658, P. O.
2148 Orenge no. 2, 5, 6, 8, 9.

[86]Ord., VI, 440 ff.

[87]A. N., KK 350; the sections titled "aultre despense" list the
petty costs of administration, including the wages of clerks.

[88]A. N., KK 350 ff. 44, 77, etc.

[89]B. N., ms. fr. 26016 no. 2579.

[90]Strayer, "Viscounts and Viguiers," final paragraph.

[91]Rey also makes this point, La Domaine, p. 197.

Chapter 5

[1] This is based upon a paper read at the 1972 meeting of the Mediaeval Academy of America.

[2] We need think only of Johann Plesner's analysis of immigration into Florence, L'émigration de la campagne à la ville libre de Florence au XIIIe siècle (Copenhagen, 1934); Emilio Cristiani, Nobiltà e popolo nel comune di Pisa (Naples, 1962); Enrico Fiumi's examinations of Tuscan city-contado relationships, of the Florentine economy, and of the economic and social history of San Gimignano and Prato, "Sui rapporti economici tra città e contado nell'età comunale," Archivio Storico Italiano [ASI], CXIV (1956), 18-68, "Fioritura e decadenza dell'economia fiorentina," ASI, CXV (1957), 385-439, CXVI (1958), 443-510, CXVII (1959), 427-502, Storia economica e sociale di San Gimignano (Florence, 1961), Demografia, movimento urbanistico, e classi sociali a Prato dall'età comunale ai tempi moderni (Florence, 1968); John Larner, Culture and Society in Italy, 1290-1420 (London, 1971); Peter Burke, Culture and Society in Renaissance Italy, 1420-1540 (London, 1972). The works of American scholars fall into the same categories, see, e.g., Gene A. Brucker, Florentine Politics and Society, 1343-1378 (Princeton, 1962) and Renaissance Florence (New York, 1969); Marvin B. Becker, Florence in Transition, 2 vols. (Baltimore, 1967-1968); David Herlihy, Pisa in the Early Renaissance (New Haven, 1958) and Medieval and Renaissance Pistoia (New Haven and London, 1967); William M. Bowsky, The Finance of the Commune of Siena, 1287-1355 (Oxford, 1970); cf. Josiah Cox Russell, Medieval Regions and their Cities (Bloomington, Ind., 1972).

[3] Hans Baron, The Crisis of the Early Italian Renaissance, 2nd ed. (Princeton, 1966).

[4] See, e.g., Peter Partner, "Florence and the Papacy, 1300-1375," in J. R. Hale, J.R.L. Highfield and B. Smalley, eds., Europe in the Late Middle Ages (London and Evanston, Ill., 1965), pp. 76-121.

[5] La Divina Commedia, Inferno, X, 85-86.

[6] Robert Langton Douglas devotes an entire chapter of A History of Siena (New York and London, 1902) to the battle; Ferdinand Schevill's even better-known volume, Siena. The Story of a Mediaeval Commune (London, 1909) lingers long and lovingly over the details of Montaperti. Two more useful recent studies are Ernesto Sestan, "Siena avanti Montaperti," Bullettino Senese di Storia Patria [BSSP], LXVIII (1961), 28-74, and Giuseppe Martini, "Siena da Montaperti alla caduta dei Nove (1260-1355)," ibid., 75-128.

[7] History of Siena, p. 141.

[8] F. Schevill, Siena, p. 199.

[9] Ibid., p. 202. The contado was that portion of the state outside

of the city and its boroughs that was most fully subject to a commune's jurisdiction.

[10]Ibid., pp. 190-191.

[11]P. Partner, "Florence and the Papacy," pp. 84-85.

[12]See ibid., p. 92, "...the danger of the mercenary companies in central Italy was to be an important factor in Florentine policy, and one which inclined her on the whole to extend and emphasize the collective security arrangements which she maintained with the other Tuscan guelfs." Also see G. Brucker, Florentine Politics, p. 140, "In the 1340's Florence no longer aspired to be the leading Guelf power in central Italy, a role which required an extensive network of alliances. Its objectives limited by its physical weakness, the commune concentrated on defense and the recovery of its territory lost in 1343. It sought protection in leagues of limited scope with neighboring communes, Siena and Perugia."

[13]P. Partner, "Florence and the Papacy," p. 86.

[14]See, e.g., W. Bowsky, Finance, p. 290; Robert Davidsohn, Forschungen zur Geschichte von Florenz, 4 vols. (Berlin, 1896-1908), IV, 557-577, "Florentiner an der Spitze auswärtiger Kommunen."

[15]Archivio di Stato di Firenze [ASF], Provvisioni [Provv.], 37, ff. 83v-85r. See also William M. Bowsky, "The Impact of the Black Death upon Sienese Government and Society," Speculum XXXIX (1964), 24 n. 136.

[16]For this paragraph on Massa Marittima, Siena, and Florence, see the documentation cited in William M. Bowsky, "Medieval Citizenship: The Individual and the State in the Commune of Siena, 1287-1355," Studies in Medieval and Renaissance History, IV (1967), 193-243, pp. 222 n. 72, 223 n. 73, esp. Sarah Cocconi, "L'espansione della Repubblica di Siena nella Maremma e la sottomissione di Massa Marittima," Archivio di Stato di Siena, MS. F. 7. [Henceforth all unpublished documentation not otherwise identified will refer to materials housed in the Archivio di Stato di Siena.] See also ASF, Provv., 26, ff. 33v-34v (July 13, 1333), 35r (July 16, 1333), 36r (July 23, 1333), 53v (Sept. 7, 1333).

[17]See Carla Dumontel, L'Impresa italiana di Giovanni di Lussemburgo, re di Boemia, Università di Torino, Pubblicazioni della Facoltà di Lettere e Filosofia, Vol. IV, Fasc. III (Turin, 1952).

[18]See ASF, Missive, Registri, 3, ff. 6r-v (Jan. 25, 1328), 19v (Mar. 16, 1328)--instructions for a Florentine embassy to Siena (dates are new style); Provv. 23, ff. 11r (Sept. 23, 1326), 32r (Nov. 26, 1326), 36v-37v (Dec. 3, 1326), 47r-48r (Dec. 30, 1326), 51v (Jan. 13, 1327), 55r (Feb. 4, 1327); Provv., 24, ff. 11r-13v (Oct. 23, 1327), 45r-48r (Feb. 26, 1328). See also Giugurta Tommasi, Dell'Historie di Siena, 2 vols. in one (Venice, 1525-1526), II, 236 (1328).

[19] See esp. William M. Bowsky, "The Anatomy of Rebellion in Four-teenth-Century Siena: From Commune to Signory?" in Lauro Martines, ed., Violence and Civil Disorder in Italian Cities, 1200-1500 (Berkeley, Los Angeles, London, 1972), pp. 229-272.

[20] ASF, Provv., 40, ff. 155r-161v (Oct. 16, 1353); Provv. Duplicati, 13, ff. 32r-v, 38v; Libri Fabarum, 32, f. 72v. This request, made on behalf of one of the Donati, was approved 148 vs. 9.

[21] ASF, Missive, Registri, 11, f. 15r (Jan. 4, 1353); cf. ibid., f. 19v (Feb. 21, 1353).

[22] ASF, Provv., 19, f. 1r, esp. "Item provido viro Lotto de Quarata pro ipso comuni Florentie transmisso ad dictam civitatem Sen. cum certam quantitatem peditum lige Chiantis in servitium et subsidium ipsius Civitatis Sen. pro ipsius Lotti salario tredecim dierum quibus ibit et stetit occasione predicta, ad rationem librarum quatuor flor-enorum parvorum pro quolibet die. In summa libras quinquaginta duas florenorum parvorum."

[23] ASF, Provv., 11, ff. 190v-191r (Feb. 6, 1303); cf. Bernardino Barbadoro, ed., Consigli della Repubblica Fiorentina, 2 vols. (Bologna, 1930-1931), I, 78-79.

[24] ASF, Provv., 15, ff. 47r-56v, esp. 51r (Apr. 5, 1317).

[25] "Cronica senese attribuita ad Agnolo di Tura del Grasso detta la cronaca maggiore" [Agnolo], in Alessandro Lisini and Fabio Iacometti, eds., Cronache Senese [C. S.], in Rerum Italicarum Scriptores, n. s., XV pt. VI (Bologna, 1931-1937), 394.

[26] Agnolo, 396. This army was possibly aimed against Pisa, Arezzo, or Castruccio Castracani, Lord of Lucca.

[27] E.g., Mar. 1317, again to halt Tolomei-Salimbeni feuding: Agnolo, 364-365. For relations between these two clans see Giovanni Cecchini, La pacificazione fra Tolomei e Salimbeni, Quaderni dell'Accademia Chigiana, II (Siena, 1942).

[28] Agnolo, 371.

[29] Agnolo, 503.

[30] ASF, Missive, Registri, 8, f. 73r (Apr. 5, 1344).

[31] Agnolo, 470, 477.

[32] See esp. Alessandro Lisini, "La contessa palatina Margherita Aldobrandeschi e il suo matrimonio con il conte Guido di Monforte," BSSP, XXXIX (1932), 1-48, p. 40.

[33] Alessandro Lisini, "La Margherita Aldobrandeschi e il cavaliere Nello di Pietro," BSSP, XXXIX (1932), 249-283, pp. 255-256.

[34]For the battle of Campaldino see Robert L. Oerter, "Campaldino, 1289," Speculum, XLIII (1968), 429-450; Robert Davidsohn, Storia di Firenze, III (Florence, 1957), 466; Giovanni Villani, Cronica di Giovanni Villani a miglior lezione ridotta, 4 vols. (Florence [Magheri], 1823-1825), Bk. VII, chap. CXXXI (for the contributions of Siena and the other communes). For Lucignano in the Valdichiana (not to be confused with Lucignano d'Arbia or Lucignano d'Asso) see Giovanni Cecchini, Le liti di confinazione fra Lucignano e Foiano, Quaderni dell'Accademia Chigiana, VII (Siena, 1944).

[35]See, e.g., F. Schevill, Siena, pp. 21-28.

[36]On the battle of Montecatini see R. Davidsohn, Storia di Firenze, IV (1960), 792-808; Agnolo, 350-356; cf. William M. Bowsky, Henry VII in Italy: The Conflict of Empire and City-State, 1310-1313 (Lincoln, Nebr., 1960), pp. 205ff.

[37]See W. Bowsky, Finance, p. 13 n. 36 and the sources there cited.

[38]Guido Pampaloni, "I trattati stipulati dal comune di Firenze nei secoli XII e XIII," ASI, CXXIII (1965), 480-523, p. 519.

[39]Ibid., 520-521.

[40]Ibid., 521-522.

[41]ASF, Provv., 12, f. 75v (Aug. 8, 1302); 13, ff. 31v, 149r (Nov. 19, 1306, Dec. 9, 1307); cf. B. Barbadoro, Consigli, I, 155, 295, II, 352.

[42]W. Bowsky, Henry VII, p. 37; Theodor E. Mommsen, ed., Italienische Analekten zur Reichsgeschichte des XIV. Jahrhunderts (1310-1378), Schriften der Monumenta Germaniae Historica, XI (Stuttgart, 1952), No. 1.

[43]ASF, Diplomatico Riformagioni [DR], cartaceo, Nov. 26, 1315 (II). Florence here was acting for herself and for the towns of Città di Castello, Volterra, Pistoia, Prato, San Gimignano, and Colle di Valdelsa. The troops were to serve for from nine months to a year, including three months of travel time from and to France.

[44]See esp. Giovanni Cecchini, "La politica di Siena durante la guerra contro Castruccio Castracani," Reale Accademia Lucchese, Atti, n. s., III (1933), 73-92.

[45]Agnolo, 412. Bologna and Perugia also belonged to this league, though Agnolo does not list their contributions.

[46]Ibid., 498.

[47]DR, June 21, 1335; see also ASF, DR, Atti Pubblici, June 16, 1340.

[48]ASF, Provv., 34, ff. 111v-112r (Feb. 19, 1347), a league "ad fortificationem et augmentum totius status partis guelfe ytalie que est

sancte matris ecclesie ymitatrix." (f. 111v). See also ASF, DR, Atti Pubblici, Mar. 14, 1346 (Florentine style), Apr. 20, 1347; and Archivio di Stato di Perugia, Contratti Diversi, Nov. 17, 1347 (cass. 34, n. 95), which tells the shares owed by each commune and names the four men to whom the captainship of the league was to be offered in turn, should there be refusals. These were the lords Alamanno degli Obizzi of Lucca, Jacopo di messer Canto dei Gabrielli of Gubbio, Simone de Battifolle count palatine in Tuscany, and one Isnuduccio... [sic] of San Severino.

[49]ASF, DR, Atti Pubblici, Aug. 19, 1351 (X); see also Archivio di Stato di Perugia, Consigli e Riformanze, No. 23, ff. 206v-207r (Sept. 2, 1351), 214r (Sept. 9, 1351), 215v (Sept. 11, 1351), 228r (Oct. 9, 1351).

[50]Concluded February 15, this league was to take effect Apr. 22, 1354: DR, Feb. 15, 1353 (Sienese style), No. 1702. An unspecified number of infantry were also to be included. The pact contained stipulations that a captain would be chosen for the league, and that he was to be accompanied by two councillors from each of the three league towns "armis expertos et vere guelfos"; no league member could enter into any other league or pact that could prejudice this one without the prior consent of the other members; new members of the league needed the approval of all three present members; for the duration of the league no member could concede reprisals against other members or their "persons" and the citizens and "districtuales" of each city in the league had to be treated by judges in civil and criminal cases as if they were citizens and inhabitants of the town by which they were being tried; any place recovered by league forces was to be understood to have been recovered for the member "cuius possessio vel quasi erat...." Any contravention of the terms of this pact was to cost the violator 20,000 gold florins--but, significantly, no mechanism was included for the operation of this clause.

[51]P. Partner, "Florence and the Papacy," p. 97.

[52]G. Brucker, Florentine Politics, p. 99.

[53]ASF, Diplomatico Volterra, July 23, 1308, Nov. 29, 1308. Even league arbitration had its limits, though, for in the following spring the matter had to be rearbitrated by the same allies: ASF, Diplomatico San Gimignano, Apr. 14, 1309.

[54]See above, no. 50.

[55]E.g., in 1297 and 1298; ASF, Provv., 7, ff. 128v, 186r-v; see also Alessandro Gherardi, ed., Le Consulte della Repubblica Fiorentina dal MCCLXXX al MCCXCVII, 2 vols. (Florence, 1896-1898), I, 616; cf. ASF, Provv., 19, f. 76r (Feb. 28, 1323). This was part of a general policy to eliminate reprisals wherever possible; see, e.g., ASF, Provv., 12, ff. 116r-v, 119v (Dec. 21, 1304), 13, ff. 165r-166r (Dec. 29, 1307), 15, f. 192v (June 30, 1318), 18, ff. 50v-51r (Jan. 18, 1319), 19, f. 30r (Aug. 18, 1322). See also Archivio di Stato di Bologna, Carteggio,

Lettere dal Comune, No. 593 (Aug. 9, 1293)--a letter sent to 46 Italian
cities, lords, and lands proposing a common suspension of reprisals
for six months and the appointment of arbitrators to settle all such
disputes (Busta 1, Reg. 6, No. 5, f. 4r-v).  These include Siena,
Florence, Milan, Parma, Piacenza, Cremona, Brescia, Lodi, Como, Novara,
Reggio, Pistoia, San Gimignano, Colle, Poggibonsi, Arezzo, Assisi,
Prato, Ferrara, Mantua, Venice, Viterbo, Rome, Ascoli, Narni, Rieti,
Forli, Cesena, Ancona, the marquis of Este, the counts of Biandrate,
and the lands of the Lunigiana.

[56]See, e.g., Quinto Senigaglia, ed., Lo Statuto dell'Arte della
Mercanzia Senese (1342-1343) (Siena, 1911) [reprinted from the BSSP],
pp. 283-284 (index, s. v. Rappresaglie); Alessandro Lisini, ed., Il
costituto del comune di Siena volgarizzato nel MCCCIX-MCCCX, 2 vols.
(Siena, 1903), II, 613 (index, s. v. Rappresaglie).

[57]Consiglio Generale [CG], 110 ff. 117r-120r (Dec. 31, 1331)--
granting the reprisal; 114, ff. 50r-52r (Oct. 3, 1333), 118, f. 26r
(Mar. 27, 1336), 121, ff. 50r-51v (Dec. 8, 1337); cf. Biccherna, 181,
f. 39v (Nov. 2, 1334).  This reprisal also was discussed in other
City Council sessions of 1333 and 1334.

[58]See esp. W. Bowsky, Finance, pp. 63-64; idem, "Medieval Citizenship," 222-223, and the bibliography there cited; Danilo Marrara,
Storia istituzionale della maremma senese (Siena, 1961); Ildebrando
Imberciadori, Per la storia della società rurale.  Amiata e Maremma
tra il IX e il XX secolo (Parma, 1971).

[59]In addition to the works cited above, notes 32, 33, 58, see
Alessandro Lisini, "La Margherita Aldobrandeschi e la dissoluzione
della grande Contea di S. Fiora e di Sovana," BSSP, XXXIX (1932),
323-357; Daniel Waley, Mediaeval Orvieto (Cambridge, 1952).

[60]See, e.g., W. Bowsky, "Medieval Citizenship," 220; idem, "City
and Contado:  Military Relationships and Communal Bonds in Fourteenth-
Century Siena," in Anthony Molho and John A. Tedeschi, eds.,
Renaissance Studies in Honor of Hans Baron (Florence, 1971), pp. 95-96.

[61]Grosseto rebelled, e.g., in 1254, 1259, 1266, 1310 (at the instance of Emperor Henry VII), 1334 and 1335 (in alliance with Pisa).

[62]Thus, e.g., when imperial forces threatened Siena during the
expedition of Henry VII the government relaxed its pressures and
followed a policy of compromise and reasonableness; after the
emperor's death and the negotiation of peace with the Ghibellines
through the offices of Robert of Naples (1316-1317) Siena again
turned forcefully against Massa Marittima, the Aldobrandeschi, the
Pannocchieschi, etc.

[63]La Divina Commedia, Purgatorio, XIII, 151-153.

[64]See W. Bowsky, Finance, pp. 23-25; ASF, Missive, Registri, 8,
f. 83r (May 13, 1344).

[65]ASF, Provv., 34, ff. 137v-138r (May 19, 1347).

[66]CG, 45, ff. 64r-v (Mar. 25, 1293), 65r-v (Mar. 29, 1293), 51, ff. 48v-49r (Feb. 2, 1297). The limitation finally was waived on Mar. 20, 1298, when the City Council agreed to give the 2,000 gold florins that Charles sought to his embassy then present in Siena: CG, 53, ff. 84v-85v.

[67]See, e.g., Mario Chiaudiano, Studi e documenti per la storia del diritto commerciale italiano nel secolo XIII, R. Università di Torino, Memorie dell'istituto giuridico, ser. II, mem. VIII (Turin, 1930); idem, "I Rothschild del Dugento: La Gran Tavola di Orlando Bonsignori," BSSP, n. s., VI (1935), 103-142; Gino Arias, Studi e documenti di storia del diritto (Florence, 1902), pp. 3-73; Armando Sapori, "Le compagnie mercantili toscane del dugento e dei primi del trecento. La responsabilità dei compagni verso i terzi," in his Studi di storia economica. Secoli XIII-XIV-XV, 3rd ed., III (Florence, 1955), 765-808; Yves Renouard, Les relations des papes d'Avignon et des compagnies commerciales et bancaires de 1316 à 1378, Bibliothèque des écoles francaises d'Athenes et de Rome, 151 (Paris, 1941), index, s.v. Bonsignori. Sienese City Council deliberations that deal with the problem of the Bonsignori, the papacy, and the interdict, include: CG, 137, ff. 5r-6v (July 22, 1345)--the arrangement for an embassy to be sent to Pope Clement VI; 139, ff. 41r-42r (Nov. 20, 1346)--arrangement for another embassy to the pope in order to raise the interdict levelled by reason of the Bonsignori Company; 140, ff. 21v-22r (Mar. 7, 1347)--the Nine are to select a commission of three men from each Terzo or major district of the city "unum videlicet de Mangnatibus alterum de gente media et reliquum de Minoribus" (f. 22r) to decide what should be done concerning letters received from the Sienese embassy at the papal court dealing with the excommunication and interdict; 140, ff. 30v-32v (Apr. 25, 1347)--provisions made against the heirs of the Bonsignori and other members and heirs of the defunct company--among them the sons and heirs of Meo di Orlando Malavolti, and various Noveschi, including the Montanini and "heredes Montanini," the heirs of Guido, Guccio and Geri [Montanini], "Buonaventura dni. Manfredi," and "filii et heredes Ture Buonamichi." The interdict was in effect in Siena and its contado, the excommunication against Sienese officials and councillors.

[68]For military and financial aid granted by Siena to Boniface VIII in 1297, see CG, 51, ff. 111r-112v (June 22), 52, ff. 25r-v (July 3), 28v-29r (July 5), 56v-58r (Aug. 19). On Apr. 3, 1298 at the proposal of messer Mino di messer Cristoforo Tolomei the City Council voted 179 to 72 to give a cup and 200 gold florins to the papal legate, cardinal Matteo of Aquasparta, and to send 75 cavalry to serve in a papal army against the Colonna: CG, 53, ff. 95v-96r. (See also Miscellanea Storica Senese, III [1895], 159-161.) On Nov. 27, 1306 the Nine proposed to the City Council that it allocate 500 gold florins for the rebuilding of Palastrina at the request of the cardinal deacon Stefano Colonna and his nephews Jacopo (Sciarra) and Giordano Colonna. Although the proposal was supported by the powerful

Noveschi noble messer Biagio di messer Mino Rossi dei Montanini, at
the advice of Frederigo di messer Renaldo Tolomei the Council declined
by the narrow margin of 118 to 114:  CG, 69, ff. 127r-128v.

[69]This subject will be treated specifically in my forthcoming study
of Siena during the regime of the Nine.

[70]Nobiltà e popolo, cited above, n. 2.  On anti-magnate legislation
in general see also Gina Fasoli, Ricerche sulla legislazione anti-
magnatizia nei comuni dell'alta e media Italia (Bologna, 1939), originally published in Rivista di storia del diritto italiano, XII (1939).

[71]Il commune di Firenze alla fine del dugento (Florence, 1926).
More recently see Guido Pampaloni, "I magnati a Firenze alla fine
del dugento," ASI, CXXIX (1971), 387-423.

[72]Interestingly it is in the few cases of disagreement among the
leading elements of Sienese political society that we find the Nine
rebuffed.  And a careful analysis of these few cases even then ordinarily does not show any simple division, such as that of the Nine
against members of excluded magnate clans.  Rather we see the Nine
disagreeing with a strong fragment of the excluded nobles, with members
of the casati themselves divided.

[73]W. Bowsky, Finance, p. 7 n. 19.

[74]Agnolo, 528.

[75]E.g., "Cronaca Senese di Donato di Neri e di suo figlio Neri,"
Alessandro Lisini and Fabio Iacometti, eds., in C. S. (cited above,
n. 25), 576.

Chapter 6

[1] I shall refer here only to Étienne Fournial, <u>Histoire monétaire de l'Occident médiéval</u> (Paris, 1970). Being little more than a history of French coinage, it is characteristic of the attitude described above. It is also supplied with abundant bibliographies.

[2] Renée Doehaerd, <u>La haut Moyen Age occidental, Économies et sociétés</u> (Paris, Nouvelle Clio, no. 14, 1971), p. 313.

[3] Philip Grierson, in <u>Karl der Grosse, Persönlichkeit und Geschichte</u> (Dusseldorf, 1965), pp. 535-536.

[4] Heinrich Beyer, ed., <u>Urkundenbuch zur Geschichte der...mittelrheinischen Territorien</u>, I (Koblenz, 1860), pp. 144 and 192.

[5] For obvious reasons, I exclude from this survey the Islamic world and even the Christian regions bordering it--which is not to say that there were no interrelations.

[6] These lines were almost completely written, when I came to read the recent book by George Duby, <u>Guerriers et paysans, VII<sup>e</sup>-XII<sup>e</sup> siècles, premier essor de l'économie européenne</u> (Paris, 1973 [an English edition is projected]). I can only rejoice that the views summarized here so often coincide with the conclusions of that excellent work. For the monetary aspect in the management of monastic estates, see pages 241 to 244.

[7] Mireille Castaing-Sicard, <u>Monnaies féodales et circulation monétaire en Languedoc (X<sup>e</sup>-XIII<sup>e</sup> siècles)</u> (Toulouse: Association Marc Bloch, 1961).

[8] Philip Grierson, "La fonction sociale de la monnaie en Angleterre aux VII<sup>e</sup>-VIII<sup>e</sup> siècles," in <u>Moneta e scambi nell'alto, VIII<sup>a</sup> Settimana di studio del Centro Italiano di studi sull'alto medioevo</u> (Spoleto, 1961), pp. 341-362. The quotation is from page 362.

[9] <u>Economic History Review</u>, 2nd series, XVIII, no. 3, Dec. 1965, pp. 475-482. The quotations are from pages 475 and 482.

[10] P. H. Sawyer, "The Wealth of England in the Eleventh Century," in <u>Transactions of the Royal Historical Society</u>, 5th series, XV, 1965, pp. 145-164.

[11] Of course, this is by no means new. Among others, see: Carlo M. Cipolla, "Currency Depreciation in Medieval Europe," <u>Economic History Review</u>, 2nd s., XV, no. 3, April 1963, pp. 413-422. But French historians as a whole are probably not enough aware of it.

## Chapter 7

[1] For the early history of this house, see Joaquím Miret y Sans, _Les cases de Templers y Hospitalers en Catalunya..._ (Barcelona, 1910), pp. 39-40, 162-165; _Els castells catalans_, ed. Rafael Dalmau, 3 vols. to date (Barcelona, 1967-1971), II, 93-98; and A. J. Forey, _The Templars in the Corona de Aragón_ (London, 1973), pp. 50, 88-91, 96, 100. "Palau-solità" is said to be the traditional name for this place (_Diccionari nomenclàtor de pobles i poblats de Catalunya_, 2d edn. [Barcelona, 1964], p. 283), but the text printed below has "Palacii salatani," a form attested in other texts, and modernized by Miret y Sans as "Palau Salatà," _Cases de Templers_, p. 167; see also p. 163.

[2] Arxiu de la Corona d'Aragó (to be cited as ACA), Cancelleria, pergamins Alfons I, 300; the _debemus_ reads in part: "propter quos inpignoramus uobis omne nostrum directum tocius decimi parroechie Sancte Marie de Palacio salatan cum nostris pariliatis quas ibi habemus simul cum nostro molendino de Lizano cum omnibus suis necessariis et instrumentis, tali pacto ut teneatis ita quod omnia expleta computetis et recipiatis pro istis .cxx. morabetinis tantum quod bene sitis paccati. Et computetis blad sicuti uenundetur de festo Sancti Michaelis usque ad festum Omnium Sanctorum. Iamdictas pariliatas laboretis bene et mittatis omne semen. In tempore messium leuate inde semen, leuato semine, accipite uos medietatem pro uestra laboracione; alteram medietatem tocius blad computate in persolucione morabetinorum...."

Guillelmus de Turre (or Torre), a substantial proprietor of the Vallès from a family of Caldes de Montbui or its near vicinity, can be traced back at least to 1171 in documents of Sant Cugat and Palau, _Cartulario de "Sant Cugat" del Vallès_, ed. José Rius Serra, 3 vols. (Barcelona, 1945-1947), III, no. 1079; ACA, perg. Alfons I, 300, 329, 462, 531, 534, extrainv. 2607; Miret, _Cases de Templers_, p. 164. Other citations are provided by Enric Moreu-Rey, _La rodalia de Caldes de Montbui. Repertori històric de noms de lloc i de noms de persona_ (Barcelona, 1961), p. 223 (and he prints perg. Alfons I, 531, Apèndixs, no. 28).

[3] ACA, perg. Alfons I, 508; printed below, pp. 99-101.

[4] The pricing in the account certainly appears to refer to marketing, but may sometimes indicate evaluation for credit to the account; see below.

[5] This presumption would be strengthened if the debtor or his son (who bore the same name) could be identified with the Brother Guillèm de Torre who was preceptor of the Templars at Miravet in 1198, _Cartas de población y de franquicia de Cataluña_, ed. José Maria Font Rius, 1 vol. in 2 parts (Madrid-Barcelona, 1969), no. 208; but this identification is doubtful. I have failed to trace Guillèm senior with certainty later than 1188 (ACA, perg. Alfons I, 462; final entry of account).

[6]Cf., e.g., ACA, perg. Ramon Berenguer IV, 233, which begins: "Hec est comemoratio totius ipsius honoris..."; or the "carta et rememoratio" of Templar rights in Cerdanya (ca. 1184), ed. Joaquín Miret y Sans, "Pro sermone plebeico," Boletín de la Real Academia de Buenas Letras de Barcelona, VII (1913), 163-164, 169.

[7]This point, and others in this paragraph, will be established in a forthcoming edition of fiscal accounts of Catalonia under Alphonse I and Peter I.

[8]ACA, perg. Alfons I, 200, extrainv. 2613, extrainv. 2616.

[9]ACA, perg. Alfons I, 361, 360, 416, 435, 453, 579, 588; perg. Pere I, 48, 8; perg. Alfons I, 568, 580, 581, 592, 603, 652, 662, 674, 672, 678. It may be added that the Templars were entitled to a tenth of royal revenues, Forey, Templars in the Corona de Aragón, p. 22, and references; but the history of this revenue in the later twelfth century remains obscure.

[10]The absence of alphabetic lettering at the top is indecisive in this regard. Such lettering might have been added only after the texts were complete; or, indeed, might have been omitted altogether. See ACA, perg. Alfons I, 300; also perg. Pere I, 206, 203, unmarked records of a royal bailiff's accounts for the honor of Berguedà (1203-1204). The central accounting (no. 203) before the comendator of Palau (among other officials) strikingly resembles the entry for 1186 in the account of Guillèm de Torre's pledge; of the former text, two copies must have been needed.

[11]Examples of debeo are very numerous; for one, see Colección de documentos inéditos del Archivo general de la Corona de Aragón, ed. Próspero de Bofarull y Mascaró, 41 vols. (Barcelona, 1847-1910), IV, no. 111. For sales or contracts of bailiwicks, see, e.g., ACA, perg. Alfons I, 25, 292.

[12]ACA, perg. Pere I, 203 (see note 10).

[13]ACA, perg. Alfons I, 361. Cf. no. 200, receipts on royal pledges to the Templars were noted on the record of debt.

[14]Entries for 1181, 1183, 1187-1188, and see Table 1. Cf. Charles du Fresne Du Cange, Glossarium mediae et infimae latinitatis, new edn., 7 vols. (Paris, 1840-1850), v. quartarium, for a quarter that was ¼ the sextarius.

[15]This is the only evidence I have yet found clearly defining the Catalonian quartana and distinguishing it from the quartera. Cf. ACA, perg. Ramon Berenguer IV, 233, passim; extrainv. 2502; and accounts of Alfons I, such as those cited above, note 9.

[16]Table 2; cf. J. F. Niermeyer, Mediae latinitatis lexicon minus (Leiden, 1954--), v. pugneria, where Du Cange's slender evidence is cited. The puniera may be found in Rius, Cartulario de "Sant Cugat," III, nos. 1128, 1218; the pojeria in Cartulaires de Douzens, ed. Pierre

Gérard and Élisabeth Magnou (Paris, 1965), A, no. 202. The _punera_
must have been a very small measure because the reckoning for
can be verified without taking account of the single _punera_ of lentils
mentioned in that year. Cf. J. A. Brutails, Étude sur la condition
des populations rurales du Roussillon au Moyen Age (Paris, 1891),
pp. 58-59.

[17] On the _maille_ and the obol, see Niermeyer, Lexicon, v. _medala,_
_obolus_; Novum glossarium mediae latinitatis ab anno DCCC usque ad
annum MCC, fascicule Meabilis-Miles (Copenhagen, 1961), v. _medalia_;
Felipe Mateu y Llopis, Glosario hispánico de numismática (Barcelona,
1946).

[18] It is for this reason that I have not attempted to calculate the
balances of 1186 and 1187-1188. E.g., if it is assumed that the price
of the morabetin in 1186 was 6s. 3d. and that the _punera_ was reckoned
at ⅕ _quartera_, then a final balance of 28 mo. 6s. 2d. can be computed--
or 9s. 11d. less than the stated balance. If the price of the morabetin in 1186 was 7s. and the _punera_ is disregarded (cf. note 16),
then we arrive at a final balance of 30 mo. 3s. 2d.m.--or 3s. 1d.m.
more than the stated balance, etc.

[19] More preponderantly so than meets the eye, for the Templars must
have routinely understated receipts in _bladum_ (see note 2).

[20] ACA, perg. Ramon Berenguer IV, 233 (text M in my edition); s.f.
16; and references in note 21.

[21] Glossarivm mediae latinitatis Cataloniae, 6 fascicules to date
(Barcelona, 1960--), cols. 493-496, v. _cibaria, cibata._

[22] According to the statement of debt (above, note 2) the mill was
at Llicà (de Vall), two kilometers north of Parets.

[23] The _saumata_, or _saumada de vindemia_, figures also in records of
the Templars of Douzens, Gérard and Magnou, Cartulaires de Douzens,
A, nos. 5, 83. It seems necessary to assume that the price de uindemia
was expressed _per somatam_, for only on that assumption can a plausible
price for millet (13d.) be deduced.

[24] E.g., ACA, perg. Ramon Berenguer IV, 233 (B and Q).

[25] Perg. Ramon Berenguer IV, 233 (Q): the count has ¾ "de decima,
preter terciam partem quam Sanctus Petrus in minuturis ipsius decimi
[sic] accipit...."

[26] Bernardus de Plicamanibus, possibly the son of Berenguer, can be
traced in numerous local texts from the 1160's to at least 1187, ACA,
perg. Ramon Berenguer IV, 326; perg. Alfons I, 77 (these pieces are
printed by Moreu-Rey, Rodalia de Caldes de Montbui, Apèndixs, nos. 22,
25); perg. Alfons I, 383, 462, extrainv. 2607; Rius, Cartulario de
"Sant Cugat," III, nos. 1066, 1079, 1108; for the family, see Moreu-
Rey, p. 133.

$^{27}$See Georges Duby, L'Économie rurale et la vie des campagnes dans
l'Occident médiéval, 2 vols. (Paris, 1962), I, 232-235; tr. Cynthia
Postan, Rural Economy and Country Life in the Medieval West (London,
1968), pp. 135-136. The evidence for Spain in our period has not yet
been marshalled, but see Jaime Vicens Vives, An Economic History of
Spain, tr. Frances M. López-Morillas (Princeton, 1969), pp. 138-152.

$^{28}$ACA, perg. Alfons I, 361. For fluctuating prices of frumentum
and barley around Nîmes toward 1182, see Claude Devic and J.-J.
Vaissete, Histoire générale de Languedoc..., new edn., 16 vols.
(Toulouse, 1872-1904), V, 30.

$^{29}$El "Llibre Blanch" de Santas Creus..., ed. Federico Udina Martorell
(Barcelona, 1947), nos. 259, 278; Rius, Cartulario de "Sant Cugat,"
III, nos. 1152, 1159; ACA, perg. Alfons I, 408.

$^{30}$The account of Palau gives no price for the morabetin in 1185
and 1186, but ACA, perg. Alfons I, 417, shows it at 7s. in 1186. See
also perg. Alfons I, 567, 635; Chronicon Barcinonense..., ed. Jaime
and Joaquin Lorenzo Villanueva, Viage literario a las iglesias de
España, 22 vols. (Madrid, 1806-1902), VIII, 230.

$^{31}$Or peses; but I cannot render this word securely.

$^{32}$Duby, Économie rurale, I, 185-187; Country Life, pp. 99-100; idem,
Guerriers et paysans... (Paris, 1973), p. 223.

$^{33}$That the brothers of Palau could store grain, and sell from reserves is suggested by an account of 1207, ACA, perg. Pere I, 261.

$^{34}$See generally, Forey, Templars in the Corona de Aragón, chap. 9;
María Vilar Bonet, "Actividades financieras de la orden del Temple en
la Corona de Aragón," VII Congreso de Historia de la Corona de Aragón,
3 vols. (Barcelona, 1962), II, 577-585; and (with little reference to
Spain) Marie Luise Bulst-Thiele, "Templer in königlichen und päpstlichen Diensten," Festscrift Percy Ernst Schramm, 2 vols. (Wiesbaden,
1964), I, 289-308.

$^{35}$It may be noted, in addition to evidence cited in notes 2 and 26
above, that Arnau, the priest of Santa Maria of Palau who served as
guarantor to the debtor in 1186, can be traced back into the 1160's,
ACA, perg. Alfons I, 43, 126 (the latter ed. Moreu-Rey, Rodalia de
Caldes de Montbui, Apèndixs, no. 26), 164. On settlement and resettle-
ment in this region, see Rius, Cartulario de "Sant Cugat," I, II, passim; cf., for the region just to the east, Anscari M. Mundó, "Domains
and Rights of Sant Pere de Vilamajor (Catalonia): a Polyptich of c.
950 and c. 1060," Speculum, XLIX (1974), 238-257.

[1]Constitutional History of England, 3 vols. (Oxford, 1874-1878), vol. II (3rd ed., 1887), pp. 138-165.  Cf. the Introductory Sketch to the Select Charters and Other Illustrations of English Constitutional History (9th ed., Oxford, 1913).

[2]See Geoffrey Templeman, "Edward I and the Historians," Cambridge Historical Journal 10 (1950), and my forthcoming historiographical article on Edward I.

[3]H. Rothwell, "The Confirmation of the Charters, 1297," English Historical Review, LX (1945), pp. 16-35, 177-191, 300-315, and his "Edward I and the Struggle for the Charters," Studies in Medieval History Presented to F. M. Powicke (Oxford, 1948); F. M. Powicke, The Thirteenth Century (2nd ed., Oxford, 1962), pp. 644-683; J. G. Edwards, "Confirmatio Cartarum and Baronial Grievances in 1297," English Historical Review, LVIII (1943), pp. 147-169, 273-300; Bertie Wilkinson, The Constitutional History of England, 1216-1399, with select documents, 3 vols. (London, 1948-1959), vol. I, pp. 187-232; Michael Prestwich, War, Politics and Finances Under Edward I (Totowa, New Jersey, 1972), chapters XI, XII.

[4]"Edward I and the Struggle for the Charters."

[5]"Edward I's Castle-Building in Wales," Proceedings of the British Academy, XXXII (1946), pp. 17-81.

[6]Ibid., quotations from pp. 16 and 65, respectively.

[7]Ibid., p. 61.

[8]Ibid., p. 62.

[9]Such as John E. Morris, for whose The Welsh Wars of Edward the First (Oxford, 1901), he expresses high praise.

[10]The History of the King's Works, general editor H. M. Colvin, 2 vols. (London, 1963), vol. I, chapters V and VI; vol. II, chapter XIII and appendices C.I, II, III contain a vast store of information on the castles and associated works.  The authors note that actually ten new castles were built (they add Ruthin and Hope to Edwards' list of eight), that four "lordship" castles (Hawarden, Denbigh, Holt, and Chirk) were begun under general royal direction, and that substantial work was undertaken at three native Welsh castles that fell into royal hands (Dolwyddelan, Bere, Criccieth), as well as at several border fortresses which had served as English bases (Chester, Oswestry, Shrewsbury, Montgomery, St. Briavel's).  See vol. I, p. 293.

[11]"Castle-Building," pp. 64-65.  This seems to echo T. F. Tout's assertion that "Edward formed so many great designs that he was always more and more in want of money.  From this perpetual indebtedness

sprang half the defects of Edward's character, and more than half of
the difficulties of his reign." Edward I (London, 1893), p. 66.

[12]Helen Cam wrote in England Before Elizabeth (Harper Torchbook edn.,
New York, 1960), p. 113: "...all through his reign he was plunging
deeper and deeper into debt. The wars of his father's reign had
bequeathed to him a deficit that he was never able to make good; his
own crusade and his wars in Wales, Scotland and France increased it,
and his attempts to realize some of the floating wealth of the realm
involved him...in disputes with his subjects without materially improving the position." The idea of cumulative indebtedness was not,
of course, first stated by Edwards, nor by Tout (see previous note).
William Stubbs wrote in 1882 that the king "inherited from his father
a poverty which his own obligations, incurred during the Crusade, increased into a lifelong burden." Chronicles of the Reigns of Edward
I and Edward II, 2 vols. (Rolls Series, London, 1882), vol. I, p. c.

[13]See Richard W. Kaeuper, Bankers to the Crown, the Riccardi of
Lucca and Edward I (Princeton, 1973) and the sources cited there,
especially Edmund B. Fryde, "Public Credit, with Special Reference
to North-Western Europe," Cambridge Economic History, vol. III
(Cambridge, 1963), chapter VII. Cf. Michael Prestwich, War, Politics
and Finance, chapter IX.

[14]See the tables and discussion in Kaeuper, Bankers to the Crown,
pp. 124-131.

[15]The quotations are taken from his introduction to Chronicles of
the Reigns of Edward I and Edward II, vol. I, pp. c-cii.

[16]The quotations appear in Chapters in the Administrative History
of Medieval England, 6 vols. (Manchester, 1920-1933), vol. II, pp.
117 and 113-114, respectively. Tout had first used the comparison
to Oriental potentates and South American republics in The Place of
the Reign of Edward II in English History (Manchester, 1914), p. 38.
He was equally negative toward the Italian companies in his earlier
biography of Edward, in which he wrote of the king's finding himself
"helplessly in the hands of the greedy companies of Lombard bankers
who had begun to push themselves into the position which had hitherto
been monopolized by Jewish usurers." Edward I, p. 66. Cf. pp. 83,
142.

[17]Public Record Office, E 101/126/1. All documentary references
will be to manuscripts in the Public Record Office.

[18]E 372/142 m. 35d.

[19]The resentment which would produce a serious drop in the yield of
taxation late in the reign had not yet begun. See F. M. Powicke,
Thirteenth Century, pp. 524-527, Michael Prestwich, War, Politics and
Finance, pp. 179-182, and the sources cited in both of these works.

[20]This is the thesis of Kaeuper, Bankers to the Crown. Cf. E. B.

Fryde, "Public Credit," p. 437, Tout, Chapters, II, p. 112, and Prestwich, War, Politics and Finance, pp. 192-193, 218.

[21] Edwards "Castle-Building," Appendix I, and King's Works, II, Appendix C.I.

[22] Books of Prests of the King's Wardrobe for 1294-5 (Oxford, 1962), p. 1.

[23] War, Politics and Finance, p. 175.

[24] "Edward I's Monetary Policies and Their Consequences," Economic History Review, 2nd ser., XXII (1969), pp. 406-416.

[25] Tout, Place of Edward II, pp. 36-38; Fryde, "Public Credit," pp. 457-458; J. G. Edwards, "Confirmatio Cartarum and Baronial Grievances in 1297," English Historical Review, LVIII (1943), pp. 157-160; Harry Rothwell, "Edward I and the Struggle for the Charters, 1297-1305," Studies in Medieval History Presented to Frederick Maurice Powicke (Oxford, 1948), pp. 322-323; Powicke, Thirteenth Century, chapter XIV; Prestwich, War, Politics and Finance, passim.

[26] See the analysis in Kaeuper, Bankers to the Crown, chapter V, section 1.

[27] Powicke, Thirteenth Century, p. 648.

[28] E 159/68 m. 86d.

[29] For what follows see Kaeuper, "The Frescobaldi of Florence and the English Crown," Studies in Medieval and Renaissance History, X (1973), pp. 45-95.

[30] Ibid., p. 72.

[31] E 372/130 mm. 5,5d.  E 101/351/10.  E 372/136 m. 33.  E 101/4/2.

[32] Of this sum approximately £103,737 was owed for Gascon trip expenses.  See Calendar of Patent Rolls, 1281-1292, p. 318, and the discussion in Kaeuper, Bankers to the Crown, pp. 95-96.  The remaining sum of £8,300 was advanced for the suppression of the revolt.  See E 372/132 m. 1, E 372/133 m. 28, E 372/134 mm. 1, 2d., E 101/4/21, and the discussion in Kaeuper, Bankers to the Crown, pp. 195-199.

[33] Kaeuper, "Frescobaldi," p. 67.

[34] Chapters, vol. II, p. 129.

[35] Kaeuper, "Frescobaldi," pp. 62-68.

[36] In The Place of Edward II, p. 38, he states unequivocally, "Probably no medieval king has left his finances in a more hopeless confusion than did the great Edward.  Certainly none of them ever handed to his successor so heavy a task with such inadequate means to discharge it."

Chapter 9

[1]I am grateful to the American Philosophical Society for a grant from the Penrose Fund which made possible my trip to Florence in April 1972, to Prof. Reinhold C. Mueller for introducing me to the Florentine archives, and to Prof. Christopher Kleinhenz and Prof. Gino Corti for bibliographical and other assistance.

[2]Il Decameron, ed. Charles S. Singleton, Scrittori d'Italia, 97 (Bari, 1965), I, 27-39, or ed. Vittore Branca, 4th ed. (Florence, 1960), 46-66. Boccaccio's portrait of the "Italian Tartuffe" influenced not only the literature of his own country but that of others as well. For instance, late in the sixteenth century Jakob Ayrer continued the Fastnachtspiele of Hans Sachs with Der Falsch Notarius mit seine unwahrhaften Beicht and Voltaire retold the story, "Saint Ciappelletto, qui avait été le plus grand fripon de son temps"; on this and other matters see Luigi Fassò, "La prima novella del Decameron e la sua fortuna," Annali della Facoltà di Filosofia e Lettere della Università di Cagliari, III (1931), 15-64, reprinted in his Saggi e ricerche di storia letteraria (Milan, 1947), pp. 33-90. For some other examples of the treatment of "Ser Ciappelletto" see Vittore Branca, Boccaccio medievale (Florence, 1956), pp. 71-99; Luigi Russo, Letture critiche del Decameron (Bari, 1967), pp. 51-68; and Aldo D. Scaglione, "Boccaccio, Chaucer, and the Mercantile Ethic," in Literature and Western Civilization, ed. David Daiches and A. Throlby (London, 1973), II, 579-600. The best-documented study of the historical Cepperello is a book by a local historian intended to restore the reputation of a fellow-citizen, Giulio Giani's Cepparello da Prato (Prato, 1915); I have not seen his Ancora due parole su Cepparello (Prato, 1916). Giani was greatly concerned with the literal truth of the story, which must owe much to Boccaccio's imagination and has antecedents which go back to Sulpicius Severus' biography of St. Martin of Tours.

[3]Paoli, "Documenti di ser Ciappelletto," Giornale storico della letteratura italiana, V (1885), 329-369.

[4]Robert Mignon, Inventaire d'anciens comptes royaux, ed. Charles-Victor Langlois (Paris, 1899), no. 1158. On the famous banker of Philip the Fair see Friedrich Bock, "Musciatto dei Francesi," Deutsches Archiv, VI (1943), 521-544. Cepperello's nephew, "Jaqueminus Caym" also worked as a tax-collector in Champagne in the 1290's; see Robert Fawtier, Comptes royaux, 1285-1314 (Paris, 1953-56), II, 98, no. 15288.

[5]Claude Faure, Étude sur l'administration et l'histoire du Comtat-Venaissin, 1229-1417 (Paris, 1909), p. 181, dates Vatican Instrum. Miscell. 1288-1295, no. 55, the document which mentions Cepperello as treasurer, as after February 1, 1297. Giani, Cepparello, pp. 96-100, dates the document to 1295. Faure erred in his assertion (p. 99) that the treasurer was always an ecclesiastic.

[6]Noffo appears in the accounts of 1288-1290, Paoli, "Documenti," pp. 346-360.  On Noffo (Arnolfo Deghi) see Abel Rigault, Le procès de Guichard, évêque de Troyes (Paris, 1896), pp. 23-24.

[7]Giani, Cepparello, pp. 61-72.

[8]Joseph R. Strayer, "Italian Bankers and Philip the Fair," in Economy, Society, and Government in Medieval Italy:  Essays in Memory of Robert L. Reynolds (Kent, Ohio, 1969), pp. 113-121, reprinted in Medieval Statecraft and the Perspectives of History (Princeton, 1971), pp. 239-247.

[9]These accounts have been re-edited in an improved form by Alfredo Schiaffini, Testi fiorentini del Dugento e dei primi del Trecento, new ed. (Florence, 1954), pp. 244-259.

[10]These accounts from the Auvergne would also benefit from a new edition by someone familiar with local place-names.  If a new edition is prepared, note should also be taken of Jean de Trie's accounts from the All Saints' term of 1287, copied in Clermont-Ferrand, Bibl. mun. ms. 623, fol. 110 ff. (which I have not seen) and partly printed by Henri Gravier, Essai sur les prévôts royaux (Paris, 1904), pp. 81-82.

[11]For what remains see Michel Nortier, "Le sort des archives dispersées de la Chambre des Comptes de Paris," Bibliothèque de l'École des chartes, CXXIII (1965), 460-537.

[12]Cesare Paoli, "Le carte dei Gondi donate all'Archivio di Stato di Firenze," Archivio storico italiano, ser. 4, t. XII (1884), 296-300.

[13]Léon L. Borrelli de Serres, Recherches sur divers services publiques du XIIIe au XVIIe siècle (Paris, 1895-1909), II, 44-45.  For other passing references to Cepperello and these accounts, see Rigault, Procès de Guichard, p. 24; Camille Piton, Les Lombards en France et à Paris (Paris, 1892-93), I, 71; Elizabeth Chapin, Les villes de foires de Champagne (Paris, 1937), pp. 93 and 173.

[14]Fawtier, Comptes royaux, III, xlviii, no. 40, noted Paoli's edition, but he did not include it in his list of accounts of the nouveaux acquêts on pp. lvi-lx.  For displaced accounts not included in Fawtier's magnificent survey, reference may be made to T. P. Voronova, "The accounts of Renaut de Sainte-Beuve for the expenses of his mission to Lyon, Feb.-March 1313" [in Russian], Srednie Veka, XXIX (1966), 260-266.

[15]In preparing this edition I have depended heavily on Alphonse Roserot, Dictionnaire historique de la Champagne méridionale (Aube) des origines à 1790 (Langres, 1942-48) and the indices of Auguste Longnon, Documents relatifs au comté de Champagne et de Brie, 1172-1362 (Paris, 1901-14).

[16]Ordonnances des roys de France de la troisième race, ed. Eusèbe de Laurière (Paris, 1723-1849), I, 303-305.

[17]For the published accounts see Fawtier, Comptes royaux, II, 315-364 and III, lvi-lx. Marie-Élisabeth Antoine-Carreau submitted a thesis on "Les commissaires royaux aux amortissements et aux nouveaux acquêts sous les Capétiens (1275-1328)" to the École des chartes in 1953; see Positions des thèses, 1953, pp. 19-22. I am grateful to Mme. Antoine for sending me an offprint.

[18]The 69 items in the ecclesiastical column of these accounts produced 844 l. of revenue, while 70 items in the lay column produced 603 l. 19s. 6d. Since churches had to pay less than the laity for the same value of property, it appears that ecclesiastical purchases were significantly more substantial. But since the lists are incomplete, no firm conclusions comparing totals can be drawn.

[19]Mignon, Inventaire, nos. 1852-1853. Mignon, as edited by Langlois, spells the place-name as Noycello. In the entry cited in the following note, the collector is called "magister G. de Noentello." In the index to the Comptes royaux, François Maillard identified the place as Nointeau in Indre-et Loire, which seems correct for a canon of Tours.

[20]Comptes royaux, ed. Fawtier, no. 15293.

[21]Mignon, Inventaire, no. 1853.

[22]In 1292 the collector for the nouveaux acquêts in the bailliage of Caux took in under 100 l. and spent over 170 l. in the process; see Fawtier, Comptes royaux, III, lvii. Prof. Strayer demonstrates the diligent fund-raising of the monarchy in 1294 in Studies in Early French Taxation (Cambridge, Mass., 1939), pp. 25-28, 44-46.

[23]Longnon, Documents, III, 119-123. The precise total is 12,631 l. if the figure for Jean Acelin of Méry (p. 123 L) is really xi; 12,660 if it should be xl. Fawtier miscalculated in his total of 12,591 l. in Comptes royaux, III, lvi. In this roll we can recognize many names which appear in Latin in Cepperello's accounts. Guillaume du Châtelet, the individual who owed the largest amount to Cepperello (200 l.), does not appear in the list of those who subscribed to the loan. He is probably to be identified as the former bailli of Troyes who was bailli of Sézanne in 1295; see Paulette Portejoie, L'ancien coutumier de Champagne (Poitiers, 1956), p. 10, n. 28.

[24]Longnon, Documents, III, 210.

[25]Comptes royaux, ed. Fawtier, II, 345.

[26]These figures have been supplied me by Dr. Evergates, who is now revising for publication his 1971 Johns Hopkins dissertation, "Feudal Society: The Bailliage of Troyes under the Counts of Champagne, 1152-1284." For a study of the aristocracy of the entire county of Champagne and their income see his articles, "The Aristocracy of Champagne in the Mid-Thirteenth Century: A Quantitative Description," Journal of Interdisciplinary History, V (1974), 1-18, and "A Quantitative Analysis of Fiefs in Medieval Champagne," Computers and the Humanities, IX (1975), 61-67.

[27]A note to one entry (158) says the _prévôt_ ought to give an accounting for it.

[28]The pouillés of all the dioceses which made up the bailliage of Troyes are edited by Auguste Longnon, _Pouillés de la province de Sens_ (Paris, 1904). For the value of the clerical tenth in the reign of Philip the Fair see _Recueil des historians des Gaules et de la France_, ed. Martin Bouquet et al. (Paris, 1738-1904), XXI, 540-545, 557-560.

[29]Ferdinand Lot, "L'état des paroisses et des feux de 1328," _Bibliothèque de l'École des chartes_, XC (1929), 51-107, 256-315; "Extenta terre comitatus Campanie et Brie" in Longnon, _Documents_, II, 9-183; "Estimation des biens ecclésiastiques au bailliage de Troyes," _ibid._, III, 124-133.

[30]Lot, "État des paroisses," p. 71.

[31]The map of the bailliage of Troyes in Roserot, _Dictionnaire_, Introduction, facing p. 44, shows Molins as an enclave surrounded by territory in the bailliage of Chaumont. The eastern boundary of the bailliage in Roserot's map differs substantially from that in the map accompanying this article.

[32]The accounts list payments by the location of the property rather than that of the recipient. Nevertheless, unless we have information to the contrary, it is reasonable to assume that most parish churches were acquiring property within their own parishes.

[33]For instance, he read _Antissiodoro_ for _Autissiodoro_, _Lenz_ for _Leuz_, _Montanigro_ for _Montaingone_, and _Unennoy_ for _Vriennon_.

[34]Dr. Rudolf Hirsch, who has catalogued those portions of the Gondi papers acquired by the University of Pennsylvania, has kindly informed me that no thirteenth-century French accounts are part of the collection; cf. _The [University of Pennsylvania] Library Chronicle_, XXXVI (1970), 79-104, and XXXVII (1971), 3-23. Prof. Gino Corti of Florence has also kindly informed me that to the best of his knowledge no missing fragments of these accounts are in the private archives of the Gondi family, and that no Regnadori papers are known to exist outside those given to the archives in the nineteenth century.


                                Appendix


[1]These words, demanded by the sense of the passage, were omitted by the copyist.

[2]Ms. torn.

[3]It is difficult to tell if the fourth letter is _n_ or _u/v_. The geographical context suggests that the word is a corruption of some

form of Brevonne.

[4]Although we would not expect to find a cleric in this list of lay people, if Decanus is an office rather than an unusual personal name, this is presumably a reference to Jacques, doyen de chrétienté of Villemaur.

[5]The ms. reads sacē.

[6]I read the second letter as t (stalat.); Paoli read it as c and expanded to scalatis. In a letter Leopold Deslisle suggested to him that this might be a stripped cloth used to cover the sacks of money; cf. Du Cange, s.v. scallatus. My interpretation is that the word refers to charges for stallage; cf. scalaticum in J. F. Niermeyer, Mediae latinitatis lexicon minus (Leiden, 1954-).

[7]The total is inexplicable.

[8]In margin: sol. .b.

[9]The ms. reads Psiaco. Paoli expanded to Prisiaco, but there is no place-name in the region which fits this reading. Plansiaco makes sense; it is possible that the canons of the collegiate church of Saint-Laurent de Plancy had a chapel south of the Aube in the territory of the castellany of Méry.

[10]In Margin: sol. .b.

[11]Apparently an error for Marine, though a chapel of Sainte-Marine is not known in the region of Ervy.

[12]In margin: lib.

[13]Total inexplicable.

[14]In margin in large writing: Prepositus debet respondere de argento.

[15]In margin: lib.

[16]Bouy-Vieux was a chapel under the care of the curate of Brienon.

[17]In margin: lib.

[18]The priory of Saint-Nicolas of Réveillon was in fact in the diocese of Auxerre.

[19]The ms. reads cetollaz, with a mark of suspension over the e which I am not sure how to expand. Paoli read Certollaz.

Chapter 10

[1] On these currents see Matthew F. Maury, The Physical Geography of the Sea (New York, 1858), pp. 150 and 154-161. The log of the U.S. ship Levant for March 1855 describes this situation as follows: "At noon stood in Almería Bay anchored off the village of Roguetes. Found a great number of vessels waiting for a chance to get to the west and learned from them that at least a thousand sail are weatherbound between this place and Gibraltar. Some of them have been so for six weeks and have even got as far as Malaga only to be swept back by the current. Indeed no vessel has been able to get out into the Atlantic for three months past." Maury, op. cit., pp. 152-153.

[2] Saga tradition indeed tells us of one such expedition from the north reaching the Mediterranean and Sicily during the period 1150-1152, that of the Jarl of Orkney on his way to the Holy Land. On this expedition as related in the Orkneyinga Saga, see Count P.-E.-D. Riant, Expeditions et pèlerinages des Scandinaves en Terre Sainte au temps de Croisades (Paris, 1865), pp. 235-261. See also T. Andersson, "Skalds and Troubadours" in Medieval Scandinavia, II (1969), pp. 11-14. Incidentally, the Orkney Jarl, like all the rest, returned from the Mediterranean overland and not by way of the Straits of Gibraltar.

[3] These sailing directions for the western Mediterranean are to be found in Roger of Hoveden, Annals, ed. W. Stubbs, III (London, 1870), pp. 46-52. Since these passages report North Africa in Moslem hands but Moslem Spain divided between Almahads and independent rulers of Jaen, Murcia, and Valencia, they must date from the period 1160 to 1172. See op. cit., p. 52.

[1]See William C. Jordan, "Saint Louis' Influence on French Society and Life in the Thirteenth Century:  The Social Content of the Crusade of the Mid-Century" (unpublished Ph.D. diss., Princeton University, 1973), pp. 78-82.

[2]As our discussion moves forward it will be necessary to refer to the map accompanying this chapter.  Didot and Didot, Nouvelle biographie générale, XXXI (Paris, 1862), "Louis IX," p. 778, talk of a general policy on péages to guarantee the safe travel of goods, but there is so much wrong in the notice that I can give no credence to their statement.  Two incidents, probably of the policy of Louis' mother, Blanche of Castile, in 1229 and 1233, show that there was a precedent for the suppression of specific péages, as e.g. when founding a new monastery; see É.-J. Lauriere, ed., Ordonnances des rois de France de la troisième race (hereinafter Ordonnances), 22 vols. (Paris, 1723), XI, 326, and E. Roussel, Inventaire-sommaire...; Oise..., série H, II (Beauvais, 1897), 153.  Louis IX, himself, in his teachings to his son, seems, in later life, to have tried to justify his conduct here by explaining to the future Philip III that policy changes with respect to tolls and taxes should not be undertaken except in urgent necessity (Jean, sire de Joinville, Histoire de saint Louis, ed. N. de Wailly [Paris, 1872], chap. cxlv).  Moreover, on the crusade, Louis was admonished for transgressing customs (Joinville, chap. xxxvi), a notion he also defended in his teachings to his son when he urged him to remove bad customs (Joinville, chap. cxlv).  It is interesting that his remarks to his son on tolls and taxes and on bad customs are in the same clause.  David O'Connell, The Teachings of Saint Louis:  A Critical Text (Chapel Hill, 1972), p. 23, suggests that the citations of the teachings by Louis' friend, Joinville, may be from a corrupt manuscript with early fourteenth century interpolations.  It is true, also, that the critical text published by O'Connell, op. cit., pp. 55-60, lacks something of the political flavor of Joinville's version.  On the other hand, the general policy of eliminating bad customs and enforcing only good ones was characteristic of Louis IX; see, e.g., Francois Olivier-Martin, "Le Roi de France et les mauvaises coutumes au moyen âge," Zeitschrift...für Rechtsgeschichte, LXXI (1938), 117-121.

[3]AD:  Gard, SS17 (Nîmes).  The petition is undated.  Two suggestions are 1248 and 1270; for the arguments see Jordan, pp. 79-80, n. 41.

[4]This charter (May, 1246) is reprinted in Alexandre Teulet, et al., eds., Layettes du Trésor des chartes (hereinafter Layettes), 5 vols. (Paris, 1863-1909), II, no. 3522, pp. 618-622.  It is the only new town charter issued in the Beaucaire sénéchaussée in the early reign of Louis IX (cf. Margaret Labarge, Saint Louis [Boston, 1968], p. 103), and its length alone emphasizes the difference between it and, say, the charters of Philip-Augustus.  There are sweeping concessions in governing the town (e.g., the consuls did not have to be approved by the king, p. 619); there were, as we noted, financial immunities ("immunes ab omnibus questis, talliis, et toltis, et mutuo coacto, et

omni ademptu coacto," etc., p. 618); and there were attempts to promote the settlement of the town by special liberties.  Yet, despite
all this, there is an extremely possessive tone in the document, unlike the charters of Philip-Augustus or even the confirmations up to
this time of Louis himself (which, by the way, are brief, uninteresting
documents).  There is' an over-long discussion of how the consuls must
serve the king and fight those who disobey him, and this is completely
beyond the usual formula that graces documents of this sort; p. 619.
A French translation of the charter will be found in Nicolas Lasserre,
Histoire populaire d'Aigues-Mortes (Nîmes, 1937), pp. 189-193; and
there is a good discussion of it in Robert Michel, L'Administration
royale dans la sénéchaussée de Beaucaire au temps de saint Louis
(Paris, 1910), pp. 269-281.

[5]Archibald Ross Lewis, "Montpellier and Its Institutions to 1294"
(unpubl Ph.D. diss., Princeton University, 1940), differentiates the
institutional structures to which these words apply.

[6]These included suppression of péages adversely affecting the town;
see, for example, Joseph Berthelé, Archives de la ville de Montpellier,
III:  Inventaire ces cartulaires de Montpellier (980-1789), etc.
(Montpellier, 1901-1907), p. 128, no. 808.

[7]The fact that Montpellier was friendly to Louis indicates its
antipathy toward the overlordship of King James of Aragon; on this,
see A. Germain, Histoire du commerce de Montpellier, 2 vols.
(Montpellier, 1861), II, 119.

[8]A. Germain, Histoire de la commune de Montpellier, 3 vols.
(Montpellier, 1851), II, 76-92, and II, "Pièces justificatives," no.
XLV.

[9]J. Rouquette and A. Villemagne, eds., Cartulaire de Maguelone, I-
III (Montpellier and elsewhere, 1912-1921), II, 655-656, no. dlxviii.
See below, n. 37.

[10]Rouquette and Villemagne, Cartulaire, II, 655-656, no. dlxviii.

[11]C.-F. Émile Boisson, De la ville de Sommières (Lunel, 1849), pp.
53-61.

[12]Boisson, Sommières, pp. 53-61; André Peyriat, Histoire de St.-
Hippolyte-du-Fort (Nîmes, 1939), p. 43 (who mixes up the narrative
of Bermond's rebellion very badly); Jean Germain, Sauve, antique et
curieuse cité (Montpellier, 1952), pp. 139, 142.

[13]Dom J. Vaissète, et al., eds., Histoire générale de Languedoc
(hereinafter HGL), 16 vols., ed. (2nd ed.), A. Molinier, et al.
(Toulouse, 1872-1904), VIII, c. 1247; and below, text to n. 34.

[14]HGL, VIII, c. 1247; Gallia christiana in provincias ecclesiasticas
distributa (hereinafter GC), 16 vols. (Paris, 1715-1865), VI,
"Instrumenta," c. 202 no. xxxi.

[15] Archives départementales (AD): Hérault, AA1, document 3 (Marsillargues)--parchment with paper transcription.

[16] (Berthelé,) Archives...cartulaires, p. 128, no. 808, p. 95, no. 669 (here the date is misprinted 1231 for 1251; Lewis, Montpellier, though helpful on many of the points in the text, erroneously accepts the inventory date, p. 117); pp. 108-109, nos. 760-764. See also, Germain, Commune, II, pp. 76-92; Germain, Commerce, I, "pièces justificatives," no. xxii; but contrast Augustin Fliche, Aigues-Mortes et Saint-Gilles, 2nd ed. (Paris, 1950), p. 7, on the naming of this péage.

[17] Thomas Millerot, Histoire de la ville de Lunel (Montpellier, 1880), pp. 61-62; Germain, Commune, II, pp. 76-92. This temporary phenomenon became permanently reactivated by 1257, as indicated in a document respecting the homage of the sires of Lunel (vidimus of 1283)--Archives municipales (AM): Lunel, AA3, 1678 (Michel, Beaucaire, p. 12).

[18] Germain, Commerce, I, "pièces justificatives," no. xxii (cf. Fliche, Aigues-Mortes, p. 6, p. 6, n. 1, p. 7, on nomenclature); see also Elisée Reclus, Nouvelle géographic universelle, II: La France (Paris, 1877), p. 249; and Germain, Commune, II, 76-92. I have consulted old maps at Lunel and Montpellier, but the exact position of the Fossa is still conjectural.

[19] AD: Gard, SS17 (Nîmes); L. Ménard, Histoire de ville de Nismes, I (Paris, 1750), "Preuves," p. 78, no. lv; Millerot, Lunel, pp. 61-62. Cf. above, n. 3, on the date. Again, the exact position of the étangs is conjectural; there has been a great deal of topographical change in 700 years.

[20] Lasserre, Aigues-Mortes, p. 189 (Layettes, II, no. 3522); Lasserre may be using a too rigid translation of gabella.

[21] AM: Lunel, AA1, 1639 (Le Livre blanc), fol. 28 recto (the sire of Lunel is restored to the péage of S. Nazaire in 1255, our text inferred from this citation). We might add that a large proportion of the supplies accumulated in Aigues-Mortes was probably to be salted meats. This certainly would add urgency to the situation. We know that Damietta was well stocked with salted pork in 1250, and it is likely that this was brought over with the crusading army. Even after Damietta was surrendered to the Moslems the salted pork was supposed to be turned over to the French (although it was destroyed instead); Joinville, chaps. lxx, lxxii.

[22] I say "finally" but in fact the issue is far from closed. Indeed, for a good many towns directly around Aigues-Mortes we know absolutely nothing about the situation of péages ca. 1245-1254. This is true for Aimargues, Gallargues-le-Monteux, S. Laurent d'Aigouze, Aigues-Vives, Mus (but cf. Jordan, pp. 83-84, n. 56), Vergèze and Codognan (conversation, adjunct archivist, Gard, December 15, 1971); see also Bessot de Lamothe and Bligny-Bondurand, Inventaire-sommaire des archives départementales, Gard, série E. supplément, vol. I: Arrondissement de Nîmes, Aiguesmortes, Aiguevives, Aimargues, Aramon (Nîmes, 1888);

and Jean Vidal, Monographie de la ville d'Aimargues (Paris, 1906?),
pp. 18-29 and p. 23, n. 1.

[23]August 16, 1249 (during the regency)--Germain, Commerce, I, "pièces
justificatives," no. xvii. This limitation does not apply to the Nîmes
area, on which see below, n. 29.

[24]J. Rouquette, "Saint Louis et le comte de Melgueil," Revue d'histoire de l'église de France, V (1914-1919), p. 195; Layettes, III, nos.
3709, 3710, 3711; Lasserre, Aigues-Mortes, "Liste des châtelains et
gouverneurs d'Aigues-Mortes," 179.

[25]Reclus, II, fig. no. 70, p. 248.

[26]Whether (and to what extent) Aigues-Mortes may have changed since
the Middle Ages is in dispute, but all authorities condemn its physical qualities (even in the Middle Ages) as a port. On this general
point, see Jordan, pp. 79-80, n. 40; cf. Reclus, II, 249; and Fliche,
Aigues-Mortes, p. 7.

[27]Moreover, Montpellier was "fed" by an important western trade
route (from the Béziers, Toulouse, Carcassonne region) which was not
as richly duplicated for Nîmes (see map).

[28]Ménard, I, text, pp. 313, 317; Michel, Beaucaire, pp. 231-239, 250.
Whether there were adequate grounds for any suspicion of Nîmes' loyalty
is doubtful (conversation October 23, 1973, with Mr. Raphael DeSoignie).

[29]Ménard, I, 317; HGL, VIII, cc. 1235-1236; this may explain why
stone from the region near Nîmes was only imported for the defensive
Tower of Constance and not for the ramparts of Aigues-Mortes (Jordan,
pp. 83-84, n. 56).

[30]One senses that the people of Aigues-Mortes were in favor of Nîmes,
fearing as they did the commercial hegemony of Montpellier; see Ménard,
I, "Preuves," p. 78, no. lv.

[31]Rouquette and Villemagne, Cartulaire, II, 655-656, no. dlxviii;
on the naming of the towns, see Dictionnaire topographique de la
France:  Gard (Paris, 1868), esp. p. 5 on Alès(t)=Alais.

[32]Naturally, finished Italian goods imported through Montpellier were
not affected by this change.

[33]AM:  Lunel, AA3, 1678.

[34]Rarely would these merchants go to Nîmes since trade with Nîmes
could more propitiously proceed from S.-Ambroix, Alès, or Anduze
directly to that town; in addition, with péage collection more ruth-
less to the east, it would have been inane to further duplicate the
merchants' costs.

[35]Boisson, Sommières, pp. 53-61; AD:  Gard, H106 fol. 59 recto.

[36](Berthelé,) Archives...cartulaires, pp. 95, 108-109, 128 (nos. 669, 760-764, 808); Germain, Commune, II, pp. 76-92; Layettes, III, no. 4092, p. 205; HGL, VIII, cc. 213-214.

[37]Rouquette and Villemagne, Cartulaire, II, 655-656, no. dlxviii: "salvo jure venerabilis patris episcopi Magalonensis de pedagio suo, quod percipiebat apud Sanctam Crucem [-de-Quintillargues]." Though the document itself does not make explicit mention of where this Holy Cross is, later usages (and geographical common sense) denote it as Sainte-Croix-de-Quintillargues (see accompanying map); see also, AD: Hérault, G1475; Dictionnaire topographique de la France: Hérault (Paris, 1895), p. 174; Prof. J. Combes, personal letter, February 13, 1972; and conversation, A. Jeanjean, January 11, 1972. Compare, however, the tempting possibility that the later usage is erroneous and that the original usage refers to the Rue Sainte-Croix in Montpellier, known in the Middle Ages as the "descente Sainte-Croix," where the wall of the town intersected a church which was later replaced by the cathedral of Montpellier, the seat of the bishop of Maguelonne, who still retailed his ancient and outmoded title "of Maguelonne." On the naming of the street, but not the theory, see Louis-H. Escuret, Vieilles rues de Montpellier, 2 vols. (Montpellier, 1956, 1964), I, 213; and J. Duval-Jouve, Les Noms des rues de Montpellier (Montpellier, 1877), p. 306.

[38]Rouquette and Villemagne, Cartulaire, II, 655-656, no. dlxviii: "...illud pedagium percipiat apud villam de Lentrescleriis." How these goods were inventoried for this collection we do not precisely know; cf. Achille Bardon, Histoire de la ville d'Alais de 1250 à 1340 (Nîmes, 1894), p. 158. Rouquette, "Saint Louis," p. 195, mentions the change in the collection of the bishop's péage as evidence of the unrestrained activity of the sénéchal of Beaucaire, but Rouquette's treatment of the question is hurried, and he does not note that the bishop's péage was simply moved not seized by the king. Michel (see his Beaucaire, pp. 183-185), is also prone to think merely in terms of the sénéchal's zeal.

[39]HGL, VIII, c. 1247.

[40]AD:  Gard:  H106 fol. 59 recto; GC, VI, "Instrumenta," c. 202, no. xxxi ("contigua via(e) quae ducit Alestum")--note grammatical emendation suggested in marginalia of GC;--Layettes, III, no. 3706.

[41]On the other possible towns on this route before and after it was diverted, there is almost nothing more. The king collected a péage at Alès; in 1254 part of the income from this péage was ceded to the Cistercians (HGL, VIII, cc. 1335-1338). Therefore, there may be something to the theory that the king had adversely affected the inhabitants by tampering with the péage (cf. Michel, Beaucaire, pp. 244, and 239-245). Personal letters and investigations of the local archives revealed very little for the towns of Quissac, Salinelles, S.-Hippolyte-du-Fort, Sauve, S. Jean-de-Crieulon, Corconne, Pompignan, Castries, Treviers, Pradès-le-Lez, Montferrier, Fontanès, Vacquières, Valflaunès, Assas. On some of these, however, HGL and Layettes have a little useful information (which we have cited where appropriate). Some of these towns are shown on the map.

[42]Rouquette and Villemagne, Cartulaire, II, 655-656, no. dlxviii--
June 1249; an alternative translation for strata publica is public
highway, but the sense in the document before us is trade route.

[43]Reclus, II, fig. no. 69 (between pp. 240 and 241) and no. 70 (p.
248). There is a pine forest on the Cordon littoral.

[44]For a general summary of the physical geography, see "France," in
Encyclopaedia Britannica, 24 vols. (Chicago, 1960), IX, 585-586.

[45]G. Droysen, Allgemeiner Historischer Handatlas (Bielefeld and
Leipzig, 1886), p. 57.

[46]The total army was between 15,000 and 25,000 but it did not leave
France at once. The 5,000 figure cited in the text is a guess. For
a discussion of the army, see Jordan, pp. 72-77.

[47]Aigues-Mortes, whose highest population in the Middle Ages as now
was about 3,500 (see Lasserre, Aigues-Mortes, "Renseignements démo-
graphiques," p. 186), must have been overwhelmed by the influx of
knights (say 1,000), an influx which continued through 1249 (Joseph R.
Strayer, "The Crusades of Louis IX" in Medieval Statecraft and the
Perspectives of History, eds. J. F. Benton and T. N. Bisson [Princeton,
1971], p. 165). Now, each knight-banneret was probably attended by 5
servants, and each bachelor by 2; "A List of the Knights Who Accompanied Saint Louis in His Expedition to Palestine," in T. Johnes, comp.
and trans., Memoirs of John Lord de Joinville (after DuCange), II
(1807), p. 224; cf. Jordan, p. 12, n. 2 and p. 74, n. 11, on this
source. Also, Layettes, III, no. 3883, shows that families accompanied
crusaders. Cf. the observations of Abbé H. Aigon in the somewhat un-
reliable Aigues-Mortes: Ville de saint Louis (Nîmes, 1908), p. 54,
and "Majus chronicon Lemovicense," Martin Bouquet, et al., eds.,
Recueil des historiens des Gaules et de la France (hereinafter HF), 24
vols. (Paris, 1738-1904), XXI, p. 766, that Louis "ad portum cum magno
exercitu et innumerabili populo et inaestimabili apparatu venit."
Francois Mahoudeau, Croisade pour Aigues-Mortes (Montpellier, privately
printed, 1969), p. 46, remarks on the crowded conditions, but he estimated the number of crusaders there at 60,000.

[48]On the original decision to depart in 1247, see Layettes, II, no.
3537. Cf. Account of Ascension, 1248, HF, XXI, 283, on naval provisions (including wood supplies of a specialized variety). As an
interesting comparison to the textual point on firewood, see Blanche's
need when she put down a winter rebellion in 1229 (Labarge, pp. 39,
40, and relevant notes).

[49]It was usual for horses to embark with the forces; "List," pp. 222-226.

[50]E. Decq, "L'Administration des...forêts," Bibl. de l'École des
Chartes, LXXXIII (1922).

[51]For example, in 1248 the king secured a 10-year lease to extensive
forests in the Orléanais in the Loire valley for 1000 l. p.; Layettes,

III, no. 3714; <u>GC</u>, VIII, c. 1506; J. Thillier and E. Jarry, <u>Cartulaire</u>
<u>de Sainte-Croix d'Orléans</u> (Paris, 1906), pp. 380-381.  Also, in August
1248 Pierre de la Brosse, the king's chamberlain (<u>Layettes</u>, IV, index
under Petrus Broc), contracted for firewood ("chaufagium") in the
Poitevin-Loire forest of Boscus-Ogerius from Sire Droco de Melluto
(<u>Layettes</u>, III, nos. 3709, 3710, 3711).  Although Pierre may have been
Droco's vassal (Quentin Griffiths, "The Counselors of Louix IX," unpub.
Ph.D. diss., University of California, Berkeley, 1964, p. 80), it is
possible that the reason for the contract was connected to the needs
of Aigues-Mortes.  Indeed, the contract was confirmed by the king while
in Aigues-Mortes in August 1248.  And later during the crusade, Louis
showed special favor to Droco when he abandoned his claims to two
castles in favor of Droco (<u>Layettes</u>, III, nos. 3834, 3951).  These
transactions (the contract for wood, the settlement of the dominion
of the castles) may simply be private affairs, but as we know something of the nature of the office of chamberlain and the locations in
which the transactions took place (Aigues-Mortes and in the East on
crusade), there may be something to the conjecture that part of the
firewood was intended for Aigues-Mortes.  On the nature of the
chamberlain's office, cf. the comments in Griffiths, "Counselors,"
pp. 8-14, 67-74.

[52]<u>Layettes</u>, III, no. 4202; "de arboribus eorum incisis circa
Sumidrium et Salve et in opera domini regis positis."

[53]<u>Layettes</u>, III, no. 4202.

[54]On the carpenters, see Michel, <u>Beaucaire</u>, p. 244 (cf. also his
general description of the king's treatment of Alès, ca. 1245-1248,
pp. 239-245).  For the sumptuary law prohibiting torchlight parades,
see Michel, <u>Beaucaire</u>, "pièces justificatives," no. 18, p. 408.

[55]Largest that is in terms of trained fighting men; cf. Strayer,
"Crusades," p. 167.

[56]Jordan, chapters 1-5.

[57]<u>Ibid</u>., chapters 7-10.

Chapter 12

[1] On trade see M. M. Postan and E. E. Rich, eds., Trade and Industry in the Middle Ages in Cambridge Economic History of Europe, II (Cambridge, 1952); E. Lipson, The Economic History of England, 12th ed., 3 vols. (London: Black, 1961), I, chs. 6, 10; M. M. Postan, Medieval Trade and Finance (Cambridge, 1973); Louis F. Salzman, English Trade in the Middle Ages (Oxford, 1931); Jules Finot, Étude historique sur les relations commerciales entre la Flandre et L'Espagne au Moyen Age (Paris, 1899), pp. 43, 59; Santos Madrazo Madrazo, Las dos Españas. Burguesía y nobleza (Madrid, 1969), pp. 73-86; María del Carmen Carlé, "Mercaderes en Castilla, 1252-1512," Cuadernos de Historia de España, XXI-XXII (1954), 237-242; Charles Verlinden, El comercio de paños flamencos y brabanzones en España durante los siglos XIII y XIV (Madrid, 1952); Verlinden, "The Rise of Spanish Trade in the Middle Ages," The Economic History Review, X (1940), 44-59; Verlinden, "Contribution a l'étude de l'expansion commerciale de la draperie flammande dans la péninsule ibérique au XIII siècle," Revue du Nord, XIII (1936), 5-20.

[2] The documents in the Calendar of the Patent Rolls (C.P.R.), Close Rolls (C.C.R.), and Fine Rolls (C.F.R.) often refer to Spain, Aragon, and Catalonia in the same sentence, with Spain being synonymous with Castile. See below.

[3] One of the limitations of the Calendars is that they consist only of royal documents.

[4] For a general background of Castilian history see Antonio Ballesteros y Beretta, Historia de España y su influencia en la historia universal, 12 vols. (Barcelona, 1918-58), III; Claudio Sánchez Albornoz, España: Un enigma histórico, 2 vols., 3d ed. (Buenos Aires, 1973); Jaime Vicens Vives, Manual de historia económica de España (Barcelona, 1959), ch. 3; also Vicens Vives, ed., Historia social y económica de España y America, 5 vols. in 6 (Barcelona: 1957-59), II, 8-162, 184-222. For English merchants settling in Castile in the late twelfth century see Luciano Serrano, El obispado de Burgos y Castilla primitiva desde el siglo V al XIII, 3 vols. (Madrid, 1935-36), II, 210-216. Also Yves Renouard, "Les voies de communication entre pays de la Méditerranée et pays de l'Atlantique au Moyen Age," Études d'histoire medievale, 2 vols. (Paris: S.E.V.P.E.N., 1968), II, 720. "Ce n'est qu'au XIIIe siècle et surtout après la reconquête de Carthagène (1245) et de Seville (1248) par les chrétiens qu'un courant régulier de navigation commerciale s'establit d'une mer dans l'autre." Robert S. Lopez, The Commercial Revolution of the Middle Ages, 950-1350 (Englewood Cliffs, N.J., 1971), pp. 144-145.

[5] For the role of the Bay of Biscay fleet in the conquest of Seville see Guillermo Ávila y Díaz-Ubierna, El primer almirante de Castilla. Don Ramón de Bonifaz y Camargo (Burgos, 1948).

[6] Ramón Menéndez Pidal, ed., Historia de España, 17 vols. to date

(Madrid, 1935 ff.), XIV (1966), pp. xv-201; Julio Valdeón Baruque, "Aspectos de la crisis castellana en la primera mitad del siglo XIV," Hispania, XXIX (1969), 5-24.

[7] For the Mesta see Julius Klein, The Mesta. A Study in Spanish Economic History, 1273-1836 (Cambridge, Mass., 1920).

[8] The treaty of Paris in 1259 settled the long standing disputes with France. Maurice Powicke, The Thirteenth Century, 1216-1307 (Oxford, England: Clarendon Press, 1953), pp. 119-128. On Lord Edward's protection of foreign merchants, Powicke, p. 619; for the period up to 1350, May McKisack, The Fourteenth Century, 1307-1399 (Oxford, England: Clarendon Press, 1959). Both Powicke and McKisack rarely mention Castilian merchants in England. For merchants in England after 1350 see Alice Beardwood, Alien Merchants in England, 1350 to 1377. Their legal and economic position (Cambridge, Mass., 1931).

[9] Powicke, pp. 644-719.

[10] Ballesteros y Beretta, III, p. 33. On the Infantes de la Cerda see A. Ballesteros y Beretta, Alfonso X. El Sabio (Barcelona, 1963).

[11] Letter from Edward I thanking Don Enrique, regent of Castile, for his offer of military aid in Gascony in Thomas Rymer, ed., Foedera, conventiones, literae... (London, 1705), II, pp. 687-88.

[12] C.P.R., 1292-1301 (London, 1895), p. 203 (9-16-1296), safe-conduct to merchants and sailors from Pontevedra, Noya, and Bayona in Galicia coming to England to trade. For the pilgrimage to Compostella see Luis Vázquez de Parga et al., Las peregrinaciones a Santiago de Compostela, 3 vols. (Madrid, 1948-49), I, 77-79.

[13] C.P.R., 1334-1338 (London, 1895), p. 554 (11-18-1337); p. 571 (1-3-1338); p. 546 (11-2-1337); C.C.R., 1349-54 (London, 1906), p. 537 (4-8-1353); C.P.R., 1350-1354 (London, 1907), p. 396 (1-30-1353).

[14] See T. F. Ruiz, "Burgos. Society and Royal Power, 1250-1350," unpubl. Ph.D. diss., Princeton, 1973, ch. II.

[15] Luis Suárez Fernández, "Evolución histórica de las hermandades castellanas," Cuadernos de Historia de España, XVI (1951), 22-23.

[16] See below for references to these towns. In English documents these names often appear under different form, e.g., Vermeu for Bermeo, Font Araby for Fuenterrabía, Plasencia for Plencia, etc.

[17] Miguel Gual Camarena, "El comercio de telas en el siglo XIII hispano," Anuario de Historia Económica y Social, Ano I (1968), 91-97; Verlinden, El comercio de paños....

[18] See Mercedes Gaibrois de Ballesteros, Historia del reinado de Sancho IV de Castilla, 3 vols. (Madrid, 1922-28), I, Apéndice documental, "Cuentas y gastos del Rey Don Sancho IV."; Cortes de los

antiguos reinos de León y Castilla, 5 vols. (Madrid:  Real Academia de la Historia, 1861-63), I, Jerez (1268), pp. 64-85.

[19]See below for the role of Castilian merchants as carriers of English goods.

[20]C.C.R., 1333-37 (London, 1898), p. 644 (1-23-1337); also same entry in C.F.R., 1337-47 (London, 1915), p. 5 (1-30-1337).

[21]C.C.R., 1337-39 (London, 1900), p. 85 (7-12-1337); C.P.R., 1334-38, p. 525 (9-25-1337).

[22]Other examples:  C.F.R., 1337-47, p. 5 (1-28-1337); C.P.R., 1292-1301, p. 234 (2-17-1297); C.P.R., 1338-40 (London, 1898), p. 5 (2-6-1338); C.P.R., 1327-30 (London, 1891), p. 250 (3-5-1328); C.P.R., 1338-40, p. 373 (1339); C.C.R., 1349-54, pp. 470-71 (3-9-1351); pp. 578-80 (1-14-1353).

[23]Cases of piracy or complaints against seamen from the Bay of Biscay. Some examples:  C.P.R., 1281-92 (London, 1893), p. 509 (10-18-1292); C.C.R., 1296-1302 (London, 1906), p. 98 (4-1-1297); C.P.R., 1301-07 (London, 1908), pp. 460-61 (7-28-1306), a truce between Bayonne, Castro Urdiales, Laredo and Santander; C.P.R., 1307-13 (London, 1892), p. 124 (8-8-1308), a merchant of Southampton robbed of his wines by Spaniards on the high seas while he traveled from Gascony to England. Ibid., p. 243 (10-1-1309), merchants of Southampton complained that their ship had been robbed by Spaniards off the coast of Brittany; C.C.R., 1307-13 (London, 1892), p. 383 (11-12-1311); pp. 488-89 (11-4-1312); C.C.R., 1313-18 (London, 1893), pp. 38-39 (1-22-1314); p. 580 (12-7-1317); C.C.R., 1330-33 (London, 1898), p. 138 (3-28-1330); p. 401 (8-26-1331); C.C.R., 1333-37 (London, 1898), p. 106 (4-24-1333), protests to Alfonso XI of piratical acts by ships from Santander off the Isle of Wight; C.C.R., 1339-41 (London, 1901), p. 512 (8-20-1340); C.C.R., 1341-43 (London, 1902), pp. 265-66 (7-26-1341); C.C.R., 1343-46 (London, 1904), p. 219 (6-4-1343); p. 231 (9-2-1343); p. 549 (2-4-1345); C.C.R., 1346-49 (London, 1905), p. 79 (6-25-1346).

[24]Salzman, pp. 103, 161; C.C.R., 1307-13, p. 112 (5-20-1309); p. 342 (2-18-1311); C.C.R., 1313-18, p. 425 (7-16-1316); C.C.R., 1330-33, p. 556 (4-13-1332); C.C.R., 1337-39, p. 379 (1-25-1338); C.P.R., 1338-40, p. 464 (4-12-1340); C.P.R., 1340-43 (London, 1900), p. 172 (4-15-1341).

[25]C.C.R., 1313-18, pp. 231-232 (5-28-1315); other examples:  C.P.R., 1292-1301, p. 234 (2-17-1297); C.P.R., 1321-24 (London, 1900), p. 175 (7-13-1322); C.P.R., 1324-27 (London, 1904), p. 16 (8-23-1324); C.C.R., 1337-39, p. 282 (1-8-1338); C.C.R., 1339-41, p. 625 (9-1-1340).

[26]C.P.R., 1334-38, p. 537 (10-8-1337).

[27]C.C.R., 1337-39, pp. 125, 143 (3-18-1337); p. 282 (1-8-1338).

[28]C.C.R., 1343-46, pp. 552-553 (3-10-1345); p. 589 (6-22-1345).

[29]Peter de Mundenar received a safe-conduct for five years in 1276 (see below). Gauselin Angevini and other Spanish merchants were granted license until Easter to take their goods to Brabant, Holland, and Zeeland. C.P.R., 1338-40, p. 5 (2-6-1338). A year was the most common period of time granted in the royal safe-conducts.

[30]See below and Salzman, pp. 14, 153.

[31]Some examples:  C.P.R., 1301-07, p. 547 (5-5-1307), John de Ispannia and other Spanish merchants were robbed of most of their goods when their ship was wrecked in the coast of Cornwall.  C.P.R., 1307-13 (London, 1894), p. 422 (9-28-1311); C.C.R., 1307-13, p. 527 (4-24-1313); C.P.R., 1313-17 (London, 1898), p. 144 (4-8-1314); C.P.R., 1317-21 (London, 1901), p. 481 (3-6-1320); pp. 605-06 (4-30-1321); C.P.R., 1334-38, p. 140 (3-25-1335); p. 367 (11-8-1336); p. 367 (11-8-1336).

[32]In 1313 Andrés Pérez de Castrogeriz was listed among the most pre-dominent citizens of Burgos.  He had lent 1,000 maravedises to the concejo of Burgos for the building of the city walls.  Archivo Municipal de Burgos (AMB) clasif. 652 (12-19-1313).

[33]C.P.R., 1292-1301, p. 450 (11-2-1299).

[34]C.P.R., 1301-07, p. 7 (12-30-1301); p. 165 (11-9-1303).

[35]Pedro Pérez was alcalde of Burgos (the most important judicial position in Castilian cities in the late thirteenth century) in 1293, 1294, and 1313.  He was also collector of custom duties in Laredo, Santander, San Vicente de la Barquera, and Castro Urdiales.  He was a member of the Sarracín family, the most important family of Burgos in the thirteenth century, and nephew of the dean of Burgos' cathedral chapter.  M. Gaibrois de Ballesteros, I, pp. vi, xcv and cxi; AMB clasif. 652 (12-19-1313); Archivo Catedral de Burgos (ACB), vol. 49, f. 68 (3-1-1291).

[36]C.P.R., 1307-13, p. 139 (10-1-1308); p. 451 (4-4-1312); C.P.R., 1313-17, p. 116 (5-17-1314).

[37]Ibid., p. 299 (6-11-1315); C.P.R., 1317-21, p. 2 (7-11-1317); p. 559 (1-30-1321); C.P.R., 1321-24, p. 266 (3-21-1323).

[38]Ibid., p. 2 (7-8-1324).

[39]On the matter of the negotiations for the wedding see C.C.R., 1323-27 (London, 1898), pp. 254-255, 334, 344-346, 351 (1325). Another entry in 1325 shows that Andrew Petri de Castro Xeriz put in his place James de Ispannia to prosecute a recognisance for 16 l. made to him in chancery by Robert de Killesey.  C.P.R., 1324-27, p. 84 (1-26-1325).

[40]C.P.R., 1324-27, p. 93 (2-16-1325).

[41]C.C.R., 1330-33, p. 423 (12-29-1331).  "To Alfonso, king of Castile, whereas the late king caused 1,000 marks sterling to be paid to Andrew

de Peritz de Castro Suriz burgess of Burgos (Burgh), and Gunsalvus
Goderitz to buy destrier-horses in Spain...."

[42] Ibid., p. 423. Communication to Alfonso XI, the heirs and executors of Andrés Pérez's will and the concejo of Burgos. Also C.P.R.,
1330-34 (London, 1893), p. 230 (12-29-1331). Arnald Garcia returned
with the horses. C.P.R., 1330-34, p. 364 (10-26-1332).

[43] C.P.R., 1324-27, p. 181 (10-12-1325).

[44] C.C.R., 1330-33 (London, 1898), p. 391 (10-15-1331).

[45] C.C.R., 1333-37, p. 308 (4-6-1334).

[46] C.F.R., 1337-47, p. 5 (1-28-1337).

[47] C.P.R., 1338-40, p. 23 (2-27-1338).

[48] Ibid., p. 10 (2-20-1338).

[49] C.C.R., 1337-39 (London, 1900), p. 539 (10-10-1338). Another
entry on Ferrand Mangeon C.C.R., 1343-46, p. 127 (7-14-1343).

[50] C.P.R., 1343-45 (London, 1902), p. 545 (8-28-1345).

[51] C.P.R., 1345-48 (London, 1903), p. 55 (2-15-1346).

[52] Ibid., pp. 201, 213.

[53] C.P.R., 1272-81 (London, 1901), p. 184 (12-8-1276). Extended for
five more years in 1285, C.P.R., 1281-92, p. 149 (1-1-1285).

[54] Salzman, pp. 412-413. "Gonzalo Martinez was sent to Portsmouth
to buy fruits from a Spanish ship for Queen Eleanor (Dec. 1289), he
bought a frail of figs of Seville, a frail of raisins, a bale of dates,
230 pomegranates, but only 15 lemons (pom-cedrin) and 7 oranges."

[55] Although the English documents do not show their family ties,
there is enough evidence in the municipal and cathedral archives of
Burgos to verify their relationship. Gaibrois de Ballesteros, I,
p. cxxvii; AMB clasif. 652 (12-19-1313); ACB vol. 50, p. 1, f. 43 (6-
29-1248); ACB vol. 49, f. 2 (1-14-1309); ACB vol. 32, f. 289 (6-5-
1302); ACB vol. 42, f. 223 (12-15-1324); ACB vol. 40, f. 251 (11-6-
1320).

[56] Finot, p. 47.

[57] C.C.R., 1307-13, p. 230 (8-17-1309). On the brotherhood of Our
Lady of Gamonal Julián García Sainz de Baranda, "Primitiva regla
escrita de la cofradía de Nuestra Señora de Gamonal," Boletín de la
Comision de Monumentos Artísticos e Históricos de Burgos, 65 (1939),
158-164.

[58] C.P.R., 1307-13, p. 486 (8-17-1312); C.P.R., 1317-21, p. 440 (4-20-1320).

[59] C.P.R., 1313-17, pp. 300, 368 (6-12 and 11-4-1315).

[60] C.C.R., 1333-37, p. 644 (1-23-1337); C.F.R., 1337-47, p. 5 (1-30-1337).

[61] C.P.R., 1334-38, p. 546 (11-2-1337).

[62] Ibid., p. 572 (1-3-1338).

[63] C.C.R., 1337-39, p. 342 (3-12-1338); p. 346 (4-7-1338); C.P.R., 1345-48 (London, 1903), p. 206 (11-8-1346).

[64] Y. Renouard, "Un sujet de recherches: l'exportation de chevaux de la péninsule ibérique en France et en Angleterre au Moyen Age," Études..., II, pp. 1113-20.

[65] Ban on exports of horses, Cortes..., I, Valladolid (1258), #12, p. 57; Jerez (1268), #14, p. 71; Haro (1288), #24, p. 105; Valladolid (1307), #25, p. 194; Valladolid (1312), #74, 75, p. 215; Palencia (1313), #17, p. 225; Burgos (1315), #17, pp. 277-278; Valladolid (1322), #43, 44, pp. 348-349; Madrid (1339), #14, pp. 465-466; León (1349), #27, pp. 635-636.

[66] The horses used by the urban knights, i.e., horses fit for warfare, set at a minimum price of 30 mrs. in 1256 (the best horse at 200 mrs.) went up to a minimum of 800 mrs. in 1338. AMB clasif. 115 (7-25-1256); Cortes..., I, Burgos (1338), #18, p. 451.

[67] Grant to Burgalese merchants to take one rocín (work horse) out of Castile. AMB clasif. 96 (11-28-1339). "...por les ffaser merced touiemos lo por bien. E mandamos alos mercaderes dela dicha Ciubdat que ffueren ffuera del nuestro Senorio como dicho es que puedan levar ssendo rrocines...."

[68] C.P.R., 1281-92, p. 11 (2-11-1282).

[69] C.P.R., 1307-13, p. 204 (1-11-1309); p. 437 (3-4-1312); p. 557 (3-15-1313); C.P.R., 1313-17, p. 162 (4-1-1314).

[70] Postan, p. 172.

[71] Salzman, pp. 409-410. Also C.C.R., 1288-96, p. 365 (8-21-1294), goods arrested from three Spanish merchants, including 1,500 quintals of iron. C.P.R., 1307-13, pp. 246-247 (11-16-1309), Martin Moygnez, merchant of Castro Urdiales, "being on a voyage to England in a ship laden with iron and other goods," wrecked on the coast off the Isle of Wight. C.P.R., 1340-43, p. 364 (11-26-1341), three great ships freighted with iron of Spain and other goods attacked by citizens of Southampton. C.C.R., 1346-49 (London, 1905), p. 213 (5-7-1347).

[72]A simple look at the Bay of Biscay custom accounts for 1293-94 will bear this out. See Gaibrois de Ballesteros, I, "Apéndice documental."

[73]Salzman, pp. 14, 254, 264, 372, 381-383, 401, 409-418. Also C.C.R., 1288-1296, p. 365 (8-21-1294); C.C.R., 1333-37, p. 118 (6-6-1333); C.C.R., 1337-39, p. 85 (7-12-1337); C.P.R., 1334-38, p. 367 (11-8-1336); C.P.R., 1350-54, p. 442 (5-10-1353); C.P.R., 1334-38, p. 443 (3-17-1337).

[74]C.C.R., 1313-18, p. 452 (1-31-1317); p. 580 (12-7-1317). "To the rulers or keepers of the realm of Spain. Request that they will permit the servants of Anthony Pessaigno of Genoa, knight, to buy and provide up to 1,000 rased bushels (rasura) of wheat in that realm...." Also Renée Doehaerd, Les relations commerciales entre Gênes, La Belgique et L'Outremont (Bruxelles, 1941), pp. 225-226.

[75]See J. Valdeón Baruque, op. cit. Also C.P.R., 1330-34, pp. 419, 487 (1333); p. 542 (1334); C.P.R., 1345-48, p. 58 (3-18-1346).

[76]C.P.R., 1334-38, p. 546 (11-2-1337); C.C.R., 1349-54, p. 537 (4-18-1353).

[77]See above. Also C.C.R., 1288-96, pp. 324-325 (7-15-1293); C.P.R., 1292-1301, p. 376 (3-7-1298); C.P.R., 1292-1301, p. 590 (4-25-1301); C.P.R., 1321-24, p. 371 (7-15-1323); Registres du Trésor des chartes, 2 vols. to date (Paris, 1966), II, part 1, #505 (6-?-1317), #1266 (3-8-1317), #1977 (12-?-1318), #2186 (1-?-1319).

[78]This represents only figures from the Calendar of the Patent, Close, and Fine Rolls. The numbers of ships and merchants going from Castile to England were probably higher in 1337 and early 1338.

[79]C.P.R., 1334-38, p. 554 (11-18-1337). The same day Arnald Tolosan and his fellow merchants of the city of Seville received the same protection as did Diagus Lopes de Arbo Lanchia.

[80]C.P.R., 1334-38, p. 554 (11-18-1337); p. 554 (11-30-1337); ibid.

[81]Ibid., p. 529 (9-28-1337). Protection and safe-conduct granted to Michael Leure. He brought a cargo of merchandise to Southampton in his ship la Seinte Katerine of San Sebastian. Ibid., p. 539 (10-8-1337); ibid., p. 537 (10-8-1337), protection and safe-conduct to Peter Viellardel, William Peres, and Hugh de Mayork, masters of la Seinte Marie. Their ship had been hired by Dinus Forcetti and other merchants of the Bardi society to carry English wool to Lombardy.

[82]C.P.R., 1334-38, p. 543 (11-2-1337).

[83]C.P.R., 1338-40, p. 3 (1-26-1338); p. 4 (2-9-1338); p. 19 (2-20-1338); p. 23 (2-27-1338). These grants covered merchants from Chieri, Piacenza and Asti.

[84] Ibid., p. 1 (1-26-1338).

[85] C.P.R., 1350-54 (London, 1907), p. 396 (1-30-1353).

[86] Ibid., p. 472 (6-20-1353); p. 442 (5-10-1353).

[87] See Doehaerd, pp. 223-224; Alfred Doren, Die florentier Wollentuchindustrie vom 14. bis zum 16. Jahrhundert (1901; rpt. Aalen, 1969),
p. 107; A. Deroisy, "Les routes terrestres des laines anglaises vers
la Lombardy," Revue du Nord, 25 (1939), 40-60.

[88] A. Ballesteros y Beretta, Sevilla en el siglo XIII (Madrid, 1913),
pp. 43-49; Carlé, pp. 230-248.

Chapter 13

[1]Representation is dealt with in every historical work on commercial law; here it will be enough to quote two good, recent works that can introduce one to the subject: for the West, F. Calasso, Introduzione al diritto comune (Milano, 1951), p. 149 ff.; for the Muslim world, A. Udovitch, Partnership and Profit in Medieval Islam (Princeton, 1970), p. 68 ff. and 134 ff.

[2]See, for instance, R. de Roover in Cambridge Economic History, III.

[3]The full text of the document was published in R. S. Lopez, La prima crisi della banca di Genova (Milan, 1956), pp. 162-163; see also p. 56 and the footnote for another document of the same kind, concerning Benedetto Zaccaria. A later document (of 1327) with a similar clause has given occasion to a brief debate between M. Chiaudano, who published it--"La costituzione di una società commerciale a Pinerolo," Bollettino Storico Bibliografico Subalpino, XLII (1940), 149 ff.--and A. Sapori, Studi di storia economica (third ed., Florence, 1955), II, 765 ff.; while essentially agreeing with Sapori, I see the validity of some of Chiaudano's remarks.

[4]Brief descriptions of this and other contracts can be found in R. S. Lopez, The Commercial Revolution of the Middle Ages (Englewood Cliffs, 1971), pp. 73 ff. and 103 ff.; see also the texts in Lopez and Raymond, Medieval Trade in the Mediterranean World (New York, 1955) and the discussion in R. de Roover, above n. 2.

[5]Most of the documents are published and briefly discussed in R. S. Lopez, "Familiari, procuratori e dipendenti di Benedetto Zaccaria," Miscellanea di Storia Ligure in onore di Giorgio Falco (Milan, 1962), pp. 211 ff., and have been reprinted in a collection of studies by the same author, Su e giù per la storia di Genova, (Genoa, 1975). Here the problem is re-examined in a wider context.

[6]There is an undoubted resemblance between this arrangement and the fraterna of Venetian sea trade, on which see F. C. Lane, "Family Partnerships and Joint Ventures in the Venetian Republic," Journal of Economic History, IV (1944). The fraterna, however, stems more clearly from the joint administration of undivided heritages; the agreement between Benedetto and Manuele was clinched while their father was still alive, and long after the brothers had separately engaged in business.

[1] Leon Ménard, Histoire civile, ecclésiastique, et littéraire de la ville de Nismes, II (Paris, 1752), preuves, pp. 45, 63 ff.

[2] Archives communales de Nîmes, HH.2, fols. 1-264; hereafter cited as HH.2.

[3] Ménard, II, preuves, p. 45.

[4] Ibid., preuves, pp. 63 ff.

[5] Ibid., preuves, pp. 88-91.

[6] Jean Combes, "Les foires en Languedoc au moyen âge," Annales: Economies, sociétés, civilisations, 13 (1958), 231-259; p. 239.

[7] HH.2, fols. $23^r$-$24^r$.

[8] II, note VII.

[9] Saint-Thibéry is mentioned only once, HH.2, fol. $93^v$; Toulouse: fols. $68^v$, $85^r$, $87^r$, $93^v$, $117^r$, $129^r$, $132^v$, $149^v$, $152^v$, $159^v$, $181^r$, $186^r$, $199^v$, $210^v$, $215^r$, $218^r$, $229^r$, $232^r$, $235^r$, $250^r$; Fanjeaux: $87^r$, $96^v$, $117^r$, $132^v$, $149^v$, $215^r$, $218^r$, $229^r$, $232^r$, $235^r$; Limoux: $186^r$, $199^v$, $229^r$, $232^r$, $235^r$; Montolieu: $117^r$, $173^r$, $176^r$, $188^r$, $199^v$, $218^r$; Carcassonne: $68^v$, $85^r$, $87^r$, $93^v$, $96^v$, $117^r$, $129^r$, $132^v$, $149^v$, $159^r$, $173^r$, $176^r$, $181^r$, $186^r$, $199^v$, $210^v$, $215^r$, $218^r$, $229^r$, $232^r$, $235^r$, $259^r$; Narbonne: $87^r$, $96^v$, $132^v$, $173^r$, $176^r$, $181^r$, $186^r$, $199^v$, $215^r$, $229^r$, $232^r$, $235^r$; Béziers: $68^v$, $88^v$, $96^v$, $117^r$, $129^r$, $149^v$, $173^r$, $176^r$, $181^r$, $186^r$, $211^r$, $218^r$, $235^r$, $259^r$; Lodève: $176^r$, $181^r$; Montagnac: $93^v$, $96^v$, $117^r$, $128^r$, $129^r$, $132^r$, $149^v$, $173^r$, $181^r$, $199^v$, $211^r$, $215^r$, $218^r$, $259^r$.

[10] Avignon: HH.2, fols. $73^r$, $83^v$, $93^v$, $96^v$, $107^v$, $121^v$, $133^r$, $144^v$, $156^r$, $164^v$, $167^v$, $176^v$, $194^v$, $205^v$, $216^v$, $259^r$; Marseille: $73^r$, $83^v$, $93^v$, $96^v$, $101^v$, $107^r$, $121^v$, $133^r$, $144^v$, $156^r$, $167^v$, $176^v$, $194^v$, $205^v$, $212^v$, $216^v$, $259^r$; Arles: $73^r$, $83^v$, $93^v$, $101^v$, $107^v$, $121^v$, $133^r$, $144^v$, $156^r$, $167^v$, $176^v$, $190^r$, $194^v$, $205^v$, $259^r$; Tarascon: $83^v$, $96^v$, $101^v$, $121^v$, $133^r$, $144^v$, $156^r$, $164^v$, $167^v$, $176^v$, $194^v$, $205^v$, $216^v$, $259^r$; Salon-de-Provence: $83^v$, $101^v$, $107^v$, $121^v$, $133^r$, $144^v$, $176^v$, $194^v$, $205^v$, $259^r$; Carpentras: $83^v$, $93^v$, $259^r$.

[11] The names of several merchants from Provence who were not Italians were given by one of the witnesses, fol. $107^{r-v}$.

[12] Avignon: HH.2, fols. $157^v$, $163^r$, $203^v$, $259^v$; Arles: $203^v$, $259^v$.

[13] Most of the witnesses mentioned Italians residing in Nîmes among those attending the fairs.

[14] Genoese merchants are mentioned in fols. $66^r$, $73^v$, $108^r$, $164^v$,

199$^v$, 210$^v$, 227$^v$, 231$^r$, 235$^v$, 240$^v$, 243$^r$, 248$^r$, 251$^v$; cf. Jean Morize, "Aigues Mortes au XIII$^e$ siècle," Annales du Midi, XXVI (1914), 313-348, on the predominant position of the Genoese in Aigues Mortes, esp. p. 345.

[15]Pisa: HH.2, fols. 66$^r$, 164$^v$, 248$^r$, 251$^v$; Lucca: 240$^v$, 243$^r$, 248$^r$, 251$^v$; Milan: 107$^v$; Pistoia: 164$^v$, 251$^v$; Savona: 66$^r$, 108$^r$, 145$^v$; Asti and Piacenza: 248$^r$.

[16]Lunel: HH.2, fols. 149$^v$, 224$^v$, 228$^r$; Sommières: 93$^v$, 109$^v$, 149$^v$, 216$^v$, 224$^v$; Aimargues: 149$^v$; Beaucaire: 190$^r$; Sauve: 93$^v$, 109$^v$, 187$^r$, 228$^v$, 231$^r$, 237$^r$; Anduze: 93$^v$, 109$^v$, 115$^v$, 117$^v$, 149$^v$, 164$^v$, 179$^v$, 187$^r$, 190$^r$, 207$^r$, 216$^v$, 228$^v$, 231$^r$, 237$^r$; Alès: 93$^v$, 109$^v$, 115$^v$, 117$^v$, 144$^v$, 149$^v$, 164$^v$, 179$^v$, 187$^r$, 190$^r$, 207$^r$, 216$^v$, 224$^v$, 231$^r$, 237$^r$; Vézénobres: 164$^v$; Uzès: 93$^v$, 109$^v$, 115$^v$, 117$^v$, 144$^v$, 149$^v$, 164$^v$, 179$^v$, 187$^r$, 190$^r$, 207$^r$, 216$^v$, 224$^v$, 228$^r$, 231$^r$, 237$^r$; Bagnols-sur-Cèze and Pont-Saint-Esprit: 149$^v$.

[17]HH.2, fols. 93$^v$, 109$^v$, 164$^v$, 179$^v$, 187$^r$, 207$^r$, 216$^v$, 224$^v$, 227$^v$, 231$^r$, 237$^r$.

[18]Robert-Henri Bautier, "Recherches sur les routes de l'Europe médiévale. I: De Paris et des foires de Champagne à la Méditerranée par le Massif Central," Bulletin philologique et historique (jusqu'au 1610) du Comité des travaux historiques et scientifiques, 1960, vol. 2, pp. 99-143; on the Via Rigordiana see pp. 111-126.

[19]Ibid., passim, and also part 2 of this study: "Le grand axe routier est-ouest du Midi de la France, d'Avignon à Toulouse," ibid., 1961, pp. 277-308. Cf. Odette Taviani, "Le commerce dans la région aixoise au milieu du XIVe siècle à travers un fragment de compte du péage d'Aix-en-Provence," Annales du Midi, LXXIV (1962), 255-285, esp. p. 257, where it is shown that the most frequented itinerary to southern France from the Aix region passed through Arles, Nîmes, and Montpellier.

[20]Ménard, II, preuves, p. 47 (letter of the "suprapositi parayrarie" of Fanjeaux to the consuls of Nîmes, dated November 13, 1322).

[21]HH.2, fol. 96$^v$. In the arrangements with the cloth dealers of Fanjeaux cited above, n. 20, it was stipulated that these dealers would treat the matter further with the consuls of Nîmes in unison with the cloth dealers of Carcassonne, Limoux, and Montolieu; the same act reveals that agents of the consuls of Nîmes had held preliminary discussions concerning this matter with representatives of the cloth dealers of Fanjeaux at the fair of Saint-Thibéry, thus suggesting that at the time of the establishment of the fairs of Nîmes the consuls were making a strong effort to attract cloth dealers from western Languedoc to these fairs. At the fairs of Champagne it was also common for groups of merchants from the same locale to lodge and trade at a designated location; see Elizabeth Chapin, Les villes de foires de Champagne des origines au début du XIVe siècle (Paris, 1937), pp. 107-118.

[22]Horses: HH.2, fols. 75$^v$, 93$^r$, 132$^v$, 135$^r$, 143$^v$, 144$^v$, 150$^r$, 155$^v$, 162$^r$, 190$^r$, 200$^r$, 206$^v$, 225$^r$, 259$^v$; other livestock: 69$^r$, 75$^v$, 132$^v$, 135$^r$, 143$^v$, 144$^v$, 150$^r$, 154$^r$, 162$^r$, 186$^v$, 190$^r$, 200$^r$, 203$^r$, 215$^r$, 218$^r$, 225$^r$, 259$^r$.

[23]HH.2, fol. 190$^r$, livestock was brought in from Uzès, Alès, Anduze, and Arles and other areas across the Rhône.

[24]Meats: HH.2, fol. 169$^v$; furs: 83$^v$, 107$^v$, 132$^v$, 135$^r$, 143$^r$, 150$^r$, 169$^v$, 200$^r$, 215$^r$, 225$^r$.

[25]Testimony of Johannes de Nemauso, HH.2, fol. 107$^v$.

[26]Iron tools: HH.2, fols. 150$^r$, 206$^v$; feathers: 84$^r$, 206$^v$; mer-seria: 132$^v$, 143$^v$, 206$^v$, 225$^r$; gold cloth: 132$^v$, 215$^r$.

[27]Pepper: HH.2, fols. 84$^r$, 164$^r$, 251$^v$, 254$^r$; ginger: 84$^r$, 164$^r$, 183$^r$, 248$^r$, 251$^v$, 254$^r$; spices in general: 75$^v$, 93$^v$, 132$^v$, 143$^v$, 155$^v$, 169$^v$, 206$^v$, 215$^r$; alum: 143$^v$, 183$^r$, 248$^r$; leather: 240$^v$, 248$^r$, 251$^v$; wax: 164$^r$, 240$^v$, 248$^r$, 251$^v$.

[28]Linens: HH.2, fols. 164$^r$, 169$^v$; sugar: 248$^r$, 251$^v$; olive oil: 240$^v$.

[29]Almost every witness mentioned purchase of cloths by Italians; direct trading for cloths: HH.2, fols. 73$^v$, 164$^r$, 200$^r$.

[30]To Italy: HH.2, fols. 97$^r$ (to Genoa), 108$^r$, 165$^v$, and 211$^r$ (to Lombardy), 243$^v$; to other parts: 108$^r$.

[31]Francesco Balducci Pegolotti, La pratica della Mercatura, ed. Allan Evans (Cambridge, Mass., 1936), gives information on the measures of cloth from Languedoc sold in Constantinople (p. 37), Famagusta in Cyprus (p. 79), Sicily (p. 109), and Naples (p. 180). Cf. the Statuto dell'Arte di Calimala (Codex of 1332), Book 2, chapter 15, which sets rules for the sale in Florence of cloths from Toulouse, Perpignan, and Carcassonne, ed. Paolo Emiliani-Giudici, Storia politica dei municipj italiani (Florence, 1851), Appendix, p. 128.

[32]Ed. cit., passim and section on Nîmes and Montpellier, pp. 224-229.

[33]HH.2, fols. 81$^v$, 84$^r$, 113$^r$, 118$^r$, 121$^v$, 142$^v$, 163$^r$, 259$^v$, 263$^r$.

[34]See above, n. 15.

[35]Most witnesses mentioned purchase of cloth by merchants from these regions. Merchants from Provence were mentioned as buying ginger (HH.2, fols. 84$^r$, 183$^r$), pepper (84$^r$), and alum (183$^r$). Cf. "Le Livre-journal de maître Ugo Teralh, notaire et drapier à Forcalquier (1330-1332)," ed. Paul Meyer, Notices et extraits des manuscrits de la Bibliothèque nationale et autres bibliothèques, XXXVI (1899), 129-170, which shows that most of the cloths sold by this Provençal draper were

from western Languedoc.

[36]For the sources on which this map is based see nn. 9, 10, 14-17 above; also HH.2, fols. 107$^r$ (Nice and Grasse), 121$^v$ (Aix-en-Provence), 149$^v$ (Saint-Quentin).

[37]HH.2, fol. 134$^v$.

[38]HH.2, fol. 183$^v$.

[39]Armando Sapori, Una compagnia di Calimala ai primi del Trecento (Florence, 1932), pp. 57-58.

[40]HH.2, fol. 159$^r$; a Neri Bertacci is mentioned as a host in Nîmes for agents of the Peruzzi in 1336 in Sapori, ed., I libri di commercio dei Peruzzi (Milan, 1934), p. 72; on the term "host" see Florence Edler, A Glossary of Medieval Terms of Business. Italian Series (1200-1600) (Cambridge, Mass., 1934), entry under "oste," p. 198.

[41]HH.2, fol. 221$^v$.

[42]Sapori, Una compagnia, pp. 57-58; a contract of May 20, 1320 quoted ibid., p. 59, shows 22 1. 10s. a fior. = 12 1. t. The cloth prices listed by Carmelo Trasselli in "Prezzi dei panni a Palermo nel XIV secolo," Economia e storia, III (1956), 88-90, show cloths of Narbonne, Carcassonne, and Toulouse costing roughly one-third to one-half as much per canna as cloth from Châlons and Bruges during this period. A large number of retail prices of cloths from Languedoc sold at Forcalquier in this period are available in "Le Livre-journal de maître Ugo Teralh," ed. cit.; their prices vary sharply, from as low as 8 s.t. to as high as 26 s.ob.t. per canna, but a price of about 20 s.t. per canna was most common; cloths from the chief cloth producing towns of western Languedoc had twelve canne per piece, according to Pegolotti, ed. cit., p. 108.

[43]HH.2, fol. 112$^r$.

[44]HH.2, fol. 186$^r$.

[45]HH.2, fol. 211$^r$.

[46]Sapori, Una compagnia, p. 72; cf. Edler, p. 102, and the Statuto dell'Arte di Calimala, ed. cit., p. 129.

[47]HH.2, fols. 166$^r$, 170$^r$, 219$^r$, 222$^r$. The royal conventions of 1278, which established the Italian merchant community of Nîmes, imposed among other sales taxes a charge of 1d. per piece of cloth bought or sold by the Italians at Nîmes; Ordonnances des roys de France de la troisième race, IV (Paris, 1734), 670.

[48]HH.2, fol. 145$^v$.

[49]HH.2, fol. 146$^v$.

[50]Further evidence that Italian companies were involved was provided by Nicholosus Falqui, a Florentine residing in Nîmes; he testified that "mercatores ytalici qui apud Nemausum morantur non tantum pro eis set etiam pro aliis mercatoribus ytalicis morantibus Avinione et per alias partes prope Nemausum cum dicte nundine Nemausi erant emebant plures pannos et plures alias merces quas eorum sociis mitebant...." (HH.2, fol. 163$^{r-v}$); cf. above, n. 43.

[51]On this duty see John Bell Henneman, Jr., "Taxation of Italians by the French Crown (1311-1363)," Mediaeval Studies, XXXI (1969), 15-43, esp. p. 18; and Jules Viard, ed., Les Journaux du trésor de Charles IV le Bel (Paris, 1917), p. xxi.

[52]HH.2, fol. 242$^v$. On December 24, 1325 the royal treasury accounted for 1200 l. p. (= 1500 l. t.) turned in by this same Bartholomeus in his capacity as collector of this tax in the seneschalsy of Beaucaire; Viard, no. 9350. This indicates that the sum of 800 l. t. cited by him could not refer to all the revenues collected by him from this tax, and that he was probably referring to his collections at the fair of Nîmes alone. Bartholomeus' brother, Marquesius Scatisse, was appointed treasurer of the seneschalsy on September 20, 1327, and for the next two years Bartholomeus acted as his lieutenant in Nîmes; Ménard, II, preuves, p. 63.

[53]Henneman, p. 18.

[54]HH.2, fols. 202$^v$, 206$^v$, 259$^r$, 262$^r$; others said they saw these fairs for seven or eight years: 214$^v$, 221$^v$, 227$^r$, 230$^v$, 238$^v$.

[55]HH.2, fol. 242$^v$.

[56]HH.2, fol. 256$^v$.

[57]HH.2, fol. 262$^{r-v}$,

[58]HH.2, fol. 156$^v$.

[59]HH.2, fol. 150$^r$, "...quod bene valuerat solum pro nundinis anni quando tenebantur quatuor milia librarum turonensium et plus, et anno isto non valuit nisi duo milia de toto anno vel circa quia nundine non fuerunt."

[60]H. Moranvillé, "Notes de statistique douanière sous Philippe VI de Valois," Bibliothèque de l'Ecole des chartes, LXIV (1903), 567-576, p. 572; for the increase in rate see Henneman, p. 24, who, however, failed to take note of Viard, no. 10312, where the higher rate is seen to have been in force by January 22, 1328.

[61]C. Piton, Les Lombards en France et à Paris (Paris, 1892), I, p. vii.

[62]Félix Bourquelot, Etudes sur les foires de Champagne, in Mémoires présentés par divers savants à l'Académie des inscriptions et belles lettres, 2d series, vol. 5 (n. d.), part 2, p. 199.

[63]Ordonnances, IV, 668. As late as November 8, 1329, Philip VI
ordered the seneschal of Beaucaire to compel the merchants subject
to the conventions to trade at Nîmes and to bring straight to Nîmes
all the wares they imported through Aigues Mortes; A. Germain, Histoire
du commerce de Montpellier (Montpellier, 1861), I, 479.

[64]In part I of the study cited above, p. 139; cf. Morize, pp. 334
ff. on the dependence of Aigues Mortes on merchants established at
Nîmes.

[65]Renée Doehaerd, Les relations commerciales entre Gênes, la Belgique,
et l'Outremont d'après les Archives notariales génoises aux XIIIe et
XIVe siècles (Brussels and Rome, 1941), I, 223-227; Léone Liagre-de
Sturler, Les relations commerciales entre Gênes, la Belgique, et
l'Outremont d'après les Archives notariales génoises (1320-1400)
(Brussels and Rome, 1969), I, p. clxx; Alfred Doren, Die florentiner
Wollentuchindustrie vom 14. bis zum 16. Jahrhundert (1901; rpt. Aalen,
1969), p. 107.

[66]See above, n. 18; cf. Sapori, Una compagnia, pp. 80-99, for itineraries of six shipments of cloth by the del Bene company, one of
which included Nîmes. An act dating from the early part of 1327 gives
a good idea of how the commercial fate of Nîmes was linked to that of
the fairs of Champagne. It consists of recommendations made to the
king of France and to his council by the guardians of the fairs of
Champagne and by merchants active at these fairs; the object of the
measures recommended was to revive the decadent fairs of Champagne.
The document also states reasons why the fairs had declined; among
them was that whereas in the past, when the fairs were thriving,
Italian merchants and others would come through the port of Aigues
Mortes and through Nîmes to the fairs of Champagne, now they took
their wares to Flanders and to England by sea, without passing
through the kingdom; Henri Laurent, ed., "Choix de documents pour
servir à l'histoire de l'expansion commerciale des Pays-Bas en
France au Moyen Age (XIIe-XVe siècles)," Bulletin de la Commission
royale d'histoire, XCVIII (1934), 335-415; no. 24, p. 380.

[67]Pegolotti, ed. cit., p. 257.

[68]Combes, pp. 244-246, lists the towns from which merchants attended
the fairs of Montagnac and of nearby Pézénas in the 1340's; the list
is largely similar to that given in this paper for the fairs of Nîmes,
and the chief object of trade was likewise cloth.

[69]The papal court in nearby Avignon seems to have purchased very
little from Nîmes; see K. H. Schäfer, Die Ausgaben der apostolischen
Kammer unter Johann XXII (Paderborn, 1911), where the only item shown
to have been bought in large quantities from Nîmes was wine (pp. 143,
146, 151, 154, 156, 158, 160, 161, 163); a large purchase of wax is
indicated on March 1, 1323, during the time of the first fair of Nîmes,
where, as has been seen, wax was one of the imported items offered
for sale (p. 478).

[1] T. F. Tout, The Place of the Reign of Edward II in English History (end ed.; Manchester, 1936), pp. 212-240; R. L. Baker, "The establishment of the English wool staple in 1313," Speculum, XXXI (1956), 444-453.

[2] C.P.R., 1307-13, p. 591. Cf. ibid., 1313-17, p. 15.

[3] P.R.O., Chancery, Patent Rolls, No. 164, m. 8; C.P.R., 1330-34, pp. 362-363; Rotuli Parliamentorum (n. p. [London], n. d. [1767-1777]), II, 246-251; ibid., II, 391; ibid., III, 379.

[4] For commissions carrying this phrase, see Patent Rolls (Supplementary, Nos. 22 & 23, passim, in which are enrolled the commissions issued to Mayors and Constables of the domestic staples during the reigns of Edward III and Richard II. Like comment is made in the returns from the port concerning the elections. See P.R.O., Chancery, Certificates of Election, Files 4-8, passim. That alien merchants did figure in the elections, at least in the early years after the establishment of home staples in 1353, is evident from returns from Newcastle and Winchester in which participating aliens are cited. Ibid., File 7, mm. 24, 25; ibid., File 8, mm. 63, 64, 66.

[5] P.R.O., Chancery, Treaty Rolls, No. 49, m. 9; ibid., No. 59, m. 11; ibid., No. 68, m. 10; ibid., File 8, mm. 63, 64, 66.

[6] T. Rymer, Foedera, ed. A. Clarke, F. Holbroke, and J. Caley (London, 1830), III, 691-692. Cf. ibid., III, 688-689.

[7] February 9, 1363. Ibid., idem.

[8] M. McKisack, The Fourteenth Century, 1307-1399 (Oxford, 1959), p. 354; G. Holmes, The Later Middle Ages, 1272-1485 (London, 1962), p. 48. This conclusion seems to have been derived from a dissertation by A. Jenckes, The Origins...of the Staple of England (Philadelphia, 1908) and given currency by Sir James Ramsay in his Genesis of Lancaster (Oxford, 1913), I, 453-454, and History of the Revenues of the Kings of England (Oxford, 1925), II, 239.

[9] Lords Committee Report...Touching the Dignity of a Peer (London, 1929), IV, 597-598, 609-610.

[10] Patent Rolls (Supplementary), No. 22, passim.

[11] The chronicler Henry Knighton spoke of the men as de valentioribus regni. Cited by McKisack, Fourteenth Century, p. 354.

[12] Ibid., idem.

[13] Rot. Parl., II, 276.

[14]Rymer, _Foedera_, III, 719.

[15]February 16, 1364.  _Ibid_., III, 722-723.  One of the merchants appointed as a Justice was Adam de Bury, one of the twenty-six.

[16]P.R.O., Exchequer, K.R. Various Accounts, Bdle. 101, Nos. 2 and 3.  No. 2 is in the form of a roll and seems a fair copy of the most pertinent documents in the collection of manuscripts that makes up No. 3.  G. Daumet, _Calais sous la domination Anglais_ (Arras, 1902), pp. 72-73, used these documents but only as they shed light on the reason for the failure of the system of government by the twenty-six.

[17]Adam de Bury excepted.  See above, note 15.

[18]The first five inquests are given in K.R. Various Accounts, Bdle. 101, No. 2, mm. 1-2, but the sixth appears only in _ibid_., No. 3, m. 14.

[19]_Ibid_., No. 2, mm. 2-3.

[20]See Appendix.

[21]The new system of government was in operation as of July 5, 1364, the date that the treasurer began to keep the accounts.  Pipe Rolls, No. 209, m. 52.

[22]_Ibid_., _idem_.

[23]One of the most frequently stated reasons for the defective nature of the Calais government was _la debate entre les deux Meirs_, and it was the consensus of the aldermen and burgesses, expressed in the second inquest, _qe la dite vill deust meltz estre gouerne par vn Meir_.  K.R. Various Accounts, Bdle. 101, No. 2, mm. 1-3.

[24]Rymer, _Foedera_, III, 768-769.

[25]On June 23, 1366, the king granted to "the community of the merchants of the staple" the right to elect the Mayor and Constables. _Ibid_., III, 795.

Chapter 16

[1]Joseph R. Strayer, "The Fourth and the Fourteenth Centuries," American Historical Review, LXXVII (1972), pp. 1-14.

[2]The best introduction to the problem, although it treats rural as well as urban unrest, is Michel Mollat and Philippe Wolff, Ongles Bleus, Jacques, et Ciompi:  les révolutions populaires en Europe aux XIVe et XVe siècles (Paris, 1970), the nearest thing we have to a survey.  However, a wealth of individual studies of individual uprisings exists; the above work includes an introductory bibliography. Städtische Volksbewegungen im 14. Jahrhundert (Tagung der Sektion Mediavistik der deutschen Historiker-Gesellschaft 1960 in Wernigerode) (Berlin, 1960), hereafter abbreviated Tagung, includes several such investigations by East German historians, largely but not entirely of German towns.  Some other important studies will be cited below. For approaches to urban violence and unrest of all kinds in this period, see Lauro Martines, ed., Violence and Civil Disorder in Italian Cities 1200-1500 (Berkeley, 1972).  Rural unrest is, of course, of at least equal importance; however, as Mollat and Wolff admit (see especially pp. 271-283), it is a very different phenomenon and thus outside the scope of this paper.

[3]See the somewhat impressionistic effort of Manuel Jorge Aragoneses, Los movimientos y luchas sociales in la baja edad media (Madrid, 1949).

[4]For example, Hans Lentze, Der Kaiser und die Zunftverfassung in den Reichsstädten bis zum Tode Karls IV. (Breslau, 1933).

[5]Robert S. Lopez, The Birth of Europe (New York, 1967), p. 398. Friedrich Lütge, Deutsche Sozial- und Wirtschaftsgeschichte (Berlin, 1960), p. 144.

[6]Marian Malowist, "Z hospodárské problematiky krise feudalismu ve XIV. a XV. století," Ceskoslovenský Casopis Historický, IV (1956), pp. 85-99.  Frantisek Graus, "Die erste Krise des Feudalismus," Zeitschrift für Geschichtswissenschaft, III (1955), pp. 552-592.

[7]Ernst Daenell, Die Blütezeit der Hanse (2v. Berlin 1905-06), I, pp. 162-163, II, pp. 501-503.

[8]Theo Mayer-Maly, "Die Kölner Gaffelverfassung und die Rechtsgeschichte der Demokratie," Österreichische Zeitschrift für offentliches Recht, n. s., VII (1955-56), pp. 208-218.  Phillippe Dollinger, "Le patriciat des villes du Rhin superieur et ses dissensions internes dans la première moitié du XIVe siècle," Schweizerische Zeitschrift für Geschichte, III (1953), pp. 248-258.

[9]Strayer (note 1), p. 10.

[10]The following review is not intended to be comprehensive; rather, it gives only representative examples of the major points of view,

drawn primarily from recent literature on German and Italian towns, where the greatest number of uprisings occurred and hence where the problem has received the greatest attention.

[11]A thorough and readily accessible review of this literature is Leopold Genicot, "Crisis:  from the Middle Ages to Modern Times," Cambridge Economic History of Europe, I (2nd ed., Cambridge, 1966), pp. 660-741, with bibliography pp. 834-845.

[12]On this point see particularly David Herlihy, "Population, Plague, and Social Change in Rural Pistoia, 1201-1430," Economic History Review, ser. 2, XVIII (1965), pp. 225-244; the works of Wilhelm Abel, for example Die Wüstungen des ausgehenden Mittelalters (2nd. ed. Stuttgart, 1955) and "Wüstungen und Preisfall im spätmittelalterlichen Europe," Jahrbücher für Nationalökonomie und Statistik, CLXV (1953), pp. 380-427; Friedrich Lütge, "Das 14./15. Jahrhundert in der deutschen Sozial- und Wirtschaftsgeschichte," ibid., CLXII (1950), pp. 161-213; Heinrich Reincke, "Bevölkerungsprobleme der Hansestädte," Hansische Geschichtsblätter, LXX (1951), pp. 1-33, LXXII (1954), pp. 88-90; and E. A. Kosminsky, "Peut-on considérer le XIVe et XVe siècles comme l'epoque de la décadence de l'economie européene?" Studi in onore di Armando Sapori (Milan, 1957), pp. 553-569.  A dissenting view on the subject of immigration is M. M. Postan, "Some Evidence of Declining Population in the Later Middle Ages," Economic History Review, ser. 2, II (1949-50), pp. 221-246.

[13]Among them Ernst Werner, "Probleme städtischer Volksbewegungen im 14. Jh.," Tagung, pp. 11-55; Ernst Pitz, "Die Wirtschaftskrise des Spätmittelalters," Vierteljahrsschrift für Sozial- und Wirtschafts- geschichte, LII (1965), pp. 347-367; Johannes Scnildhauer, "Das Anwachsen der plebejischen Schicht der Stadtbevölkerung im Ostseegebiet und deren Rolle in der frühbürgerlichen Revolution," in E. Werner and M. Steinmetz, eds., Die frühbürgerliche Revolution in Deutschland (Berlin, 1961), pp. 73-80, and, for Rostock, a student of Schildhauer's, Karl F. Olechnowitz, Rostock von der Stadtrechtsbestätigung im Jahre 1218 bis zur bürgerlich-demokratischen Revolution von 1848/49 (Beiträge zur Geschichte der Stadt Rostock, I) (Rostock, 1968), pp. 76-92.  A considerably milder statement, admitting the failure of "pleb ans" to emerge in a leadership capacity but contending that on the strength of their involvement a revolt succeeded or failed, is Konrad Fritze, "Soziale und politische Auseinandersetzungen in wendischen Hansestädten am Ende des 14. Jhs.," Tagung, pp. 147-156, and "Zur lage der hanse- städtischen Plebejer," Rostocker Beiträge, I (1966), pp. 31-44.

[14]This is especially common in older works by German local histori- ans; a particularly blatant example is Walther Mehl, Die Braunschweiger Schicht von 1374 und ihre Nachwirkung in anderen Städten (phil. diss. Berlin, 1909, pub.).

[15]See for example Mollat and Wolff (note 2), pp. 139-180, and two works dealing with the Ciompi from Nicolai Rubinstein, ed., Florentine Studies:  Politics and Society in Renaissance Florence (London, 1968): Gene A. Brucker, "The Ciompi Revolution," pp. 314-357, and Raymond

de Roover, "Labor Conditions in Florence around 1400:  Theory, Policy, and Reality," pp. 277-313.  Brucker indeed uses the term "proletarian," but not in a strict Marxist sense; on pp. 325-330 he describes a number of property-holding Ciompi leaders.  De Roover has found ownership of at least house and garden to be quite common in tax returns for a wool-workers' quarter, p. 304.  A dissenting Marxist, who finds virtually no participation by truly propertyless groups (in German towns at least), is Karl Czok; see his "Städtische Volksbewegungen im deutschen Spätmittelalter" (unpublished Dr. phil. habil. dissertation, Leipzig, 1963) (abbreviated SV), pp. 5-19, "Zur Volksbewegung in den deutschen Städten des 14. Jhs." in Tagung, pp. 157-169, and "Zunftkämpfe, Zunftrevolutionen, oder Bürgerkämpfe," Wissenschaftliche Zeitschrift der Karl-Marx-Universität Leipzig (gesellschafts- und sprachwissenschaftliche Reihe), VIII (1958-59), pp. 129-143.

[16]Suggested by Henri Pirenne in his classic Early Democracies in the Low Countries (rev. ed., New York, 1963), pp. 125-134.  Ernst Kelter, "Das deutsche Wirtschaftsleben des 14. and 15. Jhs. im Schatten der Pestepidemien," Jahrbücher für Nationalökonomie und Statistik, CLXV (1953), pp. 161-208, offers the strongest statement of this position.  See also Gerald Strauss, Nuremberg in the 16th Century (New York, 1966), pp. 49-50.  Others who have focused on guild regulation in a time of economic distress include de Roover (note 15) and Ahasver von Brandt, "Die Lübecker Knochenhaueraufstände von 1380/84 und ihre Voraussetzungen," Zeitschrift des Vereins für lübeckische Geschichte und Altertumskunde, XXXIX (1959), pp. 123-202.

[17]See the works of Abel and Lütge cited in note 12; graphs of these price disjunctions appear in Wilhelm Abel, "Hungersnöte und Absatzkrisen im Spätmittelalter," in Brunner, Kellenbenz, Maschke, and Zorn, eds., Festschrift Hermann Aubin zum 80. Geburtstag, I (Wiesbaden, 1965), p. 17.  Grain prices over a longer period appear in E. H. Phelps-Brown and Sheila Hopkins, "Seven Centuries of the Prices of Consumables," in E. M. Carus-Wilson, ed., Essays in Economic History, II (London, 1962), pp. 179-196.

[18]Erich Maschke, "Verfassung und soziale Kräfte in der deutschen Stadt des späten Mittelalters," Vierteljahrsschrift für Sozial- und Wirtschaftsgeschichte, XLVI (1959), pp. 289-349, 433-476, especially pp. 289-291 and 329-335.  Several Marxists also recognize the strong presence of commercial elements, including the aforementioned Konrad Fritze, Am Wendepunkt der Hanse (Berlin, 1967), pp. 180-252, and Karl Czok, SV, esp. pp. 72-110.

[19]William M. Bowsky, "The Impact of the Black Death upon Sienese Government and Society," Speculum, XXXIX (1964), pp. 1-34.  Marvin Becker, "The Novi Cives in Florentine Politics," Medieval Studies, XXIV (1962), pp. 35-82.  Reincke (note 12), pp. 12-14.

[20]These approaches have of course developed from the suggestion of Fritz Rörig that the merchant patriciate in Hanse towns, especially Lubeck, became a rentier patriciate by about 1370; this is stated most strongly in "Grosshandel und Grosshändler in Lübeck des 14. Jh.,"

pp. 216-246, and "Die Stadt in der deutschen Geschichte," pp. 658-680
in Paul Kaegbein's edition of Rörig's works, Wirtschaftskräfte im
Mittelalter (2nd ed., Vienna-Cologne, 1971). One should note, however,
that Rörig himself never applied this suggestion to uprisings in this
way; he believed that artisans were responsible for them. For Rörig,
the key factor in Hanseatic development was free trade; the appearance
of rentiers meant a retreat from free trade in Hanseatic policy after
the Peace of Stralsund, and thus the beginning of the decline of the
Hanse. Only incidentally this meant a general loss of prosperity which
spurred artisans and perhaps some mercers to revolt. Ahasver von
Brandt (note 16) believes that Rörig's suggestion was taken too literally, pp. 137-147. An interesting critique of Rörig's entire approach
is Gordon S. Harrison, "The Hanseatic League in Historical Interpretation," The Historian, XXXIII (1971), pp. 385-397.

[21]Karl Czok, "Zum Braunschweiger Aufstand 1374-1386," in Gerhard
Heitz and Manfred Unger, eds., Hansische Studien (Heinrich Sproemberg
zum 70. Geburtstag) (Berlin, 1961), pp. 34-55. Eva Gutz, "Zu den
Stralsunder Bürgerkämpfen am Ende des 14. Jhs.," ibid., pp. 90-102.
Martin Erbstösser, "Der Knochenhaueraufstand in Lübeck 1384," in
H. Kretzschmar, ed., Vom Mittelalter zu Neuzeit (Berlin, 1956), pp.
126-132. A similar approach, but with nuances which admit of much
more complexity in the problem, is Phillippe Dollinger, "Patriciat
noble et patriciat bourgeois à Strasbourg au XIVe siècle," Revue
d'Alsace, XC (1950-51), pp. 52-82, esp. p. 71.

[22]See for example Bowsky (note 19), pp. 27-33, Kelter (note 16),
pp. 188-191, von Brandt (note 16), pp. 125-126.

[23]On this point note particularly the works of Herlihy, Abel, and
Lütge (note 12).

[24]M. M. Postan, "The Trade of Medieval Europe: the North,"
Cambridge Economic History of Europe, II (Cambridge, 1952), pp. 119-
256, esp. pp. 172-174 and 216-222. Some excellent examples appear
in the work of Rörig himself, notably the famous "Der Markt von
Lübeck," pp. 36-133, and "Lübecker Familien und Persönlichkeiten aus
der Frühzeit der Stadt," pp. 134-145 in the collection cited in note
20.

[25]Brucker (note 15), pp. 325-333 and Florentine Politics and Society,
1343-1378 (Princeton, 1962), pp. 363-390. As a Marxist, Czok definitely prefers other interpretations, but admits the possibility in the
uprisings of Stade and Danzig; see SV (note 15), pp. 95-96. Certainly
a split within the patriciate seems indicated by the evidence for
Brunswick and Lubeck, below.

[26]Maschke (note 18), esp. pp. 291-335. Phillippe Dollinger, The
German Hansa (Stanford, 1970), p. 286. Mollat and Wolff (note 2),
p. 282. While of course much less inclined to view taxation, war,
and corruption as principal causes, the best Marxists certainly admit
their importance as immediate causes; see for example Karl Czok,
"Städtebünde und Zunftkämpfe in ihren Beziehungen während des 14.

und 15. Jh.," Wissenschaftliche Zeitschrift der Karl-Marx-Universität Leipzig, VI (1956-57), pp. 517-542 and "Die Bürgerkämpfe in Süd- und Westdeutschland im 14. Jh.," Jahrbuch für Geschichte der oberdeutschen Reichsstädte (Esslinger Studien, XII-XIII, 1966-67), pp. 40-72; also Konrad Fritze, "Der Kampf um die Demokratisierung des Stadtregiments in Wismar 1427-1430," Wissenschaftliche Zeitschrift der Universität Greifswald (gesellschafts- und sprachwissenschaftliche Reihe), XIII (1964), pp. 249-258.

[27] Strauss (note 16), p. 49. Konrad Fritze, Die Hansestadt Stralsund (Schwerin, 1961), pp. 102-105, 124-129, 158-159. Rosemarie Wiegand, "Zur sozialökonomischen Struktur Rostocks im 14. und 15. Jh." in Hansische Studien (note 21), especially pp. 416-417.

[28] Marvin Becker, "Economic Change and the Emerging Florentine Territorial State," Studies in the Renaissance, XIII (1966), pp. 7-39. William M. Bowsky, "The Medieval Commune and Internal Violence," American Historical Review, LXXIII (1967-68), pp. 1-17.

[29] Note especially Brucker, "Ciompi" (note 15); Becker, "Economic Change" (note 28), p. 7; Bowsky, "Impact" (note 19), pp. 21-22, and the works cited in note 26. Other comments on war, finance, and uprisings appear in Matthew M. Fryde, "Studies in the history of public credit of German principalities and towns in the Middle Ages," Studies in Medieval and Renaissance History, I (1964), pp. 221-292 and Edward J. Nell, "Economic Relationships in the Decline of Feudalism," History and Theory, VI (1967), pp. 313-350.

[30] Compare, for example, the comments by the Marxists Werner, Schildhauer, and others in Tagung (note 2) with Kelter (note 16) and with von Brandt (note 16), pp. 123-126, 179-181, 195-197. Most authors on the subject have either directly or unconsciously written from this assumption. A few have not; a particularly refreshing example is Brucker, "Ciompi" (note 15), who concludes on p. 356 that this revolt was simply "a characteristic Florentine imbroglio."

[31] Robert S. Lopez in "The Trade of Medieval Europe:  the South," Cambridge Economic History of Europe, II (Cambridge, 1952), p. 342, has raised the point that "if we look at these events too closely we discern only local causes and local peculiarities."

[32] Czok, SV (note 15), pp. 32-50, 93-95. Maschke (note 18), pp. 293-299. Johannes Schildhauer, "Die Sozialstruktur der Hansestadt Rostock von 1378 bis 1569," Hansische Studien (note 21), pp. 341-353. Horst Jecht, "Studien zur gesellschaftlichen Struktur der mittelalterlichen Städte," Vierteljahrsschrift für Sozial- und Wirtschaftsgeschichte, XIX (1926), pp. 48-85.

[33] Reincke (note 12), p. 21. Fritze, Stralsund (note 27), pp. 59-60.

[34] Maschke (note 18), pp. 293-299; Dollinger, "Strasbourg" (note 21), p. 66.

[35]Compare Werner Spiess, "Fernhändlerschicht und Handwerkermasse in Braunschweig bis zur Mitte des 15. Jhs.," Hansische Geschichts-blätter, LXIII (1938), pp. 49-85; Hans Nirrnheim, "Wandschneider und Kaufleute in Hamburg," Zeitschrift des Vereins für hamburgische Geschichte, XV (1910), pp. 135-165; Czok, Gutz, and Wiegand in Hansische Studien (note 21), pp. 41, 90-102 and 411.

[36]Ahasver von Brandt, "Die gesellschaftliche Struktur des spät-mittelalterlichen Lübeck," in Untersuchungen zur Gesellschaftlichen Struktur der Mittelalterlichen Städte in Europa (Konstanzer Arbeit-skreis für mittelalterliche Geschichte: Vorträge und Forschungen, XI, 1966), pp. 215-239. Adolf Laube, "Wirtschaftliche und soziale Differenzierung innerhalb der Zünfte des 14. Jhs.," Zeitschrift für Geschichtswissenschaft, V (1957), pp. 1181-1197. Becker, "Novi Cives" (note 19) includes pp. 48-58 a grocer, a druggist, an ironmonger, a ropemaker and a pork butcher among the wealthiest men in Florence.

[37]See particularly Postan, "Trade" (note 24), p. 169; Maschke (note 18), pp. 440-454; von Brandt, "Struktur" (note 36), pp. 224-225; Czok, SV (note 15), p. 54. For the examples see von Brandt, "Knochen-hauer" (note 16), pp. 149-151; Gerda Bergholz, Die Beckenwerkergilde zu Braunschweig (Braunschweiger Werkstücke, n. 17) (Brunswick, 1954); Reincke (note 12), p. 21. Further information on the lack of speci-alization in commercial activity may be found in Erich Köhler, Einzelhandel im Mittelalter (Stuttgart, 1938) (Vierteljahrsschrift für Sozial- und Wirtschaftsgeschichte, Beiheft 36).

[38]On this point note especially the thorough study of Johannes B. Menke, "Geschichtsschreibung und Politik in Deutschen Städten des Spätmittelalters," Jahrbuch des kölnischer Geschichtsvereins, XXXIII (1958), pp. 1-84, XXXIV/XXXV (1960), pp. 85-194. Somewhat more sharply pointed remarks, in part drawn from this work, are in Karl Czok, "Bürgerkämpfe und Chronistik im deutschen Spätmittelalter," Zeitschrift für Geschichtswissenschaft, X (1962), pp. 637-645 and in his SV (note 15), pp. 14-28. Some general comments on the tendency of literary sources to underreport the status of those lower than the source's author are in Frantisek Graus, "The Late Medieval Poor in Town and Countryside," in Sylvia L. Thrupp, eds., Change in Medieval Society (New York, 1964), pp. 314-324, esp. pp. 314-315 and notes 3 and 4.

[39]Menke (note 38), pp. 93-109.

[40]Rhiman A. Rotz, "The Uprising of 1374: Source of Brunswick's Institutions," Braunschweigisches Jahrbuch, LIV (1973), pp. 61-73. The inconsistencies in this document are mentioned, but handled some-what differently, by Menke (note 38), pp. 61-77.

[41]Herman Bote, Das Schichtbuch (ed. Ludwig Hänselmann; Brunswick, 1886), pp. 27-30.

[42]Joseph R. Strayer, "The Future of Medieval History," Medievalia et Humanistica, n. s., no. 2 (1971), pp. 179-188; quote from p. 185.

John B. Freed, "Urban Development and the Cura Monialum in Thirteenth-
Century Germany," Viator, III (1972), pp. 311-327. Jan Rogozinski,
"The Lawyers of Lower Languedoc 1270-1345" (unpub. Ph.D. diss., Princeton
University, 1967).

[43]Strayer, "Future" (note 42), p. 182.

[44]In Lubeck in the mid-fourteenth century, for example, the father
of a leader of the uprising of 1384 went by both Johan van Coesfelde
and Johan Paternostermacher, the first surname presumably indicating
geographic origin, the second occupation: von Brandt, "Knochenhauer"
(note 16), pp. 148-149. Later, the merchant and draper Johan Krowel
had two sons and a grandson named Johan: Wilhelm Koppe, Lübeck-
Stockholmer Handelsgeschichte im 14. Jh. (Neumünster, 1933), pp. 192-
194. In Brunswick, Eilert van der Heide named all three of his sons
Eilert: Sophie Reidmeister, Genalogien Braunschweiger Patrizier- und
Ratsgeschlechter (Braunschweiger Werkstücke, no. 12) (Brunswick, 1948),
p. 70. Concern over property or hereditary rights, however, usually
forced the individual to work out some unusual form which immediately
alerts the researcher to possibilities of identity or duplication.
In the first case, one finds several entries for "Johan Coesfelde
Paternostermacher." In the second, the sons became "Johan who married
the daughter of Danquard vamme See" and "Johan who married the daughter
of Hartmann Pepersac." (Also, since both sons were successful merchants and both fathers-in-law were councilmen, results in a study
of this type are not seriously affected; see below.) The Heide males
went all of their lives by "Eilert the eldest," "Eilert the middle,"
and "Eilert the youngest."

[45]A particularly extreme example may serve to illustrate the point.
Documentation for Cort Semelow of Lubeck, other than his role in the
uprising of 1408, shows only that he was a guardian for minors twice
and executor of a will. "Number of guardianships held" would hardly
be a useful statistical category for evaluation of an individual. It
was however the consistent practice to make relatives and/or business
associates one's executors or guardians of one's children, and knowing that one can make use of such information. Semelow was executor
for a major merchant (Johan Warmeskerke), and one of his guardianships was for the children of a member of an old patrician family
and the Circle Society (Gottschalk van Attendorn). In the latter
case, his fellow guardian was a patrician, Circle member, and future
councilman (Johan Darsow). Thus, although we know nothing of Semelow's
profession or income-producing activity, one may safely reckon that
he held a status no lower than that of a middle-rank merchant, and he
was therefore assigned to group II below. Normally, of course, one
finds more information, some of which can be submitted to at least
minimal computation.

[46]The wars and other disasters which have affected all German archives need not be enumerated here. In addition, the fire in the
Hamburg town hall in 1842 (then, as now, housing the municipal archives) and the disastrous "storage" of the Lubeck archives during
World War II, from which little returned (and that thoroughly saturated

from years in salt mines) have special relevance for the illustrations given here. A narrative of the latter tragedy is in Ahasver von Brandt, "Das lübecker Archiv in den letzten hundert Jahren," Zeit-schrift des Vereins für lübeckische Geschichte und Altertumskunde, XXXIII (1952), pp. 33-80.

[47]By Ahasver von Brandt; the work has been cited in note 16, above.

[48]Rhiman A. Rotz, "Urban Uprisings in Germany: Revolutionary or Reformist? The Case of Brunswick, 1374," Viator, IV (1973), pp. 207-223.

[49]A recent work which used prosopography to study the Brunswick annuity market, Jürgen Bohmbach, Die Sozialstruktur Braunschweigs um 1400 (Branschweiger Werkstücke, Reihe A, X) (Brunswick, 1973) confirms, pp. 17-32, that the status of some members of the opposition was far higher than literary sources would indicate, although the author has somewhat different opinions on the causes of the uprising itself.

[50]More complete narratives of the complex sequence of events relat-ing to the Lubeck uprising of 1408 may be found in Carl Wehrmann, "Der Aufstand in Lubeck bis zur Rückkehr des Alten Raths 1408-16," Hansische Geschichtsblätter, VIII (1878), pp. 101-156, and Edmund Cieslak, "Rewolta w Lubece 1408-1415," Przeglad Zachodni n. 3/4 (1954), pp. 471-525. Neither work contains a satisfactory analysis of the social forces involved. Some perceptive comments are in Fritz Rörig, "Geschichte Lübecks im Mittelalter," in Fritz Endres, ed., Geschichte der freien und Hansestadt Lübeck (Lubeck, 1926), pp. 28-56, esp. pp. 46-47; Fritze, Wendepunkt (note 18), pp. 178-181; Czok, SV (note 15), pp. 103-110.

[51]Karl Koppmann, ed., Die Chroniken der deutschen Städte, XXVI (Die Chroniken der niedersächsischen Städte: Lübeck, II) (Leipzig, 1899), p. 393. Volumes in this series hereafter abbreviated in this manner: C 26.

[52]C 26, pp. 422-423 and Wilhelm Mantels, Carl Wehrmann, et al., eds., Codex Diplomaticus Lubicensis--Lübeckisches Urkundenbuch (11v. Lubeck, 1843-1905), V, document no. 530. (Abbreviated on the follow-ing pattern: LUB 5.530). LUB 5.190, C 26, p. 432, LUB 5.541.

[53]Accomplished by E. F. Fehling, Lübeckische Ratslinie von den Anfangen der Stadt bis auf die Gegenwart (Veröffentlichungen zur Geschichte der Freien- und Hansestadt Lübeck, VII, no. 1; Lubeck, 1925).

[54]LUB 5.260, 2.667. C 26, pp. 388-390, 425-429, etc. C 28 (ed. Koppmann; Leipzig, 1902), pp. 48-49.

[55]Considering the opposition as a unit for purposes of socio-economic analysis is not intended to imply that the opposition was in all respects a political unit throughout the period from 1405 to

1416. There are three documented political "defections," and may have
been others. One early member of the Sixty (Johan Schotte) was elevated to the council in 1406, and, though he remained in town during
the uprising, was of little aid in 1408. Two other men once on the
Sixty (Siverd Vockinghusen and Hinrik up dem Orde) abandoned the
new regime after the imperial ban in 1409:  see Karl Koppmann, ed.,
Hanserezesse:  Die Rezesse und andere Akten der Hansestädte, series
I, 1256-1430 (Leipzig, 1870-97), V, documents 680 and 682.  (Abbreviated HR 5.680,682.)  Known correspondences, however, far outweigh
known defections and there seems to be no significant difference in
socioeconomic composition between the known members of the Sixty and
the later councils and committees.  My forthcoming monograph on the
uprising will deal in more detail with changes in political alignment
during the period from 1405 to 1416, local conditions contributing to
the uprising, and the nature of the compromise of 1416, as well as
other matters which can only be touched upon briefly in this review.

[56]The documentary base for this study includes the chronicles in C
26 and 28; LUB, 3 to 7, covering a period from 1350 to 1440; HR,
5 and 6; C. W. Pauli, Lübeckische Zustande zu Anfang des 14. Jh.
(Lubeck, 1847); and for evidence of commercial activity,  eorg Lechner,
ed., Die Hansische Pfundzollisten des Jahres 1368 (Quellen und
Darstellungen zur hansischen Geschichte, n. s., X; Lubeck, 1935)
(abbreviated PL); Hans Nirrnheim, ed., Das hamburgische Pfundzollbuch
von 1369 (Hamburg, 1910) (abbreviated PH 1) and Das hamburgische Pfund-
und Workzollbuch von 1399 und 1400 (Hamburg, 1930) (abbreviated PH 2)
(Veröffentlichungen aus dem Staatsarchiv der freien und Hansestadt
Hamburg, I and II); Rolf Sprandel, ed., Das Hamburger Pfundzollbuch
von 1418 (Cologne, 1972) (Quellen und Darstellungen zur hansischen
Geschichte, n. s., XVIII) (abbreviated PH 3).  Some professional and
genealogical information appears in Fehling (note 53); other secondary
sources used include W. Brehmer, "Verzeichnis der Mitglieder der
Zirkelcompagnie," Zeitschrift des Vereins für lübeckische Geschichte
und Altertumskunde, V (1888), pp. 393-455, which includes some genealogical and property information for the members of the Circle Society;
Koppe (note 44), which contains extracts from the Lubeck poundage
books of 1378, 1384-85, and 1400 (now in Potsdam); and Michail Lesnikov,
"Lübeck als Handelsplatz für osteuropäische Waren im 15. Jh.,"
Hansische Geschichtsblätter, LXXVIII (1960), pp. 67-86, which is
based on the commercial books of the Vockinghusen brothers.

[57]On the Circle Society, or Society of the Holy Trinity, in Lubeck
see especially Carl Wehrmann, "Das lübeckische Patriziat," Zeitschrift
des Vereins für lübeckische Geschichte und Altertumskunde, V (1888),
pp. 293-392; Georg Wegemann, "Die führenden Geschlechter Lübecks und
ihre Verschwägerungen," ibid., XXXI (1941), pp. 17-51; and Rörig,
"Grosshandel" (note 20), pp. 243-244 and note 36.  The precise role
of this society in Lubeck's social and political history is a matter
of much debate, but no one doubts that it drew its membership from
men of high standing.

[58]Van Alen: Fehling, pp. 56-57; Brehmer, p. 406; LUB 3.700, 4.489,
5.40.  Van Hildessem:  LUB 5.178, Lesnikov, p. 81, Koppe, pp. 178-181;

LUB 4.543, 6.48, 6.326. Lange: LUB 5.96, 223, 425; 7.684. PH 1,
pp. 48, 55, 126, 139-140, 142 (which totals to over 1500 marks' worth
of cloth and wax); LUB 5.11, 96, 223, 227, 543; 7.395, 572.
Schonenberch: Fehling, p. 64; LUB 5.485, 6.708, 7.406. Stange:
Koppe, pp. 178-179. LUB 5.592, 6.617.

[59]Only three individuals were placed in this group solely under
this qualification: Werner Hoep, a very active merchant who dealt
with the Queen of Denmark and King of Sweden, on the basis of his
gifts to each of his three sons of 1,000 marks on the occasion of his
remarriage (Fehling, pp. 58-59; Koppe, pp. 223-229; LUB 4.656, 5.168);
Otto Lenzeke and Lutke Nyestat, each of whom owned a village and three
additional manors (LUB 5.9, 248; 5.331, 360; 6.72, 169, 360).

[60]In the interest of brevity, council service, genealogical information, and Circle Society membership are from Fehling or Brehmer
unless otherwise indicated; no page references to the poundage books
are used, since there are often five or six such references and all
have excellent indexes. C is the abbreviation for councilman, m for
merchant. Only the most significant information is included. The
members of Group I are: Hermen v. Alen, above; Johan Bere, C 1416-
51 and burgomaster, Circle, m (PH 3) and father of two councilmen;
Lutke Boytin, m (PH 1-2), father-in-law of Bere. Johan Colman, m
(LUB 5.570), father of Johan: C 1428-54 and burgomaster. Hinrich
Cropelin, brother of Claus: C 1406-08 and exile. Kersten Ekhoff:
C 1433-48 (LUB 6.272). Hinrich Gerwer, m (LUB 4.517, 5.34), father
of Johan: Circle (LUB 6.292), uncle of Johan: C and Circle (LUB
4.493). Johan v. Hamelen, alderman of Bergen m (LUB 5.17), C 1416-
25. Johan v.d. Heide, m (PH 3), owner of two salt mines (LUB 6.725,
7.326); brother-in-law of Albert Arp: C 1416-36. Johan v. Hervorde,
m (PH 3), C 1416-25. Borcherd v. Hildessem, above. Johan Hitvelt,
m (LUB 5.149), father of Hermen: C and Circle. Werner Hoep, note
59. Hinrich Honerjäger, m (PH 3), two daughters both marry C (T.
Soling and W. Overdyk). Hinrik Hoveman, m (PL), father of Johan.
Johan Hoveman, C 1428-47, m (PH 2) and salt lord at Oldesloe (LUB
7.410, 741). Marquart v.d. Kyle, Circle; brother and son also Circle.
Johan Krowel, note 44. Hartwich Krukow, probably m (PH 2), son-in-
law of Bertram v. Rentelen: Circle. Ludwig Krull, m (PH 3), C 1416-
31 and Circle. Johan Lange, above. Otto Lenzeke, note 59. Hans
Luneborch, son and son-in-law of councilmen; Circle, m (PH 1); father
of Johan: C and Circle. Evert Moyelke, Circle; son-in-law of C
Johan v. Stove. Lutke Nyestat, note 59. Simon Odeslo, son-in-law
of C Danquart vamme See, income from land (LUB 4.687). Hinrich up
dem Orde, Circle, very active m (PH 2; LUB 5.127, 137, 6.75; HR 5.169;
Koppe, Lesnikov). Johan and Thomas Perzeval, brothers, sons of burgomaster Johan (1363-96), both Circle, advowsons (LUB 5.40,63; Pauli,
p. 165). Bertelt Roland, m (LUB 6.356, Lesnikov), C 1416-28, Circle.
Hinrich Schenking, m (LUB 5.34, 47, 6.359), C 1426-36. Johan
Schonenberch, m and draper (PL, p. 425, LUB 5.47), C 1416-23. Johan
Schotte, C 1406-08, Circle (LUB 4.625), m (Koppe, p. 117). Tideman
Serntin, m (LUB 5.570, 7.20), land (LUB 6.336); C 1416-37, Circle,
brother also Circle. Tidemann Steen, C 1416-27, burgomaster (expelled
after defeat by Denmark); Circle, m (LUB 5.484, 6.407), large bequest

(LUB 5.409). Detmer v. Tunen, m (PH 3), C from 1416, burgomaster from
1424 to 1432; Circle. Siverd Vockinghusen, Circle, m in Baltic (LUB
5.34) and to Venice (LUB 6.633). Hans Witick, father of Bertold:  C
and Circle.

[61]Exact profession uncertain:  Johannes Kogelndal, a fugitive serf
of the count of Limburg who came to own considerable property (LUB
7.833); probably a mercer (LUB 5.432, PH 3, p. 19). Hinrich Niendorp,
guardian of St. Giles Beguines and owner of village of Malsow (LUB
5.391, 6.221). Curt Semelow, note 45 (LUB 5.352, Koppe, p. 206).
   Merchants:  Johan Aelsteker (Koppe, p. 225); Cort Brandes, associate
of Colman family of group I (LUB 7.761); Johan tor Brugghe (LUB 5.468,
Koppe, pp. 203-210, PH 3, Lesnikov, p. 70); Hinrik Brucman, also judge
(LUB 4.543, 597); Johan Grove, alderman of Bergen m (LUB 5.17); Andreas
v. Hachede, distant cousin of C family (LUB 5.352, 6.359; PH 2-3);
Detlev Haverland (LUB 5.570); Johan Hervest (PH 3); Johan Hunt (LUB
5.178); Jacob Jerchow, judge, Lubeck magistrate in Falsterbo, Novgorod
m (LUB 4.543, 5.47, 335; PH 2, Lesnikov, p. 81); Bertelt Kreghel,
Bergen m (LUB 5.392, 501); Herbord v. Linden, probably associate of
C family v. Hereke (LUB 4.622, 5.34; Lesnikov, pp. 70-71, 81); Marquard
v.d. Molen (PL); Peter Nienborch (Koppe, p. 120); Bertelt v. Northem
(LUB 5.178, HR 5.123); Johan Oldenborch, draper, Novgorod m (LUB 4.517,
597, 5.335; PL, PH 2); Martin Osenbrugge, establishes altar (LUB 5.34,
127, 7.378; PH 3); Hermen Reterem, Scania m (Fehling, p. 61, LUB
7.422); Hermen Runge (LUB 5.127, PL, HR 5.414); Marquard Schutte (LUB
5.570, PH 2); Hartwich Semme (LUB 4.588); Timme v. Stendal (PH 1,
Koppe, p. 117); Hermen Vinck (LUB 4.597, PH 2-3).
   Commercial artisans:  Konrad Bloyebom (LUB 5.432, C 28, pp. 48-49);
Nosselman Bunstorp, brewer, commander of warship against pirates in
1405 (Fehling, p. 59, C 26, p. 394); Johan v. Cerben, amber-worker
(LUB 4.657, 674, 6.283); Hermen v. Gottingen, probably goldsmith,
steward of three religious societies (LUB 5.207, 311, 6.798, 7.150;
Koppe, p. 228); Johan Hulsey, brewer (C 26, p. 386, LUB 5.352, 355);
Johan Plote, amber-worker (LUB 4.657, 5.350); Hermen Poling, goldsmith
(LUB 5.428); Hans and Marquard Schele, brothers and goldsmiths (LUB
5.14, 256); Hinrik Schenkenberg, brewer, judge (Fehling, p. 62, LUB
5.444); Bernhard Schimmelpenninck, brewer and warship commander (C
26, p. 386, 394); Hinrik Schonenberch, above; Heine Sobbe, goldsmith
(C 28, p. 80); Eler Stange, above (placed in Group II because of
his artisan profession, although could also have been placed in Group
I on the basis of his marriage).

[62]Hinrik Bekeman, tanner, owned two large houses, steward of St.
James' Church (Fehling, p. 60, LUB 5.319). Vollant v.d. Berge, cobbler
(Fehling, p. 63). Merten Bertze, butcher (Fehling, p. 62). Bernd
Bischop, smith, owned garden (Fehling, p. 65, LUB 6.741). Tideke
Helmstede, weaver (LUB 6.733). Ludeke van dem Holme, leather-worker
(HR 6.262, p. 214). Steffen Junge, profession unknown, loaned 250
marks to the town mint, steward of St. Peters' (LUB 5.256, 6.798).
Johan v. Lense, butcher (HR 6.262, p. 214). Gerhard Marsen, purse-
maker (LUB 5.213). Detlev Meier, baker (LUB 6.280). Hinrich Melborch,
hatmaker, loaned 432 marks against cloth and jewels, steward of St.
Peters' (Fehling, p. 62, LUB 6.50, 798). Hans Punt, profession

unknown, brother a notary (Fehling, p. 65). Clawes Rubow, baker (C̲
28, p. 363, H̲R̲ 6.262, p. 210). Hinrich v. d. Springe, smith, steward
of St. George's chapel (L̲U̲B̲ 5.392, 7.534). Peter Timmerman, profession unknown, loan to town mint (L̲U̲B̲ 5.256, p. 265). Johan Witte,
candle-maker (L̲U̲B̲ 5.355).

[63]Von Brandt, "Struktur" (note 36), pp. 224-230, reviews and sum-
marizes his own and Johannes Schildhauer's work on the subject.

[64]J. M. Lappenberg, ed., Tratzigers Chronik der Stadt Hamburg
(Hamburg, 1865), pp. 130-131.

[65]P̲L̲ and P̲H̲ 1-2-3, above (note 56); Karl Koppmann and Hans Nirrnheim,
eds., Kammereirechnungen der Stadt Hamburg (10v. Hamburg, 1869-1951)
(abbreviated K̲).

[66]Tymmo Alverslo (P̲H̲ 2); Albert Barstede, also a parish juror (P̲H̲
3); Evert Bekerholt (P̲H̲ 2); Johan Berchstede (P̲H̲ 1, P̲L̲); Kersten
Berkampen, juror (P̲H̲ 2-3); Hinrik Bishorst, C 1417 (P̲H̲ 2-3); Helmborn
Blumenberch, draper (K̲ 1, pp. 311, 422); Hinrik Buxtehude, draper
(P̲L̲, P̲H̲ 1); Ludeke v. Eyzen (P̲H̲ 2-3); Johan Goltbeke, draper (P̲H̲ 1-2,
K̲ 1, p. 422); Johan Grant (P̲H̲ 1); Johan Ghultzow, C 1413-30 (P̲H̲ 2);
Heyno v.d. Hagen (P̲H̲ 2); Ghert Hals, C 1414-26 (P̲H̲ 3); Johan Hanstede
(P̲H̲ 2); Johan Hetfeld (H̲R̲ 3.347); Bernard Hune (P̲H̲ 2-3); Heyno Klese
(P̲H̲ 2); Johan Klese, C 1411-28 (P̲H̲ 2-3); Ludeke Klese (P̲H̲ 2-3); Bernt
Knubbe (P̲H̲ 3); Johan Kron (P̲H̲ 2); Titker Luneborch, juror, C 1431-58
(P̲H̲ 2); Johan v. Minden (P̲H̲ 2); Johan Nygenkerken (P̲H̲ 2-3); Peter
Scharpenberch (P̲H̲ 2); Helmich Simmensen (P̲H̲ 2); Eilard Stapelvelt,
draper (P̲H̲ 2, K̲ 1, p. 422); Hinrik Tzeghelke (P̲H̲ 2); Sander v.d.
Vechte (P̲H̲ 2); Hinrik Wulhase, C 1412-28 (P̲H̲ 2-3).

[67]Johan v. Alverding, 1416-30; Johan Bekerholt, 1411, excommunicated
for striking a beadle, municipal embassy to Pope about it costs 1000
Flemish pounds (K̲ 2, pp. 22-23, 40-47); Vicko v.d. Hove, 1416-42;
Erich v. Tzeven, 1414-50; Johan Wulf, 1414-21.

[68]Albert Grevink, 1388; Peter Mildehoved, 1402; Werner Römhagen,
1409; Johan Strote, 1408; Bernt Vermerschen, 1410; Johan Widemule,
1413; Hilmer Woldehorn, 1398.

[69]Henneke Ekhof, cooper (K̲ 1, p. 421); Clawes Koeting, cooper (K̲ 1,
p. 334, 2 p. 19); Kersten v.d. Hoye, cobbler (K̲ 1, p. 376); Hinrik
Lamspringh, goldsmith (K̲ 1, p. 261, 468; 2 p. 13); Titke Munster,
tinker (K̲ 1, p. xxxviii, note 2).

[70]Marquard Hoygerstorp (K̲ 2, p. 10); Anneke v.d. Oldeland (K̲ 1,
pp. 305, 406); Godeke v.d. Slus, holding Dutch guilders (K̲ 2, p. 3);
Hinrik Stenbeke (H̲R̲ 4.94).

[71]See for example the remarkably specific list of grievances issued
by the Sixty, L̲U̲B̲ 5.188.

[72]Von Brandt, "Struktur" (note 36), notes p. 226 that in Lubeck in
1460, the top 19% of the taxable population provided 58% of the funds
raised by the basic tax.

Chapter 17

[1] I want to express my gratitude to the American Council of Learned Societies which granted me a Fellowship in the academic year 1970-71 and to the research Board of the University of Illinois at Urbana for its continued support of my research.

[2] William Mendel Newman, Les Seigneurs de Nesle en Picardie, t.I (Philadelphia, 1971), p. 7.

[3] Louis du Bois, Recherches archéologiques, historiques, biographiques et litteraire sur la Normandie (Paris, 1843), pp. 117-118; Victor Gastebois, Les Comtes de Mortain, 995-1789 (Mortain, 1934), pp. 12-35.

[4] Du Bois, Recherches, p. 115.

[5] There has been some scholarly debate as to whether William Werlenc was Mauger's son or his grandson. Du Bois, loc. cit. emphatically states that William Werlenc was Mauger's son; but Augustus Le Prevost suggests that there was an intervening generation between the two. See his Orderici Vitalis Historiae Ecclesiasticae Libri Tredecim (Paris, 1845), p. 259, note 1. David Douglas, William the Conquerer (Berkeley, 1964), p. 25 postulates that one of Duke Richard I's bastards, Robert, may have been Count of Mortain, but this would mean that the obscure Robert and Mauger were contemporaries, unless they held the fief seriatim.

[6] Gastebois, Comtes de Mortain, p. 19. F. M. Stenton, Anglo-Saxon England (3rd ed., Oxford, 1971), p. 595 for Robert's part in the subjugation of England; pp. 615, 621-624 for Robert of Mortain as part of the Duke's "standing baronial council." Stenton has valuable material on the historical significance of the Bayeux Tapestry as a contemporary document, pp. 569-570; for the tapestry's social and artistic value, see Frank Stenton, et al., The Bayeux Tapestry (Phaidon Press, 2nd ed., Greenwich, Conn., 1965). Count Robert is pictured here but this piece of embroidery does not present a physical description of anyone that could be called accurate.

[7] Augustus Le Prevost, ed., Orderici Vitalis Historiae Ecclesiasticae Libri Tredecim, lib. quartus, cap. v, pp. 194-195, lib. septimus, cap. xvi, pp. 244-246.

[8] Du Bois, Recherches, pp. 135-140; Gastebois, Comtes de Mortain, pp. 72-74.

[9] E. P. Sauvage, ed., "Vitae BB. Vitalis et Gaufridi, primi et secundi abbatum Saviniacensum," in Analecta Bollandiana, I (1882), pp. 358-359 (hereafter Vitae).

[10] Vitae, p. 359; see also H. Sauvage, Saint Vital et l'Abbaye de Savigny (Mortain, 1895), pp. 23-24.

[11]Vitae, pp. 359-360; Auguste Laveille, ed., Dom Claude Auvry, Histoire de la Congregation de Savigny. Sociéte de l'histoire de Normandie, no. 30, vol. I (Rouen and Paris, 1896), pp. 13-30.

[12]Auvry, Histoire de la Congregation de Savigny, I, pp. 32-45; H. Sauvage, Saint Vital et l'Abbaye de Savigny, p. 24.

[13]Ordericus Vitalis, lib. octavus, cap. i, pp. 265-266.

[14]Vitae, p. 362; Acta Sanctorum, Januarius 1-15, p. 390; Auvry, Histoire de la Congregation de Savigny, p. 45.

[15]Du Bois, Recherches, pp. 141-142; H. Sauvage, Saint Vital, p. 26 here repeats the direct account of the chronicler.

[16]Vitae, pp. 362-363; Auvry, Histoire de la Congregation de Savigny, pp. 45-80 stresses Vital's zealousness in the defense of ecclesiastical discipline, no doubt a product of his training in canon law and of the influence of the ideals of the Gregorian Reform movement upon him.

[17]Vitae, pp. 363-364.

[18]Gastebois, Comtes de Mortain, p. 22; Du Bois, Recherches, pp. 124-125.

[19]Gallia Christiana, XI, 541.

[20]Guy Devailly, "Une enquête en cours:  L'Application de la réforme grégorienne en Bretagne," in Annales de Bretagne, LXXV (July, 1968), pp. 293-316; see also L. Raison et R. Niderst, "Le Mouvement érémetique dans l'Ouest de la France à la fin du XIe siècle et au début du XIIe" in Annales de Bretagne, LIII-LV (1946-48), pp. 1-45.  For Bernard of Tiron and Vital of Savigny as preachers, see Johannes von Walter, Die ersten Wanderprediger Frankreichs (Leipzig, 1906), which contains an old but still useful bibliographical discussion.

[21]Vitae, p. 363; Auvry, Histoire de la Congregation de Savigny, pp. 84-91, 105.

[22]Vitae, p. 364; Gallia Christiana, XI, 540-541.

[23]Gastebois, Comtes de Mortain, pp. 72-74; see Appendix I.

[24]Charles-Adrien Duhérissier de Gerville, Études géographiques et historiques sur le Départment de la Manche (Cherbourg, 1854), pp. 47-48, 50; see also "Etude sur les étymologies des noms de lieux et des noms de famille dans l'Avranches," in Mémoires de la Société d'Archeologie, Littérature, Sciences, et Arts des Arrondissements d'Avranches et de Mortain, XII (Avranches, 1895), p. 215.

[25]Bertrand d'Argentré, L'Histoire de Bretaigne (Paris, 1618), col. 224c.

[26]Baudrillart, Dictionnaire d'histoire et de géographique ecclésiastiques, vol. XVII (Paris, 1971), col. 1263.

[27]C. de Mas Latrie, ed., Trésor de chronologie d'histoire et de
géographie pour l'étude et l'emploi des documents du moyen âge (Paris,
1889), col. 1605.

[28]The original charter certifying the grant does not survive, nor
does the first general or royal confirmation of it. But before being
lost or destroyed, a copy of the general confirmation of Henry I,
dated March 2, 1113, was made and later printed by the editors of the
Gallia Christiana, XI, Instrumenta, col. 111; and then by J. H. Round,
Calendar of Documents Preserved in France 918-1206, I (London, 1899),
no. 792. Recently Charles Johnson and H. A. Cronne have included it
in their edition of Regesta Regum Anglo-normannorum 1066-1154, II--
Regesta Henrici Primi 1000-1135 (Oxford, 1956), no. 1015.

[29]Gallia Christiana, XI, 541. Literis cum esset apprime imbutus,
collegiatae S. Ebrulfi Moritoniensis ecclesiae canonicus et comitis
capellanus est institutus, apud quem tanta valuit gratia, ut Moritoni-
ensem elemosynam illi largitus sit Willelmus comes ad honorem sanctis-
simae Trinitatis, quam postea abbati Cadomensi donavit Vitalis de
consensu Henrici I regis.

[30]See Appendix, pp. 249-253.

[31]For a general discussion of monastic charters, see V. H. Galbraith,
"Monastic Foundation Charters of the Eleventh and Twelfth Centuries,"
Cambridge Historical Journal, IV, no. 3 (1934) and the recent valuable
discussion in David Knowles, C.N.L. Brooke, and Vera London, eds.,
The Heads of Religious Houses--England and Wales 940-1216 (Cambridge,
1972), pp. 5-15; for the gradual passing of noble lands and wealth
into the hands of the Church and the effect this had on familial fortunes, see the provocative remarks of Georges Duby, Rural Economy and
Country Life in the Medieval West, trans. Cynthia Postan (London,
1966), pp. 182-186. For monastic tithes, see the definitive study of
Giles Constable, Monastic Tithes (Cambridge, 1964), passim, and esp.
pp. 190-191 for Savigny's acquisition of tithes.

[32]Archives National, L 967, no. 108 is an undated general confirmation by Henry, Bishop of Bayeux (1164-1179), of Savigny's possessions
in his diocese; Archives National, L 968, no. 210 is the confirmation
charter of Stephen, Bishop of Rennes (1156-1178), also undated.

[33]For this document, see the Appendix, pp. 249-253.

Chapter 18

[1]This study is the first fruit of a 1973 grant from the American Council of Learned Societies for the purchase of the aerial photograph coverage of the coastal area of Languedoc. Thanks to a Ford Foundation grant administered by Amherst College, I was able to visit many of the sites mentioned here during the summer of 1969.

[2]I have taken the liberty of putting the chronicler's indirect discourse back into direct quotation. Petri Vallium Sarnaii Monachi, Hystoria Albigensis (ed. P. Guébin and E. Lyon, Paris, 1926-1939), vol. I, pp. 101-102, 112-113.

[3]Ibid., p. 94.

[4]The bibliography is now substantial. Each passing year adds further refinement to the techniques of analysis available and additional discoveries made from the air. For a general introduction see R. Chevalier, L'Avion à la découverte du passé (Paris, 1964). A striking recent example of both technical development and archeological use (primarily in the form of oblique, low-level photography) is D. Jalmain, Archéologie aérienne en Ile-de-France (Paris, 1970).

[5]I.G.N. survey 2345-2445 (1962), no. 104.

[6]Grid Zone numbers are the standard Lambert III southern zone.

[7]See Figure II.

[8]A full inventory of these indications will have to await later publication where more space is available. Pertinent traces of Roman roads incorporated into the medieval road system are shown on I.G.N. 1:50,000 type 1922 maps at G.Z. 63001090 to 63201080, 6170115 to 62301115, 60801050 to 61091053, and 58501045 to 59961012.

[9]One example among many: in 1176 a number of lords of Ventajou sold the villa of Fabas to the viscount of Beziers for 1000 sol. melg.; Société archéologique de Montpellier, ms. 11, fo 240. Fabas is now a métairie in the commune of Laure (Aude) [G.Z. 61771075]. (It is difficult to set a precise value for this sum of money, but one may note that in 1178 the viscount paid 1100 sol. melg. for five men residing at Montreal, along with their wives, children, possessions, and honores; ibid., fo 111.)

[10]The ms. 11 of the Société archéologique de Montpellier, called the "Cartulaire dit de Foix," and sometimes assumed to be the "Cartulaire, caisse 15" so often cited by the Benedictine editors of the Histoire générale de Languedoc, is primarily a collection of oaths concerning castles. I would like to thank M. Jean Claparede, president of the Société archéologique, for allowing me to consult this manuscript under the best possible working conditions.

[11]For a description of its trace see I. König, Die Meilensteine der Gallia Narbonensis [Itinera Romana, 3] (Bern, 1970), pp. 57-63, where a full bibliography will also be found.

[12]See I.G.N. map 1:50,000 feuille XXVI-44.

[13]See R. Chevalier, Les voies romaines (Paris, 1972), pp. 56-57 for the general significance of such names. I have been unable to trace the reference of "la Reine Juliette," perhaps a corruption of an earlier local name.

[14]Acad. des Inscr. et B-L., Forma Orbis Romani, fasc. 10 (ed. E. Bonnet), p. 27.

[15]See the testament of Viscount William of Beziers (990), Cl. de Vic and J. Vaissette, Histoire générale de Languedoc (ed. Privat, Toulouse, 1875), vol. V, cols. 316 ff.

[16]Ibid., cols. 425 ff.

[17]Ibid., col. 794; Soc. arch. Montpellier, ms. 11, fo 76 (for Poussan). Hist. gén. Lang., vol. V, cols. 852, 1122 (for Loupian).

[18]I hope to publish elsewhere a full inventory of these castles, the sources that mention them, and maps of their locations. Only a brief summary can be allowed in the space here provided.

[19]A detailed description and analysis of these oaths is presented by Mme. Magnou-Nortier in "Fidélité et féodalité méridionales d'après les serments de fidélité," Les structures sociales de l'Aquitaine, du Languedoc et de l'Espagne au premier âge féodal [Colloque de Toulouse, 1968] (Paris, 1969), pp. 119-128.

[20]Ibid., esp. p. 128.

[21]A. R. Lewis, The Development of Southern French and Catalan Society 718-1050 (Austin, 1965), chapters 12 and 15, and esp. p. 358.

[22]Here is a nineteenth-century description of the countryside surrounding Arifat. "Rien de plus sauvage que les bords escarpés du Dadou qui coule à une grande profondeur entre deux hautes montagnes. La chaine est remarquable par l'entassement de rochers qui s'élèvent parfois perpendiculiairement et forment des dentelures les plus bizarre." M. Bastié, Description complète du département du Tarn (Albi, 1875), p. 517.

[1]Belöw,note 19.  Philip III is said by many sources (e.g., E. Boutaric, La France sous Philippe le bel [Paris, 1861], p. 55) to have ennobled Raoul l'Orfevre; see, however, C. V. Langlois, Le Règne de Philippe III le hardi (Paris, 1887), pp. 203-205.  An earlier version of these remarks formed part of a paper delivered at the March, 1971 meeting of the Society for French Historical Studies.  I am grateful for the steadfast encouragement of Paul Hauch as well as for financial aid from the Research Foundation of the State University of New York. Abbreviations used throughout:  AD--Archives départementales; AM-- Archives municipales; AN--Archives nationales; BN--Bibliothèque nationale; AP--Actes du Parlement de Paris, ed. E. Boutaric (Paris, 1863-1867); HF--Recueil des historiens des Gaules et de la France (Paris, 1738-1904); HL--C. DeVic et J. Vaissete, Histoire générale de Languedoc, ed. A. Molinier et al. (Toulouse, 1872-1904); Mignon-- Inventaire des anciens comptes royaux dressé par Robert Mignon, ed. C. V. Langlois (Paris, 1899).

[2]The number of letters varied from reign to reign:  Francis I granted about two hundred, Louis XIV several thousand:  J. R. Bloch, L'Anoblissement en France au temps de Francois I$^{er}$ (Paris, 1935), p. 211.

[3]Histoire des institutions françaises au moyen âge, sous la direc- tion de F. Lot et R. Fawtier, II:  Institutions royales (Paris, 1958), passim.  See also R. Cazelles, "Une exigence de l'opinion depuis Saint Louis:  La réformation du Royaume," Annuaire-Bulletin de la Société de l'histoire de France Années 1962-1963 (Paris, 1964), p. 98; F. Autrand, "Offices et officiers royaux en France sous Charles VI," Revue historique, CCXLII (1969), 285-338; B. Guenée, "État et pouvoir à la fin du moyen âge," Annales Économies Sociétés Civilisations, XXVI (1971), 399; J. Henneman, "The French Ransom Aids and Two Legal Tra- ditions," Studia Gratiana, XV (1972), 615-629.

[4]G. Duby, "Une Enquête à poursuivre:  La Noblesse dans la France mediévalé," Revue historique, CCXXVI (1961), 19; "Les sociétés médiévales," Annales E. S. C., XXVI (1971), 4.  For the bourgeoisie, M. Mollat and P. Wolff, Ongles bleus, Jacques, et Ciompi (Paris, 1970), p. 60.

[5]"Sur le passé de la noblesse française:  quelques jalons de recherche," Annales d'histoire économique et sociale, VIII (1936), 374.

[6]See especially C. Nicolet and A. Chastagnol, Annales E. S. C., XXV (1970), 1220, 1224, 1229.  In his discussion in Daedalus (Winter 1971, pp. 46-79), L. Stone confounds prosopography and interpretative essays making use of prosopographical evidence.  Whatever the merit to his criticisms of Syme, Namier, and Beard, their books are not prosopography; they are interpretive syntheses of data taken from earlier historians who used numerous other techniques besides those

of prosopography.

[7]"Étude sur les lettres d'anoblissement," Revue historique nobiliaire et biographique [new series], V (1869), 193-208. Written in 1906, although it was not published until 1935, the study of J. R. Bloch (cited note 2) is limited to the reign of Francis I and adds nothing to Barthélemy's remarks about earlier centuries. Dom Carpentier has some cogent comments in the introduction to his manuscript catalogue, compiled in 1753, of many of the letters registered by the royal chancery (from 1308 to the 1600's) and by the chambre des comptes (after 1422). The complete catalogue is in the Bibliothèque nationale (ms. lat. 18345, 241 unnumbered pages); an incomplete copy made in 1882 is in the national archives (AN S-12[84]). The registers of the comptes destroyed by fire in 1737 could otherwise provide us with a much more complete list: below note 18; Fawtier, Institutions françaises, II, 183.

[8]F. Cheyette, "Suum cuique tribuere," French Historical Studies, VI (1970), 289; J. Rogozinski, "The First French Archives," French Historical Studies, VII (1971), 111-116; R. Bautier et al., Les sources de l'histoire économique du moyen âge, I (Paris, 1968), pp. viii-ix.

[9]J. R. Strayer, "The Future of Medieval History," Medievalia et Humanistica [new series], II (1971), 186; R. Fossier, Histoire sociale de l'occident médiéval (Paris, 1970), p. 362. Cf. P. Goubert in Revue historique, CCXL (1968), 183-188; and in Daedalus (Winter, 1971), pp. 113-121.

[10]E. Perroy, "Social Mobility among the French Noblesse," Past and Present, No. 21 (1962), pp. 31-32. Noble lineages seem to run a greater risk of extinction than do lower-class families: Duby, "Enquête... noblesse," p. 20; S. P. Vivian, "Some Statistical Aspects of Genealogy," The Genealogist's Magazine, VI (1934), 482-489. The disappearance of aristocratic surnames was, moreover, exceptionally rapid about 1300. See P. Feuchère, "La noblesse du Nord de la France," Annales E.S.C., VI (1951), 315; R. Fossier, La Terre et les hommes in Picardie, 2 vols. (Paris, 1968), I, 283. For southern France, R. Fédou, "Une famille aux XIVe et XVe siècles: Les Jossard de Lyons," Annales E.S.C., IX (1954), 479; J. Rogozinski, Year Book of the American Philosophical Society, 1970, p. 681.

[11]Social etiquette has received far less attention than economic or political terminology, and there is no history of nobilis to set alongside the works devoted to universitas, status, or commune. An old metaphor has it that social classes are like hotels, with guests always arriving and leaving. But the hotels themselves change, are torn down, rebuilt. Their form is not easily reconstructed. Cf. S. Thrupp, "Hierarchy, Illusion and Social Mobility," Comparative Studies in Society and History, II (1959-1960), 126-128; J. Monfrin, "A propos du vocabulaire des structures sociales du haut moyen âge," Annales du Midi, LXXX (1968), 611-620.

[12]Over five million cases are recorded in the archives of the

Parlement of Paris alone (Fawtier, Institutions françaises, II, 417);
the existing indices, dating from the seventeenth century, deal mainly
with public law: M. Langlois, Guide des recherches dans les fonds
judiciaires (Paris, 1958), p. 128. As J. R. Bloch indicates
(Annoblissement Francois I$^{er}$, p. 13), the jurists of the ancien régime
were concerned with current politics and logical elegance and had
little interest in the historical evolution of noble privileges; cf.
D. Bitton, The French Nobility in Crisis 1560-1640 (Stanford, 1969);
G. Huppert, The Idea of Perfect History...in Renaissance France
(Urbana, 1970).

[13]G. Duby, "The Diffusion of Cultural Patterns in Feudal Society,"
Past and Present, No. 39 (1968), p. 9; R. Witt, "The Landlord and the
Economic Revival of the Middle Ages," American Historical Review,
LXXVI (1971), 986.

[14]Guenée, "État et pouvoir," p. 401; Duby, "Enquête noblesse," p.
18; J. Bartier, Légistes et gens de finances au XV$^e$ siècle: Les
conseillers des Ducs de Bourgogne Philippe le Bon et Charles le
Téméraire (Bruxelles, 1955), pp. 198-199.

[15]Below, notes 106, 117. On the late development of the legal
concept of dérogeance, E. Dravasa, "Vivre noblement," Revue juridique
et économique du Sud-Ouest, sèrie juridique, XVI (1965), 135-193,
XVII (1966), 23-129.

[16]Rogozinski, "First French Archives," p. 115.

[17]F. J. Pegues, The Lawyers of the Last Capetians (Princeton, 1962),
p. 223. Nogaret's colleague Guillaume de Plaisians was ennobled by
the Dauphin of Vienne and not by Philip the Fair: L. Henry, Le Moyen
âge, V (1892), 33.

[18]I have found no letters of ennoblement in printed sources that
are not also in the chancery records. Unpublished private archives
may preserve a few others, although it is difficult to understand
why the grantee would not insist on registration to protect himself
against future challenges by lower courts. In the fourteenth century,
ennoblement was commonly sought through the Requêtes de l'hôtel, and
Philip VI ordered that all letters be sent to the chambre des comptes
for verification: A. Guillois, Recherches sur les Maîtres des requêtes
de l'hotel des origines à 1350 (Paris, 1909), pp. 59-60; Ordonnances
des roys de France de la troisième race..., ed. M. de Laurière et al.,
21 vols. (Paris, 1723-1849), II, 69.

[19]AN JJ-34, No. 71. Concevreux (Aisne, near Laon) for Curte
Superiori following Dom Carpentier (above, note 7); other translations
suggest themselves.

[20]Taillefontaine (Aisne, c$^{on}$ Villers-Côtterêts) for Talliafons:
AN J-1024, No. 47. Not in 1290 as indicated by Bloch, Anoblissement
Francois I$^{er}$, p. 131; see text, Barthélemy, "Lettres d'anoblissement,"
p. 199.

[21]Gilles de Concevreux was the son of a noble mother and a non-noble father. Jean de Taillefontaine's father was noble but his mother was a serf; and serfdom followed the status of the mother: Etablissements de Saint Louis, II, ch. 31 in Ordonnances des roys, I, 278-279. Cf. P. Guilhiermoz, Essai sur les origines de la noblesse en France (Paris, 1902), p. 353.

[22]Registres du Trésor des chartes, I:  Règne de Philippe le Bel, ed. R. Fawtier (Paris, 1958), no. 1285 (1311); Mignon, nos. 1199, 1317.

[23]Languedoc proper comprised the sénéchaussées of Beaucaire-Nîmes, Carcassonne-Bèziers, Toulouse-Albi as well as those of Périgord-Quercy and the Rouergue separated after the treaty of Bretigny in 1369:  P. Dognon, Les institutions politiques et administratives du pays de Languedoc (Toulouse, 1895), p. 216; J. R. Strayer, "Normandy and Languedoc," Speculum, XLIV (1969), 3.

[24]Reg. Ph. IV, nos. 1314 (1311), 1511 (1312).

[25]B. Guillemain, La cour pontificale d'Avignon (Paris, 1962), 61, 278, 295; G. Mollat, The Popes at Avignon (New York, 1965), 285-286.

[26]Guillemain, Cour pontificale, p. 311.  The referendary received petitions and presented them to the pope with suggested responses.

[27]After 1275 non-nobles acquiring fiefs were legally obliged to pay a fine equivalent to two years of revenue when the services furnished to the crown by the fief were diminished and four years' revenue when they were abolished by the transfer of title; the penalty was increased to a flat fee of three years' revenue (six in Languedoc) from 1291 to 1326, when the two/four requirement was restored: Guilhiermoz, Origines de la noblesse, p. 480; Ordonnances des roys, I, 745-749, 797.  These charges were not exhorbitant, and individuals and entire communities were sometimes exempted in return for financial or other assistance; thus note 111 below, and L. Ménard, Histoire civile, ecclésiastique et littéraire de la ville de Nismes, 7 vols. (Paris, 1750-1758), I, preuves, no. 37.  All fiefs received as free gifts were freed in  315 as were all those without rights of justice in 1331 (Ordonnances, I, 617; II, 68-69.  Such laws were probably most useful to the government  and most irritating to its subjects) during negotiations over taxes or forced loans when royal commissioners might threaten to impose heavy fines on or to confiscate property purportedly transferred in violation of the rules:  J. Henneman, "'Enquêteurs-Réformateurs' and Fiscal Officers," Traditio, XXIV (1968), 313-315; Royal Taxation in Fourteenth Century France:  The Development of War Financing 1322-1356 (Princeton, 1971), pp. 3, 44, 49-50; M. Carreau, "Les Commissionaires royaux aux amortissements et aux nouveaux acquêts," Position des thèses, École Nationale des Chartes (Paris, 1953), p. 20.

[28]Guillemain, Cour pontificale, p. 483; see Reg. Ph. IV, nos. 745, 1200, 1315 for other royal grants.  Property in Périgord:  AP, no. 7738.

[29]Gallia Christiana, 16 vols. (Paris, 1715-1865), I, col. 139.
Hugues Géraud's avarice ultimately led him to burn at the stake:
fearing conviction for embezzlement and simony, he sought the murder
of John XXII through poison and witchcraft; see Mollat, Popes at
Avignon, p. 12.

[30]Reg. Ph. IV, no. 1188 (1310); AP, no. 3192.

[31]HL, IX, 116, 346-347; XII, 302.  The marriage in 1317 of Bernard's
sister to the nephew of Pope John XXII provides an indication of the
family's standing (HL, IX, 418); Bernard was also allied by marriage
to the Colonna Cardinals who feuded with Pope Boniface VIII:  J.
McNamara, Gilles Aycelin The Servant of Two Masters (Syracuse, 1973),
p. 90.

[32]Bernard's father took part in the war with Aragon in 1285 together
with his cousin Bertrand de l'Isle-Jourdain:  Le Coy de la Marche,
Les relations politiques de la France avec le royaume de Majorque, I
(Paris, 1892), 247-249; Comptes royaux 1285-1314, ed. R. Fawtier, 3
vols. (Paris, 1953-1956), nos. 10260, 11931.  Bertrand, who belonged
to a cadet branch of the family, was seneschal of occupied Gascony
and of Beaucaire-Nîmes in the 1300's, a signal honor since these posts
were rarely entrusted to inhabitants of the province:  J. Rogozinski,
"The Counsellors of the Seneschal of Beaucaire and Nîmes, 1250-1350,"
Speculum, XLIV (1969), 424; F. Maillard, "Mouvements administratifs...
sous Philippe le Bel," 84e Congrès national des Sociétés savants tenu
à Dijon, 1959 (1960), p. 421; J. R. Strayer, The Albigensian Crusades
(New York, 1972), p. 167.  For Bertrand's relationship to this family,
see BN Collection de Languedoc (Bénédictins), LXXXII, fol. 42;
Registres du Trésor des chartes, II:  Règnes de Louis X et Philippe
V, ed. J. Guerout (Paris, 1966), nos. 2848, 2981.  Bernard de l'Isle-
Jourdain himself received land worth five thousand pounds in 1319
when he was appointed captain on the Flemish border together with
Constable Gaucher de Chatillon and Henri de Sully, the latter at the
height of his power as the King's favorite:  Reg. Louis X et Ph. V,
nos. 2673, 2843; Pegues, Lawyers of the Last Capetians, p. 240.
Raised to the rank of count by Philip VI, the family played an important role in the defense of Languedoc during the Hundred Years' War:
G. Dupont-Ferrier, Gallia Regia ou État des officiers royaux des
bailliages et des sénéchaussées de 1328 à 1515, 6 vols. (Paris, 1942-
1961), IV, no. 13672; HL, IX, 747, 843, 944, 994; P. Contamine, Guerre,
État et société à la fin du moyen âge (Paris, 1972), pp. 60, 166.

[33]The grant in April, 1314 (Reg. Ph. IV, no. 2156) followed by only
a month the Parlement's rejection of the transaction because of Simon's
lack of nobility (AP, no. 4257).

[34]J. R. Strayer, Les Gens de Justice de Languedoc sous Philippe le
bel (Toulouse, 1970), p. 57; Rogozinski, "Counsellors," pp. 430-431.

[35]In addition to Jean Marc and Hugues de la Porte, one other man
was ennobled (Pierre Roche:  below, note 77) of the some two hundred,
most not noble, appointed to legal offices in the five sénéchaussées

of Languedoc between 1280 and 1320; see Strayer, Gens de justice, pp.
21, 32, 34. The judicial system that was created during the reign
of Philip the Fair included a major judge (judex major), who heard
appeals from the "ordinary judges" in the local courts and received
certain cases in first instance, and at least one royal advocate and
several royal proctors to look after the interests of the crown in
each sénéchaussée: J. Rogozinski, "Ordinary and Major Judges,"
Studia Gratiana, XV (1972), 589-612.

[36] Strayer, Gens de justice, p. 26.

[37] Legum professor at the University of Montpellier and judge of the
municipal court in 1292, 1299, 1301, 1302, and 1305: Rogozinski,
"Counsellors," p. 431. The judge was appointed by the consuls and
not by the king of Majorca as stated by Strayer, Gens de Justice, p.
60; see A. R. Lewis, "Seigneurial Administration in Twelfth-Century
Montpellier," Speculum, XXII (1947), 65-66; J. Baumel, Histoire d'une
Seigneurie du Midi de la France, II (Montpellier, 1971), pp. 65-71.
Jean was held in high regard by the town's wealthiest citizens; he
acted as executor of their wills and advised them on commercial transactions and property transfers: AM Montpellier BB-1, no. 119; BB-2,
nos. 435, 458-463, 468, 499, 508-509, 568; Cartulaire de Maguelone,
ed. J. Rouquette et A. Villemagne, 5 vols. (Montpellier, 1912-1924),
III, no. 1142. With other members of the faculty, he arbitrated social
conflict in neighboring communities: AM Agde AA-1; AM Marsillargues
AA-4. Raymond Marc, major judge in the 1260's and royal enquêter in
Nîmes and the Gévaudan: AD Gard E-180; Ménard, Nismes, I, preuves,
nos. 67, 71, 79; A. Maisonobe, Mémoire relatif au paréage de 1307
conclu entre l'évêque Guillaume Durand II et le roi Philippe-le-Bel
(Mende, 1896), pp. 15-18, 491-492, 498-499.

[38] Rogozinski, "Counsellors," p. 431; he acted as lieutenant of the
seneschal in October, 1311: AN P-1397[2], no. 578.

[39] Reg. Ph. IV, no. 1273 (October, 1310). For this incident, L. J.
Thomas, "Montpellier entre la France et l'Aragon pendant la première
moitié du XIVe siècle," Monspeliensia, I (1928-1929), 8-13. E. Brown
discusses the legal issues raised by such an egregious abuse of proc-
torial powers in "Representation and Agency Law in the Later Middle
Ages," Viator, III (1972), 355-356.

[40] Thomas, op. cit., p. 15. He was removed ostensibly because of
ordinances forbidding a judge to hold office in the province of his
birth; but this rule had been ignored for half a century: J. Fesler,
"French Field Administration: The Beginnings," Comparative Studies
in Society and History, V (1966), 92; J. R. Strayer, On the Medieval
Origins of the Modern State (Princeton, 1970), p. 51 and note 44;
Rogozinski, "Counsellors," pp. 430-433. A special copy of the letter
of dismissal was sent to the consuls who also accused Marc of extortion while major judge: AM Montpellier, Grand Chartrier, no. 419;
AN X[2a]2, fol. 49[v]; AP, nos. 5046, 5157. Strayer (Gens de justice,
p. 171) has Marc in Toulouse from 1317 to 1322; he is last mentioned
in Carcassonne in 1325: C. Douais, L'Inquisition: Ses origines,

sa procédure (Paris, 1906), p. 314.

[41] Reg. Ph. IV, nos. 1488, 1509 (both 1312). Hugues' resignation as royal proctor in June, 1317 (Reg. L. X et Ph. V, no. 1103) may thus be connected to consular outrage at Jean Marc; he had acquired a good deal of property in Montpellier through the exercise of his office, which he held simultaneously with various ordinary judgeships: Strayer, Gens de justice, pp. 67, 76, 87. Guillaume de Conques as consul or mayor (bajulus) of Montpellier: A. C. Germain, Histoire de la commune de Montpellier, 3 vols. (Montpellier, 1851), I, pr. 25.

[42] Reg. Ph. IV, nos. 492, 1055.

[43] Pegues, Lawyers, pp. 101-103, 217. For Plaisians, also A. Bardon, "Listes chronologiques pour servir a l'histoire de la ville d'Alais," Mémoires de l'Académie de Nîmes, 7e série, XV (1892), 88.

[44] See, for example, no. 1482 (1311) for Honoré Firmin as Plaisian's representative.

[45] Reg. Ph. IV, no. 1043; ed. HL, X, no. 138. See Pegues, Lawyers, p. 217; and, for the Barrian family, Comptes royaux 1285-1314, nos. 9000-9001.

[46] J. R. Strayer, "Philip the Fair--A 'Constitutional King,'" American Historical Review, LXII (1956), 31.

[47] Reg. Louis X et Ph. V, no. 149 (June, 1315).

[48] Reg. L. X et Ph. V, no. 155 (May, 1315). Resident in Toulouse in the 1320's and in 1317 when royal enquêteur: AP, nos. 4557, 7865; Comptes royaux 1314-1328, ed. F. Maillard, 2 vols. (Paris, 1961), nos. 485, 1612, 3262.

[49] HF, XXIV.1, p. 203*.

[50] Ibid.; Reg. Ph. IV, no. 1915. See R. Fiétier, "Le choix des baillis et sénéchaux aux XIIIe et XIVe siècles (1250-1350)," Mémoires de la Société pour l'Histoire du Droit et des Institutions des anciens pays bourguignons, comtois et romands, XXIX (1968-1969), 270-271.

[51] Reg. L. X et Ph. V, nos. 165, 166b (June, 1315); Ménard, Nismes, VII, 631; Cartulaire de Maguelone, no. 1383.

[52] Reg. L. X et Ph. V, nos. 50, 166 (June, 1315); AP, no. 4137; Les Olim ou registres des arrêts, ed. A. Beugnot, 3 vols. in 4 (1839-1848), III, 793, no. 78. Guillaume de Mussy as royal enquêteur: Mignon, no. 1966 (1298); Reg. Ph. IV, nos. 234 (1305), 235 (1303); cf. also AP, nos. 2786-2787 (1292), 6867 (1322).

[53] The royal letters name fifty-two individuals, but twelve were directly related so that only forty-one families actually joined the nobility. Five men can not be identified: Séguin Leutart (Reg. L.

X et Ph. V, no. 311; February, 1317), Collard de Noella (no. 1840, April, 1318), Laurence Saunier (no. 2012, May, 1318), Aimeri de Martellis (no. 2883, December, 1319), Herbert Bellant (no. 3500, June, 1321). The last named was Poitevin, and Séguin Leutart also came from southern France.

[54]Reg. Ph. V, no. 1690 (January, 1318), no. 1834 (April, 1318). Raoul de Macart was guard of the fairs of Champagne as was also the son of Gaucher de Châtillon: Mignon, no. 88 (1315-1316); Reg. Ph. V, nos. 3406 (1317), 3297 (1320); cf. P. Lehugeur, Philippe le Long roi de France....Le mécanisme du gouvernement (Paris, 1931), p. 296. Under Philip the Fair, he had collected taxes for the Flemish campaign of 1298: Mignon, pp. 102, 165, 176. Jacques de La Noë was bailiff and enquêteur-réformateur for Parlement: Reg. Ph. V, no. 2881; Comptes 1314-1328, no. 231; Lehugeur, Mécanisme du gouvernement, p. 304; cf. R. Cazelles, La société politique et la crise de la royauté sous Philippe de Valois (Paris, 1958), p. 450.

[55]Cazelles, Société politique, pp. 36-37. Anseau de Joinville, son of the historian of Saint Louis, was seneschal of Champagne, an office hereditary in his family since 1152; he returned to power in the 1340's as a member with Miles de Noyers of the secret council and the chambre des comptes: Reg. Ph. V, nos. 2124, 2616; Cazelles, Soc. pol., pp. 121-126; J. Longnon in Institutions françaises, ed. Fawtier, I (1957), p. 130; R. Rider, "Vie et survie de familles illustres," Le Moyen âge, LXXIX (1973), 252-253. The family of Gaucher de Châtillon-Porcien, constable of France since 1302, was also among the most prestigious of Champagne: Cazelles, Soc. pol., pp. 285-286; Longnon, op. cit., p. 131.

[56]Reg. Ph. V, nos. 409, 1003 (March, 1317); AP, no. 6687 (1322) for accusations of violence against the cathedral chapter of Toul.

[57]Reg. Ph. V, no. 78 (May, 1317). Nos. 11, 22, 241 for the relationship to the Clermont-Nesle, correcting W. Newman, Les seigneurs de Nesle en Picardie, 2 vols. (Philadelphia, 1971), I, 79; intermarriage between the two families was frequent throughout the thirteenth century (Newman, I, 70-71; II, 335-342, no. 212).

[58]Reg. Ph. V, no. 1906 (May, 1318); Lehugeur, Mécanisme de gouvernement, pp. 314-315; A. Artonne, Le mouvement de 1314 et les chartes provinciales de 1315 (Paris, 1912), p. 210.

[59]Guilleman, Cour pontificale, p. 134; Mollat, Popes at Avignon, p. 253.

[60]Reg. Ph. V, nos. 1383-1383b (September and October, 1316). Gifts to Pierre Duèse and to the nephews of John XXII, P. Lehugeur, Histoire de Philippe le Long (Paris, 1897), pp. 201-202.

[61]Reg. Ph. V, no. 610 (September, 1317); Pegues, Lawyers of the Last Capetians, pp. 233-244.

[62]Dravasa, "Vivre noblement"; Bitton, French Nobility in Crisis (cited above, notes 12 and 15).

[63]J. B. Henneman, Royal Taxation in Fourteenth Century France (Princeton, 1971), pp. 15-16.

[64]Reg. Ph. V, no. 3146. See Rogozinski, "Counsellors," p. 436; he held the relatively unimportant judgeship of Alès from 1308 to 1311: AD Lozère G-755; AM Nîmes BB-1.

[65]For the fourteenth century, note 87, below, and Rogozinski, "Counsellors," note 77. The de Godols were judges for the counts of Toulouse in the twelfth century and took part in the local and regional assemblies that regulated matters of potential dispute: Ménard, Nismes, VII, preuves, p. 720; I, preuves, pp. 44, 68; cf. A. R. Lewis, "Popular Assemblies and the Charter of Liberties of Montpellier in 1202," Proceedings of the Society for the History of Representative Institutions (Budapest, 1972). A Guillaume de Godols jurisperitus was among the first major judges of the sénéchaussée following the conquest of Languedoc by France: Ménard, I, pr. 59; R. Michel, L'Administration royale dans la sénéchaussée de Beaucaire au temps de Saint Louis (Paris, 1910), pp. 406, 412; AM Nîmes BB-1; cf. P. Tisset, "Placentin et l'enseignement du droit à Montpellier," Recueil de Mémoires et travaux...d'histoire du droit et des institutions des anciens pays de droit écrit, II (1951), 93; E. Bligny-Bondurand, Les coutumes de Saint Gilles (Paris, 1915), p. 136. The highest judicial post was again held in 1260 by Raymond de Godols who remained a member of the seneschal's council into the 1280's (Rogozinski, "Counsellors," p. 429) when he was replaced by Guillaume de Godols legum doctor: Cartulaire de Maguelone, no. 1116; A. C. Germain, Histoire du commerce de Montpellier, 2 vols. (Montpellier, 1861), I, 405; Les Olim, III.2, p. 1136, no. 55; AM Nîmes GG-1; AM Aimargues FF-4.

[66]The letter (Reg. Ph. V, no. 3022) was addressed to Gérard Imbert, royal vicar of Uzès in 1324 (Comptes royaux 1314-1328, no. 5387), and to the sons and grandsons of Bertrand Imbert, jurisperitus and judge of Uzès in 1264, councillor of the seneschal in 1268: Ménard, Nismes, I, pr. 67; Michel, Administration royale, pr. 44; A. Eysette, Histoire administrative de Beaucaire, II (1889), pr. 11. Bertrand was consul of Nîmes in 1264, 1277, 1283, and possibly in 1293; Gérard Imbert consul in 1270: Ménard, I, pr. 67, 74; AM Nîmes FF-1, NN-1. Bernard Imbert, also jurisperitus, at the royal assizes in 1262 (AD Gard, G-760, H-167) and at those in Saint Gilles in 1266 (H-888).

[67]Reg. Ph. V, no. 3111 (April, 1320). Germain, Commerce, I, pr. 71 for Pierre at the assizes of the sénéchaussée; Rogozinski, "Counsellors," note 59 for Grunerius de Thome, advocatus regis in the 1290's.

[68]Guillaume Durand, bishop of Mende and nephew of the author of the Speculum judiciale, concluded the pariage in 1307 that definitely united the Gévaudan to the crown: A. Maisonobe, op. cit. (above, note 37); J. R. Strayer, "La noblesse du Gévaudan et le paréage de

1307," Revue Gévaudan, XIII (1967), 66-71. The family of the bishop of Montpellier, André de Frédol, were also held in high regard by the Capetians and the papacy; the bishoprics of Béziers and Montpellier and other valuable benefices went from uncle to nephew virtually as family property: Guillemain, Cour pontificale, p. 269; Histoire littéraire de la France, XXXIV (Paris, 1914), 62-68.

[69]C. V. Langlois, "Pons d'Aumelas," Bibliothèque de l'École des Chartes, LII (1891), 260.

[70]Rogozinski, "Counsellors," p. 424. Chancellor for Philip V as Count of Poitiers and royal chancellor in 1316 and 1317, Pierre d'Arrabloy became cardinal in the latter year but remained in Paris and was executor of the king's will. Pegues, Lawyers of the Last Capetians, p. 195; Guillemain, Cour pontificale, p. 197; L. Perrichet, La Grande Chancellerie de la France (Paris, 1912), pp. 533-534.

[71]Rogozinski, "Ordinary and Major Judges," pp. 608-609.

[72]Reg. Ph. V, no. 3310 (December, 1320); Jacques Enguillebert's patron was Raymond I de Baux-Avellino, not Raymond II as stated by the editor. The de Baux were involved from the 1260's in the Italian adventures of the Angevin Kings of Naples; they were connected by marriage to the Dauphin of Vienne and also to Pope Clement V and twice held the bishopric of Arles: S. Runciman, The Sicilian Vespers (Penguin: Bungay, 1960), p. 91, and note 94 below; Guillemain, Cour pontificale, p. 168; P. Fournier, Le Royaume d'Arles et Vienne 1138-1378 (Paris, 1891), p. 408; see p. 382 for Philip V's ambivalent policy toward Italy and Provence. Rogozinski, "Counsellors," p. 424 for Agout de Baux, Captain-General of Languedoc in the 1340's.

[73]Reg. Ph. V, no. 3586 (August, 1321); Ménard, Nismes, VII, 615; II, pr. 22.

[74]Pegues, Lawyers of the Last Capetians, pp. 217-218.

[75]Reg. Ph. V, nos. 3542-43 (July, 1321); Comptes royaux 1285-1314, no. 16527.

[76]Reg., no. 3166 (June, 1320).

[77]Reg., no. 1628 (December, 1317); Strayer, Gens de justice, pp. 116, 118-119.

[78]Reg., nos. 3064-66, 3076; HL, IX, 379.

[79]Strayer, Gens de justice, pp. 147-148; A. Gouron, "Diffussion des consulats méridionaux et expansion du droit romain," Bibliothèque de l'École des Chartes, CXXI (1963), 26-75.

[80]Reg., no. 2756 (June, 1319); below, note 85.

[81]Reg., no. 1971 (November, 1318); Lehugeur, Mécanisme de

gouvernement, p. 254.

[82] Reg., no. 334 (February, 1317).  Commissioned in 1315 (Mignon, no. 2022) and possibly earlier, since there are few records remaining from the first years of the customs service.  We do know that its chief officers were well paid,and Arnaud de Portal also received in 1317 a life pension of thirty pounds a year (Reg., nos. 908, 1017).  See J. R. Strayer, "Pierre de Chalons and the Origins of the French Custom Service," Festschrift Percy Ernst Schramm, I (Wiesbaden, 1964), 334-339.

[83] Le Vernet (Haute Garonne, c^on Auterive); Reg., no. 3253 (October, 1320), confirmed no. 3384.  See Mignon, no. 2535; and for the Counts of Auvergne-Boulogne:  HF, XXIV.1*; A. Bossuat in Institutions françaises, ed. R. Fawtier, I, 106-107; E. Boutaric, Saint Louis et Alphonse de Poitiers (Paris, 1870), pp. 112, 173; Dictionnaire de Biographie française, IV (1948), 757-758.

[84] Dict. de Biog. française, VI (1954), 1374.  As bishop of Tournai, Guy de Boulogne assisted with the conviction of Pierre de Latilly at a politically motivated trial so dishonest and unjust that Gilles de Aycelin, royal councillor since 1288, refused to attend lest he act as "an evil man and a prevaricator and against my conscience and honor" (Pegues, Lawyers, p. 71; McNamara, Giles Aycelin, p. 197).

[85] Reg., no. 1146; AP, nos. 4504 (1316), 5856 (1319).

[86] Viguier at a salary of 200 pounds from 1321 to 1331:  Comptes royaux 1314-1328, no. 1060; BN Collection de Languedoc (Bénédictins), LXXXI, fol. 270^v.  Béziers was the largest of the southern vicariates (it comprised the three dioceses of Béziers, Agde, and Lodève); and viguiers had important military and administrative responsibilities: J. R. Strayer, "Viscounts and Viguiers under Philip the Fair," Speculum, XXXVIII (1963), 245-246.

[87] Whatever was the case with the lower classes, most of the élite families discussed here were extended in the technical sense of that term; the urban residence of the de Godols of Nîmes, for example, witnessed in 1362 the political assassination of more than six members of the family representing at least three generations (Ménard, Nismes, II, preuves, pp. 241, 258).  They were concerned for the success of the entire lineage and placed great significance on ties through the female line.  Because of the state of the evidence, it is often impossible to trace out all the ramifications of familial influence.  As Georges Duby has shown for an earlier period (Annales E.S.C., XXVII [1972], 805), the task is made more difficult by the aristocratic tradition of repeating given names according to some code of rules "qui peut être n'étaient pas absolument contraignantes à l'époque, en tout case qui ne sont pas claires pour nous."

[88] Above, note 32.

[89] Reg., nos. 2953-54 (December, 1319):  Villebrumier (Tarn et

Garonne, arr. Montauban) was at this time attached to the jugerie of
Villelongue in the sénéchaussée of Toulouse.  Pierre Grimoard was
enquêteur into fiefs and mainmortes in 1283 (Mignon, no. 1873); Pope
Urban V came from a branch of this family that had migrated to the
Gévaudan (Guillemain, Cour pontificale, p. 162, note 375).

[90]Reg., no. 2908 (December, 1319).  It seems likely that the noble
Assalide de Noblat, mother of Guillaume Daniel, had previously been
married to a son of Bernard de l'Isle-Jourdain's grandfather and his
second wife (HL, IX, 118).  Daniel was also related in some way to
Guiraud Guy, lord of Cabanes, then seneschal of Toulouse following
F. Maillard, "Les mouvements administratifs des baillis et des sénéchaux de 1314 à 1328," Bulletin philologique et historique année
1963, II (1966), 901.  Durand Grégoire of Riom in the Auvergne, whose
mother was reputed noble, similarly received a patent in April, 1321
(Reg., no. 3476); he and his son had paid fines in 1293-1294 for
possessing noble fiefs:  Comptes royaux 1285-1314, nos. 8447-48.

[91]Reg., nos. 3180 (July, 1320), 3184,3244.  Nicholas' brother-in-
law, Pierre de Châtelus, was abbot of Saint Serge in Angers.  For
Cardinal Aimeric de Châtelus, Guillemain, Cour pontificale, pp. 188,
196, 230.

[92]Reg., no. 3544 (July, 1321); he was lord in part of Bournazel.

[93]According to Léopold Delisle (HF, XXIV.1, 203*-204*), Philip V
as Count of Poitiers named him judge of his lands in the Limousin in
1314 and appointed him bailiff or seneschal (both titles were used)
in 1315.  After the reunion of the Limousin to the sénéchaussée of
Poitou in 1316, Daniel was judge of Maumont and acted as lieutenant
of the seneschal.  See also the references (p. 190*) to Arnaud Daniel,
guard of the seal of the sub-bailiwick of Laron in 1289.

[94]Reg., no. 3284 (November, 1320):  ennoblement of Arnaud Saumade
at the request of his brother Gaillard; for the latter, Gallia
Christiana, I, 575.  Bernard Saumade, legum doctor and councillor of
the seneschal of Rouergue (Reg. Ph. IV, nos. 512, 1104; AP, no. 6428),
had earlier married the oldest daughter of Gualhard de Béral, a middling lord in the neighboring sénéchaussée of Quercy: F. Aubert,
Foreword to Guillaume de Breuil: Stilus curie parlamenti (Paris,
1909), p. ii.  Philip of Tarente was the third son of Charles of
Naples and grandson of Charles of Anjou, the brother of Saint Louis
whose ambitions in Sicily led to the Sicilian Vespers and the disastrous Crusade against Aragon; he carried on the family traditions by
paying 40,000 pounds for the Duke of Burgundy's illusory rights to
the Eastern Empire:  Guillemain, Cour pontificale, p. 245; Cazelles,
Société politique, p. 110.

[95]Reg., no. 3268 (November, 1320).  De Breuil was notorious among
the advocates before Parlement for his greed and lack of scruples;
he was related to the Saumade family through his marriage to the
younger daughter of Gualhard de Béral: Aubert, op. cit., pp. ii-v.

[96]Reg. Ph. V, no. 2785; below, note 107.

[97]Reg., nos. 2855-56, 2991, 2993. Cazelles, Société politique, pp. 107-111 for a succinct summary of the interwoven transactions of the Gayte and Chauchat. The Gayte were important financial agents for Philip the Fair: Reg. Ph. IV, passim; Artonne, Le mouvement de 1314, p. 27; L. Borrelli de Serres, Recherches sur divers services publics du XIIIe au XVIIe siècle, 3 vols. (Paris, 1895-1905), III, 214. They enjoyed the complete confidence of Philip V, who named Géraud Gayte lay master in the chambre des comptes and royal receiver for the sénéchaussées of Beaucaire-Nîmes and Champagne; his brother Mathieu and Jacques Gayte were receivers for Toulouse and the Auvergne. Unable to resist the opportunities for chicanery inherent in this accumulation of offices, Géraud was forgiven currency speculation and other irregularities in 1318 (Reg., no. 3437; Pegues, Lawyers, p. 193) and died in jail in 1322 when Philip's successor proved less generous. The Chauchat continued to enjoy favor under Charles IV but were ousted by Philip VI in 1328. Both families were later restored to office with the help of the Avignese papacy, and Mathieu Gayte was royal treasurer from 1335 to 1338.

[98]Reg., nos. 2813, 3217; below, note 105.

[99]Reg., nos. 3263-63[b], 3218. Most of these letters were issued while the king was with the council at Léry, an estate in Normandy that Philippe de Villepreux gave to the queen five months later. Guarin de Senlis as royal changer at the Louvre in 1314, receiver for Philip as count of Poitiers, and royal treasurer from 1316 to 1320: Borrelli de Serres, III, 59, 80-81; Lehugeur, Mécanisme du gouvernement, pp. 216-217.

[100]Reg., nos. 3235, 3468. During the reign of Philip the Fair, Philippe de Villepreux, also known as Philippe le Convers, bore sole responsibility for the management of the royal forests throughout the kingdom and almost singlehandedly created the forest law and administration of France. Because of this invaluable accomplishment and his relationship to the royal family (he was Philip IV's godson), Villepreux escaped the trials that brought down Marigny and others even though he was proved guilty of financial malfeasance in office. His assignments under Louis X were few and unimportant, but Philip V restored him to full power and seems to have trusted him totally: effectively the first master of the Réquêtes de l'hôtel, he ordered more letters out of the chancery than any other member of the royal council. See Pegues, Lawyers, pp. 124-140; Lehugeur, Mécanisme du gouvernement, p. 62; Guillois, Maitres des requêtes, pp. 219-221.

[101]Reg., no. 3254. Perhaps originally from Champagne, Jacques de Vertus was a citizen and property-owner in Paris when ennobled: Reg., no. 3382; Documents parisiens du règne de Philippe VI de Valois, ed. J. Viard, 2 vols. (Paris, 1899-1900), I, 267. He was a notary in the chancery under Philip IV (Reg. Ph. IV, s. v.); a list of 1316 includes him among the members of Parlement (AP, no. 4490B), perhaps erroneously since he was again active in the chancery the following year

(Lehugeur, Mécanisme, p. 99).

[102] Reg., no. 3520; Comptes royaux 1285-1314, nos. 23928, 23971, 23976-77, 23993, 24002, 24074, 24083. Bourgeois of Paris where his father Étienne Haudry founded a hospital for women in 1306: Reg. Ph. IV, s. v.; Reg. Ph. V, no. 2252.

[103] Originally from the region around Gisors, Guillaume du Bois became bailiff of Caux from 1305 to 1311 (HF, XXIV.1, p. 115*; Reg. Ph. IV, s. v.). Appointed treasurer in 1311 at the suggestion of Enguerran de Marigny, a fellow Norman of noble birth who dominated the royal administration during the last years of the reign of Philip the Fair, he shared Marigny's fortunes and was imprisoned in 1315 for peculation and treason. Unlike Marigny, he escaped hanging and was again treasurer from 1317 to 1320. Under Charles IV, he was bailiff of Meaux. See Borrelli de Serres, III, 48, 64, 70, 78; J. Favier, Un conseiller de Philippe le Bel, Enguerran de Marigny (Paris, 1963), p. 99.

[104] Pegues, Lawyers, p. 125; he was born in Villepreux, a small village not far from Paris (Reg. Ph. V, nos. 3060, 3557).

[105] The des Essarts were among the thirty-six families of hereditary "peers" controlling the municipal government of Rouen. Martin des Essarts was himself mayor in 1310; he was subsequently accused of stealing public funds but was found innocent by a royal commission composed of other members of the royal council: Reg. Ph. IV, no. 2199; Reg. Ph. V, no. 3232; A. Chéruel, Histoire de Rouen pendant l'époque communale, 2 vols. (Rouen, 1833-1844), I, 217-224. Martin was in Paris by 1313 when he became attached to the hôtel de roi through marriage to the daughter of the royal treasurer Baudouin du Roye (Reg. Ph. IV, no. 1339). He was appointed to the chambre des comptes by Philip V; his brother Pierre was receiver for the queen, royal argentier in 1325 and 1326, and master in the comptes after 1336: Cazelles, Soc. pol., pp. 68, 181, 219; Borrelli de Serres, III, 54, 208. The latter was imprisoned and fined 50,000 pounds by the Estates-General of 1347.

[106] Jean Haudry continued to furnish the royal household with cloth; Guarin de Senlis sold jewelry to the crown through his son-in-law Pierre des Essarts; and Geoffroi de Fleury put his governmental connections to good account as a money lender and tax-farmer: Comptes royaux 1314-1328, no. 13886; Cazelles, Soc. pol., pp. 182, 313, 392-393, 396. All three called themselves "bourgeois de Paris," and Geoffroy de Fleury was échevin in 1328: Cazelles, pp. 293-295; Dravasa, "Vivre noblement," p. 154.

[107] The careers of eight of the ten follow this pattern. Jean Billouart first entered the royal administration under Louis X, Geoffroi de Fleury under Philip V. Billouart was master of forests for Charles of Valois who had him appointed first royal argentier and war-treasurer in 1315 and master in the chambre des comptes in February, 1316: Borrelli de Serres, III, 208; Comptes royaux 1314-1328, nos. 13541, 13543, 14468-76; Cazeles, Soc. pol., pp. 58-59. He was

unusually competent or politically astute, for he managed to be highly regarded by all three of the last Capetians. He is called "familiar du roi" under Philip V who appointed him to Parlement in January, 1317: AN K-40, No. 11; Guillois, Maitres des requêtes, p. 264. He was treasurer almost continuously from 1319 to 1326; argentier from 1326 and 1327; and in the latter year again at the chambre des comptes: Borrelli de Serres, III, 82, 103, 208; Reg. Ph. V, no. 2823; Comptes royaux, nos. 13547, 14216-435. The career of Geoffroi de Fleury was more typically checkered. He was Philip V's argentier as count of Poitiers and was carried over to the royal household. Removed by . Charles IV, he was brought back into the royal administration by Philip VI as treasurer (1336-1339) and master in the comptes (1340): Borrelli de Serres, II, 49; III, 104, 208; Cazelles, Soc. pol., pp. 126, 295.

[108]Lehugeur, Histoire de Philippe le Long, passim; C. H. Taylor, "French Assemblies and Subsidy in 1321," Speculum, XLIII (1968), 217-218; E. Brown, "Assemblies of French Towns in 1316," Speculum, XLVI (1971), 297.

[109]Barthélemy ("Lettres d'anoblissement," p. 202) cites a grant of 1334 by the duke of Bourbon; others are known from the dukes of Bar, Burgundy, Brittany, Flanders, and Orleans: Bloch, "Quelques jalons de recherche," p. 374; G. Dupont-Ferrier, Étude sur les institutions financières, II (Paris, 1932), p. 178; cf. J. Mundy, Europe in the High Ages (New York, 1974), p. 274.

[110]Bartier, Légistes et gens de finances, pp. 195-197.

[111]The chancery registers have hundreds of examples; e.g., Reg. L. X et Ph. V, nos. 377, 386, 396, 584, 1693, 1759, 1789, 2175, 3134, 3228-29, 3308, 3381, 3407, 3582.

[112]As Dupont-Ferrier indicates (Instit. financières, II, 162-163), virtually every ordinance establishing a general tax specifically stated that nobles were not to be exempted. Toward the end of the century, nobles serving with the royal armies were occasionally exempted from some royal war taxes: Dupont-Ferrier, p. 177; Henneman, Royal Taxation, pp. 316-317; La Guerre de Cent Ans vue à travers les registres du Parlement, ed. P. C. Timbal et al. (Paris, 1961), pp. 19-24, 397. But neither the southern patricians nor the fiscal officials ennobled by Philip V had any intention of taking up arms. The available evidence suggests that noble citizens and residents held liable for municipal taxes: Timbal, Guerre de Cent Ans, p. 233; A. Bardon, Histoire de la ville de Alais de 1341 (Nîmes, 1896), pr. 22; Ménard, Nismes, III, pr. 24, p. 116; B. Guenée, Tribunaux et gens de justice dans le bailliage de Senlis (Paris, 1963), pp. 411-412; G. Espinas, Les finances de la commune de Douai (Paris, 1902), p. 48; J. Guerout, "Fiscalité, topographie et démographie à Paris," Bibliothèque de l'École des Chartes, CXXX (1972), 82-84.

[113]Dognon, Institutions de Languedoc, pp. 155-161; J. Mundy and P. Riesenberg, The Medieval Town (Princeton, 1958), pp. 57-58. Strayer,

Gens de justice, p. 34 for nobles who were royal judges.

[114]Ménard, Nismes, II, pr. 52; cf. W. M. Bowsky, "The Impact of the Black Death upon Sienese Government," Speculum, XXXIX (1964), 28; E. Kantorowicz in Twelfth-Century Europe and the Foundations of Modern Society, ed. M. Glagett et al. (Madison, 1961); Guenée, Tribunaux de Senlis, p. 413.

[115]A. R. Lewis, loc. cit., note 65 above; The Development of Southern French and Catalan Society 718-1050 (Austin, 1965), pp. 361-373; Rogozinski, "Counsellors," 426-428.

[116]HL, VIII, no. 547; Dravasa, "Vivre noblement," p. 142; cf. Ménard, Nismes, III, pr. 24.

[117]Unlike most of the financial advisors ennobled by Philip V (above, note 106), the des Essarts of Rouen did use the titles of nobility elicited from Philip V; see Cheruel, Rouen, II, 542 (1376). An heir of Jean Marc of Montpellier styled himself noble in 1329 when he recognized the bishop of Montpellier as lord over some of his lands (Rogozinski, "Counsellors," p. 433); but the title was not recognized by municipal courts, which denied him exemption from taxation five years later: AM Montpellier, Grand Chartrier, no. 3235; Actes du Parlement de Paris 1328-1350, I, ed. H. Furgeot (Paris, 1920), nos. 3974, 4494. The direct descendants of Guillaume de Conques (note 41 above) were styled noble or donzel throughout the fourteenth century, but other branches of the family continued to use the title of bourgeois: Combes, Bourgeois de Montpellier, p. 104. The Enguillebert of Beaucaire held municipal office as nobles into the fifteenth century: Eysette, Beaucaire, II, 70-72, 205, 211. In Nîmes, the nobility of the de Godols, challenged in 1328 (AM Nîmes NN-1), was fully accepted by the 1360's: M. Gouron, "Estimation des biens des nobles nîmois en 1369-1379," Mémoires et travaux...de droit écrit, II (1951), 31. Some of the Imbert were treated as nobles but not others, and all of the descendants of Pierre de Thome were enrolled among the non-noble citizens: Ménard, Nismes, II, pr. 91.

## Chapter 20

[1]John Beeler, Warfare in Feudal Europe, 730-1200 (Ithaca, 1971), pp. 219-221.

[2]Honoré Bovet, l'Arbre des Batailles, p. 123, quoted in Philippe Contamine, Guerre, état et société à la fin du moyen âge: études sur les armées des rois de France (Paris and The Hague, 1972), p. 171.

[3]F. M. Powicke and C. R. Cheney, eds., Councils and Synods, II, with Other Documents Relating to the English Church (2 vols., Oxford, 1964), II, 751-752. Cf. Gratian, Decretum, Pars IIa, causa 23, quaestio viii; and Extravagantes, III, 1, 2, 5; V, 25, 39. See also, Gabriel Le Bras, Institutions ecclésiastiques de la Chrétienté médiéval (Paris, 1959-64), pp. 165, 278. Henry Despenser, the militant bishop of Norwich (1370-1406), who led the so-called "crusade" against the Flemish adherents of the anti-pope in 1383, received a blanket dispensation from Boniface IX in 1390, since the bishop necessarily violated the canons by fighting at the head of a crusading army, Calendar of Entries in the Papal Registers: Papal Letters (hereafter, C.P.L.) (London, 1904), IV (1362-1404), 325.

[4]Contamine, p. 172, nn. 92-93, names eight bishops, an abbot, and an archdeacon who served in the French armies during the Hundred Years' War, at least two of whom served as knights banneret with other knights and archers in their private companies.

[5]Heinrich S. Denifle, La désolation des églises, monastères et hôpitaux en France pendant la guerre de cent ans (Paris, 1897-99), p. 187, quoted in Contamine, p. 171.

[6]Contamine, p. 173. Thomas Rymer, Foedera (Record Commission Edition, London, 1830), III, ii, 98 (hereafter, Foedera, Record ed.).

[7]Calendar of the Close Rolls, 1368-1374, pp. 38-39 (hereafter, C.C.R.). This entry is a good translation of the Latin writ as given by Thomas Rymer, Foedera (17 vols., London, 1704-17), VI, 631 (hereafter, Foedera).

[8]There is a change in the fixed language of the writs after that of 1400. The writ of 1400 is the last example of the form used, with only one notable exception, on every occasion since 1369, quoted above (see n. 9). The writ issued by Richard II in 1386 is not to be found in any published collections, but it is recorded in London, Guildhall MS. 9531/3, Register of Robert Braybrooke, bishop of London (1381-1404), f. 369[v] (hereafter, MS. Reg. Braybrooke [London]). It is in the form of a privy seal letter (in Franch), dated September 18, and its wording is unique, for it merely orders the bishop to come "sanz delaye" before the king, with all his clergy, armed for war. The 1415 and 1418 writs order the bishop "to assemble with all possible speed the able and fencible clergy of his diocese, regular and secular, exempt and non-exempt, within liberties and without, causing and

compelling them to be arrayed and furnished with arms according to
their estate and means, sparing none, and keeping them in array so as
to be ready to resist the malice of the enemies of the realm and church
of England and of the Catholic faith when need be...." (Foedera, IX,
253-254). The writs issued by Edward III to the prior of the Hospitallers to array his order June 18, 1373 (Foedera, Record ed., II,
ii, 986), which, except for the one issued to the Abbot of St. Albans
in 1400, is the only one issued to any prelate save a bishop or an
archbishop, and to the bishop of Winchester to array his clergy "in
the county [sic] of Southampton," June 20, 1373 (Foedera, VII, 27),
are each unique. The language of the writ issued by Henry IV on
July 14, 1402, to the archbishop of Canterbury to array his clergy
in co. Kent, to the bishop of Norwich for his clergy in co. Norfolk,
and to the bishop of Exeter for his clergy in co. Devon (Foedera, VII,
270), is also unique, although it is similar to the writs issued by
Henry V in 1415 and 1418 (and to that issued by Richard II to the
archbishop of York in 1381) in that it concludes with a little writ
of aid in favor of the bishop to whom it was addressed.

[9]Edward III: 1369, Foedera, VI, 631; 1372, Foedera, VI, 726; 1373,
Foedera, VII, 27; Richard II: 1377, Foedera, VII, 162; 1381, Foedera,
Record ed., IV, 127; 1385, C.C.R., 1381-1385, pp. 551-552; 1386, MS.
Reg. Braybrooke (London), f. 369ᵛ; Henry IV: 1400, Foedera, VIII,
120; 1402, Foedera, VII, 270; Henry V: 1415, Foedera, IX, 253-254;
1418, Foedera, IX, 60 .

[10]See Bertie Wilkinson, Constitutional History of England in the
Fifteenth Century (1399-1485) (London, 1964), pp. 366-367.

[11]Foedera, Record ed., III, ii, 961-962; and London, Public Record
Office (hereafter, P.R.O.), Miscellanea of the Chancery, C. 47/2/49,
no. 37. Cf. Foedera, Record ed., III, ii, 988.

[12]Foedera, VII, 27: ...scientes pro certo quod, si in arraiatione
cleri vestri predicti repidi vel remissi fueritis, dictum clerum per
laicos arraiari et ibidem duci faciemus, ex causa supradicta.

[13]The Reverend William Hudson, "A Commission to Arm and Array the
Clergy in 1400," Sussex Archaeological Collections, LI (1908), 153-
162.

[14]Cecil Deedes, ed., The Episcopal Register of Robert Rede, O.P.,
Lord Bishop of Chichester, 1397-1415 (2 vols., Sussex Record Society,
n.p., 1908 and 1910), I, 76.

[15]Hudson, pp. 159-162. Cf. C.C.R., 1399-1402, p. 123, and Foedera,
VIII, 123. This writ is virtually verbatim that of Richard II issued
July 25, 1377, Foedera, VII, 162.

[16]Rotuli Parliamentorum (Record Commission edition, London, n.d.),
VIII, 302 (hereafter, Rot. Parl.). Cf. T. F. Kirby, ed., Wykeham's
Register (2 vols., Hampshire Record Society, London, 1896 and 1899),
II, no. 17a, pp. 79-80.

[17]The expression "as the king is aware that the bishops and other prelates and all the clergy of the realm are bound to lay to their hands with other lieges for defense of the Church and realm," which is to be found in some form in many of the writs of array (e.g., C.C.R., 1381-1385, p. 552, and Foedera, VII, 120), may be a sort of reference to the consents granted by parliament and prelates in 1369.

[18]William Stubbs, eds., Select Charters, 9th ed. rev. by H.W.C. Davis (Oxford, 1913), pp. 181 and 466 (Old French), 468 (English).

[19]Foedera, VIII, 473.

[20]C.C.R., 1381-1385, pp. 551-552.  Cf. Foedera, VII, 27, dated June 20, 1373.

[21]Kirby, ed., III, Appendix I, p. 625.  The itinerary given by Kirby indicates that Wykeham did not leave his diocese during this period.  The army that accompanied Richard II to Scotland that summer was not, however, the ancient feudal host, but rather was a contract army of the sort then common.  See, N. B. Lewis, "The Last Medieval Summons of the English Feudal Levy," English Historical Review, LXXIII (1958), 1-56.

[22]Richard II ordered the abbot of Bury St. Edmunds to proceed in person with all his household and sufficient men at arms, hobelars, and archers to his estates on the coast of Suffolk, "as heretofore used to be done by him and his predecessors in time of war," as the king was informed that the French planned an invasion that summer with great force.  "The king has commanded the arrayers in that county and the sheriff not to trouble the abbot touching the arraying of men at arms, etc."  C.C.R., 1381-1385, pp. 542, 556-557.  Cf. Foedera, Record ed., III, ii, 953, the abbot of St. Augustine's, Canterbury, ordered to defend the Isle of Thanet; Foedera, VII, 27, the bishop of Winchester ordered to defend Southampton.

[23]C.W.C. Oman, The History of England from the Accession of Richard II to the Death of Richard III, 1377, 1485 (London, 1906), pp. 5-6; Richard Baker, Chronicle of the Kings of England (London, 1684), p. 137.

[24]Foedera, VII, 162.

[25]A. H. Davies, trans., William Thorne's Chronicle of St. Augustine's Abbey, Canterbury (Oxford, 1934), pp. 609, 658-659.

[26]Thomas Walsingham, Ypodigma Neustriae (Rolls Series, no. 28, pt. 7; London, 1876), p. 327.  C.W.C. Oman, p. 6, adds that the prior of Lewes was leading the shire levies of Sussex, as their proper chief, the earl of Arundel, had fled to safety in the city of London.

[27]Baker, p. 137.

[28]Foedera, Record ed., IV, 127.

[29]Calendar of Fine Rolls, 1383-1391, p. 125 (hereafter, C.F.R.).

[30]Ibid., p. 288.

[31]P.R.O., Ancient Correspondence of Chancery, S.C. 1/57, nos. 38-40, 43, 45, 46, 48, 50-55, 57, 58, 61A-B, 62, and 123. The return for the bishop of Hereford, 1415, and that of the bishop of St. Asaph, 1418, somehow became separated from their fellows and are now found in Miscellanea of the Chancery, C. 47/2/49, no. 46 and no. 11, respectively. The return for the bishop of Worcester, 1418, was also misplaced and is now found in Miscellanea of the Chancery, C. 270/13, no. 20.

[32]Rot. Parl., III, 526-527 (1404). See, Wilkinson, pp. 366-367.

[33]MS. Reg. Braybrooke (London), ff. 369$^v$-370$^r$.

[34]Ibid., f. 370$^v$.

[35]Deedes, ed., I, 76.

[36]James Raine, ed., Historiae Dunelmensis Scriptores Tres (Surtees Society, Durham, 1839), Appendix, No. CLXI, pp. clxxxiii-iv (the vicar-general's order for the array), and No. CLXII, pp. clxxxv-vii (the muster-list).

[37]E. F. Jacob, ed., The Register of Henry Chichele, Archbishop of Canterbury, 1414-1443 (Canterbury and York Society, 4 vols.; Oxford, 1943-47), IV, 129-130.

[38]T. S. Holmes, ed., The Register of Nicholas Bubwith, Bishop of Bath and Wells, 1407-1424 (2 vols., Somerset Record Society; London, 1913-14), I, no. 552, pp. 213-214.

[39]Ibid., I, no. 555, pp. 214-215; P.R.O., S.C.1/57, no. 52.

[40]Margaret Archer, ed., The Register of Bishop Philip Repingdon, 1405-1419 (2 vols., Lincoln Record Society; Lincoln, 1963), I, xliii-iv. The king specifically ordered the bishop of Lincoln not to array within the University of Oxford and the bishop of Ely not to do so within the University of Cambridge, C.C.R., 1413-1419, p. 218.

[41]Foedera, IX, 253-254. Lincoln, as well as other cathedrals, was (and Lincoln still is) surrounded by a defensive wall, making it capable of being held against the attack of enemies coming up the hill if adequate defenders were provided.

[42]P.R.O., S.C. 1/57, nos. 61A and 61B.

[43]Ibid., no. 62.

[44]See n. 31, above.

[45]P.R.O., C. 47/2/49, no. 11, the St. Asaph return for 1418, includes only two categories of armed men, <u>viros defensabiles competenter armatos cum lanceis, ut moris est</u>, and <u>architenentes defensabiles et ad bellum aptos et ydoneos</u>. The Ely returns for both 1415 and 1418 (P.R.O., S.C. 1/57, nos. 45 and 46) list <u>numerus vero personarum nostre diocesis plene armaturum omni lanceis comparencium</u>, as well as hobelars and archers. The Salisbury 1415 return (<u>ibid</u>., no. 123) includes only two categories, <u>viri cum suis lanceis armati</u> and archers. See also, May McKisack, <u>The Fourteenth Century, 1307-1399</u> (Oxford, 1959), pp. 239-240; and E. F. Jacob, <u>The Fifteenth Century, 1399-1485</u> (Oxford, 1969), p. 143.

[46]Usually called <u>architenentes</u>, but sometimes <u>sagittarii</u> and in the Durham, 1400, muster-list <u>sagittae</u> (literally, "arrows").

[47]P.R.O., S.C. 1/57, no. 57.

[48]P.R.O., C. 270/13, no. 20.

[49]P.R.O., S.C. 1/57, nos. 52 and 54.

[50]Ibid., no. 51.

[51]Ibid., no. 58.

[52]Ibid., nos. 50 and 51.

[53]At the time James H. Wylie wrote <u>The Reign of Henry V</u> (4 vols., London, 1914), the Rochester 1415 muster-list, now P.R.O., S.C. 1/57, no. 61B, must have been undiscovered, or else was unknown to him, for he refers to it as "not now preserved," Wylie, I, 479, n. 6.

[54]P.R.O., S.C. 1/57, nos. 61A and 61B (1415) and 58 (1418).

[55]F. C. Hingeston-Randolph, ed., <u>Register of Thomas de Brantyngham, Bishop of Exeter, A.D. 1370-1394</u> (2 parts, London, 1886, 1906), Part I, pp. 271-272.

[56]Ibid.

[57]Ibid., p. 272.

[58]London, Lambeth Palace Library, MS. Register of William Courtenay, archbishop of Canterbury (1381-1396), f. 65ᵛ. Cf. f. 331ᵛ.

[59]Ibid., ...<u>cum utriusque iuris tam divinam quam humanam pagina attestetur omnes tam clericos quam laicos ad defensionem proprie patrie et invasionum inimicorum pro viribus repellendam tueri</u>....

[60]Ibid.

[61]P.R.O., S.C. 1/57, nos. 61A, 61B, and 58.

$^{62}$Rot. Parl., III, 526-527.

$^{63}$P.R.O., S.C. 1/57, no. 61B, recto.

$^{64}$Ibid., but, oddly, the entry reads Archidiaconus Roffen' a$^{tus}$ (i.e., armatus or arraiatus ?) comparet per procuracionem....

$^{65}$Ibid., verso.

$^{66}$Raine, ed., Appendix, No. CLXII, pp. clxxxv-vi.

$^{67}$I have not seen this document in manuscript, and Raine's published version gives no indication of a change in handwriting, which would presumably be evident in the comparet, non comparet, etc., if they were added to a list prepared in advance.

$^{68}$This was the case in the so-called "musters of the clergy" in Elizabethan times and after. There is no evidence of any military arrays of the clergy of the sort discussed in this essay after that of 1418, nor any evidence that after that date any clergy appeared in person at the "musters of the clergy," even though they did provide the requisite weapons and sometimes money to hire soldiers. See, London, Lambeth Palace Library MS. 2009, The Fairweather Papers, a collection which contains a number of documents regarding musters of the clergy in the sixteenth and seventeenth centuries. See also, Joan Wake, ed., A Copy of Papers Relating to Musters, Beacons, Subsidies, etc. in the County of Northampton, A.D. 1586-1623 (Northamptonshire Record Soceity, n.p., 1925), pp. lxii, cxvi, 123, 126; Joan Wake, ed., The Montagu Musters Book, A.D. 1602-1623 (Northamptonshire Record Society, n.p., 1933), pp. xvii, xxvii, xxx, xxxi; and Great Britain, Historical Manuscripts Commission, Second Report (London, 1874), p. 73. It appears that during the reign of Henry VIII some clergy were required to serve by proxy if they held any lay tenements. Cf. in this context, B. Cozzens-Hardy, "A Muster Roll and Clergy List in the Hundred of Holt, ca. 1523," Norfolk Archaeology, XXII (1926), 45.

$^{69}$P.R.O., C. 255/2/12, formerly Miscellanea of the Chancery, C. 47/18/9, no. 23. Cf. C.F.R., 1383-1391, p. 125.

$^{70}$C.C.R., 1385-1389, p. 4. See also, C.C.R., 1399-1402, p. 82, dated March 30, 1400; the abbot and monks of St. Savior, Bermondsey, are granted an exemption from being arrayed by the arrayers of the bishop of Winchester, as the abbot will see to the arraying of his monks himself; and ibid., dated April 6, 1400, complete exemption from array granted to the prior and convent of Hurley, diocese of Salisbury.

$^{71}$C.C.R., 1399-1402, p. 150.

$^{72}$C.P.L., VI (1404-1415), pp. 53, 71.

$^{73}$Ibid., p. 71.

$^{74}$P.R.O., S.C. 1/57, no. 62.

$^{75}$P.R.O., C. 47/2/49, no. 46.

$^{76}$James H. Wylie quoted figures from some of the returns for 1415 in his book, The Reign of Henry V, but he made several mistakes in transcribing the figures. For example, he did not include all the clergy returned as arrayed in Lincoln. He recorded Lincoln as returning 292 hobelars and 3,632 archers in 1415, although in fact the return clearly states that the diocese returned 972 armed men (which in the 1418 return specifically included hobelars as well as "competently armed men") and 5,009 archers. Wylie also classified all the viri competenter armati as hobelars, which is not what the returns say and which gives a rather different impression of their armament. See Wylie, I, 479, n. 6.

$^{77}$James H. Ramsey, A History of the Revenues of the Kings of England, 1066-1399 (2 vols., Oxford, 1925), II, 289, on the basis of the number of clergy paying the poll tax of 1377, gives 29,161 as the total number of clergy in that year, beneficed and unbeneficed, in England and Wales, excluding the palatinates of Durham and Chester and also excluding the four orders of mendicants. Records of the poll tax of 1377 quoted in Edward L. Cutts, Parish Priests and their People in the Middle Ages in England (London, 1898), pp. 389-391, indicate that there were considerably more clergy paying the poll tax in each diocese in that year than there were clergy arrayed in the same diocese in either 1415 or 1418.

$^{78}$C.F.R., 1383-1391, pp. 125, 288.

$^{79}$MS. Reg. Braybrooke (London), f. 370.

$^{80}$Cutts, pp. 172-173: "...Robert Newley, rector of Whyttchurche and official of the archdeacon of Oxford (diocese of Lincoln), in his will made in 1412, leaves to his brother his 'best sword,'...and (in the diocese of Durham)...the vicar of Gaynford, in 1412, leaves his 'best suit of armor and all of his arrows;' and the rector of Scrayningham, in 1414, leaves a suit of armor; and the dean of the collegiate church at Auckland leaves his 'best sword and a complete suit of armor'." This vicar of Gaynford, Roger de Kirkby, also left household goods and corn to the value of £99 11s. 3d., and £36 13s. 4d. in money, according to Jacob, p. 285, who quotes from his will printed in Wills and Inventories (Surtees Society, Durham, 1833), p. 56. It should be noted that the Durham muster-list of 1400 shows the vicar of Gaynforth (i.e., Gaynford) and the dean of Auckland both among the clergy then armed and arrayed.

$^{81}$Herbert B. Workman, John Wyclif: A Study in the English Medieval Church (2 vols., Oxford, 1926), II, 303.

$^{82}$L. J. Daly, S.J., The Political Theory of John Wyclif (Chicago, 1962), p. 139, referring to Wyclif, De officio regis, p. 272, and to De civili dominio, II, xvii, 249-250.

[1] J. Leclercq, Saint Pierre Damien, ermite et homme d'église, Uomini e dottrine, VIII (Rome, 1960), is the basic work for any further study of Damian. Lec ercq himself discusses (ibid., p. 11) the distinction between a portrait and a biography. I have cited the sources in the following way: all references to works by Peter Damian will have one Arabic numeral, referring to a column in PL, CXLIV for the letters (Ep.) or CXLV for the treatises (Op.). Exception is made for Op. XIII, where the number refers to a page in P. Brezzi and B. Nardi, eds., De divina omnipotentia e altri opuscoli (Florence, 1943).

[2] Op. XX.v (449).

[3] O. J. Blum, "The Monitor of the Popes, St. Peter Damian," Studi Gregoriani, II (1947), 459-476.

[4] Ep. I.i (205-206).

[5] Ep. III.ii (289-290).

[6] Ibid.

[7] F. Neukirch, Das Leben des Petrus Damiani (Göttingen, 1875), pp. 91-117; reproduced with modifications by O. J. Blum, St. Peter Damian: His Teaching on the Spiritual Life (Washington, 1947), pp. 201-203, and by F. Dressler, Petrus Damiani, Leben und Werk, Studia Anselmiana, XXXIV (Rome, 1954), pp. 238-240. Cf. G. Lucchesi, "Clavis S. Petri Damiani," in Studi su San Pier Damiano in onore del Cardinale Amleto Giovanni Cicognani (Faenza, 1961), pp. 249-407; also his "Per una Vita di San Pier Damiani," in San Pier Damiano nel IX Centenario della morte (1072-1972), 2 vols. (Cesena, 1972), I, 13-161, II, 13-160. Peter said that he was working on the biography of Romuald fifteen years (tria lustra) after the latter's death; Vita beati Romualdi prol., ed., G. Tabacco, Fonti per la storia d'Italia, XCIV (Rome, 1957), p. 9. As Romuald's death is placed at the earliest in 1023 and at the latest in 1027 (ibid., pp. liii-liv), the range of possible dates for the biography goes from 1038 to 1042.

[8] A. Wilmart, "Une lettre de S. Pierre Damien à l'impératrice Agnès," Revue Bénédictine, XLIV (1932), 144.

[9] Op. LVII.v (825).

[10] Besides Leclercq, Saint Pierre Damien, consult J. Gonsette, S. Pierre Damien et la culture profane (Louvain, 1956); J. J. Ryan, Saint Peter Damiani and His Canonical Sources: A Preliminary Study in the Antecedents of the Gregorian Reform, Pontifical Institute of Mediaeval Studies, Studies and Texts, II (Toronto, 1956); and A. Cantin, "Les sciences séculières et la foi: la critique unitaire de saint Pierre Damien (1007-1072)," unpublished thesis (Paris, 1968).

[11] Op. LI.xiii (762); Op. XLII.vii (672).

[12] Wilmart, "Une lettre," pp. 133-134.

[13] The standard works are those of Leclercq, Dressler, and Blum cited above.

[14] Op. XLII.vii (672): "Memini plane, quia cum apud Parmense oppidum liberalium artium studiis docendus insisterem, dum adhuc videlicet in ipso adolescentiae flore, et nova pubertas indueret faciem, et aestus libidinis accenderet carnem, clericus quidam...." Cf. Wilmart, "Une lettre," p. 133.

[15] Op. LI.xiii (762): "Adolescentem me in Faventina urbe propter litterarum studia constitutum audire contigit quo ennaro."

[16] Vita Romualdi lxix (ed. Tabacco, p. 112).

[17] Op. XL.ix (659-660); Ep. VII.xviii (458).

[18] The earlier date for the city-wide fire was published in 1902, but the fact was placed in conjunction with Peter Damian's reference only recently. For a full discussion of the question, see Lucchesi, "Per una Vita di San Pier Damiani," I, 53-57.

[19] For Lucchesi, see ibid., p. 54; for Wilmart, see "Une lettre," p. 134.

[20] Op. XLII.vii (673): "Nam dum per quinque fere annorum lustra in hac luxuriosa voluptate vixissent ante annum cum commune ipsius urbis flagraret incendium, in una domo reperti uterque simul igne consumpti sunt." My colleague Eleanor S. Duckett (Smith College) graciously and helpfully discussed the meanings of this passage with me.

[21] H. Rashdall, The Universities of Europe in the Middle Ages, ed., F. M. Powicke and A. B. Emden (London, 1936), I, 462-463; III, 352-353.

[22] Op. XLII.vii (673): "Quid dicam? quia dum haec cernerem, titillantis luxuriae molestias pertuli, cum etiam postquam ad eremum veni, ejusdem lenocinii memoria me saepius colaphizare non destitit."

[23] John of Lodi Vita B. Petri Damiani ii (PL, CXLIV, 117): "Cumque discendi finem ex omni liberali scientia peritus fecisset, mox alios erudire, clientium turba ad doctrinae ipsius famam undique confluente, studiosissime coepit."

[24] One standard account is that by Dressler in New Catholic Encyclopedia, VII, 1059.

[25] John Vita Petri Damiani i-iv (115-121).

[26] Ibid., prol. (114).

[27]Wilmart, "Une lettre," p. 144: "ut primogenitam michi sanctae vitae germanum, quae me vice matris alverat...."

[28]Ibid., p. 132, n. 1. Note again that this has subsequently become the standard interpretation.

[29]Leclercq, Saint Pierre Damien, p. 19; Lucchesi, "Per una vita di San Pier Damiani," I, 17.

[30]John Vita Petri Damiani i (115A and 116C). Cf. Leclercq, Saint Pierre Damien, p. 17.

[31]Ep. V.ii (340-342).

[32]Leclercq, Saint Pierre Damien, pp. 126-131.

[33]Ep. VII.viii (447).

[34]Wilmart, "Une lettre," pp. 140-145.

[35]Lucchesi, "Per una vita di San Pier Damiani," I, 17, does not ask why Peter Damian did not return home more often. Instead he accepts the fact and deduces from it that Peter's home must not have been on one of the important, unavoidable streets of the city. He thus assumes that had it been more conveniently located Peter would have visited it more often.

[36]Dr. Mary Martin McLaughlin, in working on the history of childhood in the ninth through the thirteenth centuries, also found John of Lodi's account valid and immensely revealing. She gave me helpful criticism on the present essay and she kindly allowed me to read her work prior to its publication; see her "Survivors and Surrogates: Children and Parents from the Ninth to the Thirteenth Centuries," in The History of Childhood, ed., L. de Mause (New York, 1974), pp. 101-181.

[37]John Vita Petri Damiani ii (117).

[38]Wilmart, "Une lettre," p. 131, n. 1; Leclercq, Saint Pierre Damien, p. 19.

[39]John Vita Petri Damiani ii-iv (117-121).

[40]M.-D. Chenu, "The Masters of the New Theological 'Science,'" in his Nature, Man, and Society in the Twelfth Century: New Theological Perspectives in the Latin West, trans. J. Taylor and L. K. Little (Chicago, 1968), pp. 270-309.

[41]G. Post, K. Giocarinis, R. Kay, "The Medieval Heritage of a Humanistic Ideal: 'Scientia donum dei est, unde vendi non potest,'" Traditio, XI (1955), 195-234.

[42]R. W. Southern, Western Society and the Church in the Middle Ages

(Harmondsworth, 1970), pp. 277-279, 294.

[43]G. Spinelli, "La data dell'ordinazione sacerdotale di S. Pier Damiani," Benedictina, XVII (1972), 595-605. The argument is on the whole persuasive except that the author holds too rigidly to the approximate birthdate of 1007.

[44]Ibid., pp. 601-602.

[45]Ep. IV.xi (321).

[46]McLaughlin, "Survivors and Surrogates"; E. R. Coleman, "Infanticide dans le Haut Moyen Age?" Annales E.S.C., XXIX (1974), 315-335. I am grateful for the most helpful comments of Georges Duby, Jacques Le Goff, and Jean Leclercq in the seminar conducted by M. Duby at the Collège de France on the subject: "Structures de parenté et sexualité aux $X^e$-$XII^e$ siècles."

[47]Wilmart, "Une lettre," p. 131, n. 3; Blum, St. Peter Damian, p. 39.

[48]Op. XVI.i (367); Op. XIII.vi (ed. Brezzi, pp. 226-232). See the discussion by G. Miccoli, "Théologie de la vie monastique chez saint Pierre Damien (1007-1072)," in Théologie de la vie monastique: Etudes sur la Tradition patristique (Paris, 1961), pp. 469-472.

[49]Ep. III.ii (289).

[50]Op. XII.iv (255).

[51]Op. LIII.iv (793-796).

[52]Op. XXVII (503-512).

[53]Op. XXXI (529-542).

[54]Op. XXVII.ii (507). For Peter's place in the history of thought concerning the vices, see L. K. Little, "Pride Goes before Avarice: Social Change and the Vices in Latin Christendom," American Historical Review, LXXVI (1971), 16-49, especially 20 and 46.

[55]Ep. VII.vi-viii, xiv (443-447, 451-454); Op. XVIII, diss. 3 (416-424). J. Leclercq, "S. Pierre Damien et les femmes," Studia Monastica, XV (1973), 43-55.

[56]Op. L (731-750).

[57]Ep. VII.xviii (458).

[58]Op. VII (159-190).

[59]J. T. McNeill and H. M. Gamer, Medieval Handbooks of Penance (New York, 1938), pp. 103, 113, 172-173, 185, 226, 250, 252, 254, 274,

302-303, 335, 355.  Burchard of Worms <u>Decretum</u> <u>XIX</u> (<u>PL</u>, CXLII, 967-968).  Ivo of Chartres <u>Decretum</u> IX.xc-xcv (<u>PL</u>, CLXI, 682).

[60]Mansi XIX, 897-899.

[61]<u>PL</u>, CXLV, 159-160.

[62]<u>Op</u>. VII, <u>praef</u>. (161).

[63]<u>Ep</u>. II.vi (270-272).

[64]Leclercq, <u>Saint Pierre Damien</u>, p. 152.

[65]<u>Op</u>. XVIII, diss. 2 (403).

[66]<u>Op</u>. XI.xix (246-251).

[67]<u>Op</u>. XI.xx (252).

[68]<u>Ep</u>. IV.xi (321).

[69]<u>Op</u>. XL (649-660).

[70]<u>Ibid</u>. ix (658-660).

[71]<u>Ep</u>. V.ii (340-341).

[72]<u>Ep</u>. I.xx-xxi, II.vi, III.iv, vi, VII.iii (237-254, 270-272, 290-295, 437-442).

[73]<u>Op</u>. XI.xix (249).

[74]<u>Op</u>. XI.v (235).

[75]<u>Vita Romualdi</u> xxiv (ed. Tabacco, p. 51).

[76]<u>Op</u>. XIII.iii (ed. Brezzi, p. 214).

[77]<u>Op</u>. XI.xix (250); cf. Miccoli, "Théologie de la vie monastique," pp. 461-469.

[78]<u>Op</u>. XLIII (679-686).  J. Leclercq, "La flagellazione voluntaria nella tradizione spirituale dell'Occidente," in <u>Il Movimento dei Disciplinati nel Settimo Centenario dal suo inizio (Perugia 1260). Convegno internazionale:  Perugia, 25-28 Settembre 1960</u> (Perugia, 1962), pp. 73-83.

[79]<u>Op</u>. XLIII.vi (686).

[80]McLaughlin, "Survivors and Surrogates," p. 116.

[81]John of Lodi <u>Vita Petri Damiani</u> ii (117).  Cf. McLaughlin, "Survivors and Surrogates," p. 105.

[82]E. H. Erikson, Childhood and Society, 2nd ed. (New York, 1963), pp. 247-251.  M. Klein, "Some Theoretical Conclusions Regarding the Emotional Life of the Infant," in M. Klein, P. Heimann, S. Isaacs, and J. Riviere, Developments in Psycho-Analysis, The International Psycho-Analytical Library, no. 143 (London, 1952), pp. 198-236.

[83]Ep. VIII.viii (476).

[84]I am deeply grateful to Mary M. McLaughlin (see above, n. 36), Barbara H. Rosenwein (Loyola University, Chicago), and Paul H. Seton (Smith College) for their generous and learned help in formulating this interpretation.

Chapter 22

[1]I wish to express my deep appreciation to Dr. Alexander Patschovsky and my wife Erdmut for providing aid in technical and linguistic matters. Funds to help sustain research for this paper were provided by Northwestern University and the National Endowment for the Humanities; the opinions herein are my own and not necessarily those of the supporting institutions.

[2]On Lea's method of research, Edward Sculley Bradley, Henry Charles Lea (Philadelphia, 1931), pp. 261-262.

[3]The documents concerning Marguerite Porete are in Henry Charles Lea, A History of the Inquisition of the Middle Ages (New York, 1888; repr. New York, 1955), II, 575-578. These are reprinted without emendation in Paul Fredericq, Corpus documentorum inquisitionis haereticae pravitatis Neerlandicae (Ghent, 1889-1906), I, 155-160, #164-65. Lea's brief remarks on the Angel of Philadelphia are in his History, pp. 123-124.

[4]A forthright characterization of Langlois not only as "érudit impeccable" but also as a "misanthrope à l'âme solitaire et troublée" is by Charles Samarin in Recueil des travaux historiques de Ferdinand Lot (Paris, 1968-), I, 24. See also the glowing tribute by R. Fawtier in The English Historical Review, XLV (1930), 85-91. Langlois' role as organizer of studies pertaining to the reign of Philip the Fair is described by Franklin J. Pegues, The Lawyers of the Last Capetians (Princeton, 1962), pp. 28-35.

[5]"Marguerite Porete," Revue historique, LIV (1894), 295-299. Langlois also corrected here, 295-296, some of the false readings of Lea's copyist, but these corrections were incorporated neither in Fredericq (as above, n. 3) nor in the reprinted edition of Lea's History. Fredericq, II, 63-64, #37, reprinted the text edited by Langlois concerning Marguerite Porete but ignored the text concerning Guiard of Cressonessart.

[6]Charles-Victor Langlois and Charles Seignobos, Introduction aux études historiques (Paris, 1898), e.g., p. 13: "pas de documents, pas d'histoire"; and Langlois' lament, p. 15, that "on n'est jamais certain d'avoir épuisé toutes les sources d'information." There is also an English translation of Introduction by G. G. Berry, Introduction to the Study of History (New York, 1903).

[7]H. S. Denifle and E. Chatelain, Chartularium universitatis Parisiensis (Paris, 1889-97), III, 660-661. I have been unable to find any indication of how Denifle and Chatelain divided their work on this project (which Denifle supervised), and it is unclear whether either of them actually ever bothered to check layette J. 428. On Denifle, see D. Knowles, "Denifle and Ehrle," History, LIV (1969), 1-12, and the bibliography in Ingeborg Degenhardt, Studien zum Wandel des Eckhartbildes (Leiden, 1967), p. 186, n. 2. As an example of Denifle's

intolerance for unorthodox varieties of religious experience, see his
remark about the condemned sentences of Meister Eckhart cited by
Degenhardt, p. 177:  "Wem bei diesen Sätzen nicht krankhaftes Denken
auffällt, der hat selbst nie gesund gedacht."

[8] On Marguerite Porete, see my Heresy of the Free Spirit in the
Later Middle Ages (Berkeley, 1972), pp. 68-77, 200-208, and the lit-
erature there cited.  I make passing reference to Guiard in the same
work, pp. 77-78, as does Ernest W. McDonnell, The Beguines and
Beghards in Medieval Culture (New Brunswick, 1954), p. 492; H. Grundmann,
"Ketzerverhöre des Spätmittelalters als quellenkritisches Problem,"
Deutsches Archiv für Erforschung des Mittelalters, XXI (1965), 526,
n. 16; and R. Guarnieri, "Il movimento del Libero Spirito," Archivio
Italiano per la storia della pietà, IV (1965), 413.

[9] Inventaire sommaire et tableau méthodique des fonds conservés aux
Archives nationales (Paris, 1871-), I, 9.

[10] Layettes du Trésor des Chartes, 5 vols. (Paris, 1863-1909), II,
#1693-94, 1742-43, 1758, 1768, 1776, 1787, 1789, 1930, 1942.

[11] In the appendix below I edit all the texts pertaining to Guiard's
trial.  I have no intention of editing those concerning Marguerite
Porete, but this would be a worthwhile task since one is new and the
others are in need of re-editing.

[12] Lea's mistaken date of May 30, 1310, was repeated by Langlois.
Even though it was then corrected by Denifle and Chatelain (as above,
n. 7), III, 661, it was subsequently repeated by Grundmann, 524, n.
11, Guarnieri, 412, and by myself, p. 71 (all as above, n. 8).

[13] Only advice about Guiard's case is specified in J. 428 #16, but
since the judgment of canon lawyers concerning both cases followed
directly, it may be assumed that the case of Marguerite Porete was
also discussed at the meeting in March.  J. 428 #16 throws some added
light on the personnel of the University of Paris in the spring of
1310.  I report the most important conclusion--that the Cistercian
Jacobus previously thought to have been Jacques Fournier was in fact
one Jacques of Dijon--in "A Note on the University Career of Jacques
Fournier, O. Cist., Later Pope Benedict XII," Analecta Cisterciensia,
XXX (1974), 66-69.  For the further identification of the theological and legal masters involved, see the notes to my edition of J. 428
#16 in the appendix below.

[14] The fact that Guiard recanted is found explicitly only in the
Continuatio Chronici Guillelmi de Nangiaco, in Chronique latine de
Guillaume de Nangis, ed. H. Géraud (Paris, 1843), I, 380.  This is
the only contemporary chronicle report but it appears to be very well-
informed concerning Guiard's and Marguerite Porete's cases.  Grundmann,
525, has pointed out that the author of this chronicle--definitely a
monk of St. Denis--may even have been the theologian Petrus de Sancto
Dyonisio consulted in both cases or, if not, was probably directly

informed by this Peter.

[15] Continuatio Chronici, 379-380. I mistakenly dated Marguerite's execution to May 31 instead of June 1 in my Heresy of the Free Spirit (as above, n. 8), pp. 1, 72.

[16] Lea (as cited above, n. 3), II, 123. See also Guarnieri (as cited above, n. 8), 413: "Un suo simpatizzante o forse seguace."

[17] For the only possible exception, see n. 20 below. Conversely, Marguerite Porete's Mirror of Simple Souls does suggest a distinction between "Holy Church the Little" and "Holy Church the Great" (see my Heresy of the Free Spirit, p. 205) that might be seen to correspond with Guiard's ideas, but the language is different and Marguerite presents no developed theory of Church history of the sort found in Guiard's testimony. The most basic agreement between Guiard and Marguerite is their common stress on the cult of voluntary poverty, but in this they were typical of almost all high- and late-medieval heretics as a group.

[18] For what follows I rely on Guiard's testimony found in Archives Nationales J. 428 #18 (edited in the appendix below).

[19] The Latin is ambiguous here. The text could alternatively mean that the office of "Angel" had first been granted to him twenty-four years earlier in the Sainte Chapelle. On two later heretics who had intense conversion experiences in churches, see my Heresy of the Free Spirit, pp. 144, 178.

[20] "Inter diversos status Ecclesie est quidam status currencium qui omnia dimiserunt, volentes tenere rigorem evangelicum, et pretendere lucem suam per conversacionem extrinsecam, pretendentem ardorem interiorem...." The latter part of this description, the meaning of which is unclear to me, is the only portion of Guiard's testimony that may possibly be related to the mysticism of Marguerite Porete.

[21] See my Heresy of the Free Spirit, pp. 35-47, 61-68, 78-84.

[22] Ibid., pp. 67-68; text in Fredericq (as cited above, n. 3), I, 154-155, #163.

[23] Continuatio Chronici (as cited above, n. 14), 380: "dicebat quod nec cingulum pelliceum quo erat praecinctus, nec habitum quo erat indutus ad mandatum Papae deponere tenebatur, imo Papa praecipiendo peccaret, tandem incendii [timore], habitum cingulumque deponens, et errorem suum finaliter recognoscens, adjudicatus est perpetua muri inclusione praecingi."

[24] On the Augustinian use of the zona pellicea and the biblical and patristic precedents behind it, see Jordanus de Saxonia, Liber Vitasfratrum, ed. R. Arbesmann and W. Hümpfner (New York, 1943), pp. 48-57.

[25] The early Franciscan sources do sometimes refer to Francis and his followers wearing a zona or cingulum (see Analecta Franciscana, X [Quaracchi, 1926-41], 434, 533, 536, 567), the terms for belt used in reference to the outfit of Guiard of Cressonessart, but this is never said to be made of animal hide.  As the illustrations show (e.g., the early representations of Francis and his followers by Bonaventura Berlinghieri), it was clearly what we would call a cord.

[26] Joachim of Fiore, Expositio in Apocalypsim (Venice, 1527; repr. Frankfurt, 1964), fol. 39b-c.

[27] Marjorie Reeves and B. Hirsch-Reich, The Figurae of Joachim of Fiore (Oxford, 1972), pp. 61-65, and fig. 6.  See also p. 276 and fig. 39 for the same inscription in the Pseudo-Joachite Praemissiones. For Joachim's exegesis of the term "key of David," see Expositio, fol. 85b-87b.

[28] Expositio, fol. 21d-22a, 28a-29d, and Enchiridion in Apocalypsim (a mistaken title, on which see Marjorie Reeves, The Influence of Prophecy in the Later Middle Ages [Oxford, 1969], pp. 26-27), ed. J. C. Huck, Joachim von Floris und die joachitische Literatur (Freiburg/ Br., 1938), p. 292:  "Hoc enim significant quinque principales ec- clesie, quod principales tribus quinque, hoc septem tribus relique, quod ecclesie septem in Asia ab apostolis institute.  Sive etenim in quinque tribubus sive in ecclesiis quinque designantur etates seculi, ab Adam scilicet usque ad Christum....  Sane in septem tribubus et in septem ecclesiis septem novissimorum temporum designantur progenies, que sibi seriatim succedunt, et a primo Christi adventu usque in finem per successionem pertranseunt...."  On Joachim's five/seven patterns, see further Reeves and Hirsch-Reich, Figurae, pp. 13-14. It should also be added that Joachim--always eschewing simple sche- mata--saw the last Church of Asia--the Church of Laodicea--as refer- ring not to the seventh but to the sixth time; see Expositio, fol. 92c:  "due iste ecclesie...sub uno sexto tempore coartantur," and also n. 32 below.  On the superiority of the Church of Philadelphia to the Church of Laodicea, see Expositio, fol. 93a.

[29] Joachim distinguished between seven Augustinian ages (etates), seven times (tempora), of the Church and three states (status) of Father, Son, and Holy Spirit.  On the identity between his seventh tempus with his third status, see Reeves and Hirsch-Reich, Figurae, p. 12.

[30] Expositio, fol. 22a:  "A sexto tempore secundi status initiari oportet tertium statum simul et novum ordinem qui creatus est ad imaginem spiritus sancti."  On the significance of the Angel of Philadelphia, see further Expositio, fol. 82c-84d.  A typical source of confusion is that Joachim's tempora are not always the same:  for a different scheme based on the Apocalyptic vision of the seven seals, see M. Reeves and B. Hirsch-Reich, "The Seven Seals in the Writings of Joachim of Fiore with Special Reference to the Tract De septem sigillis," Recherches de théologie ancienne et médiévale, XXI (1954), 211-247.  In Joachim's Book of Figures the seven tempora do not even

begin with Christ, see Reeves and Hirsch-Reich, Figurae, p. 126.

[31] Expositio, fol. 86c: "Puto etenim quod in tempore sexto oportebit incipere claritatem istam que significata est in facie Christi"; fol. 92a: "...angelo ecclesie Phyladelphie cui datum est in spiritu scire sacramenta abscondita et rimari pre solito etiam profunda Dei."

[32] Passage from the still unpublished Enchiridion in Apocalypsim cited by Herbert Grundmann, Neue Forschungen über Joachim von Fiore (Marburg, 1950), p. 110: "Relique vero due ecclesie ad tertium transeunt statum et tamen cum secundo participant.... Secundum hoc ergo accidet et nunc in ordine monachorum sexto designato in ecclesia Philadelfie et in ordine septimo designato in ecclesia Laodicee. Duo isti ordines sub uno sexto tempore coartantur. Qui cum sint spiritales pre ceteris...."

[33] Expositio, fol. 87d: "...tempori huius angeli phyladelphie viciniores sumus...."

[34] See Joseph Ratzinger, The Theology of History in St. Bonaventure (Chicago, 1971) (translated from the original German version of 1959), pp. 24-31. Ratzinger's book is the most authoritative statement on Bonaventura's historical views and their relation to those of Joachim.

[35] Bonaventura, Collationes in Hexaemeron, in Opera omnia (Quaracchi, 1882-1902), V, coll. xx, 29 (p. 430b): "...philadelphiae, qui interpretatur, conservans hereditatem..."; coll. xxiii, 29 (p. 449b): "Hic est Angelus sextus Philadelphiae, salvans hereditatem. Hic providet frumenta contra famem futuram." The equation between the Angel of Philadelphia and Joseph is also found in Joachim, Expositio, fol. 22a. I follow Ratzinger, pp. 5-6, in preferring the version of the Collationes found in the Opera omnia to that edited by Ferdinand Delorme (Florence, 1934), which seems to represent some abbreviation. Nonetheless, it is possible, as S. Clasen has suggested in reviewing Ratzinger's book in Wissenschaft und Weisheit, XXIII (1960), 199, that some of the Joachite passages found in the Opera omnia version but not in that of Delorme may not have originated with Bonaventura.

[36] Collationes in Hexaemeron, coll. xvi, 30 (p. 408b): "Et dixit, quod adhuc intelligentia Scripturae daretur vel revelatio vel clavis David personae vel multitudini; et magis credo, quod multitudini."

[37] Ibid., coll. xx, 29 (p. 430b): "Nota, quod duodecim signationes sunt sub sexto sigillo et sub sexto Angelo...et sexto Angelo, scilicet Philadelphiae...." This is admittedly not an explicit equation of the two angels but such an equation seems strongly implied and also seems clear from Bonaventura's entire scheme of parallels between the several visions of Revelation. After writing this, I found this opinion concurred with by Brian Tierney in Origins of Papal Infallibility 1150-1350 (Leiden, 1972), p. 78: "Bonaventura apparently identified these angels with one another and certainly regarded both as figures of St. Francis."

[38] On Francis as the Angel of the Sixth Seal and the community of
144,000 as the "empirical" and "eschatological" Franciscan order,
see Ratzinger, pp. 31-55.

[39] On Bonaventura's analogies between St. Francis and Elijah and
John the Baptist, see Ratzinger, pp. 32-33.

[40] Cited by Raoul Manselli, La "Lectura super Apocalipsim" di
Pietro di Giovanni Olivi (Rome, 1955), pp. 179-180: "prima visio
literaliter et aperte tangit septem ecclesias Asye sibi contemporaneas,
allegorice vero describit septem status generales ecclesie...." As of
this writing a full critical edition of Olivi's commentary on Revelation is expected but has not yet appeared.

[41] Cited by Reeves, Influence (as above, n. 28), p. 198: "Sicut
etiam in sexta aetate, reiecto carnali Judaismo et vetustate prioris
seculi, venit novus homo Christus cum nova lege et vita et cruce,
sic in sexto statu, reiecta carnali Ecclesia et vetustate prioris
seculi, renovabitur Christi lex et vita et crux. Propter quod in
eius primo initio Franciscus apparuit, Christi plagis characterizatus
et Christo totus concrucifixus et configuratus."

[42] Ibid., pp. 196-197 on Olivi's Joachism (cf. the hesitations expressed by E. Pásztor in reviewing Reeves' book in Studi medievali,
ser. 3, XII [1971], 800). On Bonaventura's eschewal of the Joachite
three-age theory, Ratzinger, pp. 105, 117-118.

[43] Bernard Gui, De secta illorum qui se dicunt esse de ordine apos-
tolorum, ed. A. Segarizzi, Historia Fratris Dulcini heresiarche
(L. A. Muratori, Rerum Italicarum scriptores, n.s. IX, 5) (Città di
Castello, n. d. [1907]), pp. 21-22.

[44] E.g., Reeves, Influence, p. 247, and Bernhard Töpfer, Das
kommende Reich des Friedens (Berlin, 1964), p. 297. For a later
example of Italian heretical preoccupation with the Church of
Philadelphia, see John N. Stephens, "Heresy in Medieval and Renaissance Florence," Past and Present, 54 (February, 1972), 47.

[45] Papsttum und Untergang des Templerordens (Munster, 1907), I,
149. See also Georges Lizerand, Le Dossier de l'affaire des Templiers
(Paris, 1923), p. iv: "Il est plus simple de croire que le roi a
préféré s'adresser à l'inquisiteur de France, Guillaume de Paris, son
chapelain, parce qu'il croyait pouvoir compter sur sa complaisance."
The best biography of William known to me is Félix Lajard, "Guillaume
de Paris, Dominicain," Histoire littéraire de la France (Paris, 1733-),
XXVII, 140-152.

[46] Finke, I, 213.

[47] In my Heresy of the Free Spirit (as cited above, n. 8), p. 71,
I followed Lea and Langlois in mistakenly assuming that William was
still involved in the case of the Templars from 1308 to 1310. Dr.
Alexander Patschovsky has called my attention to the hitherto

unnoticed appearance of William's name in a document copied in MS
Wölfenbuttel 311 Helmstedt, fol. 30v-31r.  In this text, a formulary
for an inquisitor's handbook, William, called papal Inquisitor for
the realm of France, delegates to an unnamed person the authority to
investigate a certain unnamed heretic who supposedly maintained that
no sexual intercourse with any woman whatsoever is illicit and who
tried to persuade others of the truth of this view.  Unfortunately
the document is undated; since William claims in it that an urgent
press of business prevents him from proceeding in the case himself
it is possible that it stems from the time in 1307 when he was actively
engaged in the case of the Templars.  The document contains no further
specific information.  Dr. Patschovsky is editing it in his book, Die
Anfänge einer ständigen Inquisition in Böhmen.  Ein Prager Inquisitoren-
Handbuch aus der ersten Hälfte des 14. Jahrhunderts, soon to appear.

[48]See the codicil of Nov. 28, 1314, to Philip's will, ed. E. Boutaric,
"Notices et extraits de documents inédits relatifs à l'histoire de
France sous Philippe le Bel," Notices et extraits des manuscrits de
la Bibliothèque Impériale, XX, 2 (1862), 231:  "Item librum vocatum
Speculum Hystoriale, quem nobis dedit frater Guillelmus de Parisius,
quondam confessor noster...."  Philip's will itself surprisingly remains to my knowledge unpublished; see on it Jean Favier, Un Conseiller
de Philippe le Bel:  Enguerran de Marigny (Paris, 1963), p. 201.

[49]Auguste Castan, "L'Évêque de Paris Hugues de Besançon," Mémoires
de la société d'émulation du Doubs, ser. 4, I (1865), 250-270 (255-
256).  This is the fullest biography of Hugh known to me:  it contains much valuable information but a host of documents published
subsequently renders it highly incomplete.  The article on Hugh by
T. de Morembert in the Dictionnaire de biographie française (Paris,
1932-), VI, 305, makes no further contribution.  The obscurity of
the other canonists in Guiard's case arises from the fact that we are
sadly ill-informed about the Parisian faculty of law during this
period; see, e.g., G. Péries, La Faculté de droit dans l'ancienne
Université de Paris (1160-1793) (Paris, 1890), p. 12:  "jusqu'à la
fin du XIVe siècle, les renseignements exacts et circonstanciés sur
la Faculté sont malheureusement trop rares...."  As indicated in my
edition of J. 428 #16, I have been unable to identify the three canonists Guilelmus dictus Frater, Henricus de Bethunia, and Petrus de
Vallibus.

[50]Hugh first appears as doctor of canon law along with John of Thelu
(another canonist in the case of Guiard of Cressonessart) in a document of August 24, 1302, ed. Chartularium (as cited above, n. 7), II,
97-98, #628.  He first appears as a canon of Notre Dame in a papal
document of Nov. 16, 1305, in Regestum Clementis Papae V (Rome, 1885-
88), I, 19, #117.  He must have attained both positions at a relatively early age because in 1296 he was not yet old enough to be a priest;
see on this, Les Registres de Boniface VIII (Paris, 1907-39), I, col.
466, #1299, and the remarks by B. Hauréau, "Les Registres de Boniface
VIII," Journal des Savants (1891), p. 304.  Hugh, as this evidence
shows, was obviously a remarkably successful careerist from the start.

[51]Hugh appears as witness not only to the confession of the Grand
Master Jacques de Molay but also to the collective hearing of other
Templars on October 26, 1307. Both documents are edited by Finke (as
cited above, n. 45), II, 307-313. Clement V's order of August 12,
1308, is in Regestum Clementis Papae V, III, 318, #3522. The Tables
des registres de Clément V (Paris, 1957), 246, reveal how frequently
Hugh appeared as an instrument of papal business during the pontificate of Clement V.

[52]Castan, 257-258, who does not cite his source for this informa-
tion. That it is probably reliable can be inferred from the fact that
Hugh was an adviser to Jeanne's mother, Mahaut d'Artois; see on this,
A. Giffard, "Études sur les sources du droit français, VI: Eudes de
Sens et Jacques d'Ableiges," Nouvelle revue historique de droit fran-
cais et étranger, XXXVII (1913), 656. I have not seen Jean-Marie
Richard, Une petite-nièce de Saint Louis, Mahaut comtesse d'Artois
(Paris, 1887).

[53]Castan, 258, and Paul Lehugeur, Philippe le Long, Roi de France
1316-1322 (Paris, 1931), p. 146.

[54]C.-V. Langlois, "Les Papiers de Guillaume de Nogaret et de
Guillaume de Plaisians au Trésor des Chartes," Notices et extraits
des manuscrits de la Bibliothèque Nationale, XXXIX, 1 (1909), 215-
216, 226 (#129), 238 (#395), 241 (#460).

[55]On the activities of the two men in the spring of 1310, see Robert
Holtzmann, Wilhelm von Nogaret (Freiburg/Br., 1898), pp. 176-190. I
am unaware of any detailed work on Plaisians since A. Henry, "Guillaume
de Plaisians, Ministre de Philippe le Bel," Le Moyen Age, V (1892),
32-38.

[56]It is impossible to be certain about which of the documents belonged to which of the Williams, but I would say that item 129 of the
contemporary inventory--therein labeled "Instrumenta facta super
examinatione Margarite Porete, culpabilis de heresi"--found among the
papers of Nogaret must be the same as J. 428 #15 & 16: "Instrumenta
facta super examinacione M. Porete culpabili heresi" and "Instrumentum
factum super examinacione Margarete Porete culpabili de heresi."
Items 395 and 460--labeled in the inventory respectively "Processus
contra M. Porete, culpabilem de heresi" and "Instrumentum de respon-
sionibus illius heretici qui se dicebat angelum Filadelphie"--found
among the papers of Plaisians must refer to the residue. Item 460
must be the same as J. 428 #18 even though that document is labeled
"Processus contra M. Porete, culpabilem de heresi," a misleading
title that would more sensibly apply to J. 428 #19bis.

[57]On the other events of the spring of 1310, see Holtzmann, p. 185.

[58]Joseph R. Strayer, "Philip the Fair--A 'Constitutional' King,"
in Strayer, Medieval Statecraft and the Perspectives of History
(Princeton, 1971), pp. 208-209, reprinted from an article that first
appeared in The American Historical Review, LXII (1956), 18-32.

## Appendix I

[a]The entire document--an original notarial instrument--is labeled:
"Instrumenta facta super examinacione M. Porete culpabili heresi.
M° CC° IX°" (date in a different hand from that of the foregoing).
In this and what follows I adhere to the spelling of the MSS except
in cases which might impede fluent reading (placing the MS reading in
the notes) and except in writing v̲ for consonantal u̲.  I use the following abbreviations for the footnotes:

  CUP=H.  Denifle and E. Chatelain, Chartularium universitatis
        Parisiensis (Paris, 1889-97)

  Finke=Heinrich Finke, Papsttum und Untergang des Templerordens
        (Münster, 1907)

  Glorieux=P. Glorieux, Répertoire des maîtres en théologie de
        Paris au XIIIe siècle (Paris, 1933)

  LTK=Lexikon für Theologie und Kirche, 2nd ed. (Freiburg/Br.,
        1957-67).

[b]MS q̅m̅.

[c]MS xanctiones.

[1]Guillaume de Baufet, Bishop of Paris 1305-20; see on him Histoire
littéraire de la France (Paris, 1733-), XXXII, 469-474.

[2]This Jacobus de Virtuto (Vertus) was one of three notaries who
notarized an instrument containing the confession of the Grand Master
of the Templars, Jacques de Molay, on October 25, 1307, edited by
Finke, II, 307-309.

## Appendix II

[a]J. 428 #16--a notarized copy of a notarial instrument--is labeled:
"Instrumentum factum super examinacione Margarete Porete culpabili
de heresi."  J. 428 #17--an unofficial copy--has no label.  The text
of #17 begins at note c below and ends at note v.  In cases of vari-
ants, #17 most often has superior readings even though it is an unofficial copy; very likely it was made from the missing original.

[b]MS arrestate lacking.

[c]J. 428 #17 begins here.  J. 428 #19 is substantially the same
document issued by the same lawyers on the same date with Marguerite
Porete substituted for Guiard of Cressonessart.

<sup>d</sup>#17 Telleuz.

<sup>e</sup>#17 Bitunia.

<sup>f</sup>#17 Autissiodorensis.

<sup>g</sup>#16 fauteria.

<sup>h</sup>#17 Marguerete.

<sup>i</sup>#17 Hannonia.

<sup>j</sup>#16 nominaciones.

<sup>k</sup>#16 prestande.

<sup>l</sup>#17 ac.

<sup>m</sup>#17 pertinentibus lacking.

<sup>n</sup>#17 plane.

<sup>o</sup>#16 peticionis

<sup>p</sup>#16 procedendum lacking.

<sup>q</sup>#16 trasierit.

<sup>r</sup>#16 contumacis.

<sup>s</sup>#16 recurrens penituerit.

<sup>t</sup>#17 inquisitoris ipsius.

<sup>u</sup>#16 Pro.

<sup>v</sup>#17 ends here without notarization

[1] Glorieux #212.

[2] Glorieux #214; LTK, X, 135. Thomas' designation here as penitentiary is new information which shows that he held this office at least four years earlier than previously known.

[3] Glorieux #218. John of Ghent (de Gandavo) is not to be confused with John of Jandun (de Ganduno).

[4] Glorieux #221.

[5] Glorieux #222.

[6] I.e., Heinrich of Friemar the elder. Glorieux #406 is outdated;

see instead LTK, V, 188, and literature therein cited.

[7]Glorieux #223; LTK, V, 1071-1072.

[8]I.e., Laurence of Poulengy; Glorieux #383.

[9]Glorieux #393.

[10]Glorieux #65.

[11]Glorieux #348; LTK, V, 835-836.

[12]I am unable to identify these canonists.

[13]C. E. Bulaeus, Historia universitatis Parisiensis (Paris, 1665-1673), IV, 37, 115; CUP, II, #628.

[14]See footnotes 49-53 to text above.

[15]I.e., Alexander of Sant' Elpidio; Glorieux #408; LTK, I, 309.

[16]Glorieux #225; further bibliography in Charles H. Lohr, "Medieval Latin Aristotle Commentaries," Traditio, XXVIII (1972), 384.

[17]Overlooked by Glorieux; see instead Gallia Christiana (Paris, 1716-1865), XII, 217, and CUP, II, #809. On the significance of this identification, see my "Note on the University Career of Jacques Fournier, O. Cist., Later Pope Benedict XII," Analecta Cisterciensia, XXX (1974), 66-69.

[18]Glorieux #407.

[19]Evenus Phili appears as notary along with Jacobus de Virtuto in the document of October 25, 1307, edited by Finke, II, 307-309.


                         Appendix III


[a]The document--an unofficial copy--is labeled:  "Actum anno M°CCC° IX°.  Processus contra M. Porete culpabilem de heresi." (Second sentence in different hand from that of first.)

[b]MS quidem(?).

[c]The text from here to note g was previously edited by C.-V. Langlois, "Marguerite Porete," Revue historique, LIV (1894), 297-299. Langlois made a handful of minor mistakes in transcription which I silently correct.

[d]MS hec inserted above the line.

[e]MS vel or et inserted very lightly above the line.

[f]MS possunt(?).

[g]Langlois' edition ends here.

[h]MS has an abbreviation that is difficult to decipher:  could also
be vero or eciam.


[1]Cf. Liber sextus, 3. 17. 1.  (Religionum diversitatem nimiam), ed.
E. Friedberg, Corpus iuris canonici (Leipzig, 1879-1881), II, 1054-
1055:  "ne aliquis de cetero novum ordinem aut religionem adinveniat
vel habitum novum religionis assumat...."

[2]Gratian, Decretum, I, D. 19 c. 1 (Decretales epistola vim auctori-
tatis habent), ed. Friedberg, I, 58-60.

[3]Ibid., II, C. 25 q. 1 c. 5 (In Spiritum Sanctum blasphemunt qui
sacros canones violant), ed. Friedberg, I, 1008.

[4]Ibid., II, C. 25 q. 2 c. 18 (Anathema sit qui mandata vel decreta
Romanorum Pontificum servare contempserit), ed. Friedberg, I, 1016.

[5]Gregory IX, Decretales, 1. 1. 1. par. 3 (Una vero est fidelium
universalis ecclesia, extra quam nullus omnino salvatur), ed.
Friedberg, II, 6.

Chapter 23

[1]See the balanced assessment given by Joseph R. Strayer in "The Laicization of French and English Society in the Thirteenth Century," first published in 1940 and now reprinted in Medieval Statecraft and the Perspectives of History:  Essays by Joseph R. Strayer, ed. John F. Benton and Thomas N. Bisson (Princeton, 1971; hereafter Strayer, Statecraft), p. 265, and see also Joseph R. Strayer, "Philip the Fair--A 'Constitutional' King," first published in 1956 and now available in Strayer, Statecraft, pp. 208-210.

Special thanks are owed to Francois Maillard, who gave me invaluable help and judicious advice as I was preparing this essay.

[2]See Strayer, "Laicization," in Strayer, Statecraft, pp. 260-261, and Joseph R. Strayer, "Defense of the Realm and Royal Power in France," originally published in 1949, and now in Strayer, Statecraft, pp. 291-299; Ernst Kantorowicz, The King's Two Bodies:  A Study in Mediaeval Political Theology (Princeton, 1957), pp. 249-258; Gaines Post, "Ratio Publicae Utilitatis, Ratio Status, and 'Reason of State,'" first published in German in 1961 and now available in a revised, English version, in Gaines Post, Studies in Medieval Legal Thought: Public Law and the State 1100-1322 (Princeton, 1964), pp. 241-309. Wolf, surveying the wills of Philip Augustus from this point of view, concluded that Philip Augustus--and, he suggested, his successor Philip the Fair--was far more concerned with the needs of the state than with other matters:  Gunther Wolf, "Ein unveröffentlichtes Testament Kaiser Friedrichs II. Versuch einer Edition und Interpretion," Zeitschrift für die Geschichte des Oberrheins, CIV (1956), 42-43.

[3]For the stress laid in France on the idea of Christian kingship, particularly in the fourteenth century, see Joseph R. Strayer, "France:  The Holy Land, the Chosen People, and the Most Christian King," first printed in 1969, and now in Strayer, Statecraft, pp. 300-314; for a review of the literature relating to the king's moral obligations, particularly in France and with special emphasis on their fiscal policies, see Elizabeth A. R. Brown, "Taxation and Morality in the Thirteenth and Fourteenth Centuries:  Conscience and Political Power and the Kings of France," French Historical Studies, VIII (1973), 3-8.

[4]Cf. Petrus Jacobus, Aurea practica libellorum... (Cologne, 1574), p. 279.

[5]Brown, "Taxation and Morality," pp. 2-3.  In the early fourteenth century Pierre Jame wrote that the deaths of men perishing in unjust wars were imputed as homicide to the princes responsible for the wars:  Petrus Jacobus, Aurea practica, p. 279.  Some years earlier Vincent of Beauvais had asserted that princes who extorted money from their subjects were like thieves, although they sinned more gravely than thieves since their actions endangered public justice, which

they were instituted to uphold:  Vincent de Beauvais, <u>Speculum quad-</u>
<u>ruplex, sive Speculum maius:  Naturale, Doctrinale, Morale, Historiale</u>
(Graz, 1964-1965), III, 1287.  See also Gaines Post, "Law and Politics
in the Middle Ages:  The Medieval State as a Work of Art," <u>Perspec-</u>
<u>tives in Medieval History</u>, ed. Katherine F. Drew and F. S. Lear
(Chicago, 1963), pp. 72-73.

[6]Brown, "Taxation and Morality," pp. 25-27.

[7]Cf. Raymond Cazelles, "Une exigence de l'opinion depuis Saint
Louis:  La réformation du royaume," <u>Annuaire-Bulletin de la Société</u>
<u>de l'Histoire de France</u> (1962-1963), pp. 92-95.

[8]Brown, "Taxation and Morality," pp. 26-27.

[9]<u>Ibid</u>.

[10]<u>Ibid</u>., pp. 11-13.

[11]Cf. the cynical comments of Dossat concerning Alfonse of Poitiers'
provision in his will of 1270 for the disposal of tithes he had been
collecting which lawfully belonged to others:  Yves Dossat, "Les
restitutions de dîmes dans le diocèse d'Agen pendant l'épiscopat de
Guillaume II (1247-1263)," <u>Bulletin philologique et historique (jusqu'à</u>
<u>1610) du Comité des travaux historiques et scientifiques</u> (1962), p.
552.

[12]Writing in the early fourteenth century, Pierre Jame warned rulers
against relying on their successors to make amends for their misdeeds,
reminding them that a ruler should not expect his heir to do more than
he himself had done, and pointing out that rulers rarely did anything
at all for their predecessors:  Petrus Jacobus, <u>Aurea practica</u>, p. 279.
A quodlibet prepared in 1315 by Gui Terreni raised the question of
whether or not one could advance one's salvation by ordering an heir
to carry out restitutions which one should accomplish oneself:  Palémon
Glorieux, <u>La littérature quodlibetique de 1260 à 1320</u>, Bibliothèque
thomiste, vols. 5 and 21 (Le Saulchoir, Kain, and Paris, 1925-1935),
I, 169, quodlibet iii, 15.

[13]Henri Auffroy, <u>Évolution du testament en France des origines au</u>
<u>XIIIe siècle</u> (Paris, 1899), p. 378; Jean-François Poudret, <u>La suc-</u>
<u>cession testamentaire dans le pays de Vaud à l'époque savoyarde (XIIIe-</u>
<u>XVIe siècle)</u>, Bibliothèque historique vaudoise, XVIII (Lausanne,
1955), 129.

[14]In a quodlibet written in the late thirteenth century, Renier de
Clairmarais examined the question whether a person whose testamentary
executors deferred distributing property he had left would therefore
be forced to remain longer than otherwise in purgatory.  Renier decided that if the property had been left for purposes of restitution,
delay would not affect the length of time spent in purgatory unless
the testator had knowingly selected irresponsible executors; if, however, the testator had left the property as alms to gain forgiveness

for his sins, his release from purgatory would be delayed, although his suffering would not be increased. Renier warned that executors sinned gravely in deferring distribution of such bequests; they should, he said, be compelled to act by a superior authority and should be excommunicated if they failed to take action. The quodlibet is found in Paris, Bibliothèque Nationale, ms. lat. 15850, fol. 38v°, and cf. Glorieux, La littérature, I, 239, no. 140. See also the quodlibet of Jean de Naples, probably composed in the first decade of the four-teenth century, which discussed the question whether testamentary executors sinned mortally in not implementing the testament immedi-ately: Glorieux, La littérature, II, 159-161, especially quodlibet ii, p. 161.

On the relationship between heirs and executors, see Louis Dulac, Développement historique et théorie de l'exécution testamentaire (Toulouse, 1899), especially pp. 20 and 27.

[15]See, in general, Auffroy, Évolution, pp. 466-478, 615-627, 638-640, 665-671; see also Poudret, La succession, pp. 116-139; Robert Boutruche, "La noblesse: Aux origines d'une crise nobiliaire. Dona-tions pieuses et pratiques successorales en Bordelais du XIIIe au XVIe siècle," Annales d'histoire sociale, I (1939), 161-177, 257-273; Georges Chevrier, "Remarques sur la liberté de disposer en Bourgogne (VIIe-XV[e] siècles)," Mémoires de la Société pour l'histoire du droit et des institutions des anciens pays bourguignons, comtois et romands, XIV (1952), 251; Georges Duby, La société aux XIe et XIIe siècles dans la région mâconnaise (Paris, 1955), pp. 272-277 and 501-502 (pp. 221-224 and 379-380 of the reprinted edition of 1971); F.-J.-M. Olivier-Martin, Histoire de la coutume de la prévôté et vicomté de Paris (Paris, 1922-1930), II, pt. 2, pp. 498-501; G. Partsch, "L'apparition du testament et la capacité de disposer dans le droit valaisan du XIIIe siècle," Mémoires de la Société pour l'histoire du droit et des institutions des anciens pays bourguignons, comtois et romands, XVII (1955), 33-35; and for England the excellent book of M. M. Sheehan, The Will in Medieval England from the Conversion of the Anglo-Saxons to the End of the Thirteenth Century (Toronto, 1963), pp. 76-79, 122-123, 231-258, 288-293.

It was generally the rule that all movables, all property acquired during the testator's lifetime, and some portion of inherited proper-ty--varying from region to region--might be left to heirs of the tes-tator's choice. In thirteenth-century France, however, it was coming to be felt that, in the case of the kingdom and of some baronies held of the kingdom, no division of what might be called the "droit corps du...reaume" or of the barony might take place, and hence that those holding such territories might leave only movables or acquired prop-erty: Li livres de jostice et de plet..., ed. Rapetti (Paris, 1850), p. 224, bk. 12, sect. 3, no. 1; Philippe de Beaumanoir, Coutumes de Beauvaisis, ed. A. Salmon, Collection de textes pour servir à l'étude et à l'enseignement de l'histoire, vols. 24 and 30 (Paris, 1899-1900), I, 212, sect. 445; Pierre Chaplais, "Un message de Jean de Fiennes à Édouard II et le projet de démembrement du royaume de France (janvier 1317)," Revue du Nord, XLIII (1961), 146-148 and p. 148 for the phrase quoted in the preceding statement; Jean Richard, Les ducs de

Bourgogne et la formation du duché du XIe au XIVe siècle, Publications
de l'Université de Dijon, XII (Paris, 1954), 318-327, and especially
pp. 319 and 327 for the attempt of Robert II to establish the inalienability of the principal acquisitions made by the duke during his reign.
For Béarn, see Pierre Luc, Vie rurale et pratique juridique en Béarn
aux XIVe et XVe siècles (Toulouse, 1943), p. 52; for Navarre, Percy
Ernst Schramm, "Der König von Navarra (1035-1512)...," Zeitschrift
der Savigny-Stiftung für Rechtsgeschichte, Germanistische Abteilung,
LXVIII (1951), 153.

[16]Auffroy, Évolution, 374-375, and, for Philip Augustus' extravagant
bequests, Alexander Cartellieri, Philipp II. August, König von
Frankreich (Leipzig, 1899-1922), II, 100-104; IV, 558-560, 565-568,
653. Philip's various testamentary provisions are conveniently assembled in Florilegium Testamentorum..., ed. Gunther Wolf (Heidelberg,
1956), 29-36.

[17]Cf. the comments of Maurice Rey, Le domaine du roi et les finances
extraordinaires sous Charles VI 1388-1413 (Paris, 1965), p. 167.

[18]In explaining why kings, unlike emperors, could not as a matter
of course institute vectigalia and collecte, Pierre Jame wrote that
"reges...veniant ex successione in regno, quasi in patrimonio suo,
redditus suos habent, & largissimas obuentiones & separatas:" Petrus
Jacobus, Aurea practica, p. 278.

[19]See n. 15 above, and see also Kantorowicz, Two Bodies, pp. 347-
358 and especially p. 356.

[20]Petrus Jacobus, Aurea practica, pp. 278-279, 303; Brown, "Taxation
and Morality," 3-6; Elizabeth A. R. Brown, "Cessante Causa and the
Taxes of the Last Capetians: The Political Applications of a Philosophical Maxim," Studia Gratiana [Post Scripta], XV (1972), 565-588.

[21]Brown, "Taxation and Morality," pp. 17-25, where bibliographical
information concerning other studies of these acts may be found.

[22]Borrelli de Serres, Recherches sur divers services publics du
XIIe au XVIIe siècle, 3 vols. (Paris, 1895-1909), II, 233-235.

[23]Paris, Archives Nationales, K 39, no. 2, a notarized copy of the
act issued by Henri de Taperel, guard of the prévôté of Paris, on
March 3, 1317, on which see Jules Tardif, Monuments historiques (Paris,
1866), no. 1095; Paris, Archives Nationales, J 403, no. 20[bis] is a
rough draft of this document, and J 403, no. 20 and J 403, no. 20[ter]
are copies of the final version, the latter of which is sealed in
green wax on green and red silk laces. The act was copied in the
royal register JJ 52, fols. 25-26, no. 47, and a summary of it appears in Registres du Trésor des Chartes, vol. II, Règnes des fils de
Philippe le Bel, pt. 1, Règnes de Louis X  e Hutin et de Philippe
V de Long, ed. Jean Guerout (Paris, 1966), no. 97.

[24]For Philip's death, see the account of Yves de St.-Denis printed

in Recueil des historiens des Gaules et de la France, XXI, ed. J.-D.
Guigniaut and J.-N. de Wailly (Paris, 1858), 205-208, and the account
of Guillaume Baldrich, written for Guillaume de Canet, lieutenant of
the king of Majorca, and published by Baudon de Mony, "La mort et les
funérailles de Philippe le Bel d'après un compte rendu à la cour de
Majorque," Bibliothèque de l'École des Chartes, LVIII (1897), 5-14.
Yves de St.-Denis' account was based on information given him directly
by Philip's confessor and on his own observations, and therefore his
evidence and chronology of events seems preferable to Baldrich's,
much of whose account--as his repeated use of the phrase "ut dicitur"
suggests--was based on hearsay:  for Yves de St.-Denis' sources, Recueil,
XXI, 206, 208, and cf. Frantz Funck-Brentano, "La mort de Philippe le
Bel," Annales de la Société historique et archéologique du Gâtinais,
II (1884), 88-89, 91; for Baldrich's sources, Baudon de Mony, "La
mort," p. 12.  Baldrich's account of Philip's death is evidently
affected by his assumption that Philip was unable to speak between
November 28 and shortly before his death on the following day:  Baudon
de Mony, loc. cit.

[25]The acts of November 28, 1314, to be discussed below, seem to me
to indicate that Philip was fully conscious at that time and suggest
that it is perfectly possible that he was responsible for the act of
November 29 regulating the apanage of his son Philip.  Since Guillaume
Baldrich was not present at Philip's deathbed, there seems no reason
to accept his account in preference to Yves de St.-Denis', who was much
better informed:  see the preceding note.  For a different interpretation, see Charles T. Wood, The French Apanages and the Capetian
Monarchy 1224-1328 (Cambridge, Mass., 1966), p. 49; and also Jean
Favier, Un conseiller de Philippe le Bel. Enguerran de Marigny,
Mémoires et documents publiés par la Société de l'École des Chartes
vol. XVI (Paris, 1963), 97, but see ibid., p. 200 for a different
account of the king's condition at the time of his death.

[26]Cazelles, "Une exigence," pp. 91-95; Brown, "Taxation and Morality," p. 26; Elizabeth A. R. Brown, "Charters and Leagues in Early
Fourteenth Century France:  The Movement of 1314 and 1315," Ph.D.
diss., Radcliffe and Harvard, 1960, pp. 23-96; Elizabeth A. R. Brown,
"Charters, Leagues, and Liberties in Thirteenth- and Fourteenth-
Century England and France," Abstracts of the Papers Presented at
the Eighth Conference on Medieval Studies, April 29, 30, May 1, 2,
1973, Western Michigan University, No. 2 (Kalamazoo, 1973), pp. 64-
65; Elizabeth A. R. Brown, "Philip IV the Fair, of France," Encyclopaedia Britannica, 15th ed. (Chicago, 1974), Macropaedia, XIV, 223-
225.

[27]None of these wills has been published, but François Maillard
has informed me that he has intended for some time to edit them and
plans to do so in the near future.

[28]Paris, Archives Nationales, J 403, no. 12.  For Philip's special
ties with and dedication to Maubuisson, where Louis IX had been
raised and where he and his mother had founded a monastery, see
Adolphe Dutilleux and Joseph Depoin, L'abbaye de Maubuisson (Notre-

Dame-la-Royale).  Histoire et cartulaire (Pontoise, 1882-1885), pp.
3-23.

[29]Although the wills of Philip the Fair's predecessors differed
in details, they generally made it clear that debts, restitutions,
and bequests were to be covered by the sale of the movable property
held by the king at the time of his death.  Note that Philip Augustus
set aside a flat 50,000 livres parisis de rebus nostris for restitutions:  Layettes du Trésor des Chartes, ed. Alexandre Teulet et al.,
5 vols. (Paris, 1863-1909), I, 549, no. 1546.  Louis VIII assigned
his movables to pay his debts and restitutions, decreeing that these
were to be covered before his legacies were paid:  Layettes, II, 54-
55, no. 1710, and also in Ordonnances des roys de France de la
troisième race..., ed. Eusèbe-Jacob de Laurière et al., 22 vols.
(Paris, 1723-1849), XI, 324.

[30]The provisions of the will drawn by Louis IX in February 1270 were
strikingly like those of Philip the Fair's first will, for Louis
ordered that his legacies should be paid by selling the movables he
held in regno Francie and, if necessary, by disposing of woods; he
also bound his heir and his land for the execution of his orders:
Layettes, IV, 420-421, no. 5638; Ordonnances, XI, 345.  Shortly before
his death, when he obligated his heir to borrow and spend 100,000
livres tournois for the Crusade, he commanded that this sum be repaid
from ecclesiastical tenths and other clerical subventions, and de
redditibus et bonis aliis regni nostri:  Layettes, IV, 470, no. 5735.
The wills of Philip III, father of Philip the Fair, were less specific.
The testament prepared on October 2, 1270, at Carthage, obligated bona
nostra mobilia et immobilia et heredes nostros:  Paris, Archives
Nationales, J 403, no. 8.  But he decreed in March 1285 in his final
will that money to cover his bequests should be taken from the biens
que nous aurons au reaume de France at the time of his death:  Luc
d'Achéry, Spicilegium, sive Collectio veterum aliquot scriptorum...,
ed. Étienne Baluze et al., 3 vols. (Paris, 1723), III, 692; and on
the testament of 1270 see Le Nain de Tillemont, La vie de Saint Louis,
ed. J. de Gaulle, Publications de la Société de l'Histoire de France,
vols. 47, 50, 53, 55, 57, 66 (Paris, 1847-1851), V, 180-181.

The outlook reflected in the will of Alfonse of Poitiers, count of
Toulouse, who died without heirs of his own body, contrasts sharply
with the approach taken in the royal wills.  In his testament of
June 1270 Alfonse ordered that his bequests should be paid from his
movables and then from the issues of his lands, from which his heirs
were to receive nothing until his instructions had been completely
carried out.  He also ordered his executors to sell le quint de nostre
terre & touz nos conquez & toutes nos droitures; the proceeds, to be
divided into nine portions, were to be devoted to various charitable
purposes specified by Alfonse in the will:  Paris, Archives Nationales,
J 406, no. 4.

[31]François Maillard, who has established a complete itinerary for
Philip the Fair, believes that the will, issued at Royaumont in March
1296 and hence datable, because of the dates of Easter in 1296 and
1297, either 1296 or 1297, must have been prepared in 1297:  in March

of that year--and not in 1296--Philip was in the region of Orléans, at St.-Benoit-sur-Loire and Châteauneuf, and hence near Royaumont, where the will is known to have been completed. The itinerary printed in Recueil, XXI, 435, indicates that Philip was in Royaumont in March 1296, but the only evidence cited is the testament itself.

[32] For a comprehensive account of Philip's reaction to his father's death in 1285, see Claude de Vic and Jean-Joseph Vaissete, Histoire générale de Languedoc..., ed. A. Molinier, 15 vols. (Toulouse, 1872-1893), IX, 113-114, and X, 43-44, n. 7, and preuves, col. 233. For the account of the Continuator of Girard de Fraichet, Recueil, XXI, 7; for Guillaume de Nangis, Recueil, XX, ed. J. Naudet and P.-C.-F. Daunou (Paris, 1840), 538-539 and 570-571. See also Glorieux, La littérature, I, 80, especially n. 1; p. 91; p. 189, quodlibet viii, no. 26; and cf. p. 137, no. 58; and p. 151, quodlibet i, no. 11.

[33] For Philip and Poissy, see Recueil, XXIII, ed. J.-N. de Wailly et al. (Paris, 1876), 190-191; Denis de Ste.-Marthe, Gallia Christiana... (Paris, 1715-1865), VIII, 1339; Alain Erlande-Brandenburg, "La priorale Saint-Louis de Poissy," Bulletin monumental, CXXIX (1971), 85-112; Odette Dufourcq-Latron, "Le monastère royal de Saint-Louis de Poissy," Positions des thèses de l'École des Chartes (1929), pp. 77-87.

[34] The declaration of May 1295, issued by Philip and confirmed by his wife Jeanne, is found in Ordonnances, I, 325-326. Having proclaimed that the changes had been introduced "pro ingruentibus nostris & regni nostri negotiis," the king promised that "omnibus qui monetam hujusmodi in solutum vel alias recipient in futurum, id quod de ipsius valore, ratione minoris ponderis, alleii, sive legis deerit, in integrum de nostro supplebimus, ipsosque indemnes servabimus, in hac parte, nos et terram nostram, heredes ac successores nostros, ac nostra et eorum bona, & specialiter omnes redditus nostros et proventus quoscumque totius Normannie.... Volentes etiam ex nunc...quod dicta moneta pro pretio quod in ea appositum fuerit, a die qua currere incipiet, quo usque ad fiscum nostrum tota finaliter sit recepta, pro nostris redditibus capiatur, licet ipsam forsan antea duxerimus reprobandam, sive de primo pretio minuendam."

The corresponding section of the testament of 1297 reads as follows: "Item volumus / et precipimus omnia debita nostra solui / & restitui quecumque per Nos fuerint indebite exacta / & specialiter volumus & ordinamus restitutionem plenariam fieri omnibus dampnificandis ratione monete minoris ponderis alleii & ualoris / quam pro ingruentibus nostris & Regni nostri negotiis fecimus fabricari / & volumus & ordinamus / quod ad fiscum Regni / pro precio quo dicta moneta currere incepit / in acquitationem reddituum seu debitorum quorumcumque totaliter deducatur / nullatenus ulterius pro dicto precio exponenda / Ad predictam autem restitutionem faciendam / obligamus & obligatos esse uolumus specialiter & expresse / omnes redditus & prouentus quoscumque Regios totius Normannie / necnon Viromanden' & Ambian' balliuiarum / volentes & precipientes attente / quod executores nostri / omnes & singulos redditus & prouentus supradictos / teneant & percipiant / in restitutionem huiusmodi / per manus ipsos integre conuertendos / ac prohibentes

expresse / ne predicti redditus uel prouentus ad manus heredum uel
successorum nostrorum reuertantur / eciam de ipsorum executorum assensu
/ donec de predictis dampnis / plena & integra & publica satisfactio
sit impensa": Paris, Archives Nationales, J 403, no. 13.

For discussion of Philip's declaration of 1295, when his first money
changes were introduced, see Raymond Cazelles, "Quelques réflexions
à propos des mutations de la monnaie royale francaise (1295-1360),"
Le Moyen âge, LXXII (1966), 85 ff., and also A. Grunzweig, "Les
incidences internationales des mutations monétaires de Philippe le
Bel," Le Moyen âge, LIX (1953), 129 ff. Cf. John Bell Henneman,
Royal Taxation in Fourteenth Century France: The Development of War
Financing 1322-1356 (Princeton, 1971), p. 335.

[35]See the statement quoted in n. 34 and see n. 30 for the similar
restriction imposed in the will of Alfonse of Poitiers.

[36]Paris, Archives Nationales, J 403, no. 17; note that Philip's
first will of 1288 had been completed and dated at Maubuisson.
Philip's interest in testaments during the first decade of the fourteenth century--when he was being served by Guillaume de Plaisians,
who died in November 1313--is indicated by the fact that surviving
among Plaisians' papers are transcripts of the wills of Louis IX
and Philip III: Charles-Victor Langlois, "Les papiers de Guillaume
de Nogaret et de Guillaume de Plaisians au Trésor des Chartes,"
Notices et extraits des manuscrits de la Bibliothèque Nationale et
autres bibliothèques, XXXIX, pt. 1 (1909), p. 238, no. 374, and cf.
pp. 245-246, nos. 578 and 598 for Philip's concern with his forest
property. Item 598 shows that the king had forest holdings at "la
montainne de Chatres," probably to be identified with Mont-de-Châtre,
where he founded a Celestine house: see below at n. 44. On Plaisians,
see Abel Henry, "Guillaume de Plaisians, ministre de Philippe le Bel,"
Le Moyen âge, V (1892), 32-38.

[37]J.-É.-M. Viard, Les journaux du Trésor de Charles IV le Bel (Paris,
1914), nos. 3321 and 4915, entries dated June 25, 1323, and in
November 1323, which show that annual payments of 1000 livres tournois
were still being made by the Norman Exchequer to Poissy.

[38]See Favier, Enguerran, p. 100; Henneman, Royal Taxation, p. 343;
Harry A. Miskimin, Money, Prices, and Foreign Exchange in Fourteenth-
Century France (New Haven, 1963), p. 143; and cf. Brown, "Charters,"
p. 111; and also Elizabeth A. R. Brown, "Subsidy and Reform in 1321:
The Accounts of Najac and the Policies of Philip V," Traditio, XXVII
(1971), 423, n. 82.

[39]Note that the church of Cîteaux and the abbey of Fontevrault,
together with many other establishments, received in 1311 what they
had been given in earlier wills.

[40]For relations between Celestine and Boniface, see Heinrich Finke,
Aus den Tagen Bonifaz VIII. Funde und Forschungen (Münster, 1902),
pp. 24-43, and also Franz Xaver Seppelt, Studien zum Pontifikat Papst
Coelestins V., Abhandlungen zur Mittleren und Neueren Geschichte,

XXVII (Berlin and Leipzig, 1911), passim.  For Philip's interest in securing the canonization of Celestine V, a move evidently linked with his vendetta against the memory of Boniface VIII, see Georges Lizerand, Clément V et Philippe IV le Bel (Paris, 1910), pp. 136-137, and also Monumenta Coelestiniana.  Quellen zur Geschichte des Papsts Coelestin V, ed. Franz Xaver Seppelt, Quellen und Forschungen aus dem Gebiete der Geschichte...Görres-Gesellschaft, XIX (Paderborn, 1921), 123-134.  For the canonization of Celestine on May 5, 1313, and the negotiations preceding the move, see L.-H. Labande, "Le cérémonial romain de Jacques Cajétan.  Les données historiques qu'il renferme," Bibliothèque de l'École des Chartes, LIV (1893), 61-67.  The Celestine order was founded by Celestine, then Pietro del Morrone, some years before he became pope in 1294; the order was given papal approval in 1264 and 1274:  Philippe Schmitz, "Célestins," Dictionnaire d'histoire et de géographie ecclésiastiques, XII (1953), 102.

For Philip's foundation of the house of Mont-de-Châtre, see Guerout, Registres, no. 1695.

[41] "Testamentum regis Philippi genitoris moderni dupplicatum nullius ualoris qui postmodum per innouationem alterius reuocatum propter aliquas additiones & Diminuaciones sicut in codicillo / dispositioni presenti dupplicate anexo plenius continetur.  Verumtamen dictum testamentum cui dictus codicillus anexus est in omnibus continet istam formam":  Paris, Archives Nationales, J 403, no. 17[bis], on the fold.

[42] "Cum vero de suo testamento aliisque rebus ad ejus salutem pertinentibus ageretur, ad superna totis anhelans suspiriis, jam quantum in se erat suo reddens spiritum Creatori, suam sententiam frequentius interrumpens, sincera cordis devotione saepe et saepe dicebat illum versiculum:  'In manus tuas, Domine, commendo spiritum meum,' et cum fervore cordis hymnum illum dulcissimum, Jesu nostra redemptio, integraliter frequentissime recitabat":  Recueil, XXI, 206, the account of Yves of St.-Denis.

[43] The codicil has been printed in its entirety by Edgard Boutaric, "Notices et extraits de documents inédits relatifs à l'histoire de France sous Philippe le Bel," Notices et extraits des manuscrits de la Bibliothèque Nationale et autres bibliothèques, XX, pt. 2 (1862), pp. 229-235, no. xliv.  See also the analysis of the codicil given by Louis Douët d'Arcq, "Note sur la mort de Philippe le Bel, à propos de la communication suivante de M. J. Gauthier," Revue des sociétés savantes, 6th ser., IV (1876), 277-280.

[44] For Poissy and Mont-de-Châtre, see nn. 33, 37, and 40 above. Acts relating to Philip's foundation of Poissy and Moncel may be found in Charles-Victor Langlois, "Registres perdus des archives de la Chambre des Comptes de Paris," Notices et extraits des manuscrits de la Bibliothèque Nationale et autres bibliothèques, XL (1917), 81, 332-333, 343-344; and on Moncel, see L. Meister, "Quelques chartes inédites relatives à l'acquisition du Moncel par Philippe le Bel (1309-1314)," Mémoires de la Société académique d'archéologie, sciences et arts du département de l'Oise, XVII (1898), 593-611; and Gallia Christiana, IX, 852.

[45]"Injunxit etiam eidem de opere quod apud Pissiacum fundaverat consummando. Postmodum vero factis et confirmatis inter filios aliquibus ordinationibus, rex devotissimus se totum recollegit in unum": Recueil, XXI, 207.

[46]Boutaric, "Notices et extraits," pp. 230-231, 234. According to the codicil, at about the time of the Feast of the Epiphany (January 6) in 1314, Philippe le Convers had, at the king's command, been instrumental in preparing an ordinance for Poissy. As the codicil states, this ordinance was not sealed, and I have found no trace of it. It may have included the provision referred to in the codicil which ordained that Philippe le Convers should sell royal woods to produce 2000 livres parisis for Poissy's benefit: Boutaric, "Notices et extraits," 230, 234. See Rouen, Bibliothèque Municipale, ms. 3402 (Leber 5870, Menant 5), fols. 139-143v° for a detailed inventory of the transcripts in the Liber Rubeus of the Chambre des Comptes relating to Poissy. A microfilm copy of the entire Menant collection has recently been acquired by the University of Pennsylvania, through the Medieval Microfilm Project of the Medieval Studies Committee.

[47]Philip stated that he would be satisfied if his son Louis departed within the period of time in which he himself had promised to go. Otherwise, he stipulated, 100,000 livres tournois were to be given for the support of the Holy Land, and they were to be paid to his son Philip, or to his son Charles, or to Charles of Valois, or to Louis of Évreux, or to the count of St-Pol--to the one who would agree to set out within the prescribed time; if none would go, the money was to be given to the nearest relative who would leave after that date: Boutaric, "Notices et extraits," pp. 233-234.

For Philip's involvement with the crusade, see Lizerand, Clément, pp. 273-309 and 361-363; J. N. Hillgarth, Ramon Lull and Lullism in Fourteenth-Century France (Oxford, 1971), pp. 120-121; Ewald Müller, Das Konzil von Vienne 1311-1312. Seine Quellen und seine Geschichte, Vorreformationsgeschichtliche Forschungen, XII (Münster, 1934), 158-161, 216-218. Although Philip promised to take the cross within a year after his pledge to do so at the Council of Vienne on April 3, 1312, his promise was not kept until Pentecost of 1313: see Franz Ehrle, "Zur Geschichte des päpstlichen Hofceremonielle im 14. Jahrhundert," Archiv für Literatur- und Kirchengeschichte des Mittelalters, V (1889), 576-578, for an eye-witness account of the Council of Vienne which shows that in April 1312 Philip swore that he, his children, and his brothers would take the cross in a year and set forth on crusade within six years from March 1, 1313; cf. Regestum Clementis Papae V... (Rome, 1887-1888), no. 8964, a letter of December 21, 1312, confirming these commitments and permitting Philip to postpone taking the cross until Pentecost 1313.

For the ceremony in Paris on June 6, 1313, at which the cross was taken by Philip, his sons, and Edward of England, his son-in-law, see La chronique métrique attribuée à Geffroy de Paris, ed. Armel Diverrès (Paris, 1956), pp. 183-184; Les grandes chroniques de France, ed. Jules Viard, 10 vols. (Paris, 1920-1953), VIII, 288. Geffroy de Paris and Jean de St.-Victor, who often relied on Geffroy, report in similar

accounts that before he died Philip the Fair asked Louis not only to
make amends for his misdeeds, but also to fulfill his crusading vow,
and Philip's codicil adds credibility to these accounts:  Geffroy de
Paris, Chronique, pp. 218-219; Recueil, XXI, 659; cf. Léon Lacabane,
"Dissertations sur l'histoire de France au XIV^e siècle. I. Mort de
Philippe le Bel.--II. Avènement de Louis Hutin," Bibliothèque de
l'École des Chartes, III (1841-1842), 8; for the relationship between
Geffroy and Jean, see Natalis de Wailly, "Mémoire sur Geffroi de
Paris," Mémoires de l'Institut national de France, Académie des
Inscriptions et Belles-Lettres, XVIII, pt. 2 (1849), pp. 527-528.

[48] The ordinance of November 28, 1314, is printed inaccurately in
Louis-François du Vaucel, Essai sur les apanages ou Mémoire historique
de leur établissement (n.p., n. d., but probably Paris and before
1792), I, 134-136, no. xiii, and cf. the original, Paris, Archives
Nationales, J 975, no. 10. It seems likely to me that, had Philip
decided before completing his codicil precisely how he wished to fund
his bequests, he would have included these provisions in the codicil
itself. Note that Yves de St.-Denis indicates that the preparation of
the royal ordinances which were approved by his sons was one of Philip's
final acts:  Recueil, XXI, 206-207. The Continuator of Guillaume de
Nangis implies, however, that the drafting of the act relating to the
apanages preceded the tax cancellation and completion of the codicil:
Chronique de Guillaume de Nangis et de ses continuateurs, ed. H.
Géraud, Publications de la Société de l'Histoire de France, vols. 33
and 35 (Paris, 1843), I, 413. The information given concerning the
apanage document is grossly inaccurate, since the Continuator simply
says that Charles, who had never received any portion before, was
assigned the county of la Marche, and there seems to be no reason to
accept his chronology.

In form this document can be distinguished from an ordinary testament, and Richard has suggested, following a notation in a cartulary
of the dukes of Burgundy, that such an act as this should be referred
to, technically, as an ordinatio. Since Philip the Fair's act includes provisions relating directly to the execution of his testament,
however, it differs from those documents dealing solely with property
division; it is also noteworthy that Louis alone, rather than all
Philip's sons, is said to have approved the division:  Jean Richard,
"La diplomatique du testament bourguignon (XIII^e-XV^e siècles),"
Mémoires de la Société pour l'histoire du droit et des institutions
des anciens pays bourguignons, comtois et romands, XVII (1955), 80; cf.,
however, n. 62 below. Although in some areas the tendency to mingle
bequests and property arrangements became increasingly strong in the
late thirteenth and early fourteenth centuries, Louis VIII's will of
June 1225 had contained a divisio of property to prevent discord among
his heirs, as well as ordinary bequests; Ordonnances, XI, 324;
Layettes, II, 55; cf. Richard, loc. cit. In his will of February
1270 Louis IX mentioned the portiones assigned to his sons, but, as
he noted there, they were fully described in other letters:  Ordonnances, XI, 345; Layettes, IV, 421; cf. Layettes, IV, 468, no. 5730
for Louis IX's codicil of July 1270, in which he referred to his
ordinationes concerning these portiones, which he distinguished from
his testamentum. See Vaucel, Essai, I, 132-133 for a similar ordinatio

made by Philip III on February 28, 1285, dividing lands among his sons.

[49]Vaucel, Essai, I, 134.

[50]See n. 29 above for similar provisions made by Louis IX in August 1270, shortly before he died.

[51]See Wood, The French Apanages, p. 30, n. 56, and pp. 50-51 for a discussion of this arrangement, which reduced by 8000 livres the amount originally assigned to Philip of Poitiers.

[52]Elsewhere, discussing 40,000 livres of this sum which he acknowledged having appropriated, he said they had been needed for his besoignes pour certennes causes: Paris, Archives Nationales, JJ 46, fol. 94, no. 162, and cf. Registres du Trésor des Chartes, vol. I, Règne de Philippe le Bel, ed. Robert Fawtier et al. (Paris, 1958), no. 1441.

[53]For the agreement of December 28, 1311, which stipulated that the annual payments be kept in Arras and be guarded by Mahaut, Enguerran, Thierri d'Hireçon, and Gui Florent, see Favier, Enguerran, pp. 102, 117-118, who did not, however, mention the arrangement concluded on November 28, 1314, now being discussed, despite Enguerran's involvement in it. See Fawtier, Registres, no. 1440.

[54]Philip's act assumes that the entire dowry was Charles' alone, which perhaps indicates that the dowry had been subject to de facto confiscation when the adultery convictions took place: cf. Favier, Enguerran, pp. 118-119.

[55]See Fawtier, Registres, no. 1440. Favier indicates that Blanche's dowry amounted to only 100,000 livres tournois, since he focuses on the agreements of 1311, which involve only that half of the 200,000 livres which was intended to be used to buy lands and annuities for Blanche and the children she bore Charles: Favier, Enguerran, 102, 117-118. In the elaborate agreement concluded between Philip and Mahaut in September 1307 the other half was clearly stated to be intended to pass to Charles outright after the marriage: Fawtier, Registres, no. 895, and cf. nos. 301 and 748-749; a vidimus of this agreement, dated February 17, 1309, is found in Pas-de-Calais, Archives Départementales, A 53, no. 34 (no. 2736).

The four men who were to counsel Enguerran and Hugues concerning the disposition of the money had served as guarantors of the agreement of September 1307, and on November 29, 1314, Philip appointed them to determine the dowries of any daughters of Philip of Poitiers, in case, in the absence of male heirs, his county of Poitiers should revert to the king: Fawtier, Registres, nos. 748[bis] and 895; Favier, Enguerran, pp. 96 and 232; Wood, The French Apanages, p. 50.

[56]For Jeanne's wills, see the next note.

[57]In a will drawn on April 1, 1304, Jeanne stated that her bequests were to be paid with the 40,000 livres tournois allotted her by Philip, in addition to all her movables: Paris, Archives Nationales, J 403,

no. 15. This will was approved by Philip alone, and he and the count
of St.-Pol were two of the queen's executors. In the will she drew
up on March 25, 1305, soon before her death, she was able to dispose
of 40,000 livres parisis (equivalent to 50,000 livres tournois) as
well as her movable property, and, in addition, since these sources
did not suffice for her bequests, with the assent of Philip and their
eldest son Louis she assigned the revenues of Champagne and Brie for
three years to her executors: César Égasse Du Boulay, Historia Vni-
versitatis Parisiensis..., 6 vols. (Paris, 1665-1673), IV, 74-75,
and cf. p. 80 for the executors, who still included the king and the
count of St.-Pol. Louis sealed the will to signify his approval.
Jeanne included pledges of restitution in the codicil drafted on
March 31, 1305, the day before her death: Du Boulay, Historia, IV,
80-81. This codicil, too, was specifically sanctioned by Louis. See
also Du Boulay, Historia, IV, 81-82 for a document dated March 31,
1305, in which Philip the Fair testified that Louis had sworn on the
Gospels to observe the provisions of Jeanne's will; for the assent
of Philip and Louis to the act by which Jeanne founded the Collège
de Navarre, dated March 25, 1305, see Du Boulay, Historia, IV, 84-85.

Evidence that the revenues of Champagne were collected by Jeanne's
executors from April 2, 1304 to April 2, 1308 appears in Inventaire
d'anciens comptes royaux dressés par Robert Mignon sous le règne de
Philippe de Valois, ed. Charles-Victor Langlois, Recueil des historiens de la France, Documents financiers, I (Paris, 1899), no. 87.
The Collège de Navarre was functioning by 1315: Du Boulay, Historia,
IV, 87-96.

[58] Brown, "Taxation and Morality," p. 19, n. 67; Brown, "Charters
and Leagues," pp. 163-164, 175-176.

[59] Brown, "Taxation and Morality," pp. 18-19 and especially n. 65;
see also Elizabeth A. R. Brown, "Philip IV and the Morality of Taxation," in John Bell Henneman, The Medieval French Monarchy (Hinsdale,
1973), pp. 111-119.

Geffroy de Paris, Jean de St.-Victor, and Guillaume Baldrich all
attribute to the dying king regret for his financial policies, although
none of them records that he cancelled the tax of 1314 on his deathbed. Baldrich's account is vague and general, for he simply says that
Philip told his son Louis that "the greatest avarice had reigned in
him, and he asked his son to free himself from all avarice": "Incusa-
vit autem se ipsum idem rex quod summa avaricia regnavit in ipso,
rogavitque filium suum ut a se omnem avariciam abdicaret": Baudon
de Mony, "La mort," p. 12. Geffroy and Jean are much more specific.
Jean states that Philip expressed sadness at having unjustly burdened
many men through his taxes, extortions and frequent coinage changes,
and that he asked his son, generally, to make amends for his misdeeds:
"multos gravavi injuste talliis et extorsionibus, et frequenti muta-
tione insolita monetarum.... Rogo te ergo, fili, supportes et suscipias
onus meum et forefacta mea, quantum poteris emendando et votum crucis
quod habeo persolvendo": Recueil, XXI, 659 and cf. n. 47 above.
Geffroy asserts that, in response to baronial complaints, Philip
abolished all males tostes, tailles, and susventions while he was

still at Poissy, before being taken to Fontainebleau to die; Geffroy
de Paris, Chronique, p. 217, lines 6706-6709.  According to Geffroy,
immediately before he died Philip was stricken with despair because
of his taxes and prises, and, convinced that restitution would be
necessary for his salvation, instructed his son Louis to implement it:
Geffroy de Paris, Chronique, pp. 218-219, lines 6759-6779.  Geffroy's
polemical intent in inserting these words into the mouth of the king
seems undeniable.  He, like many others, surely hoped that, although
Philip had not pledged restitution of the proceeds of the tax of 1314,
his son Louis would follow the example set in 1313 and restore all
money that had been collected:  cf. Brown, "Charters and Leagues,"
pp. 148-164 and 175-176, and Brown, "Cessante Causa," pp. 576-579.

Yves de St.-Denis' statement that in his last days Philip was taking
thought for things pertaining to his salvation might be interpreted
broadly as referring to the tax cancellation; on the other hand, the
Continuator of Guillaume de Nangis' chronicle, interested in the
"unjust exaction" of 1314, explicitly connects Philip's concern for
his soul with his deathbed order that it should be halted:  see n. 43
above for Yves de St.-Denis.  The Continuator, having reported the rumor
that the tax had been imposed by Philip's counselors, goes so far as
to say that it was only on his deathbed that the king learned of the
tax:  "Sed de salute animae suae attentius cogitans, exactionem
maletoltae, quae jam ad aures ejus insoluerat, et ei multum displicebat,
cessare fecit penitus et omnino":  Chronique de Guillaume de Nangis,
I, 413 and cf. pp. 412-413.  See also Brown, "Charters," pp. 102-103
and especially n. 19.  The Continuator indicates that the cancellation
followed the endowment of Charles with the county of la Marche and
preceded the completion of the codicil, but cf. n. 48 above for comments on the reliability of this chronology.

[60]As has been seen (above at nn. 35 and 37), Philip's wills of 1297
and 1311 both stated that certain specific provisions concerning the
revenues to be used to execute the testaments could not be altered
even with the consent of the executors, and this stipulation could
have been argued to apply to the provisions included in the testamentary ordinance of November 28, 1314.

[61]"Condidit etiam testamentum in quo, ut dicitur, mirabilia con-
tinentur.  Et rogavit heredem suum eidemque precepit ut contenta in
dicto testamento et omnia alia que verbo sibi injuxerat [sic] celeriter
adinpleret, quod si faceret benedicebat cum benediccione paterna;
alioquin vocavit dictum heredem ad divinum judicium, rogans Deum quod,
in illum casum, dictus heres suus ipsum celeriter sequeretur":  Baudon
de Mony, "La mort," p. 12.  The Continuator of Guillaume de Nangis
gives a shorter account, but he too indicates that Philip threatened
Louis with divine and paternal condemnation if he should fail to carry
out his orders:  "Tandemque testamento suo multa cum maturitate
relecto, et sapienter pariter et prudenter, quam fieri commode potuit,
ordinato; domino Ludovico, suo primogenito, jam Navarrae regi, salu-
bria salutis monita sapienter impendens, et eidem efficaciter adim-
plenda et sub minitatione divinae pariter et paternae maledictionis
imponens":  Chronique de Guillaume de Nangis, I, 413. Yves de St.-Denis
supporting Baldrich's statement, says that before relating his final

wishes to Louis, Philip warned him to keep his commands "under every curse a father can lay on a son, so that unless you observe them, you will incur God's curse and mine": "Et haec sunt quae vobis mando et servanda praecipio sub omni maledictione quam pater potest inferre filio, ita quod nisi ea servaveritis maledictionem Dei incurratis et meam": Recueil, XXI, 206. Unlike Baldrich, Yves de St.-Denis does not state that Philip associated this curse with his testamentary provisions, although Yves does say that Philip later enjoined Louis to complete the work he had begun at Poissy and then made certain arrangements which were confirmed by his sons: Recueil, XXI, 207 and cf. n. 46 above.

[62]"Presentem autem ordinationem nostram, testamentum principale, ac codicillum eidem annexum et omnia contenta in eis carissimus Ludovicus primogenitus noster per fidem corporalem manu nostra per eum prestitam promisit se fideliter tenere, servare et integraliter adimplere.... Per dominum regem et de consensu domini regis Navarre": Boutaric, "Notices et extraits," p. 235.

For the significance of the terminology employed in this clause, and particularly of the word ordinatio, see n. 48 above.

[63]Vaucel, Essai, I, 136.

[64]See n. 57 above, and cf. n. 34 for the confirmation which Philip secured from his wife Jeanne in May 1295.

[65]"Et pour la promesse que il li a faite que bien et leaument il consoillera son fil le roy et mettra peine a asseuir li execution bonnement": Rouen, Bibliothèque Municipale, ms. 3401 (Leber 8700, Menant 4), fol. 113v°. This entry, from a treasury roll relating to the years 1312-1317, records Philip's gift of 10,000 livres to Gaucher de Châtillon on November 28, 1314, for his good services, for costs incurred in connection with an exchange of land made with the king, and for the promise described above. See n. 70 below.

[66]See Boutaric, "Notices et extraits," p. 211, for an ordinance concerning projected income and expenditures of 1314, in which it is noted that the five bailliages of Normandy were expected to produce 100,000 livres tournois, not including the fouage, a special tax paid there every three years. In contrast, 80,000 livres tournois were anticipated from the seneschalsies of Toulouse, Rouergue, Quercy, Périgord, and Saintonge, and from the bailliages of Auvergne and Limousin.

[67]See above, at nn. 37 and 50.

[68]See Brown, "Cessante Causa," pp. 578-580, and, for the low yield of the war tax of 1314, Joseph R. Strayer, "Consent to Taxation under Philip the Fair," in Joseph R. Strayer and Charles H. Taylor, Studies in Early French Taxation (Cambridge, Mass., 1939), pp. 87-88, but note, first, that the surviving records indicate the yields of only some parts of the kingdom, and also that the value of money was far less inflated in 1314 than it had been in 1304, the year to which

Strayer compares it.

[69]Estimation of royal revenue in the early fourteenth century is
exceedingly difficult, and the figure given in the text represents
the roughest sort of estimate:  see Charles-Victor Langlois, "La
comptabilité publique qu XIIIe et au XIVe siècle," Journal des
Savants (1905), pp. 146-148; Henneman, Royal Taxation, pp. 348-353;
and John F. Benton, "The Revenue of Louis VII," Speculum, XLII (1967),
91 and especially n. 64.

[70]Baudon de Mony, "La mort," pp. 6-7.  For money spent in connection
with Philip's funeral ceremonies, see Rouen, Bibliothèque Municipale,
ms. 3401 (Leber 8700, Menant 4), fol. 112, and see Comptes du Trésor
(1296, 1316, 1384, 1477), ed. Robert Fawtier, Recueil des historiens
de la France, Documents financiers, II (Paris, 1930), xxi, nn. 1-2,
and see ibid., pp. xx-xxiii for a full discussion of the treasury roll
in which the entries appear, referred to in n. 65 above.

In a letter which the archbishops of Reims, Rouen, and Sens addressed
on July 28, 1315, to the ecclesiastics of the province of Bourges,
they emphasized the many expenses occasioned by his father's death
and by his own coronation which Louis had had to meet:  Aveyron,
Archives Départementales, G 10, fol. 66.

[71]These executors were named in Philip's will of 1311 and in the
codicil of November 28, 1314.  Thirteen men were named in the will
of 1311, and the codicil added five executors and replaced five of
the original executors, four of whom had died:  Paris, Archives
Nationales, J 403, no. 17; and Boutaric, "Notices et extraits," pp.
234-235.  Sance de Charmoye, canon of Noyon, and active in royal
fiscal affairs, was named an executor in 1311 but was not mentioned
in the codicil.  Although an entry in the treasury accounts for 1316
suggests that he was still involved in the king's affairs in that
year, Borrelli de Serres states that he was not living in 1314:
Comptes du Trésor, p. 19, no. 374, and especially n. 1; Borrelli de
Serres, Recherches, I, 313, n. 3.

[72]See above, at n. 65.

[73]The letter is simply dated in the month of December 1314 at
Vincennes.  Louis is known to have spent Christmas at Bois de
Vincennes, and since there is no evidence that he was there earlier
in the month, I have hypothesized that the agreement was completed
at Vincennes at about that time:  Recueil, XXI, 464.

[74]The copy of this act which appears in the royal registers omits
from the list of reserved assets le tresor, so that the phrase concerning the treasuries reads "lancien tresor et les Ioiaus dou louure":
Paris, Archives Nationales, JJ 52, fol. 25, and cf. Guerout, Registres,
no. 97.  Later in this transcription, however, "le tresor du louure"
is specifically mentioned with the ancien tresor as having been set
aside for Louis' use, which shows that the earlier omission of the
phrase was inadvertent:  Paris, Archives Nationales, JJ 52, fol. 25v°.

A rough draft of the agreement shows that this section was the product of serious discussion and that it was originally planned that the
king should retain only the two treasuries, the war tax, and the last
tenth granted for the Holy Land, giving the executors the right to
dispose of all tenths already collected and all arrears of these taxes.
The prior of Poissy may have intervened to protect the nunnery's
interests, and the executors may have pointed out to the king that
Philip's ordinance of November 28, 1314, had specifically stated that
ecclesiastical tenths intended for the crusade should not be used to
pay his bequests: see above at n. 50.

See Paris, Archives Nationales, J 403, no. 20bis, labeled on the
dorse "Transcriptum conuentionum habitarum inter Regem ludouicum &
Exequtores testamenti philippi Genitoris sui." In this draft the
following clause was cancelled: "Exceptez lancien tresor / le tresor
du louure / les deniers qui sont leuez & deuz pour ceste derreniere
Subuention & le derrenier disieme otroie pour la terre saincte les
queles choses exceptees nous demouront." Then appears the following
statement, into which several words, indicated by parentheses, were
inserted by a different hand, and of which some portions, indicated
by brackets, were cancelled: "Tout ce qui est en depos des (toz)
autres disiemes [par deuant otroiez par quelconque cause que ce Soit]
(exceptez ceux qui peuvent apartenir a la terre sainte si comme
dessus est dit) & touz les arrerages qui [en] sont deuz (des diz
disiemes excepte ceux de la terre sainte)." At the top of the act
is found the following new clause, drafted to replace the cancelled
portion: "(Excepte lancien tresor • le tresor & les Ioiaux du louure)
fors tant comme il en apartient / a lesglise des sereurs de poissi
pour le Reson du don que nostre (chier) Segneur & pere leur fist [ou
temps que il viuoit] (en son testament) • les deniers / qui sont leuez
& deuz pour cause de ceste darreniere subuencion • & exceptez le
[tresor] (& disiesmes qui) Qui / peuent apartenir a la terre sainte
[pour cause des diziesmes] / des quell, se lan an auoit Riens oste •
li exequeteur seroient tenuz a restablir / les queles choses exceptees
nous demourront."

The only other major change involved the order in which the names
of Philip's executors were listed: a notation on the draft agreement
indicated that the names of Denis de Sens and the executors listed
after him, through Pierre d'Étampes, should precede rather than follow
the name of Enguerran de Marigny.

[75]For the loan, see Thomas Frederick Tout, The Place of the Reign
of Edward II in English History, ed. Hilda Johnstone, 2nd ed.,
Manchester Historical Series, XX (Manchester, 1936), 196, n. 4; and
cf. Favier, Enguerran, pp. 125-126 for other sums borrowed by Edward
from Enguerran de Marigny to cover the expenses of his trip. See
Viard, Journaux...Charles IV, nos. 426, 613, 1032, 1056, 1251, 2193,
2791, 4051, for the eventual repayment of the debt.

[76]See n. 66 above. A statement made by Philip's executors in 1319
shows clearly that in 1314 they anticipated being able to draw on all
Norman revenues and that Louis' assignment of the revenues of the
three seneschalsies was made instead of, rather than in addition to

the Norman income, in contravention of the provisions of the will of
1311: "Sachent tuit que comme Autre foiz de la uoulente & du con-
santement de nostre Treschier seigneur loys Iadis Roi de france & de
Nauarre / cui dieux Absoile / pour certaines causes & Iustes Nous
eussiens deleissie au dit nres le Roi loys la Terre de Normandie
qui Nous estoit Assignee A faire lexecucion du testament dudit Roy .
Philippe.. pour recompensacion souffisant que il Nous en fit cest A
sauoir en nous baillant la Seneschaucie de Beauquaire auecques autres
Seneschaucies & terres": Doubs, Archives Départementales, B 24.  In
this act, dated at Paris on March 21, 1319, the executors approved
the acts by which Philip V assigned his wife Jeanne a part of her
dowry on the duchy of Normandy, and 7000 livres annually on the seneschalsy of Beaucaire, and they acknowledged the compensation Philip
had given them from the seneschalsy of Toulouse. See also the letter
issued by Philip at Paris in March 1319, which grants the executors
7000 livres tournois worth of land, to be drawn from the profits of
the seneschalsy of Toulouse: Doubs, Archives Départementales, B 24;
and in Guerout, Registres, nos. 2209, 3400. The royal letter describes more precisely than the executors' act the assignment given
them in place of Normandy, specifying that they were granted the
income of the seneschalsies of Beaucaire, Carcassonne, and Rouergue.
On the executors' act and the special executory seal attached to it,
see Jules Gauthier, "Note sur un sceau inédit des exécuteurs testa-
mentaires de Philippe le Bel. 1319, 21 mars," Revue des sociétés
savantes, 6th ser., IV (1876), 280-282.

[77]See the act quoted in the preceding note.

[78]See the document in the Appendix, pp. 381-383.

[79]Brown, "Cessante Causa," pp. 578-580.

[80]See, for a general treatment, Borrelli de Serres, Recherches, II,
219, 233-235; III, 75-76. In February 1315 the executors agreed to
delegate their functions to four of their nubmer, the abbot of St.-
Denis, the prior of Poissy, Pierre d'Étampes, and Pierre, seigneur of
Chambly: Paris, Archives Nationales, J 403, no. 19[bis]; Paris,
Bibliothèque Nationale, ms. n.a.f. 7111 (Brienne 140), fols. 83-85;
cf. Favier, Enguerran, pp. 205-206. By the end of June 1315 the process of tampering with the revenues available to the executors, discussed in n. 76 above, had already begun: Paris, Archives Nationales,
J 403, no. 21, and see Elizabeth A. R. Brown, "Gascon Subsidies and
the Finances of the English Dominions, 1315-1324," Medieval and
Renaissance Studies, VIII (1971), 151-152, especially n. 22.

For the executors' involvement in 1315 and 1316 in the collection
of the knighting aid of Louis of Navarre, levied in 1313 but still
being collected after Philip's death and considered Philip's property,
see Emmanuel Lemaire, Archives anciennes de la ville de Saint-Quentin
(Saint-Quentin, 1888-1910), I, 233, no. 242, and also Paris,
Bibliothèque Nationale, Clairambault 228, pp. 949, 955, 957, 961.

Evidence of the executors' activities in 1315 and 1316 appears in
Comptes royaux (1314-1328), ed. François Maillard, Recueil des

historiens de la France, Documents financiers, IV (Paris, 1961), pt. 2, pp. 122-123, especially nos. 13535, 13537; and in Paris, Bibliothèque Nationale, ms. n.a.lat. 184 (a collection of extracts from treasury accounts made by François Blanchard in the early eighteenth century), fol. 103. For similar activities between 1317 and 1322 see Paris, Bibliothèque Nationale, ms. fr. 20691 (extracts from Registers of the Chamber of Accounts made in 1648-1650 by Nicolas-Charles de Ste.-Marthe), pp. 885-887. Additional evidence concerning the execution of Philip's will may be found in Guerout, Registres, nos. 331, 485, 1663, 1706, 1788, 1846, 3012, 3483; Viard, Journaux...Charles IV, nos. 3321, 4915, 5048, 6985; Paris, Archives Nationales, JJ 62, fol. 38v°, no. 68; Paris, Bibliothèque Nationale, ms. fr. 2755, fol. 390; Paris, Bibliothèque Nationale, ms. fr. 21857, fols. 110, 148; Rouen, Bibliothèque Municipale, ms. 3402 (Leber 5870, Menant 5), fols. 139-143v°, 158v°-159; J. Rouquette and A. Villemagne, Cartulaire de Maguelone (Montpellier, 1912-1926), IV, no. mcccclxxx, pp. 475-476. Philip's living executors were still at work in the late 1320's: Léon Dessalles, "Le Trésor des Chartes, sa création, ses gardes et leurs travaux, depuis l'origine jusqu'en 1582," Mémoires présentés par divers savants à l'Académie royale des inscriptions et belles-lettres, 1st ser., I (1844), 395-396.

[81]Louis assigned the house the income to recover three golden cloths, two of which Clement V had given Philip and one of which had come to him from the Hospitallers, and a great precious stone called "camaheu." The act is dated July 1315: Guerout, Registres, no. 276, and cf. Boutaric, "Notices et extraits," 231 for the bequest. For Louis' love of gold cloths, see his will, where he ordered that all matters connected with his burial, whether lights, gold cloths to be put in different places, or alms to be distributed, should be attended to by his executors: Paris, Archives Nationales, J 403, no. 22.

[82]See n. 32 above. According to Girard de Fraichet, before he died Philip III made his son swear to help his brother Charles acquire Aragon; immediately after his father's death, however, Philip returned to France, abandoning Philip III's crusade against Aragon: Recueil, XXI, 7, and cf. Joseph R. Strayer, "The Crusade against Aragon," first published in 1953 and now available in Strayer, Statecraft, pp. 107-108, 119-122.

[83]Although I maintained in "Charters and Leagues," p. 482, esp. n. 54, that Louis died on June 7, 1316, it is clear that his death actually occurred on June 5: Maillard, Comptes royaux, pt. 2, p. 189, no. 14448, and Ralph E. Giesey's unpublished study, "The Double Funeral of Louis le Hutin, 1316." The will is dated simply June 1316: Paris, Archives Nationales, J 404A, no. 22.

[84]"Premierement quant a acomplir le testament nostre / treschier Pere / nous Voulon et ordenon / que selonc lordenance que nous auon faite Aueuques les Executeurs du dit nostre chier Pere / le testament soit acompli / quant a toutes choses contenues v testament par les executeurs nostre chier Pere. Et ne voulon que nul y meite aucun empeechement. Ainz voulon que se aucun empeechement y estoit miz /

que noz executeurs leura [sic] aident a deliurer tant comme il pour-
ront et il apartendra a eulz": Paris, Archives Nationales, J 404A,
no. 22.

[85]See the clause quoted in the last note.  In some respects Louis'
testament differs notably from his father's.  Instead of attempting
to specify precisely how his bequest for the Holy Land should be spent,
Louis made a firm grant of 50,000 livres tournois to be disbursed for
the first general passage overseas by the archbishop of Rouen, the
bishop of Paris, and the abbot of St.-Denis, "pour conuertir en genz
darmes pour la terre sainte / par leur mains du conseill de noz executeurs / ou daucunz deputez diceuz":  Paris, Archives Nationales,
J 404A, no. 22.  Louis was even more careful than his father had been
to specify the sources from which his legacies were to be paid.  His
executors were to have control of the revenues of the county of
Champagne and of all the "fruiz rentes et issues dicele et toutes
les forfaitures / soient muebles ou heritages / escheues des le temps
que nous receumes le gouuernement du Royaume et toutes les autres qui
escherront deci en auant Iusques a laccomplissement de cest present
testament / Excepte la Somme de vnze Mil liures la quele somme est
assignee suz la seneschaucie de thoulouse a nostre chier frere charles
conte de la marche pour certaine cause / et certaine conuenance eue
entre nous et li / Seil les veut prendre / Et se il ne les vouloit
prendre nous voulon que toutes les dites forfaitures enterinement
soient conuerties en accomplissement de ces [sic] present testament.
Item tout ce que nous apartient et puet apartenir des forfaitures
toutes les queles eschairent v temps nostre tres chier pere / Item
toutes les deptes qui nous sont deues par tout le Royaume de quel
personne que ce soit / et de quel cause que ce soit / et par tout le
Royaume de Nauarre aussi.  Item touz noz biens muebles et Iouauz /
cheuauz / armeures / & autre hernoiz quel que il soit.  Item deuz
disimes les quieuz nous sont otriez de lordre de cluni / toutes ces
choses ici nommees et deuisees / nous ordenon et obliion a lacomplissement de cest present testament":  Paris, Archives Nationales,
J 404A, no. 22.

[86]See n. 83 above.

[87]Note Philip V's announcement in 1317 that he intended to have
his own debts and those of his father and brother fully paid:  Brown,
"Subsidy and Reform," p. 422, and especially n. 79.

[88]"Sane pro parte tua fuit nobis et fratribus nostris expositum
quod tam propter executiones testamentorum clare memorie Philippi
genitoris et Ludouici germani tuorum francie regum quam propter alia
nonnulla debita que ingruentibus multis necessitatibus pro conserua-
tione presertim et gubernatione utili christianissimi Regni francie /
te post illius suscepta gubernacula subire oportuit eris alieni sar-
cina multipliciter oppressus existis":  Paris, Archives Nationales,
J 716, no. 6, a bull issued by Pope John XXII on January 15, 1318.

[89]Paris, Archives Nationales, JJ 56, fol. 79, no. 166, dated April
1318; cf. Guerout, Registres, no. 1788.

[90]Philip assigned the royal income from Champagne and Brie, and, if necessary, from "nostre contee" of Toulouse for this purpose:  Paris, Archives Nationales, J 404A, no. 26, dated August 26, 1321.

[91]To execute his will, Philip set aside all his movable property except the movables of his churches and chapels and the old treasury of the Louvre, and he obligated his heir and all his land to carry out his provisions, mentioning especially the assignment of the revenues of Champagne and Brie and Toulouse made earlier in the will: Paris, Archives Nationales, J 404A, no. 26, and cf. n. 90.  The same attention to specific bequests and restitution seen in this testament is also evident in the codicil Philip prepared on January 2, 1322, where he deals with sums wrongly obtained by both Louis X and himself: Paris, Archives Nationales, J 404A, no. 27.

[92]For the attempts to remedy this confusion made by Charles IV, Philip the Fair's youngest son and the last direct Capetian ruler, see Borrelli de Serres, Recherches, II, 233-234.  Charles' concern over the problems caused by his predecessors' testaments did not lead him to adopt a new approach to legacies.  Like those of his father and brothers, his testament began with the order that payment of debts, restitutions, and amendment of wrongs should be attended to by his executors, and he took even greater pains than had his predecessors to describe the proper procedure to be observed in dealing with complaints.  Then he turned to his father's and brothers' wills, commanding that whatever remained undone at the time of his own death should be carried out by his successors, and charging the souls of his successors with responsibility for implementing these testaments:  Paris, Archives Nationales, J 404A, no. 29 (now AE II, 333 in the museum of the Archives Nationales), dated October 1324.  The codicil Charles drafted in January 1328 also demonstrates Charles' interest in his predecessors' bequests, and the provision he made in the codicil concerning damage done in his forests shows that he had been affected by the stipulations they had made:  Paris, Archives Nationales, J 404A, no. 29bis (AE II, 333).

## Appendix

[1]The notarized copy of this act (Paris, Archives Nationales, K 39, no. 2) contains the following phrase, found neither in the royal register JJ 52 nor in the draft of the act (Paris, Archives Nationales, J 403, no. 20bis):  "dou quel Nous vsons v temps que nostre chier seigneur et pere viuoit."

Chapter 24

[1]This article grew out of a paper, "Royal Adultery in England and France: A Comparative Approach," given at the Eighth Conference on Medieval Studies sponsored by the Medieval Institute of Western Michigan University, Kalamazoo, May 1, 1973. For comments and criticisms I am particularly indebted to Fredric L. Cheyette, Elizabeth A. R. Brown, William H. Dunham, and fittingly, Joseph R. Strayer.

[2]Ernest Lavisse, Histoire de France (Paris, 1901-1902), III², 212-216.

[3]May McKisack, The Fourteenth Century 1307-1399 (Oxford, 1959), pp. 83-92.

[4]Rotuli Parliamentorum (London, 1776-1777), II, 53.

[5]McKisack, p. 102.

[6]E.g., Martin Bouquet et al., Recueil des historiens des Gaules et de la France (Paris, 1738-1904), II, pp. 609-610, 691; XXI, 40-41, 151, 197, 658-659, 806. The only reticence I have found comes in an interpolation added to the Anonymous Chronicle of Saint Martial of Limoges (XII, 806, n. 7), which says that the d'Aunays "transgressed against the king in ways that ought not to be disclosed." Hereafter cited as H. F.

[7]William Stubbs, The Constitutional History of England (Oxford, 1880), II, 388, n. 1.

[8]Joseph Strayer, Medieval Statecraft and the Perspectives of History (Princeton, 1971), p. 384.

[9]Charles Wood, The French Apanages and the Capetian Monarchy 1224-1328 (Cambridge, Mass., 1966), pp. 48-65.

[10]H.F., XXI, 197.

[11]Wood, pp. 57-63; Gabrielle Spiegel, "The Reditus Regni ad Stirpem Karoli Magni: A New Look," French Historical Studies, VII (1971), 156, 163.

[12]Paul Viollet, "Comment les femmes ont été exclues de la succession à la couronne de France," Mémoires de l'Institut de France, XXXIV² (1895), 131-148.

[13]H. F., XXI, 663. The chronicles are much more explicit about the problem of illegitimacy than are official documents, which never mention it. Until the succession question was resolved, Jeanne's paternity was officially no more than "hidden agenda" about which no records were kept.

[14] Stubbs, II, 388.

[15] Charles Wood, "Personality, Politics, and Constitutional Progress: The Lessons of Edward II," Studia Gratiana [Post Scripta], XV (1972), 524-525.

[16] Jehan Froissart, Chronicles of England, France, Spain, and the Adjoining Countries (London, 1839), I, 13.

[17] Galfridus le Baker de Swinbroke, ed. Giles, Chronicon Angliae Temporibus Edwardi II et Edwardi III (London, 1847), p. 95; Wood, "Personality," 524-525.

[18] Chalfont Robinson, "Was King Edward the Second a Degenerate?" American Journal of Insanity, LXVI (1909-1910), 455, n. 27.

[19] I am indebted to Elizabeth A. R. Brown, who kindly did the appropriate chronological calculations and checked the itineraries of both king and queen.

[20] Lavisse, III$^2$, 214.

[21] McKisack, p. 93.

[22] Thomas F. Tout, "The Captivity and Death of Edward of Carnarvon," The Collected Papers of Thomas Frederick Tout (Manchester, 1934), III, 145-190.

[23] McKisack, pp. 80-81, 83, 85, 93.

[24] Frederick Pollock and Frederick W. Maitland, The History of English Law, 2nd ed. (Cambridge, 1968), II, 396-397; André Esmein, Cours élémentaire d'histoire du droit francais (Paris, 1925), p. 236.

[25] Selden Society, Year Books of Edward II (London, 1903), I, 186.

[26] Ibid., I, 187.

[27] Pollock and Maitland, II, 398.

[28] W. C. Bolland, The Year Books (Cambridge, 1921), p. 76. I am indebted to William H. Dunham for this citation and, more generally, for drawing the interest of the common law to my attention.

[29] McKisack, pp. 90-91.

[30] Carl Stephenson and Frederick G. Marcham, Sources of English Constitutional History, rev. ed. (New York, 1972), I, 192.

[31] Fritz Kern, Kingship and Law in the Middle Ages (Oxford, 1956), pp. 12-13; Henry G. Richardson, "The Coronation in Medieval England," Traditio, XVI (1960), 116.

[32]Robert Fawtier, <u>The Capetian Kings of France</u> (London, 1960), pp. 48-49; in the case of England, I am thinking primarily of William I's selection of Rufus; Henry I's of his son William; the agreement to Henry II during Stephen's reign; and, finally, Henry II's crowning of his son Henry in 1170.

[33]Kern, pp. 54-55.

[34]Ernst Kantorowicz, <u>The King's Two Bodies</u> (Princeton, 1957), pp. 328-330; Marc Bloch, <u>The Royal Touch</u> (Montreal, 1973), p. 127.

[35]Ralph Giesey, "The Juristic Basis of Dynastic Right to the French Throne," <u>Transactions of the American Philosophical Society</u>, new series, Part 5, LI (1961), 5.

[36]Bloch, pp. 1-4.

[37]Achille Luchaire, <u>Histoire des institutions monarchiques de la France sous les premiers Capétiens (987-1180)</u>, I, 66.

[38]Spiegel, 145-146, 152, 160-162.

[39]The whole of Professor Spiegel's article is relevant here. I should add, however, that my interpretation of the sources differs from hers insofar as I take most seriously the likelihood that they were written to legitimate dynastic thinking whereas she stresses their importance to later territorial ambitions. In citing her article here and in the footnotes that follow, my references are more to her sources than her interpretation of them. In this regard, my own thinking has been heavily influenced by Andrew W. Lewis, "Royal Succession in Capetian France: Studies of Familial Order and the State" (a 1972 Harvard doctoral thesis), and especially by its fourth chapter, "The Growth of Capetian Dynasticism."

[40]Spiegel, 151.

[41]Georgia Sommers [Wright], "Royal Tombs at St. Denis in the Reign of Saint Louis" (1966 Columbia doctoral thesis, copyright 1967), pp. 94-100.

[42]Spiegel, 145-146.

[43]Bloch, pp. 127-128.

[44]Spiegel, 160-162.

[45]Spiegel, 155, 172.

[46]Spiegel, 170-173.

[47]Kantorowicz, pp. 252-253; Strayer, pp. 302-303, 305-308, 312-313.

[48]Robert Branner, "The Montjoies of Saint Louis," <u>Essays in the</u>

History of Architecture Presented to Rudolf Wittkower, ed. D. Fraser et al. (London, 1967), I, 15-16.

[49]Henri F. Delaborde, ed., Oeuvres de Rigord et de Guillaume le Breton (Paris, 1882), I, 164.

[50]Philippe de Beaumanoir, ed. Salmon, Coutumes de Beauvaisis (Paris, 1889-1900), I, 146, no. 294.

[51]Kern, p. 20, n. 4.

[52]Translated in Charles Wood, ed., Philip the Fair and Boniface VIII, 2nd ed. (New York, 1971), p. 65.

[53]Strayer, pp. 300-314.

[54]Kantorowicz, p. 333.

[55]David C. Douglas, ed., English Historical Documents (New York, 1953), II, 142-144, 146, 214, 215-216, 217, 221, 224, 230-231, 285.

[56]In June 1119 William Adelin attested a royal charter as "Dei gratia rex designatus"; Regesta Regum Anglo-Normannorum, II, Regesta Henrici Primi, 1100-1135, ed. Charles Johnson and H. A. Cronne (Oxford, 1956), no. 1204. I am indebted to C. Warren Hollister for this citation.

[57]Rufus, Henry I, and Richard had no legitimate sons that survived them; deaths are almost too numerous to mention.

[58]I am thinking primarily of the struggles of Henry I, Robert Curthose, and William Clito; of Stephen and the Angevins; and of Henry II and his sons. Without developing the point, it seems apparent that these cross-Channel conflicts confused the succession and undermined royal legitimacy.

[59]Spiegel, 152.

[60]Bloch, p. 346, n. 73.

[61]Bertie Wilkinson, Constitutional History of Medieval England 1216-1399 (London, 1948), I, 68-98.

[62]Kern, p. 55, n. 33.

[63]A hard point to prove, given the relatively scant attention paid to the subject in France. But cf. Richardson, 161-174, and Robert S. Hoyt, "The Coronation Oath of 1308: The Background of 'Les Leys et les Custumes,'" Traditio, XI (1955), 235-257. That the French had an entirely different approach to charters of liberties, and totally different reasons for granting them, was brilliantly suggested in a paper, "Charters, Leagues, and Liberties in Thirteenth- and Fourteenth-Century England and France," given by Elizabeth A. R. Brown at the same conference from which the present article derives.

[64]Kantorowicz, p. 380.

[65]Bloch, p. 133.

[66]Bloch, pp. 137-139.

[67]Viollet, 139-141.

[68]H. F., XX, 645.

[69]Bloch, pp. 275-282; Kantorowicz, pp. 218-223.

[70]Fawtier, p. 57; Kantorowicz, pp. 221-223.

[71]Richardson, 145-146, 150.

[72]S. B. Chrimes, English Constitutional Ideas in the Fifteenth Century (Cambridge, 1936), p. 24, n. 1.

[73]Chrimes, p. 7, n. 2.

[74]Chrimes, p. 7; Bloch, p. 139; Bertie Wilkinson, Constitutional History of England in the Fifteenth Century (1399-1485) (New York, 1964), p. 196.

[75]Quoted in Chrimes, p. 32. Chrimes (pp. 22-32) takes the Yorkists' claims of dynastic legitimacy with the utmost seriousness as the major prop of their authority; Wilkinson, on the other hand (Fifteenth Century, pp. 138-142, 162-163), properly points out that all of them in practice had to rely on parliamentary support to such an extent that it undercut their purely hereditary claims. See also my forth-coming study, "The Deposition of Edward V," Traditio, XXXI (1975), which strengthens Wilkinson's case significantly.

[76]Professor Strayer has cautioned me that much more is involved in the deposition of kings, or the lack thereof, than differences in theories of kingship. In particular, he cites the differing political organizations of the two countries and the contrary geographic ways in which power was organized. I agree. My intent is simply to add a complementary mite to his vastly greater contributions to the subject.

[77]P. S. Lewis, Later Medieval France: The Polity (London, 1968), p. 114.

[78]Ibid., p. 61. But for proof that not all agreed with Charles and Joan, see Bloch, p. 144.

Chapter 25

[1]This little study originated in my examination of the Questiones in Libros Ethicorum, in the Bibl. Nationale, Paris, MS. Lat. 14698, a MS. of the later thirteenth century. My remarks about Professor Joseph R. Strayer and his devotion to learning and citizenship alike (in Medieval Statecraft, Essays by Joseph R. Strayer, Princeton, 1971, p. xv) were based in part on the Questiones. I feel now that I should offer a fuller study of the Questiones as a contribution to these essays in his honor. (Most of the essays are by his students. I was merely a colleague, either as a fellow disciple of Charles Homer Haskins, or in recent years as a member of the Department of History, Princeton University. I am happy to say, however, that I also am one of Strayer's students.)

[2]I. Th. Eschmann, O.P., "A Thomistic glossary on the Principle of the Preëminence of the Common Good," in Mediaeval Studies, V (1943), 132-165, esp. 137 ff. No doubt the pope assumed that the bishop was in no real danger of damnation.

[3]Helene Wieruszowski, "Ars dictaminis in the Time of Dante," in Medievalia et Humanistica, I (1943), 95-108; now in Politics and Culture (Storie e letteratura, 121), Rome, 1971, pp. 359-377. See also Hans Baron, "Cicero and the Roman Civic Spirit in the Middle Ages and the Early Renaissance," Bulletin of the John Rylands Library, XXII, i (1938), 11 ff.

[4]G. Post, "The Theory of Public Law and the State in the Thirteenth Century," in Seminar (Annual Extraordinary Number of The Jurist), VI (1948), 42-59; now in Studies in Medieval Legal Thought (Princeton, 1964), pp. 6-24.

[5]Gloss to the Peace of Constance, ad v. civitatem, in Paris, BN, Ms. lat. 5415-A, fol. 14r; in my Studies, p. 444, n. 33.

[6]See Eschmann, Med. Studies, V, 141-165.

[7]See G. de Lagarde, "La philosophie sociale d'Henri de Gand et Godefroid de Fontaines," in Archives d'hist. doctrinale et litt. du moyen âge, XIV (1943-45), 73-142; also p. 101, ref. to Remigio de Girolami, De bono communi: "Si non es civis, non es homo."

[8]"Trois commentaires 'Averroistes' sur l'Éthique a Nicomaque," AHDLMA, XXIII (1948), 292-293.

[9]M. Grabmann, Mittelalterliches Geistesleben, II, 200-224.

[10]"Trois commentaires 'Averroistes,'" AHDLMA, XXIII, 224-229, 270-271, 275, 282, 292-293, 296.

[11]Ibid., p. 275.

[12](Fol. 130, c.1) "Quamvis scriptum sit ab alexandro, quod viri
philosophici et dantes se studio et contemplationi sint naturaliter
virtuosi..., et delectationes non prosequentes, tamen secundum com-
munem hominum opinionem non est ita, licet ita sit secundum veritatem.
Immo creditur a multis, quod viri philosophici...sunt pravi, viri
increduli et non obedientes legi. Propter quod merito expellendi
sunt a communitate, ut dicunt. Et super hoc omnes dantes se studio
et contemplationi philosophice sunt defamati et suspecti." The whole
text on this subject, on fols. 130^V c. 1-130 c. 2, is given by
Gauthier, AHDLMA, XXIII, 226-227. I have quoted these passages
directly from the MS. My reading of a few words differs from
Gauthier's; e.g., he has sub hoc and diffamati in this passage. (The
relevance to contemporary suspicion of intellectuals is obvious.)

[13](Fol. 130 c.1) "Unde philosophia sicut dicitur in decimo huius
affert mirabiles delectationes puritate et firmitate. Delectatio
autem intellectualis potior est et excellentior delectatione sensuali,
quanto intellectus est potior et excellentior sensu. Propter quod
non est verisimile quod viri philosophici...maiorem delectationem
amittant pro minori."

[14](Fol. 130 c.2) "Et hoc est quod dicit commentator in prologo
octavi physicorum, quod cum homines incipiunt speculari veritatem in
philosophicis spernunt omnem aliam delectationem."

[15](Fol. 130 c.2) "Quia quicumque faciunt bonum in communitate et
nituntur ad hoc, liil debent esse pars civitatis, et non expellendi
a civitate. Immo tales sunt honorandi et elegendi. Sed viri philosophici nituntur ad bonum civitatis," and should be a pars civitatis.

[16](Fol. 130 c.2) "Et quamvis in philosophia sint aliqui errores,
tamen videtur esse expediens quod huiusmodi errores legantur et
audiantur, non quia homines eis credant, sed ut homines sciant eis
adversari secundum viam rationis per philosophiam. Et ideo expediens
est, quod philosophia legatur et exponantur errores, non quod homines
eis credant."

[17](Fol. 137 c.2-137^V) Utrum unius hominis possunt esse plura
optima--because felicitas is duplex, civilis, and contemplativa.
Then follows the discussion summarized above.

[18](Fol. 138^V c.1) Utrum felicitas sit bonum per se sufficiens.

[19](Fol. 138^r c.2-138^V c.1) "Queritur utrum vita contemplativa
sit principalior et excellentior et perfectior quam vita civilis et
activa." Contra: "illa vita que invenitur in hominibus superioribus
sicud in prelatis et in potestatibus constitutis, illa videtur esse
melior et excellentior. Sed vita activa et felicitas civilis
reparantur in talibus. Tales enim homines versantur contra agibilia,
ergo, etc. Preterea. Homo non debet dimittere maius bonum pro
minori bono. Sed quasi omnes dimittunt vitam contemplativam pro vita
activa. Unde aliqui fiunt prelati qui retrahuntur a speculatione at
contemplatione. Cum igitur omnes homines accipiant vitam" activam,

et dimittant vitam contemplativam, videtur quod vita activa sit melior et excellentior quam vita contemplativa.... Sed vita civilis precipit vite contemplative et ipsam ordinat; vita enim activa quales artes speculative debent legi, et usque ad quot tempus debent audiri.... Vita activa tendit ad bonum commune totius communitatis; vita autem contemplativa tendit ad bonum unius hominis; quod autem est bonum toti communitati et civitati est maius bonum quam est bonum uni." (Note that above there is a reference to statutes of the university which determined the curriculum.)

[20] (Fol. 138ᵛ c.1) "Hec enim vita (contemplativa) debetur homini secundum quod in eo existit aliquid divinum, ut pote intellectus.... Illa vita per quam homo maxime assimilatur deo et intelligentiis et efficitur eis amantissimus, est excellentior et principalior. Vita speculativa est huius(modi), quia per vitam contemplativam assimilatur homo deo et intelligentiis et efficitur eis amantissimus, sicut dicit philosophus in .Xᵒ. Ergo, etc." The emphasis on the intelligences comes chiefly from neo-platonizing Aristotelianism.

[21] (Fols. 138ᵛ c.1-139ʳ c.1) "Immo illud quod est bonum uni sicut contemplatio et speculatio veritatis est melius et honorabilius quam bonum toti civitati, licet non utilius."

[22] See Eschmann, Med. Studies, V, 158, no. 167; St. Thomas says that the contemplative life is dignior, the active or political life utilior.

[23] (Fol. 139ᵛ c.1) "Utrum divitie vel habundantia bonorum exteriorum requiratur ad felicitatem." Who this Tholomeus is is uncertain-- Ptolemy Chennos, Ptol. Claudius? In a Com. on Bk. X of the Ethics the name is associated with that of Heraclitus, G. Post, "Petrarch and Heraclitus," Speculum, XII (1937), 343-350. I plan to publish the Commentary with my own commentary.

[24] (Fol. 141ᵛ c.1) "Felicitas est optimum in genere humane nature. Propter felicitatem homo maxime assimilatur deo. Per felicitatem enim civilem homo assimilatur, quia sicut deus regit multa, sic etiam homo felix felicitate civili regit multos. Et iterum per felicitatem con- templativam homo assimilatur deo, quia per ipsam efficitur homo divinus et deo amantissimus, sicut dicitur in .Xᵒ. Et ideo sicut deo debetur honor, ita felicitati debetur honor in genere humane nature."

[25] (Fol. 146 c.1-c.2) Utrum contigat in istis (homicide, theft, and adultery) ratione agere.

[26] A familiar maxim in the two laws; see my Studies, Index, ad v. "vim vi repellere," esp. p. 263.

[27] (Fol. 146 c.1) "Secundum quod alibi scriptum est, licitum est vim vi repellere...; quod ordinat legislator propter bonum civitatis, illud est bonum; sed ipse ordinat quod latrones interficiantur et suspendantur."

[28]A reflection of the canon lawyers, who frequently argued that it is not so serious a sin to steal when a man or his family is starving--with Biblical references, of course; see my Studies, p. 21.

[29](Fol. 146 c.1) "Idem arguitur de adulterio, scilicet, quod in adulterio contingat recte agere.... Ponamus quod sit aliquis tyrannus, qui intendit destruere communitatem et bonum communitatis, et nesciatur intentio eius in hoc casu. Videtur quod bonum sit accedere ad uxorem eius, ut aliquis possit extorquere ab ea intentionem eius; et hoc est adulterium. Ergo videtur quod aliquando bonum sit facere adulterium."

[30](Fol. 146 c.2) I hasten to say that not even those accused of spying and plotting in the recent "Watergate" scandal have been accused also of committing adultery for reasons of civil or national security.

[31](Fol. 146 c.2) "Ad rationes ad primam dico, quod interficere latronem bonum est, non a quocumque sed ab eo qui habet potestatem publicam, scilicet, a ballivo vel preposito. Ad aliam rationem dico, quod ordinatur quod latrones interficiantur ab eo qui habet potestatem publicam, et non a quocumque; et hoc non est homicidium proprie...." As for adultery with the wife of a tyrant, "non est bonum nec licitum," if it is not done frequently; "sed si ita contingeret, ut in pluribus et frequenter, quod homo posset extorquere intentionem mariti ab uxore, licitum est." An astounding conclusion.

[32]See the studies by Richard Kay, Kimon Giocarinis, and G. Post, "The Medieval Heritage of a Humanistic Ideal," in Traditio, XI (1955), 195-234, esp. the section by Giocarinis.

INDEX

# Index

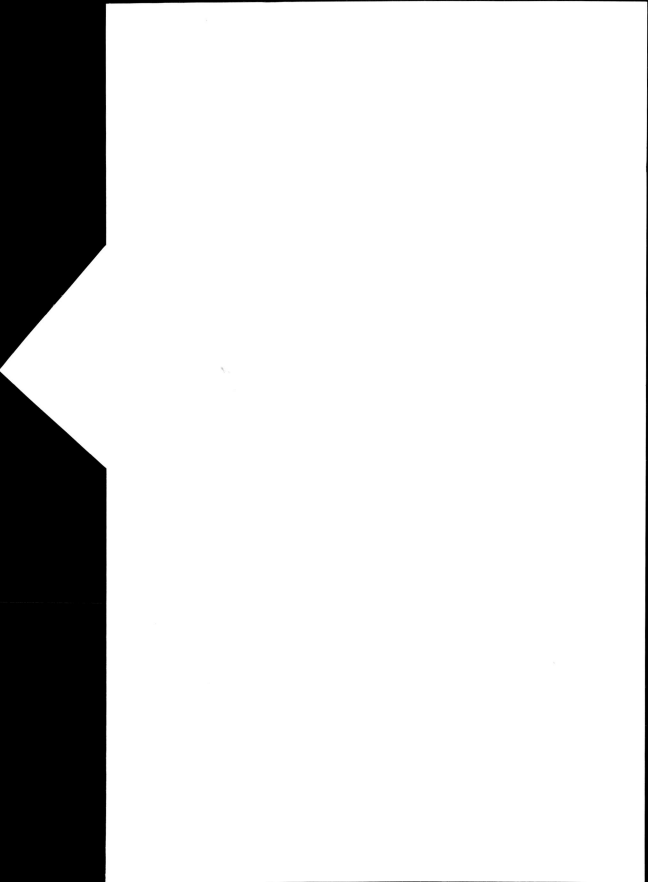

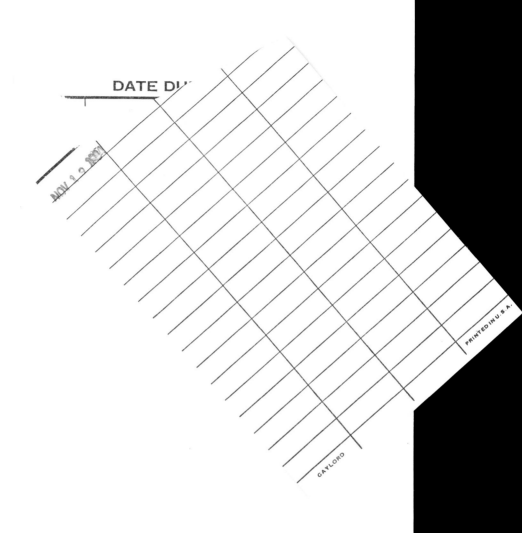

DATE DUE

NOV 1 2 1981

GAYLORD

PRINTED IN U.S.A.